To Evan. I love you to the moon and back.

consumer behavior & insights

DIANE M. PHILLIPS
Saint Joseph's University

NEW YORK   OXFORD
OXFORD UNIVERSITY PRESS

Oxford University Press is a department of the University of Oxford.
It furthers the University's objective of excellence in research, scholarship,
and education by publishing worldwide. Oxford is a registered trademark of
Oxford University Press in the UK and certain other countries.

Published in the United States of America by Oxford University Press
198 Madison Avenue, New York, NY 10016, United States of America.

© 2021 by Oxford University Press

Cataloging-in-Publication Data is on file with the Library of Congress.

ISBN: 978-0-19-085713-4

9 8 7 6 5 4 3 2 1
Printed by LSC Communications, United States of America

Brief Contents

Contents

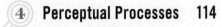

⑧ Decision-Making and Involvement   278

Part 3 Consumption: A Macro Perspective

⑨ Patterns of Buyer Behavior   318

Preface

The Goal of this Book

This book is designed to help students develop an in-depth appreciation and understanding of the complex processes involved in consumer decision-making and behavior. It elucidates how both internal and external factors influence how consumers think about themselves, their role within a society or culture, and the various processes and activities associated with being a consumer. These models and theories are powerful and effective. The goal is to encourage students to use the resources contained within these pages for several purposes. First, the knowledge gained within these pages should help you better understand what impacts you, so that you can be a smarter and more empowered consumer. If you know about your own tendencies or biases for decision-making, as well as how the broader environment influences your interpretations and behaviors, you will simply be able to make better decisions and be a more empowered consumer. Second, this book should broaden your perspective such that you will consider the vast array of consequences that are related to consumption behaviors, such as the impact on the environment and other people, including people who live in different parts of the world and people who will follow after us in the future. Finally, this book should spark a curiosity in you so that you will be inspired by the study of consumer behavior. Sure, it can sometimes be frustrating. Consumers are often unpredictable and fickle; they do not always do what we expect them to do. At the same time, however, the study of consumer behavior is fascinating *because* it is so unpredictable and dynamic. Sometimes, our predictions are wrong. As one of the executives said in an Insights from the Boardroom feature, "We were proven wrong; the best project is when this happens!" With the study of consumer behavior, there is always something new and surprising to discover or try. The study of consumer behavior is just as fun and fascinating as it is frustrating, because the study of consumers is also the study of *us*.

In support of this goal, the textbook is written so that the focus is on the theories and models of consumer behavior, as well as the insights that are derived from consumer research. These insights are indispensable in bringing the material to life because they answer the "So what now?" kinds of questions in the readers' minds. These insights provide a hands-on application of the chapter material and were selected to be particularly relevant to university students. Indeed, there are discussions of tailgating behaviors, relationships, study-abroad, and social media behaviors. Consumer-focused issues and problems are explored in the Insights from the Field sections; top-level executives share their experiences and advice in the Insights from the Boardroom sections; and cutting-edge research projects that connect the chapter content to current, relatable research findings are provided in the Insights from Academia sections. An important part of what makes this textbook engaging is that it is inclusive, global, and diverse. The executives who were interviewed are from a variety of backgrounds and perspectives, the case studies and other insights illustrate a wide and diverse variety of global topics, and a vast array of examples are given throughout about companies, consumers, and decision-making situations.

◉ Why is Consumer Behavior so Important?

From the moment we get up in the morning to the time we go to bed at night, we are consuming things. We brush our teeth, take a shower, get dressed, and head off to work or school. In that short period of time, we've used toothpaste and shampoo, consumed a cup of coffee, and checked the weather report. If you think about it, consumption is something that occurs throughout most of the day, every day, all year long. In cultures all around the world, individuals consume products and services throughout the day too. Just imagine the various products and services that are used in the vastly different morning routines for consumers all around the world! Then, imagine the vastly different products and services that are used for other consumption situations, such as the birth of a baby or a wedding. Because consumer behavior is such a central part of a person's life in everyday settings as well as on special occasions, we need to better understand this important phenomenon.

Today's business and marketing students are tomorrow's business and marketing decision-makers. As such, they must have a comprehensive understanding of consumer behavior to be able to shape and influence consumer behavior in different environments, as well as to find ways to provide consumers with the products, services, and experiences they desire. As we will learn, a variety of forces impact consumer behavior, and each one provides a unique and compelling view of the reality of the consumer's consumption experience. This book will explain and describe the most important theories and models in the fascinating field of consumer behavior. After studying these theories and models, students should start to develop a deep understanding of the various influences on consumers. This understanding is strengthened and expanded with insights from academics, executives, and marketing researchers. We will see that some of our theories and models sometimes provide conflicting predictions about what the consumer might do. That's ok! Consumer decision-making and behavior is a complex process and even the experts don't always get it right. Hopefully in the end, you will find what thousands of other students have discovered throughout the years—that consumer behavior is a dynamic and exciting field of study!

◉ How this Book is Organized

This book relies on two key analogies to help readers understand the key concepts and theories in consumer behavior. First, as the material is presented and builds on previous chapters, it is useful to think of a bicycle (see Figure P.1).

Establishing a framework

Part 1 is represented by the *framework* of the bike, which provides a strong supporting structure for what comes later. Part 1 is composed of three chapters that highlight the historical and contemporary perspectives of consumer behavior and provide an in-depth look at the consumer research process. Chapter 1 provides a *historical perspective* on consumption by revealing how researchers and commentators throughout the centuries and across cultures have viewed consumption. It also provides a basis by which we can see how our understanding of consumers has evolved. In Chapter 2, some *contemporary perspectives on consumption* are presented to assist in building the framework for our understanding of how consumers behave in the early twenty-first century. Chapter 3 provides a solid foundation for understanding the *consumer research* process and a basic understanding of how researchers build theories and models to better understand consumers. Most of our discussion throughout the text refers back to consumer research studies, so a clear understanding of the research process is essential. The objective of Part 1 is to create a strong framework for our later, more in-depth analyses.

Consumption: a micro perspective

Part 2 can be viewed as one of the wheels of the bicycle that is connected to the framework and moves in a forward direction. It consists of five chapters that encompass the *micro perspective*. In this part of the book, the focus is on the individual consumer and all of the internal processes and phenomena that occur, such as memory, learning, attitude formation, and the decision-making process. To start, Chapter 4 focuses on *perception* and the perceptual process as the vehicle by which individuals internalize information from the external environment. Next, Chapter 5 considers the processes of *learning and memory*, including the different approaches to learning theory and how they impact consumption decisions. In Chapter 6 we turn to *personality, self, and motivation* to examine how they impact consumption, as well as the interrelationships between these concepts. In Chapter 7 we consider *attitudes and behaviors*, one of the most widely used concepts in marketing. The importance of this topic is reinforced with numerous examples of how attitudes are utilized by both marketers and policy makers. Finally, in Chapter 8, we focus on *consumer decision-making*, especially the five-step consumer decision-making process, where consumers start with recognizing that they have a problem and then proceed through a series of steps to find a solution to that problem.

Consumption: a macro perspective

Part 3 can be thought of as the other bicycle wheel that is connected to the framework. It is just as important as the first wheel and also helps propel us in a forward direction. This part of the textbook represents the *macro perspective* of consumer behavior because the focus is on all of the external influences on the consumer. Here, consumer behavior is examined in a broader context, from how a consumer's patterns of behavior function as a whole within the marketplace to how that person may operate in groups and as part of a larger culture. To start, Chapter 9 is a complement to Chapter 8, in that it considers decision-making. Here, however, rather than looking at the individual, the chapter utilizes data from consumer panels to focus on the macro aspects of *patterns of behavior* for large groups of consumers. In Chapters 10 and 11 the focus is shifted to examine important group, cultural, and social influences on the consumption experience. Chapter 10 looks at the structure and processes of different *social groups* and Chapter 11 considers how *culture* shapes consumption. As with any bike, both wheels need to be strongly connected to the framework and work in coordination with one another. In the study of consumer behavior, both the micro perspective and the macro perspective need to be supported by a common framework to develop a deep understanding of the phenomenon of consumption.

Where do we go from here?

Part 4 answers the question, "Where do we go from here?" Now that all of the necessary components of the bicycle are in place, through the careful study of Parts 1–3, the bicycle is ready to go with handlebars that can steer us forward. Although Part 4 is located at the end of the book, it is important to realize that issues of ethics, social responsibility, and future trends are interwoven throughout the entire book. Part 4 is made up of two chapters and focuses on ethics, social responsibility, and a variety of future trends in consumer research. To provide a solid foundation for understanding *ethical decision-making and social responsibility*, Chapter 12 begins with an in-depth look at two ethical perspectives. Then, it identifies several trends that raise ethical questions or dilemmas, as well as some trends that are a reaction to ethical questions or dilemmas. In the final chapter, Chapter 13, a variety of future trends in consumer behavior are investigated by examining *what's trending in consumer behavior*. This chapter highlights three key trends: trends in consumer research, consumer trends, and technological trends.

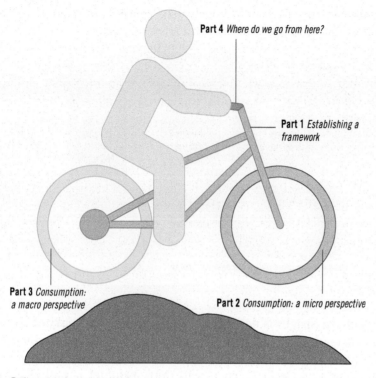

Part 4 *Where do we go from here?*

Part 1 *Establishing a framework*

Part 3 *Consumption: a macro perspective*

Part 2 *Consumption: a micro perspective*

● **Figure P.1** *How this book is organized*

Now that each component of the bicycle is in place and secured together by a sturdy framework, the last part is you, the reader, who will power the bicycle and move it forward to navigate the often bumpy landscape of creating and delivering value to consumers.

◉ The Essential Nature of Insights

This book also relies on another important analogy to help readers understand the process by which consumer research leads to insights, which then lead to a rich understanding of the phenomenon of consumer behavior. Here, it is useful to think of a building that has a strong foundation, three supporting pillars, and a roof (see Figure P.2).

To be clear, an *insight* takes the data and information that are gathered from the consumer research process and then creates an interpretation that is useful for marketing managers. Consumer researchers know that "the goal of consumer research is to generate consumer insights" (Hamilton

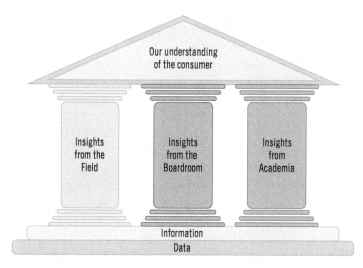

● **Figure P.2** *The three pillars of consumer insight*

2016, 282)[1]. An insight is not just a conclusion or a summary of a research finding. Instead, it represents a deeper level of understanding about the consumer's history, context, and experience. Insights are built on a deeper knowledge and understanding of who your customer is and what makes him or her tick. Importantly, an insight is actionable—it gives the marketing manager direction about what to do. Over time, the most valuable insights are those that are generated from multiple research studies. Insights are not static. They are refined and improved over time as more data and information become available.

Data and information

As depicted in Figure P.2, each of these three pillars is indispensable to our understanding of the phenomenon of consumer behavior; the roof would not be as solid or sturdy without insights from each of these three important constituents. You may notice that each pillar rests on a firm foundation of data and information. As we will discuss later in Chapter 3, *data* are the numerical and nonnumerical descriptors of a phenomenon, while *information* is data that are presented in an organized format. Both data and information are generated from research studies in consumer behavior as well as in disciplines such as psychology, sociology, public policy, anthropology, and ethics. Information builds on data, provides context, and is therefore indispensable in the development of good insights.

[1]Hamilton, R. 2016. *"Consumer-Based Strategy: Using Multiple Methods to Generate Consumer Insights That Inform Strategy."* Journal of the Academy of Marketing Science *44:281–85.*

Insights from the Field

The first type of insight is referred to as Insights from the Field. These insights are generally developed by marketing researchers or other experts. They are generated from important information about consumption trends, habits, or other consumption-related phenomena. Insights from the Field are generated, for example, when observers notice interesting patterns in how consumers respond to advertising, how they search for information, or how they incorporate products into their own lives. These insights are valuable because they are based on how consumers actually behave as they go about their lives. Within this book, a diverse set of topics for these insights include, for example, how consumer activists brought about the microbead ban, how social media is used to increase engagement in museums, how to get more men to study abroad, and how a beer company uses artificial intelligence to create the perfect-tasting beer.

Insights from the Boardroom

The second pillar that supports our understanding of consumer behavior is referred to as Insights from the Boardroom. Here, top-level executives delve into their years of experience to share their own insights about what makes consumers tick. These executives have successfully faced many marketing challenges head-on and have shared these insights with us.

Importantly, these insights come from the kind of firsthand, inside knowledge that is rarely shared with others or publicly disclosed. Executives from organizations such as the Denver Broncos, Tourism Fiji, Campbell's, McCormick, and the Philadelphia Flyers all provide their real-world interpretations and their own insights into the theories and models in each chapter.

Insights from Academia

The third pillar of insights is generated from professors and research scientists who have made it their careers to study consumer behavior. Very often, these individuals work in universities and research institutes and dedicate years or even decades to investigating just one narrow dimension of the consumer experience. The research process is complex and thorough, and a manuscript is reviewed by multiple editors and other scientists before it can be published in research journals. It is not uncommon for an academic to spend several years working on a research article before it is finally published. Insights from Academia bring some of the most recent, cutting-edge research to our understanding of consumer behavior. These research findings appear in the top consumer research journals in the field and provide a glimpse into some of the biggest concerns, important findings, and breakthrough research that is currently taking place. Importantly, these insights are located within the chapters so that they complement the material that is discussed in those sections. In addition, these insights were selected so that they are especially surprising, interesting, and relevant to a student audience. In Chapter 1, for example, we examine a research study on what motivates individuals to engage in extreme sports and other activities like Tough Mudder.

One of the important objectives of this book is to underscore the practical implications of consumer behavior theory—to make these theories and models come alive. Therefore, heavy emphasis is placed on the development of key insights for each chapter, including insights from the field, from the boardroom, and from academia. These insights are timely, relevant, and closely connected to the content in each chapter. Importantly, they demonstrate how consumer research creates data and information, which then can be used to build insights that are relevant for marketing managers.

Our understanding of the consumer

So what happens next, after the insights are created and we now have a better understanding of consumers? First, marketers are able to make more well-informed decisions about product features, pricing strategies, distribution, and communications. Marketers and consumers both reap benefits when products and services are better able to satisfy the needs and wants of consumers. Second, when well-crafted insights lead to a better understanding of consumer behavior, there are benefits to other stakeholders, such as consumer rights advocates, nonprofit organizations, and public policy officials. These stakeholders can use their better understanding to assist in their efforts to lessen the chances of consumers being cheated, deceived, or otherwise exploited. When these unfortunate events do happen, this better understanding of consumer behavior may help ensure that those who are responsible will be brought to justice. Finally, a better understanding of consumer behavior helps *all* consumers better navigate their own role as consumers.

Guided Tour Of The Book

◉ Identifying and Defining

Learning objectives

At the start of each chapter, learning objectives are provided to help students follow the material and navigate their way through the chapter. Chapter concepts, examples, and insights tie back into the leaning objectives, which are then revisited in the chapter summaries.

Glossary of key terms

Each key term is defined and thoroughly described within the chapters, and a comprehensive glossary of key terms is provided at the end of the book. A quick look at the glossary can refresh a student's understanding and comprehension of key terms.

◉ Consumer Behavior in Practice

Insights from the Field

Every chapter contains several Insights from the Field that explore a wide variety of issues, such as online social networking platforms, the benefits to the brain of being bilingual, and chief executive officers behaving badly. These insights can be thought of as mini cases. Such well-known companies and organizations as LEGO, Coca-Cola, Pez, and Chipotle are included. Importantly, these insights focus on fascinating characteristics of consumers, decision-making tendencies, or behavioral patterns of consumers. These insights help illustrate how consumer behavior theories and models are utilized by marketers and, consequently, help students better connect to the material.

Case studies

At the end of each chapter, a case study provides additional depth and understanding of the concepts that are discussed in each chapter. A wide variety of organizations and topics are highlighted, such as sneakerheads and their quest for the rarest sneakers, TerraCycle and its mission to reduce "the idea" of waste, Google Glass and its successful targeting of a new market, and the privacy concerns associated with companies such as AncestryDNA. Each of these case studies brings together the themes discussed in the chapter and helps students connect with the material at a deeper level.

👁 Application of Understanding

Insights from the Boardroom

The real-life experiences and insights from marketing executives help illustrate how they have faced a variety of marketing challenges. These insights focus on aspects of consumer behavior that are closely tied to the chapter content. Topics range from neuroimaging and fan engagement to the use of search experience optimization. These insights help build an understanding about how consumer behavior theories and models shape the decisions that are made by some of the top marketing decision-makers in the early twenty-first century.

Review questions

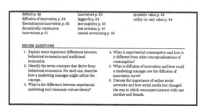

Each chapter concludes with a set of review questions to test the student's knowledge of the chapter's key concepts. These questions are invaluable in helping to clarify the chapter's most important concepts, theories, and models.

👁 Stretching and Expanding

Insights from Academia

Each chapter also includes several Insights from Academia, which coincide with the chapter topics and highlight some of the latest research findings on those topics. The research studies utilize a variety of methodologies, and the insights that are derived from these projects stretch and expand student understanding of the theories and models by applying this understanding to their own lives or to the work of marketing managers. For example, did you know that it's a bad idea to go shopping after a scary movie? How about the fact that the color blue is perceived as more "green" than the color green? Did you know that the royal family can be seen as a brand? Read these research insights to find out how and why.

Discussion questions

At the conclusion of each chapter, a set of discussion questions is provided to help students dive into the chapter topics more deeply and hone their analytical and reasoning skills by wrestling with these challenging questions. These discussion questions are a great resource for initiating thought-provoking in-class discussions and expanding further study.

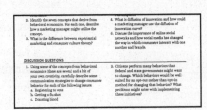

Teaching and Learning Tools

Oxford Learning Link

www.oup.com/he/phillips

This site is your central hub for a wealth of engaging digital teaching and learning tools. For self-study, students can access chapter-level study tools like PowerPoint Slides, Flashcards, Key Terms Quizzes, Chapter Quizzes and Exams, Videos, Web Activities and Web Links. Instructors will find an Instructor's Manual, Test Bank, Art and Lecture PowerPoint Slides, and course cartridges for use within many popular learning management systems.

Format Choices

Oxford University Press offers cost-saving alternatives to meet the needs of all students. This text is offered in ebook format through Redshelf and VitalSource and in a loose-leaf format at a 30 percent discount off the list price of the text. You can also customize our textbooks to create the course materials you want for your class. For more information, please contact your Oxford University Press representative or call 800.280.0280.

Acknowledgments

◉ Author's Acknowledgments

Diane M. Phillips would like to thank the executives who took valuable time out of their demanding schedules to share their insights with the next generation of marketing decision-makers: Jen Drexler (Connects the Dots), Josefa Wivou (Tourism Fiji), Joan Hoenninger (Wawa), Alice Ping (Campbell's), Adriane Randolph, PhD (nurltec), Anne Ryan (the Brownstein Group), Marta Insua (Alma), Cindy Stutman (the Philadelphia Flyers), Dennis Moore (the Denver Broncos), Andrew Speyer (Airbnb), A. Bruce Crawley (Millennium 3 Management), Bill Simon (McCormick), and Ryan Wall (Idea Evolver).

The author would like to thank the team at Oxford University Press for its support and guidance throughout the entire development and editorial process. In particular, Jennifer Carpenter and Ishan Desai-Geller deserve sincere, heartfelt thanks for their expertise and talent in guiding her through the entire process. Special thanks also go out to Caitlyn Phillips, Stephanie Hammond, and Jillian Bodemer for their assistance in developing the supplements for this text.

Diane M. Phillips would like to thank her students and colleagues at Saint Joseph's University, as well as the university itself for providing her a well-timed sabbatical leave to finish the book. She would also like to thank numerous friends, family, and colleagues for their interest, enthusiasm, and support of this project. Finally, and most important, the author would like to thank her husband for his unwavering support and faith in the process, and daughter for her excitement and encouragement throughout the many months of research and writing. You both inspire me.

The following reviewers gave generously of their time and expertise:

Ebru Ulusoy Akgun, Farmingdale State College
Kelly Atkins, East Tennessee State University
Lee Boggs, West Virginia University
Shaheen Borna, Ball State University
Monica Dee Guillory, Winston-Salem State University
Stephen Hersh, Northwestern University
Rika Houston, California State University—Los Angeles
Hwa-young (Ysabella) Lee, University of Ottawa
Chrissy Mitakakis Martins, Iona College

John M. McGrath, University of Pittsburgh—Johnstown
Deirdre T. Guion Peoples, North Carolina Central University
Linda Tuncay Zayer, Loyola University Chicago

◉ Publisher's Acknowledgments

The publisher would like to thank the practitioners and professionals who gave their time to provide us with an insight into how consumer behavior theories play an important role in the real world.

The publisher would also like to thank the very long list of people who kindly granted permission and supplied the images to illustrate this textbook.

Every effort has been made to contact copyright holders, but in some instances this was not possible. We will be pleased to clear permission with any copyright holders we were unable to contact in the first instance.

About the Author

Diane M. Phillips, PhD, is a professor of marketing at Saint Joseph's University in Philadelphia. Dr. Phillips is also a Guest Professor at the Institute for Retail Management at the University of St. Gallen, Switzerland. She received her PhD from Penn State University and focuses her research in the broad area of consumer psychology. More specifically, she examines consumer attitudes, satisfaction, emotional responses, and consumer decision-making. Her research has been presented at a variety of international conferences and published in a variety of international publications. She is a frequent speaker at national and international conferences, civic organizations, businesses, and universities. Each semester, Dr. Phillips teaches several classes at the graduate and undergraduate levels and frequently leads international study tour trips with her students.

consumer behavior & insights

Historical Perspectives on Consumption

◉ Introduction

If you think about it, most of our day is spent consuming something or making decisions about what to consume and how to consume. From the time we first open our eyes in the morning to the time we go to sleep at night, we are consuming something. We get up, wash, dress, and get ready to start our day. This involves many consumption behaviors: using soap, shampoo, toothpaste, and clothing. The first few minutes of our morning routine also involve many decisions: Eggs or cereal for breakfast? Which jacket to wear? Is it a good idea to bring an umbrella? Should I bring my laptop? In just the first hour of every day, most consumers make a series of consumption-related decisions and enact a large number of consumption-related behaviors without really thinking about it. The rest of the day will also revolve around consumption decisions and behaviors, right up until we rest our heads on a pillow and call it a night—consumer behavior is a critical part of our lives.

Who needs to understand consumer behavior? Marketing practitioners need to know about it so that they can create better ways to meet the needs and expectations of consumers. Policy makers need to know about consumer behavior so that they can develop programs and policies to protect consumers and encourage certain behaviors. Finally, *we all* need to know more about consumer behavior. If we are better informed about our own decision-making tendencies as well as how we are impacted by cultural and other environmental forces, we will make decisions that are better for ourselves, our families, and society.

Consumption occurs when individuals or groups acquire, use, and dispose of products, services, ideas, or experiences (Arnould, Price, and Zinkhan 2004). An important point here is that consumption is not just about consuming a product, like a Coke or a new pair of Nikes. Consumption also includes *services*, like the dentist or your college education. It includes *ideas*, like "don't drink and drive" and "remember to get your flu shot." It includes *people*, such as a celebrity or a certain political candidate. It also includes *places*, like Disney World or the new restaurant

Consumption occurs when individuals or groups acquire, use, and dispose of products, services, ideas, or experiences.

Consumer behavior is a field of study that examines the behaviors of consumers, as well as the motivations behind those behaviors.

Psychology is the "scientific study of the behavior of individuals and their mental processes" (American Psychological Association 2017).

Sociology is a field of study that examines all the external influences on a consumer, such as social class, gender, and family.

in town. Finally, it includes *experiences*, like a study tour trip or a concert. Because consumption is such an important part of our daily lives, we must understand its foundations to better understand all its influences.

Consumer behavior is certainly about the *behavior* we can easily see consumers perform. However, it is about so much more than that. Consumer behavior is also about the different motivational forces that are behind those behaviors. Have you ever wondered why people do different things? For example, have you ever wondered why your friend got that new tattoo? Have you ever wondered why someone would want to go skydiving? How about learning a new language or standing in line for twelve hours to get the new iPhone? Have you ever wondered why *you* just bought that new jacket or pair of jeans? Have you ever wondered why you just wasted the whole day binge-watching Netflix? The study of consumer behavior will help us develop a better understanding of all these things by giving us frameworks and models for understanding many of the consumption choices we make.

The study of consumer behavior is based in large part on principles of psychology and sociology. Psychology is an area of study that deals with the internal workings of the human mind. According to the American Psychological Association, an organization that was founded in 1892 to promote the understanding of psychology in everyday lives, **psychology** is the "scientific study of the behavior of individuals and their mental processes" (American Psychological Association 2017). Principles of psychology can be utilized in a variety of contexts, including human health, child and family studies, sports, media, and law. Here, we will rely on principles of psychology to help inform us about how individuals process information, make decisions, and behave. Consumer behavior also taps into a wealth of knowledge from the discipline of sociology. The American Sociological Association was founded in 1905 and works with researchers and professionals to promote continued research and the application of that research to help society. The discipline of **sociology** examines the external influences on individuals and includes a myriad of topics such as gender, race, aging, social class, and family dynamics. It then applies those findings to better understand the reaction of a person or a social group to, for example, climate change, public health issues, politics, and the workplace (American Sociological Association 2017). For our purposes, we will use principles of sociology to understand how these external influences might impact a variety of consumer decisions. Psychology and sociology are not the only disciplines from which consumer behavior pulls important concepts. Consumer behavior also taps into the collective wisdom of research in a variety of disciplines such as economics, anthropology, and biology. As you can see, consumer behavior is a complex and dynamic discipline. This book will give you an appreciation for how a better understanding of consumer behavior can shape a variety of business and marketing decisions. Further, this book will also help you appreciate how consumer behavior is an important part of *your* day-to-day life.

◉ Before We Get Started

Why are we studying consumer behavior and not buyer behavior? It is easy to study buyer behavior. Researchers can look at sales receipts and easily determine what consumers are purchasing. They can see how effective coupons are by looking at coupon redemption rates, they can see how effective online ads are by looking at click-through rates, and they can assess how effective new product features are by looking at how many people try or even adopt new products. In short, it is easy to determine what people *do*. This is **buyer behavior**.

Unfortunately, it is not always easy to see *why* consumers do the things they do. Consider someone who is buying a new pair of Nikes. If we just studied buyer behavior, we would know nothing more than what they bought, where and when they bought it, and how much they paid for it. The problem is that, while this information is useful in telling us what has already happened, it is not very useful in helping marketers predict what consumers may do next. Buyer behavior tells us nothing about the underlying motivations of the consumer when purchasing the shoes. Perhaps the consumer wanted to purchase the shoes because of a desire to get fit. Maybe the consumer saw the shoes as a fashion statement. Alternatively, the consumer may have purchased the shoes as a backup because his or her favorite brand was out of stock. As you can imagine, each of these motivations tells us something different about the reasons behind consumer decision-making, and that is why we focus our efforts here on understanding consumer behavior rather than buyer behavior. A careful study of consumer behavior will help marketers understand why consumers do what they do. This, in turn, will help us predict what they may do next so that marketers can create better products and services to meet their needs. It will also help marketers design better pricing, distribution, and promotional strategies.

Similarly, we focus our efforts on consumer behavior much more than we do on customer behavior. **Consumers** are the individuals who actually consume a product, while **customers** are the ones who buy the product. Consider a common scenario in many American households: a daughter asks her dad to buy her a new Nokona softball glove because she is moving up to the school's varsity softball team. In this situation, the consumer is the girl who is going to use the glove to make fantastic plays on the field and the customer is the dad because he is the one who is buying the new glove. Admittedly, it is important to understand the motivations of both. The dad certainly needs to share his own expertise in picking the best option for his rising softball star. However, in

Buyer behavior (also behavioral research) is a field of study that examines what consumers do. It does not account for the underlying motivations for those behaviors.

Consumers are individuals who use a product.

Customers are individuals who purchase a product.

this scenario, what we really want to know (because it will help us predict what the daughter may do next) is *why* she wants this particular glove. Does she like the glove because of its performance and reputation? Because all of her friends also have this glove? Is it because of the celebrity spokesperson in the new ad campaign? In the end, our main goal is to predict what consumers will do next, and that is why we study *consumer behavior*.

In the beginning: early consumption practices

To gain a solid appreciation of consumer behavior, it is important to first look to the past to understand how people thought about and practiced consumption and to think about how this has influenced the ways we consume in the early twenty-first century. Indeed, individuals have traded and exchanged things since the beginning of time. More organized trading routes, along with a variety of trade customs and rules, became established in some of the earliest great civilizations. The Spice Route was an incredibly complex network of roads and shipping lanes that connected China and countries in the East, through India and the Middle East, to different cultures and consumers in the West. As early as 2000 BCE, spices such as cinnamon from Sri Lanka were being traded to ports and markets all along the route. Soon, other items were being traded, like metals, ivory, gems, and other "special" items. Indeed, the word *spice* originates from the Latin *species*, which refers to an item of particular or "special" value (UNESCO 2017). Ancient Rome was an important port along the Spice Route and had a thriving economy, with producers making a variety of products that were exchanged with other producers thousands of miles away (see Photo 1.1).

● **Photo 1.1** *Shopping in Ancient Rome*

Salt was another one of the early products that was traded along the Spice Route. Because of its ability to preserve food, salt was worth the same per ounce as gold, and many workers were paid in bags of salt for their labor. Indeed, *salary* is derived from the word for salt, and the common saying that someone is "not worth their salt" derived from these early Roman days when workers had their salaries of salt cut if they did not put in a full day of hard labor (TIME Staff 1982). In addition to products moving along the Spice Route, information and knowledge were also passed along (UNESCO 2017). Traders exchanged information with one another on the latest news about politics, war, and new discoveries.

The concept of exchange remains just as important in understanding consumer behavior in the early twenty-first century. **Exchange** happens when one entity gives up something to get something from another entity. Most of the time in marketing, we talk about giving up money for a product or service. Thus, for example, consumers give up $1,000 in exchange for a new iPhone. However, there are also other kinds of exchange. Consumers could give up their time and attention in exchange for the information and perhaps entertainment of a new television advertisement, for example. Remember that each party gives up something and gets something. In an increasingly popular situation where two people barter services and/or products, one person could provide lawn care services, for example, in exchange for some help with dog-sitting. In the United States in the year 2020, there were over 1,100 websites offering extensive networks of individuals with products and services to barter. Customers benefit because they save money. Some even use a type of currency called *barter bucks* to make the exchanges easier (Burton 2015). Bartering, however, is not new. Even though money was widely available at the time, bartering and sharing were common practices up through the Middle Ages.

> **Exchange** is the process of giving up something of value and getting something of value in return.

However, once people started to produce products not just for their own use, but also for others to buy and consume, the idea of consumption took an important step forward. There was now a relationship between the producers who manufactured, raised, or supplied the products and the consumers who consumed those products. Producers learned what consumers wanted or needed and began to specifically make products and create services that addressed those needs and wants. For their part, when consumers saw value in these products and services, they exchanged currency for them. Exchange was thus made a lot easier for both producers and consumers when money could be used to facilitate the process.

It is not an exaggeration to say that consumption has been inextricably connected to the growth and development of human civilization. The development of global trading routes and the movement of products along those routes has played an important role in how cultures have developed and evolved over the millennia. Products such as sugar and tobacco started to be consumed in Europe after early trading routes with the New World opened up in the seventeenth century. It was Christopher Columbus who introduced sugar to Europe in 1493, setting the stage for the development of vast sugar plantations in the southern states. Columbus also brought tobacco to Europe and described it as having medicinal qualities. In one of the first early descriptions of smoking, he wrote that the natives "drank smoke" (Penn 1901). Back in Europe, to keep up appearances, many in the upper class started to consume these and other new products. At the same time, a middle class began to emerge, made up of individuals who had enough extra money to afford some small luxuries of their own.

For those lucky enough to be in the highest echelons of society, very important consumption rules dictated the kinds of products that were required and the ways in which these products were consumed. Many of the rules were based on a shared understanding of what these items represented or meant to other people. Those who frequented the English court of Queen Elizabeth I, who ruled from 1558 to 1603, would see a monarch who was impeccably dressed by a team of women in order to solidify her image as a virgin queen. Each color, cut of fabric, styling flair, and piece of jewelry were carefully selected to convey important meaning to the members of the court, foreign dignitaries, and her citizens (Howey 2009). Even if you weren't the monarch, you still had to follow strict rules regarding dress and consumption. If you happened to be a fashion-forward young man living in sixteenth-century England, for example, you could never be caught in public without your small sword or dagger (MacGregor 2012). For centuries, most royal courts throughout the world had very strict sets of rules for behavior and dress, and to maintain the favor of the court, individuals were required to spend vast sums of money buying and displaying their purchases (see Photo 1.2). By the eighteenth century, consumption of what were previously considered luxury goods, such as tea and coffee, was much more widespread (McCants 2007). Consumption of all sorts of products increased dramatically among the middle class and provided a key stimulant to the Industrial Revolution and therefore, arguably, the rise of contemporary mass consumerism. The **Industrial Revolution** occurred in the early nineteenth century in the United States and coincided with innovations in fuel, transportation, and technology. During this time, large numbers of workers shifted their efforts from working on farms to working in factories. Factories and transportation systems started to be powered by coal and steam, allowing for mass production and easy transportation to urban centers. In most industrialized economies, a well-established middle class regularly purchased a growing quantity of consumer goods (Loftus 2011).

As individuals started to consume at higher rates, some observers launched criticisms about consumption and its associated problems. Throughout the centuries, critics of consumerism have focused their ire on a variety of consumption-related

Industrial Revolution refers to the period when the economy transitioned from agriculture to manufacturing. Experts generally agree that this transition happened in the late 1700s and early 1800s in the United States.

● **Photo 1.2** *Portrait of Queen Elizabeth I*

attitudes and behaviors. Most recently, distaste in the ills associated with modern consumerism has resulted in anticonsumption movements and lifestyles, such as the voluntary simplicity movement. Over the centuries, some of these anticonsumption sentiments have been codified into anticonsumption laws. One such set of laws that date back to some of the earliest cultures are referred to as **sumptuary laws**, which are designed to "regulate expenditure, especially with a view to restraining excess in food, dress, equipage, etc." (Oxford English Dictionary 2013). Sumptuary laws exist across many periods in human history and in a variety of cultures around the world. They seek to regulate citizens' expenditures and discourage conspicuous consumption. Some of history's earliest sumptuary laws date back to the Qin dynasty in China (221 BCE) and the early Roman Empire. In medieval Europe, sumptuary laws helped individuals signify the social class to which they belonged. These rules codified into law which clothing or accessories were allowed to be worn by individuals of different social classes and reinforced a social hierarchy that was understood by all. For example, aristocratic women in fourteenth-century Italy were restricted from wearing low necklines and jeweled sable furs (Killerby 2002), knights in fifteenth-century England were prohibited from wearing any gold or ermine fur on their armor (Berry 1994), and *no one* in sixteenth-century England was permitted to wear purple unless he or she was a member of the monarchy (Hayward 2009). While some of these laws might seem silly now, sumptuary laws were created, in part, because of a concern about the role that consumption should play in the lives of consumers. These concerns are still quite relevant. Although some consumers may engage in excessive, wasteful, or conspicuous consumption, others are much more mindful of their consumption behaviors. These more mindful consumers might consider, for example, how their consumption choices impact the workers who labor to manufacture their products or the health of the planet. They might also be concerned about the impacts of their consumption choices on their own well-being and that of their families. As consumption has evolved throughout time and across cultures, we notice one thing that is constant: the ever-present tug-of-war between what are believed to be appropriate and inappropriate ways to consume. The following section introduces several philosophers and economists who have been pivotal to our understanding of humankind's relationship with and understanding of consumption.

> **Sumptuary laws** are laws that attempt to control and regulate permitted consumption activities.

Developing an understanding of consumption

In 1776, while Americans were declaring their independence and fighting for freedom on one side of the Atlantic, Scottish philosopher and economist Adam Smith was on the other side of the Atlantic thinking about the topic of consumption. He believed that consumption played an important role in the economy, the process of production, and the creation of a democratic political system. His book, *The Wealth of Nations*, described these processes and relationships and has been pivotal to our understanding of the modern consumer (Kroen 2004). In the late eighteenth century, most economists focused their efforts on finding more efficient methods of production. Smith, however, noticed important connections between the production and consumption of products, writing that "consumption is the sole end and purpose of all production; and the interest of the producer ought to be attended to, only in so far as it may be necessary for promoting that of the consumer" (A. Smith [1776] 1981, 660). Because of these new insights, Smith became concerned about social justice and the equitable distribution of wealth. One area of particular concern to Smith was the welfare of workers, who may have few opportunities because of physical needs, no education, and limited access to resources. In *The Wealth of Nations*, Smith discussed the risks of concentrating wealth among an elite class and promoted the idea of a more equalized distribution of wealth among a nation's citizens. His work led him to the conclusion that consumption could promote economic growth. However, too much consumption or consumption of frivolous or luxury products should only be encouraged to prevent economic stagnation (A. Smith [1776] 1981).

A few decades later, British economist and philosopher John Stuart Mill also studied the connection between production and consumption, with a particular focus on luxury consumption. He thought that this type of *unproductive* consumption by anyone in a society ended up hurting the working class (Mill [1848] 2004). As a solution to luxury consumption, Mill proposed that all citizens in a society should be *productive consumers* and consume products that helped individuals in the working class, who would then have the means to purchase products and improve their own conditions. The topic of luxury consumption can still provoke debate. Luxury brands and popular brands are certainly not necessary for a consumer's well-being, but they do help consumers gain access to and fit in with different social groups (Elliott and Leonard 2004).

By the nineteenth century, our understanding of consumption had shifted again. German philosopher and economist Karl Marx focused much of his effort on trying to understand social class and the plight of workers, who had to labor to produce products for other people's consumption (Marx [1867] 2000). As workers moved away from their homes to work in factories in the cities, they were often exploited because wealthy factory owners had complete control over their working conditions and wages. The situation is not all that different for early twenty-first century workers in developing countries, who work long hours in difficult conditions for low wages just to make products for consumers in the developed world.

Marx theorized that once a product was manufactured in great quantities and distributed widely, consumers no longer recognized or cared about the methods or purpose of production. Marx referred to this change of perception as the **fetishism of commodities** (Marx [1876] 1976), which is "the disguising or masking of commodities whereby the appearance of goods hides the story of those who made them and how they made them" (Lury 1999, 42). **Commodity products** are those items that are mass-produced and are not distinctly different from one another. For example, most of us see gasoline as a

Fetishism of commodities refers to the domination of objects or things in the market and relates to the idea of masking the human activity that is critical to, and lies behind, the production of consumer goods and services.

Commodity products are those products that are mass-produced and are not distinctly different from one another.

commodity product because, regardless of which brand you use to fill up your car, one brand is not distinctly different from another. The important point here is that when products are mass-produced, there is very little connection between the producer and the consumer.

Philosophers and economists refined their understanding of consumption even further as a result of the First World War, which forced consumers in many countries to ration, or severely cut back on, their consumption. Basic necessities were scarce and people wanted to support their countries in the war effort. In addition, governments stepped in and instituted wage restraints, tariffs, and *buy national* campaigns (de Grazia 2005). By the 1920s, the war was over and British economist John Maynard Keynes theorized that if the wages of workers were increased, the economy would flourish. He believed that when an economy experienced a downturn and factories laid off workers, the whole economy was at risk of a downward spiral. Since workers could no longer bring home a paycheck, they would cut back on their spending. Consequently, local restaurants, appliance stores, and clothing stores, for example, would have fewer customers and they would suffer too, perhaps even laying off workers. This downward spiral could be far-reaching and long-lasting. Keynes referred to the connection between consumer purchasing power and the strength of the economy as the **consumption function**.

This consumption function demonstrated that, compared to other members in a society, wealthy individuals consumed relatively less. Think about it. No matter how wealthy a person is, he or she still is likely to only need one stove, one refrigerator, etc., for his or her house. So, rather than giving tax breaks to the rich, it made better sense to distribute the wealth of a country among the people, so that many people are purchasing stoves, refrigerators, and a host of other things for their homes. The overall economy will perform better when more money is in the hands of working people. To prevent a downward economic spiral when a factory must lay off workers, Keynes recommended that the best way to get the economy moving again was government intervention. So, for example, it made sense to have the government invest in projects to build new roads or bridges. This way, the workers on these projects would have money in their pockets and would then spend that money at restaurants, appliance stores, and clothing stores. The people who worked at these stores, in turn, would be employed and make money, which they, in turn, could also spend in the local economy. This continuing spending and respending of money would improve and grow an economy (Keynes 1964).

Revolutionary advancements in consumption

As our understanding of the relationship between production and consumption was continuing to evolve, another development was happening in parallel to these advancements: the Industrial Revolution. Products were manufactured more efficiently and prices dropped, making more consumer products accessible to more consumers. In addition, sophisticated marketing strategies began to develop.

Consumption function maps the relationship between disposable income and level of wages.

As we have already learned, before the Industrial Revolution, most production and consumption were small-scale and local, and a great deal of buying and selling took place at outdoor markets that were set up in village squares or other centralized locations. By the seventeenth and eighteenth centuries, stand-alone shops and storefronts started to appear (see Photo 1.3) (see Table 1.1). As these new retail stores started to thrive, our understanding of marketing started to develop too. Shop owners realized that they could entice customers with interesting window displays, colorful signs, and advertising in local publications.

Advancements in manufacturing and automation, as well as expansion of global trade, meant that by the late 1800s, consumers had an increasing array of choices. Consumers were buying more and with greater regularity. To keep consumers buying on a regular basis, marketers introduced new fashions in clothing and home decor, new options in personal care, and new advancements in technology. For urban consumers, department stores started to emerge in downtown areas, while for rural consumers, mail-order companies delivered a wide range of products. Indeed, the Sears catalog, dating back to 1888, provided customers around the country a way to purchase a wide variety of products in the latest styles at guaranteed low prices (Sears Archives 2017).

The Industrial Revolution also ushered in a wide range of innovations in technology that influenced the kinds of products that were produced and the ways in which consumers shopped. Researchers and engineers created new innovations in materials such as plastic, rayon, nylon, and viscose, which, in turn, inspired product designers. Innovations in transportation also changed the way we consumed and shopped by introducing an array of new and sometimes exotic options to consumers. At the same time, household appliances and electronic devices multiplied, revolutionizing even the most mundane household chores and tasks (see Insights from the Field 1.1). Perhaps one of the most important innovations has been the high-powered interconnectivity of electronic devices that has resulted in consumers being continuously connected to one another and to the global marketplace. For all the good that social media has done, new research has found that this constant connection is not always positive. For example, in a survey of eighteen- to twenty-nine-year-olds, 42 percent of those in a serious relationship say their partner has been distracted by his or her phone while they were together,

● **Photo 1.3** *Levi Strauss advertisement from the 1880s*

Table 1.1 Oldest retail stores in the United States

ESTABLISHED	STORE NAME	SPECIALTY
1818	Brooks Brothers*	Men's clothing
1826	Lord & Taylor	High-end department store
1851	Kiehl's	Luxury skin care products
1858	Macy's	High-end department store
1861	Bloomingdale's	High-end department store
1867	Saks Fifth Avenue	High-end department store
1872	Von Maur	High-end department store
1873	Barnes & Noble	Books
1885	Havertys Furniture	Furniture
1886	Sears	General merchandise department store

Source: Skorupa (2008).

* After years of faltering sales, Brooks Brothers declared bankruptcy in 2020, citing the economic slowdown caused by the global coronavirus pandemic (Maheshwari and Friedman 2020).

18 percent have argued with a partner about the time one of them spent online, and 8 percent say they have been upset by something his or her partner was doing online (Lenhart and Duggan 2014).

Important innovations in materials, technology, and transportation have resulted in products that better meet the needs of consumers. They have also resulted in **planned obsolescence**, the situation where a product is designed to have a limited life span, and therefore consumers are forced to replace the product on a regular basis. Planned obsolescence means that the manufacturer of the product "plans" for the product to break or become obsolete because of a variety of factors, such as unavailable software updates or parts. The idea is that the product should last just long enough to keep a customer happy, but should not last "too long." **Perceived obsolescence** is different, but the outcome is the same: to get customers to replace their products more quickly. Here, products are "believed" to be out of date because of changes in style or design. Cars, clothing, and electronics manufacturers are especially guilty of this. Manufacturers change the color, cut, or styling of the product every few months to motivate consumers to replace the product because it is out of date. Many consumers are more than happy to comply; compared to previous generations, modern consumers regularly update their clothing, phones, and household decor as soon as they seem out of style.

Planned obsolescence happens when products are designed to break down or become out of date before they should.

Perceived obsolescence happens when a product goes out of date because of its fashion or style.

INSIGHTS FROM THE FIELD 1.1

A revolution in the kitchen

Let's face it: with school, work, and family, quick and easy meals are just a part of modern-day life. A truly revolutionary innovation occurred in the 1920s in the American kitchen when frozen foods were introduced in the United States. At the same time, consumers started to have small refrigerators in their homes, and transportation systems and grocery stores developed such that frozen food could be kept cold when it was shipped and displayed for sale (Rhodes 2012). These innovations meant that families could easily store food for a longer period of time. They could also try a greater variety of food and were not limited to eating only food that was in season. Another consequence of this was that women no longer had to spend hours each day shopping and cooking meals for the family. Instead, they could pursue other interests and work outside the home.

By the 1980s, convenience foods were being used all around the world, including India, where Maggi brand instant noodles made cooking easy for busy mothers, as well as fun for children. Innovations such as the microwave meant that meals could be heated quickly, and different members of the family could easily cook their meals at any time of the day. By 2017, 70.5 percent of American mothers and 92.8 percent of

American fathers worked outside the home (US Bureau of Labor Statistics 2017), which meant that the job of preparing meals was everyone's responsibility. At the same time, convenience foods became fresher and more nutritious. Simply look at the success of Blue Apron, one of several delivery services that provides boxes of fresh ingredients in the correct measurements and proportions to make it as easy as possible for anyone in the family to cook a healthy and nutritious meal. Blue Apron promises an efficient and environmentally friendly food delivery system (Blue Apron 2019). Its success is apparent: Blue Apron sells over eight million meal kits per month, employs four thousand workers, and is worth over $1 billion (Kell 2016).

Questions

1. Are convenience foods good or bad for the modern American family? Why? Support your answer with evidence from the text and elsewhere.
2. Take a look at the *slow food movement*. Why do you think this movement is happening? What is the main benefit for consumers?

Sources: Kell (2016); Rhodes (2012); US Bureau of Labor Statistics (2017); Blue Apron (2019).

Too much consumption?

Conspicuous consumption is a pattern of consumer behaviors where products are utilized by some consumers as a way to compete in the social sphere and gain social recognition.

In his book *Theory of the Leisure Class*, the American economist Thorstein Veblen introduced the concept of **conspicuous consumption**, which theorized that products were utilized by some consumers as a way to compete in the social sphere and gain social recognition (Veblen [1899] 2007). Veblen focused his research on the consumer behaviors of the very wealthy and how they compared themselves to their social groups through the purchase of extravagant items such as artwork, mansions, and other goods. Within this leisure class of consumers, certain products signified social status and individual value. One sure-fire way to solidify an individual's social status and value was to be extravagant and wasteful, paying large sums for clothes

INSIGHTS FROM THE FIELD 1.2

Status and consuming

In our modern consumer culture with constant communication with our social networks, it is becoming more important to consume products and brands that are socially acceptable and even admired within our networks. One thing that is especially important is the unique or specialized knowledge some people have about certain products, brands, or events. In the context of consumption, the **statusphere** refers to the process by which consumers communicate their specialized consumption knowledge or expertise to one another to attain status within their social group. For example, a consumer could talk up their ecofriendly consumption credentials, their specialized knowledge of the latest bands, or other product-related knowledge and skills. Demonstrating unique knowledge and skills helps the consumer gain recognition and admiration among others in the social group.

Services can also help consumers demonstrate status, such as when a consumer embarks on a once-in-a-lifetime trip around the world. Posting about the trip establishes status, as does displaying a special purchase from the trip, like a hand-carved wooden bowl or a hand-woven scarf (see Photo 1.4). In the early twenty-first century, apps help to facilitate the statusphere process. Users of Songkick, for example, can find where their favorite bands are performing, track up-and-coming artists, and connect to social media via Spotify and Facebook. Street Art Cities is an app that helps tourists and art lovers find the best examples of graffiti and murals in cities around the world. Then, once consumers engage in these experiences, they pass on their newfound knowledge to their social networks.

● **Photo 1.4** *A special purchase from a trip to Nepal*

Questions

1. It is easy to think about products that communicate status, but how about services? In what ways might consumers use a service to signify status to others? In what ways might it be more difficult to communicate status with the consumption of a service, as opposed to a product?

2. Some consumers might use *not* consuming as a status symbol. How might a marketer interact with one of these consumers compared to a consumer who does choose to use products as status symbols?

Sources: Veblen ([1899] 2007); Trend Reports (2010).

that were rarely worn or food that was not consumed (Veblen [1899] 2007). Concerns about conspicuous consumption are still relevant. Some of the most desperately poor countries in the world are understandably dismayed at the consumption patterns in more developed countries. For developing countries, such as many of those in South America, Asia, Africa, and eastern Europe,

Statusphere refers to the process by which consumers communicate their specialized consumption knowledge or expertise to one another in order to attain status within their social group.

consumers are playing a bit of a catch-up game with their consumption behaviors to access products and enjoy the same kinds of consumption experiences as those in the developed world. It is not surprising that these new consumers become angry at any criticism of their consumption habits, especially when it is directed at them from people in developed countries who have been overconsuming for so long.

The evolution of the shopping experience

Stand-alone shops in city and town centers were common by the mid-1800s, but a new innovation occurred when department stores and shopping malls were introduced. These stores offered one-stop shopping for consumers who could examine a variety of products all under one roof. Importantly, shoppers could also examine a variety of products that they were not necessarily considering, but just might be interested in seeing. Photo 1.5 shows an advertisement encouraging holiday shoppers to visit the John Barker department store, where they could, presumably, get all of their shopping done in one place. From the consumer's perspective, this new format provided more choices and more convenience. The rise of suburban shopping malls, with their climate-controlled, music-infused, artificial settings, was the next big development in the consumer experience and shopping. The first suburban, fully enclosed mall in the United States opened in 1956 and was called Southdale Center.

● **Photo 1.5** *1898 ad for the John Barker department store*

Located outside Minneapolis, the mall allowed customers to park their cars outside and then walk in comfort and ease from shop to shop without having to brave the cold Minnesota winters. Advertisements for the mall promised an "eternal spring" for the very appreciative winter-weary shoppers (Marshall 2015). Unfortunately, with the explosion of online shopping and free delivery, shopping malls may now be a thing of the past. Experts estimate that by 2022, one quarter of America's malls will close (Sanburn 2017).

The rise of the empowered shopper

As the department store and shopping mall concept started to gain popularity with customers, they began to pop up all around the world. One of the most important characteristics of this new format was the anonymity of the shopper. In earlier generations, customers were well known to the shop owners; shop owners and assistants greeted their customers and helped them make their purchases. In department stores and malls, customers selected their own items and only rarely interacted with shop assistants; customers never interacted with the department store owners.

Grocery stores are the food equivalent of department stores. Customers continued to be anonymous, have a wide variety of choices, and make their own selections without help. This new concept of food shopping first made its appearance in the 1930s in the United States. In a way that is very similar to department stores, customers were tempted to consider other products that they may not have planned to buy. Shoppers could browse a variety of different packages and check the ingredients and labels of those products without the pressure of a salesperson hovering close by. Interesting point-of-sale displays and well-designed packaging caught the eye of customers, and oversized shopping carts encouraged unplanned impulse purchases.

Over the decades, consumers started to change their attitudes about the role that shopping played in their lives. In the past, consumers would *do the shopping*, which was a "necessary task" and involved purchasing specific products that were, more than likely, on a list. By 2000, consumers *went shopping*, which was much more leisurely, "open-ended," and "a diversion" (Bowlby 2000). This shift in the role of the consumer in the shopping experience meant that shopping could often be considered a leisure activity, rather than a chore. This anonymity of the customer has continued with online and mobile shopping.

Downtown shops, farmers' markets, consignment shops, shopping malls, art studios, department stores, convenience stores, supermarkets, and of

● **Photo 1.6** *Roadside stand in rural Panama*

Consumers can buy some surprising things from vending machines

In an increasingly busy world where consumers have very little time for shopping, the vending machine can help make life a little easier. Most people don't know that the earliest recorded vending machine goes back to the first century in Alexandria, Egypt. In return for a coin, this machine dispensed holy water at religious sites (E. Smith 2015). In the early twenty-first century, vending machines will dispense almost anything you can imagine. Are you in need of a gold nugget? Go to the Emirates Palace hotel in Abu Dhabi and the "To Go Gold" vending machine will satisfy your desire. Craving some live crabs? Simply go to the subway station in Nanjing, China, and buy a few. Did you forget to bring your Kindle and are about to board a plane? No worries. Travelers in Las Vegas can pick up a new Kindle with all the accessories at the Kindle vending machine. Feel like making the world a better place? In exchange for an empty plastic bottle, a vending machine in Turkey will dispense a bowl of water and cup of dog food to help out the local stray dog population (Business Insider 2014). In France, consumers can pick up a freshly baked baguette (Knutson 2013), and in South Korea, time-strapped commuters in subway and bus stations can examine pictures of grocery products and scan the QR (quick-response) codes with their phones. These vending machines are operated by the British grocery giant Tesco. The products are delivered rapidly to consumers' homes, just after the consumers arrive home. Customers like the added flexibility and convenience of these vending machines because it feels like "real" shopping, with the added bonus that time spent waiting for the train does not feel like a waste of time. Tesco refers to these vending machines as "virtual stores" and has credited them with helping to increase its online presence in South Korea by 130 percent (Staff 2011) (see Photo 1.7).

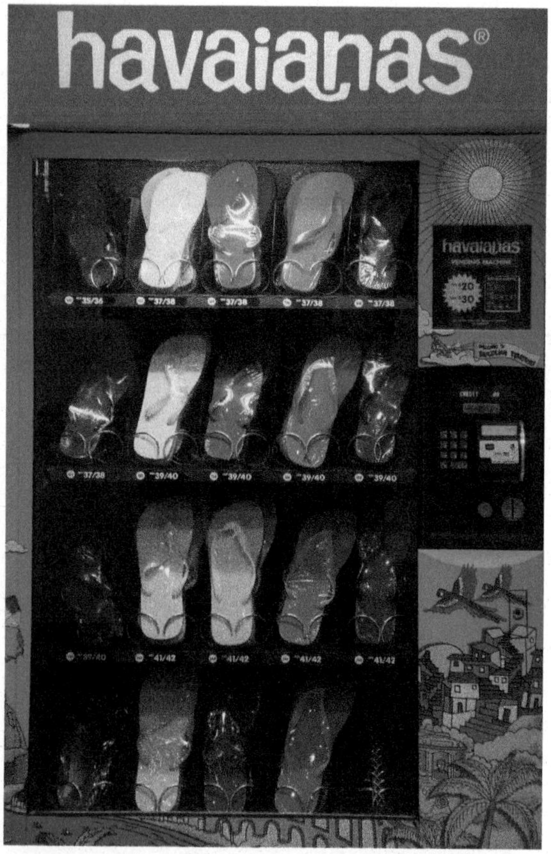

Questions

1. With advances in mobile technology that give consumers the ability to shop for groceries anywhere, are Tesco's virtual stores destined for failure? Why or why not?
2. What conclusions can you draw about when consumers need convenience and when they might not need convenience? Are there any drawbacks to convenience?

● **Photo 1.7** *Customers can buy flip-flops from a vending machine in Sydney, Australia*

Sources: Business Insider 2014; Knutson 2013; E. Smith 2015; Staff 2011.

course the online environment are all alternatives for shoppers in the early twenty-first century. These formats are also available to shoppers in some of the most far-flung places around the world, even at a tiny roadside stand in Panama advertising food and drinks to passers-by (see Photo 1.6). The city of Dubai in the United Arab Emirates is known for its over-the-top shopping malls that house attractions such as an indoor ski slope, complete with snowboarding area and chairlifts. Consumers in Dubai have a significant amount of disposable income and have developed a taste for products coming from the European Union and the United States. To meet this emerging demand, a variety of artisan food shops and organic farmers' markets have become very popular there (Hirsch 2013). Technological breakthroughs in vending machines have brought a surprising range of products to new locations and new customers. Increasingly, technological advances are helping to innovate how we shop, as highlighted in Insights from the Field 1.3.

Pop-up shops are another phenomenon that provide additional interest and variety to shoppers, thus putting power into their hands. Pop-ups are often found in empty storefronts or short-term temporary locations like tents or stands. The benefit for consumers is that the different products that are available provide surprises and novelty. Because the stores are only open for a limited time, pop-up consumers may feel motivated to make an immediate purchase, rather than wait. The benefit for the retailer, especially a new retailer, is the chance to test the market and see what products might be popular with customers because retailers can open a pop-up without committing to the cost of full-scale operations. The popularity, scale, and variety of pop-ups have been growing to include artisan food, single-brand outlets, and even virtual reality experiences.

One big trend in pop-ups is the efforts by marketers to allow consumers the ability to connect with their products on a more experiential level, such as Jim Beam's Honey whiskey pop-up in the Munich airport. The displays provide honey-themed interactive displays and aesthetics with the slogan, "it was worth every sting" (Byers 2015). Another trend is exclusivity, in which pop-ups are open on a members-only basis, like online retailer Revolve. Revolve, a high-end style and beauty brand, opened a members-only pop-up in Los Angeles for two weeks in 2017 and offered curated collections and boxes of items for influencers to examine and purchase (Perez 2017). Finally, another trend in pop-ups is the pretend pop-up. For those consumers who have become accustomed to seeing marketing messages and pop-ups in unusual locations, the pretend pop-ups play little tricks on consumers to get the point across, such as the Loblaws bakery in Montreal, where the offerings are so good, consumers are surprised to find that all of the bakery items are gluten free (Brown 2016).

As some big brick-and-mortar retailers have started to experience financial difficulties and even bankruptcy filings, many landlords have turned to pop-ups as a solution to fill empty storefronts. Indeed, seasonal pop-up stores that specialize in Christmas and Halloween, for example, have found many

● **Photo 1.8** *Halloween store pop-up in a vacant retail space*

opportunities to rent inexpensive space for a short time to offer products and a shopping experience that are both unique and fun (Barry 2018) (see Photo 1.8). As we can see, the increasing variety of shopping experiences provides consumers with more choices and power. Consumers no longer need the assistance of a shopkeeper, they can easily compare prices and options, and they do not have to settle for a limited set of consumption choices or experiences.

◉ Research Perspectives

There are currently three broad perspectives in consumer research: behavioral, cognitive, and motivational.

Behavioral research—a focus on what consumers do

In the early part of the twentieth century, consumers had little choice about products and product features. Manufacturers produced and sold products that a factory could easily and efficiently produce. Manufacturers put very little thought into finding out what consumers actually wanted. Therefore, consumers usually had only one or two choices when they went to a store. Indeed, Henry Ford was famous for saying that the customers who purchased Ford cars could have any color they wanted, "as long as it was black." It was during this time that early research focused on the behaviors that consumers performed—what they purchased, how much they paid, etc. In the early twenty-first century, **behavioral research** has been expanded to encompass investigations into how consumers use a product and how often they use it. Behavioral research would reveal, for example, consumers who are heavy users versus light users or consumers who use a product for certain reasons (e.g., a new iPad for gaming vs. for schoolwork). Behavioral research is still conducted quite often because it is easy to assess via sales data or click-through rates. Further, tools like data analytics help researchers easily sort through data and draw preliminary conclusions about what consumers do.

> **Behavioral research (also buyer behavior)** is an approach to consumer research that examines what consumers do. It does not account for the underlying motivations for those behaviors.

Cognitive research—a focus on how consumers process information

Consumer researchers also want to know what consumers think, and **cognitive research** provides a set of methods and analytical tools for developing a better understanding of how consumers learn, remember, retrieve information, process information, and form conclusions. Much of this research is based on the notion that the human brain is much like a computer. It is capable of storing, retrieving, and processing data. In conducting cognitive research, researchers create carefully designed research studies that are often conducted in a laboratory setting.

> **Cognitive research** is an approach to consumer research that focuses on how consumers learn, remember, retrieve information, process information, and form conclusions.

Motivational research—a focus on a consumer's desires and feelings

In the 1920s, advancements in manufacturing brought large-scale production to the United States. Products were rolling off production lines at an ever-increasing rate, bringing more variety and lower prices to war-weary consumers. American marketers tried to develop a better understanding of consumer motivations and found that important advancements were being made by Sigmund Freud, the Austrian founder of psychoanalysis. These marketers utilized Freud's research techniques and findings to help predict why consumers behaved as they did. Before this, when products were scarce and money was tight, there were few options and consumers generally purchased necessities. There was no need to understand a consumer's underlying motivations. However, mass production meant that marketers and businesses had to start competing for buyers. **Motivational research** recognizes the importance of desires and emotions in consumer decision-making. See Insights from Academia 1.1 for a description of an interesting research study on what motivates some consumers.

> **Motivational research** is an approach to consumer research that focuses on underlying influences on consumer behavior, such as desires and emotions.

INSIGHTS FROM ACADEMIA 1.1

When the going gets tough, the tough go shopping for . . .

Bleach, cleaning products, and screwdrivers. Say what? A bad breakup, a job loss, or financial difficulties can often make consumers feel like they are losing control. When this happens, consumers try to gain back control of their lives by buying functional and practical products like cleaning supplies, cooking ingredients, and tools. These products are associated with problem-solving and give consumers back their sense of control. This insight provides important information to marketers as they craft messages for consumers who are sometimes facing difficult situations.

Chen, C. Y., L. Lee, and A. J. Yap. 2017. "Control Deprivation Motivates Acquisition of Utilitarian Products." Journal of Consumer Research 43 (6): 1031–47.

Motivational research gains a following

Sigmund Freud's research was very influential, in part, because it established a firm foundation upon which other researchers built theories and models of motivation. Freud theorized that all behavior, including consumer behavior, was a tug-of-war between a person's irrational and unconscious motives and his or her socialized inhibitions (Berlin 2011). A **socialized inhibition** is a behavior that society tells you is inappropriate, such as kissing your cousin. Freud's research found that a person's unconscious thoughts were just as important as their conscious ones. Over the years, numerous researchers built on Freud's theories to better understand what motivated consumers to buy or not buy certain products. Freud's work has important implications for consumer researchers for a variety of reasons, one of which concerns how research itself is conducted. Because Freud believed that the unconscious and conscious minds both played a role in motivating consumer behavior, researchers could not ask straightforward questions about a particular behavior, but instead needed to ask a series of indirect and nuanced questions to ascertain the real reasons for the behavior.

Researchers have known for a long time that consumers do not often reveal what they're really thinking. Sometimes, consumers tell researchers what they *think* they want to hear. For example, *The Hidden Persuaders*, by Vance Packard, described the trouble a brewery was having in trying to better understand the characteristics and motivations of consumers in their two target markets: regular beer drinkers and light beer drinkers. Researchers started out by asking consumers the very simple question of which beer they drank; this is where the problem started. The findings revealed that light beer drinkers significantly outnumbered regular beer drinkers by a three-to-one margin. The problem is, these findings could not be accurate because the brewery produced and sold nine times more regular beer than light beer! Why the disparity between what consumers *said* they bought and what they actually

Socialized inhibition refers to a behavior that society tells you is inappropriate.

bought? Building on Freudian theory, Packard concluded that there were both unconscious and conscious processes at work. Consumers simply didn't want to admit that they were drinking the "regular stuff" and wanted to appear that they had more "refinement and discriminating taste" (Packard 1957, 38). Uncovering the underlying motivations of consumers can be very challenging!

In the 1930s, Austrian American psychologist Ernest Dichter was at the forefront of trying to apply some of Freud's theories to the emerging field of consumer research (see Insight from Academia 1.2). Dichter often used **in-depth interviews** in which the research participant is asked detailed and probing questions by the interviewer to identify underlying motivations for a variety of consumption-related behaviors. Dichter's research uncovered many fascinating insights into the inner workings of the consumer mind. For example, Dichter found that women viewed their daily bathing routine as anything but "routine." Instead, women saw this time as a few moments of indulgence in which they had private time away from the demands of work and family.

In-depth interviews are a descriptive consumer research method where a single interviewer discusses a topic with a consumer.

Dichter found that women viewed the Ivory brand of soap as pure, while the competing brand Camay was perceived as seductive (Samuel 2010). In another project, Dichter utilized motivational research techniques to find out why Plymouth Chrysler may have been experiencing a slump in sales. He found that men viewed convertible cars as representing freedom, youth, and even a bit of sexiness, so placing a convertible car in the dealership's display window resulted in many more visits to the showroom by men ("Retail Therapy" 2011) (see Photo 1.9).

Limitations of motivational research

As we learned earlier in this chapter, concerns about consumerism have appeared throughout the centuries. As more sophisticated marketing strategies were developed and implemented after the Second World War, observers grew concerned that consumers were buying products that they neither needed nor wanted. Some marketers were using a variety of psychological techniques to unfairly tempt consumers and some unscrupulous marketers did indeed take advantage of consumers. Critics argued that consumers

● **Photo 1.9** *Advertisement for Alfa Romeo using sexual innuendo Image Courtesy of The Advertising Archives*

INSIGHTS FROM ACADEMIA 1.2

Why we want busy people around us

Some products are very exclusive; they're hard to find and it takes some effort to acquire them. When this happens, consumers value them more and might even pay more money to get them. Think about a first-edition book or an antique watch. These items are special and prized, in part, because they're so hard to get. The same thing happens with busy people. When people are busy with work, school, and other obligations, it's hard to get even a few minutes of their time. So, busy people are often seen by the rest of us as being special and prized. Think about the implications this insight has for marketers, especially in customer service encounters.

Bellezza, S., N. Paharia, and A. Keinan. 2017. "Conspicuous Consumption of Time: When Busyness and Lack of Leisure Time Becomes a Status Symbol." Journal of Consumer Research 44, no. 1 (June): 118–38.

were purchasing products in a vain attempt to achieve a consumerist lifestyle. These critics further argued that in the end, the effect of these increasingly persuasive advertising messages was that consumer welfare suffered (Packard 1957).

Although motivational research has had its criticisms, it has continued to be used by many researchers to help companies develop better products to better meet the needs of consumers. In the end, why would it make sense for companies to offer products and services unless there was a fairly good chance that consumers would be interested? Doing so would be a big waste of time and money for both consumers and companies. Motivational research has assisted countless marketers in understanding the needs of consumers so that they can create and deliver better products and services for them. In this way, motivational research has indeed made an important contribution to understanding consumer behavior (Tadajewski 2006).

The Rise Of Consumerism

As consumption started to become a more central part of our daily lives in the nineteenth and twentieth centuries, consumers began to fill their lives with more consumer products. At the same time, another development was occurring in parallel with this trend. Consumers started to become even more empowered and consumer advocates started to voice their concerns with more force. The result was that the political establishment started paying attention to the rights and safety of consumers.

In those early days, consumers and manufacturers alike operated under a theory of **caveat emptor**, or *buyer beware*, where it was the customer's responsibility to be cautious and aware of any product flaws. If a customer got hurt using a product, that was too bad. That customer should have been more careful. The term *consumer sovereignty* was first coined in the 1930s (de Grazia 2005) and was an important advancement in how our thinking about consumption evolved. The idea was that consumers, not manufacturers, were the best judges of which products were the most appropriate, useful, or enjoyable. It was also at this time that marketers started to evolve their thinking and operate under a different theory: **caveat venditor**, which means that the seller should beware. Under caveat venditor, manufacturers needed to make sure that their products were safe and free of flaws. Consumers should not become sick or hurt as a result of using the product. If they did, it was the manufacturer's fault. A variety of consumer advocacy organizations operate around the world, such as the Consumers' Association in the United Kingdom, the Consumers' Federation of Australia, and the National Consumer Union of Italy. In addition to most European countries having their own consumer protection agencies, the European Union also has the European Consumer Centres Network, a group of offices that provides advice and assistance to consumers in every EU country. The goal of each of these organizations is the same: to protect consumer rights.

In 1914 in the United States, the Federal Trade Commission (FTC) was founded to protect the rights of consumers by "preventing anticompetitive, deceptive, and unfair business practices, enhancing informed consumer choice and public understanding of the competitive process, and accomplishing this without unduly burdening legitimate business activity" (Federal Trade Commission 2019). Within the FTC is the Bureau of Consumer Protection, which specifically works to protect consumers from unsafe and unlawful practices by organizations. The bureau has a set of rules for the operation of a fair marketplace and it educates consumers about their rights and responsibilities. When necessary, it takes complaints about scams and frauds and then enforces the law to ensure consumers are treated fairly (Federal Trade Commission 2019). One big issue for the FTC is the use of phone calls, emails, texts, and posts by unscrupulous sellers. The FTC has a "do not call" registry for those who do not wish to be bothered by annoying phone calls and it is cracking down on many unscrupulous sellers by issuing fines, but there is still a lot of work to do.

In 1934, the US Federal Communications Commission was founded to regulate interstate and international communications within the United States and its territories. This covers all communications by radio, wire, wireless, television, satellite, and cable. The purpose of the Federal Communications Commission is to promote investment, innovation, and competition when it comes to the use of these communication tools. It ensures, for example, that consumers are protected against unauthorized charges on their cell phone bills and exorbitant charges for the early

Caveat emptor is an approach to the buyer/seller relationship that says that the buyer should beware.

Caveat venditor is an approach to the buyer/seller relationship that says that the seller should beware.

INSIGHTS FROM THE BOARDROOM 1

Getting deep insights takes some creativity

● *Jen Drexler*

Jen Drexler knows how difficult it is to get consumers to open up and be honest. Drexler is the founder of Connects the Dots, a boutique consumer research firm that engages in "radical consumer intimacy and full-frontal consumer research panels," according to Drexler (2017). For more than twenty years, she has worked with a long list of some of the most well-respected brands, including Westin Hotels, Johnson & Johnson, Mondelez, A&E Networks, Viacom, and Bioré.

Drexler spends her days designing research studies to identify deep consumer insights. She has interviewed so many consumers that she "stopped counting at 40,000" (Drexler 2017). The purpose of what she's doing is not "disaster relief" research or figuring out what went wrong after the fact. She also doesn't like to do research on "what ad do you like and why?" Instead, Drexler likes to do research much earlier in the process, "so it is foundational and iterative" (2017). From the beginning of her career, Drexler had a profound dissatisfaction with how traditional consumer research had been conducted using sterile one-on-one interviews between a researcher and a consumer. She asked, "Why would anyone tell you anything if

you put them in a setting where they are being treated like a witness in a criminal trial?" (2017). Instead, she believed that the setting in which an interview is conducted is critical to getting good results. The more comfortable, the better.

Several years ago, for example, Drexler and her team were working on a project for the global cosmetics and beauty company Elizabeth Arden. The company wanted to find out how consumers might react to several new lotions and oils that would be used in spa treatments. Drexler wanted to find the best way to get women to open up and think about the topic in depth, so she and her team decided to invite small groups of women into the interview center. Once there, she invited them to dress up as if they were going to the spa. She provided a huge wardrobe filled with plush terrycloth robes and comfortable slippers, and the women were invited to change out of their regular clothes and get comfortable. They were then brought into a room that had a tranquil setting with soft music and muted lighting. Once they were comfortable, the women were asked to share their expectations, thoughts, and impressions about a variety of spa treatments and products. Drexler gets consumers to share some very personal information. She says, "Clients tell me all the time that participants will never talk to me about X. Watch me!" (2017).

Another recent project involved a very well-known breakfast brand that was exploring new opportunities to better connect with busy families. The primary question centered around consumers' expectations. That is, what did consumers really want out of a breakfast brand—something that was fun, faster, more nutritious, or something else? Drexler and her team decided that they would conduct a series of "breakfast ethnographies" in which they would see firsthand what busy families did in the morning. So, they made arrangements to visit consumers all over the country at six o'clock in the morning. The whole team showed up—interviewers, camera crew, support staff—to record what busy families did to get ready in the morning. She described one of their visits: "I'll never forget, we were in rural Texas doing this one interview with a family and their 2-year old kid climbed out the 'doggie door' and was gone! We were so worried about him and started running after the kid, but they reassured us, 'He always does that!' We gave him an iPad and a cookie. That kept him busy and in one place for the rest of the time!" (2017).

Drexler understands that to get consumers to open up, "the methodology is just as important as the insights." Because of this, one of her newest pursuits is integrating mobile technology into her research designs. One recent example of this is a "selfnography" project for a well-known skin care company. Women were asked to apply the skin care treatments and then give their impressions of the results over a period of several days. Critical to the research design was the use of mobile "pings" that were sent out to the participants throughout the day, which allowed the women to record themselves applying the treatments, observing the results in the morning, and reflecting on the results throughout the day. Drexler then embedded short segments of these videos

in her report back to the client, which she says are "100 times more impactful than a bunch of PowerPoint slides" (2017). Drexler's clients appreciate these deep insights: "We get such different insights than anyone else out there because the environment we've created allows me to do that."

What's next for Drexler? In the end, she says, it's about making research participants feel comfortable enough to open up and discuss issues from the heart. Customers shouldn't try to tell researchers what they think researchers want to hear. Instead, they should be a caught a little off guard so that they open up and are honest about what they really think and feel. Most of this depends on the research setting, and sometimes, "the wackier, the better. The only thing I haven't done yet is under water, but don't put it past me!" (2017).

connects the dots
strategy in context

termination of a wireless plan. In the end, the goal is to make sure there is unrestricted access to the free flow of communications and ideas (Federal Communications Commission 2019).

The Consumer Product Safety Commission, founded in 1972, has a mandate to protect the public from "unreasonable risks of injury or death associated with the use of thousands of types of consumer products under the agency's jurisdiction." One of its earliest efforts was to protect children and babies from unsafe cribs. By 2017, "deaths, injuries, and property damage from consumer product incidents cost the nation more than $1 trillion annually." On its website, the Consumer Product Safety Commission has a list of current and recent product recalls. It also has a variety of tools consumers can use to ensure they and their families are protected. Because of its efforts on behalf of consumers, the rate of injuries and death that can be attributed to products has declined dramatically (US Consumer Product Safety Commission 2019).

In 2011, the US Consumer Financial Protection Bureau was founded to ensure that "banks, lenders, and other financial companies treat you fairly." The bureau provides a variety of consumer and educational tools to ensure that consumers are not victimized by unscrupulous and aggressive lenders. The bureau can issue warning letters and even bring an organization to trial for not properly following the laws that are already in place to protect consumers. By 2018, the Consumer Financial Protection Bureau helped over thirty-one million customers and recovered $12.4 billion for consumers who were harmed by unlawful and predatory actions by financial lenders (Lew 2019).

In addition to government agencies, many other people and organizations are actively involved in campaigning for better, safer products and safer working environments. American consumer advocate Ralph Nader has been at the forefront of several efforts to make companies more accountable for shoddy products and misleading advertisements. In his 1965 book entitled *Unsafe at Any Speed*, Nader accused the car industry of putting profits ahead of passenger safety. At the time, American car manufacturers did not have a number of safety features, including seat belts. Nader has continued his campaign for passenger safety and has worked with lawmakers to pass several federal laws to that effect (Jensen 2015). Naomi Klein is a more recent advocate for consumer rights. Her book, *No Logo*, paints a stark portrait of corporate greed and misdeeds as it uncovers some of the most appalling labor practices perpetrated by some of the most well-known multinational companies (Klein 2000). Filmmaker Morgan Spurlock's 2004 documentary, entitled *Supersize Me*, chronicles his surprisingly rapid weight gain, health complications, and psychological problems after spending just thirty days eating food exclusively from McDonald's. The documentary also highlighted the fast-food industry's pervasive influence on the nutrition and health of the American public (Spurlock 2004). In addition to these more well-known examples of consumer advocacy, everyday consumers have also banded together to share information and advocate for their own rights. Technology has allowed consumers to easily monitor the actions of organizations and has facilitated information sharing and activism.

Classifying Consumers

Marketers, consumer advocates, government officials, and others sometimes utilize insights to create categories, or typologies, of consumers. Some classification systems use demographic characteristics such as age, race, gender,

Table 1.2 A typology of consumers based on money

CONSUMER TYPE	DESCRIPTION
Flourishing Frugal (31.5% of Americans)	These consumers are in the top income bracket, make an average annual income of $78,100, and are not feeling any particular financial distress. They are slightly older than the other types, with a mean age of 52.6, and are likely to be college graduates and/or retirees. Although they don't need to be frugal, many are motivated to be smart shoppers. These individuals still enjoy an occasional impulsive purchase and a purchase that signifies status.
Comfortable Cautious (27.5% of Americans)	Individuals in this category have a mean annual income of about $20,000 less than the Flourishing Frugals and a mean age of 41.7. Although objectively these individuals are doing well, they report high levels of stress about money and finances. These individuals have a fairly high level of impulse and status-oriented purchases, which might be one of the main reasons why they also report high levels of financial guilt and stress.
Financial Middle (21.0% of Americans)	Individuals in this group only feel moderately secure from a financial perspective. More than 30% of these individuals are students and 57% make less than $40,000 per year. On the upside, this group is not likely to purchase products impulsively or for status purposes. These consumers plan their purchases and feel pride in being smart shoppers.
Financially Distressed (20.0% of Americans)	This is the smallest category of consumers, with the lowest average annual income ($39,636) and highest likelihood of unemployment. Despite their difficult financial situation, these consumers do not always exercise self-control in spending, which sometimes makes their economic situation even more stressful.

Note. Totals in the left-hand column do not add up to 100% because of rounding errors.

Source: Adapted from Hampson et al. (2018).

or income. Other classification systems use more subjective or psychographic characteristics such as attitudes, opinions, and interests. There are many classification systems and a decision-maker will select one based on the question of interest. A classification system exists for nearly every purpose. For example, classification systems exist for green consumers, family decision-making, and familiarity with technology. To illustrate the depth and types of information available in a typology, see Table 1.2, a classification based on consumer attitudes about money. This typology utilizes a combination of demographic and psychographic factors to create four separate dimensions (Hampson et al. 2018).

Another classification system based on psychographic criteria divides consumers into one of four types, depending on where they are located along two key dimensions: materialistic/nonmaterialistic and individualistic/collectivist. The resulting four categories or "faces" of the consumer identify and describe important consumption-related motivations (see Table 1.3 and Figure 1.1) (Dagevos 2005).

Table 1.3 The four faces of the consumer

	MATERIALISTIC	NONMATERIALISTIC
Individualistic	The *calculating* consumer. This consumer is rational, mainstream, efficient, and effective in decision-making and consumption. Further, this consumer is concerned with convenience and wants to keep up with the latest fashions and trends.	The *unique* consumer. This person engages in conspicuous consumption, is fun and impulsive, and seeks variety. The unique consumer really likes new things and is concerned with status and distinction.
Collectivistic	The *traditional* consumer. This person is conformist, cost-conscious, self-disciplined, fearful of new things, and community oriented.	The *responsible* consumer. This consumer is highly involved in consumption, altruistic, informed, environmentally aware, and cares little for keeping up with the latest fashions and trends.

Source: Adapted from Dagevos (2005).

Consumer typologies are based on insights, but also *provide* valuable insights to decision-makers by identifying important differences between consumers that can later be utilized in marketing strategy decisions. We will learn more about ways to classify and segment consumers later in this text. See Insights from Academia 1.3 for another interesting insight.

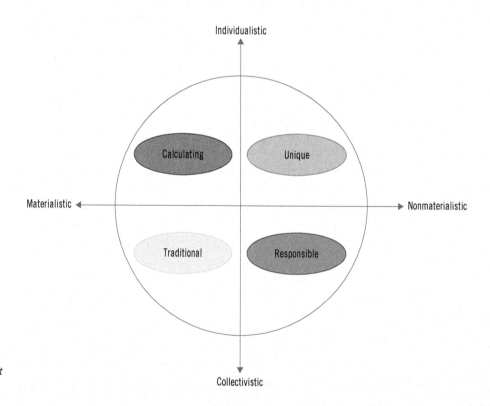

● **Figure 1.1** *Consumer images*

Source: Dagevos (2005), Copyright © 2005, Elsevier.

INSIGHTS FROM ACADEMIA 1.3

So, this is your idea of fun?

Extreme experiences like Tough Mudders and Polar Plunges are becoming increasingly popular, especially for individuals who are not "extreme" sports athletes. So, why on earth would a seemingly normal person want to pay $100 to endure the pain of fire, freezing water, and electric shocks? It turns out that some people need an escape from the grind of their daily lives. These experiences help them to rediscover themselves and become more self-aware. When they leave with scars and pain, their experiences help create stories that they can tell others about their adventurous and fulfilling lives. Insights like this help illustrate the fact that consumers have different motivations for different consumer decisions.

Scott, R., J. Cayla, and B. Cova. 2017. "Selling Pain to the Saturated Self." Journal of Consumer Research 44 (1): 22–43.

The Postmodern Consumer

With the rise of many pro-consumer sentiments, we also find an important new concept emerging: the postmodern consumer (Firat and Venkatesh 1995; Goulding 2003; Simmons 2008). The important thing to remember about postmodern consumers is they are almost impossible to clearly characterize and describe. Rather than easily being classified (as, for example, in a typology), the postmodern consumer defies classification and behaves in different ways in different situations. Unlike other consumers, the choices that postmodern consumers make do nothing to express a single, unified, static identity. Indeed, a singular identity is not something that a **postmodern consumer** seeks. Rather than seeking a unified theme to their consumption, these consumers explore different and separate identities that match fragmented markets and different products. The postmodern consumer can be a different person at work, at home, or with friends and can consume different products to support these identities. The postmodern consumer brings us back full circle to a removal of the barriers that were erected between producers and consumers during mass production and the Industrial Revolution. Thus, depending on who a consumer wants to be for a given situation, a postmodern consumer will adopt products to fit that identity and might even engage in the production process. Similarly, with the postmodern consumer, a single product can enhance or support multiple identities (Firat and Schultz 1997).

Unlike in earlier centuries, consumer researchers can no longer predict what consumers will do based on demographic information such as social class or income. Indeed, it is just as easy to find a Fortune 500 chief executive officer driving a Ford truck as it is to find an unemployed person driving a

Postmodern consumers do not seek a unified theme to their consumption but instead explore different and separate identities that match fragmented markets and different products.

BMW (Cova 1999). Some experts in consumer behavior suggest that postmodern consumption tears apart old patterns of consumer behavior and erases the existing price, image, and brand boundaries (Fassnacht 2007), such that a postmodern consumer might grab a quick lunch from a food truck, but dine at a Michelin five-star restaurant for dinner. The boundaries of what is acceptable or predictable behavior fall apart when we examine the postmodern consumer.

Post postmodernism

Some researchers have suggested that postmodernism has ended (e.g., Cova and Maclaran 2012) and that we are now in a post postmodern world. New fields of interest in consumer research, such as consumer culture theory (Arnould and Thompson 2005) (to be discussed in Chapter 2) and neuromarketing (to be discussed in Chapter 13), have captured the attention of consumer researchers and marketing managers. While the jury is still out on this, what is clear is that new theories will continue to be developed to help keep pace with the challenging job of understanding how consumers navigate their role in the marketplace.

◉ Creating Insights About Consumers

Insights are useful interpretations of the data that are gathered from the consumer research process.

You will notice that we talk a lot about insights in this book. For the record, an **insight** is a useful interpretation of the data that are gathered from the consumer research process. An insight is not just a research finding or an important discovery about a consumer; it represents a deeper level of understanding about the consumer's history, context, and experience. Also, an insight doesn't come from just one research study or one experience; insights are created and refined over time so that they represent a deeper knowledge and understanding of who your customer is and what makes him or her tick. An example from the world of financial services might help. Many parents have a variety of savings accounts set up, including a retirement account. A simple data analysis could tell us what types of retirement accounts people prefer. It could also tell us what kinds of features these investors prefer, such as interest rates or the ability to withdraw funds. However, an *insight* will tell us what this retirement account really means to the consumer. It could tell us, for example, that the retirement account represents a set of dreams—a beach house, a trip to Europe, or opening a new retirement business, such as a small bakery. Simply put, "the goal of consumer research is to generate consumer insights" (Hamilton 2016). When marketers are equipped with consumer insights, they can do a much better job of creating products and services, as well as communicating with consumers about them.

There are three types of insights that, together, help us better understand the reality of a consumer's consumption-related decisions and experience: insights from the field, insights from the boardroom, and insights from academia. As depicted in Figure 1.2, we can see that each of these three pillars is indispensable to our understanding of consumers. You will also notice that each of the insights sits on a firm foundation of data and information, which decision-makers use to create their insights. As we will discuss more thoroughly in Chapter 3, **data** refer to numbers or other nonnumerical descriptors that are used to define a phenomenon; **information** refers to data that have already been organized and analyzed. Information also provides context and is therefore more useful for managers in developing insights. It is on this foundation of data and information that the insights sit. Like columns holding up a roof, each of these pillars provides a strong supporting structure for understanding consumers.

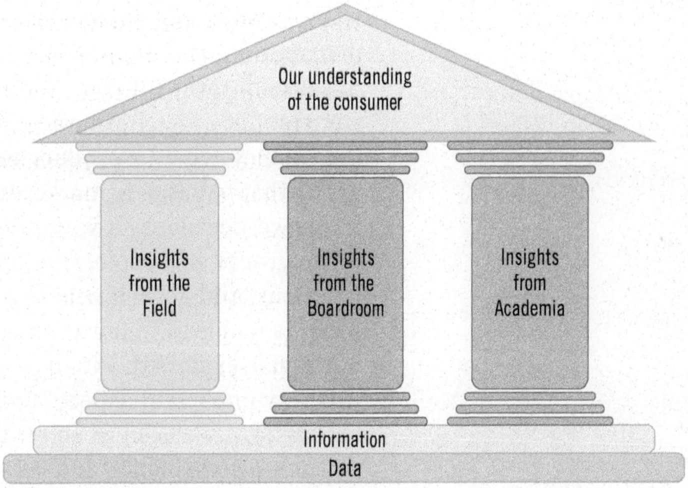

The first pillar is referred to as *insights from the field*. These insights are generated when researchers uncover important information about consumption trends, habits, or other consumption-related phenomena. These kinds of insights are generated, for example, when we observe how consumers react to advertising or other communications, how they shop, or how they go about their daily lives consuming stuff. The value of insights that come from the field is that we get to observe how consumers are actually behaving. The next pillar in our understanding of consumers is *insights from the boardroom*. Here, top-level executives tap into their years of experience to delve into the minds and hearts of their consumers. These insights come from firsthand and inside knowledge about what makes their customers tick. Insights from the boardroom are rarely shared with others or publicly disclosed because they often represent proprietary information gathered from years of experience. Finally, *insights from academia* are generated from professors and other scientists at research institutions who make it their life's work to better understand consumers. These individuals may spend years or even decades studying specific dimensions of the consumer experience and then publishing the results of their findings. These research publications are carefully reviewed by other experts in the field before they are published and are often read by marketers, executives, and other academicians.

What do marketers do with these insights and this so-called better understanding of consumers? First, these insights help marketers who are trying

● **Figure 1.2** *The three pillars of consumer insight*
Source: Diane M. Phillips

Data refer to numbers or other descriptors that are used to define a phenomenon.

Information refers to data that have already been organized and analyzed.

to make well-informed decisions about product features, pricing strategies, distribution, and communications. We do this because it simply makes a lot of sense in terms of time and money for both the organization and the consumers. Let's face it, marketers and consumers alike are wasting their time and money when a product or service doesn't hit the mark. Since no one wants that to happen, marketers utilize insights so that they can make better-informed decisions. A very important second purpose of insights is to assist other groups of people, such as consumer rights advocates, nonprofit organizations, and government officials who make public policy. Hopefully, these insights will lead to fewer instances of consumers being cheated, deceived, or otherwise exploited. Finally, insights are used to help us better understand this very important aspect of *our own* lives. If consumption is an activity that occurs 24/7, we need to better understand our own consumption-related tendencies, biases, habits, and vulnerabilities.

◉ Summary

This first chapter of *Consumer Behavior & Insights* started out by arguing for the centrality of consumption in our daily lives. Important *concepts in economics and philosophy informed our understanding of consumer behavior* and were instrumental in helping that understanding evolve over time. Some interesting historical facts about consumption illustrated how consumption has been an indispensable part of the development of human civilization and cultures. In particular, we learned that the technological advancements that brought about the *Industrial Revolution* exerted a strong influence on *consumption and conspicuous consumption*. For centuries, observers have voiced concerns about the moral implications of consumption and we discussed how that concern has been manifested in the creation of advocacy organizations that protect the rights of consumers. Case Study 1 provided an in-depth look at consumer activism and how it sparked a change in the formulation of an important, everyday product—body scrubs.

We learned that the *connection between production and consumption* has evolved over the years, from being closely linked, to being separated, to becoming closely linked again. Bartering systems, which harken back centuries, are becoming more popular in the early twenty-first century as some consumers seek a closer connection to those who produce products. The ways in which shopping has evolved over the years illustrate how this connection between production and consumption has changed. Insights from the Field 1.1 described how advancements in food technology have changed family roles and relationships. Insights from the Field 1.2 delved into the concept of the statusphere and how individuals signal status to others by, for example, demonstrating unique or specialized knowledge about fashion, technology, or travel.

We introduced the *three broad perspectives in consumer research*: behavioral, cognitive, and motivational. Insights from the Boardroom 1 introduced us to Jen Drexler, founder of a research firm that specializes in developing insights for some of the top brands in the world. These three perspectives will be revisited again later in this text, but for now, we stressed the importance of motivational research as a well-rounded method for understanding consumer behavior.

As consumers became more savvy about marketing tactics and more empowered by the wide variety of choices available to them, we saw the rise of *postmodern consumption*, a form of consumption that is quite difficult to define and easily categorize. Since one of the primary goals of marketers is to predict consumer behaviors, the postmodern consumer's tendency to defy predictability makes the marketing decision-maker's job especially difficult.

The end of the chapter discussed the role of insights in helping to craft a deep understanding of consumers and described the importance of each of the *three pillars of consumer insights*: insights from the field, insights from the boardroom, and insights from academia. Together, these insights build a strong foundation for our understanding of the consumer. In the end, we hope you agree that consumer behavior is an exciting and dynamic field of study. Indeed, it can be argued that consumers are the most important asset to any organization—no organization can function without consumers. Therefore, a careful and precise understanding of what makes consumers tick is critical to the continued success of any organization.

KEY TERMS

behavioral research p. 21
buyer behavior p. 5
caveat emptor p. 25
caveat venditor p. 25
cognitive research p. 21
commodity products p. 10
conspicuous consumption p. 14
consumer behavior p. 4
consumers p. 5
consumption p. 4

consumption function p. 11
customers p. 5
data p. 33
exchange p. 7
fetishism of commodities p. 10
in-depth interviews p. 23
Industrial Revolution p. 8
information p. 33
insight p. 32
motivational research p. 21

perceived obsolescence p. 13
planned obsolescence p. 13
postmodern consumers p. 31
psychology p. 4
socialized inhibition p. 22
sociology p. 4
statusphere p. 16
sumptuary laws p. 9

REVIEW QUESTIONS

1. Why do we study consumer behavior? Why is it more important to study consumer behavior than it is to study buyer behavior? What is the difference between a consumer and a customer?

2. Using important concepts from economics and philosophy, trace the development of our current understanding of consumer behavior.

3. What do we mean when we say that the connection between production and consumption has evolved over the years?

4. There are three primary areas of focus for consumer behavior research: behavioral, cognitive, and motivational. Describe some key differences between them. Why do researchers tend to favor the motivational research approach?

5. Consumer researchers know that many consumers don't always reveal what they really think or do. Why? What could a researcher do to remedy this problem?

6. How do the three pillars of consumer insights relate to one another and to our understanding of the consumer?

DISCUSSION QUESTIONS

1. To what extent is conspicuous consumption still an issue? Is it possible for conspicuous consumption to occur with services? How might social media play a role?

2. Do we still have a need for consumer activism? Why or why not?

3. Select either Table 1.2 or Table 1.3 for a classification system of consumers. Then, find an advertisement for each of the four categories (four ads in total). For each of the four ads, describe why each ad represents that category of consumers.

4. Let's say we want to develop a better understanding of the green consumer, someone who is interested in living a sustainable lifestyle. To build this understanding, find one insight from the field, one insight from the boardroom, and one insight from academia. Discuss each of these insights in detail. How are the insights different from one another? How might these insights be combined to provide a clearer understanding of the green consumer?

For more information, quizzes, case studies, and other study tools, please visit us at **www.oup.com/he/phillips**.

CASE STUDY 1

Consumers Push for Microbead Ban

Consumers sometimes focus their attention on issues that, rationally speaking, are not as important as other, more pressing, issues. The cosmetics and personal care industry's proactive reaction to an emerging environmental issue demonstrates that both the issue itself and how consumers interpret it are equally important to understanding what consumers might do. These insights can then be used by the marketing team to develop an appropriate strategy.

Most Americans have a plethora of products cluttering their bathrooms and showers. Some of those products are likely body washes, body scrubs, and facial scrubs. Twenty-one percent of Americans (25 percent of women and 16 percent of men) use body scrubs when they take a shower. The usage rates are even higher for young people—32 percent of Americans aged twenty-five through thirty-four use body scrubs on a daily basis (Mintel 2015). Clearly, these products are a big part of our daily routines. Some of the leading health and beauty companies that have these scrubs in their product line are L'Oreal, Johnson & Johnson, Procter & Gamble, and Unilever. When they were first introduced, these products included natural ingredients like ground coconut shells or pumice to act as scrubbing agents. Simply rub the product on your skin and the tiny scrubbers will whisk away dead skin, clear out pores, and leave skin feeling extra clean and clear. Soon, scrubbing agents found their way into other products, like toothpaste and household cleaning products (Steinmetz 2014a).

Manufacturers soon found two important problems with these natural ingredients. The most important issue was that some of the natural ingredients had problems staying inert and not reacting to the material in which they were suspended. Sometimes the color would change, the texture would change, or the material would simply degrade. Another problem that quickly became even more pressing was that some individuals with nut allergies were experiencing a growing sensitivity to the scrubs that, in extreme cases, could cause life-threatening reactions. These problems proved quite a challenge for manufacturers until chemists and researchers developed an innovative solution: plastic microbeads. These propylene beads, which could be produced in any size, could easily replace the natural ingredients, were completely inert in the suspension material, and proposed no risk of allergic reaction.

Consumers and manufacturers seemed satisfied with the switch to microbeads, that is, until 2012, when a series of scientific reports emerged that raised serious health and environmental questions related to the use of microbeads in products. When consumers use these products, the microbeads are washed down the drain

and, because they are too small to be filtered out by municipal water treatment facilities, the microbeads then make their way into lakes, rivers, and oceans. Once this happens, the microbeads absorb a variety of toxic substances that have also been washed into these bodies of water, such as pesticides and fertilizers. Because they are so small, the microbeads are consumed by fish, birds, and turtles, who mistake the tiny beads for bits of food (Worland 2015). Once ingested, the plastic microbeads and the toxins they've absorbed enter the food chain. This problem became especially pronounced in the Great Lakes region and all along coastal communities in the United States (Steinmetz 2014a). In New York State alone, microbeads have been found in 75 percent of water treatment plants (Worland 2015) and an astounding 663,000 floating pieces of plastic per square mile are estimated to be floating in the area of New York City. One million small pieces of plastic per square mile were found in some parts of the Great Lakes region (Foderaro 2016). In both locations, an estimated 60 to 85 percent were five millimeters in size or smaller, including microbeads (Foderaro 2016).

Nongovernmental organizations like Greenpeace started to pick up on the story, the media began to report on the problem, and consumers became outraged. Led by a group of environmentalists, some consumers stopped purchasing the products and others found more natural alternatives on social media and other do-it-yourself websites. Donations and funding began to pour in to environmental advocacy groups fighting for microbead bans in different states. The Beat the Microbead campaign urged consumers around the world to boycott these products and was supported by one hundred nongovernmental organizations in forty-two countries (Beat the Microbead 2019). According to one top research organization, 19 percent of Americans were aware of the issue and tried to avoid products containing microbeads (Mintel 2015).

Admittedly, microbeads are a very serious problem and consumers should be concerned. However, microbeads comprise a tiny fraction of the problem of plastics in our oceans. Indeed, one report often cited by environmentalists says that there are five trillion pieces of plastic floating in the world's oceans. Just in the North Pacific, one environmentalist says there is "20 times the amount of plastic . . . as there are stars in the Milky Way" (Steinmetz 2014b). So, although the presence of microbeads in our oceans is troubling, the overall presence of plastic is a much bigger and more pressing problem. Single-use plastic, like coffee cup lids, straws, and plastic bags, poses a much more critical problem for the world's waterways and wildlife (Shoe 2018).

Despite this, at numerous corporate headquarters across the world, personal care and cosmetics companies were planning their response to the public outrage over microbeads. When the scientific reports began to emerge and social media started to react to the microbeads issue, the marketers at these companies knew that they had to do something. Three key issues would help these marketing managers find the best way to manage the microbead problem. First, if forward-thinking companies tried to wait until the controversy blew over or if they tried to launch a scientific counterargument directed to consumers to persuade them that microbeads were not as harmful as the other plastic in the ocean, managers knew the effort could backfire. Consumers would likely be unresponsive and might even lash out against the company. What mattered is that the issue of microbeads was important to consumers. Second, marketing managers also recognized that once several states and countries around the world passed bans on microbeads, the product would need to be completely reformulated—they couldn't sell one version of the product to some locations and another version to other locations. Finally, most personal care and cosmetics companies fiercely protected their public images as innovative, caring companies with strict quality control standards. Managers at these companies knew that whatever strategy they implemented needed to stay consistent with, and even build on, that reputation.

Because of these three issues, it made sense to be proactive about efforts and develop a strategy to address the issue of microbeads in their products. Generally speaking, Johnson & Johnson and Procter & Gamble were at the forefront of meeting this challenge head-on. The first step was to stay ahead of the rest of the cosmetics and personal care industry so that they could have a competitive advantage in their own product formulations. Together, these companies were among the first manufacturers to proactively respond to the consumer outcry by replacing microbeads with natural abrasives (Shoe 2018), such as sugar and salt. Changing the formulation of their products before the competition had a chance to do so meant that they would be among the first to put their new formulations into the hands of customers and would build on their reputations as trusted brands (see Photo 1.10).

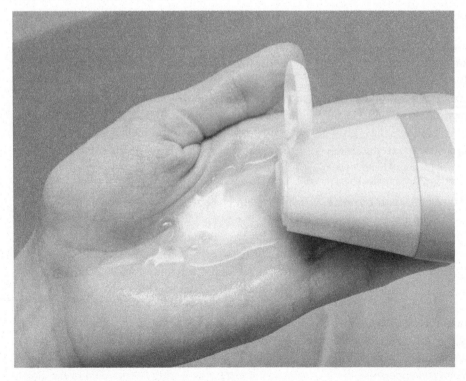

● **Photo 1.10** *Consumers demanded microbead-free bodywash*

In a victory for the environment, industry, and consumers, the Microbead-Free Waters Act, which was signed into law in 2015, required that companies stop the use of plastic microbeads in their products by July 2017 (Foderaro 2016). Although some environmentalists hailed the new law, many were still concerned about the sheer volume of plastics in our waterways. One scientist noted, "Its common sense. We can't keep using this stuff for a few minutes and then throwing it out and having it end up in our waters" (Foderaro 2016). Still, this legislation is an important step in the right direction for reducing the amount of plastic in our environment. It is also an important demonstration of the power of consumers in influencing change in the law and in business.

Sources: Foderaro (2016); Mintel (2015); Shoe (2018); Steinmetz (2014a, 2014b); Worland (2015); Beat the Microbead (2019).

QUESTIONS

1. The issue of microbeads in our waterways is important, but it is not as important as the overall issue of plastic in our waterways. Why do you think consumers focused their attention on microbeads and not on the overall issue of plastic?

2. Marketing managers in the cosmetics and personal care industry decided that it would not make sense to launch a scientific counterargument with consumers to say that microbeads were not a significant problem. Do you agree with this decision? Why or why not?

3. Consumers sometimes base their decisions on emotions and other times on rational thinking. Sometimes, consumer decisions are based on both! What are some emotional issues that consumers might consider here? What are some rational issues?

REFERENCES

American Psychological Association. 2017. Accessed May 20, 2017. https://www.apa.org.

American Sociological Association. 2017. Accessed May 20, 2017. https://www.asanet.org.

Arnould, E. J., L. Price, and G. M. Zinkhan. 2004. *Consumers.* 2nd ed. New York: McGraw–Hill/Irwin.

Arnould, E. J., and C. J. Thompson. 2005. "Consumer Culture Theory (CCT): Twenty Years of Research." *Journal of Consumer Research* 31 (4): 868–82.

Barry, E. 2018. "How Vacant Spaces Are Becoming Pop Up Opportunities for Landlords, Retailers." CNBC. October 27, 2018. https://www.cnbc.com/2018/10/26/vacant-spaces-become-pop-up-shops-for-retailers-landlords.html.

Beat the Microbead. 2019. "Impact." *Plastic Soup Foundation.* Accessed August 9, 2019. https://www.beatthemicrobead.org/impact.

Berlin, H. A. 2011. "The Neural Basis of the Dynamic Unconscious." *Neurophsychoanalyis* 13 (1): 5–71.

Berry, C. 1994. *The Idea of Luxury: A Conceptual and Historical Investigation.* Cambridge: Cambridge University Press.

Blue Apron. 2019. "We're Building a Better Food System." Accessed August 9, 2019. https://www.blueapron.com/pages/vision.

Bowlby, R. 2000. *Carried Away by Shopping.* London: Faber & Faber.

Brown, D. 2016. "Loblaw Pop-up Proves Gluten-Free Doesn't Mean Taste Free." *Canadian Grocer.* March 31. https://www.canadiangrocer.com/top-stories/loblaw-pop-up-proves-gluten-free-doesnt-mean-taste-free-63450.

Burton, N. 2015. "Bartering in the Modern Day: How People Are Swapping Skills and Services . . . for Free." *Forbes,* July 20, 2015. https://www.forbes.com/sites/learnvest/2015/07/20/bartering-in-the-modern-day-how-people-are-swapping-skills-and-services-for-free/#6669a4ff17ed.

Business Insider. 2014. "30 Bizarre Vending Machines from around the World." Accessed May 30, 2017. http://www.businessinsider.com/most-unique-vending-machines-2014-11#in-taiwan-customers-can-buy-medical-face-masks-from-vending-machines-these-were-especially-popular-during-the-bird-flu-outbreak-3.

Byers, R. 2015. "This Jim Beam Honey Display is an Immersive Pop-up Display." *Trend Hunter.* September 3. Accessed September 6, 2020. https://www.trendhunter.com/trends/jim-beam-honey.

Cova, B. 1999. "From Marketing to Societing: When the Link Is More Important Than the Thing." In *Rethinking Marketing,* edited by D. Brownlie, M. Saren, R. Wensley, and R. Whittington, 64–83. London: Sage.

Cova, B., and P. Maclaran. 2012. "Rethinking Consumer Culture after Postmodernism: In Search of a New 'Turn.'" Presented at McDonald's Consumer Culture Theory Conference, University of Oxford, August 2012.

Dagevos, H. 2005. "Consumers as Four-Faced Creatures: Looking at Food Consumption from the Perspective of Contemporary Consumers." *Appetite* 45 (1): 32–39.

de Grazia, V. 2005. *Irresistible Empire: America's Advance through 20th Century Europe.* Cambridge, MA: Belknap Press.

Drexler, J. 2017. Personal interview. July 10, 2017.

Elliott, R., and C. Leonard. 2004. "Peer Pressure and Poverty: Exploring Fashion Brands and Consumption Symbolism amongst Children of the 'British Poor.'" *Journal of Consumer Behavior* 3 (1): 347–60.

Fassnacht, M. 2007. "Postmodern Shopper." Marketing Geek, January 28, 2007. http://marketinggeek.blogspot.co.uk/2007/01/postmodern-shopper.html.

Federal Communications Commission. 2019. "About the FCC." Accessed August 9, 2019. https://www.fcc.gov/about/overview.

Federal Trade Commission. 2019. "About the FTC." Accessed August 9, 2019. https://www.ftc.gov/about-ftc.

Firat, A., and C. Shultz. 1997. "From Segmentation to Fragmentation: Markets and Marketing in the Postmodern Era." *European Journal of Marketing* 31 (3/4): 183–207.

Firat, A., and A. Venkatesh. 1995. "Liberatory Postmodernism and the Reenchantment of Consumption." *Journal of Consumer Research* 22 (3): 239–67.

Foderaro, L. W. 2016. "Study Shows the Buildup of Plastic in Waterways." *The New York Times*, Late Edition (East Coast), Section A, Column 0, Metropolitan Desk, p. 28, February 19, 2016.

Goulding, C. 2003. "Issues in Representing the Postmodern Consumer." *Qualitative Research* 6 (3): 152–59.

Hamilton, R. 2016. "Consumer-Based Strategy: Using Multiple Methods to Generate Consumer Insights That Inform Strategy." *Journal of the Academy of Marketing Science* 44:281–85.

Hampson, D. P., A. Grimes, E. Banister, and P. J. McGoldrick. 2018. "A Typology of Consumers Based on Money Attitudes after Major Recession." *Journal of Business Research* 91

(October): 159–68. https://doi.org/10.1016/j.jbusres.2018.06.011.

Hayward, M. 2009. *Rich Apparel: Clothing and the Law in Henry VIII's England.* Surrey, England: Ashgate.

Hirsch, J. 2013. "Dubai's First Farmers Market." *Modern Farmer*, July 17, 2013. http://modernfarmer.com/2013/07/dubai-farmers-market/.

Howey, C. L. 2009. "Dressing a Virgin Queen: Court Women, Dress, and Fashioning the Image of England's Queen Elizabeth I." *Early Modern Women*, 4 (Fall), 201-208.

Jensen, C. 2015. "50 Years Ago, 'Unsafe at Any Speed' Shook the Auto World." *The New York Times*, November 26, 2015. https://www.nytimes.com/2015/11/27/automobiles/50-years-ago-unsafe-at-any-speed-shook-the-auto-world.html.

Kell, J. 2016. "Meals in the Mail: How Blue Apron Got Started and Where It's Heading." *Fortune*, September 11, 2016. http://fortune.com/2016/09/11/blue-apron-meal-delivery/.

Keynes, J. M. 1964. *General Theory of Employment, Interest, and Money: The Classic Work and Foundation of Modern Day Economics.* New York: First Harvest/Harcourt.

Killerby, C. K. 2002. *Sumptuary Law in Italy 1200-1500.* Oxford: Oxford University Press.

Klein, N. 2000. *No Logo.* London: Flamingo.

Knutson, A. 2013. "24 Vending Machines You Won't Believe Exist." *Buzzfeed Food*, January 14, 2013. http://www.buzzfeed.com/arielknutson/vending-machines-you-wont-believe-exist.

Kroen, S. 2004. "A Political History of the Consumer." *Historical Journal* 47 (3): 709–36.

Lenhart, A., and M. Duggan. 2014. "Couples, the Internet, and Social Media: How American Couples Use Digital Technology to Manage Life, Logistics, and Emotional Intimacy within Their Relationships." *Pew Research Center: Internet & Technology*, February 11, 2014. http://www.pewinternet.org/2014/02/11/couples-the-internet-and-social-media/.

Loftus, D. 2011. "The Rise of the Victorian Middle Class." BBC History, February 17, 2011. http://www.bbc.co.uk/history/british/victorians/middle_classes_01.shtml.

Lury, C. 1999. *Consumer Culture.* Cambridge, MA: Polity Press.

MacGregor, N. 2012. *Shakespeare's Restless World.* London: Allen Lane.

Maheshwari, S. and Friedman, V. 2020. "Brooks Brothers, Founded in 1818, Files for Bankruptcy." *The New York Times.* July 8., https://www.nytimes.com/2020/07/08/business/brooks-brothers-chapter-11-bankruptcy.html#:~:text=Brooks%20Brothers%2C%20the%20retailer%20known,apparel%20and%20sales%20shifted%20online.

Marshall, C. 2015. "Southdale Center: America's First Shopping Mall—A History of Cities in 50 Buildings, Day 30." *The Guardian*, May 6, 2015. https://www.theguardian.com/cities/2015/may/06/southdale-center-america-first-shopping-mall-history-cities-50-buildings.

Marx, K. (1867) 2000. "The Culture Industry: Enlightenment as Mass Deception." In *The Consumer Society Reader*, edited by J. B. Schor and D. B. Holt. New York: New Press.

Marx, K. (1876) 1976. *Capital: A Critique of Political Economy.* Vol. 1. Chicago: Kerr.

McCants, A. E. C. 2007. "Exotic Goods, Popular Consumption, and the Standard of Living: Thinking about Globalization in the Early Modern World." *Journal of World History* 18 (4): 433–62.

Mill, J. S. (1848) 2004. *The Principles of Political Economy.* New York: Prometheus.

Mintel. 2015. *Personal Care Consumer—US.* London: Mintel Group.

Lew, J. J. 2019. "Progress and Challenges After the Financial Crisis." In *Ten Years After the Crash: Financial Crises and Regulatory Responses.* O'Halloran, S. and Groll, T., eds. New York: Columbia University Press.

Oxford English Dictionary. 2013. *Oxford English Dictionary.* 11th ed. Oxford: Oxford University Press.

Packard, V. 1957. *The Hidden Persuaders.* London: Penguin.

Penn, W. A. 1901. *The Soverane Herb: A History of Tobacco.* London: Grant Richards.

Perez, O. 2017. "E-Commerce Giant REVOLVE Launches First-Ever Beauty Pop Up." *Forbes.* December 4. Accessed September 6, 2020. https://www.forbes.com/sites/

oliviaperez/2017/12/04/e-commerce-giant-revolve-launches-first-ever-beauty-pop-up/#55bf88de6e89

"Retail Therapy: How Ernest Dichter, an Acolyte of Sigmund Freud, Revolutionised Marketing." 2011. *The Economist* 401 (8764): 119–23.

Rhodes, J. 2012. "Clarence Birdseye: The Man behind Modern Frozen Food." *Smithsonian Magazine*, May 16, 2012. http://www.smithsonianmag.com/arts-culture/clarence-birdseye-the-man-be-hind-modern-frozen-food-95808503/.

Samuel, L. R. 2010. *Freud on Madison Avenue*. Philadelphia: University of Pennsylvania Press.

Sanburn, J. 2017. "Why the Death of Malls Is about More Than Shopping." *Time*, July 20, 2017. http://time.com/4865957/death-and-life-shopping-mall/.

Sears Archives. 2017. *History of the Sears Catalog*. Accessed May 22, 2017. http://www.searsarchives.com/cata-logs/history.htm.

Shoe, D. 2018. "The U.K. Has Banned Microbeads. Why?" *The New York Times*, January 9, 2018. https://www.nytimes.com/2018/01/09/world/europe/microbeads-ban-uk.html.

Simmons, G. 2008. "Marketing to Postmodern Consumers: Introducing the Internet Chameleon." *European Journal of Marketing* 42 (3/4): 299–310.

Skorupa, J. 2008. "Top 10 Oldest US Retailers." *Retail Info Systems*, August 19, 2008. https://risnews.com/top-10-oldest-us-retailers.

Smith, A. (1776) 1981. *An Inquiry into the Nature and Causes of the Wealth of Nations*. Indianapolis, IN: Liberty Press.

Smith, E. 2015. "The History of Vending Machines Goes Back to the 1st Century." *Atlas Obscura*, August 3, 2015.

Spurlock, M., producer and director. 2004. *Supersize Me* (film). New York: Roadside Attractions, Samuel Goldwyn Films, and Showtime Independent Films.

Staff. 2011. "Tesco Builds Virtual Shops for Korean Commuters." *The Telegraph*, June 27, 2011. https://www.telegraph.co.uk/technology/mobile-phones/8601147/Tesco-builds-virtual-shops-for-Korean-commuters.html.

Steinmetz, K. 2014a. "States Are Cracking Down on Face Wash." *Time*, May 7, 2014. https://time.com/74956/states-are-cracking-down-on-face-wash/.

Steinmetz, K. 2014b. "Environmentalists Go to Battle over Face Wash." *Time*, December 11, 2014. https://time.com/3628392/microbead-ban-states/.

Tadajewski, M. 2006. "Remembering Motivation Research: Toward an Alternative Genealogy of Interpretive Consumer Research." *Marketing Theory* 6 (4): 429–66.

TIME Staff. 1982. "A Brief History of Salt." *Time*, March 15, 1982. http://time.com/3957460/a-brief-history-of-salt/.

Trend Reports. 2010. "Statusphere: Consumers Are Finding Increasingly Diverse Ways to Get Their Status Fix. Are You Ready?" Trendwatching.co. Accessed May 29, 2017. http://www.trendwatching.com/trends/statusphere/.

UNESCO. 2017. *Silk Road: Dialogue, Diversity and Development*. Accessed May 19, 2017. http://en.unesco.org/silkroad/content/what-are-spice-routes.

US Bureau of Labor Statistics. 2017. "Employment Characteristics of Families—2016." Press Release USDL-17-0444. Thursday, April 20, 2017.

US Consumer Product Safety Commission. 2019. "About CPSC." Accessed August 9, 2019. https://www.cpsc.gov/About-CPSC/.

Veblen, T. (1899) 2007. *The Theory of the Leisure Class*. Oxford: Oxford University Press.

Worland, J. 2015. "The Face Wash Ingredient in Your Fish." *Time*, September 18, 2015, pN.

Contemporary Perspectives on Consumption

◉ Introduction

In contrast to Chapter 1, which discussed historical perspectives of consumer behavior, this chapter will discuss more contemporary perspectives in the field of consumer behavior. In all, five big themes will be introduced. First, we will discuss behavioral economics and how this field of study has influenced the creation of new perspectives and methodologies that uncover key insights into an individual's consumption decisions and experiences. These behavioral perspectives have been adopted and used extensively by marketing experts. Second, we will introduce the notion of experiential marketing, which places a strong emphasis on the emotional (rather than just the rational) benefits of an experience. Using experiential marketing perspectives, we can better understand the benefits consumers get from, for example, a scary movie or an exciting overseas trip. We will then discuss consumer culture theory, which places a strong emphasis on the social and cultural aspects of consumption. The fourth topic that we will introduce is innovation and how different consumers try out and adopt new innovations. Finally, we will discuss the importance of social networks and social media in influencing consumer perceptions and behaviors.

The field of consumer behavior continues to develop as researchers search for and utilize new perspectives to investigate this important phenomenon. In the early twenty-first century, there is a shift away from a purely rational approach to consumer behavior, where we conclude that consumers make decisions for purely logical reasons, such as an assessment of product benefits and price. Instead, researchers take a much more balanced approach and propose that consumer decisions are often a blend of both rational and emotional factors. There is an appreciation for the entire consumption experience, as well as an appreciation of how the experience changes over time, how it is integrated into a consumer's life, and how it might shift depending on the context.

👁 Behavioral Economics

If you've ever taken an economics class, you know that traditional micro- or macroeconomic theories treat consumers as very logical and rational decision-makers. They propose that consumers make very cool-headed consumption decisions that are based on attributes such as price and product features. Most of the rest of us know that this is not how consumers make decisions! Luckily, **behavioral economics** is a branch of traditional economics that proposes that an individual's behavior is complex and is influenced by rational, emotional, contextual, and sociocultural factors. An important feature of behavioral economics is that it takes into account the **contexts of decisions**, which recognizes that the circumstances and the environment where a decision takes place are critical to the decision itself. Behavioral economics also takes into account the consumer's consumption history, cultural influences, and emotions. With the behavioral economics perspective, there is a recognition that different contexts of consumption will result in different behaviors. To better understand how behavioral economics can be used to improve our understanding of consumer behavior, we first must grasp a few important concepts: exchange and value, automatic and reflective modes, mental accounting, loss aversion, norms, defaults, and priming.

Value and exchange

There are several ways to think of value, but perhaps the most common way is **exchange value**, which is how much a product is worth to a consumer, usually expressed as the product's price. In a competitive market, the price is a balance between the maximum consumers will pay and the minimum suppliers will accept, so exchange value is critical in how markets function. **Utility (or use) value** is another notion of value and is a measure of what function the product performs for the consumer. It is related to the satisfaction consumers get from a product, which is usually thought of as being determined by a set of product attributes; for example, for a car, these attributes might include fuel economy, acceleration, and styling. A **product attribute** is a feature of the product, usually seen in the description of the product (a product attribute for a sweater could be that it is made with 100 percent wool; a product attribute for a hotel could be that it has free Wi-Fi). Utility value, therefore, can be described as the value of a product to a consumer in terms of the tangible benefits (or usefulness) it provides. Utility value is necessary for exchange value, but can be above or below the exchange value for an individual buyer or seller. As an example, most homeowners do not have their house on the market; the home's *utility value* to them is higher than its *exchange value*. You might decide not to buy a jacket because it is too expensive, meaning that its exchange value is higher than its utility value to you. These traditional economic concepts treat consumers as self-contained and unconcerned about how others view them.

However, we also talk about the **symbolic value** of a product, which is a collection of deeper meanings consumers attach to products. Here, consumption is a signal to others about a consumer's identity and place in social relationships.

Behavioral economics is a branch of traditional economics that proposes that an individual's behavior is complex and is influenced by rational, emotional, contextual, and sociocultural factors.

Contexts of decisions recognizes that the circumstances and the environment where a decision takes place are critical to the decision itself.

Exchange value is how much the product is worth to the consumer, which is usually expressed as the product's price.

Utility (or use) value is a measure of what function the product performs for the consumer.

Product attribute is a feature or characteristic of the product.

Symbolic value is the collection of deeper meanings consumers attach to products.

This can turn the traditional categories of value upside down, so that a higher price is a symbol that a product is exclusive. This exclusivity may make the product especially attractive, even if in traditional functional terms its utility value may be similar to an alternative that is cheaper (i.e., has a lower exchange value).

Imagine the actual cost of making a high-end designer wallet, such as Louis Vuitton or Hermes, compared with the price for which it can be sold in a designer store. The exchange value of that wallet does not represent its utility value, because the function of the wallet could just as easily be accomplished with a much cheaper alternative. However, the *symbolic value* of such a wallet is probably higher for those who purchase it than either the exchange value or the utility value. For many consumers, the products we consume are defined as much by their symbolic value as by their utility value. For marketers, it is vitally important to understand how consumers perceive these different kinds of value.

Two modes of thinking: automatic and reflective

According to researchers in behavioral economics, consumers engage in two modes of thinking: automatic and reflective. Consumers who are operating in the **automatic mode** do not deliberately or consciously think before they behave. Instead, the reactions and behaviors are automatic, such as smiling at a puppy or jumping at a loud sound. In automatic mode, a tired student may automatically walk over to Starbucks after a long day of classes without even thinking about it and may even order the same extra shot of espresso. Consumers using the **reflective mode** of thinking, however, exert deliberate effort to their thoughts and decision-making before they behave. It is more effortful and controlled (see Photo 2.1).

> **Automatic mode** of thinking means that individuals do not deliberately or consciously think before they behave.

> **Reflective mode** of thinking means that individuals exert deliberate effort to their thoughts and decision-making before they behave.

An example may help illustrate the difference between the two modes of thinking. Try to remember back to when you were learning how to drive a car. You most likely were very careful about every move you made, such as which pedal to use, how fast to accelerate, and when to use your turn signal. The whole driving experience may even have been a bit stressful, especially if you had a parent sitting next to you in the passenger seat! At this early point in the learning process, you were using a reflective mode of thinking. You were carefully thinking about each and every part of the driving experience. After a few weeks of practice, however, you became much more comfortable and familiar with the whole process. You had a better sense of the driving experience and could almost drive to familiar places like school, work, and home automatically. It was at this point that you switched to automatic mode.

Examples of organizations trying to get individuals to transition to a reflective mode of thinking are all around us. One

● **Photo 2.1** *Reaching for a cup of hot coffee on a cold day after class is an example of using the automatic mode of thinking*

● **Photo 2.2** *Cigarette recycling bins from TerraCycle*

example is a newly implemented strategy by some cities around the country to find a way to deal with the problem of cigarette butt waste. In 2014, New Orleans became the first city in the United States to offer its citizens and visitors an especially easy way to recycle their cigarettes. The initial installation of fifty "Recycle Your Butts" receptacles was a welcome sight for some local citizens of New Orleans who were tired of the huge volume of discarded cigarettes on their streets (New Orleans Convention and Visitor's Bureau 2014). According to Keep America Beautiful, cigarette waste is the most littered item in the United States and across the globe; 65 percent of all cigarette butts end up as litter (Keep America Beautiful 2020). It is hoped that when smokers see the receptacles, they will move from an automatic mode to a more reflective mode of thinking and recycle their cigarette butts (see Photo 2.2).

Strategies like these are increasingly being utilized by governments and policy makers who are concerned about finding the most effective ways to change people's behavior in areas such as saving enough for retirement, getting the proper vaccinations, or not drinking or eating too much.

Because it has an impact on consumer decision-making, consumer researchers would like to know which mode of thinking consumers are using. Knowing which mode of thinking consumers are using helps marketers design strategies to tap into those modes. For example, sometimes marketers would like consumers to maintain an automatic mode, for example, when they grab a Snickers bar in the grocery store checkout aisle. These marketers want to make sure their candy is available and easy to reach in as many places as possible. Marketers may also want to encourage more thoughtful, or reflective, modes of thinking. If this is the case, marketers may *nudge* consumers toward a behavior by altering the environment in which the decision is being made. Marketers do this by carefully constructing the **choice architecture,** or the presentation of two or more choices, which influences consumers to make the "preferred" choice. One example of the use of choice architecture is how fast-food outlets, cafeterias, and restaurants are now adding information on calories and fat content to their menus. Rather than automatically picking a burger and fries, the presence of this information may result in some customers being nudged to make healthier choices. Another example can often be seen with your restaurant bill. At the end of the meal, when your bill is presented, some restaurants provide a list of suggested tips at the bottom of the bill in increments of 15, 18, or 20 percent. This architecture of choice means that the customer will be nudged to at least give the waiter or waitress a 15 percent tip!

Mental accounting

Mental accounting occurs when individuals allocate assets, such as their finances, into separate categories to which they assign different levels of utility. An example may help explain this. After getting their paycheck at the end of the week,

Choice architecture describes how marketers may influence the choice context by presenting two or more choices such that consumers make the "preferred" choice.

Mental accounting occurs when individuals allocate assets, such as their finances, into separate groupings to which they assign different levels of utility.

many people mentally put that money into different categories—specific amounts may go for rent, bills, food, and fun. Individuals use mental accounting to help organize their lives. A person will think very carefully before spending so much money on "fun" that there is not enough left over for rent, bills, or food. People also allocate their time, for instance, spending an hour at the gym, an hour on social media, and then the rest of the night studying. Why do we use mental accounting? Because individuals have certain cognitive limitations, it helps frame their decisions and make those decisions easier. Simply put, it makes the consumption environment easier to navigate by helping consumers organize and keep track of lots of things. It also gives them a sense of control and empowerment.

Loss aversion

Another important notion from behavioral economics is **loss aversion**, which is the tendency of individuals to dislike losses more than gains of an equivalent amount. Organizations and governments often try to change individual behavior through the use of incentives and rewards. Some of these efforts would be much more successful if they used principles of behavioral economics, such as loss aversion. This is because the concept of loss aversion predicts that obtaining an incentive is not as motivating as avoiding a loss. One study, for example, tried to find ways to reduce obesity by giving individuals financial rewards for losing weight. Not surprisingly, very few individuals were able to achieve, let alone maintain, their weight loss (Paul-Ebhohimhen and Avenell 2008). However, *reverse* incentives, or the fear of losing money, can be very motivating. In another weight-loss study, study participants made small monetary deposits into an account. If they met their weight-loss targets, the money was returned to them—with a bonus. If they did not meet the targets, the money would be lost. After several months, study participants achieved and maintained their weight-loss goals (Volpp et al. 2008). Loss aversion has been applied to numerous contexts, but the general result is always similar: avoiding a loss is more motivating than achieving a gain.

The concept of loss aversion can even result in consumers making less than rational decisions. Take the example of cellular phone bills. Chances are, with your phone bill you get a fixed number of minutes or data per month. If you go over those limits, you are charged a higher price. Many consumers are quite bothered by this kind of penalty charge because they experience it as "losing money." In fact, they would rather buy a plan that gives them far more than enough minutes or data so that they never get hit with a charge, even if they end up paying far more for that plan. These consumers would rather have a known, higher expense with the costlier contract than a surprise "loss" from a penalty charge.

One important characteristic of loss aversion is the **endowment effect**, which is the tendency for individuals to value the things they own. In a classic experiment, student research participants were given a free coffee mug that was decorated with their university's crest. Each person was then asked to sell the new mug to another student who did not own one. The concept of the endowment effect would predict that individuals who owned a mug would be

Loss aversion describes the fact that most people dislike losses more than gains of an equivalent amount.

Endowment effect is the tendency for individuals to value the things they own.

somewhat reluctant to part with the mug, and that is exactly what happened. Specifically, mug owners required about *twice* as much money to sell their mug as the other students were prepared to pay. Once someone owns an item, he or she generally does not like the idea of giving it up (Thaler and Sunstein 2009). This experiment has been repeated many times with many kinds of items over the years. Simply owning the object gives it a special significance and makes the owner less willing to part with it. A fascinating follow-up to these original studies found that the endowment effect was much stronger in Western cultures, which are much more individualistic than the much more interdependent Eastern cultures (Maddux et al. 2010).

Norms

Norms are a set of informal rules that society imposes to guide individual behavior.

Another important concept of behavioral economics is **norms**, which refer to a set of informal rules that a society imposes to guide individual behavior. Because norms are strongly tied to culture and specific social situations, they are well known to most members in those social or cultural groups. Norms help individuals understand and derive meaning from the kinds of behavior they see around them. For example, even the simple act of greeting someone from a different culture can be fraught with difficulty unless a person knows the correct social norms. In some countries, such as Italy or France, it is customary to give a loose embrace and a kiss to each cheek; in the Netherlands, you get three kisses (first cheek, second cheek, and the first cheek again). In contrast, people in the United States and the United Kingdom are a bit more formal and shake hands. In Asia, you bow, but you had better be sure about the type of bow—China requires a nod or bow, Japanese protocol calls for a bow from the waist, and Koreans give a slight bow. Social norms around the world regarding the exchange of a business card are even more complicated!

Social norms work to exert peer pressure on individuals by providing information they can use to help guide their decisions (see Insights from Academia 2.1). This information is needed if we are to successfully navigate new contexts. Think about it: if we learn that a number of people are doing something, we may incorporate this information into our own decision-making and conclude that we want to also engage in that behavior. Seeing a lot of people at a restaurant or a long line at the movie theater might influence you to go to that restaurant or see that movie too. Peer pressure works best when the opinion of others really matters to us. In Chapter 10, we will learn much more about groups and social pressure. One example of how social norms and peer pressure can influence behavior is reusing towels in hotel rooms. One study found that when a hotel room had a sign in it saying that most (75 percent) of the guests who stayed in the hotel room reused their towels to help save the environment, 44 percent of guests reused their towels. If the sign simply asked clients to reuse their towels to help the environment, only 35 percent reused their towels (Goldstein, Cialdini, and Griskevicius 2008). Norms and peer pressure work!

INSIGHTS FROM ACADEMIA 2.1

Pay your taxes on time. Your neighbor did!

No one likes to pay taxes, but in the United Kingdom, social norms are used to encourage people to pay their taxes on time. The old method to get people to pay their taxes on time involved threats of legal action. When threats were used, 68 percent complied and paid their taxes on time. However, when a message was sent out saying that 93 percent of the "people in your town pay their taxes on time," the rate at which people paid on time went up to 83 percent. Compare this compliance rate to other social norm–based appeals, such as "people in your postcode" (79 percent compliance) and "UK citizens" (73 percent compliance). The especially interesting thing to note here is that the more *precise* the social norm (i.e., people in your town), the higher the compliance rate.

Martin, S. 2012. "98% of HBR Readers Love This Article." Harvard Business Review *(October): 23–25.*

Information that is generated around social norms can influence both positive and negative behaviors. In a study of three hundred US households, homeowners were given information on their own energy consumption as well as the average consumption in their area. Over the next few weeks, homeowners used this information to adjust their energy usage. The above-average users decreased their use, but unfortunately, the below-average users increased their energy usage (Schultz et al. 2007). This phenomenon is known as the *boomerang effect* and indicates that there can be very tangible downsides when individuals see that their behavior is better than social norms.

Defaults

Sometimes it is just easier to keep using the same product or service. A **default** is a preselected option that a consumer makes without active thought or consideration. Default decisions and behaviors rely on the fact that it is often more of a bother to change than it is to continue with the same decision or behavior. Unfortunately, consumers often use defaults to their own detriment. For example, many consumers are unwilling to change their phone and data plans, even when there are better options elsewhere. Because of defaults, companies know that they can often entice consumers to sign up for subscription services with a limited-time "free" offer. These organizations know that consumers are unlikely to cancel and will then start paying for the subscription after the limited-time offer expires.

This behavioral economics tendency of default behavior has produced an important insight about how inertia will prevent individuals from dropping out of a program for which they are already signed up. Indeed, the concept of *opting in* and *opting out* resulted from this insight. If individuals are automatically registered into a program and have to consciously think

Default is a preselected option that a consumer makes without active thought or consideration.

Nudging consumers toward healthier decisions

Nudging happens when subtle cues are used to help consumers or citizens make choices that are better for them or their families. Behavioral economic principles are often behind these nudging strategies. One example revolves around the efforts to help curb the obesity problem that is plaguing the United States. Countless restaurants and fast-food chains now offer calorie information for consumers in an effort to "nudge" them toward better food choices.

Childhood obesity is of particular concern. According to the Centers for Disease Control, the percentage of children who are obese has tripled since 1970; obesity now impacts about 18.5 percent of US children. Obese children have more chronic health conditions; suffer from social isolation, depression, and low self-esteem; and are likely to also have chronic health problems once they reach adulthood (Childhood Obesity 2019). We know that even subtle cues can influence the kinds of choices that kids make when snacking. Even the size and weight of a cartoon character, for example, can make a difference. When children view overweight cartoon characters like Homer Simpson or Chris on the TV series *Family Guy*, for example, they are more likely to overeat. By contrast, children who view normal weight cartoon characters do not overeat (Campbell, et al. 2016).

Because of this, there has been increased scrutiny on these environmental influences and experts have enacted efforts to nudge children to make better consumption choices and to become more active. Overall, if healthy options like fruit and vegetables, water, and salad bars are *easily* available in school cafeterias and unhealthy items are *less* available, students will shift their choices to the healthy options. Unfortunately, if school lunch lines are long and the time for lunch is limited, nudging doesn't work and children are more likely to select less healthy options (Frerichs et al. 2015) (Photo 2.3).

Nudging and choice architecture can also help individuals make choices for a healthier planet. Some environmentally-minded retailers are eliminating the most environmentally unfriendly options in their product assortments, essentially giving customers a choice of products that range from only slightly unfriendly to very environmentally friendly. In a similar vein, rather than

● **Photo 2.3** *Nudging kids toward healthier food choices*

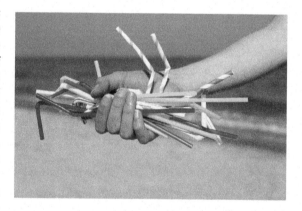

● **Photo 2.4** *Nudging can be used to get consumers to use fewer plastic straws, which are harmful to marine life*

automatically giving patrons a drinking straw, some restaurants are starting to only provide one when asked (Photo 2.4).

Questions

1. Your task is to nudge individuals in the eighteen- to thirty-five-year-old age bracket to get a flu shot. How might you use social norms to accomplish this? Be specific.
2. Altering the choice architecture can limit a consumer's free choice. Do you agree or disagree? Why?

Sources: Frerichs et al. 2015; Cabinet Office (2010); Childhood Obesity (2019).

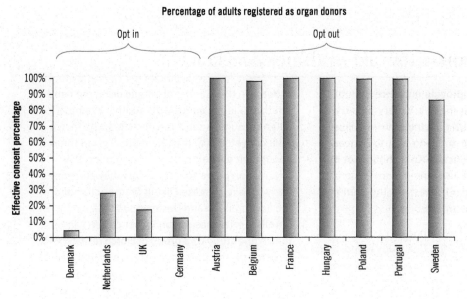

Percentage of adults registered as organ donors

Figure 2.1 *Comparison of organ donation registration in opt-in and opt-out systems*
Source: Johnson and Goldstein (2003).

about and exert effort to opt out of the program, they are very unlikely to do so. On the other hand, individuals are not likely to expend the time or effort to opt in to a program, even though it might be beneficial to them. Some countries around the world automatically register their citizens into an organ donation database and it is up to the individual to opt out. Others leave it up to their citizens to opt in to an organ donation program. We can see the difference in the number of people who are registered organ donors, depending on whether the opt-in or opt-out strategy is used (see Figure 2.1).

Nudging happens when subtle cues are used to help consumers or citizens make choices that are better for them or their families.

Priming

Priming is the last concept from behavioral economics that we explore for now. Think about how certain people, images, or things make you feel. Seeing a puppy or a kitten makes you feel happy; hearing some music from your teenage years makes you feel nostalgic. Look at Photo 2.5. Do you feel happy? This effect on our feelings and behaviors is called priming and has been studied quite extensively in consumer behavior because it has the potential to influence

Photo 2.5 *Seeing a puppy primes consumers to feel happy*

INSIGHTS FROM THE FIELD 2.2

Priming in action

Behavioral economics can provide guidance to public officials in helping people make a variety of better choices. For example, the UK government has utilized these strategies to reduce smoking and to increase organ donation (Cabinet Office 2010). It should not be surprising that companies use priming to influence consumers too. Of particular interest are the priming effects of words, sights, and smells.

1. **Words:** The spoken and written word can be very powerful in altering behavior. One study found that after research participants read a list of words that are associated with the elderly (e.g., *wrinkles*), they walked more slowly and had a poorer memory, compared to other people who read a different list of words. The researchers concluded that the people who were primed with an elderly stereotype reacted accordingly (Dijksterhuis and Bargh 2001). Priming can also help individuals react in a positive way. In another study, research participants who were primed with words such as *fit*, *lean*, *active*, and *athletic* were much more likely to use the stairs rather than the elevator (Wryobeck and Chen 2003).
2. **Sights:** Visual cues can also influence behavior. When a hospital installed a picture of two eyes over a hand sanitizing station (as in, "we're watching you"), there was an 18.3 percent increase in the number of people using the hand sanitizer (King et al. 2016). As another example, when consumers see ads with actors who match their own ethnicity, they are more likely to think about their own ethnicity as they process the information in the ad. In addition, they are more likely to have increased liking for the actors and the ad (Forehand and Deshpande 2001).
3. **Smells:** Certain scents can influence behavior too. In one study by a group of Dutch researchers, research participants were exposed to the "clean" scent of an all-purpose cleaner as they ate in the cafeteria. Compared to those who had not been exposed to the scent, those who had been exposed were more likely to keep their tables clean (Holland, Hendricks, and Aarts 2005).

Questions

1. Using what you have learned about priming, carefully describe how you might get children to read more during the summer months.
2. How would a pharmaceutical manufacturer use priming tactics to encourage consumers to stock up on their products during cold and flu season?

Sources: Dijksterhuis and Bargh (2001); Wryobeck and Chen (2003); Holland et al. (2005); Cabinet Office (2010).

Priming is a phenomenon in which exposure to a stimulus, such as words, images, or sounds, alters an individual's response, without conscious awareness.

our behavior. **Priming** is a phenomenon in which exposure to a stimulus, such as words, images, or sounds, alters an individual's response, without conscious awareness. Consumers who are first primed with certain cues can change their behavior. Much of this happens without them being consciously aware of the effects (see Lench, Flores, and Bench 2011 for a review). See Insights from the Field 2.2 for more detailed information about the kinds of stimuli that have been used to prime behavior.

Priming is especially powerful because individuals are often not aware of its influence (see Insights from Academia 2.2). Because most consumers are unaware of the priming effect, we need to be especially careful that it is not used to manipulate consumers.

INSIGHTS FROM ACADEMIA 2.2

So cute I could eat it up!

Priming has an especially powerful influence on a variety of consumption behaviors, including eating. When participants were primed with whimsically cute products, mental representations of fun were cued. Further, when consumers think about fun, they're less likely to carefully consider calories, diets, and weight loss. One part of the study had participants take either a cute ice cream scoop with a funny face on it or a regular ice cream scoop. Those who used the cute scoop took bigger scoops of ice cream—and consumed more ice cream—than those who used the regular scoop. Thus, as one of the core concepts in behavioral economics, the concept of priming demonstrates that consumers are influenced by a variety of external and contextual factors.

Nenkov, G. Y., and M. Scott. 2014. "So Cute I Could Eat It Up:" Priming Effects of Cute Products on Indulgent Consumption." Journal of Consumer Research *14, no. 2 (August): 326–41.*

Political leaders, activists, and nongovernmental organizations may also use priming to try to influence the behaviors of citizens or voters. At first glance, Photo 2.6 appears to be a picture of some tasty pieces of sushi. However, it quickly becomes apparent that there is something seriously wrong. After looking more closely and reading the ad copy, the effect is one of revulsion. The message is that plastics in the ocean results in plastic in our food. The simple imagery not only grabs our attention with a bit of shock and emotion, it also conveys an important message by priming us to think about a very serious issue. Further, it exhorts us to become more informed and involved in efforts to keep our oceans and beaches clean.

WHAT GOES IN THE OCEAN GOES IN YOU.

A RECENT STUDY FOUND THAT 35% OF FISH SAMPLED OFF THE WEST COAST HAD INGESTED PLASTIC. FIND OUT HOW YOU CAN HELP. VISIT WWW.SURFRIDER.ORG MAKE THE PLEDGE. BAN THE BAG.

SURFRIDER FOUNDATION

● **Photo 2.6** *Plastic Sushi Ad from Surfrider Foundation*

👁 Experiential Marketing

Experiential marketing builds on concepts from behavioral economics and is a different way of thinking about consumer behavior. It is a shift in conceptualizing the consumer as a rational decision-maker to thinking of the consumer as an experience-seeker. According to this perspective of consumer behavior, consumers often want to engage in activities that are creative, exciting, and new (Holbrook and Hirschman 1982). By studying how individuals consume music, dance, theater, and entertainment, as well as other travel and leisure activities, marketers concluded that there were important *sensory* and *hedonic* aspects of consumer behavior.

Experiential marketing is a way for researchers to better understand marketing. It is a shift in emphasis from the consumer as a rational decision-maker to a model where the consumer is viewed as an experience seeker.

What is the authentic Fiji experience? It depends on who you ask.

● *Josefa Wivou*

Josefa Wivou is the director of niche marketing for Tourism Fiji. He has a tough job: encouraging tourists to visit Fiji. Wivou is a native of Fiji, but has spent his life traveling around the world and working for companies like Priceline and Qantas. He knows that certain tourists are looking for more than just a relaxing time on the beach. Instead, they're looking for something much more experiential—something where they can challenge themselves, learn about the culture, make a difference, and leave with stories to tell their friends.

Fiji is located in the Pacific Ocean, about four hours northeast of Sydney, Australia; about three hours north of Auckland, New Zealand; and about eleven hours from Los Angeles. Fiji is made up of 333 small islands, about 100 of which are uninhabited. The main island of Viti Levu is where most of the tourists go because that is where the international airport is located. Tourism Fiji is a small branch of the Fijian government tasked with increasing visits to Fiji, but doing so in a sustainable manner. To do this, Wivou has tried to uncover more about what visitors expect from their Fiji experience.

Before Wivou started his job, the only thing that Tourism Fiji knew about tourists was the total number of visitors per year. They didn't know where they were coming from, how much money they spent, what they did, or where they stayed. Now, Wivou knows what visitors are doing and what they're seeking when they arrive. He uses data analytics to look at trends and then develops models for understanding the behaviors of tourists. Using these models and insights, he can then market to tourists in a way that fulfills their expectations for their own idea of the ideal Fijian experience.

Searching for the experience

Approximately 800,000 people visit Fiji each year, which is quite a lot when you consider that the entire population of Fiji is approximately 936,000 (Central Intelligence Agency 2020). Wivou has found that 70 percent of tourists to Fiji come from Australia and New Zealand, while 14 percent come from North America, mainly from the West Coast. According to Wivou, these three markets "could not be more different" in what they want out of a vacation trip to Fiji (2017). Wivou and his team developed customer profiles of three primary segments to find out what their expectations were for their Fijian experience:

- *Australia*: These tourists want to have fun, relax, and drink some tropical drinks. Their main motivation is a hassle-free, relaxing time on the beach. They're very likely to spend the whole time in a resort close to the airport and are very unlikely to venture out to see other parts of Fiji.
- *New Zealand*: These tourists have a much stronger cultural interest. Historically, New Zealanders have a much stronger connection to their native Maori culture (as compared to Australians and the Aboriginals). New Zealand does a lot to integrate and celebrate its native culture, which helps define the overall identity of the nation. Tourists from New Zealand want to find some common points of interest when they visit Fiji. They're interested in cultural experiences, hiking, and visiting the native villages.
- *North America*: This is called the *long-haul* market and, because they are traveling from so far away, they want to make the trip worth it. These tourists are very concerned about carefully planning each part of their trip and generally spend a bit more than tourists from other places. For example, they are very interested in scuba diving, perhaps because Fiji is the soft-coral capital of the world and has some excellent shark diving experiences. North American tourists want to stay active and

want to see as much of Fiji as they can. Unlike the Australians, it would be difficult to find a North American tourist spending his or her entire vacation in a resort by the beach.

Matching expectations with the experience

What's next for Tourism Fiji? Based on the profiles, Wivou and his team developed different initiatives to meet the expectations of the different segments:

- *Australia*: In the near future, the focus will be on families, because the current Australian youth market is not that interested in Fiji right now. These younger tourists are looking to go to Southeast Asia and Europe because they have a little more time on their hands. Families are generally price-conscious, so Tourism Fiji encourages hotels to offer discounts to coincide with the school holidays, which happen in October. They also encourage hotels to promote babysitting services and children's activities so that the adults can relax.
- *New Zealand*: Tourism Fiji is aggressively going after the youth and backpacker market from New Zealand. Fiji is a very safe country; it is very family and community oriented. In addition, English is one of the three main languages spoken in Fiji. Although the New Zealand market does not have a lot of money, Tourism Fiji is trying to get them to play "a leading role in sustainability" by volunteering for projects such as farming programs and beach or reef restoration programs.
- *North America*: One of the biggest efforts with this group is to provide better information about bookings and other adventures that these tourists can experience. Like the New Zealanders, these consumers show a strong interest in volunteering. They want to make a difference and climate change is a very important issue for them. "It's a key part of their demographic profile," Wivou explains (2017).

Wivou has only been on the job for a few years, but he is happy with the progress he has made in opening up the possibilities of his small island nation to the rest of the world so that they can fulfill their own dreams and expectations of a "true Fiji experience."

Sources: Central Intelligence Agency (2020); Wivou (2017).

Sensory aspects of consumption involve the experience of sensations that enter one's consciousness through one of a consumer's five senses (i.e., see, smell, taste, touch, or hear). **Hedonic aspects of consumption** involve multiple senses, emotions, and even some fantasy. Think about the last time you went to the theater to see a movie. It likely involved multiple senses (sights, sounds, smells, etc.), it involved emotions (it was funny or it was scary), and it involved some fantasy (for example, that situation could never happen in real life!). Watching a movie is an act of *hedonic consumption*.

Experiential marketing is a perspective that views consumers not as rational decision-makers, but as participants in an experience who reap a variety of practical and emotional benefits from that experience. Think about the last time you got tickets to see your favorite singer or band. It is easy to see that the entire

Sensory aspects of consumption involve the experience of sensations that enter one's consciousness through one of a consumer's five senses (sight, smell, hearing, touch, taste).

Hedonic aspects of consumption involve multiple senses, emotions, and even some fantasy. Consumption is designed to provide pleasure, fun, or enjoyment.

consumption experience incorporates so much more than just rational thoughts and reasoning. Indeed, emotions are incorporated at each step of the process, from the purchase of the tickets all the way until the concert is over and you are telling your friends about it. What are you really consuming when you see your favorite singer or band? Sure, you are experiencing the band members, the venue, and many of your favorite songs. In addition, this type of consumption is a shared experience with everyone else there; the audience shares in this unique experience together. Most consumption experiences, even mundane ones like going to the dentist or bringing your car in for service, have important rational and emotional components. There are four key stages in the consumption of an experience (Arnould, Price, and Zinkhan 2002; Szmigin and Piacentini 2015):

- Stage 1: the preconsumption experience—searching for, planning, and imagining the experience;
- Stage 2: the purchase experience, which includes the choice process and the interaction with the service setting;
- Stage 3: the core consumption experience, which involves the sensation of consumption and whether we feel good about it or not;
- Stage 4: the remembered consumption and the nostalgia experience, which is about reliving the past experience and classifying the experience among other experiences.

In many consumer decisions, the experiential part of consumption is incredibly important. Think about what is involved in planning for and then going on a vacation (see Insights from the Boardroom 2). The impact of behavioral economics and experiential marketing has been enduring in how marketers see consumers because it shifts the emphasis away from consumers as simply buyers to a focus on consumers as participants in experiences.

Advances in behavioral economics spurred marketers and other observers to acknowledge experiential dimensions of consumption. In addition, they motivated consumer researchers to conceive of consumption more holistically and to develop new research techniques to study this phenomenon (see, for example, Belk, Sherry, and Wallendorf 1988; Belk, Wallendorf, and Sherry, 1989; Rook 1988; and O'Guinn and Faber 1989).

◉ Consumer Culture Theory

Consumer culture theory (CCT) is a broad collection of models, perspectives, and research methods for studying the social and cultural aspects of consumption.

Built on principles of behavioral economics, **consumer culture theory** (CCT) is a broad collection of models, perspectives, and research methods for studying the social and cultural aspects of consumption. The CCT approach seeks to understand the role that consumption plays in the lives of consumers. It attempts to understand how consumers form individual and collective identities around consumption, as well as the interactions between these identities, consumption communities, and the broader sociocultural environment (Arnould and Thompson 2005). For example, researchers using a CCT approach to investigate voting attitudes and perceptions might focus on the various ways in which individuals learn about issues and candidates, how certain issues become more or less important to them, or how they form connections of trust with candidates. A CCT approach might also investigate voting behavior by studying practices around registering to vote, influencing others to vote, and family dynamics around politics. All of this is meant to develop a contextually rich understanding of voting so that candidates and campaign managers can derive useful insights from those findings. Consumer culture theory can be sorted into four main themes (Arnould and Thompson 2005) (see Table 2.1 and Insights from Academia 2.3).

Another important aspect of the CCT approach is that it has developed new research methods designed to better understand the complexities of consumption culture. Some of the research approaches now being used are detailed in Table 2.2.

Academic researchers often use an experiential approach with its associated research methods to understand a wide variety of consumer behaviors (see Insights from Academia 2.4). These methods have become more widely used in marketing practice, with a majority of Fortune 500 companies including them in their research repertoire.

Table 2.1 Themes of consumer culture theory

CONSUMER CULTURE THEORY THEME AND EXPLANATION
1. *Consumer identity projects.* This research has focused on consumers seeking to develop their identity through their consumption behavior. Identity projects relate to the idea that throughout our life we are engaged in a process of constructing a story (or narrative) of ourselves and use consumption to mark this story. Jewelry often serves this function for consumers. The Danish jewelry company Pandora markets its charms and charm bracelets with the promise, "You're certain to find one for each of your special moments."
2. *Marketplace cultures.* This research theme focuses on how consumers interact with the marketplace, how their particular consumption needs are served by it, and how consumers become influencers and producers of culture. Nightclubs provide a good illustration of a marketplace culture—the fashions and trends in music, styles of dancing, clothes worn, and drinks and drugs consumed are influenced and shaped by both clubbers and club promoters.
3. *The sociohistoric patterning of consumption.* This strand looks at how consumption experiences are influenced by the institutions and social structures in our lives, such as gender, social class, and ethnicity. The overall goal is to develop a deep understanding of consumer culture and consumption experiences, as well as how they have evolved and changed over time. Efforts to understand sociocultural influences on men's eating habits, for example, may systematically analyze representations of men, food, eating, and health in various media over a historical period.
4. *Mass-mediated marketplace ideologies and consumers' interpretive strategies.* This research strand is concerned with how consumers make sense of marketing messages and develop responses to them. From this perspective, consumers are active agents, engaged with meaning-creating activities. Examples of this type of activity may focus on the ways that consumers connect to form grass-roots movements encouraging businesses to be more environmentally friendly or socially just.

Source: Szmigin and Piacentini (2015).

INSIGHTS FROM ACADEMIA 2.3

How many "likes" can I get for losing five pounds?

Who knew that one way to drop a few pounds was to go online? This study examined the comments that were made by participants in two online weight-loss forums and concluded that when individuals participate in the forum, they form important relationships with people who are going through the same thing. Importantly, the friends they make and the support they get become an important part of their own social identity. So, when people commit online to a weight-loss goal, because this commitment is now intertwined with their own identity, it is more likely that they will achieve that goal. Online community interactions like these can be extremely helpful to consumers, and consumer culture theory helps us understand this fascinating aspect of consumer behavior.

Bradford, T. W., S. A. Grier, and G. R. Henderson. 2017. "Weight Loss through Virtual Support Communities: A Role for Identity-Based Motivation in Public Commitment." Journal of Interactive Marketing *40 (November): 9-23.*

Table 2.2 Some research methods favored in the consumer culture theory approach

METHOD	EXPLANATION
Ethnography	The goal of this research method is to create a deep understanding of a culture or cultural phenomenon, including its knowledge and meaning systems. To create this understanding, researchers engage in deep immersion in the culture, which involves a researcher spending extensive time in, or even living in, a culture to fully understand it.
Introspection	A method whereby participants engage in self-reflection and give careful and detailed descriptions of their own thought processes.
Narrative analysis	A method that asks participants to tell stories about their lives and experiences. Based on a careful analysis of the stories, researchers then try to better understand the consumers' life experiences and underlying motivations.
Discourse analysis	A method that studies spoken and written forms of communication, as well as their patterns and frequencies. The goal is to identify overall themes of communication between individuals and groups.
Netnography	A method for studying online communities that investigates communications between individuals and how relationships and meaning are developed and shared.

INSIGHTS FROM ACADEMIA 2.4

Tailgating at the big game

Have you ever seen those elaborate college football tailgates in which happy fans set up a table, chairs, and even some of other comforts of home like rugs, lighting, and big-screen televisions? As it turns out, the consumers who do this are bringing their very private world into a very public space in which they interact with friends and strangers. This creates a fascinating phenomenon in which strong relationships are forged and strengthened with others who are doing the same thing. Using methods of consumer culture theory research, the researchers found that fans have a sense of ownership of their spaces and take personal pride in their setups, their hospitality, and their shared experiences (see Photo 2.7).

Williams Bradford, T., and J. F. Sherry. 2015. "Domesticating Public Space through Ritual: Tailgating as Vestaval." Journal of Consumer Research *42 (June): 130.*

● **Photo 2.7** *College Football Tailgate Party*

◎ Innovation And Consumer Behavior

Another contemporary perspective on consumption concerns the role that technology and innovation play in influencing choice and consumption. Technology is an important driver of social change, and as new innovations are introduced at an increasingly quick pace, the consumption experience itself begins to shift and change.

The sociocultural context of technology

Developments in technology have fundamentally altered almost every dimension of business and the marketplace. They have also dramatically altered almost every dimension of our lives as consumers. Are advancements in technology a logical *result* of changes in consumer needs or are these advancements *responsible* for changes to consumer needs?

Some technological advances are a result of changes in consumer needs. The history of contact lenses, for example, goes all the way back to Leonardo da Vinci, who first proposed the idea in 1508. In 1887, contact lenses were made of glass and covered the entire eye. Over time, design improvements were made because of innovations in materials, but also because consumers increasingly demanded more comfort and performance out of the product. In response to these demands, contact lenses started to be manufactured out of softer plastics by 1939, and by 2010, consumers could get custom-manufactured lenses made from silicone hydrogel ("A brief history" 2019). This example illustrates how changes in consumer needs and wants can spur technological innovation.

By contrast, technological advancements are sometimes responsible for changes to consumer needs and wants. When smartphones were first introduced around 2001, very few people could have predicted the ways in which this new technology changed the nature of human interactions and consumption. The technology has changed the way in which consumers shop, communicate, search for information, and date. Consumers use their phones to keep up with the news, their favorite sports teams, one another, and their classes. Perhaps you are even reading this book on your phone! Advancements in the speed of downloading and streaming have prompted cellular service providers to adjust their pricing, speed, and access. One unexpected outcome of increased speed and access is that consumers have developed an expectation for immediate and personalized responses from companies. These expectations have carried over to other service encounters, as further discussed in Insights from the Field 2.3. Advancements in technology can sometimes be a *result* of changes in consumer needs and can sometimes be *responsible* for changes to consumer needs. For now, the debate is not settled. However, no one can debate the fact that the changes are dramatic. Intuitive researchers know, however, that the study of consumer behavior is an ongoing process and that consumer perceptions, attitudes, and behaviors will be measured by marketing teams to create insights to help predict how consumers will react to the next new innovation.

Types of technological innovations

Continuous innovations are innovations that tend to create little change in consumption patterns and generally involve the introduction of a modified product rather than a completely new one.

For our purposes, innovations are best classified according to the effect they have on consumer behavior. In essence, how much will this new product alter a consumer's consumption patterns and practices? **Continuous innovations** are small, incremental improvements in products that tend to create very few

The technologically empowered customer

Consumers are becoming more empowered in every aspect of the consumption experience, in part because technology has enabled consumers to have more information about products and pricing. It has also made it easier for consumers to band together and demand justice when somethings goes wrong. In effect, a consumer's phone not only provides instant access to a variety of price and product comparison sites, but also functions as a calendar, map, library, health/lifestyle assistant, and credit card (Rosenbaum 2015). Because retailers and brands keep information on every aspect of consumer search activity and because consumers are *aware* of this, consumers have expectations about how they wish to be treated. Retailers and brands had better remember previous purchases and then use that information to more precisely target consumers in their next communication. Did the retailer forget about the fact that I returned my last purchase? This consumer is moving on, thank you very much! What is a beleaguered retailer or brand to do when consumers seem to be holding all the cards? Here are some suggestions (Rosenbaum 2015):

1. Make sure to connect with consumers on the technology platform of their choice. Also, the interface should look the same and have the same capabilities, regardless of where or how the customer accesses it.
2. Provide a platform for the biggest fans of your brand to interact with one another; this could provide a source of incredibly valuable data that could then be used to develop new product attributes or service opportunities.
3. Make sure that the content that is delivered is contextually relevant; look at the data and communicate in a way that is meaningful to consumers' lives.
4. Use data analytics to more precisely develop messages, to target those messages, and to deliver those messages to your target customers.
5. Creatively connect and engage customers across multiple points of contact (or touchpoints).

Interacting with empowered consumers certainly presents more challenges for brand managers, but it also provides fascinating opportunities for strengthening relationships and more targeted communications with those consumers.

Questions

1. Imagine that you own a small, local microbrewery and you want to have a local band perform at your facility on Friday night. How could you use the five points above to make sure you have a big crowd? Be specific.
2. From the marketing manager's perspective, what are some disadvantages to having more technologically empowered consumers?

Source: Rosenbaum (2015).

---

changes to consumption patterns. Examples are new safety features in your car or a new software update for your phone. The essential behaviors of driving and using your phone are the same. **Dynamically continuous innovations** are new products or features that create some changes in behavioral patterns for consumers. However, consumers can generally utilize their previous consumption experiences to help them figure out any new consumption behaviors that are needed. For example, using Apple Pay or Google Pay for purchases at stores and restaurants is easier and faster for consumers. However, some

Dynamically continuous innovations create some change in behavioral patterns, but the magnitude of change is not very big.

● **Photo 2.8** *Discontinuous innovation—the future of transportation?*

Discontinuous innovation has a disruptive effect and will require the establishment of new behavioral patterns by consumers.

new learning and behaviors are involved because these platforms require some initial setup on the part of the consumer and some new behaviors at checkout.

The final type of innovation is **discontinuous innovation**, which is a product that is so disruptive to a consumer's established consumption patterns that completely new consumption behaviors need to be learned. Discontinuous innovations are revolutionary. One example is the Internet, which radically changed the way we communicate, while another is wearable health/fitness trackers, which put a host of tools and data into the hands (and wrists!) of consumers to give them greater control of their own health and wellness. The *driverless car* is another discontinuous innovation. Manufacturers claim that there will be fewer accidents and traffic jams. Consumers seem to like the idea of using the time in the car for other pursuits like entertainment, work, or catching up on social media. However, questions remain about how likely consumers will be to accept a ride from a driverless taxi or Uber. Although the technology is rapidly improving, accidents will still happen. Will an accident driven by a driverless car be judged more harshly because it was powered by artificial intelligence rather than human intelligence? Speaking of this technology, what safeguards are there against outsiders hacking into the software and taking over cars? All these questions must be answered before driverless cars become more mainstream (Chopra 2017). What will be the next new discontinuous innovation? It's hard to predict, but wouldn't it be fun to strap on a jetpack for your commute to work or school every morning (see Photo 2.8)?

From a marketing perspective, it is important for the success of any new innovation to have a system of support for the new product as soon as it enters the market. Going back to the driverless car example, proper road markings and sensors would need to be installed, charging stations for the cars will need to be easily available, and consumers will probably want to see a variety of safety features, such as the ability for a passenger to hit the brakes.

Adoption of new innovations

When comparing how quickly new innovations are adopted by a group of people, experts often use a benchmark of fifty million users. Looking back, it took the radio thirty-eight years, television thirteen years, the Internet four years, and Facebook approximately three and a half years to reach that fifty-million-user benchmark. The world was shocked when it took the Angry Birds Space app thirty-five days to reach fifty million users, that is, until Pokémon Go did it in ten days (KPMG 2016). Most new innovations will not experience such a quick rate of adoption, and it is important to remember that adoption rates for these socially based technologies are facilitated by other technological advances: increased processing and connection speeds.

What makes consumers adopt innovations and new ideas? New innovations are diffused, or spread, throughout a group of people because these people interact with, communicate with, and influence one another. This social system of consumers watches and listens to its members and, over time, different types of consumers adopt a new innovation until all the consumers in a given market have adopted it. Researchers have identified five categories of adopters, based on the extent to which these consumers are ready to incorporate the new innovation into their lives: innovators, early adopters, early majority, late majority, and laggards. This model has been used in a variety of contexts over the years and has helped marketing managers develop insights about consumers and their likelihood of accepting new innovations and products (see Rogers 1995).

As shown in Figure 2.2, the first people to adopt a new product are referred to as **innovators** and make up 2.5 percent of all the consumers who will eventually adopt the product. These consumers are especially important because they get the ball rolling. They're willing to take risks and to pay a little more for the product to get it first. Next to adopt the product are the **early adopters,** who make up 13.5 percent of the total number of consumers. They don't need to be the first consumers to get their hands on the product, but they are definitely willing to give it a try. The early adopters provide the volume of sales to convince the next group, the **early majority** (34 percent), that adopting this product would be a good idea because they don't want to be left behind. Next come the **late majority** consumers, making up another 34 percent of the population of consumers who will eventually adopt the new innovation. These consumers are motivated to purchase the product

Innovators are visionary imaginative individuals who are technology enthusiasts. They want to be the first to get new technological products.

Early adopters genuinely enjoy the process of discovering new technologies and love talking to others about it. They are likely to embrace new social technologies before most people do.

Early majority consumers deliberate a little longer over adoption and take their cues from innovators or early adopters they know personally. They tend to look for innovations offering incremental predictable improvements on existing technology. They do not like risk, care about the reputation of the innovator, are fairly price sensitive, and like to see competitors entering the market so that they can compare features.

Late majority consumers are conservative, somewhat skeptical, and cautious of new products and progress, preferring and relying on tradition. They fear high-tech products and usually adopt new technologies only when forced to do so.

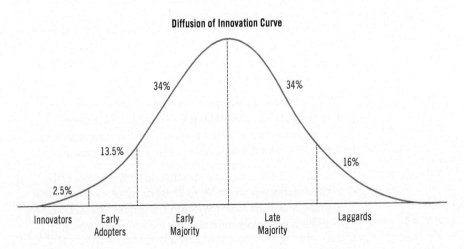

Diffusion of Innovation Curve

2.5%   13.5%   34%   34%   16%

Innovators   Early Adopters   Early Majority   Late Majority   Laggards

● **Figure 2.2** *The Diffusion of Innovation Curve*
Source: Rogers, 1995

Laggards are consumers who exhibit similar characteristics to the late majority (traditional, skeptical), but even more so. Likely to be found among older consumers and consumers with lower socioeconomic status.

Diffusion of innovation is a model that is used to describe the way in which a new innovation is accepted and spread throughout a group of consumers.

because just about everyone else has one and prices are dropping. Finally, the **laggards** (16 percent) are the last group of consumers to make the leap and adopt the new innovation. These individuals are primarily motivated to adopt the product because there are few other alternatives available to them. These are the people who are buying their first touchscreen cell phones now, probably because flip phones are no longer available. This entire process is called the **diffusion of innovation** because it refers to how new innovations are accepted and spread throughout a group of consumers.

Table 2.3 provides an overview of the characteristics of consumers at each stage of the diffusion of innovation process.

The diffusion of innovation curve is used extensively in marketing. Because marketers *know* that consumers adopt a new product at different points in time and because marketers *know* some important characteristics of these individuals, they can adjust their marketing strategies to meet the needs of those consumers (see Table 2.4).

Table 2.3 Characteristics of consumers at different stages of the diffusion of innovation curve

CATEGORY	CHARACTERISTICS
Innovators (2.5%)	These individuals are visionaries and technology enthusiasts. They enjoy being the first to get new technological products and will even pay a little more money to get them.
Early adopters (13.5%)	These consumers genuinely enjoy the process of discovering new technologies and embrace new social technologies before most people do. They are opinion leaders within their social groups and enjoy sharing their ideas about products with others.
Early majority (34%)	These consumers carefully watch what innovators or early adopters do before they will commit to a purchase. They tend to prefer innovations offering incremental improvements on existing technology. They do not like risk, are somewhat price sensitive, and like to compare product features.
Late majority (34%)	Conservative and skeptical about new products and progress, these consumers will only adopt a new innovation when almost everyone else has done so. These consumers are very bound by tradition and may even fear high-tech products.
Laggards (16%)	Laggards exhibit characteristics that are similar to those of the late majority, but even more so. These consumers will only adopt a new innovation when they are forced to do so. These consumers are likely to be older and have a low socioeconomic status.

Sources: Based on Rogers (1995); Huh and Kim (2008); Hoyer and MacInnis (2008); Szmigin and Piacentini (2015).

Table 2.4 Marketing strategy implications for the different stages of the diffusion of innovation curve

CATEGORY	MARKETING STRATEGY IMPLICATIONS
Innovators (2.5%)	The strategy here is to energize and motivate these very creative and innovative consumers so that they will then energize the early adopters. No need to worry too much about difficult-to-understand product attributes yet because these "true believers" will be able to easily figure out any technologically complex features. The price should be high—to recover initial development costs and because innovators are willing to pay it. Distribution should be very limited and promotion should be limited to trade or tech media outlets with the message focusing on *exclusivity* or being the first to own the product.
Early adopters (13.5%)	The strategy with early adopters should be to encourage this critical mass of consumers that this is the product to adopt, thus creating a *tipping point* in the market where it is desired by the early majority. Product attributes should be simplified for the mainstream, the price should be lowered slightly, and distribution should expand. Promotion should focus on product benefits and being *ahead of the curve* compared to other consumers.
Early majority (34%)	With this group, the strategy is to achieve mass market penetration so that your product is the one that is preferred over that of the competition, which is likely entering the market now. Product attributes should be easy to use for the mass market, the price should drop slightly, and mass market distribution should be achieved. Promotion should focus on encouraging consumers to establish a strong connection with the brand.
Late majority (34%)	The strategy for the late majority group is to convince this significant share of the marketplace to adopt your product, despite the fact that they haven't done so yet. The strategy should also attempt to keep the competition at bay. Additional product attributes can be added, price discounts can be attempted, mass market distribution should be maintained, and promotional strategies should get creative with contests, celebrity endorsers, etc. The goal is to make it as easy as possible for this reluctant group of consumers to come on board.
Laggards (16%)	The strategy for the laggard group needs to be developed with the realization that everything that has been attempted so far to encourage the laggards has not worked. Reduce the number of product attributes; there is no need for many different varieties of the product. Plus, it will save costs. The price can either be discounted even further to encourage sales or increased because consumers will have fewer choices in the marketplace and so will have to pay a higher price. Limit distribution and promotional efforts to further reduce costs.

The impact on consumption

There are at least three factors influencing the way in which a new innovation impacts consumption. One major issue relates to how disruptive the innovation is to the existing sociotechnical context. In other words, what changes need to be made to support this new innovation? Technological innovations could prompt a wide network of changes, including the existing infrastructure, regulations, customers, and other stakeholders. A key question regards how each of these elements would need to change for the innovation to succeed. The previous example of the driverless car illustrates the extensive changes that sometimes need to be made to support such a groundbreaking innovation.

A second factor that influences widespread acceptance of a new technological innovation is the impact exerted by the external environment, such as the local culture, economic conditions, political conditions, and history of a group of consumers. The Nano car by Tata Motors was positioned as the world's cheapest car when it was introduced in 2009. Produced in India, this bare-bones car had no air conditioning, electric windows, or power steering. In 2013, the base price was about $2,250. The Nano seemed like a great option for consumers who were looking to buy their first car in place of a motorbike or scooter (Thottam and Perera 2011). Unfortunately, the marketing strategy did not take into account the various problems that arose from the external environment, including environmental critics who were concerned about increasing traffic congestion and pollution, political protests because of disagreements about wages, and a safety scare (Thottam and Perera 2011). Thus, in predicting the likelihood of widespread acceptance among consumers, it is incredibly important to carefully understand the pressures of the external environment. As you can see in Insights from the Field 2.4, even when innovations are developed in response to pressures from some part of the external environment (here, climate change), balancing all of the external stakeholder interests can be a difficult task.

A third issue that influences widespread acceptance of a new technological innovation is its unanticipated social and economic consequences, which are not always positive. For example, online travel platforms allow individuals to book their own vacation hotels, transportation, and activities. Tourists can check ratings to ensure they are making smart choices and can refer to countless websites and blogs for specialized advice. Because of these innovations that are putting more power in the hands of tourists, many full-service travel companies have experienced severe financial difficulties. The difficulties at the Thomas Cook travel firm were some of the most visible. The firm was founded in 1841 in the United Kingdom; in 2019, after years of declining profits and share prices, it abruptly went bankrupt and 22,000 people lost their jobs. The bankruptcy was so abrupt that the company immediately ceased all operations in September of that year, leaving 150,000 travelers stranded in various holiday destinations around the world. The UK's Civil Aviation Authority was forced to hire a fleet of jets to bring these stranded citizens home in what was called the country's "biggest peacetime repatriation." One expert blamed the fact that customers were making their own travel arrangements and the company was not flexible enough to accommodate these important changes in consumer behavior (Staff 2019). Organizations must not only keep pace with technological change, but also anticipate how consumers might respond. Admittedly, it is sometimes difficult for businesses to predict with 100 percent accuracy how consumers will behave. However, careful monitoring of the external environment and regular interaction with consumers will help in creating useful insights for managers on how to handle these changes.

INSIGHTS FROM THE FIELD 2.4

Some people are just not "blown away" by wind

By 2019, US wind power capacity reached 98 giga-watts and there were over 57,000 wind turbines operating in forty-one states, enough to power 26 million homes and account for 6.5 percent of the country's electricity needs, avoiding 201 million metric tons of CO_2 emissions. Wind energy currently is responsible for more than 114,000 jobs in the United States ("Wind Facts" 2019). The popularity of wind energy has spread around the world as individuals and governments have become more concerned about the climate crisis.

Despite their benefits, wind farms can sometimes spark heated debates and, as such, illustrate how widespread acceptance of innovations is strongly influenced by social and cultural factors. Those in favor of wind farms argue that wind turbines provide a carbon-free source of energy; they create jobs for those who manufacture, install, and maintain them; the energy they generate can be stored in batteries for later use; the price per kilowatt hour is *less than* that generated by traditional methods; and they reduce our reliance on foreign oil.

Members of local communities, however, are often not so enthusiastic about wind farms. These critics argue that wind farms disrupt the natural beauty of the landscape; they are noisy and cause potential health effects for people living close by (Crawford 2014); they can cause disruption to television and radio signals; and birds and bats might fly into the blades and be killed (Bryce 2016).

Clearly, the arguments are not expressed purely in terms of climate impact, but rather reflect the complexity of external environmental issues involved, as well as the stakeholders affected, when introducing such a disruptive new technology.

Questions

1. Using the diffusion of innovation curve and its associated marketing strategies, what would be the best way to encourage communities that are on different stages of the curve to install a local wind farm?
2. Identify two other technological innovations that sparked heated debates when they were introduced. Briefly discuss the issues and nature of the debates. Refer to the three ways in which a new innovation impacts consumption and identify which ones were at work for each of these innovations.

Sources: Bryce (2016); Crawford (2014); "Wind Facts" (2019).

Online Social Networks

In this section we will examine online social networks and how these platforms have changed the way in which consumers perceive themselves, products, and the overall consumption experience. Social networks have significantly changed the ways in which consumers and marketers interact, as well as how consumers interact with one another. In short, the power of online social networks is one of the most important contemporary topics in consumer behavior. Social media has completely changed modern-day social interaction. Facebook is the world's most popular social media site, with about 1.2 billion people logging in every day. Snapchat, however, is used much more by younger consumers, indicating that it might someday come close to, or even surpass, Facebook in global popularity (Moreau 2017; Shaban 2019). From a

INSIGHTS FROM THE FIELD 2.5

LEGO and social networking

Be honest. Is there a box of LEGOs somewhere in your house? If so, you're like millions of other American families! LEGOs, the small plastic building bricks, are a staple toy for most kids. The LEGO Company was founded in Denmark in 1932 by Ole Kirk Christiansen and the company is still in the hands of his grandson. The name LEGO is an abbreviation of *leg godt*, which means "play well" (Mortensen 2015). Despite having some financial difficulties in the early 2000s, LEGO has turned things around, relying quite heavily on online social networks to achieve this feat. By some experts' estimates, the privately held firm has seen a "supernatural" annual growth rate that more than tripled its net income between 2010 and 2015 (Wienberg 2017). Management at LEGO is hoping for a more realistic 6 percent annual growth rate over the next few years, with some restructuring as well as expansion of their facilities in China and Mexico (Wienberg 2017). Nevertheless, in 2015, LEGO beat out the likes of Red Bull, Rolex, Ferrari, and Nike to be named the world's most powerful brand (Apple was the world's most valuable brand) (Hobbs 2015) and it holds a commanding 65 percent share of the market (Schmidt 2015), 570 stores worldwide, and annual revenue growth of about 6% (The LEGO Group 2020).

Why are LEGOs so popular? Sure, kids like the product because they enjoy the challenge and creativity involved in playing with it. You can build anything you want—the Taj Mahal, the Titanic, Jurassic Park, the Harry Potter castle, or the Millennium Falcon from Star Wars—the possibilities are only limited by the imagination. Parents and relatives also love to buy the product because it makes a great gift for kids. An important trend that LEGO is riding right now is the focus on science, technology, engineering, and mathematics (STEM) programs for kids. Whether it is a stronger emphasis on these programs in schools, summer camps, or specialized charter schools, STEM is seen as an important way for children to stay competitive on the world stage in technology and innovation. In their nonschool hours, parents and other guardians encourage kids to ditch their electronics and engage in educational play. Last, adults like LEGOs almost as much as kids do. For adult fans, LEGO provides a variety of more difficult and expensive sets, like the $500 Star Wars–themed set with five thousand pieces. For them, it's about the nostalgia and challenge of putting together an especially difficult set.

What ties all three groups together—kids, parents, and adult fans—is social networks, some of which have developed on their own. YouTube, for example, has thousands of videos of LEGO projects and people sharing their thoughts and design ideas. A Jurassic Park stop-motion video has close to 4.9 million views. The creators claim to use $100,000 in LEGO pieces for the three and a half–minute video! LEGO also supports social networking with its own interactive website, where fans can blog, share ideas, play games, upload photos, and interact with one another. Those who are especially creative can even purchase their own original sets from the company—they just need to specify their size and color choices. LEGO also created its Ambassador Program, a group of forty people around the world between the ages of nineteen and sixty-five years old, who can be described as superfans of the product. LEGO has built strong relationships with these ambassadors and frequently turns to them for ideas and advice.

LEGO no longer sees itself as just a toy manufacturer—LEGO now is also in the entertainment business. *The LEGO Movie*, which was released in 2014, made $469 million, and *The LEGO Batman Movie*, which was released in 2017, made $312 million worldwide (Box Office Mojo 2019). LEGO also has more than fifty iPhone and iPad apps to further engage with customers. What's next for LEGO? Again, the possibilities are limited only by the creativity of the people who really love this product. One new Silicon Valley startup, Pley, now rents LEGO sets to customers who want the challenge of putting together a set, but don't want to store it. The company cleans and sanitizes everything and replaces any missing pieces when the sets are returned. Pley currently has fifty thousand monthly subscribers of all ages. According to the owner, "It's a brand that spans generations" (Schmidt 2015). So, next time you're home, take out that LEGO set and join the fun with the online LEGO community.

Questions

1. Check out the LEGO website and the different opportunities that consumers have to interact with one another. What does LEGO's interactive site do to help facilitate social networking for each of the three key customer groups—kids, parents/guardians, and adult fans?

2. If you think about it, LEGO is encouraging its customers to forge strong relationships with each other as well as with the brand. From LEGO's perspective, what are some important benefits when customers form strong relationships with each other?

Sources: Box Office Mojo (2019); Hobbs (2015); Schmidt (2015); Wienberg (2017).

consumer behavior perspective, social media has changed not only our social interactions, but also a variety of consumption-related behaviors, such as recommending or complaining about products and services. For their part, companies monitor what consumers say to one another and often respond to comments. They also create platforms to engage with their consumers, to find out more about them, and to offer them new products and services (see, for example, what LEGO is doing in Insights from the Field 2.5). Table 2.5 demonstrates the clear popularity of Facebook, but identifies other popular social networking sites around the world.

Online sites such as Yelp and TripAdvisor are some of the most frequently used sites that encourage consumers to provide honest feedback on a company, product, or experience. This community of reviewers provides a good indication to new consumers about what to expect from the consumption experience. Research shows that 88 percent of consumers trust online reviews as much as personal recommendations, which is quite surprising given the fact that these reviews are submitted by total strangers (DeMers 2015). The benefits of these sites and a company's own sites are twofold. First, the sites provide a great way for consumers to act as advocates or champions for the product. Written by consumers with real experience with the product and no obvious financial incentive to write the review, these reviews are much more meaningful than an advertisement from the company. Second, the sites provide valuable information to organizations about what consumers like and don't like about the product. This feedback can then be incorporated into the company's next new product innovation.

Company-sponsored social networking sites facilitate a different type of interaction with current and potential customers. Consumers can become more engaged in the brand when they play games, complete quizzes, or enter competitions via social media. Social media sites have opened up more ways for two-way communication (back and forth between company and consumer) and

Table 2.5 Preferred social network site by country

COUNTRY	NO. 1 SOCIAL NETWORK	NO. 2 SOCIAL NETWORK
Australia	Facebook	Instagram
Belgium	Facebook	Instagram
Brazil	Facebook	Instagram
Canada	Facebook	Reddit
China	QZone	None
Denmark	Facebook	Instagram
Finland	Facebook	Instagram
France	Facebook	Instagram
Germany	Facebook	Instagram
India	Facebook	Instagram
Italy	Facebook	Instagram
Japan	Facebook	Twitter
Netherlands	Facebook	Instagram
Norway	Facebook	Reddit
Portugal	Facebook	Instagram
Russia	V Kontakte	Odnoklassniki
South Africa	Facebook	Twitter
Spain	Facebook	Twitter
Sweden	Facebook	Instagram
United Kingdom	Facebook	Instagram
United States	Facebook	Instagram

Source: World Map of Social Networks (2020).

provide a convenient way for consumers to share information with one another, such as tips for using products or reviews of products. At the time of this writing, there were over 126 million daily Twitter users in the world, compared to 1.2 billion for Facebook and 60 million for Snapchat (Shaban 2019). Importantly, compared to traditional advertising, with online social networks the consumer engages in more personalized and frequent interaction with the brand.

Behavioral economics has formed the foundation for many of our contemporary perspectives on consumer behavior. This shift away from a purely rational approach to a more balanced approach to studying consumer behavior sets the stage for a thorough exploration of consumer research, which will be discussed in the next chapter.

◉ Summary

This chapter examined how experts such as marketing managers, academics, and executives viewed the phenomenon of consumer behavior. Because it forms the foundation for the other contemporary perspectives, we engaged in a detailed discussion of *behavioral economics* and a variety of related concepts, such as exchange and value, automatic and reflective modes, mental accounting, loss aversion, norms, defaults, and priming. In Insights from the Field 2.1, we described several examples of how the behavioral economics concept of nudging can be used to encourage healthy choices. We also looked at how experts have utilized insights to predict how consumers may respond to messages about reusing towels in hotels and paying taxes on time.

Next, we introduced the concepts of *experiential consumption* and *consumer culture theory* and illustrated some key differences between them. Insights from the Boardroom 2 focused on the ways in which different tourists have expectations for one very experiential event—a vacation to Fiji—and how these expectations resulted in different messaging strategies for these consumer groups.

Another development in our understanding of consumer behavior is the model of the diffusion of innovation and, more generally, the *role that innovation and technology* play in modern-day consumption. The *nature of innovations* and the *diffusion of innovation curve* were explored in depth and we described how marketing strategy can change, depending on where a consumer fell along the diffusion of innovation curve. We also discussed the importance of understanding the extent to which a new technology will disrupt established patterns of consumer behavior. As a part of this discussion, we introduced the debate about whether advancements in technology are a *result* of changes in consumer needs or whether they are *responsible* for changes to consumer needs. In addition, we provided several fascinating insights from the field, such as Insights from the Field 2.3, where we discussed how the technologically empowered consumer is presenting challenges to marketing managers, and Insights from the Field 2.4, where we illustrated the case of wind farms and how social and cultural factors might sometimes slow the spread of innovation.

The last topic we covered in contemporary perspectives was online social networks and *social media*. We considered the example of LEGO's efforts in promoting social networking in Insights from the Field 2.5 and we took an in-depth look at embedded virtual reality and how it is changing the shopping experience in Case Study 2. Because social media is used differently by different consumer groups, it offers many opportunities to connect and enhance the consumer's relationship with the brand. An important takeaway from this chapter is a recognition that there is no single uniform model or theory of consumer behavior. Marketing decision-makers need to derive insights from the field, from academics, and from experts in the boardroom to create better strategies to reach their consumers.

KEY TERMS

automatic mode p. 45
behavioral economics p. 44
choice architecture p. 46
consumer culture theory
(CCT) p. 56
contexts of decisions p. 44
continuous innovations p. 60
default p. 49
diffusion of innovation p. 64
discontinuous innovation p. 62
dynamically continuous
innovations p. 61

early adopters p. 63
early majority p. 63
endowment effect p. 47
exchange value p. 44
experiential marketing p. 53
hedonic aspects of
consumption p. 55
innovators p. 63
laggards p. 64
late majority p. 63
loss aversion p. 47
mental accounting p. 46

norms p. 48
nudging p. 50
priming p. 52
product attribute p. 44
reflective mode p. 45
sensory aspects of
consumption p. 55
symbolic value p. 44
utility (or use) value p. 44

REVIEW QUESTIONS

1. Explain some important differences between behavioral economics and traditional economics.
2. Identify the seven concepts that derive from behavioral economics. For each one, describe how a marketing manager might utilize the concept.
3. What is the difference between experiential marketing and consumer culture theory?
4. What is *experiential consumption* and how is it different from other conceptualizations of consumption?
5. What is diffusion of innovation and how could a marketing manager use the diffusion of innovation curve?
6. Discuss the importance of online social networks and how social media has changed the way in which consumers interact with one another and brands.

DISCUSSION QUESTIONS

1. Using some of the concepts from behavioral economics (there are seven) and a bit of your own creativity, carefully describe some communication strategies to change consumer behavior for each of the following issues:
   a. Registering to vote
   b. Getting a flu shot
   c. Donating blood
2. Citizens perform many behaviors that federal and state governments might want to change. Which behaviors would be well suited for an opt-out rather than opt-in method for changing that behavior? What problems might arise with implementing these initiatives?

3. Using the four stages of an experiential consumption experience (Arnould, Price, and Zinkhan 2002), describe a recent purchase you made. Now, imagine you are a marketing manager who is trying to appeal to consumers just like you. Create two insights to help the marketing manager.

4. Ethnographic research is often a search for finding the "hidden obvious." Watch a short video on how ethnography was used to try to discover the "obvious" parking problems that many people have: https://www.youtube .com/watch?v=nV0jY5VgymI. What are the benefits of using ethnographic research in a situation like this? What are the limits of using ethnographic research?

5. Think about a recent new innovation you adopted. When you purchased the product, in what stage of the diffusion of innovation curve were you? How do you use this product now? In what ways have you engaged with the company or other consumers of this product?

For more information, quizzes, case studies, and other study tools, please visit us at **www.oup.com/he/phillips**.

CASE STUDY 2

Virtual Reality Brings Consumption Closer

Experiential marketing acknowledges that consumers engage in product experiences for both rational and emotional benefits. In the increasingly fast-paced world of marketing and technology, one innovation is allowing consumers to get a better sense of what actual consumption will be like by allowing them to "feel" and "see" themselves in simulated consumption situations.

Picture yourself sitting on the beautiful white-sand beaches of Aruba. Imagine the palm trees swaying in the breeze, your toes in the soft white sand, and a frosty tropical drink in your hand. Now you don't have to just imagine these things: you can "see" them for yourself using embedded virtual reality (VR).

Embedded VR is an innovation that is catching on with a growing group of consumers and marketers. Basically, marketers are doing several things to better engage their consumers with VR technology. The overall goal is to build a stronger connection between consumers and the brand. It's referred to as *embedded* because it becomes part of the overall brand experience; the VR experience is not a stand-alone, enjoyable, and informative encounter. These experiences can range from simply providing a simulated environment, like home improvement giant Lowe's does with its embedded VR of new kitchen and bath renovations for do-it-yourselfers. Homeowners can better picture what a real renovation will look like in their own homes and how they can use Lowe's products to make it happen (Stanley 2016).

At the other end of the technological continuum, the VR experience completely fuses the brand and the customer together into one experience. Coca-Cola, for example, has directions on its twelve-pack boxes of Coke cans that allow consumers to fold the cardboard box a certain way, download an app, insert

● **Photo 2.9** *McDonald's Happy Goggles*

their phone, and then "experience" Coke in a VR setting. Another simple example is what McDonald's is doing in Sweden. Swedish consumers can refold their Happy Meal boxes and experience a downhill skiing run. Called Happy Goggles (see Photo 2.9), this promotion was launched in collaboration with the Swedish ski team (Jardine 2016). One of the important features of these examples is the do-it-yourself assembly for these VR viewers, which serves two purposes. First, there is a well-known phenomenon that when consumers own something or make something themselves, they place a higher value on that item (the endowment effect) (e.g., Thaler and Sunstein 2009). Perhaps they might even use the item for more than one occasion. Second, the newly assembled viewers give the product packaging a second life. So, rather than going directly into the trash and landfill, the boxes get to be reused to provide some entertainment for a while (Jardine 2016).

An even more sophisticated VR experience is provided by Google. It allows users of Android and iOS to take a 360-degree view of any setting, allowing users to capture and share fun experiences, like a concert or a vacation. These images can then be uploaded and shared on social media. It also allows users to experience a variety of other three-dimensional, 360-degree images. From a marketing standpoint, VR provides the ability to more clearly depict what an experience may be like, from the more mundane, like a hotel room, to the more adventurous, like a scuba diving trip. Google's VR technology is not limited to real-life images. Indeed, it has the ability to create computer-generated imagery depictions of anything imaginable. Want to

"walk" around the Alamo in Texas in 1836 right before the Mexican attack? No problem. Want to "see" yourself as one of the blue alien characters in the movie *Avatar*? VR can do that.

Embedded VR has been particularly helpful to the fashion industry. Studies show that 71 percent of US consumers still want to buy products from retail stores, even if the same products are available online. Why do they want to do this? Eighty-five percent of these consumers reply that they want to "touch and feel" the product before purchasing it (Stanley 2016). Few retailers have incorporated VR technology as successfully as high-end designer Rebecca Minkoff. By partnering with eBay to install and run the technology, the designer has embedded VR technology in various aspects of her stores. Although you can buy a very fashion-forward handheld viewer, customers do not require handheld VR viewers to see what it would be like to wear a new Minkoff dress (Segran 2015). Instead, consumers can interact with mirrors with VR capabilities on the showroom floor as well as in the dressing rooms. They can watch a 360-degree depiction of various styles on the runway, request a variety of clothing to be delivered to the dressing room, and even order a cold beverage if they are thirsty. One feature that shoppers particularly like about the interactive, touchscreen technology in the dressing rooms is that it allows them to see a picture of their sales associate, preventing them from having to search around the store for someone who can help. It also allows shoppers to communicate with their sales associate to get assistance and even provides an estimated wait time for when the associate will return with the items requested. Because each item in the store is embedded with an ID tag, once the associate enters the changing room with the new items, the items automatically pop up on the dressing room mirror's display, complete with information about the fabric, where it was made, and the price (see Photo 2.10).

After the installation of the interactive mirrors and embedded VR, sales associates noticed an influx of competitors coming into their stores to check out the new technology. To stay one step ahead of their competitors, the fashion house has signed an exclusive long-term

● **Photo 2.10** *Embedded VR Technology Allows Customers to Experience the Product Before Buying It*

contract with eBay such that Rebecca Minkoff will always have the latest version of the VR technology and older versions can be sold to other retail stores. Indeed, "the beautiful thing about our relationship with eBay is that it is a long-term contract and we're always first in." The competitors can have similar technology, but they will always be "at version 1 while we will be at version 1.2," says Minkoff (Segran 2015).

One of the big benefits to this technology is that managers at Rebecca Minkoff get real-time data on the entire decision-making process, including what items consumers are trying on, the order in which they are trying them on, and what items are being paired with one another. If it turns out that customers don't want to purchase the items just yet, they can be added to an online shopping cart and the store can send periodic push reminders about completing the purchase at a later time. The technology also allows the store to keep track of its customers' preferences so that the next time they shop, they can be offered a variety of options that appeal to their own style and size.

Minkoff understands that customers don't go into a store just to be wowed by technology and that the products still need to be able to speak for themselves. We're "looking at the data, but we always have to be innovative" with the styles and designs, confirms Minkoff as she talks about what may be next for the company. What they are doing is "taking this data, solving a problem with it," and then trying to anticipate the next big thing that customers might not even know they want. Then, the executive team strategizes about what "we could do that would make them excited," says Minkoff (Stanley 2016).

Has there been any uptick in sales at Rebecca Minkoff stores? You bet! In dressing rooms with the interactive mirrors, 30 percent of customers are asking for additional items and Rebecca Minkoff is selling "three times the amount of apparel." This is also in part a result of the push notifications that customers receive after they leave the stores to make purchases later. Indeed, year over year, sales have risen by 50 percent in stores with the technology (Dishman 2015).

QUESTIONS

1. Experiential marketing recognizes that consumers make decisions that are both emotional and rational. How does embedded VR help bring the emotional and rational together?

2. On the one hand, we can see from this case that embedded VR technology can help consumers better engage with the product. On the other hand, Rebecca Minkoff suggests that consumers don't go into a store to be "wowed by the technology." Is it possible for managers to find the correct balance? How?

Sources: Dishman (2015); Jardine (2016); Segran (2015); Stanley (2016); Thaler and Sunstein (2009).

REFERENCES

Arnould, E., L. Price, and G. Zinkhan. 2002. *Consumers*. New York: McGraw–Hill.

Arnould, E. J., and C. J. Thompson. 2005. "Consumer Culture Theory (CCT): Twenty Years of Research." *Journal of Consumer Research* 31 (4): 868–82.

Belk, R. W., J. F. Sherry, and M. Wallendorf. 1988. "A Naturalistic Inquiry into Buyer and Seller Behavior at a Swap Meet." *Journal of Consumer Research* 14 (4): 449–70.

Belk, R. W., M. Wallendorf, and F. J. Sherry, Jr. 1989. "The Sacred and the Profane in Consumer Behavior: Theodicy on the Odyssey." *Journal of Consumer Research* 16 (June): 1–38.

Box Office Mojo. 2019. *Lego Movies. Box Office Mojo, an IMDb Company.* Accessed August 10, 2019. https://www.boxofficemojo.com/showdowns/chart/?id=legomovies.htm.

"A Brief History of Contact Lenses." 2019. GP Contact Lenses. Accessed October 31, 2019. https://www.contactlenses.org/timeline.htm.

Bryce, E. 2016. "Will Wind Turbines Ever Be Safe for Birds?" Audubon Society. Accessed July 28, 2017. http://www.audubon.org/news/will-wind-turbines-ever-be-safe-birds.

Cabinet Office. 2010. "Applying Behavioural Insight to Health." *Discussion Paper, Cabinet Office Behavioural Insights Team*, London, December 31, 2010. https://www.gov.uk/government/publications/applying-behavioural-insight-to-health-behavioural-insights-team-paper.

Campbell, M. C., K. C. Manning, B. Leonard, and H. M. Manning. 2016. "Kids, Cartoons, and Cookies: Stereotype Priming Effects on Children's Food Consumption." *Journal of Consumer Psychology*, 26 (2), 257-264.

Central Intelligence Agency. 2020. *The World Factbook*. Accessed September 6, 2020. https://www.cia.gov/library/publications/resources/the-world-factbook/geos/fj.html.

Childhood Obesity. 2019. "Childhood Obesity Causes & Consequences." Centers for Disease Control and Prevention. Accessed August 9, 2019. https://www.cdc.gov/obesity/childhood/causes.html.

Chopra, A. 2017. "What's Taking so Long for Driverless Cars to Go Mainstream?" *Forbes*, July 22, 2017. http://fortune.com/2017/07/22/driverless-cars-autonomous-vehicles-self-driving-uber-google-tesla/.

Crawford, A. 2014. "Bad Vibes in Kingston, Mass." *Boston Magazine*, January 28, 2014. http://www.bostonmagazine.com/news/article/2014/01/28/wind-turbines/4/.

DeMers, J. 2015. "How Important Are Customer Reviews for Online Marketing?" *Forbes*, December 28, 2015. https://www.forbes.com/sites/jaysondemers/2015/12/28/how-important-are-customer-reviews-for-online-marketing/#5dd3b9891928.

Dijksterhuis, A., and J. A. Bargh. 2001. "The Perception–Behavior Expressway: Automatic Effects of Social Perception on Social Behavior." *Advances in Experimental Social Psychology* 33:1–40.

Dishman, L. 2015. "Inside LA's New Futuristic Store—Magic Mirrors Included." *Fortune*, October 8, 2015. http://fortune.com/2015/10/08/rebecca-minkoff-technology/.

Forehand, M. R., and R. Deshpande. 2001. "What We See Makes Us Who We Are: Priming Ethnic Self-Awareness and Advertising Response." *Journal of Marketing Research* 38 (3): 336–48.

Frerichs, L., J. Brittin, D. Sorensen, M. J. Trowbridge, A. L. Yaroch, M. Siahpush, M. Tibbits, and T. T. Huang. 2015. "Influence of School Architecture and Design on Healthy Eating: A Review of the Evidence." *American Journal of Public Health* 105, no. 4 (April): E46–57.

Goldstein, N. J., R. B. Cialdini, and V. Griskevicius. 2008. "A Room with a Viewpoint: Using Social Norms to Motivate Environmental Conservation in Hotels." *Journal of Consumer Research* 35 (3): 472–82.

Hobbs, T. 2015. "'Everything Is Awesome' for LEGO as It Overtakes Ferrari as Most Powerful Brand." *Marketing Week*, February 17, 2015. https://www.marketingweek.com/2015/02/17/everything-is-awesome-for-lego-as-it-overtakes-ferrari-as-most-powerful-brand/.

Holbrook, M. B., and E. C. Hirschman. 1982. "The Experiential Aspects of Consumption: Consumer Fantasies, Feelings and Fun." *Journal of Consumer Research* 9 (2): 132–40.

Holland, R. W., M. Hendriks, and H. Aarts. 2005. "Smells Like Clean Spirit, Non-conscious Effects on of Scent on Cognition and Behavior." *Psychological Science* 16 (9): 689–93.

Hoyer, W. D., and D. MacInnis. 2008. *Consumer Behavior*. Boston: Cengage Learning.

Huh, Y. E., and S. H. Kim. 2008. "Do Early Adopters Upgrade Early? Role of Post-adoption Behavior in the Purchase of Next-Generation Products." *Journal of Business Research* 61 (1): 40–46.

Jardine, A. 2016. "McDonald's Turns a Happy Meal Box into a Virtual Reality Headset." *AdAge*. March 1, 2016. https://adage.com/creativity/work/happy-goggles/45754.

Johnson, E. J., and D. Goldstein. 2003. "Medicine: Do Defaults Save Lives?" *Science* 302 (5649): 1338–39.

King, D., I. Valaev, R. Everett-Thomas, M. Fitzpatrick, A. Darzi, and D. J. Birnbach. 2016. "'Priming' Hand Hygiene Compliance in Clinical Environments." *Health Psychology* 35 (1): 96–101.

KPMG. 2016. "Customer Adoption: How to Predict the Tipping Point." November 2016. https://assets.kpmg.com/content/dam/kpmg/uk/pdf/2016/11/open-minds-consumer-adoption-predicting-tipping-point.pdf.

The LEGO Group. 2020. "The Lego Group Delivered Top and Bottom Line Growth in 2019." Press Release. March 3. Accessed September 6, 2020. https://www.lego.com/en-us/aboutus/news/2020/march/annual-results/.

Lench, H. C., S. A. Flores, and S. W. Bench. 2011. "Discrete Emotions Predict Changes in Cognition, Judgment, Experience, Behavior, and Physiology: A Meta-analysis of Experimental Emotion Elicitations." *Psychological Bulletin* 137 (5): 834–55.

Maddux, W. M., H. Yang, C. Falk, H. Adam, W. Adair, Y. Endo, Z. Carmon, and S. Heine. 2010. "For Whom Is Parting with Possessions More Painful? Cultural Differences in the Endowment Effect." *Psychological Science* 21, no. 2 (December): 1910–17.

Moreau, E. 2017. "The Top Social Networking Sites People Are Using." *Livewire*. Last modified February 24, 2020. https://www.lifewire.com/top-social-networking-sites-people-are-using-3486554.

Mortensen, T. F. 2015. "LEGO History Timeline." LEGO. January 9, 2015. https://www.lego.com/en-us/aboutus/lego-group/the_lego_history.

New Orleans Convention and Visitor's Bureau. 2014. "City of New Orleans First in the US to Launch Cigarette Butt Recycling Program." Last modified October 31, 2017. https://www.neworleans.com/articles/post/city-of-new-orleans-first-in-the-us-to-launch-cigarette-butt-recycling-program/.

O'Guinn, T. C., and R. J. Faber. 1989. "Compulsive Buying: A Phenomenological Exploration." *Journal of Consumer Research* 16 (2): 147–57.

Paul-Ebhohimhen, V., and A. Avenell. 2008. "Systematic Review of the Use of Financial Incentives in Treatments for Obesity and Overweight." *Obesity Reviews* 9 (4): 355–67.

Keep America Beautiful. 2020. "Litter in America: Key Findings: Cigarette Butts." Keep America Beautiful.

Accessed September 6, 2020. https://kab.org/wp-content/uploads/2019/09/LitterinAmerica_FactSheet_CigaretteButtLitter.pdf.

Rogers, E. M. 1995. *Diffusion of innovations.* 4th ed. New York: Free Press.

Rook, D. W. 1988. "Researching Consumer Fantasy." *Research in Consumer Behavior* 3:247–70.

Rosenbaum, S. 2015. "The New World of the 'Empowered Consumer.'" *Forbes*, July 16, 2015. https://www.forbes.com/sites/stevenrosenbaum/2015/07/16/the-new-world-of-the-empowered-consumer/#58be76144aab.

Schmidt, G. 2015. "LEGO'S Success Leads to Competitors and Spinoffs." *New York Times*, November 20, 2015. https://www.nytimes.com/2015/11/21/business/legos-success-leads-to-competitors-and-spinoffs.html.

Schultz, S. P., J. M. Nolan, R. B. Cialdini, N. J. Goldstein, and V. Griskevicius. 2007. "The Constructive, Destructive, and Reconstructive Power of Social Norms." *Psychological Science* 18:429–34.

Segran, E. 2015. "Rebecca Minkoff Takes Fashion Tech to the Next Level with Virtual Reality Headsets." *FastCompany*, September 3, 2015. https://www.fastcompany.com/3050771/rebecca-minkoff-takes-fashion-tech-to-the-next-level-with-virtual-reality-headsets.

Shaban, H. 2019. "Twitter Reveals Its Daily Active User Numbers for the First Time." *The Washington Post*, February 7, 2019. https://www.washingtonpost.com/technology/2019/02/07/twitter-reveals-its-daily-active-user-numbers-first-time/?noredirect=on.

Staff. 2019. "Thomas Cook Collapses as Last-Ditch Rescue Talks Fail." *BBC News*, September 23, 2019. https://www.bbc.com/news/business-49791249.

Stanley, T. L. 2016. "5 Trends That Are Radically Reshaping ShopperMarketing." *AdWeek*, June 19, 2016. http://www.adweek.com/brand-marketing/5-trends-are-radically-reshaping-shopper-marketing-171960/.

Szmigin, I., and M. Piacentini. 2015. *Consumer Behaviour.* Oxford: Oxford University Press.

Thaler, R. H., and C. R. Sunstein. 2009. *Nudge: Improving Decisions about Health, Wealth and Happiness.* London: Penguin Books.

Thottam, J., and A. Perera. 2011. "The Little Car That Couldn't." *Time International (Atlantic Edition)* 178 (16): 39–41.

Volpp, J., L. K. John, A. B. Troxel, L. Norton, J. Fassbender, and G. Lowenstein. 2008. "Financial Incentive-Based Approaches for Weight Loss: A Randomized Trial." *JAMA* 330 (22): 2631–37.

Wienberg, C. 2017. "LEGO Calls on Batman to Save the Day." *Bloomberg*, March 9, 2017. https://www.bloomberg.com/news/articles/2017-03-09/lego-girds-for-slower-growth-as-toymaker-s-u-s-sales-stagnate.

"Wind Facts at a Glance." 2019. Wind Energy in the United States, American Wind Energy Association. Accessed August 10, 2019. https://www.awea.org/wind-101/basics-of-wind-energy/wind-facts-at-a-glance.

Wivou, J. 2017. *Personal interview*, July 12, 2017.

World Map of Social Networks. 2020. Vincos Blog. Accessed September 6, 2020. http://vincos.it/world-map-of-social-networks/

Wryobeck, J., and Y. Chen. 2003. "Using Priming Techniques to Facilitate Health Behaviors." *Clinical Psychologist* 7 (2): 105–8.

3 Consumer Research

⊚ Introduction

Marketers want to know how consumers make decisions, what is important to them, and how products fit into their lives. This includes not just knowing what consumers are doing right now or what they have done in the past. Indeed, marketers want to predict what consumers might do in the future. We engage in consumer research for two primary reasons. First, we conduct consumer research to provide useful information to marketing decision-makers. Marketing managers want to effectively predict how consumers might react, for example, to a new product, a new product feature, or a new advertising campaign. Thus, the first goal of consumer research is to generate useful information so marketers can create insights about how consumers will react to product features, pricing strategies, distribution, and communications. A second reason is that we want to provide information to other groups of people, such as consumer rights advocates, nonprofit organizations, and government officials who make public policy. These people can form insights about programs and initiatives that, hopefully, will result in fewer consumers being cheated, deceived, or otherwise exploited.

Remember that the data and information provided by consumer research provide the raw ingredients for the three pillars of insights: from the field, from the boardroom, and from academia. These insights, in turn, form the foundation for our understanding of consumer behavior. This chapter is organized into two sections. First, we will discuss the research process, which will describe in detail the five-step process by which we try to answer very important research questions. This chapter will then dive deeper into the techniques and research procedures used to gather the data that help us develop information and insights. At the end of the day, we want to understand consumers so we can make better predictions about what they will do.

⊚ The Consumer Research Process

In Chapter 1, we learned that there are three key research perspectives: behavioral, cognitive, and motivational. Behavioral research describes what consumers *do* and includes, for example, research about

LEARNING OBJECTIVES

Having read the chapter, you will be able to:

1. Describe each part of the five-step *consumer research process*, as well as the importance of each step.

2. Understand and describe the differences between *data, information*, and *insights*.

3. Describe the differences between *primary* and *secondary data* as well as the differences between *qualitative* and *quantitative research*.

4. Explain the reasons why researchers want to reduce *various forms of bias* in their data collection and analysis.

5. Discuss the three *research perspectives* and several *research methods* that could be used for each perspective.

what products consumers buy, when they buy them, where they buy them, and how much they pay for them. Cognitive research is designed to uncover how consumers process information, or how they *think*. The questions that are asked in cognitive research studies include, for example, how do consumers use information that is stored in memory versus information that is on a product label to evaluate a product? Motivational research is a broader perspective than the first two. It certainly incorporates important information about behaviors and cognitive processing, but it also takes into account a consumer's *emotions* and consumption *experience*. We will discuss these three perspectives in much more detail in the second half of this chapter.

First, we will discuss the research process. Regardless of whether a researcher engages in behavioral, cognitive, or motivational research, the five-step process of conducting a consumer research study is the same. The **consumer research process** is a deliberate series of steps designed to answer key questions about consumer behavior to develop insights that will be helpful to marketing managers. Remember that an **insight** is a useful interpretation of the data that are gathered from the consumer research process.

Why conduct consumer research?

As costly as it is to conduct research, it is often costlier to a firm to *not* engage in research. All of the costs, indeed, must be carefully considered. Not only is there a cost to pay the research firm to conduct the study or to have your own marketing department conduct the study, but also there are costs involved in the delayed time it might take to launch a new product or communications campaign, as well as the cost of potentially tipping off your competitors about your plans. Many managers, often those with less marketing experience, have some mistaken ideas about the usefulness of marketing research. Table 3.1 depicts some misguided myths as well as the realities of properly constructed consumer research.

The history of marketing and failed product launches also illustrates the dangers of not properly conducting research. For example, when Tropicana, the iconic orange juice company, decided it needed to freshen up its packaging in 2009, it removed the well-known image of an orange with a straw sticking out of it, an image that conveyed the idea that the product was picked at the peak of freshness. Consumers who were used to scanning the orange juice section at the grocery store for that image and putting the carton in their shopping carts were confused. The brand lost $33 million and sales dropped by 20 percent in just two months before the packaging was quickly redesigned again, with the orange and straw returned to the front of the carton (Zmuda 2009). Burger King made a mistake a few years ago when it introduced the King mascot. In advertisements, the mascot surprised consumers by turning up unexpectedly in their homes, cars, etc. Some simple consumer research would have told managers at Burger King that the King was a bit creepy. Sure, the King caught the attention of consumers; he just didn't motivate people to run out and get a Whopper. Burger King dropped from the number two to

Table 3.1 Consumer research myths and realities

CONSUMER RESEARCH MYTH	CONSUMER RESEARCH REALITY
The big-decision myth: *A firm should only engage in research when there is a big decision to be made.*	In reality, managers need to do a careful cost–benefit analysis for every project to determine whether the insights provided by the research will be worth the lost time, money, and opportunities.
The survey myopia myth: *Doing research means you are doing surveys.*	Research can occur in many ways, from the simple "How was our service today?" cards that you find at restaurants to much more sophisticated multimethod approaches.
The big-bucks myth: *Research is too expensive for any but the wealthiest firms.*	With new technologies, the cost of research can be quite low and some free research is available from government and nonprofit organizations.
The sophisticated researcher myth: *Only trained experts can conduct research.*	In reality, all managers should know the basics of data analysis, statistics, and research design. They don't need to be experts, however.
The most research is not read myth: *Most research is irrelevant and only confirms what a manager already knows.*	The reality is that a well-planned and executed research project should produce deep insights for managers. It is up to the manager to utilize those insights to the benefit of the organization.

Source: Adapted, in part, from Andreasen (1983).

the number three fast-food retailer in the United States (James 2012). Even Apple, Inc., is not immune. In one of Tim Cook's first efforts as chief executive officer in 2012, he introduced the new iPhone 5, which included a new mapping app. Some early research on consumer usability would have revealed that the app had countless mistakes, such as airports being located in the middle of oceans, directions that were wildly wrong, and important landmarks that were incorrectly located (the Brooklyn Bridge looked like it was melting into the East River). Cook quickly came out and apologized, but the event is sometimes still referred to as *Mapplegate* (Kurtzleben 2012).

Consumer research is especially critical in the international arena. The cosmetics and beauty company L'Oreal found out that sometimes consumers don't do what you expect them to do. In India, a market of 1.35 billion people, consumers very often purchase small packets of single-use shampoos and are not interested in trading up to bigger bottles of shampoo, as they do in other developing countries. L'Oreal found that in other large, developing countries, such as China and Brazil, sales of these single-use packets account for less than a third of sales volume because consumers trade up to the bigger bottles. However, throughout India, more than 50 percent of shampoo is sold in these small packets. So, although consumers in some developing countries

Hot dogs, popcorn, or grasshoppers?

With the global population expected to top 9.7 billion people by 2050 (United Nations 2017), there will be increased pressure on finding sources of nutrition and protein to feed all those people. Although bugs still have a decidedly strong "ick" factor for many Western consumers, 2 billion people across the globe currently include insects as a regular part of their diet. Mealworms, for example, have the same amount of protein, vitamins, and minerals as fish, as well as high levels of unsaturated omega-3. Crickets are a "complete protein" with nine essential amino acids needed to build and repair protein tissues in the body. Aside from the nutritional benefits, another benefit to consuming insects is that, compared to other sources of protein, insects mature more quickly, require fewer resources, and have fewer environmental hazards (LaMotte 2019).

Recently, Mohammed Ashour set out to find out if Western consumers would be open to the idea of eating bugs. Ashour is the chief executive officer of Aspire, a company that raises and sells a variety of insects across the country. While a student at McGill University in Montreal, he started his company after winning the top prize of $1 million for a business proposal that was both viable and socially responsible. The Hult Prize enabled Ashour to focus on making insects a viable, nutritious option for people in developing countries and, more generally, people in need (Peters 2017). One of his first priorities was attempting to automate the process so that he could bring down the cost to consumers. Clearly, the product must be affordable if it is to fulfill its promise of helping those in need. Ashour engaged in a multitude of updates and technological innovations to bring the price down from twenty dollars per pound to about ten dollars per pound (Peters 2017) (see Photo 3.1).

The next big hurdle was gaining consumer acceptance. Ashour knew that there would be substantial resistance to his idea from consumers in more developed countries, so he set out to understand what was on their minds in an attempt to convince them to give bugs a try. His research indicated that consumers were much more likely to accept insects if they were presented whole (such as roasted on a stick) than if they were ground up in another food. Consumers wanted to be fully aware of what they were eating. These insights helped Ashour forge a partnership with the Seattle Mariners (Peters 2017) and in early 2017, the Mariners launched a new product at its ballpark concession stands: fried grasshoppers in a spicy Mexican seasoning with a splash of lime (Vinh 2017). Fans lined up and paid four dollars for a four-ounce cup of fried grasshoppers. The delicacy created such a buzz that the stadium sold eighteen thousand bugs in just the first three games of the season. If you don't get yours by about the fourth inning, they will likely be sold out (Vinh 2017). Next time you go to a baseball game, forget the hot dog. Get a bowl of grasshoppers!

Questions

1. Do you think grasshoppers at a baseball game is a short-lived fad or do you think it could turn into a long-term trend? Why? Are there other occasions in which it might be acceptable to eat grasshoppers? Describe.

● **Photo 3.1** *Dinner anyone?*

2. Social influences play a big role in whether a consumer may be willing to try a bowl of grasshoppers. How might marketers try to get social pressures to work in their favor and push for more consumption?

3. Consumers were more willing to try insects when they could see them versus when the insects were ground up in another product. If you were a marketing manager, what additional information would you want to know about food consumption behaviors or ballpark behaviors to help you create an insight about this?

Sources: LaMotte (2019); Peters (2017); United Nations (2017); Vinh (2017).

eventually trade up to bigger shampoo bottles, consumers in India are not interested in doing so. Because of this finding, L'Oreal now has expanded its use of the single-use format and also sells single-use packets of men's face wash and hair color. It hoped to capture 150 million customers in India by 2020, approximately 10 percent of the market (Rana 2016).

When the Japanese electronics manufacturer Panasonic decided to launch a new touchscreen monitor for its PCs into the US market, it chose Woody the Woodpecker as a likeable mascot. However, the product itself was called "The Woody" and the touchscreen feature was called the "Touch Woody." Luckily, just days before the campaign was launched, one of the American partners noticed the problem (James 2012). A simple investigation of American cultural slang would have revealed the concern with the names. Insights from the Field 3.1 illustrates the importance of consumer research when introducing a completely new product to a group of baseball fans.

Two broad research orientations

The **positivist approach** to consumer behavior emphasizes the objectivity of science and the consumer as a rational decision-maker (Calder and Tybout 1989). This approach sees the world as having an external objective reality, and the goal of research using this perspective is to understand consumers in terms of theories that have been rigorously tested and that can explain this external reality. Methods from this perspective often focus on examining relationships between key factors (or variables) that explain some aspect of consumer behavior and research tools that allow relationships to be observed and quantified in some way. For this reason, most methods involved in this approach to consumer research tend to be quantitative (involving numbers and formulas), with qualitative methods being used in a limited supporting role. Many commercial companies use this approach, and typical techniques include structured questionnaires, experiments, and consumer panels. With the positivist perspective, the main goal of the research study is to uncover an "objective truth" about why, for example, consumers prefer one ad or one product over another.

Positivist approach emphasizes the objectivity of science and the consumer as a rational decision-maker.

Interpretivist perspective stresses the subjective meaning of the consumer's individual experience and the idea that any behavior is subject to multiple interpretations rather than one single explanation.

The **interpretivist perspective** stresses the subjective meaning of the consumer's individual experience and the idea that any behavior is subject to multiple interpretations rather than a single explanation. This approach is driven by a need to develop a deep understanding of people's lives and behaviors, recognizing that the researcher interprets these data in terms of a particular system of ideas and assumptions about the nature of reality. This approach recognizes that reality is socially constructed and that the researcher is an active participant in the research process (rather than an objective bystander). The interpretivist perspective uses qualitative research such as unstructured in-depth interviews, allowing the researcher to adopt a flexible approach to the interview and to probe more deeply into areas of particular interest. Other methods include ethnography, personal introspections, participant observations, and narrative analyses. With the interpretivist perspective, there are very few predictions about what will emerge from the research findings. Instead, the main goal of a research effort is to "see what the research reveals" about the question of interest.

Overview of the five-step consumer research process

The five steps in the consumer research process are as follows: identify the problem, select the perspective, collect the data, analyze the data, and, finally, develop consumer insights. It is important to realize that even when a consumer research project is "finished," it is not really finished. That is, smart consumer researchers use the insights that were gathered from the research process to give them direction about the next research project that can be designed, to find out even more about consumers. No smart researcher would start with a blank slate each time a new problem needs to be answered. Indeed, there is a feedback loop that brings valuable insights back to the start of the process for the next project (see Figure 3.1).

Identify the problem

The first step in the consumer research process is the careful identification of the research problem. This is a very important step in the process because if a manager does not know the correct question, it will be impossible to answer

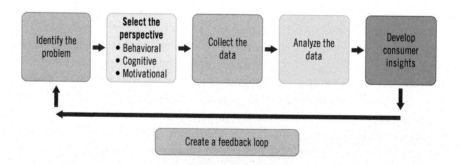

● **Figure 3.1** *The consumer research process*

that question, regardless of the amount of data collected later. **Problem identification** involves the careful articulation of the exact question a consumer researcher needs to answer. The question cannot be too broad or too narrow.

To determine the most appropriate depth versus breadth of the research question, the manager must first consider whether the research effort requires exploratory work or a confirmatory approach. With **exploratory consumer research**, the researcher is interested in finding out broad trends or patterns of behavior. Perhaps the product is completely new to the consumer. That is, perhaps the consumer is in a target market that is completely new for the organization and therefore the consumer knows very little about the product, its attributes, or its proposed benefits. Alternatively, perhaps the consumer is already a loyal customer of the organization, but the organization is interested in introducing a novel product or launching a completely new communications campaign. If this is the case and an organization is interested in some general ideas about what consumer reactions might be or how the product might be incorporated into the consumer's life, exploratory consumer research is the appropriate way to go. Alternatively, suppose the firm already has an established relationship with the consumer and is interested in adding a new feature. What if the firm and the product are both well known and the firm is interested in reactions to a new celebrity spokesperson, for example? If this is the case, **confirmatory consumer research** is warranted because it seeks to find a specific answer to a specific

Problem identification is the first step in the consumer research process. It involves the careful articulation of the exact question a consumer researcher needs to answer.

Exploratory consumer research is interested in finding out broad trends or patterns of behavior.

Confirmatory consumer research seeks to find a specific answer to a specific question.

INSIGHTS FROM ACADEMIA 3.1

Marketers learn more from brains than from people

Several new techniques have arisen in consumer research that try to reveal what a consumer is really thinking. One technique is electroencephalography (EEG), which measures electrical activity across different regions of the brain. Another technique is functional magnetic resonance imaging (fMRI), which measures oxygen levels in the brain; the more oxygen that is seen in one part of the brain, the more that part of the brain is working (see Photo 3.2). In a recent study, researchers wanted to find out which techniques were more effective in helping to predict consumer memories of and favorability toward a variety of television ads. They also wanted to find out how these neurotechniques compared to traditional techniques, such as asking consumers to rate favorability, desirability,

etc., for the product. In the end, the researchers determined that the EEG and the fMRI techniques were much better at predicting favorability than consumers' own verbal responses. Why? The researchers concluded that the ratings consumers provide might be influenced by a host of other social and contextual factors and biases. However, with an EEG or fMRI scan, there is no hiding the brain's work in processing and storing information.

Venkatraman, V., A. Kimoka, P. A. Pavlou, K. Vo, W. Hampton, B. Bollinger, H. E. Hershfield, M. Ishihara, and R. S. Winer. 2015. "Predicting Advertising Success beyond Traditional Measures: New Insights from Neurophysiological Methods and Market Response Modeling." Journal of Marketing Research *52 (4): 436–52.*

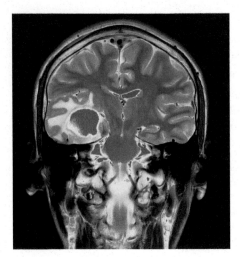

● **Photo 3.2** *A functional magnetic resonance image of a brain*

question. Since the team is dealing with a well-known product and target market, previous research studies likely have already given the research team some early indications about how consumers might respond. With confirmatory consumer research, the research team is seeking to confirm an expectation that it might already have. Insights from Academia 3.1 describes one study that used brain imaging technology to confirm that consumers do not always tell researchers what is on their minds.

Experts recommend that good research questions should account for three separate dimensions of the consumer–organization relationship. First, a good research question should address *what a consumer brings* to the encounter. Such questions could focus on what the consumer goals might be in consuming the product, key memories that are evoked when consuming the product, and emotions they might feel when consuming the product. Second, good research questions could touch on *what a consumer encounters* during the decision or during consumption. Examples include questions about how easily they can process information in an advertisement, how sensory factors (like smell, taste, or sound) impact processing, and how social influences work when a consumer is making a decision. Finally, a good research question could assess *what consumers do* during shopping, purchase, and consumption. For example, how much do they search for information beforehand, what do they do when they actually pay for the product, and what happens during postpurchase (Dholakia et al. 2010)? All in all, identifying the key research problem as well as a set of research questions will help guide the entire process by providing a concrete goal that everyone on the research team will need to work toward.

To clarify the difference between a research problem and a research question, consider the case of the "soda tax" in Philadelphia. After years of opposition by beverage company giants like PepsiCo and Coca-Cola, the city of Philadelphia enacted a new soda tax in early 2017. Sweetened beverages were taxed an extra 1.5 cents per ounce. The original rationale was admirable: City schools were underfunded because of budget cuts and the revenues from the tax ($39.7 million) would be used to fund kindergarten and prekindergarten programs throughout the city. There was also an added health benefit in that some people might consume fewer sweetened beverages. At the time the tax was implemented, Berkeley, California, was the only other city in the country to have implemented such a tax. Beverage sales at convenience stores, restaurants, grocery stores, and fast-food outlets in Philadelphia dropped immediately after implementation of the tax. In this example, a manager at a chain of convenience stores would likely want to find out more about the impact of the tax on consumer behaviors (Burdo 2017). Table 3.2 provides some specific examples of well-articulated research problems and questions, including some for our convenience store manager.

Table 3.2 Examples of well-articulated research problems and questions

RESEARCH PROBLEMS	RESEARCH QUESTIONS
Sales of soda have dropped at our convenience stores in the past six months.	Is the drop in sales the result of a long-term trend away from sweet beverages? Is the drop in sales a result of the increased price of the soda? Are our consumers buying their soda somewhere else?
Visits to our online store have dropped over the past three months.	Have the online behaviors of our consumers changed over the past few months? Do consumers still see value in our products and services?
Over the past year, fewer customers are opting for the insurance coverage when they rent our cars.	Do our customers clearly understand our marketing and the benefits of the optional insurance? Do consumers have coverage from another source, such as their own auto policies?

Select the perspective

Selecting the appropriate perspective depends entirely on the first step in the research process: identifying the research problem. Once the problem is clearly identified, the researcher can select how the team will go about obtaining the data that will help determine an answer to the problem. As we learned in Chapter 1, the three research perspectives are behavioral, cognitive, and motivational. These three perspectives will be discussed in detail in the second half of this chapter. For now, it is enough to say that if the research questions center around issues of what consumers *do*, a behavioral perspective is appropriate; if the questions focus on how consumers *think*, a cognitive perspective is appropriate; and if the questions focus on how consumers *feel*, the social or family factors that influence consumers, or how they are motivated, a motivational approach is best.

Collect the data

During this phase of the research process, the research team will launch the project and start collecting the data. There are several decisions that need to be made during this phase. First, the research team must decide whether they can use data that are already available or need to collect new data. **Secondary data** have already been collected for another purpose, and some researchers can find that data quite useful in gathering information for important insights. Secondary data have the advantage of being very quick and comparatively inexpensive. A host of government, university, and research institutes provide free or low-cost data. For example, the US Census Bureau provides extensive data on US citizens that can be sorted by many factors, such as age, ethnicity, income, and where they live (see US Census Bureau 2019). The World Bank provides extensive economic and social data on each country around the world, including literacy rates, life expectancy, population, and even carbon dioxide emissions (see World Bank 2019).

Secondary data have already been collected for another purpose.

"We're dog people. Crazy dog people."

Sixty-seven percent of American households own a pet, which equates to 84.5 million homes. Dogs can be found in 63.4 million homes and cats can be found in 42.7 million homes. Together, American pet owners spent approximately $97.5 billion on their pets in 2019. For those households who do own a pet, 48 percent own a dog and 38 percent own a cat (American Pet Products Association 2019-20). The biggest spenders? People who have attended college, people who have more money, and millennials. Yes, despite having comparatively less money to spend, one study found that millennials are more likely than those in other age groups to spend it on premium pet food (Riley 2017). Many people treat their pets like family and go to extreme lengths to provide their pets with the best of everything. An astounding two-thirds of car buyers "considered their pet's comfort" when purchasing a car (Riley 2017). Drawn-out, nasty divorce feuds often center around who gets custody of the couple's pet. One famous case involved a California woman who spent $146,000 on her divorce case, which centered around custody of her beloved dog (she got the dog!). Perhaps because of this case and others, more than 150 North American law schools now teach *animal law*, including how to handle disputes over pet custody (Riley 2017).

Despite the cost, there are big medical benefits to owning a pet. According to WebMD, the five key benefits include the following (Davis 2017):

- Having pets at home can reduce your risk of allergies.
- Pets can help you meet people and strengthen your social relationships.
- For elderly people, having a pet around decreases anxiety and increases the likelihood of exercise.
- Pets help us lower our blood pressure and lower the likelihood of depression.
- Pets are good for our hearts—one study found that heart attack patients survive longer when they have a pet at home.

Bark & Co. was founded in 2012 to help dog owners express their love for their dogs. Once a month, Bark will send a box of all-natural treats and fun toys for your special dog to enjoy. The monthly subscription service starts as low as $22 per month. To date, Bark has shipped boxes to over two million homes and has more than six hundred thousand regular customers across the United States and Canada. Revenue is currently estimated at $200 million (Bark 2019) (see Photo 3.4 for a look at the typical BarkBox contents and the reaction from a very happy consumer). A recent study commissioned by Bark surveyed more than one thousand dog owners (eighteen years old and older) in a nationally representative sample of Americans. The results indicated that Americans are absolutely in love with their dogs. Indeed, some of the more interesting findings are as follows (Bark 2019):

- Seventy-one percent say their dog has made them happier people.
- Forty-nine percent share a bed with their dog and thirty-six percent say they would sleep in an uncomfortable position so their dog could sleep next to them.
- Forty-five percent admit to dressing their dog in clothing.
    - Thirty-four percent sometimes take their dog on a date.
    - Twenty-two percent have given their dog a birthday party.

Bark & Co. has used both primary and secondary data to help understand its

● **Photo 3.3** *The Bark & Co. people are crazy dog people*

customers and their needs and to connect with them in a variety of ways to create a lifestyle brand. Bark & Co. boasts 7.5 million followers across all of its social media platforms, and BarkShop allows customers to purchase a variety of treats and products. Bark's next big venture is BarkPark, which promises to be an "ultra-fun dog park" and "hip human hangout" (Bark 2019).

Questions

1. *Lifestyle brands* are designed to motivate and inspire customers in such a way that they help consumers with their social relationships and even self-definition. Ideally, lifestyle brands become an integral part of a customer's day-to-day life. In what way is Bark & Co. attempting to become a lifestyle brand for its customers? What else could they do?
2. Look at the results from the study sponsored by Bark & Co. and the results of the WebMD study. What insights could Bark & Co. generate from this

● **Photo 3.4** *Happy BarkBox consumer*

information to help strengthen (a) their connection to customers, (b) the connections customers have with one another, and (c) the connections customers have with their dogs?

Sources: American Pet Products Association (2017–18); Davis (2017); Martin (2016); Riley (2017); Bark (2019).

The United States also provides a host of other data sets that are available on a wide range of topics that fall under fourteen broad headings, including local government, agriculture, health, climate, and education (see Data.gov 2019). These resources are just a small sampling of the total number that are available for free to anyone who would like to use them. Secondary data can also be purchased from research organizations that compile reports and sell them to businesses. Examples include Nielsen, Mintel, and Information Resources, Inc. Reports from these organizations start at several thousand dollars each.

However, if the research team decides that the questions they need to answer are more complex than can be answered in a report that has already been prepared, the team will likely opt for primary research. **Primary data** come from a specifically designed research effort that seeks to answer a very specific question at hand. Researchers engage in primary research when, for example, they need to answer questions about their product, their advertising, or their particular target market. Primary research is much more focused and precise than secondary research. Insights from the Field 3.2 illustrates how both primary and secondary research can be used by companies like BarkBox to better understand pet owners (see Photo 3.3).

Primary data are collected to specifically answer the question at hand.

Qualitative data describe qualities of a situation, product, consumer, etc.

Quantitative data use numbers, ratios, and other measurements to describe a situation, product, consumer, etc.

Second, the research team needs to decide whether the data that will be collected should be qualitative or quantitative. As the name indicates, **qualitative data** is the term for nonnumerical data. The key feature of this type of data is that they approximate and characterize the phenomenon of interest. This type of data can take many forms, such as words or images, and are generally collected through methods of observations, one-to-one interviews, focus groups, and other similar methods. For example, when describing the millennial group of consumers (individuals born after 1980), a researcher might conclude that they are confident, connected, and open to change. These are characteristics of who these people are and describe the essence of what it is like to be a millennial (Pew Research Center 2010). **Quantitative data**, by contrast, utilize numbers, ratios, and other measurements to describe a situation, product, consumer, etc. If we are talking about millennials again, we could use quantitative data to say that 61 percent of millennials in the United States are White, 19 percent are Hispanic, and 14 percent are Black (Pew Research Center 2010). Other characteristics also set them apart from previous generations. For example, there are currently about fifty million millennials in the United States. Only about 60 percent were raised by both parents, a scant 2 percent of males have served in the military, and about 40 percent have a college education (Pew Research Center 2010).

Qualitative data are generally collected at the beginning of a research project, when the researchers are still trying to understand the phenomenon of interest. They are also used when researchers need to understand the issue at a deep and profound level. Have a look at Insights from Academia 3.2 for a description of qualitative research with children. Quantitative data are generally collected later in the process, when researchers need to examine specific relationships between variables, such as the price of a product and its sales. Because they are numerical, quantitative data let the researcher perform a variety of statistical analyses and make predictions about what consumers might do.

A third question that must be addressed during the data collection phase of the research process is *who* will be the target of the investigation. For example, would a researcher like to talk to women or men? Consumers who are early adopters or laggards? Consumers who live in Texas or California? Consumers who are heavy users of social media or those who are light users of social media? A clear articulation of the research problem should help the researchers answer this question. As soon as the research team determines who they eventually want to target with a marketing strategy, they need to determine the research **sample**, which is a smaller group of consumers who represent the actual target market.

Sample refers to a smaller group of consumers who represent the target market and are used in a research study.

Researchers select a sample of consumers because it would simply be too difficult to speak with everyone in the target market. There are many methods for determining the size and scope of a research sample. Of course, a large part of these decisions has to do with the cost—in terms of time, money, and lost opportunity—of conducting the research study. The cost

INSIGHTS FROM ACADEMIA 3.2

"Obviously, all the cool kids have iPhones"

It is especially difficult to conduct research on children because consumer researchers must go to great lengths to ensure that children's rights are protected when they are asked questions. Early consumer researchers cautioned that children should not be allowed to make consumer-related decisions until they are cognitively mature enough to interpret ads and make decisions about the costs versus benefits of product use. However, younger consumers in the early twenty-first century seem to be quite savvy. One recent study attempted to look at how children are pressured to fit into their peer groups with products like designer clothing and electronics. To find out more, the researchers conducted a series of in-depth interviews and focus groups with eight- to thirteen-year-olds in the United Kingdom. Then, after the transcripts from the interviews were examined, they created a set of broad themes about how these children consume products like designer clothing and electronics. The researchers found that consumption is a part of the normal, everyday lives of these kids. They think about it, are concerned about it, and use consumption in a variety of ways to fit into a social hierarchy. Even at this young age, these children have already developed three very specific consumption-related skills:

● **Photo 3.5** *School kids texting before class*

1. Recognition—they understand that a social hierarchy exists, whether or not they like it.
2. Performance—they have a desire to have a place in the social group near the top, or at least not near the bottom, of the hierarchy.
3. Communication—they understand that there are rules about what can and cannot be talked about in relation to consumption. For example, they don't want to talk about their stuff too much or they might be called *spoiled*.

Knowing more about the process of how children become skilled consumers helps parents, teachers, and policy makers (see Photo 3.5 for a very typical scene of kids before class).

Nairn, A., and F. Spotswood. 2015. "'Obviously in the Cool Group They Wear Designer Things': A Social Practice Theory Perspective on Children's Consumption." European Journal of Marketing 49 (9/10): 1460–83.

for a typical research study for a consumer product can start at $10,000 and take a few days, or it could cost up to several hundred thousand dollars and take several months to complete. As much as possible, a research team will want to construct a sample that is **representative** of the actual target market, which means that they have the same core set of characteristics

Representative research samples have the same core set of characteristics as the larger group of consumers.

as the bigger group of consumers. For example, the team would want to make sure that the research sample has the same values or lifestyle habits as the target market, as well as the same ratio of men and women, ethnicities, income brackets, etc., as the larger target market. It is important to note that the more variables that are used to define the research sample, the higher the cost to create this sample.

Why is representativeness so important? Because it allows us to **generalize** our findings to the larger group of consumers when the results are in. We must ensure that our sample is representative of all consumers in our target market so that we can extend our research conclusions to that broader group (see Photo 3.6). What would happen, for example, if the beauty products manufacturer L'Oreal wanted to test a new shampoo with 100 percent organic ingredients to see how much consumers would like the formulation but only included consumers who lived close to their research headquarters in Paris? How representative of the entire population of consumers is that sample strategy? How generalizable would those findings be? If the study has a representative sample, it is far more likely that the results will be generalizable.

A fourth key question or consideration that needs to be answered in the data collection phase of the research process focuses on the rights of the individuals in our research sample. The people who participate in the research study are referred to as **research participants**. These participants have certain rights, and it is the responsibility of the researchers to make sure that

Generalizing the findings of a research study means that the researcher is able to extend the findings from the smaller research sample to a broader group of consumers.

Research participants are the group of consumers who take part in a research study.

● **Photo 3.6** *Researchers want to make sure that their research sample is representative of the target audience*

these rights are not violated. After some blatant violations came to light in the 1960s and 1970s, the US government enacted a series of laws designed to protect the health and welfare of any participant in a research study.

Although there were many violations over the years, perhaps two of the most infamous cases were the Milgram experiment and the Stanford prison experiment. The Milgram experiment was originally designed to see how susceptible individuals were to strong authority figures. Psychologist Stanley Milgram at Yale University designed the study after the end of World War II and the Holocaust to try to better understand how seemingly normal people could inflict such cruel and horrific harm on other people. In the study, research participants were asked to provide electrical shocks to a stranger in another room in an effort to "teach" them. With a strong authority figure standing over them, the participants gave a series of increasingly stronger and more painful electric shocks to the stranger in the other room. Participants could hear the stranger screaming in pain, until, eventually, the screams stopped. Luckily, the study was a ruse and everyone was an actor (except the participant administering the shocks!). Unfortunately, later, many of the participants suffered significant emotional and psychological trauma knowing that they were capable of inflicting such harm on another person (cf., A. G. Miller, Collins, and Brief 1995). In the Stanford prison experiment, psychologist Philip Zimbardo took a group of healthy young men and split them into two groups: one group would be the "prisoners" and one group would be the "prison guards" in a simulated jail. It only took a few days before the research participants were fully playing out their parts. The guards enacted cruel and sadistic punishments on the prisoners, while the prisoners became depressed and exhibited extreme stress. The experiment was supposed to last two weeks, but was abandoned after just six days because of the extreme effects the participants were experiencing (cf., G. Miller 2011).

These kinds of studies would not happen today because strict rules designed to protect research participants are now in place. The American Psychological Association created the **Belmont Report**, which described the ethical principles and guidelines for the protection of research participants (1979). As a result of this report, there are now strong federal laws that regulate what can and cannot happen during a research study. The Belmont Report established three key ethical principles for conducting research with people:

Belmont Report (1979) describes the ethical principles and guidelines for the protection of research participants.

1. Respect for persons—individuals are capable of making their own decisions about their personal goals and are free to act according to their own judgment. For people who may be less capable of making their own decisions (children, the elderly, disabled individuals), extra protection and consideration are required to ensure their rights.

2. Beneficence—people will be treated in an ethical manner by not only respecting their rights to self-determination, but also making efforts to

secure their well-being. Any research should: (a) do no harm and (b) maximize possible benefits while minimizing possible harms.

3. Justice—research participants should all be treated equally and have the same random chance of receiving different research treatments, procedures, or manipulations (Belmont Report 1979).

Institutional review board is a group of people in an organization whose purpose is to review all research studies before they are conducted to ensure the rights of research participants.

In the early twenty-first century, any institution (e.g., university, research firm, government) that conducts research using people must have an **institutional review board**, whose purpose is to review all research studies before they are conducted to ensure the rights of research participants. The three core ethical principles just mentioned guide the board's deliberations and decisions. The institutional review board is generally composed of research scientists and those who are very familiar with the research process. In the end, researchers want to have useful data that will help them develop insights. In addition to being unethical, if research participants are hurt or traumatized, the data will not be useful for decision-makers.

An important caveat when collecting data is that researchers should always collect the amount of data they need to answer the research question—no more and no less. If a researcher collects less data than is needed to answer the problem, the data will reveal an incomplete picture of what is happening and incorrect insights might be developed. If a researcher collects more data than needed, the effort on those extra questions is a waste of time and money. Many times, researchers fall into the trap of adding just a few more questions to a survey, focus group, or experiment. If the questions were important enough to add to the research effort, they should be stand-alone research questions in their own right, not afterthoughts or add-ons.

Analyze the data

Data refer to numbers or other descriptors that are used to define a phenomenon.

Information refers to data that have already been organized and analyzed.

During the data analysis phase of the research process, researchers combine the data they have received into formats that are usable for managers. **Data** refer to numbers or other nonnumerical descriptors that are used to define a phenomenon; **information** refers to data that have already been organized and analyzed. Information also provides context and is therefore more useful for managers in developing insights.

If the research is qualitative, researchers will transcribe transcripts of interviews and focus groups. They will code the data, analyze it, and summarize key findings that they have made during their observations of what consumers do, for example, while shopping, cooking, examining a label, or navigating a web page. All of this *information* will then be combined into several themes about consumers and their decision-making processes and behaviors. If the research is quantitative, researchers will conduct a series of statistical analyses and look for patterns in the data to help them develop conclusions about consumer decision-making and behavior. This *information* will then be provided to marketing managers.

Data visualization is an important graphical tool to help managers see patterns in data.

With both types of data analysis—qualitative and quantitative—**data visualization** is an important tool to help managers see patterns in the data that might be difficult to visualize by simply looking at the raw data. Data visualization tools are especially useful when there are a lot of data to digest, and with interactive data visualization tools that allow users to hover a cursor over the graphic, some tools allow managers to drill down and obtain more detailed information on very specific pieces of information. There are many tools for data visualization, but the goal of this technique is the same: to convey important findings and information in a way that is easy for others to understand (see Photo 3.7).

There are several ways in which researchers must be particularly careful about biases that may be present during the analysis of the data. A bias refers to a systematic error in the data collection or the analysis of the data that skews the results. **Confirmation bias** happens when researchers look at the results of the data analyses as a way to confirm a conclusion they had already made. Sometimes, researchers are selective in what they see or don't see in the data and, because of this, draw conclusions that already fit with what they expected to happen. This bias is particularly troublesome because it is how most of us think. To avoid this, always look for alternative explanations for the results and do not try to explain away results that don't fit your expectations (Dooley 2013). **Irrational escalation** happens when new data conflict with a decision that has already been made. The marketing team decides, for example, to roll out a new product launch even though troubling information about the product has come back from the marketing research study. Once committed to a project, some managers may be reluctant to admit they are wrong and will ignore any conflicting data. However, sometimes it may be smarter to cut your losses than to continue down a losing path. **Social desirability bias** happens when research participants provide answers that make themselves look good or that they think the researcher might want to hear. No research participant wants to admit to embarrassing behavior or thoughts, so responses may be altered accordingly. To avoid this problem, researchers might want to assure participants that their responses will remain anonymous. **Framing** is another bias that researchers need to consider. The bias of framing happens when the setting or context alters the answers a participant might give. The order in which the questions are asked could also alter how participants respond. To avoid framing effects, researchers can make sure that the research context is the same for every participant and that the order of the questions is randomized. Finally, researchers need to be aware of **knowledge bias**, the tendency for participants to prefer a product, advertisement, or even celebrity spokesperson with which they are familiar compared to one that is unfamiliar. The research team will want to do whatever it can to design the research study, construct the questions, and analyze the data to reduce the chance of bias. The team wants to ensure that the data are as accurate as

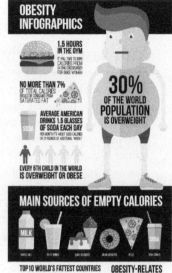

● **Photo 3.7** *Data Visualization of the Global Obesity Epidemic*

Confirmation bias happens when researchers look at the results of the data analyses as a way to confirm a conclusion they have already made.

Irrational escalation happens when new data happen to be in conflict with a decision that has already been made and managers are reluctant to "cut their losses."

Social desirability bias happens when research participants provide answers to make themselves look good or provides answers they think the researcher might want to hear.

INSIGHTS FROM ACADEMIA 3.3

You saw that, right?

An innovative new way for consumer researchers to collect data is through a variety of mobile apps. There are several advantages to collecting data via apps: researchers can obtain huge amounts of data, they can gather it quite cheaply, and they can measure things that might otherwise be difficult to measure in a laboratory setting. Information gathered from one app ended up offering surprising insights that were put to use in national security and healthcare. Airport Scanner is a game that allows users to simulate the job of an airport Transportation Security Administration agent and do visual searches of "luggage" for "unsafe items." As it turns out, users are very good at finding common items that are banned, like guns or knives. However, they do not do well at identifying rare items that might be just as dangerous, like cannonballs, for example. Although an object might be quite big on the screen, it is rare for such items to appear. Often, users either report that they never saw the item or they ignore it. This information about how users interpret a visual image can have important implications for marketing as well as other applications. First, the findings have already been shared with the Transportation Security Administration, which can perhaps retrain its agents to look for these rare items. The findings have also been shared with medical professionals to warn them, for example, that it might be difficult for a doctor to visually inspect an X-ray and notice a very rare form of cancer. From a marketing standpoint, advertisers must be careful about inserting unusual or "rare" images in an advertisement—consumers might never even notice them.

Mitroff, S. R., A. T. Biggs, E. W. Dowd, J. Winkle, and K. Clark. 2015. "What Can 1 Billion Trials Tell Us about Visual Search?" Journal of Experimental Psychology: Human Perception and Performance *41 (1): 1–5.*

Framing describes how a consumer makes a decision within different contexts; it is the perspective from which the consumer considers the decision.

Knowledge bias is the tendency for participants to prefer a product, advertisement, or spokesperson with which they are familiar over one that is unfamiliar.

possible, with no systematic shifting or skewing of the results. Because bias will lead to incorrect data and information, it will also lead to incorrect insights. Read Insights from Academia 3.3 for a description of a study that revealed what consumers are likely to see and not see in an ad.

Develop consumer insights

During this part of the consumer research process, the research team combines its research findings from the data analysis phase and develops insights that help answer the research question that was originally posed in the first stage of the process. During this phase of the research process, the team generally reports the findings of its research project with a written report or presentation. An important part of reporting the findings is developing insights. Insights take the information that is generated, connect it with information that may be available from other sources like data visualization tools, and form conclusions.

An example of the difference between data, information, and insights will illustrate the differences between these three concepts. Research tells us that people have a difficult time sorting through information that is available online and often find their information from websites, social media, or "news reports" that provide slanted or even incorrect information about political parties, government initiatives, and political candidates. If we are to have an informed population, we must make sure that citizens have access to correct and unbiased information so they can vote for candidates who will represent their best interests. The problem of sorting through all this information is made worse with the massive amounts of information available online, as well as the ability for search engines to "learn" a person's search behavior and provide information that is already consistent with their preexisting beliefs. Mintel, one of the global leaders in providing secondary research to organizations, conducted a study on this topic in 2017. In this example, the *data* would be the reams of spreadsheets that would result from hundreds of research participants providing scores to a variety of questions. *Information* would be the following findings: 54 percent of US consumers say it's difficult to tell if the information they're getting online is accurate and 63 percent of Americans say technology gives them so many choices it's hard to pick the best one. Finally, a key *insight* could be as follows: "Disruption is more important than ever before as curated information 'bubbles' leave consumers with a lack of diverse content and viewpoints" (Mintel 2017). In this example, the insight offers a glimpse into the consumer's experience and hints at a recommendation to the marketing manager—use something that will surprise consumers and jolt them out of the habit of looking at information that only confirms what they already know or believe.

Create a feedback loop

It is important to remember that the goal of consumer research is to answer important questions that managers or others may have about how to better connect or engage with consumers. Because consumers, the marketplace, and the overall context in which consumer behavior takes place are always changing, the consumer research process must be a continuous process. Managers cannot be satisfied with simply answering questions. Instead, they need to create a more complex, nuanced, and continuously evolving portrait of the consumer. The insights that are developed from one research project should always feed into the next project. Therefore, a feedback loop provides important conclusions from one research project and makes them available to managers as they identify the next big research problem (see Insights from the Boardroom 3).

◉ Consumer Research Perspectives

For the purpose of clearly explaining each of the research perspectives, we will present them one at a time. However, remember that more than one research perspective can be utilized at a time (as in the Wawa case) to provide deeper and more meaningful insights into consumer behavior. Indeed, sometimes it makes sense to tackle a problem using several methods and

INSIGHTS FROM THE BOARDROOM 3

Sometimes a research project needs to be tackled with multiple methods

● *Joan Hoenninger*

Selecting the right research method for a project can sometimes be tricky, but Joan Hoenninger knows how to do it. In the end, using the correct research method for a given project allows her to uncover important consumer insights. Hoenninger is the customer insights manager for Wawa, a privately held chain of convenience stores in the mid-Atlantic region and Florida. The company was founded in 1865 as a dairy operation; in 1902, it became increasingly successful because of the quality and purity of its milk. Currently number thirty-six on the Forbes list of the largest privately held companies, with $9.1 billion in annual revenue, Wawa has more than 750 stores and 30,000 associates in New Jersey, Pennsylvania, Delaware, Maryland, Virginia, and Florida (*Forbes* 2017).

What research methods does Wawa use? "It depends entirely on our needs," reports Hoenninger, again confirming the importance of clearly defining the research problem as the first step in the research process. For example, explained Hoenninger, "We used focus groups when we revamped our Sizzli® packaging (a Sizzli® is a grab-and-go hot breakfast sandwich). It was important to show customers what the options looked like so that we could see how they reacted and get their impressions. We wanted them to touch, feel, interact with, and see the product. We wanted to see what cues customers looked at on the packaging when selecting what variety of Sizzli® they wanted. The designer initially wanted brighter colors and we also wanted to assess drawings vs. photos of the product." For the question about which color to use, she noted, "We found that red was associated with frozen products—a lot of frozen foods use red. It was not perceived as 'made fresh' and when red was used on all of the varieties, customers could not easily distinguish which variety was which." So, it was out with red. Wawa settled on a variety of more muted colors. For the question about graphics, Hoenninger stated, "We found that customers like pictures much more than words because they're easier to understand when they're in a hurry. So, for example, instead of writing 'bacon' on the packaging, we added a picture of bacon" (Hoenninger 2017). See Photo 3.8 for the new Sizzli® packaging.

To ensure that all Wawa-branded products are top quality, the company utilizes sensory methods (involving taste, aroma, visuals) for gathering data. For example, Hoenninger noted, "We had a project a few years ago when we investigated how consumers would react if we changed the presentation of our coffee from glass pots to thermal containers." There were two big issues that needed to be investigated. First, she said, "We knew that coffee in the glass pots had a shelf-life of 20 minutes while the shelf-life in the thermals was closer to 2 hours. When the glass pots start to get empty and are sitting on the burner for a little too long, about 30 mins, the taste is affected. We wanted to ensure that there was a consistent taste for the customers and we thought that there was just too much variation sometimes with the glass pots. Second, temperature is also critical to the sensory experience. The coffee needs to stay at the ideal temperature that is hot and pleasant, but won't burn the taste buds of the customers." In the end, the sensory data provided the insight that gave Wawa the confidence to switch to thermal containers. Since then, Wawa has seen positive results.

Hoenninger and her team deftly handle the seemingly continuous stream of research questions that come in to the department. When they needed to determine which label was most preferred for the Wawa-branded bottled water, they conducted the study online. When they needed to determine what customers thought about a new concept for a store layout, they did store intercepts with customers both before and after the redesign. "We actually got the same people to come back. We walked with them through the store and asked questions along the way. We needed to be in the store to do that project and get their natural reactions," said Hoenninger. The team has started to utilize a variety of mobile and digital research methods too.

Whether it is focus groups, sensory studies, store intercepts, online, or mobile methods, determining the right research method requires skill

● **Photo 3.8** *Wawa's updated Sizzli® packaging*

and expertise. However, according to Hoenninger, the overall goal is to still "look at the consumer perspective in all of the decisions we make. Also, we need to think about what works for the store associates. Depending on the business needs, we try to provide research to enable day-to-day as well as more strategic decisions" (2017). Sizzli® anyone?

Sources: Forbes (2017); Hoenninger (2017).

perspectives, such as in-depth interviews, surveys, and ethnographic research. Multimethod approaches like these have the benefit of looking at a concept from different angles, while at the same time overcoming the weaknesses of some perspectives and building on the strengths of others. When the research team arrives at the second step in the research process, it must determine what perspective it will take. Much of this decision depends on how the problem was identified and how the research question was formulated. There are three options: behavioral, cognitive, and/or motivational. These will be discussed in detail.

A common method by which consumer researchers develop a deeper understanding of consumers is with **experiments**. Experiments are widely used in behavioral, cognitive, and motivational research. Generally speaking, researchers are interested in finding out about the relationship between independent variables and dependent variables. On the one hand, **independent variables**, as the name implies, do not depend on other factors in the experimental setup. Typical independent variables would be a person's age or gender. Other independent variables could be a customer's previous experience with or knowledge about the product. **Dependent variables**, on the other hand, actually depend or rely on other factors in the experimental setup. For example, a dependent variable could be a consumer's likelihood to live-stream the Super Bowl; this likely depends, in part, on age, gender, and if the customer has experience with live-streaming other sports events. The main purpose of experimental research is for the researcher to carefully control as much as possible to get a very precise assessment of how consumers might react if changes are made to one or more independent variables. The kinds of questions that consumer researchers could assess with experiments are almost limitless. It might seem ironic at first that experimental research, which is supposed to provide insights about consumer behavior, only sometimes measures actual behavior (Morales, Amir, and Lee 2017). Indeed, researchers also often examine other dependent variables, such as attitudes and intentions. However, remember that the purpose of experimental research is to more carefully study the relationship between independent variables and dependent variables. Once a research team develops a better understanding of the relationship between variables, it can then use a multimethod approach to expand that understanding. In each of the sections below, we will discuss experiments in more detail.

Behavioral research

Behavioral research starts with a desire to understand what consumers are currently doing. A variety of methods can be employed, but they all fall under the heading of **observational methods**, or observing the actual behaviors of consumers or the results of those behaviors. Perhaps the most obvious observational method is simple **observation**. Researchers simply watch and record what customers do. For example, observation can happen at a retail store, where researchers could record how many products customers examine, how much time they spend examining each product, and how many customers look at the product labels. Researchers could observe almost anything customers do, even behaviors that happen at home, like cooking a meal, getting the kids ready for bed, or cleaning the house, as long as they have permission from the customer to do so.

Experiments carefully control everything in a laboratory environment to obtain a precise assessment of the relationship between independent and dependent variables.

Independent variables in consumer research change on their own and are not dependent on other factors.

Dependent variables in consumer research change because of the influence of another factor (the independent variable).

Observational methods describe a broad set of methods to observe the actual behaviors of consumers or the results of those behaviors.

Observation in research occurs when researchers simply watch and record what customers do.

Scanner data are another measure of what customers do. Scanner data are generated when a consumer's purchases are electronically scanned at the checkout line at a retail store. These data can provide a lot of high-level information to retailers about regional patterns of purchases or store-level patterns of purchases. Scanner data can also provide data on the purchases of individual customers, such as "the basket" of purchases they make at a single stop, which coupons they use, how they pay (cash, credit card, etc.), and how all this connects to previous purchases. Target, Inc., received a great deal of criticism a few years ago when its scanner data determined a teenager was pregnant even before she told her parents. Based on purchases like cotton balls, vitamins, unscented soaps/lotions, and hand sanitizers, Target can surmise with somewhat alarming accuracy when someone is pregnant and sends coupons to these women for additional products. That's what got them in trouble. When one teenager in Minneapolis received a booklet of these coupons, her father paid a visit to the store and yelled at the manager. The unsuspecting manager apologized profusely. A few days later, when the manager called the father to apologize again, the father was embarrassed to admit that he had made a mistake, saying, "It turns out there's been some activities in my house I haven't been completely aware of. She's due in August. I owe you an apology." Although Target still collects the data and sends coupons to women it suspects may be pregnant, it adds a few other coupons to the mix, like coupons for wine glasses and lawn mowers, so as not to arouse too much concern (Hill 2012) (see Photo 3.9).

Scanner data is an observational research method that collects data from products scanned at a retail store's checkout counter.

● **Photo 3.9** *Data are collected from scanners every time you buy something at the store*

Online behavior is an observational research method that assesses behaviors such as click-through rates, time spent on a site, search terms used, how a customer navigates through a site, and where the customer went after leaving the site.

Cognitive research is an approach to consumer research that focuses on how consumers learn, remember, retrieve information, process information, and form conclusions.

Physical methods of cognitive research examine the functions and reactions of the brain.

Nonphysical methods of cognitive consumer research attempt to map the thought processes of consumers to infer, or draw conclusions about, the consumer's cognitive processes.

Online behavior is another area of interest for consumer researchers. They can assess click-through rates, how much time the consumer spends on the site, which search terms are used, how the customer proceeds through the site, where the customer came from before getting to the site, and where the customer went after leaving the site. A recent study confirmed what a lot of us probably have experienced with online shopping—if searching through the site or checking out is difficult, we will abandon the purchase. The study of over seven thousand online customers tried to find the key drivers in making customers "sticky"—likely to follow through with online purchases, become loyal, and even recommend the product to others. The evidence overwhelmingly pointed to *decision simplicity* as the key driver—the "ease with which consumers can gather trustworthy information about a product and confidently and efficiently weigh their purchase options" (Spenner and Freeman 2012).

Another way that researchers using a behavioral approach might observe what consumers do is by conducting an experiment. An example would be to attempt to determine whether a new ecofriendly claim on a product's packaging would increase or decrease the amount of time a consumer picks up and examines the product. Researchers could place the different packages in a retail store and then observe how consumers examine the package as well as the amount of time they hold the package. Here, the independent variable is the presence or absence of the ecofriendly label. The dependent variables are which parts of the label are examined and the amount of time consumers spend examining the label (see Figure 3.2 for a depiction of behavioral research methods).

Cognitive research

Cognitive research is the study of the human mind, its structure, and its processes. It is designed to help researchers understand, for example, what people think, how they remember, and how they process information. Cognitive research methods can be broken down into two main categories. The first is **physical methods**, which examine functions or reactions of the brain. Brain scans are one of the most commonly used methods here, and as we learned in Insights from Academia 3.1, the information obtained from brain scans is often more predictive of behavior than a consumer's own verbal comments (Venkatraman et al. 2015).

The second broad type of methods in cognitive research is **nonphysical methods**, which are used to infer, or draw conclusions about, different cognitive processes. Most often, research methods occur in a controlled laboratory setting. The goal of these methods is to map the thought processes of consumers to something similar to the workings of a computer. Research participants are often asked to look at a series of words or images and are asked if they recognize them. Their response times are tracked, and if the research participants respond quickly, the researchers conclude that the word/image is easily accessible in memory and will be used in helping to form a decision. Cognitive research works from the assumption that consumers

● **Figure 3.2** *The Behavioral Research Perspective and Methods*

make decisions in a purely rational and logical manner. Most researchers, however, understand that this is not a very realistic way to think about consumers and their decision-making processes. Most researchers have concluded that a consumer's cognitions *and* emotions are both quite important to their decisions. Further, the laboratory environment itself is artificial and it is difficult and sometimes unrealistic to use these data to make predictions about how customers might behave, for example, in a retail setting (Morales, Amir, and Lee 2017).

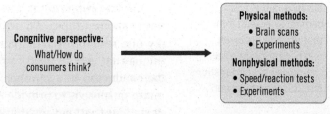

● **Figure 3.3** *The Cognitive Research Method and Perspectives*

With both physical and nonphysical methods, cognitive researchers commonly utilize experiments to reveal relationships between independent and dependent variables. Research participants are exposed to words, pictures, or sounds (all independent variables) and then the effects are measured on dependent variables, such as the location and intensity of brain activity, the speed of information processing, or the use of different pieces of information in processing (see Figure 3.3 for a depiction of cognitive research methods).

Motivational research

Most consumer researchers engage in motivational research, with is far more comprehensive than behavioral or cognitive research. Rather than taking a very narrow perspective on either what consumers do or how they think, **motivational research** recognizes that consumers are complex, sometimes unpredictable beings and are influenced by a myriad of internal and external factors. Motivational research covers how consumers feel, how they go about making a variety of consumption decisions, and how they are influenced by social and cultural factors. A wide range of research techniques and methods fall under the broad heading of motivational research.

As the name implies, **descriptive methods** are used to describe a group of consumers or their perceptions about a product, an advertisement, a store, etc. As an example, one group of consumers that is gaining in size and influence is the *lifestyles of health and sustainability* segment. These people make up 20 percent of the population in Europe and about 19 percent in the US, they are early adopters and influencers on "green" issues, they are active environmental stewards, they care deeply about their own health and that of the planet, and they are the heaviest purchasers of green products (Szakaly, et al. 2017). Keep in mind that descriptive methods can provide researchers with information about more *emotional* states of being, like feelings and values, as well as more *rational* information, like the number of consumers in this target market. There are several ways in which descriptive data can be gathered. One technique is **in-depth interviews**, where a single interviewer discusses a topic with a consumer. These interviews generally last thirty to sixty minutes and the interviewer asks a series of very detailed and probing questions. Another technique is a **focus group**. Here, a group of eight to ten

Motivational research is an approach to consumer research that focuses on underlying influences on consumer behavior, such as desires and emotions.

Descriptive methods in consumer research are used to describe a group of consumers or their perceptions about a product, an advertisement, a store, etc.

In-depth interviews are a descriptive consumer research method where a single interviewer discusses a topic with a consumer.

Focus groups are a descriptive consumer research method where a group of eight to ten people sit around a table with one interviewer and answer a series of questions about a topic.

Surveys are a descriptive consumer research method that provide research participants with a very structured set of questions that they must answer.

Ethnographic studies are a descriptive consumer research method that provides an in-depth, comprehensive description of a group of people, culture, or situation.

Emotional methods of consumer research are designed to assess consumer feelings and emotional states.

Galvanic skin response test measures electrostatic changes in the skin.

Pupil dilation test measures the extent to which a participant's pupils dilate, or open up and become bigger.

people sit around a table with one interviewer and answer a series of questions about a topic. An advantage of a focus group is that comments made by one research participant can spark ideas in others. Still another technique that can be used to provide descriptive data is a survey. **Surveys** can be conducted in a number of ways (face to face, online, by mail), but their main purpose is to provide research participants with a very structured set of questions that they must answer. The responses are generally quantified (they are turned into numbers) and statistically analyzed. Still another technique is an **ethnographic study**, which goes much further than any of the previous descriptive or observational methods and provides an in-depth, comprehensive description of a group of people, a culture, or a situation. Sometimes researchers will spend years interacting with people in the group and might even live with people to better understand them (see Photos 3.10 and 3.11). Refer again to Table 2.2 for a listing of a wide variety of qualitative research methods that can be used in motivational research.

Emotional methods are another broad category of methods and are designed to assess consumer feelings and emotional states. Once again, we have physical methods, which work from the assumption that a consumer's emotions can be experienced in the body.

Researchers can then draw conclusions about a consumer's reaction to a product, a celebrity spokesperson, etc., by carefully measuring the body's physical reaction to a stimulus. Several techniques can be used to assess the body's physical reaction to a stimulus. A **galvanic skin response test** measures electrostatic changes in the skin. As in a lie detector test, when participants feel more excitement or stress, in a galvanic skin response test there are more electrostatic changes to the skin. Further, research has shown that excitement or stress leads to changes in consumer attitudes (cf. Bettiga, Lamberti, and Noci 2017). A **pupil dilation test** measures the extent to which a participant's pupils dilate, or open up and become bigger. The underlying assumption is that people's pupils dilate when they see something they like. As the name implies, a **heart rate test** measures a participant's heart rate; when the heart rate goes up, the participant is more excited or stressed. When it goes down, he or she is more mellow and calm. As with the previous physical measures, more excitement or stress can lead to changes in attitudes. **Eye tracking** is another test that can be used to measure emotions and liking. As participants look at an advertisement, for example, researchers can monitor the movements of the eyes and determine what images consumers like.

● **Photo 3.10** *Consumer researcher conducting a focus group*

If a consumer spends a lot of time looking at the celebrity spokesperson, for example, and not a lot of time looking at the product name, researchers will know that the advertisement was successful in capturing attention and perhaps even liking, but it might be unsuccessful in getting consumers to know the brand name of the product.

A consumer's emotional response can also be measured using nonphysical methods. One nonphysical technique is surveys, which can ask participants to report the types of emotions they are feeling as well as the strength of those feelings. For example, participants could be given a long list of emotions such as cheerful, happy, joyful, lighthearted, and pleased.

● **Photo 3.11** *Ethnographic studies could involve a researcher coming into the home of a family and learning what they do as they prepare meals together*

Participants would be asked to rate on a scale of 1 to 7 the extent to which they felt each of these emotions. An example of another method that is used to measure emotions is a device called the **warmth monitor.** The warmth monitor is a knob or device like a joystick; as research participants are looking at a product or an ad, they are asked to move the monitor to the right if they are feeling positive emotions or to the left if they are feeling negative emotions. Although these techniques are much less intrusive than the physical methods described previously, they do suffer from the criticism that participants often have a difficult time translating their feelings into words, numbers, or directions on a joystick.

Experiments are used quite often by researchers using a motivational approach. Typical independent variables are the age, gender, or geographic location of a consumer. They could also include images, music, product attributes listed in an ad, or a customer's previous experience with or knowledge about the product. Independent variables could also be different pricing or distribution strategies. There are almost endless possibilities! Typical dependent variables include purchase intentions, attitudes, click-throughs, and actual purchases. If, for example, researchers for the beauty brand Neutrogena wanted to see if Katy Perry would be an influential spokesperson, they would first want to see what effect Katy Perry would have on liking for the ad and the brand. In this case, the independent variable would be an ad that either does or does not include Katy Perry. The dependent variable would be attitudes toward the ad and attitudes toward Neutrogena (see Figure 3.4 for a depiction of the motivational research perspective and methods).

It is not uncommon for a consumer research team to use a variety of research perspectives and methods to help answer a single research problem. Remember that the overall goal of consumer research is to provide a set of

Heart rate test measures a participant's heart rate; when the heart rate goes up, the participant is more excited or stressed. When it goes down, he or she is more mellow and calm.

Eye tracking is a test in which researchers monitor the movements of the eyes and determine what images consumers like.

Warmth monitor is a knob or device like a joystick that is used to measure emotions.

Captain Kirk to Trekkies: Get a life!

In 1986, *Saturday Night Live* aired a skit in which Captain Kirk told a group of avid Star Trek fans to "get a life!" The episode poked fun at the dedication and passion that some fans have for the Star Trek franchise (*Saturday Night Live* 1986). However, this level of dedication and passion for a brand is something most marketers would envy. The year 2016 marked the fiftieth anniversary of the first episode of *Star Trek*, a science fiction television series that takes place in the twenty-third century and that promised "to explore strange new worlds, to seek out new life and new civilizations," and to "boldly go" where no one had gone before (Star Trek 2019). Over the years, there have been five television series, thirteen movies, and millions of dedicated fans globally who like to refer to themselves as *Trekkies* (see an especially avid fan in Photo 3.12).

Why the intense dedication to a television series from the 1960s? *Star Trek* celebrated ethnic diversity, different

● **Photo 3.12** *A fan dresses up like Star Trek character Mr. Spock*

viewpoints, and an optimistic future. A Black woman was the communications officer, an Asian man was a helmsman, a Russian man was a navigation officer, and a half alien–half human man was the first officer. "Infinite diversity in infinite combinations" was a common mantra, and this value was demonstrated over and over again in the experiences and challenges the crew faced. The first interracial kiss ever shown on television happened on *Star Trek* (Cavna 2016). Even for people who are not avid Star Trek fans, the Star Trek culture has seeped into our everyday language. We talk about "raising our shields" when we feel threatened or we want to protect ourselves; we say we're working at "warp speed" when we're rushing to get something done. The phrase "Beam me up, Scotty" is sometimes used when we want to get out of an uncomfortable situation.

To better understand the Star Trek phenomenon, one consumer researcher conducted an ethnographic study of Star Trek fans. He spent twenty months attending conventions, visiting fan meetings, interviewing sixty-seven people, and trying to understand what made these fans so dedicated and passionate about Star Trek. After this deep immersion into the Star Trek culture, the researcher found that the one key, overarching theme that resonated with fans was the depiction of an optimistic, brighter future. Many fans were incredibly motivated by the vision of a futuristic society where there was an appreciation for diversity, equality of women, trust in science, democracy, and honesty and integrity. Star Trek and the future that it represented were seen almost as a utopian refuge or even something close to a religion (Kozinets 2001).

Most marketing managers would love to have a group of customers who are as loyal and passionate as the Star Trek fan group. Megastars Mila Kunis, Ben Stiller, Seth MacFarlane, Rosario Dawson, and Richard Branson are among the proud group of fans who call themselves Trekkies (Acuna 2015). So, rest assured, even if you don't want to admit it to your closest friends, it's OK to be a Trekkie too!

Questions

1. This ethnographic study was conducted several years ago, in 2001. Would it be appropriate to conduct another ethnographic study to find out about what motivates Star Trek fans today? What other research perspectives or methods might be appropriate?

2. In fall 2017, a new television series premiered, *Star Trek: Discovery*. The show promised Klingons, Vulcans, lots of action and drama, and the same view of diversity and a better future. What research perspectives or methods would you recommend to help you predict the success of this new series?

3. Take a quick look online and you will see thousands of Star Trek–themed products, from toasters to towels, baby products to bathroom remodels. There are even Star Trek–themed cruises. Imagine that you are the manager of a new restaurant in Chicago and you would like to hold a Star Trek–themed dinner one night. What questions would you want to answer in the *problem identification* phase of the research process?

Sources: Acuna (2015); Cavna (2016); Kozinets (2001); Saturday Night Live (1986); Star Trek (2019).

consumer insights to marketing managers. Since insights are often more complete when they come from multiple research findings, it often makes sense to utilize a multimethod, multiperspective approach. Over time, the research team will develop a deep, rich understanding of their target customers and how their product fits into those consumers' lives.

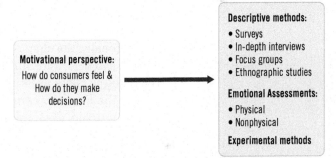

● **Figure 3.4** *Motivational research perspective and methods*

◉ Summary

This chapter started by presenting a compelling rationale for why it makes sense for researchers to engage in consumer research. In fact, despite the cost of conducting research, we found that it is often more expensive *not* to conduct research. The five-step *consumer research process* was introduced and each step was described in detail. We learned from Insights from Academia 3.1 about an innovative way that researchers can scan the brains of consumers and that these scans often provide more accurate information about a consumer's liking for a product than a consumer's own verbal reports of liking. We also examined several examples of research problems versus research questions.

As the discussion of the five-step consumer research process progressed, we discussed the differences between *data*, *information*, and *insights*. We found that the overall goal of any research effort was to provide usable insights to managers to help them answer their research questions. We can also use these insights to help improve public policy and consumer welfare.

As we dove deeper into the discussion of data collection and analysis, we learned when it would be useful to utilize *secondary data*, which are already available from other sources, and when it would be more appropriate to gather *primary data*, which derive from our own research efforts. Insights from the Field 3.2 about Bark & Co. illustrated how consumer researchers can take information that is gathered from primary and secondary research, create insights about how meaningful dogs are to people's lives, and then use those insights to create a lifestyle brand. We learned about *qualitative research*, which provides rich, contextual descriptions to help us understand an important phenomenon, and *quantitative research*, which assigns numbers to people, situations, and contexts so that they can be analyzed and compared to one another. Next, we discussed the *various forms of bias* that can be present during data collection and analysis, as well as why it is important for researchers to reduce that bias.

The more in-depth discussion of the three *research perspectives*—behavioral, cognitive, and motivational—provided a variety of examples of research methods that would be appropriate to use for each perspective. Insights from the Boardroom 3 discussed Wawa and a few of their research projects on coffee and breakfast sandwiches. It illustrated the importance of sometimes employing a multimethod research approach to uncover some of the best insights. Finally, the chapter wrapped up with a case study of Google Glass and how researchers were surprised by the initial reaction of some people to the Glass and to Glass users. The case illustrated the importance of carefully following the five-step consumer research process and clearly understanding what consumers need, want, and expect from such a product.

KEY TERMS

REVIEW QUESTIONS

1. Why is it important to conduct consumer research?
2. Explain the differences between data, information, and insights.
3. Describe the five-step consumer research process. What are the purpose and importance of the feedback loop?
4. What are some positive aspects and some negative aspects to using secondary data? Primary data?
5. When would a research team use qualitative data and when would it prefer to use quantitative data? Give two to three examples for each type of data.
6. What do we mean when we say that researchers need to recruit a representative sample of participants? Why is it important to have a representative sample?
7. What is the purpose of the Belmont Report and institutional review boards?
8. Carefully describe the forms of bias that can occur during data collection and analysis. Why is it important to reduce the likelihood of bias?
9. What is the overall purpose for each of the three consumer research perspectives?
10. For each of the three consumer research perspectives, describe several research methods that would be appropriate for a research team to use.

DISCUSSION QUESTIONS

1. Imagine that you are just about to start a new job and you want to really make a great impression on your new boss. The problem is, it's a small, family-owned company and it has never conducted consumer research. Using what you know about the importance of conducting research, develop a strong and compelling argument to present to your new boss about why the company should conduct consumer research.
2. One of the problems with Google Glass seems to be that, at the outset, it did not have a well-articulated research problem or set of research questions. Indeed, engineers developed the product and then management and marketing tried to figure out how to sell it. What would have been some appropriate research questions that managers at Google could have asked?
3. Selecting a college or university to attend is a big decision. When you were making this decision, you probably looked at both qualitative and quantitative data. Give some examples of qualitative and quantitative data you gathered and considered.
4. Imagine you are doing a research study on cheating in college. Your goal is to recruit several students to answer a series of questions about whether they know someone who has cheated, whether they have cheated, and, if they have cheated, different techniques they have used. How could you reduce or eliminate social desirability bias?
5. Globally, professional soccer (or *football* to the rest of the world) is an incredibly popular sport. It does not, however, have the passionate following in the United States that it does abroad. Imagine that a research team would like to find out more about how likely US consumers would be to become loyal and passionate soccer fans. Proceed through each part of the five-step consumer research process and describe what you might recommend at each step.

For more information, quizzes, case studies, and other study tools, please visit us at **www.oup.com/he/phillips**.

Google Glass

The research process is supposed to start with the clear identification and definition of a question a manager needs to answer. In the case of Google Glass ("Glass"), engineers worked in secret to develop an innovative new product. It is undeniable that the product represented a quantum leap forward in technology and innovation—Glass was unlike anything the world had seen before. However, a very important question still needed to be asked: Who were the target customers and what would they do with it?

The original development of Glass was a top-secret endeavor, even for people who worked at Google. Indeed, a small group of specially selected engineers worked on the product in a restricted laboratory in corporate headquarters for about eighteen months in 2010 and 2011. To maintain secrecy, the project was dubbed Google X. As the team developed some of the early prototypes, there were still some technological glitches that needed to be worked out, as well as the bigger question of how consumers would use the product. Would it be a daily wearable item or something just used for specific tasks? How would Glass help users interact with others? How would Glass be incorporated into consumers' lives? To answer these questions, the team engaged a small group of techie innovators and had them play around with the product in their day-to-day lives to provide feedback. These people were called *explorers* by the product development team because they were about to embark into unknown territory. These explorers even paid $1,500 for the privilege of doing this for Google (Bilton 2015).

However, word got out about the product before all of the kinks were properly worked out and before Google had a chance to clearly identify its target market or answer any questions about how customers would use it. News organizations and other techies were inundating Google with requests to get their hands on the new product. Sergey Brin, cofounder of Google, decided to ride the wave of enthusiasm and, at a Google developers conference in June 2012, officially unveiled Glass by having skydivers wearing the new product drop onto the roof of the conference center and ride BMX bikes into the auditorium. The skydive and the bike ride were streamed live into the auditorium from the jumpers who were wearing Glass, and the crowd roared in thunderous approval. This reaction encouraged a very enthusiastic marketing department at Google to get Glass into the hands of some key opinion leaders; fashion designer Diane von Furstenberg wore Glass at a New York fashion show (as did all of her models) and Prince Charles was seen sporting a pair in England (Bilton 2015). Beyoncé, Sarah Jessica Parker, and other celebrities tried out Glass (Naughton 2017). As other techies eventually got their hands on Glass, at $1,500 per pair, scathing reviews started to come in about the technology. They complained about the usability of the apps, the poor battery life, and awkward navigation (Bilton 2015) (see Photo 3.13).

Another important concern was that people who were wearing Glass had their attention divided between what was happening in front of them in real life and what was happening on the screen. One explorer relayed the indignant reaction he received from his wife when he suggested wearing Glass for the birth of their first child. He thought it would be a great idea—hands-free picture taking. She, however, did not think the idea was so great. At the time, part of the problem may have been that consumers were simply not used to the idea of wearable technology. It made them uncomfortable, probably because its wearers seemed out of the moment. Mobile phones were bad enough in taking a person's attention away from a conversation, but at least other people knew when someone was using a phone. When someone was wearing Glass, it was almost impossible

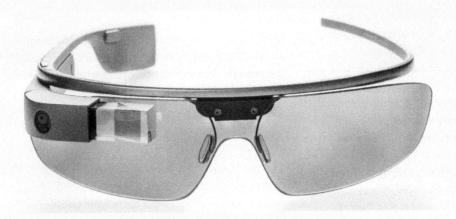

● **Photo 3.13** *Google Glass*

for others to know if that person was answering emails or surfing the Internet (Honan 2013).

Even more important, privacy issues started to arise. For example, what happens when you're wearing Glass while using the restroom? What about having a conversation with a colleague that you don't want others to hear? Other people who were with Glass users quickly became concerned because they didn't like the idea that Glass users could secretly record conversations or other things that were happening (Bilton 2015; Honan 2013). Because of these privacy concerns, Glass was banned from bars, restaurants, casinos, and other places where clients and managers did not want people recording their surroundings (Bilton 2015). It did not take long for public opinion to sour. *The Simpsons*, *Saturday Night Live*, and a host of other comedians made fun of Glass, and soon, people who were seen wearing them were called *Glassholes* (Honan 2013). In early 2015, Google Glass was pulled from the market (Reynolds 2015).

At first glance, Google did a lot of things right. It engaged a group of innovators (see the discussion of diffusion of innovation in Chapter 2), it relied on public relations to help get the word out, and it got Glass into the hands of some key opinion leaders. However, Google did make a few missteps, primarily having to do with marketing. First, as word of the Glass project leaked out, the marketing and management team jumped on the opportunity and "introduced" the product with tremendous fanfare. However, the marketing plan was ill-thought out and rushed. A real product launch would have been much more controlled and would have, at the very least, included important details such as how the product would be distributed, when it would be available, and where it would be available for sale. The Glass launch did not (Reynolds 2015). Also, although it is impressive that Glass got a lot of free public relations, there is very little control over the message when public relations is utilized. Indeed, what shows up on the evening news or in a tech blog does not allow Google to control it using a carefully crafted message or a description of a set of benefits. Paid advertising allows a business to control the message, but inexplicably, there was no advertising for Glass (Reynolds 2015).

Perhaps the biggest mistake that the marketing team at Google made was that there seems to have been no determination of the needs of the target market. Judging from their efforts to get the product into the hands of explorers, it seems as if Google thought their target market should have been consumers on the cutting edge of technology who wanted to be opinion leaders in technology issues. The problem is, there is no evidence to suggest that any research was done on what such customers would do with Glass and how they would be able to incorporate it into their lives. The reaction of other people to Glass seems to have been a surprise for Google's marketing team as well.

What a difference two years and a trip back to the drawing board can make. In July 2017, the 2.0 edition of Glass was reintroduced, now called Google Enterprise Edition (Google EE). Instead of being targeted as a consumer product, it was designed as a tool for the workplace. Indeed, some of the original explorers who were using Glass had already retooled and adapted Glass for this market. Google now referred to these techies as *Google partners* and worked with them closely to put some of the finishing touches on the Google EE. Factory and warehouse workers can use it to access diagrams and user manuals; they can also get real-time data so that, for example, as a worker is assembling a product, the Google EE will show the next step. Google EE is also safer and more comfortable than some virtual reality applications currently being promoted for the workplace. Google EE saves time and money because of greatly improved efficiencies. Some important kinks have also been worked out: workers can easily remove the "pod" from the glasses frame and, for example, connect it to safety glasses; the battery will last for a full eight-hour shift, it has a faster processer, better Wi-Fi, it works with prescription lenses, and it is lighter and more comfortable than Glass. The next step is to promote Google EE for medical and military applications (Levy 2017). Manufacturing and distribution companies, such as GE, Boeing, DHL, and Volkswagen, use the Google EE (Fiegerman 2017), and as of the date of this writing, a second version of the product, the Google EE2, has been introduced with better functionality, more fashionable styling, and a lower price (Haselton 2019).

QUESTIONS

1. One of the most important research questions for Glass concerned how consumers were going to use the product. What might be wrong with the sample Google selected to help answer these questions?

2. How much of the problem with Glass was a result of consumers not being used to the idea of wearable technology?

3. The marketing team at Google seemed quite surprised by the reaction that other people had when people were wearing Glass; there were questions about divided attention and about privacy. Could Glass have done a better job at addressing these concerns? How?

4. Do you think Google EE2 will ever be able to be marketed for consumer use? What would have to happen first before there would be wide consumer acceptance of the product? Aside from medical and military applications, what other uses might there be for Google EE2?

Sources: Bilton (2015); Fiegerman (2017); Haselton (2019); Honan (2013); Levy (2017); Naughton (2017); Reynolds (2015).

REFERENCES

Acuna, K. 2015. "7 Celebrities Who Love Star Trek More Than You." *Business Insider*, February 27, 2015. http://www.businessinsider.com/celebrity-star-trek-fans-2015-2.

American Pet Products Association. 2019-20. *APPA National Pet Owners Survey.* American Pet Products Association: Greenwich, CT.

Andreasen, A. R. 1983. "Cost-Conscious Marketing Research." *Harvard Business Review* 61, no. 4 (July/August): 74.

Bark. 2019. "By Dog People, for Dogs (and Their People)." Accessed August 11, 2019. https://www.bark.co.

Belmont Report, The. 1979. "The Belmont Report: Ethical Principles and Guidelines for the Protection of Human Subjects of Research." *National Commission for the Protection of Human Subjects of Biomedical and Behavioral Research*. April 18, 1979. https://www.hhs.gov/ohrp/regulations-and-policy/belmont-report/index.html.

Bettiga, D., L. Lamberti, and G. Noci. 2017. "Do Mind and Body Agree? Unconscious versus Conscious Arousal in Product Attitude Formation." *Journal of Business Research* 75 (June): 108–17.

Bilton, N. 2015. "Why Google Glass Broke." *The New York Times*, February 4, 2015. https://www.nytimes.com/2015/02/05/style/why-google-glass-broke.html.

Burdo, A. 2017. "With June Revenue in, Philadelphia's Soda Tax Falls Just Short of FY17 Projections." *Philadelphia Business Journal*, July 24, 2017. https://www.bizjournals.com/philadelphia/news/2017/07/24/philly-soda-tax-pbt-june-17-revenue.html.

Calder, B. J., and A. M. Tybout. 1989. "Interpretive, Qualitative and Traditional Scientific Empirical Consumer Behavior Research." In *Interpretive Consumer Research*, edited by E. C. Hirschman, 199–208. Provo, UT: Association for Consumer Research.

Cavna, M. 2016. "How Star Trek Embraced Diversity 50 Years Ago—and Continues to Do So Today." *Washington Post*, July 20, 2016. https://www.washingtonpost.com/news/comic-riffs/wp/2016/07/20/how-star-trek-embraced-diversity-50-years-ago-and-continues-to-do-so-today/?utm_term=.e7922c9a98e6.

Data.gov. 2019. Accessed August 11, 2019. https://www.data.gov.

Davis, J. L. 2017. "5 Ways Pets Can Improve Your Health." WebMD. Accessed August 29, 2017. http://www.webmd.com/hypertension-high-blood-pressure/features/health-benefits-of-pets#1.

Dholakia, U. M., B. E. Kahn, R. Reeves, A. Rindfleisch, D. Stewart, and E. Taylor. 2010. "Consumer Behavior in a Multichannel, Multimedia Retailing Environment." *Journal of Interactive Marketing* 24 (2): 86–95.

Dooley, R. 2013. "The Most Common (and Dangerous) Market Research Mistake." *Forbes*, August 21, 2013. https://www.forbes.com/sites/roger-dooley/2013/08/21/market-research-mistake/#38ab6e373fe1.

Fiegerman, S. 2017. "Google Is Taking Another Stab at Reviving One of Its Most High-Profile Flops." *CNN Tech*, July 18, 2017. http://money.cnn.com/2017/07/18/technology/gadgets/google-glass-returns/index.html.

Forbes. 2017. "America's Largest Private Companies." Accessed August 12, 2017. https://www.forbes.com/companies/wawa/.

Haselton, T. 2019. "Google Unveils New $999 Smart Glasses for Businesses, Undercutting Microsoft's HoloLens on Price." CNBC. May 20, 2019. https://www.cnbc.com/2019/05/20/google-glass-enterprise-edition-2-announced-price.html.

Hill, K. 2012. "How Target Figured Out a Teen Girl Was Pregnant before Her Father Did." *Forbes*, February 16, 2012. https://www.forbes.com/sites/kashmirhill/2012/02/16/how-target-figured-out-a-teen-girl-was-pregnant-before-her-father-did/#57e82e266686.

Hoenninger, J. 2017. *Personal interview*, August 11, 2017.

Honan, M. 2013. "I, Glasshole: My Year with Google Glass." *Wired*, December 30, 2013. https://www.wired.com/2013/12/glasshole/.

James, G. 2012. "Top 9 Brand Blunders of All Time." *Inc.*, April 10, 2012. https://www.inc.com/ss/geoffrey-james/top-9-brand-blunders-all-time.

Kozinets, R. V. 2001. "Utopian Enterprise: Articulating the Meanings of Star Trek's Culture of Consumption." *Journal of Consumer Research* 28 (June): 67–88.

Kurtzleben, D. 2012. "What 'Mapplegate' Says about Apple." *US News & World Report*, September 28, 2012. https://www.usnews.com/news/articles/2012/09/28/what-mapplegate-says-about-apple-the-company-shows-a-rare-stumble-in-its-maps-app-heres-what-it-tells-us-about-the-tech-behemoth.

LaMotte, S. 2019. "The Food That Can Feed, and Maybe Save the Planet: Bugs." CNN Health, October 25. Accessed September 6, 2020. https://www.cnn.com/2019/10/25/health/insects-feed-save-planet-wellness/index.html.

Levy, S. 2017. "Google Glass 2.0 Is a Startling Second Act." *Wired*, July 18, 2017. https://www.wired.com/story/google-glass-2-is-here/.

Martin, E. 2016. "The Company That Wants to Build 'Disney for Dogs' Is Starting with an Office Full of Toys, Treats, and Canine Coworkers." *Business Insider*, August 3, 2016. http://www.businessinsider.com/bark-and-co-barkbox-office-tour-2016-8.

Miller, A. G., B. E. Collins, and D. E. Brief 1995. "Perspectives on Obedience to Authority: The Legacy of the Milgram Experiments." *Journal of Social Issues* 51 (3): 1–19.

Miller, G. 2011. "Using the Psychology of Evil to Do Good." *Science* 332, no. 6029 (April 29): 530–32.

Mintel. 2017. *North America '17: Consumer Trends*. London: Mintel.

Morales, A. C., O. Amir, and L. Lee. 2017. "Keeping It Real in Experimental Research—Understanding When, Where, and How to Enhance Realism and Measure Consumer Behavior." *Journal of Consumer Research* 44 (2): 465–76.

Naughton, J. 2017. "The Rebirth of Google Glass Shows the Merit of Failure." *The Guardian*, July 23, 2017. https://www.theguardian.com/commentisfree/2017/jul/23/the-return-of-google-glass-surprising-merit-in-failure-enterprise-edition.

Peters, A. 2017. "This Giant Automated Cricket Farm Is Designed to Make Bugs a Mainstream Source of Protein." Fast Company. August 21, 2017. https://www.fastcompany.com/40454212/this-automated-cricket-farm-is-designed-to-make-bugs-a-mainstream-source-of-protein.

Pew Research Center. 2010. *Millennials: A Portrait of Generation Next*. February 2010. http://www.pewsocialtrends.org/files/2010/10/millennials-confident-connected-open-to-change.pdf.

Rana, P. 2016. "L'Oreal Shrinks Packages in India." *Wall Street Journal*, Eastern edition, June 9, 2016, B6.

Reynolds, S. 2015. "Why Google Glass Failed: A Marketing Lesson." *Forbes*, February 5, 2015. https://www.forbes.com/sites/siimonreynolds/2015/02/05/why-google-glass-failed/#7429fc7151b5.

Riley, K. 2017. "Puppy Love: The Coddling of the American Pet." *Atlantic*, May 2017. https://www.theatlantic.com/maazine/archive/2017/05/puppy-love/521442/.

Saturday Night Live. 1986. "Trekkies." December 20, 1986. http://www.nbc.com/saturday-night-live/video/trekkies/n9511?snl=1.

Spenner, P., and K. Freeman. 2012. "To Keep Your Customers, Keep It Simple." *Harvard Business Review*, May 2012. https://hbr.org/2012/05/to-keep-your-customers-keep-it-simple.

Star Trek. 2019. Accessed August 11, 2019. https://www.startrek.com.

Szakaly, Z., J. Popp, E. Kontor, S. Kovacs, K. Peto, and H. Jasak. 2017. "Attitudes of the Lifestyle of Health and Sustainability Segment in Hungary." Sustainability. 9 (10), 1763. doi: https://doi.org/10.3390/su9101763.

United Nations. 2017. *World Population Prospects: 2017 Revision*. New York: UN Department of Economic and Social Affairs.

US Census Bureau. 2019. Accessed August 11, 2019. https://www.census.gov.

Venkatraman, V., A. Dimoka, P. A. Pavlou, K. Vo, W. Hampton, B. Bollinger, H. E. Hershfield, M. Ishihara, and R. S. Winer. 2015. "Predicting Advertising Success beyond Traditional Measures: New Insights from Neurophysiological Methods and Market Response Modeling." *Journal of Marketing Research* 52, no. 4 (August): 436–52.

Vinh, T. 2017. "Get Your Fried Grasshoppers Here: The Big Hit at the Mariners Home Games." *Seattle Times*, April 17, 2017. http://www.seattletimes.com/life/food-drink/get-your-fried-grasshoppers-here-the-big-hit-at-mariners-home-games/.

World Bank. 2019. Accessed August 11, 2019. https://www.worldbank.org.

Zmuda, N. 2009. "Tropicana Line's Sales Plunge 20% Post-rebranding." *AdAge*, April 2, 2009. http://adage.com/article/news/tropicana-line-s-sales-plunge-20-post-rebranding/135735/.

4 Perceptual Processes

◉ Introduction

Going for a walk down any city street can be an assault on the perceptual system. The sidewalk might be crowded with people on their way to work or going about their shopping. You will notice signs and window displays, as well as cars, taxis, and busses going by. You might even smell the flowers as you pass by the florist shop or the fresh-baked cinnamon rolls as you walk by the bakery. You may feel the blast of hot exhaust from the city bus or bump into someone else who is walking down the sidewalk but is looking at their phone. You may stop for a coffee or even get to taste a free sample of cake while at the coffee shop. You may hear music, honking horns, and people talking as you make your way down the sidewalk. All of this happens without much conscious awareness, but our senses pick up stimuli and transfer meaning to our perceptual processing system. Clearly, it is not possible to pay attention to each and every stimulus that crosses our path. It would simply be too much to pay attention to every sight, smell, touch, taste, and sound because you would be completely overloaded.

The perceptual processing system is very important for furthering our understanding of consumer behavior because it describes the way in which individuals perceive a stimulus, pay attention to it, and interpret it. The perceptual process model helps marketers predict how consumers may respond to virtually anything that can be picked up by the perceptual system, including product features, advertisements, store layouts, or websites. Perception of a stimulus depends on objective features such as its size, color, and where it is located. Perception also depends on subjective criteria such as the consumer's current situation, preferences, and previous experiences. Importantly, a consumer must be willing and able to pay attention to and interpret the stimulus. Part of a marketing manager's job is to construct marketing strategies that facilitate perception, attention, and interpretation of the message. In the end, the perceptual process model is a vital tool that marketers can use to help build successful and effective marketing strategies that connect with consumers in a way that is both relevant and meaningful.

LEARNING OBJECTIVES

Having read this chapter, you will be able to:

1. Describe how each of the *five senses* picks up information from the environment and makes that information available for the attention step of the *perceptual process*.

2. Differentiate the important conceptual differences between *exposure*, *attention*, and *interpretation*.

3. Discuss the concepts of *exposure*, *selective exposure*, and *subliminal exposure*.

4. Discuss the important contribution that *Gestalt* psychology has made to the field of marketing.

5. Sketch a *positioning map* for a product or service and describe how marketers can draw important insights from a positioning map.

6. Explain how marketers have utilized several important tools from perception: *perceived risk*, *perceptual/ positioning mapping*, *repositioning*, *price perception*, and *semiotics*.

● **Figure 4.1** *The perceptual process*

<o> The Perceptual Process

Perception is the process
through which information
from a stimulus is received
by the senses and is then
organized, interpreted, and
experienced.

Perception is the process through which information from a stimulus is received by the senses and then organized, interpreted, and experienced. In the first section of this chapter, we will discuss the process by which we perceive information from the environment (see Figure 4.1). Next, we will discuss several ways in which marketers use insights into the perceptual process to reach out to consumers.

Exposure

Exposure means that the
stimulus had the ability
to be detected by the
individual.

Stimulus is a piece of
information that is available
for the consumer to pay
attention to and later
interpret.

The perceptual process starts with exposure to a stimulus—any information that is picked up from one of the five senses: sight, sound, smell, taste, or touch. In the context of marketing, consumers are constantly exposed to a barrage of sensory information. A trip to an amusement park or a county fair is an excellent example. Consumers are exposed to the smell of popcorn, the sights of the lights, the sounds of music, the feel of the breeze as the roller coaster goes by, and perhaps even the taste of a hot dog (see Photo 4.1).

Exposure simply means that the stimulus has the ability to be detected by the senses. That is, it is big enough to see, loud enough to hear, strong enough to feel, etc. A **stimulus** is a piece of information that is available for the consumer to pay attention to and later interpret. At this stage of the perceptual process, stimuli have simply come in contact with the individual. They have not yet been noticed, interpreted, or analyzed. From a marketing perspective, it is important to realize that a consumer cannot pay attention to, interpret, or respond to a stimulus if that consumer isn't first exposed to the stimulus. That's why marketers try to get their products and messages in as many places as possible: to increase the chances of exposure. Much to the consternation of consumers, advertisers are always finding new and different ways to increase the

● **Photo 4.1** *The Minnesota State Fair at Dusk*

chances that consumers will be exposed to their messages. In fact, consumers around the world are getting so frustrated with messages such as pop-up ads that they are increasingly paying extra money for ad-blocking solutions. In fact, each year, the number of individuals blocking ads increases by more than 40 percent over the previous year. Thirty-seven percent of Greeks block ads, as do 25 percent of Germans, 20 percent of Canadians, 21 percent of Portuguese, 18 percent of Australians, and 15 percent of Americans (PageFair 2015).

Selective exposure is the act of purposely seeking or avoiding exposure to stimuli. Think about your behavior when watching a live broadcast of a sporting event like the World Series. During commercial breaks, you may talk with your friends, go to the kitchen for some food, or check your phone. Selective exposure can sometimes be detrimental as when, for example, we read or follow certain sites that agree with our strongly held opinions and avoid those that disagree with our opinions. Two concepts related to selective exposure are perceptual vigilance and perceptual defense. **Perceptual vigilance** occurs when an individual determines that a stimulus may or may not be personally relevant. Perceptual vigilance varies by person, situation, and stimulus. Someone about to go on a trip to Europe may intentionally seek out advertisements for cameras or luggage, but once the trip is over, the relevance of these items diminishes. The point is that consumers will allow or even seek out exposure to topics and products in which they may be interested. **Perceptual defense** is also a way for consumers to engage in selective exposure. It occurs when a consumer avoids exposure to potentially threatening or unpleasant stimuli. People who are overweight may avoid fast-food ads and smokers may avoid government health warnings.

The **mere exposure effect** is a well-known phenomenon that says that the more often you are exposed to a stimulus, the more you will like it. You have probably had the experience of hearing a song for the first time and not liking it very much. However, after you are exposed to it again and again, you start to develop some familiarity and liking for the song. This is the mere exposure effect in action! It is important to remember that you first must be exposed to the song before the rest of the perceptual process can take place. While we're talking about exposure, let's discuss the often-controversial topic of subliminal exposure. **Subliminal exposure** to a stimulus means that the stimulus occurs at a level that is *below* the level at which it can be consciously perceived. That is, for example, the sound is too quiet to be picked up by the human ear, the image is displayed too quickly to be seen, or the smell is too faint to be consciously detected. Take the example of visual perception. For a message to be displayed so fast that it cannot be seen, it needs to flash in front of a consumer's eyes for less than 0.003 seconds. Thus, consumers can't consciously perceive subliminal messages. This controversy erupted after a 1957 study in an American movie theater showed subliminal images of "Drink Coca-Cola" and "Eat popcorn" during a movie. The authors claimed that sales of Coca-Cola and popcorn increased after movie-goers were exposed to these messages. The problem was, despite many attempts, the results could never

Selective exposure is the act of purposely seeking or avoiding exposure to stimuli.

Perceptual vigilance occurs when an individual determines that a stimulus may or may not be relevant.

Perceptual defense is when a consumer avoids exposure to potentially threatening or unpleasant stimuli.

Mere exposure effect happens when the more often you are exposed to a stimulus, the more you will like it.

Subliminal exposure occurs at a level that is below the level at which it can be consciously perceived.

be replicated and the authors eventually admitted that they had been fabricated. Despite this, close to three-quarters of Americans still believe that subliminal advertising messages occur and that they influence our behavior (Zimmerman 2014).

Can subliminal messages impact behavior? Perhaps, but only in a very limited way. It is difficult enough under normal circumstances for marketers to attract the attention of consumers and get them to do something when the typical consumer in a developed economy is exposed to 5,000 advertising messages per day. Thus, marketers must compete with approximately 4,999 actual messages (not subliminal messages) to make sure that consumers pay attention to, interpret, and respond to *their* message. It is a difficult job indeed. However, there is a very interesting and consistent finding that connects the mere exposure effect to subliminal messaging. When individuals are repeatedly exposed to a message—even a subliminal message—they increase their liking of that message (Zajonc 2001). Despite this, most researchers have concluded that although some of these messages may be picked up by our subconscious and may marginally increase liking, they have very little, if any, influence on actual consumer behaviors such as purchases.

Sensation and the perceptual process

Individuals receive information through their five sensory receptors—eyes, ears, nose, mouth, and skin—but marketers are particularly interested in what consumers *do* with that information in order to make sense of it (see Insights from Academia 4.1). If marketers know that consumers have preferences for certain stimuli, such as favorite colors, tastes, or smells, they can adjust their strategies to better resonate with those preferences. The colors used in retail stores, for example, can certainly impact consumer purchases. When shopping, consumers react most favorably to stores with a cool color palate such as blue, as compared to warm colors such as orange. These preferences, however, can be subtle and can depend on other factors, such as lighting intensity (e.g., Babin, Hardesty, and Suter 2003). The color red can speed up behavior and could be used in fast-food restaurants where the management wants to get customers in and out quickly (Bellizzi, Crowley, and Hasty 1983). This happens in the online environment too. A variety of sensory stimuli can influence search, cognitive effort, and the shoppers' enjoyment (Eroglu, Machleit, and Davis 2003). Our discussion of perception will now proceed through the five senses.

Sight

About 80 percent of the information that comes from the external environment and makes up our perception comes from our sight (Levine 2000). Given this central role, we will spend some time discussing how colors, the shape and size of an object, and the context of an object influence the perceptual process. Colors have deeply rooted cultural meanings and marketers need to be very careful about using the correct colors to connote the correct

INSIGHTS FROM ACADEMIA 4.1

Want to look taller? Wear a bright color!

The *saturation* of a color refers to the color's purity. Think of the bright red of a stop sign or the bright yellow of a school bus. These objects are painted a "pure" saturated color—not a muted or dusky color—because psychologists know something about how the human eye reacts to color saturation. When something is painted with a saturated color, we perceive it as being bigger than when it is painted with a muted color. Why does this happen? In a carefully controlled set of six experiments, researchers found that saturated colors make us feel good, which attracts our attention to the object, which makes us judge the object as bigger (see Photo 4.2 for an example). So, the next time you want to look a little taller, wear a saturated color!

● **Photo 4.2** *Coffee cups in a saturated color look bigger*

Hagtvedt, H., and S. A. Brasel. 2017. *"Color Saturation Increases Perceived Product Size."* Journal of Consumer Research *44 (2): 396–413.*

meanings. Colors can be used to signify gender, as when blue indicates male and pink indicates female. Incidentally, this use of pink and blue only began in the 1940s in the United States (Paoletti 2012). Colors can also stimulate a variety of emotions. Researchers have found that red, for example, is associated with passion, excitement, and energy. Companies who want consumers to associate these emotions with their brand often use red. ESPN uses a red logo, as do Disney, Toyota, and Coca-Cola. The meaning of red, however, changes across cultures. In China, the color red is associated with luck, joy, and celebration. Invitations to special events are always delivered in red envelopes and Chinese brides often wear a red wedding dress.

Interpretations of colors also depend on the context. When we're talking about food products, different colors signify different things. For example, one study found that yellow, blue, green, and red were seen as healthy, whereas heather, pink, and celadon (pale green) were seen as artificial and unhealthy (Wasowicz and Stysko-Kunkowsa 2015). Colors can also be used to signify certain roles or occupations. White, for example, signifies cleanliness and is therefore often worn by healthcare workers like doctors, nurses, and pharmacists. By contrast, dark colors like blue and black are associated with authority and

● **Photo 4.3** *Gourmand skincare product*

competence and are often worn by judges or members of the military. Someone who wants to be perceived as serious and capable is likely to wear a dark-colored suit to a job interview. Gourmand skincare and beauty products are available exclusively at Urban Outfitters. They come in white packaging in order to convey not only an upscale image, but also to convey both the purity of the ingredients and the manufacturing process. All of the items in the product line follow strict sustainability standards, are cruelty-free, and most are made with vegan ingredients (see Photo 4.3).

Colors even become associated with political and social movements. For example, in the United States, Democrats use the color blue, while Republicans are associated with red. Since the early 1990s, pink has been associated with breast cancer awareness campaigns (Labrecque and Milne 2012) and we often talk about the "green movement" to refer to efforts to save the environment. Most colors have different meanings in different cultures and mistakes are easily made by those who are not aware of these meanings. For example, never wear white to a celebration of any kind in Asia because of that color's strong associations with death and mourning. It would also be a big mistake to pick black for your sports' teams color in India because of the color's association with weakness (Aslam 2006).

Aside from color, there are other dimensions of sight that influence the information individuals receive from the environment. One of these dimensions is the shape, layout, and spacing of key features of the item. These physical product features influence a consumer's expectations about the product. Research by Nestlé, for example, has found surprising differences in how consumers of dark chocolate are influenced by the shape of the candy. Indeed, consumers reported that the flavor and texture of the chocolate are better when the pieces were either round or rectangular, whereas wing-shaped chocolate pieces were reported to be the most flavorful (Lenfant et al. 2013). Insights from Academia 4.2 emphasizes the importance of the interplay between a consumer's visual perceptions and later interpretation of that visual information.

In a related vein, the size and shape of a product within a given context also influence perceptions. Something especially large or small for the context would be unique and would capture a consumer's attention. For example, the BMW Mini utilizes its uniquely small size in its communications strategies by showing up in unexpected places and making smallness a virtue (see Photo 4.5). Here, a full-sized Mini was attached to the outside of a Mini dealership in London. It is easy to see how the size and the context attract attention.

Speaking of context, marketers must be especially careful about selecting the most appropriate environments for their products and advertisements (see Insights from the Field 4.1). Marketers for luxury brands like Prada and Burberry know that their brands need to be available at upscale locations such as Le Bon Marché in Paris or Saks Fifth Avenue in New York because

INSIGHTS FROM ACADEMIA 4.2

It's just too pretty!

Can a food product be too beautiful? Apparently, it can. Attractive food products, like those shown in Photo 4.4, have a positive impact on preconsumption evaluations and even product choice. Using a variety of techniques, such as a field study, online simulations, and laboratory experiments, the researchers found consistent evidence that consumers appreciate and like things that are attractive. Surprisingly, attractive products have a negative impact on actual consumption and postconsumption evaluations. Why? Consumers appreciate that a significant amount of work and effort went into the creation of an attractive product, and when they eat it, that effort is destroyed. So, not only do consumers feel bad about destroying something pretty because of the effort that someone else put into making it, but also they feel bad because they are destroying something that is intrinsically attractive.

● **Photo 4.4** *Some products can be too pretty*

Wu, F., A. Samper, A. C. Morales, and G. J. Fitzsimons. 2017. "It's Too Pretty to Use! When and How Enhanced Product Aesthetics Discourage Usage and Lower Consumption Enjoyment." Journal of Consumer Research 44 (3): 651–72.

the upscale environment of the store is consistent with the upscale image of the brand. Similarly, advertisers are careful to place ads within broadcast, streaming, print, or online environments to ensure there is a fit between the brand and the programming. Mobile gaming offers a new opportunity to place ads, logos, and coupons in front of customers. Mobile apps are incredibly engaging: they account for 23 percent of all active apps on iTunes, and these games are so pervasive that a recent survey found that 27 percent of respondents said that playing a game was the "most annoying" thing people do mid-conversation on their phones (Tepfer 2016). This high number of people who are annoying their friends means that it must be happening a lot! Gaming represents an interesting opportunity to target marketing messages to the audiences who are playing the games. Gamers who are into *Call of Duty* are likely quite different from those who are playing *Candy Crush Saga* and would be interested in different kinds of products. Therefore, to attract the attention of their target markets, marketers know that they first must expose them to those messages. Carefully targeting messages or images via mobile gaming is one more way to do that (Tepfer 2016).

● **Photo 4.5** *Using size to get attention*

Spotting your favorite coffee shop

In most cities around the world, it is quite easy to find a coffee shop. Given the variety and volume of coffee shops around the world, how can a coffee shop compete for the attention of consumers? One way is to make sure that consumers are exposed to, correctly perceive, and pay attention to the brand (see Photo 4.6). The distinctive green logo of Starbucks is known whether it is in Dubai or Dallas, consumers know what to expect. From the perspective of visual perception, it is therefore critical that the logo stands out among the clutter and is consistent, regardless of the context.

Marketers know, however, that even though they need to keep the brand image consistent to get consumers in the door, there also needs to be some bit of uniqueness that speaks to the local market. The idea is to give customers the comfort of knowing that they will get a great-tasting cup of coffee, but to also have an authenticity and connection to the local market. To do this, Starbucks has engaged in an ambitious program to update its stores around the world to reflect the style and personality of the local markets. Starbucks has two hundred retail store designers in eighteen design studios around the world, fourteen of which are in the Americas. For example, they have a jazz theme, complete with a brass instrument chandelier, at the

Canal Street store in New Orleans. In its Brooklyn, New York, store, Starbucks has furniture made out of the reclaimed wood from the basketball court at the Barclays Center (Stinson 2014).

Even more interesting than some of the design changes to appeal to the local neighborhoods are the changes that Starbucks has made to its stores based on research it has done on the unique consumption habits of its customers. In China, for example, customers go to Starbucks in bigger groups, so Starbucks stores there have lots of movable chairs and stools. In contrast, customers in large US cities come in pairs or alone. In these stores, you will be more likely to find a collection of smaller tables as well as a big community table, where customers can sit alone or together (Stinson 2014). Costa Coffee, the number two coffee shop in the United Kingdom, certainly has its set of challenges in keeping up with Starbucks. The UK-based coffee shop is working hard to convince a tea-drinking nation that it needs to make the switch to coffee. Indeed, the United Kingdom ranks forty-third in the world for coffee consumption. It might be a tough sell, but Costa has had some recent success in its global ventures in Poland and China, as well as in its initiatives to bring in more innovative and upscale products (Gerrard 2017). Time will tell, but one thing is sure: customers will use their sense of sight, touch, smell, taste, and hearing to interpret these intriguing coffee environments.

● **Photo 4.6** *No matter where you are, it is easy to spot the Starbucks' logo*

Questions
1. Find logos for at least two coffee shops, one local and one national or global. How do they use color and design to capture consumer attention?
2. Aside from color, other visual elements are also important to a consumer's perceptual process. What other visual cues do retailers use to cut through the clutter and capture a consumer's attention?

Sources: Gerrard (2017); Stinson (2014).

Sound

One feature of modern life is that we are bombarded with sound as we go about our daily lives. A short walk down a city sidewalk can mean an assault on your ears from traffic, people talking or yelling, doors slamming, machinery, or a myriad of other sounds. At this very early point in the perceptual process, our auditory sensory receptors pick up just about everything. How do our brains decide which sounds are worthy of our attention? Previous research studies give us some insights. First, screams grab our attention because they are an easily identifiable signal of distress. In essence, if someone is screaming, he or she is afraid, and maybe you should be too. Screams occupy such a "privileged niche" in our sensory systems that our nervous systems are wired to filter out other sounds and tune in to screams and other loud, scream-like noises, such as sirens and alarms (Arnal et al. 2015). Slamming car doors, loud crashes, and breaking glass also are picked up by the sensory receptors and grab our attention. From a marketing perspective, what grabs our attention? A recent series of research studies tested a wide variety of sounds for automatic reactions like pupil dilation, changes in heart rate, and galvanic skin response. The one sound that beat all others by a landslide was the sound of a baby giggling. The second-place finisher was the buzzing of a cell phone, which was closely followed by the sounds of a bank machine dispensing cash, a sizzling steak, and a soda can being popped and poured (Lindstrom 2010). When these sounds are inserted into advertisements, they may be especially successful in cutting through the clutter of other sounds and attracting the attention of consumers.

Although sound is critical to the sensory reception and attention stages of the perceptual process, it is important to the other parts of the process as well. A special song can grab a consumer's attention, but it can also enhance or change his or her mood and even encourage purchase. Shoppers spend 38 percent more time in a grocery store when slow music is played as compared to when fast music is played (Milliman 1982). Shoppers also seem to purchase products that are congruent with (or fit with) the music. When classical music is played, consumers activate other related concepts in memory, such as expensive, sophisticated, and formal. When this happens, they are more likely to purchase—and pay more money for—products that are also expensive, sophisticated, and formal (North, Sheridan, and Areni 2016). However, retailers need to be careful with how often they play famous or popular songs. One study found that although customers liked to be in a store when a popular song was played, while they listened to the song customers had a reduced number of thoughts and paid less attention to in-store cues like sales signs (Petruzzellis, Chebat, and Palumbo 2014).

Smell

Compared to the other four senses, smell elicits the strongest emotions. This is because the brain processes smells in the limbic system, which is the primitive part of the brain that is unable to engage in higher processing or language, but is instead responsible for emotion and has strong connections to memory and motivation. Smells can trigger emotions in people, particularly in relation to memory; we feel nostalgic for the smell of our grandma's kitchen or our grandpa's cabin by the lake. The most commonly used terms that we use to describe smells are floral, herbal, fruity, sweet, green, woody, spicy, animal, and citrus (Milotic 2006). Consumers have strong expectations for particular smells; they appreciate the unique smell of a new car, the lemony smell of a clean house, and the fresh smell of clothes that have just been washed. Research on smell has been useful to marketers, who use it in a variety of different ways. To entice daily commuters to come in, bakeries often blow the smell of freshly baked bread and pastries onto the busy sidewalk. Real estate agents use a well-known technique to ensure that the house they are showing to potential buyers smells "homey." They simply place a few drops of vanilla extract in a heated oven to make the house smell like fresh-baked cookies.

ScentAir, a company located in Charlotte, North Carolina, specializes in providing customized scents and delivery systems to a variety of organizations. They have over 2,400 scents from which clients can select, and clients can even create a custom scent. For example, Bloomingdale's disperses the scent of coconut in the swimsuit section and baby powder in the baby section. Marriott Hotels uses a variety of scents in its lobbies and other common areas: citrus and cinnamon to evoke feelings of happiness, white tea and thyme to invigorate, and wood and leather for an upscale feeling. The overall goal for retailers is to make shopping experiences richer, more enjoyable, and more meaningful, all for as little as $100 per month. Retailers are not the only ones using scent marketing. Organizations such as doctor's offices, sports stadiums, apartment buildings, and car dealerships are just some of the places that use scent to increase overall mood and loyalty (MSNBC 2017). Scent marketing is starting to gain traction globally. The Standard Chartered Bank in Hong Kong, for example, has created its own specialty fragrance to convey an upscale, high-quality, and warm feel for its customers, thus enhancing the customer experience and ultimately strengthening brand loyalty (Faure-Field 2013).

Although scented retail stores and other places are becoming more common, researchers have found that product scent (for example, lavender-scented tissues) is more important than ambient scent (lavender-scented air in the store) because consumers connect the scent more closely to the product. When a scent is connected to an actual product, rather than to the store or the many other products that happen to be in the store, consumers have stronger memories for the product and its attributes. Later, these memories can be used in evaluations and purchases of the product (Krishna, Lwin, and Morrin 2010).

Touch

The sense of touch provides important information to consumers about the quality of the products they're considering. Very often, consumers want to pick up and feel products before they purchase them (Underhill 2009), which presents some difficulty for online brands (see Insights from the Field 4.2).

One aspect of touch is texture, and many advertisements discuss this important product feature. Just think about the ads you see for cars that have smooth handling, ice cream that has chunky pieces of candy, or even mattresses that have adjustable firmness settings. Mars recently used the slogan "Why have cotton when you can have silk?" in the United Kingdom for its Galaxy chocolate line, emphasizing the distinctive smooth texture of the chocolate.

Consumers also have expectations about the feel or weight of an item. One research experiment conducted with electronics and sound system manufacturer Bang & Olufsen asked participants to judge the quality of a sound system by holding and examining different remote controls, one of which was heavy and one of which was lightweight. Participants had a strong preference for the heavier remote control, even after researchers explained that the lightweight control was completely functional. Regardless, participants thought the lightweight control was broken or had fewer features. These findings emphasize the importance of acknowledging that while some product evaluations are made using a consumer's knowledge about the product's attributes and memories of previous experiences with the product, others are based on more subjective perceptions (Lindstrom 2010). Retailers know how important the sense of touch is for consumers and often design their stores with the intention of getting consumers to pick up or touch their products. Retail giants Bed, Bath, & Beyond and Barnes & Noble are great examples of this. Touching products not only increases the psychological value of the product, but also, in some instances, can even increase the amount of money consumers are willing to pay for an extended product warranty (Lessard-Bonaventure and Chebat 2015).

Taste

The senses of taste and smell are strongly reliant on one another. Have you ever had a cold with a clogged-up nose and had a hard time tasting your food? That's because most of our taste is dependent on us being able to smell the food (Jacewicz 2017). Taste preferences are highly specific to individuals and cultures. Our favorite brands are often offered with different flavors in different parts of the world. In Japan, Kit Kat sells a candy bar flavored with green tea. Don't look for a Big Mac in any McDonald's restaurants in India; instead, you will have to get a Chicken or Veggie Maharaja Mac. Our taste preferences also change as we grow older. We are born with approximately nine thousand taste buds, but by age forty or fifty, they start to diminish. Our sense of smell also gets worse as we get older. These changes mean that it is more difficult to distinguish and enjoy tastes and smells as we age, and it might explain why your grandpa likes to put Tabasco sauce on everything (Jacewicz 2017)! The bottom line is that individual and cultural differences in preference ensure that food product manufacturers have their work cut out for them when they market their products around the world.

Ethical issues abound when it comes to food, health, and wellness. Many developed countries have the problem of obesity because of, among other things, the easy access to cheap, highly processed food. Critics accuse

Are you a high need-for-touch consumer?

Touching products while shopping, or tactile shopping, is an especially important activity because it provides important product-related information to consumers and is one of the few opportunities that we have to touch things without inhibition. In marketing, we know that some consumers prefer to touch products before they buy them. You know you are a high need-for-touch (NFT) consumer if you answer yes to questions like, "When walking through stores, I can't help touching all kinds of products" and "Touching products can be fun" (Peck and Childers 2003). There are strong individual differences here—some people are high-NFT and some are low-NFT consumers. High-NFT consumers derive important information from touching a product and have stronger feelings of trust when they can touch a product (Peck and Childers 2003). When products are offered online or are sealed in packaging, high-NFT consumers feel especially deprived of this important sensory experience.

Hence, marketers and retailers must understand the needs of high-NFT consumers and plan accordingly. Many online retailers are responding to this and are getting much better at simulating touch for their high-NFT consumers by allowing interactive positioning, examination, and movement of the product image. Brick-and-mortar retailers are designing their stores so that high-NFT consumers are able to sample and touch products. Globally, managers at brick-and-mortar stores are also becoming increasingly aware

of differences between *high-touch cultures* like France. where it is common for a stranger to touch you on the arm or hand, and *low-touch cultures* like Germany, where touching strangers is uncommon. These retailers can make sure that their sales staff are aware of these customs and that they react accordingly. In one recent study, it was found that if a salesperson placed a "fleeting touch" on a customer's shoulder, that customer would have an increased sense of trust and more positive product evaluations. This effect on trust and product evaluations was especially effective with very high-NFT consumers and for consumers who were from very low-touch cultures (because it was so unusual for them to be touched by a salesperson) (Orth, Bouzdine-Chameeva, and Brand 2015). By utilizing this insight about the needs of the high-NFT consumer, retailers are changing the way we all experience products.

Questions

1. How could a new nature park and resort in Australia appeal to high-NFT customers from around the world to encourage them to book a visit?
2. Imagine you are opening a new pet supply store. How would your knowledge of sensory perception influence how you would design the store?

Sources: Peck and Childers (2003); Orth, Bouzdine-Chameeva, and Brand (2015).

food manufacturers of creating food products with especially appealing tastes and textures, which consumers crave. When was the last time you ate just one potato chip? The special yumminess of this processed food is called *hyperpalatability*, which is the flavor and texture profile that stimulates addictive-like eating behavior (Pursey et al. 2014). Foods with ingredients like fat, sugar, and salt and crunchy or chewy textures create what experts call *mouth feel*. Critics say that the public health damage caused by these heavily processed foods can be likened to that caused by addictive drugs (Gearhardt et al. 2011).

Surprisingly, most people cannot pick out their favorite brands in blind taste tests (where they don't see the product label). Experts in this field of research know that a consumer's taste perception is built on the actual taste profile (sweet, sour, bitter, savory, or salty) as well as other factors like texture, temperature, and the way the product is presented. A consumer's previous history, knowledge, and expectations also influence a consumer's perceptions (Montague 2006). Insights from the Boardroom 4 provides an inside look at the extensive process involved when researchers at Campbell's make the perfect-tasting soup.

Sensory thresholds

Humans are limited in how well our senses are able to detect certain stimuli. The **absolute threshold** is the smallest level of stimulus that can be picked up by our senses; the sound has to be loud enough to hear, the aroma has to be strong enough to be detected, etc. Building on what we know about sight perception, in order to ensure that their communications can be perceived, advertisers need to make a multitude of decisions, including determining, for example, the ideal level of background music and the right size print. The **differential threshold** is the point at which we notice a difference between two stimuli. This concept is very similar to that of the absolute threshold, but with the differential threshold, individuals are examining two different stimuli and trying to see if they can detect a difference. As in the Campbell's discussion, if a new soup recipe is introduced, can consumers tell the difference?

One marketing-related application of the differential threshold is the phenomenon of *grocery shrink ray*, the practice of some marketers to slightly reduce the size of their products over time. Because consumers are paying the same price for less product, they are in effect paying more. Importantly, because the differences are often very small and occur over a period of time, they are rarely noticed by customers. Grocery shrink ray is becoming a major issue for consumer advocates. One British consumer organization called this phenomenon an "underhand(ed) way to raise prices" and called for clearer labeling (Allen 2012). The British Office for National Statistics found that there were over 2,500 products in the United Kingdom that were hit by the grocery shrink ray in a five-year period, including the beloved Toblerone chocolate bar that shrunk its distinctive triangle-shaped pieces, causing substantial consternation among fans (Northrup 2017). Similarly, Twix candy bars have lost 13.8 percent of their weight and Kit Kat candy bars have lost 16.7 percent of their weight since 2014. In the United States, ice cream used to be sold in half-gallon (sixty-four-ounce) containers and is now being sold in forty-eight-ounce containers, there are approximately 14 percent fewer sheets of toilet paper on a typical roll, and at least fifteen brands of breakfast cereal now come in smaller sizes (Greenwood 2018).

Building on the concept of the differential threshold, the **just-noticeable difference** is the minimum difference needed for a stimulus to be noticed by the majority of people. How can marketers determine the magnitude of

Absolute threshold is the smallest level of stimulus that can be picked up by our senses.

Differential threshold is the point at which we notice a difference between two stimuli.

Just-noticeable difference (JND) is the minimum difference needed for a stimulus to be noticed by the majority of people.

Guess who is coming to dinner?

● *Alice Ping*

Alice Ping is certainly one of the most interesting dinner guests you will ever have. After you find out what she does for a living, you will be quite intimidated to imagine what she might think of that new French fusion recipe you have been looking forward to trying out! Ping is the senior program manager for the sensory and consumer science function of Campbell's USA. Ping has spent twenty years doing research about how human beings perceive information through their senses. One of her areas of expertise is taste. She applies her extensive knowledge and expertise on taste to find the ideal combination of salt, sweet, bitter, sour, and savory tastes for all of Campbell's products.

Ping conducts sensory and consumer research; she sees her role as the bridge between product development and consumers. As Ping explains it, "we use the human senses to measure consumer liking and product sensory characteristics, then use that information to develop products that consumers will like" (2017). Each part of a consumer's perceptual experience is important—what a consumer sees, smells, feels, hears, and tastes.

Although taste is king in her work, other product dimensions are very important as well. For instance, the visual appearance of the product is critical because it is the first step in the consumption experience. Ping noted, "One thing we found was that the shape and size of the chunks of meat and vegetables in a package of soup can cue 'homemade' or 'natural' thoughts" (2017). So, during processing, chunks are cut unevenly to meet these expectations.

Ping and her team utilize different tools to learn as much as they can about how consumers perceive a product. Take the example of a recent research project on removing artificial flavor from a product and replacing it with natural flavor, a move that was directed by Campbell's "Real Food" philosophy. Ping and her team started the project with an "analytical sensory" tool called a "discrimination test or difference test . . . we use discrimination tests to see if consumers can detect the difference between 2 different recipes," she explained (Ping 2017). Ping noted, "Ideally we want to make sure they can't tell the difference, especially if it is a product that has a loyal consumer base." If consumers do perceive a difference, the team would need to understand whether they like it more, less, or about the same.

Another analytical tool often used is descriptive analysis. Ping (2017) explains, "Here, we engage in expert tasting. We recruit a group of consumers who are selected based on their sensory aptitude, and we train them to be expert tasters. Their job is to detect the fingerprint of the product—we call this sensory profiling." There are five key dimensions that allow the research team to precisely describe the sensory profile: aroma, appearance, taste/flavor, texture, and aftertaste (see Figure 4.2, showing the sensory profile difference of two products).

For each of these dimensions, the expert tasters carefully separate and quantify each of the perceptions. Ping (2017) says, "For example, if we're looking at a bowl of chicken noodle soup, the experts give ratings on intensity of chicken aroma, veggie aroma, herbal aroma, etc. We move through each of the dimensions

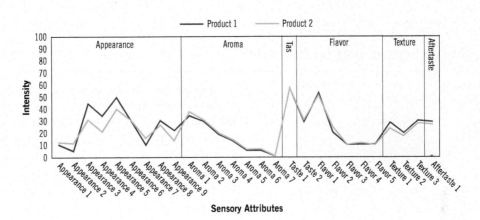

● **Figure 4.2** *Example of product sensory profile differences for two products*

Source: Campbell's R&D

this way." Ping notes, "At the end, you will have a sensory fingerprint of the product." Constructing a taste profile is a long and difficult process, but it provides valuable information.

One of the next steps in the research process is to combine the analytical sensory data with consumer research. Ping (2017) explains that "consumers give us information on their preferences for several samples of the soup. Consumers generally can't give us very good details; they can only tell us which one tastes better." This is where the research team combines the sensory profiles provided by the expert tasters with consumer preferences: "The expert tasters explain to us *why* consumers like one recipe over another. We can build a statistical model to understand whether there are different consumer preference groups which we call consumer segmentation, and what the strongest drivers are for each segment" (Ping 2017). Ping elaborates: "When we combine the analytical sensory data and consumer data with the statistical tools, the result is powerful."

Ping and her team recently completed a project where they tested two products that were both spicy. After trying the product for themselves, "half of our team said one was hotter and the other half said the other product was hotter! We knew that for this target market, consumers preferred the hotter one. The problem is, we really were not sure which was the hotter one until we took it to the lab!" (Ping 2017). Ping and her team asked consumers to break down the experience of the spice and to rate the spiciness throughout the entire taste experience. As it turns out, there are five stages of spice perception: the beginning (where it first touches your tongue), the middle, the end, the throat burn, and the lingering heat. Ping and her team found that the *end* of the consumption experience leads to more dominant perceptions of heat for consumers: the end, the throat burn, and lingering heat. Because of this finding, the product development and marketing teams were able to identify the reason for the preferred heat level of one recipe and potential optimization opportunities for the other recipe.

Who knew so much work went into a simple bowl of chicken soup? Alice Ping, that's who!

The Home
Plate

W. K. Kellogg
LOOK FOR THIS SIGNATURE

● **Photo 4.7** *The packaging for Kellogg's Corn Flakes has changed in the last 100 years*

the just-noticeable difference? Nineteenth-century psychologist Ernst Weber found that the just-noticeable difference is related to the magnitude of the initial stimulus. Specifically, **Weber's law** says that the stronger the initial stimulus, the more difference would be required for the change to be noticed. So, for example, consumers should be just as likely to notice a price change from fifty-eight cents to fifty-nine cents as they would be to notice a change from fifty-eight dollars to fifty-nine dollars. It's not the size of the price change (one cent versus one dollar), but the magnitude of the change in relation to the original price. In addition to changes in price and product size, Weber's law has also been used to explain how consumers do not generally notice small changes in packaging design that are made by marketers on a yearly basis, but will easy detect these changes over a longer period of time. Look at the 1912 ad for Kellogg's Corn Flakes in Photo 4.7. Over more than a century, design teams have made small changes to the packaging such that today's box of Corn Flakes bears little resemblance to the early one depicted here. By the way, the game of baseball has also changed! Insights from Academia 4.3 describes how the human body experiences information from the five senses differently and how that information might be used by marketers to predict behavior.

 INSIGHTS FROM ACADEMIA 4.3

If you could *feel* or *taste* the color red, you might just purchase more red stuff!

But you can't, so you won't. Advertisers try to activate as many consumer senses as possible. So, when advertisers try to motivate consumers to imagine an upcoming consumption situation, they categorize the senses in terms of what is more proximal (close) or distal (far away). Taste and touch are proximal because they are actually *experienced* by the body. Seeing, hearing, and smelling are distal because they are only perceived by the body, not experienced in it. When advertisements activate distal senses (sight, sound, and smell), consumers are more likely to delay their purchases. However, when advertisements activate proximal senses (taste and touch), consumers are more likely to purchase quickly. The next time you go to a store, see if you can determine which proximal and distal senses are being activated.

Elder, R. S., A. E. Schlosser, M. Poor, and L. Xu. 2017. "So Close I Can Almost Sense It: The Interplay between Sensory Imagery and Psychological Distance." Journal of Consumer Research 44 (4): 877–94.

Adaptation

Adaptation is the extent to which an individual's sensitivity to a stimulus diminishes over time. Sensory adaptation occurs when we get used to a certain stimulus over time; our sensory receptors become less sensitive to it. Imagine a situation where, in the dead of winter, you find a great deal and book a flight to Aruba for the week. You step off the plane and are suddenly hit with a blast of hot tropical air. After immediately bursting into a serious sweat, you enthusiastically put on some flip-flops, short sleeves, and shorts as soon as you get to your hotel. While the initial heat may have been a shock to your system, over the week, your body adapts to the heat and you find yourself becoming quite comfortable with the hot, humid air. This example of sensory adaptation illustrates how the initial strength of the stimulus lessens over time. It will take a stronger stimulus, perhaps a heat wave in paradise, to break through the exposure threshold. The four areas in which sensory adaptation happens most often are sight, touch, smell, and sound. Smart marketers are aware of sensory adaptation and utilize various communications tactics to ensure consumers are not experiencing sensory adaptation.

Attention

The next step in the perceptual process is **attention**, which is focusing mental concentration on a given stimulus. That is, consumers spend a fleeting moment (or sometimes more) focusing their mental activity on something they hear, see, taste, smell, or touch. One important characteristic of attention is that it is selective, because we can't pay attention to all of the stimuli that come our way. From a marketing perspective, consumers are exposed to thousands of ads, logos, slogans, and images each day and must carefully select which things deserve their attention. What determines selective attention? An important consideration is a consumer's processing goals. For example, when the consumer's goal is to evaluate a new product, the consumer will pay more attention to the textual information on the package and less attention to the graphics (Pieters and Wedel 2007).

Selective attention also comes into play when consumers purposely divide their attention, as when they simultaneously use multiple screens to consume content. Consumer multitasking behavior is increasing, especially with different forms of media. A recent study by Accenture, a global management consulting firm, found that 87 percent of Americans use a second screen while watching TV. Owning and using multiple devices is not just an American phenomenon. In the United States, the average household has 10.37 devices that are connected to Wifi, cable, or landline. The UK follows close behind with about 9.16 devices per household (see Figure 4.3)(Statista 2020). As Wifi enabled devices become more integrated into our daily lives, paradoxically, some tech companies are making an effort to wean their consumers off their devices. These forward-thinking companies believe that the increasing saturation of these devices into our home, work, and leisure may soon present a consumer backlash. Instead, in an attempt to give consumers

Weber's law suggests that the stronger the initial stimulus, the more difference would be required for a change to be noticed.

Adaptation is the extent to which an individual's sensitivity to a stimulus diminishes over time.

Attention is focusing mental concentration on a given stimulus.

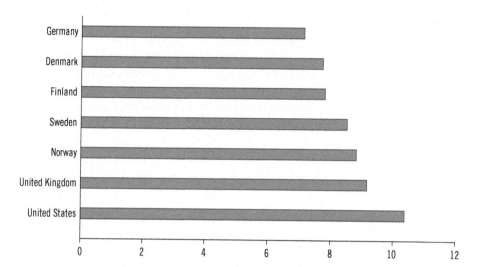

● **Figure 4.3** *Average number of connected devices per household*

Source: Adapted from Statista 2020

a break, these companies are designing their devices to easily switch to "do not disturb" time and easily pause Wifi. Many are designed for seemless integration with a customer's other devices, so the customer does not have to spend a lot of time syncing their new devices. As part of its "Digital Wellness" Program, Android's 2018 operating system update came with a variety of features that helped consumers reduce digital distractions and improve their lifestyles (Ares 2018).

Owning multiple devices is one thing, but using them simultaneously is quite another. The proportion of individuals who rely solely on TV for their media needs seems to be dropping quickly. Indeed, 57 percent of consumers simultaneously use a TV and a smartphone, 50 percent simultaneously use a TV and a laptop or desktop, and 25 percent simultaneously use a TV and a tablet. There are also big differences in how individuals in different age groups use media. For example, in the eighteen- to thirty-four-year-old group, 71 percent simultaneously use a TV and a smartphone, while only 42 percent of those in the forty-five- to fifty-four-year-old group do so (see Table 4.2) (Mann et al. 2015). With more media and programming options than ever before, more screens, and more multitasking, marketers must find ever more creative ways to cut through the clutter and grab the attention of consumers (see Insights from the Field 4.3).

Attracting attention

It can be very challenging for a marketer to find new, creative ways to attract the attention of a consumer. One way to attract attention is with movement, especially when it is unexpected. A neon cowboy in Las Vegas with a movable arm has been attracting tourists since 1951 to visit a casino there (see Photo 4.8). Today, digital displays in shopping centers, office buildings, or tourist hubs are used to attract attention. Billboards and other outdoor advertising use movement too.

Table 4.2 Multitasking by device and age

AGE OF CONSUMER	SIMULTANEOUSLY USE TV AND SMARTPHONE (%)	SIMULTANEOUSLY USE TV AND LAPTOP OR DESKTOP (%)	SIMULTANEOUSLY USE TV AND TABLET (%)
14–17	74	44	35
18–34	71	49	26
35–44	59	48	29
45–54	42	53	23
55+	27	50	18

Source: Adapted from Mann et al. (2015).

One particularly innovative campaign from British Air used movement to attract attention up and toward its planes that were passing overhead. The ad depicted a small child running and pointing to airplanes as they flew overhead saying, for example, "Look, it's flight BA475 from Barcelona" (check out https://www.youtube.com/watch?v=GtJx_pZjvzc). In case you're wondering, yes, the actual flights that were going overhead were identified in the ad. The campaign was so innovative, it won the Grand Prix award at the Cannes Film Festival (Klaassen 2014). Faster-than-normal or slower-than-normal movement in an ad can also be attention grabbing. Such approaches disrupt our expectations of the world around us, expectations that are based on schemas, beliefs, and feelings that we build up over time and through learning about our environment.

Another way to attract the attention of consumers is to present them with something novel. **Novelty** is something that is unexpected and out of the ordinary, based on your previous experiences and knowledge of that stimulus or event. If a consumer has not seen something before or if the item is in an unusual context, it will be perceived as novel. The human brain is particularly well equipped to identify and pay attention to novel stimuli (Berns, Cohen, and Mintun 1997). Thus, another technique to cut through clutter is to place something in an unusual or unlikely setting. Because of their ability to attract attention, novel and unique products are more likely to get noticed (Schomaker and Meeter 2015). Building on the concept of novelty, contrast may also be used to gain an individual's attention, such as the use of black-and-white advertisements where we are expecting to see color. An unexpected

● **Photo 4.8** *Neon cowboy sign in Fremont Street, Las Vegas*

Novelty is something that is unexpected and out of the ordinary, based on previous experience and knowledge of that stimulus or event.

Step one in selling men's deodorant: attract the attention of women

In 2011, Old Spice engaged in an innovative ad campaign. The company wanted to increase its fan base on YouTube, Facebook, and Twitter to re-energize a campaign that was originally launched in 2003. At that time, marketers for Old Spice targeted both men and women in its campaign for a new men's body wash. In the campaign's 2011 reboot, a much more forceful attempt was made to target women and to utilize social media. In searching for something to attract the attention of women, the advertising team identified American actor Isaiah Mustafa, an individual with plenty of presence, style, and charisma. Mustafa would become known as "The Man Your Man Could Smell Like." If you man doesn't *look* like the sexy Mustafa, at least he could *smell* like him. Marketing managers at Old Spice wanted to differentiate their brand in an industry that was starting to become crowded by creating an interactive and much more personalized experience. In addition, it wanted to launch a direct attack against its biggest competitor, the Dove Men+Care body wash that appeared in a Super Bowl ad that year. The Old Spice team worked with advertising powerhouse Wieden+Kennedy to create and manage the campaign (Fernandez 2011).

How did the agency do this? They began by utilizing YouTube, because it already had an established following for Old Spice and, importantly, the platform allows viewers to comment on video clips. The team identified social media mentions of Old Spice and then posted 185 videos that depicted Mustafa personally responding to those comments. At first, Mustafa responded to comments from celebrities, influencers, and superfans of Old Spice. However, overall, about 70 percent of his comments were targeted to everyday, average consumers. The ad agency even had Mustafa on stand-by in front of a green screen so that he could record real-time responses to some of the questions and comments posed by fans. The effort spread across multiple media platforms, including Twitter and Facebook. Thanks to these multimedia efforts, cross-platform conversations about Old Spice accelerated.

YouTube posted 5.9 million views on the first day of the campaign and 40 million by the end of the week. Compare this to just 1 million views for the Dove Men+Care Super Bowl ad! Twitter followers increased by 2,700 percent, Facebook fan interactions went up 800 percent, and the number of YouTube subscribers more than doubled, from 65,000 to 150,000. In the first three months following the campaign's launch, it captured 76 percent of online buzz. Importantly, sales increased by 125 percent after the launch (Fernandez 2011).

An important insight made by the marketing team was essential to the success of this campaign—more than 60 percent of body washes are purchased by women. Therefore, the campaign needed to appeal to women and to men (Fernandez 2011). In the videos, Mustafa spoke directly to women by saying, for example, "Look at your man, now back at me." Marketing managers know that successful viral advertising follows four steps (Nobel 2013):

1. Attracting viewers' attention
2. Retaining their attention
3. Getting viewers to share what they have seen with others
4. Persuading viewers

In the case of Old Spice, an important insight about who does the majority of the purchasing for men's body wash encouraged the marketing team to make women the focus of the campaign. The creative, sexy, funny execution grabbed and retained their attention, encouraged them to share the videos, and then persuaded them to buy it.

Questions

1. When you see an ad or product information online, what makes you want to share that information? Who do you generally share the information with? Why? Be specific.
2. Using the four-step process described by Nobel (2013), describe an example of an advertising campaign that was not successful. What happened? What step of the process was particularly troublesome? Why?

Sources: Fernandez (2011); Nobel (2013).

or contrasting sound is another way to grab attention, as when you hear the sound of a doorbell or ringtone during an ad.

Since the beginning of time, sex has been used to attract attention. Although it can be quite effective, marketers need to ensure that attention is directed at the brand, not just the sexual content of the ad. Sexual innuendo can be effectively utilized, as in the recent "Let's Get Zesty" print campaign for Kraft salad dressing featuring a male model. Although the campaign received much unwanted attention by some religious groups, it was backed by strong consumer support for the ad. Kraft responded by saying the campaign was "a playful and flirtatious way to reach our consumers. People have overwhelmingly said they're enjoying the campaign and having fun with it" (Nudd 2013). Another way to attract attention is with emotion. Certain images, sounds, and scenarios resonate with our emotions. Anheuser–Busch is famous for pulling at the heartstrings of consumers with its Super Bowl ads, which often feature heartwarming scenes of the brand's famous Clydesdale horses and puppies.

Advertisers also often use a combination of sound and visually appealing images to capture attention and assist in the interpretation process, the next step in the perceptual process. The financial services company Capital One recently used actor Samuel L. Jackson to sing the Al Green hit "Let's Stay Together" for its initiative with the Quicksilver credit card and Spotify. The combination of the appealing song and popular actor, as well as the lyrics, grabbed the attention of consumers and solidified in song the new connection that Quicksilver had forged with Spotify (Parisi 2017).

Using shock to attract attention

Beliefs about what is shocking or controversial change over time. Simply look at some old cigarette advertisements, with headlines such as "More doctors smoke Camels than any other cigarette" and "To keep a slender figure, no one can deny . . . Lucky Strike!" Those slogans would definitely cause controversy today. The use of shock can certainly be effective in attracting attention. Research studies have confirmed that shock can increase attention, strengthen memory, and influence behavior (Dahl, Frankenberger, and Manchanda 2003). However, this tactic needs to be used carefully because it can often backfire by angering or alienating individuals. The fashion brand Benetton regularly uses shocking images in its advertising campaigns. Since the 1980s, Benetton has sought to provoke conversation about a variety of social justice issues. The brand has done this with ad campaigns designed to stir controversy by depicting shocking images of, for example, a nun kissing a priest, a dying AIDS victim surrounded by his family, and a Black woman breastfeeding a White baby. Over the years and around the world, the ads have provoked responses varying from praise to outrage. For example, the ad with the nun and priest received strong condemnation in many Catholic countries.

More recently, Benetton ran a series of ads as a part of its "Unhate" campaign showing a variety of world leaders kissing one another, including an image of US president Barack Obama kissing Venezuelan president Hugo

Chavez and former French president Nicolas Sarkozy kissing German chancellor Angela Merkel. Benetton's goal is to ignite global debate about tolerance. All of these images were created; they're not real photographs. They work, however, because they challenge our expectations. The "Unhate" campaign itself was so well received and executed that it won the top prize at the Cannes Film Festival in France (Nudd 2012). Several years ago in the United Kingdom, one TV advertisement claimed the distinction of being the most complained-about ad ever. It showed women in a call center singing with their mouths full of delicious KFC food. Complaints flooded in to the UK's Advertising Standards Authority claiming, among other things, that the ad encouraged bad table manners in children (Advertising Standards Association 2017).

Interpretation

Interpretation involves attaching meaning to the stimulus; consumers understand the message and are likely to connect this new information to other information they already know.

Schemas are cognitive frameworks that are used to organize and interpret information.

Once consumers have attended to a stimulus, they attempt to understand it. **Interpretation** is the next step in the perceptual process and involves attaching meaning to the stimulus; consumers understand the message and are likely to connect this new information to other information they already know. Ideally, the newly acquired information will be categorized and stored in a schema. **Schemas** are cognitive frameworks that are used to organize and interpret information. Schemas help us to categorize our world and interpret stimuli. Schemas also help us interpret new stimuli because we can easily store the new information in a category that already exists. We have schemas for all sorts of things, such as how people should dress for work, what to bring to the beach, and what a retail store should look like. Our experiences help us make these schema categorizations and, importantly, help us interpret new objects or contexts. So, for example, if you are in Bangkok and need to take a taxi, you will easily be able to figure out that it would be just as useful to hail a tuk-tuk, a small three-wheeled vehicle.

Because everyone has different experiences and schemas, the interpretation step of the perceptual process will result in individuals interpreting stimuli quite differently. In addition, in some cases, interpretation may be primed or facilitated by other stimuli associated with the brand, such as the red script of Coca-Cola or the iconic Apple symbol. Interpretation will also depend on the personal relevance of the stimulus. If you're thinking about going to graduate school, you will pay attention to and interpret information on universities and graduate programs differently from someone who is not interested in graduate school. Regardless of how attention grabbing a stimulus is, if an individual is not interested in the product category, there will be little likelihood of the message being successfully interpreted. Finally, interpretation also depends on an individual's preexisting preferences—consumers interpret information that confirms their beliefs more readily than information that counters their beliefs (Chernev 2001).

It is important to remember that the perceptual process occurs within a context and environment that is full of stimuli vying for exposure and attention. The overall perceptual process is also influenced by our experiences and memories. One method that is used to make sense of our environment is a search for completeness. **Gestalt** psychology explains how the human brain looks for completeness and is another way in which the interpretation step is facilitated. *Gestalt* is a German word meaning "whole" and describes the tendency of the human brain to identify meaning and patterns in the environment. The connection between Gestalt and consumer behavior was originally forged in the late 1800s and early 1900s by a group of German psychologists who examined the differences in how individuals interpreted the "big picture" versus individual features of a stimulus. Their goal was to understand how the brain organized stimuli for completeness and, in turn, how this facilitated interpretation. The work of these early Gestalt psychologists and their creation of several key principles still influences how marketers understand and communicate with consumers.

● **Figure 4.4** *The principle of closure*

Principle of closure

The principle of **closure** says that individuals experience a psychological tension that motivates them to fill in the "missing" elements of an incomplete picture. Figure 4.4 shows several black shapes with a lot of white space, but it is easy to complete this image in our minds and see a soccer ball. Marketers use the principle of closure to increase consumer involvement and to assist storage in memory. An example of visual closure is seen in an Audi campaign (Photo 4.9). Auditory or sound closure can also be utilized, as when consumers are presented with well-known lyrics or slogans with words missing that they will be motivated to complete.

● **Photo 4.9** *This Audi advertisement provides a good example of the principle of closure*

Principle of similarity

The human brain is adept at grouping objects together that are physically similar. In Gestalt psychology, **similarity** refers to how items that have similar physical characteristics will be perceived as belonging together. In Figure 4.5, it is easy to see the shape of a T at the center of the image because it is made of similar shapes that seem to belong together. Similarity can be based on shape, size or color. Marketers use the principle of similarity when they use the same graphics and colors on all of their product packaging and advertising, so that consumers can easily see that they belong together.

Principle of proximity

When visual stimuli are located close together, the brain often categorizes them into a group. The **principle of proximity** finds that items that are close together are perceived to be more similar than items that are farther apart. In Figure 4.6, because they are sitting next to one another, most people see three dog and cat pairs, rather than three dogs and three cats. In marketing practice, retailers tend to group products together that complement one another,

Gestalt means "whole" and refers to how people look for meaning and patterns in the stimuli in the environment as a whole, rather than in terms of the individual part.

Closure is the tendency for people to fill in the "missing" elements of an incomplete picture.

Similarity refers to how items that have similar physical characteristics will be perceived as belonging together.

Principle of proximity states that things we see close together are perceived to be more related than things that are seen as farther apart.

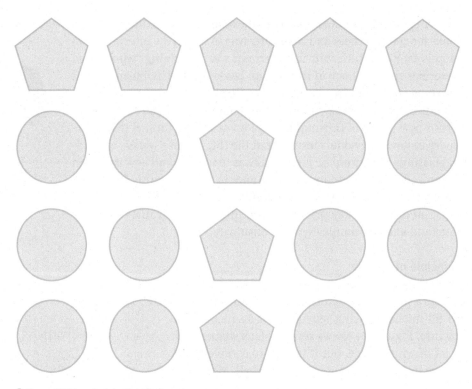

● **Figure 4.5** *The principle of similarity*

● **Figure 4.6** *The principle of proximity*

such as socks next to shoes in a department store or mustard and ketchup next to buns and a cooler of hot dogs in a grocery store.

Principle of figure and ground

As they are organizing stimuli during the interpretation phase of the perceptual process, individuals often focus on what may be prominent in the environment. The **principle of figure and ground** states that we are more likely to notice things when they stand out from the background in which they are placed. The item that is prominent is referred to as the figure, while the context is referred to as the ground. A careful look at the FedEx logo in Photo 4.10 reveals a forward-pointing white arrow. The arrow is the figure, which is contrasted against the red background in which it sits.

The principle of figure and ground helps explain why it is so important for advertisers to ensure that their message (the figure) is not overshadowed by the context or ground (the story, the setting, or the celebrity spokesperson).

Principle of figure and ground states that we are more likely to notice things when they stand out from the background in which they are placed.

To increase engagement with the ad, some marketers may wish to make interpretation of the ad a little difficult. The hope is that it may encourage consumers to think more deeply about the message. The World Wildlife Fund used this principle to blend the figure and ground in one ad showing parched earth and an outline of a parrot (see Photo 4.11) to say "Tropical trees never die alone." This ad illustrates the connection between the rainforest and its creatures with a powerful image that utilizes the Gestalt principle of figure and ground.

● **Photo 4.10** *The principle of figure and ground*

Response

The final step in the perceptual process is the consumer's response. There are inward types of responses, such as storing the information in memory for later use, updating an attitude, or experiencing an emotion. There are also outward, or behavioral, types of responses, such as clicking on an ad, visiting a store, telling a friend, or making a purchase. It is important for marketing managers to fully understand the consumer's perceptual process because it is the first point at which an individual comes in contact with their product and message. Exposure, attention, and interpretation are essential for a consumer to engage in a response to the marketing efforts. In the next section, we will discuss when the perceptual process is especially critical to marketing managers.

◎ Marketing and Perception

Marketing managers are particularly interested in understanding the nature of perception because it helps them develop better strategies to connect to consumers. In the following section, we will examine five areas in which marketers have utilized the concept of perception: perceived risk, perceptual or positioning maps, repositioning, price perception, and semiotics.

● **Photo 4.11** *Tropical trees never die alone*

Perceived risk

There is a certain amount of objective risk when a consumer chooses to go scuba diving or skydiving, but many everyday consumer decisions are also influenced by perceived risk. **Perceived risk** is the amount of uncertainty or

Perceived risk is the amount of uncertainty or doubt that a consumer has when buying a product or service.

doubt a consumer has when buying a product or service. Beliefs about the perceived risk of a purchase depend on uncertainty (how likely is it that something bad will happen?) and adverse consequences (if it happens, how bad is the outcome?) (Bauer 1960). A consumer's mood can have a substantial influence on perceived risk. Specifically, consumers in a positive mood are less risk averse—they will take more chances—than consumers who are in a negative mood (Fedorikhin and Cole 2004). Perceived risk also depends on the individual traits of the consumer, as well as how he or she perceives the information provided. Consumers are likely to perceive higher levels of risk in the following situations:

- The product or service is completely new to the market. Perceived risk will likely be higher because consumers have no previous experience with the product, so they cannot pull on memories, experiences, or the advice of experts or friends to help make a purchase decision.

- There is very little information available. Maybe few consumers have had experience with the product so there are few reviews, or perhaps the product information is in another language. Regardless, perceived risk will likely be higher.

- There are significant differences among brands. Perceived risk will likely be higher here because there is a very real chance of making an inferior choice.

- The consumer is a novice and has limited experience. Perceived risk will be higher for a twenty-something buying a new car for the first time than for a more experienced consumer who has purchased several cars over his or her lifetime.

- The consumer is likely to be judged by others for the purchase decision. Perceived risk will be higher for the purchase of a new interview suit than for a new outfit to wear when you're just hanging out with your friends.

Often, marketers want to reduce risk perceptions for consumers, such as when a financial services firm sells loans, stocks, or mutual funds. In these cases, the financial services firm will want to assure consumers that their investments are safe. In other cases, marketers may want to heighten risk perceptions for consumer. It is common for marketers of toothpaste, deodorant, and haircare products to inject a little fear into their advertisements to encourage purchases of their products so that consumers will avoid the risk of looking and smelling bad. Insights from Academia 4.4 presents some surprising findings about *incidental fear* and consumption.

Financial risk is the perception of a likely economic loss.

Different types of perceived risk influence consumer behavior. **Financial risk** is the perception of a likely economic loss. It should not be surprising that financial risk is relative; in a given situation, consumers with very little disposable income may perceive greater financial risk than those with greater amounts of disposable income (Bertrand, Mullainathan, and Shafir 2006).

INSIGHTS FROM ACADEMIA 4.4

Don't go shopping after a scary movie!

Sometimes consumers feel incidental fear that is unrelated to the consumer decision. Perhaps they are naturally more inclined to be afraid or perhaps something just happened to make them afraid, such as having a near miss in the car, reading about some bad news online, or seeing a scary movie. Researchers conducted a series of six experiments to examine how incidental fear impacts consumer decision-making. They found that incidental fear adds a bit of tunnel vision to our perceptions and encourages us to make purchases now, rather than putting them off until later. So if you're feeling a little fearful, put that credit card away until tomorrow!

Coleman, N. V., P. Williams, A. C. Morales, and A. E. White. 2017. "Attention, Attitudes, and Action: When and Why Incidental Fear Increases Consumer Choice." Journal of Consumer Research 44 (2): 283–312.

Buying a new pair of boots is an insignificant decision for some consumers, but for others it represents a major financial outlay and, therefore, higher levels of financial risk.

Performance or functional risk is the perception of how well the product will perform its expected task. These perceptions may concern the technical aspects of a product, such as a face wash that claims to deep clean the skin or a hand sanitizer that claims to kill 99.9 percent of bacteria. Companies offer money-back guarantees to consumers to help reduce perceived performance risk. These perceptions may also concern some intangible aspect of the product, such as the extent to which a new suit will make you feel confident or the extent to which a massage at the spa will lower your stress level.

Physical risk is the perception of bodily harm that a product or service might have. Many parents are reluctant to buy certain products for their children because of a concern about physical risk. These concerns will also prompt them to insist on their child wearing a helmet when riding a bike and proper equipment when playing sports. Many products have extensive warnings, safety labels, and instructions. This is especially true with prescription and over-the-counter drugs. Food marketers attempt to reduce perceptions of physical risk by, for example, adding labels to packaging with "use by" or "best before" dates.

Social risk is the risk of damaging your standing in your social community. This could occur if you had the "wrong" product or brand in the eyes of other people. Young people often believe that they need to have the "right" brand of phone or clothing, and this fear of social risk even extends to products like bike helmets. Copenhagen, Denmark, has a big biking culture; people ride to work and school, to do their shopping, and for leisure. Young people in Copenhagen dislike wearing bike helmets because they are often unstylish and therefore pose a social risk. Enter the Nutcase company, which

Performance or functional risk is the perception of how well the product will perform its expected task.

Physical risk is the perception of harm that a product or service might have.

Social risk is the risk of damaging your standing in your social community.

● **Photo 4.12** *The nutcase logo and model wearing nutcase helmet*

Psychological risk is the risk that reflects the potential to damage an individual's self-perception.

Time risk is the risk embodied in the uncertainty regarding the amount of time required to buy or learn to use a product.

Perceptual (or positioning) maps are visual representations of the marketplace from the consumer's perspective.

makes great-fitting and great-looking helmets in a variety of fun and colorful styles. Nutcase launched its innovative "Outdoor Fitting Room" campaign in Copenhagen to address the issue of social risk. A series of light posts and poles were indented with a helmet. People were invited to try the helmets on and encouraged to post a photo to the Nutcase Denmark Facebook page in exchange for the chance to win a free helmet (see Photo 4.12). This innovative campaign was successful in reducing social risk and, with more people wearing the helmets, it also reduced physical risk.

Psychological risk reflects the potential to damage an individual's self-perception. It reflects how well purchases or behaviors fit with a consumer's self-perception (discussed in more depth in Chapter 6). Basically, does the purchase fit your value system and your self-identity? Many consumers, for example, try to live their lives according to a set of ethical standards, but sometimes consume products that were made using questionable ethics, like child labor. From a marketing perspective, psychological risk occurs when consumers realize this conflict (Szmigin, Carrigan, and McEachern 2009) and how this realization might alter self-perceptions and efforts to balance any inconsistencies.

Time risk is the risk embodied in the uncertainty regarding the amount of time required to buy or learn to use the product. Many products and services are time-bound; some consumption experiences like a sporting event cannot be delayed to another day or time. Many products and services also require the consumer to devote a significant amount of time just to use the product. For example, there is a greater time risk associated with spending the time to cook a meal than for choosing fast food (Usunier and Valette-Florence 2007). When purchasing a new laptop, people may stick with what they already know—PC or Mac—because of the time and effort involved in learning a new operating system. Consumers do not want to waste their time.

Perceptual/positioning maps

Perceptual (or positioning) maps are visual representations of the marketplace from the customer's perspective. They effectively provide managers with a visual depiction of how consumers view the products and brands in the market in comparison with other brands. Importantly, they also provide vital information about the differences in how consumers see brands and how a company sees its own brands. By examining this visual representation of the brands in the marketplace, managers can clearly ascertain where their brands line up against the competition on at least two dimensions (Kim, Kim, and Han 2007;

Nestrud and Lawless 2008). Perceptual (or positioning) maps are developed by asking consumers a series of questions. First, consumers are asked, "What are the most important criteria you use when selecting this product?" If consumers are considering visiting a coffee shop, the majority of consumers might, for example, select the following two attributes: the store environment and the price. These will be the two dimensions on which the perceptual map is constructed; one will be the X axis and one will be the Y axis. Next, once these two important attributes are identified, consumers are asked to rate some brands on those attributes with questions such as, "On a scale of 1 to 10, how pleasant is the store environment at Starbucks?" The researcher will get responses for each brand on the environment attribute. After that, the researcher will move to the second attribute, price, and ask consumers, "On a scale of 1 to 10, how expensive is a Starbucks coffee?" The important thing to remember is that these questions are asked for *each* attribute and for *each* brand under consideration. Finally, the numbers are compiled and the brands are positioned on a two-dimensional space (see Figure 4.7).

The results of perceptual (or positioning) mapping are sometimes surprising, but can reveal some interesting strategic insights for brand managers. First, they are a visual representation from the consumer's rather than the company's perspective of brands and their relations with other brands. Managers will easily be able to see if there is a mismatch between what they know about the product and what consumers interpret with regard to the

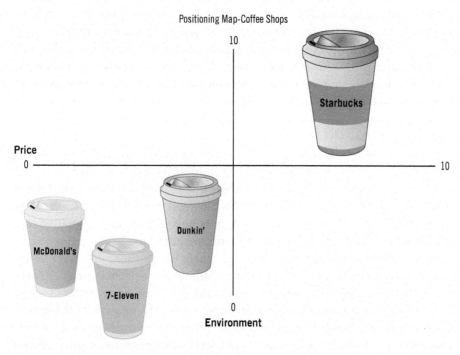

Positioning Map-Coffee Shops

● **Figure 4.7** *Perceptual/positioning map for coffee shops*

Source: Image courtesy of Kim Richmond, richmondmarketing+communications

product. Second, they can show potential gaps in the market for new product development. For example, in Figure 4.6, there is currently no competition in the low-price/more appealing environment sector of the market. Maybe some consumers would be interested in visiting a coffee shop with these characteristics! Finally, by showing managers where their brand is positioned compared to the competition, they can consider changes to their brand that might improve its position. These changes may be real in the sense of product improvements or they could be just a matter of crafting a better message to communicate important attributes about the brand. For example, in Figure 4.6, brand managers at McDonald's might be happy that their brand is perceived as the most reasonably priced option, but might also want to work to improve the store environment, so that it surpasses some competitors on two dimensions, not just one. Alternatively, sometimes a product *already does* outperform the competition on a given dimension and the "problem" may simply be one of communication. In this case, brand managers might want to launch a communications campaign to boost perceptions of this particular product attribute.

Repositioning

Brand perception is a phenomenon that exists in the minds of consumers, and companies often invest substantial money over time to manage brand perceptions using tools like positioning maps. Once brand perceptions are solidified in the minds of consumers, however, it can be quite difficult for marketing managers to change or alter how consumers perceive their brands. Sometimes repositioning is necessary because the needs of the target market have changed, a new technology has been introduced, or the product has been improved or changed. Whatever the reason, a key aspect of brand management is repositioning, or shifting the existing consumer perceptions of a brand (see Insights from the Field 4.4).

Price perception

The topic of price perception is another way in which our understanding of perceptual processes can be utilized in marketing. Have you heard of the phrase, you get what you pay for? There is a reason why we say that. People often believe that there is a correlation between the price and the quality of a product. There is a connection not only between price and quality perceptions, but also between price and store perceptions. When a marketing manager places a product in an upscale store, where there are many other high-priced products, consumers will conclude that the product belongs there and is also deserving of a high price. Retailers may even try to attract special lines of designer products to increase the prestige of the store and to encourage consumers to accept higher prices on other items in the store. In an attempt to appeal to the mid-market consumer, well-known designer brands Lilly Pulitzer and Isaac Mizrahi are carried at Target stores at a lower price than what is available elsewhere. These brands offer exclusive product lines that can only be found at Target stores. Such a move has the potential to backfire, however, because price perceptions can work both ways. While a top designer may reduce prices for a mid-range retailer in an attempt to capture a larger share of the market, such a move may damage the brand's perceived value. Consumers would undoubtedly wonder why they are paying such high prices for these brands in other stores when they can get them at Target for a fraction of the price.

Semiotics

Semiotics is a field of study that interprets "objective" reality in the context of subjective cultural codes (Oswald 2012); it is one more marketing topic that relies heavily on consumer perceptions. **Semiotics** is concerned with exploring the links between signs and symbols and the meanings they signify and convey. Importantly, semiotics takes into account the strong impact that our culture and context play in how we interpret the world. Thus, one way to understand marketing communications from an organization is through the signs or symbols we are exposed to, pay attention to, and interpret. These signs and symbols come from logos, graphics, a celebrity spokesperson, and even the layout of a retail store. In order to interpret the world, individuals rely on mental shortcuts, which are often triggered by signs and symbols. These shortcuts are derived from preexisting knowledge and experience, as well as important sociocultural practices and preferences. Over time, many of these meanings become deeply embedded in a culture and are difficult to change.

> **Semiotics** is concerned with exploring the links between signs and symbols and the meanings they signify and convey.

Semiotics helps us understand how meaning is taken from the overall cultural environment and becomes connected to symbols and objects. The origins of modern-day semiotics were developed by many philosophers, linguists, and theorists over the years, but one person in particular, the American philosopher Charles Sanders Peirce, was particularly influential in advancing the theory of semiotics. Peirce proposed that the process of semiotics relied on three elements: an object, a sign, and an interpretant. These elements were connected to one another in a triadic relationship (see Figure 4.8).

Think about Christmas—what images come to mind? First, we might imagine certain colors, such as red, green, and gold. We also might think about the social aspects of the holiday, such as a big meal with family and friends. Years of carefully planned marketing campaigns have successfully linked Coca-Cola with Christmas. In 1931, the Swedish American artist Haddon Sundblom painted Santa Claus for Coca-Cola's Christmas ads. The color of Santa's suit and other aspects of his appearance were no accident because marketers at Coke wanted to forge a strong connection between Coca-Cola, family values, and Christmas. Santa was portrayed as grandfatherly, his suit was red, and an icy bottle of Coke was an important part of the scene (see

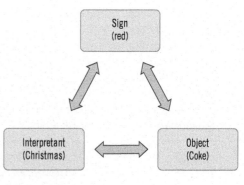

● **Figure 4.8** *The semiotics triad*

Repositioning for health and fitness

Lucozade has been a popular drink in the United Kingdom for about a hundred years. It was invented by a chemist in the industrial town of Newcastle in the 1920s and was marketed as a health drink for people with digestive problems because it contained liquid glucose (sugar) that could be easily absorbed by the body. Throughout most of the following decades it was marketed as a drink for sick people. In the mid-1980s, consumers started becoming more interested in drinks that would provide energy and stamina for people on the go. The lives of many consumers were becoming busier and they wanted an easy, healthy, refreshing, on-the-go drink. At the same time, another target market emerged with athletes who were starting to consume these drinks as a way to replenish essential vitamins and electrolytes. After a long workout or particularly grueling game, athletes needed something more effective than water. Between 2010 and 2015, the compound annual growth rate was about 16 percent in the United States for the energy drinks sector and even higher in several countries in South America. Marketers across the energy and sports drink category saw an opportunity (Datamonitor 2007).

Lucozade research revealed that energy loss and dehydration were the two biggest factors that negatively impact athletic performance. To address this need, the product development team at Lucozade created new formulas to provide hydration as well as long-term release of energy. With the introduction of the new formulas came new flavors, as well as a new promotional campaign. Lucozade's social media platforms now provide expert advice to athletes as well as links to further expert and medical opinions. The strategy also includes sports sponsorships, a general promotion of sports and exercise, and endorsement deals for some of the world's top athletes. At the same time, the drink is still promoted to busy, on-the-go consumers as a delicious, refreshing energy drink (Datamonitor 2007) (see Photos 4.13a and 4.13b).

● **Photo 4.13a** *Lucozade before repositioning*

With a target market of consumers between the ages of sixteen and twenty-four, the brand has strengthened this new position in the energy drink sector. In the United Kingdom, consumers perceive it to be positioned close to the global powerhouse brands Red Bull and Powerade. The brand has also introduced several low-calorie options and sports waters. To support its positioning, sports and entertainment superstars are used in its advertising. In addition, it recently launched a new "made to move" campaign in the United Kingdom designed to entice one million people to become more active and fit (Roderick 2017). From a perceptual perspective, the marketing

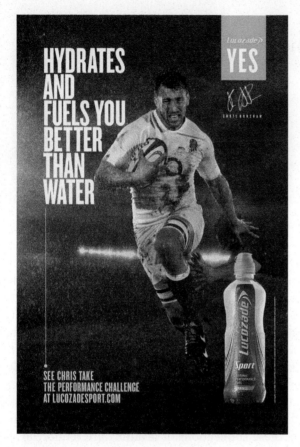

HYDRATES AND FUELS YOU BETTER THAN WATER

YES

SEE CHRIS TAKE
THE PERFORMANCE CHALLENGE
AT LUCOZADESPORT.COM

● **Photo 4.13b** *Lucozade after repositioning*

managers at Lucozade successfully shifted perceptions of the drink from one that is used for medical reasons to one that revives energy and enhances athletic performance.

Questions

1. What other brands have attempted to reposition themselves? Why do you think they may have engaged in repositioning? How were the brands repositioned? To what extent do you think the efforts were successful?
2. Construct a two-dimensional perceptual map for the energy drink market. If you were developing a brand for this market, how might you position it against existing brands in the market? Explain.

Sources: Smith (1992); Roderick (2017).

Photo 4.14). The color red is not just the color of Coca-Cola, it is also the color of Christmas. For many Americans today, Coca-Cola represents tradition and American values (Oswald 2012). To understand how these connections were forged in this decades-long effort, we can break down the symbolic connections using semiotics.

A sign is a symbol that is available for interpretation, such as a word, a color, a smell, or a flavor. The sign stands alone until it is connected to a meaning. When it is connected, a *sign* always stands for something in the minds of an individual. It is important to recognize that this meaning will change, depending on context or culture. Once this meaning is established, a link to the interpretant is made. Red is just a color, but it may symbolize different things for different people, such as danger, stop, hot temperature, or Christmas. Red is

● **Photo 4.14** *Coca-Cola Christmas advertising*

a sign in someone's mind, and the understanding of this sign is the interpretant of the sign. Thus, the *interpretant* is the meaning developed in someone's mind (Christmas). Finally, the *object* is Coke. Over time, these meanings are transformed into a shared language and understanding throughout the rest of the social group (Mick 1986). Smart marketers know which signs and interpretants are important for different cultures. That's where Coca-Cola and the work of its marketing team come into play. Marketing managers at Coca-Cola skillfully connected their product to this semiotic structure by creating ads with the red-suited Santa Claus drinking a Coke. As you can see in Figure 4.8, meaning moves back and forth between the sign, the object, and the interpretant, so that over time, these connections of meaning are reinforced and strengthened. In this example, red = Christmas = Coke is a strong culturally specific meaning. The symbolic function of a product depends on context and culture. When the diamond company De Beers first entered China in 1994, consumers did not associate diamonds with love and romance. In fact, the Chinese concept of marriage is more closely related to the concept of persistence and commitment than it is to love and romance. To address this new cultural context, De Beers positioned the diamond ring to Chinese men as a symbol of their reliability, rather than of their romantic love. De Beers engaged in a successful repositioning campaign based on this culturally relevant symbolism of persistence and commitment. A diamond ring associated with these values was needed to grow this market (Oswald 2012). Diamonds have quite another cultural meaning for some consumers in Western countries, where there are deep concerns about *blood diamonds,* or diamonds that are mined or processed in areas of the world where there is civil war, ethnic strife, and human rights abuses. Even though the world became aware of these issues at the start of the twenty-first century and safety measures have been put in place, there are still parts of Africa, such as the Central African Republic and Zimbabwe, where violence is very prevalent (Wojcik 2017). Because of this, many Westerners are becoming increasingly concerned about buying ethically

INSIGHTS FROM ACADEMIA 4.5

Would you ever sell your grandma's wedding ring?

Probably not—it is something that you will probably save and keep in a very special place. This study relied on experiential research methods such as interviews and in-depth interpretations of visual sources and media documents. The researchers found that heirlooms are not just filled with important meanings of family identity and stability; they are also objects that represent our evolving personal identities and life changes. Many people take heirlooms and infuse them with their own personal meanings. For example, an old copper cooking pot can become a new place for a plant or a special ring can be put on a chain and worn around your neck. Objects like these represent an important connection to your own past, and when you interact with these objects and make them your own, they also represent an important aspect of your present-day self.

Ture, M., and G. Ger. 2016. "Continuity through Change: Navigating Temporalities through Heirloom Rejuvenation." Journal of Consumer Research *43 (1): 1–25.*

sourced diamonds. As you can see, the same product can have vastly different culturally defined symbolic meanings, and those meanings can change over time, as further illustrated in Insights from Academia 4.5.

Understanding the consumer perceptual process is a very important first step to being able to apply that understanding to marketing. Marketing decision-makers can take what they know about the perceptual process and apply it to how consumers perceive risk and how consumer perceptions about products can be mapped. Oftentimes, marketers will find that efforts need to be taken to reposition a product in the minds of consumers. Consumer price perceptions are also an important consideration for marketers, especially with respect to the connection between price and value. Finally, the perceptual process helps managers better understand the process of semiotics, or how consumers derive culturally specific meaning from an object (such as a product) and a sign (such as a color or music). In all, our goal is to help marketing decision-makers reach out to and connect with consumers in a way that is relevant and meaningful.

◉ Summary

This chapter started with an in-depth exploration of the *perceptual process* and examined the stages of the process. We explained how important each of the five senses were to picking up information from the environment and then making it available for the attention phase of the perceptual process. We discussed the importance of *exposure* to the perceptual process, as well as how it is used by marketers. We also discussed selective exposure as a strategy for consumers to limit the sheer volume of messages they experience and we debunked the idea that subliminal exposure exerts a strong influence on consumer behavior.

In our discussion of the five *sensory receptors,* we examined the impact of each one on the perceptual process. In Insights from the Field 4.1, we examined ways in which the senses could play a role in helping consumers identify a favorite coffee shop. Insights from the Boardroom 4 provided us with an in-depth look at how researchers at Campbell's utilize a variety of sensory research techniques to create the perfect bowl of soup.

When discussing the *attention* step of the perceptual process, we learned about the fully integrated marketing campaign for Old Spice and how one important insight about targeting women was crucial for the brand's successful reboot of its social media campaign (Insights from the Field 4.3). The *interpretation* step of the perceptual process was examined next, and some basic principles of *Gestalt psychology* were described and illustrated.

In the second half of the chapter, we described some marketing-related implications and techniques that are derived from the lessons of perception. We carefully examined the concept of *perceived risk* and discussed the example of how the campaign by Nutcase biking helmets encouraged individuals to refocus their attention on the very real risk of not wearing a helmet. We discussed the importance of **perceptual** (*positioning*) **mapping** by discussing how to create a map and how marketers derive important insights from them. Brand management sometimes involves *repositioning* of a brand, and we examined the successful repositioning efforts of Lucozade in Insights from the Field 4.4, where brand perceptions were shifted from a drink that is used for medical reasons to one that revives energy and enhances athletic performance. In the final two sections of the chapter, we examined price perception and *semiotics*, the process by which important, culturally defined symbolic meanings are interpreted and transferred between an object, interpretant, and sign. As illustrated in the case of sneakerheads at the end of the chapter, marketers use insights from the perceptual process to help us forge a deeper understanding of consumer behavior and predict how consumers might react to a variety of marketing stimuli.

KEY TERMS

REVIEW QUESTIONS

1. For each of the five senses, discuss how a consumer who is exposed to a marketing stimulus might proceed through the perceptual process from sensory receptors to response.
2. Describe the criteria that are necessary for successful exposure, attention, and interpretation.
3. What is the difference between exposure, selective exposure, and subliminal exposure? Why are experts not worried about the effects of subliminal exposure?
4. In what way has Gestalt psychology influenced marketing and advertising?
5. The chapter identified five ways in which the perceptual process model has influenced marketing. Describe each of them.

DISCUSSION QUESTIONS

1. What are your school colors? What are the colors of your school's biggest rival? Describe what these colors communicate about the "brand" for each school. How else does your school use these colors? Are these the most effective colors to use to help people proceed through the perceptual process? Explain.
2. Select a print ad from Benetton's "Unhate" campaign and think about the perceptual process. What response were managers at Benetton trying to elicit from consumers who were exposed to this image? In what ways might the use of shock to gain attention be a good idea? In what ways might it be a bad idea?
3. For each type of perceptual risk, identify an example of a communications tactic (such as a tag line, logo, image, or celebrity endorser) that might help and another example that might hinder efforts by marketing managers to reach out to and connect with consumers in a way that is relevant and meaningful. Explain each of your examples.
4. Draw your own perceptual (or positioning) map for at least five brands of sneakers, making sure to identify the horizontal and vertical axes. What are some similarities and differences between the brands? Describe at least two insights that a marketer could create from your map.
5. Identify each of the three elements that might exist in a semiotic triad for each of the following signs: *blue*, *Italian*, and *silk*. Be creative! For each of the three triads that are created, be sure to provide an example of a product where this triad would be relevant and briefly discuss each connection you propose.

For more information, quizzes, case studies, and other study tools, please visit us at **www.oup.com/he/phillips**.

CASE STUDY 4

Challenge to all sneakerheads: get the next limited-edition Air Jordans and avoid the fakes

Would you take $1,200 for those sneakers, sir? The global mania around high-end sneakers is a fascinating example of the perceptual process and brand symbolism. Counterfeit and authentic brands both convey meanings to important social groups. Luckily, sneakerheads are very good at identifying the counterfeits.

The market for high-end fashion brands is massive and seems to be almost immune to economic downturns. Globally, the market for high-end personal luxury goods in 2018 was $287 billion, up 6 percent from the previous year. This number is expected to grow to between $353 and $403 billion by the year 2025. Shoes have the highest year-over-year growth rate, at 7 percent. More than ever before, consumers of these luxury products are young, diverse, and shop online (D'Arpizio et al. 2019).

High-end and limited-edition sneakers are a fascinating segment of this market. A group of people referred to as sneakerheads are at the center of much of the mania surrounding these products. Sneakerheads are "unabashed fanatics" of limited-edition and rare sneakers. They will wait in line for hours when a new shoe is being premiered or "dropped" for the first time; they will strike up friendships with owners of sporting goods stores; they will hunt for shoes in secondhand stores or their parents' garage; and they will even scour the basements of mom-and-pop shoe stores in some of the most remote corners of the country in an attempt to find a hidden gem under the dust (Wasserman 2009). Once they get their hands on the shoes, they will sell and trade them online or at events such as Sneaker Con. Sneakerheads collect and trade sneakers as a hobby and some even make a lot of money at it. These people are passionate and knowledgeable about the topic.

The trend of collecting and trading sneakers can be traced back to the 1970s when New York City street ballers were given free shoes by the top brands. These sneakers stretched the conceptions of style with eye-catching and sometimes outlandish styling, colors, and stitching. Brands started to sign exclusive agreements with star players as well as up-and-coming players and began designing exclusive sneakers just for them. The effect was that everyone wanted to have the shoes that their favorite players wore. By the 1990s, the Internet allowed collectors to more easily buy and trade sneakers with other passionate collectors. Superfans could find almost any size and style they were seeking, as long as they were willing to pay the price. Soon, big brands like Nike started to collaborate with celebrities, musicians, and artists to create limited-edition sneakers. These collaborations created sneakers that were especially desirable among the collecting community (Powell 2014).

To limit the quantity of shoes available, some manufacturers severely restrict the number of shoes produced; a run of only one hundred shoes is not uncommon. These manufacturers lose money on the sneakers because of setup costs and the high cost of special material for the shoes. However, limited-edition runs are an important part of the brand-building strategy because of the buzz and excitement generated by sneakerheads. The brand's mystique, and therefore its desirability, is strengthened. These limited-production runs increase desire for the products so much that prices often skyrocket to several thousand dollars per pair. Many sneakerheads attend conventions like Sneaker Con, a traveling convention for sneaker fanatics, to buy, sell, and trade their beloved brands. In 2017, the New York Sneaker Con hosted five hundred vendors and nineteen thousand sneaker fans (Nikas 2018). Similar conventions are held throughout the year all around the world (see Photo 4.15).

Who are these people? According to one study by a Chicago ad agency, most are men who are a "little nerdy" and a bit antisocial. They are also likely to be fans of the game Dungeons & Dragons (Wasserman 2009). The most dedicated sneakerheads can collect thousands of pairs of sneakers and often keep them in climate-controlled rooms. Many have massive social media followings and some sneakerheads will even pay up to $30,000 for the right pair. Nike Air Mags, the

● **Photo 4.15** *The Spizike sneaker by Nike was designed by Michael Jordan and Spike Lee*

shoes from "Back to the Future" that automatically snap shut, can go for $60,000 on eBay. To these most dedicated fans, the shoes are an investment (Nikas 2018). One thing sneakerheads know a lot about is how to spot a fake, and Yeezys by Adidas are one of the most frequently counterfeited sneaker brands. Sneakerheads recommend buying from a reputable dealer, whose reputation can easily be damaged if they sell a fake. It is also important to check the quality of the stitching, the size label on the inside of the shoe, and the box, which must have the correct labels and stickers (Nikas 2018). Close scrutiny will reveal several differences, mainly in terms of the quality of material used and attention to detail in production.

We know from this chapter that consumer perception is critical in identifying and deriving meaning from brands. For many consumers who cannot afford the high prices of authentic brands, counterfeit brands are an attractive option. Why do consumers purchase fake or counterfeit products? It is not just about the money. Researchers have found several varying motivations that influence a consumer's purchase of a counterfeit product (Agarwal and Panwar 2016):

- *Status consciousness*: Consumers who are motivated by status consciousness believe that authentic brands offer high status and will always seek to purchase them, rather than counterfeit products. To these consumers, counterfeit products are "a total no" and they would not risk their reputation by buying them.

- *Value consciousness*: These consumers generally feel that authentic brands are priced too high, so counterfeits are a good substitute. However, these consumers also believe that the counterfeits should have at least a minimal level of quality, otherwise the purchase would be a "total waste."

- *Uniqueness and novelty seeking*: Consumers motivated by uniqueness and novelty believe that counterfeits damage the exclusivity of authentic brands, making them seem ordinary and even "too common." These consumers seek brands that do not have counterfeits in circulation because

they want to be the ones seen wearing these unique and novel brands.

- *Susceptibility to interpersonal pressures*: Two different forces are at work on the consumer here. The first is that, depending on whether or not a consumer's social group approves of counterfeit products, consumers will either feel quite comfortable or not at all comfortable with consuming counterfeits. The second is how willing the consumer is to go along with the pressures exerted by the social group. Thus, a consumer's awareness of the pressure and willingness to comply with that pressure influence the extent to which a consumer will purchase a counterfeit.

Sneakerheads are a fascinating group of consumers who are incredibly passionate and knowledgeable. They use this knowledge to help build their collections, engage with other consumers, share their expertise, and make money. The case of sneakerheads illustrates the connection between the perceptual process model and the marketing implications of that model.

QUESTIONS

1. Imagine that you are attending a Sneaker Con for the first time. Describe what might happen to you as you proceed through each step of the perceptual process.

2. Check out this video of a visit by a news crew to the fake sneaker capital of China (https://www.youtube.com/watch?v=KxAW3t423rg). Do marketers sometimes encourage counterfeits by only making a limited number of sneakers? What could a marketer do to discourage counterfeits?

3. As discussed in this chapter, there are several types of perceived risk. Provide a description of the types of perceived risk associated with (a) authentic high-end brands and (b) counterfeit brands.

4. Sketch out a semiotic triad for counterfeit sneakers, making sure to label each part. Describe each part of the triad.

Sources: Agarwal and Panwar (2016); D'Arpizio et al. (2019); Nikas (2018); Powell (2014); Wasserman (2009).

REFERENCES

Advertising Standards Association. 2017. Accessed November 5, 2017. https://www.asa.org.uk/About-ASA/Our-history.aspx.

Agarwal, S., and S. Panwar. 2016. "Consumer Orientation towards Counterfeit Fashion Products: A Qualitative Analysis." *IUP Journal of Brand Management* 13 (3): 55–74.

Allen, E. 2012. "Supermarket 'Shrink Ray': How Shoppers Are Paying the Same for Ever Smaller Products." *Daily Mail*, April 19, 2012. http://www.dailymail.co.uk/news/article-2131927/Our-shrinking-foods-How-manufacturers-making-everyday-products-smaller-keeping-prices-same.html.

Ares, L. P. 2018. "When Less is More: How Tech Companies are Thriving by Getting us Off Our Devices." *Accenture. Technology and Innovation Blog*. August 14. Accessed September 8, 2020. https://www.accenture.com/us-en/blogs/technology-innovation/lara-ares-customer-centric-tech-innovation.

Arnal, L. H., A. Flinker, A. Kleinschmidt, A. Giraud, and D. Poeppel. 2015. "Human Screams Occupy a Privileged Niche in the Communication Soundscape." *Current Biology* 25 (15): 2051–56.

Aslam, M. M. 2006. "Are You Selling the Right Color? A Cross-Cultural Review of Color as a Marketing Cue." *Journal of Marketing Communications* 12 (1): 15–30.

Babin, B. J., D. M. Hardesty, and T. A Suter. 2003. "Color and Shopping Intentions: The Intervening Effect of Price Fairness and Perceived Effect." *Journal of Business Research* 56 (7): 541–51.

Bauer, R. A. 1960. "Consumer Behavior as Risk Taking." In *Dynamic Marketing for a Changing World*, edited by R. S. Hancock, 389–98. Chicago: American Marketing Association.

Bellizzi, J. A., A. E. Crowley, and R. E. Hasty. 1983. "The Effects of Color in Store Design." *Journal of Retailing* 59 (1): 21–44.

Berns, G. S., J. D. Cohen, and M. A. Mintun. 1997. "Brain Regions Responsive to Novelty in the Absence of Awareness." *Science* 276: 1272–75.

Bertrand, M., S. Mullainathan, and E. Shafir. 2006. "Behavioral Economics and Marketing in Aid of Decision Making among the Poor." *Journal of Public Policy & Marketing* 25 (1): 8–23.

Chernev, A. 2001. "The Impact of Common Features on Consumer Preferences: A Case of Confirmatory Reasoning." *Journal of Consumer Research* 27 (4): 475–88.

Dahl, D. W., K. D. Frankenberger, and R. V. Manchanda. 2003. "Does It Pay to Shock? Reactions to Shocking and Nonshocking Advertising Content among University Students." *Journal of Advertising Research* 43 (3): 268–80.

D'Arpizio, C., F. Levato, F. Prete, E. Del Fabbro, and J. de Montgolfier. 2019. "The Future of Luxury: A Look into Tomorrow to Understand Today." Bain & Company. January 10, 2019. https://www.bain.com/insights/luxury-goods-worldwide-market-study-fall-winter-2018/.

Datamonitor. 2007. "Lucozade & Red Bull Case Study: Repositioning Energy Drinks to Meet Consumers' Needs." Datamonitor. Reference Code: CSCM0146. November. 1-6.

Eroglu, S. A., K. A. Machleit, and L. M. Davis. 2003. "Empirical Testing of a Model of Online Store Atmospherics and Shopper Responses." *Psychology & Marketing* 20 (2): 139–50.

Faure-Field, S. 2013. "Why Customer 'Sensation' Is Important in Asian Retail and Premium Banking (Part 2)." Asian Banking and Finance. September 11, 2013. http://asianbankingandfinance.net/retail-banking/commentary/why-customer-sensation-important-in-asian-retail-and-premium-banking-part-0.

Fedorikhin, A., and C. A. Cole. 2004. "Mood Effects on Attitudes, Perceived Risk and Choice: Moderators and Mediators." *Journal of Consumer Psychology* 14 (1/2): 2–12.

Fernandez, J. 2011. "How the Old Spice Hunk Took over the World." Marketing Week. September 14, 2011. https://www.marketingweek.com/how-the-old-spice-hunk-took-over-the-world/.

Gearhardt, A. N., C. Davis, R. Kuschner, and K. D. Brownell. 2011. "The Addiction Potential of Hyperpalatable Foods." *Current Drug Abuse Reviews* 4:140–45.

Gerrard, B. 2017. "Costa Coffee Boss Wants Chain to Be 'Famous for Innovating' and Insists Hangups about Machine Coffee Are No Longer Justified." *The Telegraph*, August 19, 2017. http://www.telegraph.co.uk/business/2017/08/19/costa-coffee-boss-wants-chain-famous-innovating-insists-hang.

Greenwood, V. 2018. "The Food You Buy Really Is Shrinking: What Makes Downsizing So Hard to Swallow?" BBC Worklife. May 13, 2018. https://www.bbc.com/worklife/article/20180510-the-food-you-buy-really-is-shrinking.

Jacewicz, N. 2017. "Why Taste Buds Dull as We Age." *National Public Radio*. May 5, 2017. http://www.npr.org/sections/thesalt/2017/05/05/526750174/why-taste-buds-dull-as-we-age.

Kim, D. J., W. G. Kim, and J. S. Han. 2007. "A Perceptual Mapping of Online Travel Agencies and Preference Attributes." *Tourism Management* 28:591–603.

Klaassen, A. 2014. "British Airways 'Magic' Billboards Win Direct Grand Prix at Cannes." *AdAge*. June 16, 2014. https://adage.com/article/special-report-cannes-lions/british-airways-magic-billboards-win-direct-grand-prix/293730.

Krishna, A., M. O. Lwin, and M. Morrin. 2010. "Product Scent and Memory." *Journal of Consumer Research* 37 (1): 57–67.

Labrecque, L. I., and G. R. Milne. 2012. "Exciting Red and Competent Blue: The Importance of Color in Marketing." *Journal of the Academy of Marketing Science* 40 (5): 711–27.

Lenfant, F., C. Hartmann, B. Watzke, O. Breton, C. Loret, and N. Martin. 2013. "Impact of the Shape on Sensory Properties of Individual Dark Chocolate Pieces." *LWT-Food Science and Technology* 51 (2): 545–52.

Lessard-Bonaventure, S., and J. Chebat. 2015. "Psychological Ownership, Touch and Willingness to Pay for an Extended Warranty." *Journal of Marketing Theory and Practice* 23 (2): 224–34.

Levine, M. W. 2000. *Levine and Shefner's Fundamentals of Sensation and Perception*. 3rd ed. Oxford: Oxford University Press.

Lindstrom, M. 2010. *Buyology: Truth and Lies about Why We Buy*. New York: Random House.

Mann, G., F. Venturini, R. Murdoch, B. Mishra, G. Moorby, and B. Carlier. 2015. *Digital Video and the Connected Consumer*. Ann Arbor, MI: Accenture.

Mick, D. G. 1986. "Consumer Research and Semiotics: Exploring the Morphology of Signs, Symbols, and Significance." *Journal of Consumer Research* 13 (2): 196–213.

Milliman, R. E. 1982. "Using Background Music to Affect the Behavior of Supermarket Shoppers." *Journal of Marketing* 46 (3): 86–91.

Milotic, D. 2006. "The Impact of Fragrance on Consumer Choice." *Journal of Consumer Behavior* 3 (2): 179–91.

Montague, R. 2006. *Why Choose This Book? How We Make Decisions*. New York: Dutton.

MSNBC. 2017. "Dollars & Scents: The Sweet Smell of Success." MSNBC, Open Forum, Your Business TV. July 16, 2017. https://www.youtube.com/watch?v=OfzIFJtnPUk.

Nestrud, M. A., and H. T. Lawless. 2008. "Perceptual Mapping of Citrus Juices Using Projective Mapping and Profiling Data from Culinary Professionals and Consumers." *Food and Quality Preference* 19:431–38.

Nikas, J. 2018. "Tips from Sneaker Heads on Scoring the Hottest Shoes and Keeping Them Fresh." *New York Times*, January 2, 2018. https://www.nytimes.com/2018/01/02/style/sneakercon-shoe-care-tips-shopping.html.

Nobel, C. 2013. "Advertising Symbiosis: The Key to Viral Videos." Harvard Business School Working Knowledge. June 17, 2013. http://hbswk.hbs.edu/item/7267.html.

North, A. C., L. P. Sheridan, and C. S. Areni. 2016. "Music Congruity Effects on Product Memory, Perception, and Choice." *Journal of Retailing* 92 (1): 83–95.

Northrup, L. 2017. "United Kingdom Discovers 2,529 Products Hit by Grocery Shrink Ray, Calls It 'Shrinkflation.'" Consumerist. July 28, 2017. https://consumerist.com/2017/07/28/united-kingdom-discovers-2529-products-hit-by-grocery-shrink-ray-calls-it-shrinkflation/.

Nudd, T. 2012. "Press Grand Prix Goes to Benetton's Kissing Ads from Fabrica, 72andSunny." *Adweek*, June 20, 2012. http://www.adweek.com/brand-marketing/press-grand-prix-goes-benettons-kissing-ads-fabrica-72andsunny-141244/.

Nudd, T. 2013. "Kraft Salad Dressing Ad Gets Best Present Ever: A Slap from One Million Moms." *Adweek*, June 17, 2013. http://www.adweek.com/creativity/kraft-salad-dressing-ad-gets-best-present-ever-slap-one-million-moms-150412/.

Orth, U. R., T. Bouzdine-Chameeva, and K. Brand. 2015. "Trust during Retail Encounters: A Touchy Proposition." *Journal of Retailing* 89 (3): 301–14.

Oswald, L. R. 2012. *Marketing Semiotics: Signs, Strategies, and Brand Value*. Oxford: Oxford University Press.

PageFair. 2015. "The Cost of Ad Blocking." PageFair and Adobe 2015 Ad Blocking Report. Accessed October 13, 2017. https://pagefair.com/blog/2015/ad-blocking-report/.

Paoletti, J. B. 2012. *Pink and Blue: Telling the Boys from the Girls in America*. Bloomington: Indiana University Press.

Parisi, P. 2017. "Samuel L. Jackson Shows He Can Sing Like a 'Motherf—er' in New Capital One Ad." *Billboard*, August 18, 2017. http://www.billboard.com/articles/news/7934125/samuel-l-jackson-shows-singing-capital-one-hitmans-bodyguard.

Peck, J., and T. Childers. 2003. "To Have and To Hold: The Influence of Haptic Information on Product Judgements." *Journal of Marketing* 67 (2): 35–48.

Petruzzellis, L., J. Chebat, and A. Palumbo. 2014. "'Hey Dee-Jay Let's Play That Song and Keep Me Shopping All Day Long': The Effect of Famous Background Music on Consumer Shopping Behavior." *Journal of Marketing Development and Competitiveness* 8 (2): 38–49.

Pieters, R., and M. Wedel. 2007. "Goal Control of Attention to Advertising: The Yarbus Implication." *Journal of Consumer Research* 34 (2): 224–33.

Ping, A. 2017. Personal interview, September 5, 2017.

Powell, M. 2014. "Sneakernomics: Are Sneakerheads Important?" *Forbes*, May 21, 2014. https://www.forbes.com/sites/mattpowell/2014/05/21/sneakernomics-are-sneakerheads-important/#45cf9c743694.

Pursey, K. M., P. Stanwell, A. N. Gearhardt, C. E. Collins, and T. L. Burrows. 2014. "The Prevalence of Food Addiction as Assessed by the Yale Food Addiction Scale: A Systematic Review." *Nutrients* 6 (10): 4552–90.

Roderick, L. 2017. "Lucozade Sets Up In-House Agency to Make Its Marketing Work Harder." *Marketing Week*, August 25, 2017. https://www.marketingweek.com/2017/08/25/lucozade-brings-creative-inhouse/.

Schomaker, J., and M. Meeter. 2015. "Short and Long-Lasting Consequences of Novelty, Deviance, and Surprise on Brain and Cognition." *Neuroscience and Behavioral Reviews* 55:268–79.

Statista. 2020. "Average Number of Devices Residents Have Access to In Households Worldwide in 2020, by Country." Statista. Accessed September 8, 2020. https://www.statista.com/statistics/1107307/average-number-connected-devices-households-worldwide/

Stinson, L. 2014. "With Stunning New Stores, Starbucks Has a New Design Strategy: Act Local." *Wired*, January 8, 2014. https://www.wired.com/2014/01/starbucks-big-plan-to-be-your-cozy-neighborhood-coffee-shop/.

Szmigin, I., M. Carrigan, and M. McEachern. 2009. "The Conscious Consumer: Taking a Flexible Approach to Ethical Behavior." *International Journal of Consumer Studies* 33:224–31.

Tepfer, B. 2016. "Is the Gaming Industry the Next Big Marketing Channel?" *Adweek*, September 26, 2016. http://www.adweek.com/digital/ben-tepfer-adobe-campaign-guest-post-gaming-marketing/.

Underhill, P. 2009. *Why We Buy*. New York: Simon & Schuster.

Usunier, J.-C., and P. Valette-Florence. 2007. "The Time Styles Scale: A Review of Developments and Replications over 15 Years." *Time and Society* 16 (2/3): 333–66.

Wasowicz, G., and M. Stysko-Kunkowska. 2015. "The Meaning of Colors in Nutrition Labeling in the Context of Expert and Consumer Criteria of Evaluating Food Product Healthfulness." *Journal of Health Psychology* 20 (6): 907–20.

Wasserman, T. 2009. "Sneakerheads Rule." *Adweek* 50 (37): 10–14.

Wojcik, N. 2017. "Conflict Diamonds May Not Be on the Radar, but They're Still a Worry for Some." CNBC. Last updated January 13, 2017. https://www.cnbc.com/2016/11/04/conflict-diamonds-may-not-be-on-the-radar-but-theyre-still-a-worry-for-some.html.

Wu, F., A. Samper, A. C. Morales, and G. J. Fitzsimons. 2017. "It's Too Pretty to Use! When and How Enhanced Product Aesthetics Discourage Usage and Lower Consumption Enjoyment." *Journal of Consumer Research* 44 (3): 651–72.

Zajonc, R. B. 2001. "Mere Exposure: A Gateway to the Subliminal." *Current Directions in Psychological Science* 10 (6): 224–28.

Zimmerman, I. 2014. "Subliminal Ads, Unconscious Influence, and Consumption." *Psychology Today*, June 9, 2014. https://www.psychologytoday.com/blog/sold/201406/subliminal-ads-unconscious-influence-and-consumption.

5 Learning and Memory

◉ Introduction

When Amazon introduced the Alexa home assistant device, the company engaged in considerable effort helping consumers learn how to use it, with videos, apps, blogs, and guides. In-store and online ads showed close-ups of the device and highlighted its functionality. At the time, the Alexa represented a completely new product category and if Amazon wanted to achieve mass-market penetration, it needed to help consumers easily sync the device with their other smart home devices. Amazon also needed to help consumers develop the knowledge and capabilities to get Alexa to engage with other frequently used devices such as fitness trackers and phones. This chapter is focused on the various processes involved in learning and memory. Learning can sometimes be quite easy, as when someone learns which fork to use at a fancy dinner; it can also be quite difficult, as when someone is trying to master a new language.

Marketing managers rely on consumers remembering basic information about their brands, such as brand names, product attributes, what prices are reasonable or expected, and any previous experiences with the brand. Consumers might also remember information about advertising, a celebrity spokesperson, or other communications. For consumers to use information from memory, consumers must have first learned something about the brand and then successfully stored that information in memory. In short, to effectively deliver the value proposition, marketers need to know how consumers learn, how they store information in memory, and how they recall information that is stored in memory. The processes of learning and memory are critical to understanding most other topics that are frequently discussed in the field of consumer behavior. In fact, a marketer would be hard-pressed to identify a topic in consumer behavior that is *not* strongly linked to learning and memory.

◉ Learning

In psychology, **learning** is the relatively permanent change in behavior that occurs as a result of studying, practicing, or experiencing something. Individuals demonstrate that they have successfully

LEARNING OBJECTIVES

Having read this chapter, you will be able to:

1. Describe the benefits and drawbacks of *behavioral learning and cognitive learning*.

2. Explain the differences and similarities between *classical and operant conditioning*.

3. Discuss how marketers have utilized insights from each of the three types of cognitive learning to better meet the needs of consumers.

4. Sketch the five-step *information processing model*, explain what occurs at each step, and describe the role that memory plays throughout the process.

5. Describe what happens to a stimulus and the data it contains as it proceeds through *sensory memory, short-term memory, and long-term memory*.

Learning is the relatively permanent change in behavior that occurs as a result of studying, practicing, or experiencing something.

learned something when their behavior changes. Thus, we will know you have learned French if you can speak French; we will know you have learned how to ride a unicycle if you ride your new unicycle around the block. In marketing, learning often results in changes to attitudes, beliefs, or behavior. Marketers will know if consumers have learned something about the brand if their perceptions have shifted, their attitudes have changed, they believe something different about the brand, or their brand-related behaviors have changed. Harkening back to our Alexa example, a new brand-related behavior could be successfully using Alexa to lock the doors or check the video feed at the front door. The two most commonly researched categories of learning are behavioral learning and cognitive learning (see Figure 5.1).

Behavioral learning is concerned with changes in behavior that occur as a result of changes in the environment. This model of learning rejects the notion that internal mental processes such as thoughts and feelings are important. According to the behavioral learning approach, learning happens without any complex thoughts or processes from the consumer. A behavioral view of learning proposes that a consumer's previous experiences with a stimulus will result in automatic responses the next time the consumer encounters that stimulus. Thus, consumers who have had a nice, delicious cup of coffee from Starbucks in the past will go inside for another cup when they see a Starbucks again. The decision is automatic. This model of learning dates back to the 1950s and certainly has some limitations, but marketers and advertisers in the early twenty-first century still utilize some of its principles.

In contrast to behavioral learning, **cognitive learning** occurs as a result of internal mental processes and conscious thought. Cognitive learning theories propose that learning is a process of mental activity and deliberation. One form of cognitive learning, information processing, relies entirely on mental

Behavioral learning is concerned with changes in behavior that occur as a result of changes in the environment.

Cognitive learning occurs as a result of internal mental processes and conscious thought.

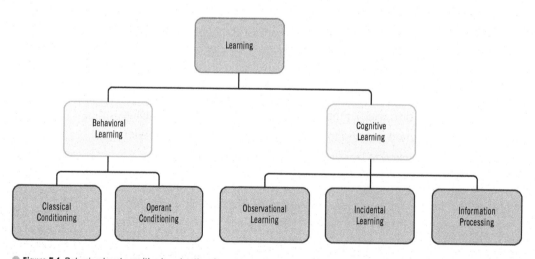

Figure 5.1 *Behavioral and cognitive learning theories*
Source: Szmigin & Piacentini (2015)

INSIGHTS FROM ACADEMIA 5.1

Too much information—I quit!

A huge benefit to online shopping is the ability to offer a wide variety of options to consumers. However, online retailers sometimes have such a wide assortment of products that a consumer has trouble processing the information, gets frustrated, and delays the purchase. What do researchers suggest marketers do to help consumers accurately perceive and store information in memory? First, the online assortment must be organized and easy to navigate. Second, graphics like thumbnails help consumers make navigation less complex (words are less effective). Finally, filtering and categorization tools (such as enabling a search for products that are less than $100) help consumers navigate large assortments. In the end, the goal is to have consumers effectively process information in a complex online environment. How easy is it to navigate *your* favorite online store?

Kahn, B. 2017. "Using Visual Design to Improve Customer Perceptions of Online Assortments." Journal of Retailing *93 (1): 29–42.*

processes and conscious thought. A consumer contemplating the purchase of a new car might engage in a process of carefully examining ads, checking consumer reviews, talking with people, and weighing the car's attributes before selecting the best option. This type of cognitive learning—information processing—represents what might happen during a high-involvement decision and will be discussed more thoroughly in Chapter 8. With cognitive learning, consumers typically need to search for and evaluate information from their memories of previous experiences (internal information) as well as from new information in the external environment (external information). Navigating through the volume of external information can sometimes be quite difficult, as we see in Insights from Academia 5.1.

Behavioral Learning

There are two types of behavioral learning, classical conditioning and operant conditioning. Both are based on the premise that, when making a decision, consumers do not engage in thoughtful, deliberate consideration of information.

Classical conditioning

First, we will examine classical conditioning and examine the concepts of first-order conditioning and higher-order conditioning, as well as stimulus generalization and discrimination. **Classical conditioning** is a theory of behavioral learning that occurs when an individual learns a connection between two stimuli that are paired with one another. This theory was originally developed

> **Classical conditioning** is a theory of behavioral learning that occurs when an individual learns a connection between two stimuli that are paired with one another.

by Ivan Pavlov, a Russian physiologist who was conducting research on the digestive processes of dogs. It seems odd that a physiologist ended up developing one of the most famous psychological theories, but that is exactly what happened when Pavlov identified a fundamental principle that is now referred to as classical conditioning. Pavlov noticed that when his assistant entered the dogs' room, the dogs began to salivate because they had formed a connection in their minds between the assistant and feeding time. Salivation is a reflexive reaction and is not able to be controlled by the dog (or by humans, for that matter). Imagine coming back to your apartment after a long day of work and school and smelling the dinner your roommate is making; your stomach starts to rumble and you start to salivate as you smell the wonderful food that is cooking. This reaction is similar to the reaction of Pavlov's dogs. After living in the laboratory for a while, the dogs began to salivate each time the assistant entered the room, regardless of whether they got any food. This reaction could not be explained physiologically. Luckily for the field of psychology, Pavlov started to look for other explanations. He rang a bell each time food was presented and found that the dogs salivated. After ringing the bell each time food was presented for several days, he then rang the bell with no food. The dogs still salivated, suggesting that the salivation process had been conditioned by the presence of the bell. This finding led Pavlov to develop his theory of classical conditioning.

Let's take this one step at a time. First, before anything happens at all, the unconditioned stimulus (US), the food, leads to the unconditioned response (UR), salivation. Dogs see food and they salivate. At this stage of the process, before any conditioning is happening, everything is referred to as *unconditioned*. Second, while the conditioning process is happening, the researcher connects a neutral stimulus (NS), such as a bell, to the process and repeats the process several times. Here, each time he gave the dogs food (US), Pavlov also rang the bell (NS), and the dogs salivated (UR). The third and final step of the process happens when the researcher does not present any food, but instead just rings the bell and the dogs salivate. At this point, conditioning has been successful and each time the bell rings (conditioned stimulus, CS), salivation occurs (conditioned response, CR). Now that conditioning has occurred, we refer to the bell as the CS and to the response as the CR. Figure 5.2 provides an explanation of this three-step process.

First-order conditioning occurs when a conditioned stimulus acquires motivational importance by being paired with an unconditioned stimulus that is already seen as positive (like food) or negative (like pain).

First-order conditioning
The simple example with Pavlov's dogs is known as **first-order conditioning**. Before the process of learning

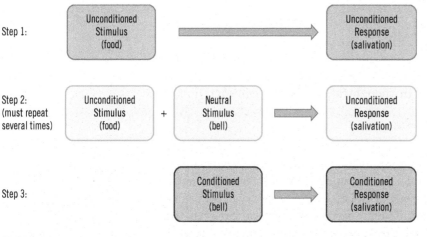

● **Figure 5.2** *Producing a conditioned response*

begins, the selection of stimuli is quite important. In Pavlov's case, an NS (bell) acquired motivational importance because it is was paired with a US that was already intrinsically motivating (food) (Gewirtz and Davis 2000). In first-order conditioning, the NS (the bell) needs to be paired directly with the US, which is often a biological stimulus (such as food, sex, or pain) that naturally elicits a physiological response. Findings from classical conditioning studies explain why sexual images are so effective in advertisements. When these images are utilized, advertisers try to connect a sexy model (US) with, for example, a sports car (NS). Sex is a basic biological instinct and the marketer is trying to make a connection by linking these two stimuli in the advertisement. Essentially, driving this expensive car will make you feel and appear sexy. Using sex appeals in advertising is certainly not new and recent research confirms that it works. In particular, when two stimuli are congruent with one another (they go together), such as grooming products (NS) and a sexy model (US), consumers are more likely to pay attention to the ad. However, if the products are incongruent, like lawn care products (NS) and a sexy model (US), there is no positive impact on attention. In terms of attitudes, men generally like the use of sex in ads more than women do (Wirtz, Sparks, and Zimbres 2017).

Over the long term, successful classical conditioning depends on reinforcing the connection between the CS (sports car) and the US (sexy model). If the US is removed from the CS, over time, the response will eventually stop. When the response stops, extinction has occurred. After a while, if Pavlov had continued to ring the bell and not produced food, the dogs would have stopped salivating because the connection between the bell and food would eventually cease to exist. This finding suggests that marketing managers need to continue to periodically connect two stimuli in ads, so that consumers can continue to connect them in their own minds. Successful classical conditioning is contingent on many factors (Bitterman 2006) and although it is still useful in understanding consumer behavior, its use in marketing and advertising is somewhat limited (Pornpitakpan 2012; Wirtz, Sparks, and Zimbres 2017).

Higher-order conditioning

We know that first-order conditioning occurs when a connection is established between the US and NS. **Higher-order conditioning** occurs when two CS are paired. Importantly, the individual already knows about and has a learned response to both stimuli. Higher-order conditioning occurs when a CS (CS1) acquires associative strength by being connected to a second CS (CS2) (rather than a US) (Gewirtz and Davis 2000). Music is a great example of the use of higher-order conditioning. In the media, the practice of connecting two CSs is called *synchronization* and reflects the appropriate pairing of song and brand (*The Economist* 2003). When the iPhone 7 (CS1) was introduced a few years ago, it was accompanied by an ad campaign featuring the song "Down" (CS2), by Marian Hill. Most consumers in the target already had positive feelings about the iPhone brand as well as the song. The connection between CS1 and CS2 was made with an ad campaign entitled "Stroll," which featured arresting images of

Higher-order conditioning occurs when two conditioned stimuli are paired.

people strolling down the street and performing impossible acrobatic feats as the music enveloped them. The message was that the new iPhone provided increased flexibility in its features in a smooth and seamless integration. For examples about how higher-order conditioning can be used with celebrities, see Insights from the Field 5.1.

Stimulus generalization

Stimulus generalization occurs when a stimulus that is similar to a conditioned stimulus elicits a similar conditioned response.

When individuals are exposed to similar stimuli, they often respond in a similar fashion. **Stimulus generalization** occurs when a stimulus that is similar to a CS elicits a similar CR. The concept of stimulus generalization explains what happens when consumers are quick to adopt a brand's product extensions. Thus, when an established brand with well-known imagery (colors, logos, design elements) stretches its product portfolio by introducing a new product to the mix, existing consumers will easily be able to recognize the imagery. Based on their previous experiences with the brand, consumers will generalize, or extend, their impressions and judgments to the new product. There is always a certain amount of risk involved when a company introduces a product extension, but the risk is reduced when consumers already have positive feelings about the parent brand that can be easily transferred to the extension. Stimulus generalization is the mechanism for this broadening of evaluations (Till and Priluck 2000), and it is more likely to happen when there is similarity between the existing products and the product extension (Broniarczyk and Alba 1994).

An example will help our understanding of this somewhat complicated process. Girl Scouts USA has engaged in several collaborative agreements over the past decade to bring the much sought-after taste of Girl Scout cookies to a variety of other products. Lip Smackers introduced a line of lip balms in 2011 and a line of lip glosses in 2012. The collection featured six of the most popular cookie flavors (Oliver 2017). From 2012 through 2014, global food giant Nestlé offered several limited-edition Nestlé Crunch bars in three flavors: Thin Mint, Peanut Butter Crème, and Caramel and Coconut (Press Release 2014). Dunkin' Donuts offered two limited-edition cookie-themed coffee flavors in 2018: Thin Mint and toasted Coconut Caramel, as well as a shortbread-flavored coffee in 2019 (C. Anderson 2019). From the perspective of both the Girl Scouts and their corporate partners, an important key to success is the clear Girl Scout–related imagery that is placed on the product. Images of the cookies, the colors, and the distinctive Girl Scouts USA logo and font are front and center on the product packaging and other marketing materials. Many Girl Scout cookie fans are familiar with these images and have strongly positive attitudes about the product's quality. The marketing teams at these partner companies know that these positive attitudes associated with the cookies are generalized to their products by the process of stimulus generalization. If Girl Scouts USA introduces any new products in the future, the phenomenon of stimulus generalization provides consumers with the confidence that the product is manufactured with high standards of taste and quality (see Photo 5.1).

● **Photo 5.1** *Girl Scouts USA and Breyers successfully utilized stimulus generalization*

INSIGHTS FROM THE FIELD 5.1

Matching celebrity endorsers to products

One insight that can be derived from classical conditioning is how to make the best use of celebrity endorsers in advertising. The match-up hypothesis uses principles of classical conditioning and finds that consumers can be conditioned to like a product when there is a strong "match" between the celebrity and the product (Till and Busler 2000; Till, Stanley, and Priluck 2008). Singer and songwriter Cardi B, for example, would be an unlikely endorser for Trek bicycles. However, the US Olympic gold medal winner for cycling, Kristin Armstrong, matches up, or is "congruent," with the product, and therefore makes her endorsement credible. Most sports brands make extensive use of celebrity endorsements, but few are as lucrative as the lifetime endorsement deal signed by Nike and LeBron James, who will reportedly receive $1 billion for his work on behalf of the brand (see Photo 5.2).

● **Photo 5.2** *The LeBron 10 Basketball Shoe*

Although there are many benefits to using classical conditioning to help consumers connect a celebrity to a brand, there can be some drawbacks. One is the possibility of a strong connection interfering with the ability to establish other connections. If a strong connection has been established between a celebrity and a brand, it may be difficult to use the same celebrity for another brand (Pornpitakpan 2012). For some celebrities, however, the UR is easily extended from one brand to another. Jennifer Aniston is a well-liked star and has endorsed the luxury brand L'Oréal, but also has endorsed a variety of upscale and mid-market brands, including Diet Coke, Smartwater, Emirates Airlines, Elizabeth Arden fragrances, and Aveeno. Thus, over time, Jennifer Aniston (CS), has established strong classical conditioning effects with a variety of other well-regarded brands (CSs) (Tschinkel 2019). Another potential drawback to using celebrities to classically condition responses is the danger in selecting a celebrity endorser who is considered edgy or who may end up getting into legal trouble. Such news of a celebrity gone bad can damage a brand,

and it is not surprising that brands quickly drop their celebrity spokesperson when scandals occur. For example, Bill Cosby made millions from his endorsement deals and from syndication of his TV sitcom, *The Cosby Show*. All those endorsements stopped, however, after allegations came to light that he sexually assaulted many women over the years (Feldman 2017).

Questions

1. Select three brands that are promoted by celebrity endorsers—pick brands from different product categories and make sure to select at least one service. For each one, discuss how well the celebrity matches up, or is congruent, with the brand.
2. Select a broad product category that has different celebrity endorsers for different brands. How does each endorser communicate something different or unique about his or her brand?
3. Aside from matching, what other qualities of the celebrity are important? Are there any celebrity–brand mismatches? Discuss.

Sources: Feldman (2017); Till and Busler (2000); Till, Stanley, and Priluck (2008); Tschinkel (2019); Pornpitakpan (2012).

Don't even try it: passing off can land a company in big trouble

Passing off is the marketing of a product in a way that enables it to be mistaken for another brand; it relies on the phenomenon of stimulus generalization. When your brand is the one that is being copied, it is time to become very concerned. Luckily, there are strong protections in US law for these companies. From a legal standpoint, when a copycat brand takes advantage of the goodwill of another brand to gain market share, profits, or customers, the company suffers financial harm and the copycat must pay for that harm. Passing off occurs because customers mistakenly associate the benefits of a well-known brand with the copycat brand that looks similar because of stimulus generalization (Warlop and Alba 2004). This is not an accident; the intention is to confuse consumers. Typically, the copycat brand uses perceptual elements from the brand it is imitating, such as color, shape, and imagery (Miceli and Pieters 2010).

● **Photo 5.3** *Verdicts in trademark cases can come with very large settlements*

A company carefully protects its **trademark**, the distinctive words, phrases, logos, and other symbols that consumers use to identify one product from another. Trademarks are legally protected. Think of Apple's distinctive logo or Nike's "Just do it" slogan. Trademark infringement happens when one company uses the trademark of another company without their permission. Trademark infringement can cost a company between $120,000 and $750,000, plus years of time and valuable human resources. It is definitely something that a company wants to avoid. Despite the potential costs, some organizations still engage in these kinds of shady strategies. Some examples of cases are as follows (TrademarkNow 2016):

- China: 3M versus 3N—the 3M company of St. Paul, Minnesota, sued a division of Huawei Advanced Materials in China for using a 3N mark to acquire customers and gain market share. Both companies were operating in a similar industry, so it was easy for customers to make the mistake, thinking they were dealing with the American 3M company. The terms of the final verdict are undisclosed, but the court ruled in favor of 3M.

- South Korea: Louis Vuitton versus Louis Vuiton Dak—executives at luxury brand Louis Vuitton were understandably shocked when a South Korean fried chicken restaurant chain decided to model their name, logo, and other imagery after the luxury brand. The fried chicken chain was ordered to pay a multi-million-dollar settlement as well as a follow-up fine of $14.5 million for noncompliance.

- United States: Lucky 13 versus Taylor Swift—when Taylor Swift started to sell fan merchandise marked "Lucky 13" and launched a Lucky 13 sweepstakes, the real owners of Lucky 13, Blue Sphere (a clothing company), had understandably had enough. Swift settled out of court for an undisclosed figure and stopped using Lucky 13.

Passing off can be "effective" for small companies who want to benefit from another company's well-earned good reputation. Unfortunately, consumers are deceived, and when these violators are brought to justice, there are sometimes severe penalties to pay.

Questions

1. Choose three separate private-label brands from a grocery store that you believe are similar to leading brands. Identify the design elements that are similar (e.g., size, shape, colors, name). What is the price difference between the private-label brands and the real brands? Are these private-label brands guilty of passing off? Why or why not? Discuss.

2. Put yourself in the shoes of a manager of a small regional company that makes organic yogurt. Defend your decision to develop a new marketing campaign that uses some design elements from the one of the biggest brands in the market. Discuss.

Sources: Miceli and Pieters (2010); Roberts (2012); Warlop and Alba (2004).

The concept of stimulus generalization can also be applied to private-label marketing. Private-label products are manufactured or packaged under the retailer's name, rather than a manufacturer's name. To compete with more well-known brands, these private-label products often use colors, fonts, and other images that are similar to those of the more well-known brands. Because the products look so similar, consumers may accidentally pick up the private-label brands. Further, because of the phenomenon of stimulus generalization, private-label brands may simply benefit from the positive evaluations that are associated with the well-known brands.

Some of the most well-known companies in the world have been involved in lawsuits to protect their brands from copycats who have tried to benefit from their brand's positive position in the marketplace (see Insights from the Field 5.2). Is it worth the effort to go to such lengths to defend your brand like this? Absolutely! First, think about all the effort a marketing team must exert to create a brand that is ideally positioned to meet the needs of its target market. Why should a copycat benefit from all that work? Second, when your customers purchase a copycat brand thinking that it is your brand, it is quite likely that the copycat will not perform as well and your own consumers could become dissatisfied with *your* brand. In addition, if customers mistakenly purchase a copycat brand and decide they *do* like it better than your brand, your brand's sales will suffer. Finally, copycat brands do indeed confuse consumers. When copycat brands are placed next to genuine brands, consumers take a longer time distinguishing between the two brands. One-third of shoppers admit that they have purchased the wrong brand because of packaging that looked too similar (Roberts 2012), indicating that the problem is fairly widespread.

Stimulus discrimination

Just as consumers learn to generalize from one stimulus to another, they also learn to discriminate between stimuli. **Stimulus discrimination** occurs when an individual can distinguish between two stimuli. For example, you can probably easily discriminate between a nice ripe apple and an apple that is a little past its peak, even though both are about the same size, shape, and color. A sommelier

Passing off is the marketing of a good in a way that enables it to be mistaken for another brand; it relies on the phenomenon of stimulus generalization.

Trademarks are the legally protected and distinctive words, phrases, logos, and other symbols that consumers use to identify one product from another.

Stimulus discrimination occurs when an individual can distinguish between two stimuli.

is a wine expert who can easily distinguish the quality of wine based on its taste, color, body, aroma, etc. If you are really serious about wine, you might consider becoming a master sommelier, a process that typically takes decades and multiple exams, demonstrating proficiency with all aspects of wine and its production. Since 1969, only 240 people across the globe have achieved the status of master sommelier (Court of Master Sommeliers 2017), indicating that it is sometimes not very easy to distinguish between stimuli!

How can consumers learn to discriminate one stimulus from another? If a CS is not connected to a US, over time, the response will decline. Going back to the original discussion of classical conditioning, learning happens when individuals respond to the intended stimulus, but not to other stimuli. An example might help. If we accidentally buy a private-label product and discover that its quality is inferior to the branded product, we are likely to notice what went wrong and switch back to the manufacturer's brand. The next time, we will be sure to carefully discriminate between the two labels. Manufacturers can make it easier for consumers to recognize their brand with slogans, such as Tetley's "The original and the best," or with a consistent color scheme in their packaging. Photo 5.4 depicts a can of Heinz Beanz, highlighting the fact that it now contains less sugar and no artificial sweeteners, but it is still the brand "your kids love." Notice the similarities and dissimilarities in the current label with other Heinz-branded products. This product has a blue label while other labels are typically red, but the current product retains the keystone shape as well as the distinctive font seen on the other products in the line.

Operant conditioning is a theory of behavioral learning that occurs when an individual's behavior is changed through reinforcement that follows a desired response.

Positive reinforcement in operant conditioning occurs when an individual learns as a result of noticing that their previous behavior has produced a positive outcome.

Negative reinforcement in operant conditioning occurs when something unpleasant is removed following a behavior.

Operant conditioning

Operant conditioning is the second type of behavioral learning. It is also referred to as instrumental learning (Skinner 1953). **Operant conditioning** is a theory of behavioral learning that occurs when an individual's behavior is changed through reinforcement that follows a desired response. Operant conditioning takes a long-term approach by examining a series of behaviors. B. F. Skinner, the scientist who developed this theory, found that pigeons would continue to press a lever in their cage to get food; they had learned that the behavior led to a positive outcome, so they continued to do it. The idea is that, over time, individuals will modify or change their behavior based on the outcomes of previous behaviors. Marketers can use principles of operant conditioning to strengthen or weaken a consumer response.

Imagine that a new Chinese restaurant has opened up in town. On your way home from work one day, when you are too tired to cook, you decide to try it and you are happy to find that the food is very fresh, good tasting, and reasonably priced. A week later, you go there again. Congratulations—you have learned as a result of noticing that your previous behavior has produced a positive outcome. This is called **positive reinforcement**. Sometimes, individuals learn through **negative reinforcement**, which occurs when something unpleasant is removed following a behavior or where

● **Photo 5.4** This Heinz Beanz label uses stimulus generalization and stimulus discrimination

you behave in a certain way to avoid something unpleasant. When Jake takes out the garbage, he is doing so because he doesn't want his dad to yell at him; he is removing something unpleasant (the yelling) from the situation by behaving in a desired way. This is an example of negative reinforcement. Remember that both kinds of reinforcement are designed to increase the likelihood of behavior. Also, remember that negative reinforcement is taking something negative *away* from the experience, like an aspirin that adds a buffer to its formulation. Here, the negative experience of a stomachache is removed from the experience of taking an aspirin. Generally speaking, marketers want to create positive reinforcement for their brands, so they try to make sure the product is of high quality and satisfying. Free samples are a useful way to encourage consumers to try products and, if consumers have a positive experience, work as a form of positive reinforcement. Jägermeister, the German liquor, makes extensive use of free samples with a young-adult audience to encourage this positive reinforcement.

Some responses decrease the likelihood of repeating the behavior and lead to a weakening of the response. If you buy a new flavor of ice cream and neither you nor your roommates like it, you are effectively being punished for your choice and are unlikely to purchase it again. **Punishment** occurs when something negative happens after you perform a behavior. Finally, if a behavior is repeated but no longer leads to a positive outcome, **extinction** will occur and the behavior will be less likely to continue. Extinction occurs when the desired behavior is no longer reinforced (your favorite store no longer gives you 10 percent off because you are a loyalty club customer) or when the reinforcement is no longer motivating to the individual (the 10 percent off is no longer motivating because another store just opened that gives 20 percent off). See Table 5.1 for more examples of strengthening and weakening desired behaviors in marketing.

Punishment in operant conditioning is a way to decrease behavior by applying a negative response to the undesired behavior.

Extinction in operant conditioning occurs when the desired behavior is no longer reinforced or when the reinforcement is no longer motivating.

Table 5.1 Marketing applications of operant conditioning

	CONDITION	BEHAVIOR AND RESPONSE	OUTCOME
Strengthens response	Positive reinforcement	While going on a weekend trip with friends, you decide to try out Airbnb. The whole process is very easy and the rental is clean and comfortable.	The next time you go on a trip, you will use Airbnb again.
	Negative reinforcement	Your bank credit card eliminates its fees on international transactions.	The next time you travel abroad, you bring the credit card so that you can avoid the extra fees.
Weakens response	Punishment	Your new raincoat turns out to be anything but waterproof and the zipper breaks.	You will not buy that brand of outerwear again.
	Extinction	The gas station that once offered a free car wash with every ten fill-ups stopped offering that service.	Over time, you eventually stop visiting that gas station.

Sometimes the likelihood of a behavior doesn't increase or decrease—the likelihood stays the same. Perhaps the behavior was not important enough or the response was neutral. Imagine going to a new restaurant that just opened in town. The food, atmosphere, and service are just all right; they're not great, but they're not terrible. The waitress didn't drop a tray of dishes on you, but the experience was not memorable in a positive way either. Because there was nothing particularly good or bad about the restaurant, you might not remember it the next time you go out for dinner. However, since it has convenient hours,

● **Photo 5.5** *Operant conditioning in action: using free delivery and returns to reinforce purchasing*

you just might go. This is referred to as a **neutral operant**.

Marketing managers try to ensure that their brand is high quality and provides other positive attributes too. Many online retailers offer free delivery and returns, especially around the holidays. The combination of the high-quality product and the extra features works as a strong positive reinforcement, especially if they are offered all the time or according to a regular schedule, as in the case of many online retailers, such as Girotti shoes (see Photo 5.5). Product returns are often costly for retailers and some have started to use principles of operant conditioning to encourage customers to make fewer returns (see Insights from Academia 5.2).

Neutral operants in operant conditioning are responses from the environment that neither increase nor decrease the probability of a behavior being repeated.

Reinforcement schedules

For both positive and negative reinforcement, an important consideration is how often the reinforcement is applied to the behavior. The purpose of reinforcement schedules is to control the timing and frequency of the reinforcement, all in an effort to encourage the desired behavior. An additional benefit to using a schedule of reinforcement is that costs for the company are lowered because the reinforcement is not offered every time. In a marketing context, reinforcement schedules almost always apply to positive reinforcement—providing a reward. Reinforcement schedules can be either fixed (continuous) or variable.

Fixed ratio schedule in operant conditioning applies reinforcement after a specific number of responses.

- A **fixed ratio schedule** applies reinforcement after a specific number of responses. After every ten purchases, for example, you receive 20 percent off your next purchase. Loyalty programs offer clear guidelines about how many behaviors are required before the reward is provided. Most retailers now track behaviors and give rewards via apps, often showing progress toward the next reward (see Photo 5.6).

Fixed interval schedule in operant conditioning is when reinforcement is provided after a specific, known period of time.

- A **fixed interval schedule** is being utilized when the reinforcement is provided after a specific, known time frame, for example, on the first day of every week, month, or quarter. A retailer, for example, might have three to four big sales each year. Unfortunately, some customers wait to make purchases only during these sale periods.

INSIGHTS FROM ACADEMIA 5.2

To return or not return?

Have you ever wanted to return a product that you purchased online? Very often, online retailers offer lenient return policies to encourage purchases. However, when customers actually do return products, costs for the retailer can be quite high. Some retailers are now using operant conditioning to discourage online shoppers from returning their purchases. By giving customers a reward such as "$10 off your next order if you keep all of your items in this order," customers are much more likely to keep the products they ordered and to place another online order. The coupon acts as a positive reinforcement for the desired behavior (keeping the items). This strategy works particularly well with consumers who frequently shop online, because they know they will use the reward. This is something to keep in mind as you do your holiday shopping!

Gelbrich, K., J. Gathke, and A. Hubner. 2017. "Rewarding Customers Who Keep a Product: How Reinforcement Affects Customers' Product Return Decision in Online Retailing." Psychology & Marketing *34 (9): 853–67.*

- **Variable ratio schedules** occur when the reinforcement is provided after an unknown and often changing number of responses. Gamblers are particularly susceptible to the effects of variable ratio schedules. With most games of chance, the individual has no control over the timing or the amount of the reward; it is completely random. Social media has also taken some cues from operant conditioning and variable ratio schedules. Since you never

Variable ratio schedules in operant conditioning occur when the reinforcement is provided after an unknown and often changing number of responses.

● **Photo 5.6** *Many retail stores offer customer loyalty programs to reinforce behavior*

know when your feed will be updated or when you will receive a like, match, etc., you are constantly motivated to keep checking (Knorr 2017). This schedule of reinforcement is the least likely to lead to extinction.

Variable interval schedules in operant conditioning occur when the reinforcement occurs at some unknown but consistent rate.

- Finally, a **variable interval schedule** is when the reinforcement occurs at some unknown but consistent amount of time. For example, a reinforcement is made, on average, every thirty days. Your parents send you a care package, on average, once a semester. This motivates you to keep studying hard and making good grades. In marketing, a retail store might run a sale, on average, every two months. Of course, it depends on what other events and holidays are happening, but the store would run the sale on average about every sixty days. This motivates shoppers to keep visiting the store on a regular basis.

Learning history

Behavioral learning acknowledges that individuals have a history of learning that has been developed from experiences they have had in the past. When individuals encounter something new, they call on these previous experiences to guide their behavior and adopt appropriate new behaviors (Foxall, Goldsmith, and Brown 1998). Marketers know that when consumers are facing a new consumption experience, they need to make it easy for consumers to draw on their previously learned experiences. For example, airports around the world have a similar basic design and layout that makes it easy for travelers to navigate entry, customs, and baggage claim. Travelers can rely on their learning history to figure out any small differences, regardless of where in the world they may find themselves.

◉ Cognitive Learning

Whereas behavioral learning involves how individuals adapt to and learn from the external environment, cognitive learning involves learning that is the result of internal mental processes. Because of the profound complexities of the human brain, the cognitive learning approach explains much more complex decision-making processes than the behavioral approach. Cognitive learning theories are based on the assertion that human beings are rational creatures and use information that is available in the environment and their memories to make decisions. Cognitive learning encompasses a variety of mental processes, including searching, interpreting, storing, and processing information. Aspects of cognitive learning impact most parts of our day-to-day lives and, as such, marketers utilize lessons from cognitive learning in a variety of applications.

There are two key elements of cognitive learning theory. First, because researchers cannot directly observe the inner workings of the human mind, they make inferences about what happens based on the individual's behavior.

For example, we can see a consumer look at the nutrition label on a package and infer that the consumer is incorporating important nutrition-related information into the decision-making process. The second key element of cognitive learning theory is that consumers create knowledge based on their own experiences. You can read an ad about a trip to Costa Rica, or you can go on the trip and experience it yourself. Your own experience creates a depth of knowledge that is impossible to obtain from reading about the trip or hearing about it from others. In the following sections, we will discuss the three types of cognitive learning: observational learning, incidental learning, and information processing.

Observational learning

Have you ever heard the phrase *monkey see, monkey do*? This is what social learning or observational learning is all about. People watch what others do and, because humans are social creatures, they try to imitate the behavior. Much of our learning occurs in a social setting, where we observe the behavior of others and learn from it. **Observational learning (or social learning theory)** says that behavior is learned from the environment when we watch what other people do and the outcomes they receive (Bandura 1965, 1969). If the other person ("the model") receives a positive outcome, we will likely repeat that behavior ourselves. If the outcome is negative, we are unlikely to repeat it. Social learning theory is particularly relevant to the way in which young children learn. If you want your child to eat healthy, then you should eat healthy yourself and have a lot of nutritious food around the house; if you want your child to read, let them see you reading, enjoying books, and going to the library. Parents who model these behaviors will likely see them in their child too. The same works with modeling bad behaviors. Any child who watches an adult swear, become violent, or be disrespectful to others is much more likely to pick up on those behaviors.

Observational learning (or social learning theory) says that behavior is learned from the environment when we watch what other people do and the outcomes they receive.

Observational learning is often used in marketing because consumers regularly learn the specifics of how to do something by observing others. If you are in a new country and want to use the bus, you may first observe what others are doing. Similarly, if you are using an automatic ticketing machine at a train station, you learn by observing others around you (see Photo 5.7). That we are prepared to learn like this is important, because it means that consumers will do some of the work for marketers and it may even mean that businesses can reduce staff costs when customers can help themselves. Consumers observe many kinds of

● **Photo 5.7** *Observational learning occurs by watching others*

INSIGHTS FROM ACADEMIA 5.3

That restaurant always has long lines . . . it must be good!

Have you ever gone to a restaurant, found that it was mostly empty, and then left because you thought that there must be something wrong with the place? You're not the only one. We can learn a lot from watching others, as observational learning demonstrates. This influence is especially strong when "novice" consumers are observing "expert" consumers. Specifically, when novice consumers observe a very short line of expert consumers waiting for a product, those consumers are much less likely to follow through and purchase; they simply walk away. Why wouldn't a consumer be happy to wait in a short line? For the uninformed consumer, wait times are a signal of product quality. If a lot of expert consumers are waiting in line, the product must be good; if there are very few people waiting, the product must be bad. Because of this, managers might want to think twice before they try to speed up the lines at their stores!

Kremer, M., and L. Debo. 2016. "Inferring Quality from Wait Time." Management Science *62 (10): 3023–38.*

behavior. When the James Bond film *Spectre* was released, fans got to see their dashing hero (played by Daniel Craig) taking a sip from a bottle of Heineken, driving an Aston Martin, and wearing an Omega watch. When he wore a Barbour jacket in one scene, the $520 jacket immediately sold out and was soon selling on eBay for $2,600 (Barber 2015). Although most of us don't have the finances to drive 007's car or wear his watch, we *can* try his beer. If consumers have a positive opinion about 007, retain these images, and become motivated to replicate his consumption behaviors, millions of dollars' worth of product placement investment will have been worthwhile. In essence, marketing managers certainly need to worry about educating consumers, but consumers can often learn just as much by watching others, as we see in Insights from Academia 5.3.

Incidental learning

Incidental learning is the nonpurposeful acquisition of knowledge.

Sometimes learning happens on its own, particularly if we are involved in an activity. **Incidental learning** is the nonpurposeful acquisition of knowledge. A child might, for example, be very interested in playing baseball, but may also be learning about teamwork and cooperation without even realizing it. Some gaming apps help students learn because they provide more varied and enjoyable ways to learn. Again, students may feel that what they are doing is entertaining, but they may incidentally be learning vocabulary, math, or some other important concept. The important thing to remember with incidental learning is that the learning just happens; it is not a deliberate effort. See Insights from Academia 5.4 to find out about one situation where intentional learning is much more important than incidental learning.

Have you ever had an earworm? Sometimes when a piece of music plays, it gets stuck in your mind and you just cannot seem to get it out. This is called

INSIGHTS FROM ACADEMIA 5.4

For green consumption, the *type* of learning matters!

When consumers are especially concerned about the environment, they often reduce their overall level of consumption. Instead of buying many superfluous items to clutter their lives, they purchase fewer items that are meaningful, more useful, or last longer. Because there are fewer purchases, each purchase "counts more" in making a positive environmental impact, so consumers want to get those decisions right. Consequently, these consumers are much more likely to engage in *intentional learning* than in *incidental learning* because they want to purposely seek out the information needed to make the decision that will make a positive environmental difference. An important insight for managers of ecofriendly products is that in order to promote intentional learning, it makes sense to provide plenty of information when and where the consumer needs it.

Newton, J. D., Y. Tsarenko, C. Ferraro, and S. Sands. 2015. "Environmental Concern and Environmental Purchase Intentions: The Mediating Role of Learning Strategy." Journal of Business Research 68 (9): 1974–81.

an earworm and researchers say that this phenomenon happens to 90 percent of us on a regular basis. Songs can get stuck in our heads for a variety of reasons, but it seems to happen more often when we have heard the song recently, when we are familiar with the song, when the song is associated with a certain memory, or when the song matches our current mood (i.e., an upbeat song for an upbeat mood) (Jakubowski 2016). This is another example of incidental learning. Because we hear the song a lot and because we actually rehearse it by playing it again and again in our minds, we end up learning the song. See Table 5.2 for the most common songs that are difficult to get out of your head.

Table 5.2 Top ten songs that get stuck in your head

RANKING	SONG AND ARTIST	RANKING	SONG AND ARTIST
1	"Bad Romance," Lady Gaga	6	"California Gurls," Katy Perry
2	"Can't Get You Out of My Head," Kylie Minogue	7	"Bohemian Rhapsody," Queen
3	"Don't Stop Believing," Journey	8	"Alejandro," Lady Gaga
4	"Somebody That I Used to Know," Gotye	9	"Poker Face," Lady Gaga
5	"Moves Like Jagger," Maroon 5	10(tied)	"Single Ladies," Beyoncé "Rolling in the Deep," Adele

Source: Jakubowski (2016).

Information processing

The information processing model falls under the category of cognitive learning and is one of the most widely used models in consumer behavior. Decades of research have contributed to the development of this information processing approach. One of its most important contributions is that it provides details about the processes involved in information interpretation, storage, and retrieval. Researchers often use references to computers, using terms such as *files*, *storage*, and *retrieval*, to describe how the human mind works and processes information (cf. Bettman 1970; Newell and Simon 1972).

Another important contribution of the information processing approach is the information processing model, which has concluded that when individuals are exposed to a stimulus, they proceed through a series of distinct steps to make sense of and store that information in memory. This five-step cognitive process ideally ends with the new piece of information being stored in memory. Think about when you were trying to decide which college to attend. This was a high-involvement decision and it likely took several months to decide what to do. However, as you were exposed to new information (for example, your dream school offers summer classes close to your home), you likely thought about it and stored that information in memory with other information that was already there. When someone is highly involved with a product or a decision (including the decision to attend a college), new information proceeds through a series of steps where the consumer is exposed to it, pays attention to it, comprehends it, accepts or rejects it, and then stores it in memory. At the same time, information from memory can be brought in at any step. The five-step information processing model is summarized in Figure 5.3 using the example of a consumer, Tyler, who is trying to figure out what to do for spring break. You will notice that the first three steps, exposure, attention, and comprehension, are the same as the first three steps of the perceptual process model from Chapter 4. In the information processing model, however, the process does not end with an immediate response to the stimulus. Instead, the process ends with efficient encoding of the piece of information into memory.

Exposure means that the stimulus had the ability to be detected by the individual.

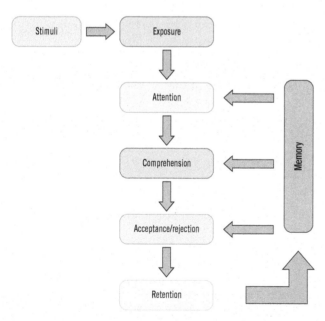

● **Figure 5.3** *The five-step information processing model*
Source: Szmigin and Piacentini (2015)

• **Exposure** occurs when the sensory system (seeing, smelling, tasting, hearing, or touching) detects information from the environment.

Tyler wants to go somewhere hot and tropical for spring break, and as he walks to class and surfs online, he is exposed to many online and print ads.

- **Attention** occurs when the cognitive system focuses on the stimulus, even if only for a brief moment. Tyler doesn't notice most of the ads and flyers to which he is exposed, but one day while he is sitting in class, he notices a small poster on the bulletin board advertising spring break trips to Aruba.

- **Comprehension** occurs when consumers interpret and understand the meaning of the information. Tyler takes a picture of the flyer and then goes to the travel company's website to find out more information about pricing and accommodations.

- **Acceptance/rejection** happens when the consumer elaborates on the information and considers any existing choice criteria. A **choice criterion** is a rule or a standard by which a decision will be made. For example, if the trip costs more than $2,000, Tyler can't go. After checking out the pricing and dates and confirming some details on TripAdvisor, Tyler decides that this trip would be a very good option.

- **Retention** occurs with the successful storage of the new piece of information; success can be measured by the ability to retrieve the information for future use. Tyler has learned several details—pricing, dates, accommodations, and reviews. He will retain much of this information in memory so that it can be retrieved later when he talks to his friends.

To make it into long-term memory, information must proceed through the stages in the information processing model. There is a special note here about the start of the process, the exposure and attention parts of the model. Successful exposure and attention are more likely to happen when the stimulus is congruent with (or fits) an existing memory, is easy to understand, and relates to our current needs. Sometimes, however, individuals also are exposed to and pay attention to information that is simply novel or interesting. Although the service or product may not be relevant to the consumer's needs, he or she might focus attention on an advertisement that is especially unusual, funny, or thought-provoking. The problem occurs in the later steps of information processing, because this kind of information might be more difficult to comprehend and accept. If that is the case, it will also be more difficult to be successfully retained and stored in long-term memory. In short, although novel stimuli may be successful in gaining the consumer's attention, it might not survive information processing to the point where it is successfully stored in memory. In Insights from the Boardroom 5, Adriane Randolph discusses several research projects involving brain scans and consumer reactions to marketing stimuli.

Attention is focusing mental concentration on a given stimulus.

Comprehension occurs when the consumer interprets and understands the meaning of the information.

Acceptance/ rejection occurs when the consumer considers existing choice criteria and elaborates on the information received to reach a point of acceptance or rejection of the information.

Choice criterion is a rule or a standard by which a decision will be made.

Retention has occurred with the successful storage of a new piece of information; success can be measured by the ability to retrieve the information.

What consumers *say* they're thinking is often quite different from what they're *really* thinking

● *Adriane Randolph*

Adriane Randolph, PhD, would love to stick some electrodes on your head to find out what you're *really* thinking. This is because Randolph knows that what individuals *say* they're thinking can sometimes be quite different from what they're really thinking. Randolph is the executive director of the BrainLab and a professor of information systems at Kennesaw State University, as well as the chief executive officer of Nurltec, a small research firm in Atlanta that connects research on memory and the mind to real-world applications.

Randolph does indeed like to stick electrodes on people's heads. She finds that when individuals are processing information, different parts of the brain are activated. By carefully examining brain scans, Randolph and her team can determine how information is being processed. She has engaged in a wide range of studies, but most of her work focuses on the differences between what individuals say they are thinking versus what they actually are thinking. "People have conscious and unconscious thoughts and processing. We ask people their feelings in a conscious state and then see what is actually happening in an unconscious state," says Randolph (2017).

Information processing and memory go hand in hand because "how information is stored in memory is critical to how people process information and make decisions" (Randolph 2017). Randolph says, "Organization in the brain is ultimately what is driving behavior. Sometimes when we're doing something, the habit is deeply ingrained," and it is not something that an individual consciously thinks about. Take the example of someone who habitually buys the same brand of peanut butter, but is asked by a researcher to describe why he likes that peanut butter so much. In looking at brain scans, there is often a mismatch between the reasoning consumers provide ("I buy this brand because it tastes the best and it has the best price") and the information that is provided by the brain scan, which indicates that it is a habitual purchase with very little, if any, thought involved. Although the consumer can provide some reasoning for the purchase when asked, the reality is that the behavior is so automatic, there is little or no information processing going on.

One area of research in which Randolph and her team have worked is eyewitness testimony in criminal trials. Eyewitness recall is notoriously unreliable because every time the witness recounts what happened, the memory gets changed slightly and then rewritten into memory. Over time, after recounting what happened multiple times, the original memory is completely overwritten so that what the eyewitness says happened bears very little resemblance to what actually happened. It all comes down to what Randolph calls *cognitive pollution*, which results from all the other thoughts that come up when a person is trying to process information. One way to help memory is "when multiple senses are engaged," says Randolph (2017).

Thus, when the memory is tied to two or more senses (sight, sound, smell, taste, and touch), the memory is encoded in multiple areas of the brain (one location for each sense). When this happens, the memory is easier to recall later because it is stronger and it is stored in multiple locations.

Randolph and her team also work on a variety of marketing-related projects. One particularly interesting study confirmed again that there is often a mismatch between individuals' conscious and unconscious processing of information. In this study, Randolph and her team examined consumer reactions to Super Bowl ads. On the day after the Super Bowl, multiple polls provide listings of the viewers' favorite ads. Randolph tried to see if there was any sort of mismatch between what consumers said they liked and what they actually liked. When Randolph collected the data in 2014, the top-rated ad was the Budweiser "Puppy Love" ad, which showed a heartwarming story of a dog whose best friend was a Clydesdale horse. When the study participants entered the lab, the electrodes went on. They were asked to watch several ads, rate them on some scales, and then describe what they liked or didn't like about each ad. First, study participants agreed with national rankings that the "Puppy Love" ad was a favorite. However, when participants were asked to describe why they liked each ad, Randolph and her team uncovered some very interesting findings. Although men said that they liked the "Puppy Love" ad, their brains actually liked one of the bottom-ranked ads, entitled "Cool Twist" by Bud Light, which showed a new beer bottle with a resealable twist cap. This ad was near the bottom of the list that year, according to *USA Today*. According to Randolph, when the male participants watched the "Cool Twist" ad, their brain scans showed "an orchestra of different activated areas" (Randolph 2017). Women showed much more consistency in what they said they liked and what their brains indicated they liked. Why did this happen? According to Randolph, demographics and social influences "matter a lot" when we discuss our opinions.

◉ Memory

Once a consumer has been through a behavioral or cognitive learning process, it is important that the information is retained in memory so that it can be used later. The function and structure of memory is an especially important topic in marketing. One reason is that marketers expend an extraordinary amount of effort and money so that consumers will remember important information about their brand. In the following sections, we will discuss memory structure and storage, as well as memory retrieval. See Figure 5.4 for a simplified depiction of how memory works.

Memory is a system and a process whereby information is received, sorted, organized, stored, and retrieved at a later time. Memory is critically

Memory is both a system and a process whereby information is received, sorted, organized, stored, and retrieved at a later time.

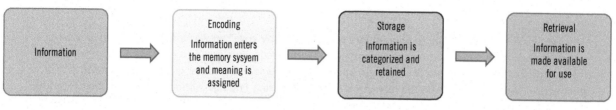

Figure 5.4 *How memory works*

important to our understanding of consumer decision-making. Consumers need to remember information about products in order to be able to make a decision about whether or not to purchase those products. However, retrieval of that information is not always easy for the consumer, especially if there was a time lag between when the consumer was exposed to the information and when it needs to be retrieved. For this memory process to work to its best advantage, marketers need to ensure that important product information is successfully encoded, stored, and retrieved. They can facilitate this process in numerous ways.

Encoding refers to how information enters the memory. During this step, consumers assign meaning to and comprehend the information. While advertising that is novel and distinctive might result in accolades and awards from the advertising industry, these ads often do little in helping a brand's message be properly comprehended during the encoding step. Encoding can, however, be facilitated with a number of techniques such as brand names that reflect the main benefit of the product, like Mr. Clean household cleaner or Beats headphones. Encoding can also be facilitated with well-known music or images, such as the bullseye target logo used by Target stores. The logo itself is a symbol for the name of the store. Generally speaking, information that is simple and avoids any ambiguity is more easily comprehended and encoded.

Storage refers to how the encoded information is retained in memory. There are numerous ways in which a piece of information can be organized, categorized, and filed away with other information that is already in storage. This intermingling with existing memories influences the ease with which the new information will eventually be retrieved. Memory structures and systems are very complex, but some characteristics of memory facilitate efficient storage. Our memories include a multitude of facts, as well as details of important experiences such as birthdays, holidays, or life events (Wildschut et al. 2006). Sometimes, individuals will engage in *strategic memory protection* to make sure their important memories remain as accurate as possible. For example, photographs and mementos help individuals remember important experiences. These "memory pointers" help us remember some specific details that might be easy to forget. Another type of strategy is *avoidance*, which protects the special memory against contamination by new information. For example, individuals may avoid driving by the house where they grew up because the changes made to the house over the years by the new owners may tarnish their happy childhood memories (Zauberman, Ratner, and Kim 2008).

Encoding refers to how information enters the memory.

Storage is how the encoded information is retained in the memory.

BLUE YELLOW ORANGE PURPLE RED GREEN BLACK

● **Figure 5.5** *The Stroop Test*

As we have learned, for memories to be retrieved, they must first be successfully encoded and stored. Many researchers have spent their entire careers investigating how this process works. For example, one line of research investigates how the process of encoding and storage can be disrupted. The Stroop test is one way for researchers to determine whether individuals are distracted when they process and store information. It involves having individuals read a list of words (blue, black, red) that are presented in a different color than the actual word (see Figure 5.5). Individuals are directed to read the color, not the word, as quickly as possible. This test has been put to a variety of uses, including understanding processing speed, working memory, and flexibility. It has even been used to test the extent of damage in individuals with traumatic brain injuries (cf., Scarpina and Tagini 2017). Later in this chapter, we will learn about how marketers assist consumers in retrieving information from memory. See Insights from the Field 5.3 for more information on one way you can benefit *your* brain: learn another language.

Memory systems

We can't point to a specific area of the brain and say that is where your memories of elementary school are located. We can, however, utilize some theories and models to better understand memory. One model is the multiple store model of memory, which identifies three distinct levels of memory: sensory, short term, and long term.

Sensory memory

In the sensory memory system, sensory information is received (sights, smells, touches, tastes, or sounds) and retained for only a brief, fleeting moment before it is moved to short-term memory. Imagine that you were lucky enough to get seats at an NFL football game and are sitting in the stadium with some friends. You will encounter a multitude of exciting sights, smells, and sounds. You may indulge in the taste of a hot dog and feel the stadium rumble when the home team scores a touchdown. All these sensory moments are fleeting because no attention or interpretation occurs. The next day, as you are describing the experience to your friends, chances are you will only remember a handful of sensations from the event, which were transferred to short-term memory. Unfortunately, you will forget most of the other sensations because, as we have mentioned, sensations only last a brief moment; visual information is only remembered for about half a second and auditory information is only remembered for about two seconds (Jansson-Boyd 2010).

INSIGHTS FROM THE FIELD 5.3

Bilingualism and the brain

With an increasingly interconnected world, there are certainly benefits to being bilingual (or even multilingual). Bilinguals can better navigate the sometimes difficult situation of trying to figure out train stations, restaurants, and hotels in a foreign land. Bilingual individuals can be open to new experiences and can better understand cultural nuances than someone with only monolingual capabilities. For example, it says something quite different about a culture when its typical response to a sneeze is "bless you" versus "gesundheit" ("good health" in German) versus nothing (in China, because there it is believed that when you sneeze, someone is talking about you). Compared to monolinguals, bilinguals are much better at picking up on these small differences in cultural meaning. Further, this better understanding allows them to adjust their behavior in a variety of culturally appropriate ways. In business, discussions and negotiations will be less likely to hit bumps of misunderstanding when a bilingual is involved, and important mistakes in translation and meaning are more likely to be caught before it is too late.

In addition to important cultural, social, and business benefits, there are also benefits to the brain. Recent scientific studies have confirmed that bilingual children perform better on cognitive tasks than their monolingual counterparts. Further, bilingual children are more capable of first making sense of a variety of cultural contexts and then providing an appropriate response. That is, they can enact an appropriate behavior based on a better understanding of the needs of other people in the situation (Kinzler 2016). There is strong and compelling evidence of the benefits of learning a second language early.

These benefits extend into adulthood. It seems that the bilingual brain is better at a variety of "executive functions," such as working memory, processing, flexibility, and processing conflicting information. These increased cognitive abilities are developed, in part, because for bilinguals to easily toggle between languages, they must focus their concentration and tune out extraneous distractions (Bialystok et al. 2004). A bilingual could be an important asset to a project that requires flexibility of thought or depth of concentration. Bilingualism can even benefit aging adults; research shows that it delays the onset of age-related cognitive decline. Bilingual older adults are able to maintain their strong executive functions in the brain much better than are monolinguals (Bialystok et al. 2004). In all, evidence suggests that information processing and memory work more efficiently in the bilingual brain than in the monolingual brain.

Questions

1. What could marketers do to ensure that their communications are accurately understood by a variety of consumers with different cultural backgrounds and different languages?
2. Compared to the brains of monolinguals, the brains of bilinguals are better at many executive functions. How could a marketing manager use this insight and adapt a communications strategy for the bilingual brain?

Sources: Bialystok et al. (2004); Kinzler (2016).

Short-term memory

Short-term memory is where current sensory information is briefly processed. Short-term memory is limited because it is only capable of handling small amounts of information for a very short period of time, such as a few seconds or minutes. Because of these limitations, most people can only remember about seven pieces of information at a time (Miller 1956). **Chunking** is a strategy that helps individuals overcome this limitation by grouping together similar or meaningful pieces of information (MacGregor 1987). Individuals can remember about

Chunking is the grouping together of similar or meaningful pieces of information.

seven chunks of information, just as they can remember seven pieces of information (Vanhuele, Laurent, and Drèze 2006). Regardless of the size of a chunk, as long as it is meaningful, it will be remembered. If you happen to see a phone number that looks like 2041566543, it might be fairly difficult to remember the numbers and their sequence. However, if it is organized into bigger chunks, such as 204-156-6543, it would be much easier for you to process and remember the number. The same is true with your social security number, your credit card number, and your student ID. It is simply easier to remember chunks.

Long-term memory

Long-term memory can potentially store information forever. First, however, information must get there, which few pieces of information do. Long-term memory takes some short-term memories and stores them away for later retrieval. This function of long-term memory is beneficial because if every piece of information from short-term memory was stored in long-term memory, our memories would be overloaded with mostly useless information. Successfully storing information into long-term memory can be helped by a variety of factors, such as an **engram,** which is the trace of the memory in the brain. It is the encoding of neural tissue in the brain that is often located within a neural network (Schacter 1996). An engram is strengthened when it is rehearsed in short-term memory and linked with information that is already stored in long-term memory. An engram for a brand would contain previously stored information about the brand attributes, advertising, pricing, and any other experiences with the brand. The result is not just the new engram of information, but a network of interconnected information (Heath 2012). Insights from Academia 5.5 illustrates a surprising downside to having a good memory.

Engrams are the trace of the memory in the brain; the encoding of the neural tissue that is often located within a neural network.

INSIGHTS FROM ACADEMIA 5.5

Your great memory means you are more likely to be bored

Do you have a great memory? Some people are simply much better at remembering information, and research has shown us that much of our ability to remember depends on our working memory capacity. People with "good memories" utilize a large portion of their working memory capacity. When they think about an experience, it is processed and encoded into memory much more deeply. What does this have to do with consumption? We know that each consumption experience brings up memories of past experiences. Consumers with good memories are able to remember many more previous experiences with a product. That can be a problem for them because each new consumption experience doesn't really seem *new*, so it is much easier for these consumers to get bored. By contrast, consumers with poor working memory capacity encode fewer memories and therefore can recall fewer previous consumption experiences. For these individuals, each consumption experience seems like a new and exciting experience.

Source: Nelson, N. M., and J. P. Redden. 2017. "Remembering Satiation: The Role of Working Memory in Satiation." Journal of Consumer Research *44 (3): 633–50.*

Successful storage into long-term memory can also be affected by the amount of effort that the individual spends on processing the information. More effort and deeper processing are more likely to result in the successful storage of information into long-term memory. It is important to realize that, although we talk about them as two distinct systems, long-term and short-term memory are complementary systems with considerable movement between the two. Think of memory as a collection of files of information that are connected by linkages. Experts refer to this as an **associative network** (J. R. Anderson 1993). Each file in the network is referred to as a node and generally includes a single concept such as an object, person, or place. A node can also include sensory information, such as taste or smell, as well as a memory. Some nodes are strongly interconnected within the associative network, with multiple connections, while other nodes are not as well connected. See Figure 5.6a for an example of an associative network someone might create when thinking about what to have for breakfast. Importantly, when one part of the network gets triggered, other parts of network that are closely located also get triggered. If you are thinking about eggs, through the process of *spreading activation*, you might also think about other closely connected concepts such as omelets,

Associative network is a collection of files of information that are connected by linkages.

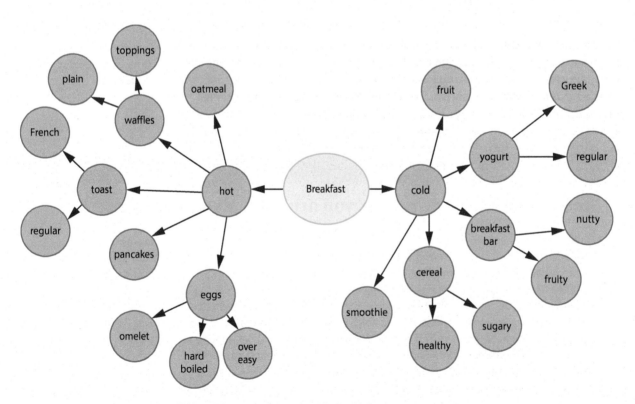

● **Figure 5.6a** *An associative network for breakfast*

hard-boiled eggs, over-easy eggs, and maybe even other hot options.

Memory also contains more comprehensive files of information called **schemas**, which are cognitive frameworks that help individuals organize and interpret information. There are many types of schemas a person could create, such as a self-schema, which would contain information about the self, as well as schemas for a variety of other concepts. For example, we may have a "going to the movies" schema, which contains information on the ticket booth, the tasty popcorn, and opinions about the ideal seats in the theater. It might also contain other information, such as the last movie we saw and

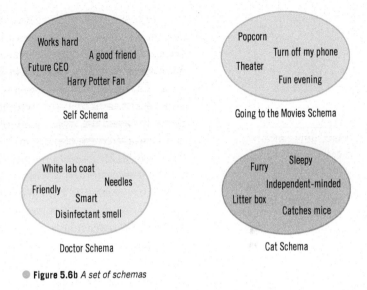

● **Figure 5.6b** *A set of schemas*

the impression that going to the movies is a fun way to spend the evening. Some schemas are "how to do things" schemas and specifically contain information on what to do in certain situations. A **script** is a type of schema that contains information on how to behave in certain situations, such as what to do when you visit the dentist (give the receptionist your name, sit down in the waiting room, etc.) or what to do when you attend class at a university (find a seat, get your notebook out, etc.). This knowledge may have developed over time from our learning history (see the previous section on operant conditioning). See Figure 5.6b for an example of several schemas that an individual may have created. When a schema is retrieved from memory, all of the information in the schema becomes available for use. So, if an individual retrieves their "cat" schema, they will think about all of the associated cat concepts, including the fact that cats are independent-minded, catch mice, are furry, sleepy, and use a litter box. Further, just like nodes are linked in an associative network, schemas can be linked to one another too.

How can marketing researchers use information about the structure and content of memory to create actionable insights about their customers? As with most marketing research endeavors, it all starts with data. First, researchers can use a technique called the response-time method. Research participants are presented with a long list of statements about a product, to which they agree or disagree. Their response times to these statements are also recorded. The data provided by this technique can help researchers visually map out the relationships in a two- or three-dimensional space. Data from the response times will also be incorporated into the depiction, with shorter times represented by stronger, close connections in the network and longer times represented by weaker and more distant connections.

Schemas are cognitive frameworks that are used to organize and interpret information.

Script is a type of schema that contains information on what to do in certain situations.

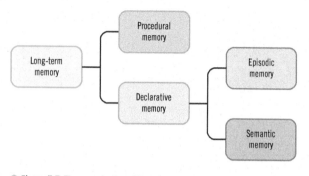

● **Figure 5.7** *The organization of long-term memory*

Source: Szmigin and Piacentini (2015)

Another technique used by marketing research-ers to find out about the structure and content of an associative network is the Kelly repertory grid (Kelly 1955). With this method, consumers are given three brand names and are asked to identify which one is different from the others. For exam-ple, if the focus of the research was consumer per-ceptions of vacation destinations, one set might include Miami Beach, South Padre Island (Texas), and New York City. Most people would identify New York as the one that is different; it is a city/cultural trip, rather than a beach trip. Using this technique, researchers ask consumers to complete multiple comparisons. The data are then compiled and data visualization software is used to create a depiction of an associative network for marketers to use. Regardless of which technique is used to create a visual depiction of the associative net-work, marketers find them quite useful and can derive important insights from them regarding brand perceptions and associated concepts.

Organization of long-term memory

As you can see, there are several ways in which researchers can represent the structure and content of memory. Each of these representations help mar-keters develop better insights. There are two types of long-term memory: procedural memory concerns how to do things and declarative memory is spe-cifically about knowing facts and events (see Figure 5.7).

Procedural memory is memory involved with knowing how to do things.

Declarative memory consists of a collection of facts and events. It is made up of two types of memory systems, episodic memory and semantic memory.

Episodic memory refers to our memories of specific events and experiences that have formed our autobiographical timeline.

Semantic memory consists of specific details, facts, and knowledge about the world.

- **Procedural memory** consists of knowledge that allows us to perform certain behaviors, like raking leaves or boiling an egg. As children, we learn many tasks and continue to learn as we get older and encounter new situations. Oftentimes, procedural knowledge becomes so automatic that it is hard for us to explain it to someone else. Think about some-one who wears a necktie every day to work. The process of tying a tie becomes so automatic that it might be difficult for that person to break down the steps to explain it to someone else.

- **Declarative memory** consists of a collection of facts and events. It is made up of two types of memory systems: episodic memory and seman-tic memory. **Episodic memories** contain details, emotions, and other information about own our past. We remember details about important life events, such as our high school graduation or the time the whole family got together for grandma's birthday. An important part of episodic memory is the context in which everything takes place, such as other people who were there, the weather, the time, and the location. Think of it as a mini video that we can play in our minds. **Semantic memory** consists of specific details, facts, and knowledge about the world. It can

● **Photo 5.8** *Much of our procedural and declarative memory is developed during childhood*

include factual knowledge, such as the name of the first US president, the boiling point of water, or the capital of Thailand. Semantic memory can also contain abstract or culturally specific knowledge, such as the words to a well-known song or the deeply held meanings associated with the date 9/11 (see Photo 5.8).

Marketers have derived several important insights from what we know about the structure and content of memory. One insight suggests that the reason why it might be difficult for consumers to remember specific advertisements is that they involve episodic memory, which requires more thorough encoding than semantic memory. Because episodic memory is much more complex and detailed than semantic memory, it is less likely to be encoded (Heath 2012). Because of this, advertisers sometimes use nostalgia in their advertisements to link their brands with happy memories from the consumers' past. Research shows that nostalgia works particularly well with millennials, who are often overworked and overstressed. They appreciate a reminder of simpler, more carefree times. Importantly, when a brand can forge a connection between a present-day brand and a consumer's memories, that brand can become particularly meaningful to the consumer (Friedman 2016). Have a look at Insights from the Field 5.4 to learn about how Horrible Histories has made learning fun using funny stories and catchy songs that are easy to remember and recall.

Horrible Histories makes learning fun

Originally targeted to children, the Horrible Histories series of books was first published in 1993. The premise was simple: encourage children to learn about history in a way that is entertaining and a little bit gross. Each book in the series focused on a specific historical period and had titles such as *Rotten Romans*, *Groovy Greeks*, *Terrible Tudors*, and *Vile Victorians*. The books are full of entertaining illustrations and funny dialogue. In *Terrible Tudors*, for example, readers learn about the Tudors' penchant for chopping people's heads off, as well as Queen Elizabeth's obsession with her looks and her tendency to use heavy makeup and wigs to hide her pockmarked skin and bald head. The philosophy of author Terry Deary is that the books had to be "horrible, funny, and accurate." At the same time, the books are irreverent in poking fun at presidents, kings, and queens. They challenge authority and often ask young readers to think about whether certain aspects of modern life are any less horrible than the past. Because of its popularity among children, adults started to pay attention too. Now, the books appeal to two very distinct target markets: school-aged children and adults who are not necessarily big fans of history, but who like the creative and engaging approach of the books (Jeffries 2018) (see Photo 5.9).

In 2009, the Horrible Histories television series, aimed at the six- to twelve-year-old audience, premiered in the United Kingdom. Just like the book series, the TV series soon attracted the attention of its other target market: adults. Indeed, the adult market has demonstrated that it has just as loyal a following as the children's market. The series aired after school and contained many of the same stories as the books, but added funny sketches and catchy songs. All of this was accomplished with the work of some of the UK's top writing, production, and acting talent. The series has won numerous educational and entertainment awards. Critics realized the important cultural impact

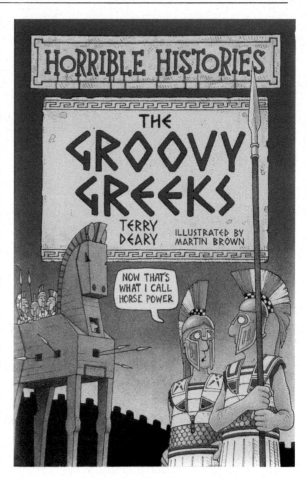

● **Photo 5.9** *Horrible Histories makes learning fun*

of the series when it crossed over to a mainstream audience and won an award for "best sketch" at the coveted British Comedy Awards, the first children's program to achieve such an honor. The show is incredibly engaging, with a good touch of the gross stuff that kids love, like slime, blood, and other goo. Importantly, the show doesn't talk down to kids. Experts call it a good introduction to history and admit that just a small bit of creative license has been taken on some of the historical details, such as the dialogue (Hickman 2011).

Horrible Histories has had a live stage production for several years and, in the summer of 2019, it released its first movie, *Horrible Histories: The Movie. Rotten Romans* (Jeffries 2018). The success of the Horrible Histories franchise is certainly a result, in part, of how it presents the material in a way that is fun and engaging, thus making it easier to encode into memory. One of the actors reflected on the success of Horrible Histories: "If someone getting wee poured over them helps people learn some facts, we're doing our job right" (Jeffries 2018).

Questions

1. The songs from this series can definitely cause earworms for some people. Watch this video: https://www.youtube.com/watch?v=XTWQzF1027I. For each step of the information → encoding → storage → retrieval process in Figure 5.4, identify what happens when a person hears this song.
2. Check out Horrible Histories online to learn more about the franchise. Are the memories that are encoded best described as episodic or semantic? Defend your answer with details from the text and elsewhere.

Sources: Hickman (2011); Jeffries (2018).

Retrieval of Memory

Retrieval is the process whereby we gain access to stored memories. These memories are pulled up from storage so that we can utilize them in decision-making. The three ways in which memories are accessed are recollection, recognition, and relearning.

Retrieval is the process whereby we gain access to our stored memories.

- **Recollection** is the simple act of retrieval of a piece of information from memory. Imagine you are taking a walk and hear some music. You may recall a specific memory about a friend who really likes that band and might remember that he drives a Ford truck. With recollection, because we spontaneously recall something without any assistance, the memory is stronger. On the day after an advertisement runs, media agencies often contact viewers to see what ads they recall seeing the night before. They might ask questions like, "What ads do you recall seeing last night?" These agencies are particularly interested in high recall numbers and would be very happy to hear consumers say they remember seeing an ad for Ford, which indicates that the ad was successfully encoded and then retrieved from memory.

Recollection is the simple act of retrieval of a piece of information from memory.

- **Recognition** occurs when a memory is retrieved because it was experienced again. In essence, consumers need a hint for the memory to be accessed. Imagine you are shopping online and come across a brand that you saw advertised during a show the previous night. Unfortunately, the memory is not as strongly encoded because you had to see the brand first before you could remember it. Turning again to advertising, after media agencies determine recall scores, the next set of questions they ask will

Recognition requires the memory to retrieve information by experiencing it again.

be about recognition. For example, "Did you happen to see an ad for Ford last night?" High recognition scores give advertisers reason to be somewhat pleased. They indicate that consumers partially encoded and then retrieved the memory of the Ford ad.

Relearning occurs when information that was previously stored in memory has been forgotten after a certain amount of time and the individual needs to relearn the material.

- **Relearning** occurs when information that was previously stored in memory has been forgotten after a certain amount of time and the individual needs to relearn the material. Luckily, relearning takes less time and effort the second time. Although you may have taken French in high school, it has been several years since you have used it. However, when you do a study-abroad trip to France, you start to relearn some of the words and phrases you have forgotten. The more often you use the language, the easier it is to retrieve the correct words and phrases you need. Media agencies that check how well an advertisement was encoded and then remembered by consumers have their work cut out for them when dealing with relearning. By the time relearning is necessary, both recall and recognition tests have failed and the advertiser might be best advised to go back to the drawing board and develop a new ad.

Sometimes, organizations would prefer that customers forget things because memories can interfere with the ability to learn new information. *Proactive* interference occurs when, for example, the memories of an older version of the product interfere with learning new features of a product. After driving around in your car for several years, you know exactly how to work the sound system, heating and cooling systems, and cruise control. However, if you trade in the car for a new one, your previous memories of how your old car worked could get in the way of figuring out your new car's features. Marketers want consumers to intentionally forget information that is no longer useful. Similarly, *retroactive* interference occurs when new information you must learn disrupts previously encoded information that is still important to know. Ideally, consumers can find the right balance by remembering the most important old *and* new information (Shapiro, Lindsey, and Krishnan 2006).

Explicit and implicit memory

It is informative to know whether or not a given memory is intentionally recalled. **Explicit memory** is the intentional, conscious recollection of information, such as class material for your next exam; it requires a purposeful effort to access the information from memory. In marketing, consumers use explicit memory through recall and recognition of ads. Marketers can assist consumer efforts to use explicit memory by using consistent colors, logos, and other design elements on product packaging (Photo 5.10).

Explicit memory is the intentional, conscious recollection of information.

Implicit memory is remembering without conscious awareness. Without our being consciously aware of it, information that is stored in memory influences our decision-making or behaviors. We may not even be aware of ever being exposed to the information. Imagine you were doing some online shopping for your dad, browsing through the sports section of L. L. Bean. You were

Implicit memory is remembering without conscious awareness.

● **Photo 5.10** *Recognition in action at the grocery store*

not specifically looking for shoes, but a week later when your friend asks you where he might buy some hiking boots, you remember some items you saw online. Implicit memory can potentially exert a strong influence on consumers who already have strong brand preferences. Further, a strong or dominant brand in the product category will be more easily accessed from memory (Lee 2002). Going back to our example, although you may have been exposed to several brands of hiking boots as you were doing your online search, you are most likely to remember a well-known brand like Merrell. Smart marketers know that although exposure to some marketing stimuli is often only momentary, consumers will still be influenced by the exposure (Holden and Vanhuele 1999).

Techniques to help memory retrieval

The significant time, effort, and monetary investment that is made to build a brand or communicate information about a brand will largely be wasted if consumers are incapable of remembering much about the brand during decision-making. Memories are notoriously bad, as can be seen in Insights from Academia 5.6. The good news is that researchers have found several techniques to help consumers retrieve information from memory.

Repetition and spacing

If consumers are exposed to a message multiple times, the likelihood of recall will increase. Advertisers generally say that consumers need to be exposed to an ad seven times before they can remember it. Interestingly, consumers do not need to see the same ad for this effect to work. Indeed, slight differences in

INSIGHTS FROM ACADEMIA 5.6

The trouble with eyewitnesses

Our memory for important events is almost always wrong. This is especially true when the events evoke strong emotions, like being an eyewitness to an accident, crime, or tragedy. Humans have evolved to pay particular attention to shocking events because knowledge and memory of these events help individuals prepare for future events. However, one problem with recalling an emotionally laden event is that "neutral objects" that were not relevant to the original event are sometimes "selectively enhanced" and take on greater importance when we later recall the event. Take the example of trying out a new gym. For a few weeks, you go to the gym, do your workout, and then go home. The next time you go, you hear

that the gym was robbed by the newly hired assistant manager. Suddenly, you start to remember all your previous interactions with the new assistant manager; the neutral interactions become selectively enhanced and take on more importance once they're remembered. Later, when eyewitnesses provide statements, they often give greater importance to nonimportant facts, which adds to greater confusion about what really happened.

Dunsmoor, J. E., V. P. Murty, L. Davachi, and E. A. Phelps. 2015. "Emotional Learning Selectively and Retroactively Strengthens Memories for Related Events." Nature 520: 345–48.

the message and execution can improve recall (Unnava and Burnkrant 1991). Variation in the spacing of an ad also assists recall. Spacing here refers to how regularly the consumer is exposed to the ad. Research indicates that consumers who are exposed to an ad message that is spaced out over a period of time may be more likely to encode the message into memory than consumers who are exposed to an advertising message rapidly, over a shorter period of time.

Duration and position

The duration and position of the advertisement may also help recall. Most TV ads today are fifteen or thirty seconds in duration. Studies show that better recall happens when ads are more than twenty seconds long (Martin-Santana, Reinares-Lara, and Reinares-Lara 2016). In TV advertising, when we discuss the position of an ad, we are talking about where the ad appears during the TV program or where it is placed during the commercial break. Ads that are aired in the middle of a program have better recall than ads that are aired at either the beginning or the end of programs (Martin-Santana, Reinares-Lara, and Reinares-Lara 2016). Generally speaking, the first and last commercials in a break have a recall advantage over those in the middle of the break (Pieters and Bijmolt 1997). **Primacy effects** describe the phenomenon where it is much more likely for an individual to remember the *first* piece of information provided, such as the first ad in a series of ads. By contrast, **recency effects** describe the phenomenon where it is much more likely to remember the *last* piece of information provided, as is the case with the last ad in a series of ads. Because of the memory advantages provided by primacy and recency

Primacy effects describe the phenomenon where it is much more likely for an individual to remember the first piece of information provided.

Recency effects describe the phenomenon where it is much more likely for an individual to remember the last piece of information provided.

effects, it is no surprise that advertisers pay more to place their ads first or last in a commercial break!

Pictorial and verbal cues

When individuals are exposed to a visual stimulus, such as an advertisement, they first perceive the images and then perceive the text (Kroeber-Riel 1986). The visual and textual elements of an advertisement, however, are complementary—they go together such that the meaning of the visuals is enhanced by the text and vice versa. For a variety of reasons, pictures are easier than words to retrieve from memory. Some words, however, can evoke vivid images in the consumer's mind. Words like *beach* and *beer* have much higher *imagery value* than words like *peace* or *equality*. High-imagery words have the advantage of being encoded both verbally and visually into memory, thus making them easier to recall at a later point in time (Richardson 1980). Marketers have used this insight from academic research to create advertisements that utilize a combination of verbal and visual cues to encourage both verbal and visual encoding. For example, the TAG Heuer watch advertisement with the prominent #DontCrackUnderPressure message and visual image of a monster wave about to wipe out a surfer certainly attract a consumer's attention. Importantly, the visual and textual elements work together to reinforce the message about the durability of the watch, as well as its suitability to accompany the wearer on any adventure (see Photo 5.11). Dual messages like these increase the chances that the message will undergo dual encoding and greatly increase the chances for the message to be retrieved later (Unnava and Burnkrant 1991).

● **Photo 5.11** *Visual and textual elements work together to strengthen encoding and later retrieval*

◉ Summary

Marketing decision-makers utilize insights about learning and memory to help design products, establish effective pricing, determine optimal distribution strategies, and construct effective communications materials. Although *behavioral learning* rejects the notion that internal factors like thoughts and emotions are relevant to the learning process, we acknowledged that learning can happen because of learned responses to and learned connections with a stimulus in the environment. *Classical conditioning* and *operant conditioning* have some important differences and similarities and are utilized in marketing today. In Insights from the Field 5.1, we learned that classical conditioning can occur when marketers effectively match the qualities of a celebrity with the qualities of the product. In discussing operant conditioning, we learned how different reinforcement schedules can be utilized in different marketing applications.

Our discussion of the *cognitive learning* approach introduced three models of learning: observational, incidental, and information processing. As we discussed these three approaches, we illustrated ways in which marketers have utilized insights from these approaches to better meet the needs of consumers. Insights from the Boardroom 5 focused on how cognitive research is conducted and then applied to marketing by examining the case of consumer reactions to Super Bowl ads. Indeed, the ad that some consumers said they liked best was not the same ad that their brains indicated they liked the best! Importantly, we introduced the *five-step information processing model*, which describes how a piece of information moves from exposure to retention in memory.

We engaged in a thorough examination of the structure and content of memory in the second half of the chapter. We found that stimulus information proceeds through *sensory memory*, *short-term memory*, and *long-term memory*. Memory storage structures such as associative networks and schemas were introduced and we briefly described what happens when a memory is activated in each of these structures. Throughout this section of the chapter, numerous examples were presented to reinforce the point that the concepts of learning and memory are not only linked to one another, but also critically important to our understanding of consumer behavior. For example, we discussed how the Horrible Histories series of books made learning fun in Insights from the Field 5.4. Case Study 5 focused on the often maligned, but intriguing FiveFinger Vibram shoe and demonstrated how marketers used insights about human learning and memory to develop and then reposition the shoe. The structure and content of memory, as well as the processes involved with encoding, storage, and retrieval, are critically important in building our understanding of consumer behavior.

KEY TERMS

acceptance/rejection p. 175
associative network p. 182
attention p. 175
behavioral learning p. 158
choice criterion p. 175
chunking p. 180
classical conditioning p. 159
cognitive learning p. 158
comprehension p. 175
declarative memory p. 184
encoding p. 178
engrams p. 181
episodic memory p. 184
explicit memory p. 188
exposure p. 174
extinction p. 167
first-order conditioning p. 160

fixed interval schedule p. 168
fixed ratio schedule p. 168
higher-order conditioning p. 161
implicit memory p. 188
incidental learning p. 172
learning p. 157
memory p. 177
negative reinforcement p. 166
neutral operant p. 168
observational learning (or social learning theory) p. 171
operant conditioning p. 166
passing off p. 190
positive reinforcement p. 184
primacy effects p. 190
procedural memory p. 184
punishment p. 167

recency effects p. 190
recognition p. 187
recollection p. 187
relearning p. 188
retention p. 175
retrieval p. 187
schema p. 183
script p. 183
semantic memory p. 184
stimulus discrimination p. 165
stimulus generalization p. 162
storage p. 178
trademark p. 165
variable interval schedule p. 170
variable ratio schedules p. 169

REVIEW QUESTIONS

1. What are some important benefits and draw-backs of behavioral learning and cognitive learning? What is the most important difference between the two?
2. Explain several important differences and similarities between classical conditioning and operant conditioning.
3. Carefully describe the five-step information processing model and what occurs at each stage. What role does memory play throughout the process?
4. Explain what happens to information from a stimulus as it proceeds through sensory, short-term, and long-term memory.

DISCUSSION QUESTIONS

1. Successful encoding of product information can occur if the individual engages in dual encoding. Describe this concept and provide at least two examples from advertising that utilize dual encoding. Discuss.
2. Imagine that you own a bakery and are trying to attract more customers during your "off hours" of weekday mid-afternoons. For each step in the information processing model, describe what you might be able to do to help facilitate the process for potential customers. Be creative!
3. For each of the four reinforcement schedules in operant conditioning, find a specific example from marketing or advertising. Describe in detail how each schedule is utilized and estimate its likelihood of success.
4. Sketch out an associative network for your dream vacation spot. Describe the nodes and connections. Next, sketch out the following schemas: your self-schema, your dream vacation schema, your college schema, and your family schema. Describe the content of your schemas. Which representation, the associative network or schemas, would be more useful to marketers of vacation destinations? Why?

For more information, quizzes, case studies, and other study tools, please visit us at **www.oup.com/he/phillips**.

CASE STUDY 5

Will Consumers Accept Vibram's FiveFinger Shoe as Casual Wear?

The strange, slightly goofy-looking Vibram FiveFinger shoe was poised to be another example of a fad that had come and gone. However, in 2019, marketers at Vibram decided to retool their strategy and pursue the "athleisure" market. What do consumers really know about the brand and how has that knowledge changed over the brand's history? Smart marketing managers must manage the process by which consumers acquire knowledge, encode it, store it, and then retrieve it. They also must be ready to adapt when new market opportunities arise.

The Vibram company traces its history back to 1937 in Italy when an avid mountain climber patented a unique sole for mountain climbing boots that had superior grip and durability. Over the years, the company partnered with a number of different manufacturers of hiking and climbing boots. The yellow, hexagonal-shaped Vibram logo became a sought-after mark of quality for the most serious climbers and outdoor enthusiasts. In 1954, Italian hikers conquered K2, the second highest mountain in the world, after Mount Everest. In 1965, Vibram partnered with Quabaug Rubber Company, which became the exclusive manufacturer of the soles in North America. As the company continued to expand into different markets and offer new product lines, not only did the soles continue to offer superior grip and durability, but also the company continued to innovate by offering improvements in new materials and designs. In 2014, Vibram first started to incorporate wearable technology into their products to wirelessly communicate with smartwatches, fitness trackers, and other devices ("History" 2019).

Vibram's US headquarters in Concord, Massachusetts, had been providing soles for other branded hiking and climbing boots to the North American market for over sixty-five years when the marketing team determined that it was time for Vibram to offer its own branded shoe. The product development team created the FiveFinger shoe, the company's first-ever shoe for the US market in 2005. The shoe definitely made a splash with its design. With very little support or padding, the shoe had a distinctive tread on the bottom as well as individual pockets for each of the five toes to give them the ability to work and stretch independently. The shoe itself was supposed to simulate walking barefoot, with the added benefit of protection of the foot (Carofano 2005) (see Photo 5.12).

The marketing team thought that the shoe had a good chance of making a splash in the US market. The first indication was that a very small, limited-edition supply of three thousand shoes was released in Italy in May 2005 and immediately sold out. Customers were drawn to the funky look and were intrigued by the barefoot running fad that seemed to be spreading among

● **Photo 5.12** *Vibram's FiveFinger Shoe*

some of world's elite runners. Barefoot running is supposed to be more natural and allows for the feet, ankles, and calves to be strengthened. Pundits claimed the shoe allowed its wearers to run on asphalt, trails, and other surfaces without fear of injury. Thus, they could simulate the effect of barefoot running without the risk of injury. The US marketing team decided to introduce a mere fifteen thousand FiveFinger pairs of shoes in a select group of eighty retailers across the country at about $70 per pair at retail. The limited distribution strategy was specifically designed to make sure that the shoes appeared alongside other high-end shoes at some of the most progressive footwear and outdoor stores in the country (Carofano 2005).

In the years that followed the introduction of the FiveFinger shoe, a growing group of barefoot running enthusiasts ditched their Nikes and New Balances to run with the minimalist FiveFinger. Other athletic shoe manufacturers jumped on the bandwagon and runners found that they were able to run more naturally, with their weight primarily on the front of the foot rather than the heel. By contrast, shoes with heavy padding and support encourage runners to strike the ground heel first. Unfortunately, the benefits of barefoot running seemed to be overblown and runners started to experience injuries when wearing the shoes. In 2014, Vibram agreed to pay $3.75 million to settle a class action lawsuit brought by runners who claimed they were deceived into thinking that the shoes were good for their feet (Harrison et al. 2014).

In 2015, Vibram acquired its long-time business partner, Quabaug, which had manufactured the rubber soles for the shoes since 1965. At the time of the acquisition, the combined company employed 750 individuals, 300 of whom were in the United States. The goal of the acquisition was to spur innovation in new materials and new products, as well as speed up the introduction of these new products to the marketplace. The newly formed company, Quabaug Vibram Innovation (QVI), announced its intention to expand into other sports such as snowboarding and golf. In addition, the marketing team was hoping to crack into a variety of other markets, such as women, children, and pet care (Scott 2015).

By 2019, QVI was hoping to leverage the "athleisure" trend that seemed to be growing in some of the developed markets in which the company operated. Athleisure describes the trend toward wearing athletic and leisure wear for nonathletic purposes. For example, some individuals may wear athletic items like yoga pants for casual occasions. Athleisure accounts for about half of athletic footwear sales, and only 16 percent of consumers who buy sports footwear use them for sports. Because fashion and design seem to be just as important as performance, many performance shoes were starting to add interesting and eye-catching design elements to their shoes. Consumers wanted to have comfortable athletic shoes, but also wanted to make a fashion statement while wearing them; shoes needed to be aesthetically appealing *and* high performing. Marketers at QVI believed they could leverage this insight by offering a shoe with all

of the performance capabilities customers expected, but with the added benefit that the shoe was capable of transitioning to casual, urban settings. The marketing team at QVI understood that the shoe still needed to appeal to its primary target: the group of customers who are using the product for its intended purpose. However, expanding the shoe into the athleisure market offered room for growth and decision-makers at QVI were very optimistic about its future (Streets and Verry 2019).

Sources: Carofano (2005); Harrison et al. (2014); History (2019); Scott (2015); Streets and Verry (2019).

QUESTIONS

1. Carefully discuss how a consumer may proceed through the processes of (a) operant conditioning and (b) classical conditioning to learn about some important product attributes for the FiveFinger shoe. Which of these learning theories is more useful? Why? Defend your answer with information from the chapter.

2. Relying on your own knowledge, information from the case, and any extra research you may conduct, sketch out (a) an associative network and (b) at least three schemas for the FiveFinger shoe. For each sketch, provide a brief, one-paragraph explanation for some of the main elements of the sketch.

3. The marketing team had its sights on the athleisure market and was hoping to position the FiveFinger brand as a "performance casual" brand. Using what you know about the structure and content of memory, create an argument for why you think this effort will be successful or not successful.

REFERENCES

Anderson, C. 2019. "The Story behind Our NEW Girl Scout Cookie Inspired Coffee Flavor—Trefoils Shortbread." *Dunkin'* (blog). February 1, 2019. https://news.dunkindonuts.com/blog/blog_custom-20190130-6741136.

Anderson, J. R. 1993. *Rules of the Mind*. Hillsdale, NJ: Erlbaum.

Bandura, A. 1965. "Influence of Models' Reinforcement Contingencies on the Acquisition of Imitative Responses." *Journal of Personality and Social Psychology* 1:589–95.

Bandura, A. 1969. *Principles of Behavior Modification*. New York: Holt, Rinehart & Winston.

Barber, N. 2015. "Does Bond's Product Placement Go Too Far?" *BBC*, October 1, 2015. http://www.bbc.com/culture/

story/20151001-does-bonds-product-placement-go-too-far.

Bettman, J. R. 1970. "Information Processing Models of Consumer Behavior." *Journal of Market Research* 7 (3): 370–76.

Bialystok, E., F. Craik, R. Klein, and M. Viswanathan. 2004. "Bilingualism, Aging, and Cognitive Control: Evidence from the Simon Task." *Psychology and Aging* 19 (2): 290–303.

Bitterman, M. E. 2006. "Classical Conditioning since Pavlov." *Review of General Psychology* 10 (4): 365–76.

Broniarczyk, S. J., and J. W. Alba. 1994. "The Importance of the Brand in Brand Extension." *Journal of Market Research* 31:214–28.

Carofano, J. 2005. "High Five." *FN: Footwear News* 61 (40): 25.

Court of Master Sommeliers. 2017. Accessed November 11, 2017. http:www.courtofmastersommeliers.org.

Economist, The. 2003. "The Death of the Jingle." February 6, 2003. http://www.economist.com/node/1570553.

Feldman, D. 2017. "Cosby on Trial: How Sexual Assault Allegations Cost Him a Fortune." *Forbes*, June 8, 2017. https://www.forbes.com/sites/danafeldman/2017/06/08/a-look-into-how-the-criminal-case-against-bill-cosby-is-costing-him-a-fortune/#7df6601741ad.

Foxall, G. R., R. E. Goldsmith, and S. Brown. 1998. *Consumer Psychology for Marketing.* 2nd ed. London: International Thomson Business Press.

Friedman, L. 2016. "Why Nostalgia Marketing Works So Well with Millennials and How Your Brand Can Benefit." *Forbes*, August 2, 2016. https://www.forbes.com/sites/laurenfriedman/2016/08/02/why-nostalgia-marketing-works-so-well-with-millennials-and-how-your-brand-can-benefit/#82a3aca36364.

Gewirtz, J. C., and M. Davis. 2000. "Using Pavlovian Higher-Order Conditioning Paradigms to Investigate the Neural Substrates of Emotional Learning and Memory." *Learning and Memory* 7:257–66.

Harrison, S., B. Kenealy, M. Lerner, K. Shepherd, and S. Veysey. 2014. "Five-Toed Sneakers Costly for Maker." *Business Insurance* 48 (11): 00030.

Heath, R. 2012. *Seducing the Subconscious.* Chichester, UK: Wiley–Blackwell.

Hickman, L. 2011. "How Horrible Histories Became a Huge Hit." *The Guardian*, March 17, 2011. https://www.theguardian.com/culture/2011/mar/17/horrible-histories-huge-hit.

"History." 2019. *Vibram Company History.* Accessed November 26, 2019. http://us.vibram.com/company/about/history/.

Holden, S. J. S., and M. Vanhuele. 1999. "Know the Name, Forget the Exposure: Brand Familiarity versus Memory of Exposure Context." *Psychology and Marketing* 16:479–96.

Jakubowski, K. 2016. "Why Some Songs Get Stuck in Your Head More Than Others." *The Independent*, November 6, 2016. http://www.independent.co.uk/arts-entertainment/music/why-some-songs-get-stuck-in-your-head-more-than-others-a7401116.html.

Jansson-Boyd, C. V. 2010. *Consumer Psychology.* Maidenhead, UK: Open University Press.

Jeffries, S. 2018. "How We Made Horrible Histories." *The Guardian*, December 11, 2018. https://www.theguardian.com/tv-and-radio/2018/dec/11/how-we-made-horrible-histories-jess-ransom.

Kelly, G. A. 1955. *The Psychology of Personal Constructs.* New York: Norton.

Kinzler, K. 2016. "The Superior Social Skills of Bilinguals." *The New York Times*, March 11, 2016. https://www.nytimes.com/2016/03/13/opinion/sunday/the-superior-social-skills-of-bilinguals.html?_r=2.

Knorr, C. 2017. "How to Resist Technology Addiction." CNN. November 9, 2017. http://www.cnn.com/2017/11/09/health/science-of-tech-obsession-partner/index.html.

Kroeber-Riel, W. 1986. "Die inneren Bilder der Konsumenten: Messung, Verhaltenswirkung, Konsequenzen für das Marketing." *Marketing ZFP* 8:81–96.

Lee, A. Y. 2002. "Effects of Implicit Memory on Memory-Based versus Stimulus-Based Brand Choice." *Journal of Marketing Research* 39:440–54.

MacGregor, J. N. 1987. "Short-Term Memory Capacity: Limitation or Optimization?" *Psychological Review* 94:107–8.

Martin-Santana, J. D., P. Reinares-Lara, and E. Reinares-Lara. 2016. "Spot Length and Unaided Recall in Television." *Journal of Advertising Research* 56 (3): 274–88.

Miceli, G., and R. Pieters. 2010. "Looking More or Less Alike: Determinants of Perceived Visual Similarity between Copycat and Leading Brands." *Journal of Business Research* 63:1121–28.

Miller, G. 1956. "The Magical Number Seven, Plus or Minus Two: Some Limits on Our Capacity for Processing Information." *Psychological Review* 63:81–87.

Newell, A., and H. A. Simon. 1972. *Human Problem Solving.* Englewood Cliffs, NJ: Prentice Hall.

Oliver, D. 2017. "Girl Scout Cookie Lip Smackers Collection." *Huffington Post*, December 7, 2017. https://www.huffpost.com/entry/girl-scout-cookie-lip-smackers_n_1074522.

Pieters, R. G. M., and T. H. A. Bijmolt. 1997. "Consumer Memory for Television Advertising: A Field Study of Duration, Serial Position, and Competition Effects." *Journal of Consumer Research* 23:362–72.

Pornpitakpan, C. 2012. "A Critical Review of Classical Conditioning Effects on Consumer Behavior." *Australasian Marketing Journal* 20:282–96.

Press Release. 2014. "Award -Winning Nestle Crunch Girl Scout Candy Bars to Return This Summer." *Nestlé USA.* May 21, 2014. https://www.nestleusa.com/media/pressreleases/award-winning-nestl%C3%A9%C2%AE-crunch%C2%AE-girl-scout-candy-bars-to-return-this-summer.

Randolph, A. 2017. *Personal interview,* October 26.

Richardson, J. T. E. 1980. *Mental Imagery and Human Memory.* London: Macmillan.

Roberts, J. 2012. "What You See Is Not Always What You Get." *Marketing Week*, June 28, 2012. https://www.marketingweek.com/2012/06/28/what-you-see-is-not-always-what-you-get/.

Scarpina, F., and S. Tagini. 2017. "The Stroop Color and Word Test." *Frontiers in Psychology* 8 (April 12): 557. https://doi.org/10.3389/fpsyg.2017.00557.

Schacter, D. L. 1996. *Searching for Memory.* New York: Perseus Books.

Scott, M. 2015. "Vibram Acquires Longtime Distributor, Forms New Firm." *Rubber & Plastics News* 44 (24): 00014.

Shapiro, S., C. Lindsey, and H. S. Krishnan. 2006. "Intentional Forgetting as a Facilitator for Recalling New Product Attributes." *Journal of Experimental Psychology: Applied* 12:251–63.

Skinner, B. F. 1953. *Science and Human Behavior.* New York: Free Press.

Streets, M., and P. Verry. 2019. "Athleisure's Popularity Is Bad News for the Performance Footwear Market." FN: Footwear News. June 21, 2019. https://footwearnews.com/2019/business/retail/athleisure-performance-footwear-industry-vibram-boa-1202795584/.

Till, B. D., and M. Busler. 2000. "The Match-Up Hypothesis: Physical Attractiveness, Expertise, and the Role of Fit on Brand Attitude, Purchase Intent and Brand Beliefs." *Journal of Advertising* 29:1–13.

Till, B. D., and R. L. Priluck. 2000. "Stimulus Generalization in Classical Conditioning: An Initial Investigation and Extension." *Psychology and Marketing* 17 (1): 55–72.

Till, B. D., S. M. Stanley, and R. Priluck. 2008. "Classical Conditioning and Celebrity Endorsers: An Examination of Belongingness and Resistance to Extinction." *Psychology and Marketing* 25 (2): 179–96.

TrademarkNow. 2016. "9 Nasty Trademark Infringement Cases—And How to Avoid Them." *TrademarkNow.* September 6, 2016. https://www.trademarknow.com/blog/9-nasty-trademark-infringement-cases-and-how-to-avoid-them.

Tschinkel, A. 2019. "Jennifer Aniston Is Worth a Reported $240 Million—Here's How She Built Her Fortune." Insider.com. January 2, 2019. https://www.insider.com/jennifer-aniston-net-worth-2018-12.

Unnava, H. R., and R. E. Burnkrant. 1991. "An Imagery-Processing View of the Role of Pictures in Print Advertisement." *Journal of Marketing Research* 28 (May): 226–31.

Vanhuele, M., G. Laurent, and X. Drèze. 2006. "Consumers' Immediate Memory for Prices." *Journal of Consumer Research* 33 (2): 163–72.

Warlop, L., and J. W. Alba. 2004. "Sincere Flattery: Trade-Dress Imitation and Consumer Choice." *Journal of Consumer Psychology* 14 (1/2): 21–27.

Wildschut, T., C. Sedikides, J. Arndt, and C. Rotledge. 2006. "Nostalgia: Content, Triggers, Functions." *Journal of Personality and Social Psychology* 91:975–93.

Wirtz, J. G., J. V. Sparks, and T. M. Zimbres. 2017. "The Effect of Exposure to Sexual Appeals in Advertisements on Memory, Attitude, and Purchase Intention: A Meta-analytic Review." *International Journal of Advertising* 38 (2): 168–98. https://doi.org/10.1080/02650487.2017.1334996.

Zauberman, G., R. K. Ratner, and B. K. Kim. 2008. "Memories as Asset: Strategic Memory Protection in Choice over Time." *Journal of Consumer Research* 35 (February): 715–28.

6 Personality, Self, and Motivation

◉ Introduction

"A man should be what he can do." —*From Here to Eternity* (1953)

Just a few decades ago, people were defined by their occupations. Just look at some old movies from your grandparents' day and you can see that people were depicted according to what job they performed—there was the police officer, the teacher, the coach, the doctor, etc. Now, like it or not, consumption plays a central role in an individual's sense of identity. Each time we use a product, we not only reinforce our own beliefs and values, but we also communicate important information to others about ourselves. Indeed, our own self-perceptions and our beliefs about how others see us influences which brands we use, how we use them, and how we respond to marketing communications.

Unlike previous chapters that discussed various dimensions of consumer behavior from an often rational, analytical perspective, this chapter's perspective acknowledges that consumers are influenced by emotional and often nonrational processes. This chapter starts with an examination of personality and the self, two concepts that are linked and that motivate individual behavior. We illustrate numerous ways in which marketers utilize their understanding of personality and the self in a marketing context. Because personality and self are closely linked, our discussion also intertwines the two. In the second part of the chapter, we examine the concept of motivation. In doing so, we consider how values can be a guiding force for consumer behavior. Importantly, we examine key concepts of motivation theory, ways in which marketers discover how consumers connect product attributes to values, motivational conflict, and some intriguing methods for researching motivation.

◉ Different Perspectives On Personality and Self

Smart marketing managers know that consumption decisions are often influenced by a consumer's self-perceptions as well as their beliefs about how others perceive them. Are you the kind of person who

Having read this chapter, you will be able to:

1. For each of the two *main perspectives on personality and self*, discuss the different definitions of personality and self, as well as the different implications for consumer researchers.

2. Describe the differences between the single-trait perspective, multitrait perspective, and the *multiplicity of self*.

3. Identify various ways in which concepts of *personality and self are utilized by marketing managers*, including symbolic consumption, values, and psychographics.

4. Describe several key concepts of *motivation*, including needs and wants, conflict, and Maslow's hierarchy of needs, and research.

5. Demonstrate an understanding of some basic qualitative research methods.

takes bottled water with you to class every day or do you bring a refillable bottle? Even this simple decision is meaningful. It says a lot about how you want to live your own life and what issues are important to you. It also says a lot about how you would like others to see you. Marketers work hard to match their brand's image with the self-image of consumers in their target market so that, for example, the rugged, outdoors image of Patagonia fits with the rugged, outdoors self-concept of the people who wear Patagonia gear. This is not a simple undertaking for a marketer and is full of potential pitfalls. One reason is that a consumer's identification with a brand can often be based on that consumer's own self-perceptions both now and in the past, as well as how the consumer imagines they might be in the future. **Personality** is a person's identity, which can be viewed from either a psychological or a sociological perspective, while the **self** represents a person's beliefs, feelings, knowledge, and attitudes *about* his or her own identity. Researchers have identified several theories and models of personality and self, but for our purposes, these models generally fall into two broad domains: individual psychological perspectives and socially oriented perspectives. Each approach provides a different perspective on the role of personality and self in motivating individual behavior, and thus each one can generate unique insights for marketing managers.

Personality is a person's identity, which can be viewed from either a psychological or a sociological perspective.

Self is a person's feelings, beliefs, knowledge, and attitudes about his or her own identity.

Psychological perspectives on personality

The **psychological perspective on personality** argues that an individual's persistent and characteristic reactions to environmental stimuli make up an individual's distinctive identity (Kassarjian 1971). These reactions can be emotional, cognitive, or behavioral. Importantly, an individual's personality is fairly stable over time. The psychological perspective encompasses psychoanalytic theories and trait theories.

Psychological perspective of personality argues that an individual's persistent and characteristic reactions to environmental stimuli make up an individual's distinctive identity.

Psychoanalytic theories

Psychoanalytic theory is based on the premise that strong and persistent unconscious inner forces are responsible for directing individual behavior. Austrian neurologist Sigmund Freud is the founder of psychoanalytic theory (1923). According to Freud, the human mind operates according to conscious and unconscious processes. Conscious processes, as the name implies, include everything of which we are consciously aware, the information and active memories we are thinking about and processing. Unconscious processes include everything that is below our conscious awareness, such as feelings, thoughts, urges, and memories. Freud argued that both the conscious and the unconscious drive all human motivation. Over the years, Freud's approach has stirred much controversy and debate. However, important insights can still be derived from his theories. One of his most important contributions is his theory that personality is influenced by three separate forces: the id, the ego, and the superego.

Id is a force that focuses attention and energy on primary needs, immediate gratification, and pleasurable acts without regard to the consequences.

- The **id** is a force that focuses attention and energy on primary needs, immediate gratification, and pleasurable acts without regard to the consequences. Much of the power of this force comes from biological urges, such as hunger, pain, or sex. Think about the id as a set of instinctive and primal urges that motivate an individual toward pleasure and away from pain.

- The **ego** is the human consciousness that attempts to look out for the interests of the individual by balancing the demands of the id and the constraints of the superego. Think about it as the regulatory force between the id and the superego.

- The **superego** reflects the rules, values, and norms imposed by society and works to prevent the id from seeking selfish gratification. The superego represents a societal force and is the opposite of the id. Think about it as a moral authority that regulates and controls all of the person's desires.

● **Photo 6.1** *The ego helps us balance and control the desires of the id and the superego*

Photo 6.1 represents a struggle many of us have had between the id (which would rather go to the beach) and the superego (which knows that there is an important report to complete). The ego helps balance and control these competing desires.

In the early twenty-first century, Freudian theory exerts only a minor influence on marketing and consumer research. Its biggest contribution is the set of research tools that it has developed, such as in-depth interviewing techniques, that help researchers identify and understand important, sometimes unconscious, motivations. Some theorists have used psychoanalytic theory as a foundation and further developed theories of personality and the self. The Swiss psychiatrist Carl Jung developed the concept of **archetypes**, which are characters that represent people, personalities, or behaviors that are constant across time and place. In all, there are twelve archetypes, such as the caregiver, the rebel, and the explorer, each of which is recognizable across cultures (Woodside 2010). Archetypes are reinforced by their depictions in popular culture in TV shows, movies, and songs. Further, regardless of culture, individuals react to archetypes in a similar way. Author Tom Clancy has sold millions of books worldwide and one of his most popular characters is Jack Ryan, a sympathetic hero archetype who always saves the day. Oprah plays the role of the sage archetype, doling out important advice at home and abroad. Indeed, Oprah is particularly popular with Saudi Arabian women, who view her as an inspiration and trusted advisor (Zoepf 2008). Archetypes are frequently used in advertising and marketing to create brand stories that resonate with consumers (see Photo 6.2). Whether using archetypes or not, depicting people in advertising can sometimes be quite tricky, as one ad industry executive has found (see Insights from the Boardroom 6).

Ego is the human consciousness that attempts to look out for the interests of the individual by balancing the demands of the id and the constraints of the superego.

Superego reflects the rules, values, and norms imposed by society and works to prevent the id from seeking selfish gratification.

Archetypes are the stable characters that capture basic ideas, feelings, fantasies, and visions that seem constant and frequently re-emerge across times and places.

The trait-based view of personality

Psychoanalytic theories provided a strong foundation for important research on personality. However, trait-based theories take those findings a step further

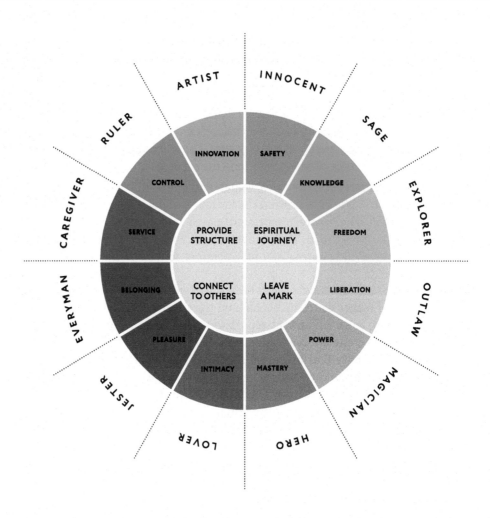

● **Photo 6.2** *Jung's twelve archetypes*

Trait-based approach (to personality) suggests that personality is the sum of an individual's traits or qualities, which can be used to predict or explain a variety of different behaviors.

by examining the effect of personality on consumption. According to the **trait-based approach**, personality is the sum of an individual's traits or qualities, which can be used to predict or explain a variety of different behaviors. This view of personality is based on the idea that traits can be assessed and evaluated. These traits are just a part of who we are, for example, conscientious, frugal, and shy. Individuals can usually be described in terms of a particular combination of these traits. Some traits are common to many individuals, but the exact combination is what we define as the individual's personality. Consistent with the psychological perspective of personality, traits are relatively stable and exert fairly consistent effects on behavior, regardless of environment.

Generally speaking, most researchers agree that an individual's personality can be described as existing along five key dimensions, sometimes called the "Big Five." These dimensions are (McCrae and Costa 1990):

- Extroversion—outgoing, talkative, and sociable
- Agreeableness—working well with others, empathizing, and being optimistic

- Conscientiousness—organized and goal-directed
- Neuroticism—emotionally unstable, moody, and anxious
- Openness—accepting of new ideas, imaginative, and engaging in abstract thinking

Marketers and other researchers have used this model in a variety of settings, including assessments of customer service (Harris and Fleming 2005), smoking (Adams and Nettle 2009), and the likelihood of taking medicine (Axelsson et al. 2011). Product development and marketing communications teams can use the Big Five model of personality to create connections that fit with a consumer's personality profile.

If consumer researchers find that a more finely tuned approach to personality is necessary, they might utilize either a single-trait or a multitrait approach in studying consumers. The **single-trait approach** presumes that in a given situation, a single personality trait will be the predominant force. Although the other personality traits play a minor role, the single-trait approach suggests that one trait takes the leading role. For example, a consumer researcher may be trying to understand the links between vegetarianism and personality. In doing so, the researcher may examine the effect of the personality trait *materialism* on preferences for eating a meat-based versus non-meat-based diet. See Table 6.1 for some frequently used personality traits in consumer research.

Single-trait approach (to personality) presumes that in a given situation, a single personality trait will be the predominant force.

Table 6.1 Examples of consumer-based personality traits

PERSONALITY TRAIT	DEFINITION
Materialism	The tendency to be overly concerned with physical objects and material goods (Richins and Dawson 1992)
Innovativeness	An appreciation for ideas, products, or experiences that are new and original (Goldsmith and Hofacker 1991)
Ethnocentrism	The opinion that a person's own group or culture is superior to others; this may lead to a strong preference for buying domestic, rather than foreign products (Shimp and Sharma 1987)
Frugality	The tendency to be restrained in acquiring products and to be resourceful in using products to achieve long-term goals (Lastovicka et al. 1999)
Spending self-control	"The ability to monitor and regulate one's spending-related thoughts and decisions in accordance with self-imposed standards" (Haws, Bearden, and Nenkov 2012, 696)

Source: Adapted, in part, from Szmigin and Piacentini (2015).

INSIGHTS FROM THE BOARDROOM 6

Don't even think about portraying older Americans as "old"

● *Anne Ryan*

Take a moment to picture a typical advertisement that is directed toward a retired person. Someone with gray hair is playing cards with friends or baking cookies with the grandkids. Now, rip up that picture and toss it out the window.

Anne Ryan is the director of brand strategy at the Brownstein Group and knows better than to use such outdated depictions when developing her brand strategies. Ryan has worked on several projects that focus on how older Americans see themselves. Located in Philadelphia, the Brownstein Group is a boutique branding agency that knows that good research leads to deep insights, which in turn lead to messaging strategies that resonate with consumers (see Figure 6.1). Ryan believes that the advertising industry has a "categorical black eye" in how it depicts older Americans. Indeed, how advertising depicts older Americans is completely different from how older Americans see themselves.

Older Americans (anyone fifty and older) make up 44 percent of the US population, but they control 70 percent of the country's disposable income. Many of them have both time and money on their hands. These individuals account for 49 percent of the nation's spending on consumer packaged goods, 40 percent of spending on wireless services, and 41 percent of spending on Apple computers. Inexplicably, only 5 percent of advertising is directed toward them (Nielsen Company & BoomAgers 2012). When advertisers do focus their efforts on this group, the depictions are out of

sync with how these consumers see themselves. If one were to look at current advertising, it would be easy to conclude that retirement is all about card games, comfortable shoes, and a slow physical decline. If you believe current advertising, "you're incapable of making your own decisions, you're sedentary, and you're plagued by health problems" (Ryan 2017).

This generation of older Americans grew up in the 1950s and 1960s, which was a time of optimism and hope. The American economy led the world, and its technological and social advances were a model for the rest of the world. This generation saw a man walk on the moon and the introduction of the birth control pill; they experienced the sexual revolution, marched for civil rights, dabbled in Eastern religions, and partied at Woodstock. But, according to Ryan, advertising doesn't talk about a better future for these people. "Their whole life is one thing and now the future is boring," says Ryan (2017).

This mismatch between advertising depictions and their own self-concepts is a recipe for a lot of dissatisfaction with product choices. Enter Ryan and her group, who worked on a recent study for a client that was planning to introduce a personal emergency response system, similar to the Fitbit device. The product category also includes the "I've fallen and I can't get up" devices. This one is different, though, because it tracks healthy living with exercise and nutrition apps. The client wanted to pitch this as a *lifestyle brand*, and initially, the researchers in Ryan's office thought the key motivator for older Americans would be *independence*. After getting the results, however, the research team was surprised to learn that independence was not important. Ryan (2017) recalls, "We were proven wrong; the best project is when this happens!"

The first step for Ryan's team was to design research that would provide data and information into the self-concepts of older Americans (see Figure 6.1). Researchers did home visits where they sat with individuals aged sixty-five to eighty-four and asked a

● **Figure 6.1** *The Research Process at the Brownstein Group*

series of in-depth questions. They asked participants to show them their homes and tell them about their hopes, their dreams, and their fears. The researchers showed imagery of a variety of ads, products, etc., and asked people to describe what they thought about or felt. "We showed pictures of 'typical' old people. . . they said, 'This is not me!'" "Then, we showed pictures of wine tastings, outdoor activities, etc.. . . they said, 'This is me!'" (Ryan 2017). The researchers also talked to the loved ones of the research participants—kids and spouses—and asked them to answer journal questions, upload photos, and complete some survey questions. This process allowed the researchers to triangulate their findings (**triangulation** of research happens when the findings from several different research techniques all lead to the same conclusion).

The second step in the research process was to develop deep insights. Ryan's group was surprised at how deep and meaningful the insights were. Some of the researchers were moved to tears by the stories they heard about different experiences. These research participants used to be groupies for bands and for jazz musicians. Now they were alone. One woman wore an emergency life alert button because one of her children made her. She hated it. Inside, she felt as if she was thirty. In the end, their goal was to be who they already are. They were not seeking independence. Instead, they were seeking to just maintain a strongly held self-concept of an interested, aware, and capable member of society.

The third step in the research process was the campaign execution. Ryan's group developed a proposal to show people as they are. Adoption of the product would just be another part in taking on a new chapter in their lives. Going back to the original prediction that the key motivator would be independence, the insights indicated that independence isn't supplemented by something like a device. Older Americans were not trying to achieve independence. The new device should not be portrayed as telling them how to live; it's not the "angel next to you." Instead, the device can help them keep going with what they're already doing now. "Keep going and moving": that was the key motivator.

One research study found an important connection between the personality trait innovativeness and pro-environment behaviors. Sometimes, despite having very strong pro-environment attitudes, consumers do not follow through and enact pro-environment behaviors. Why is there sometimes a mismatch between pro-environment attitudes and behaviors? The consumer-based personality trait of innovativeness held the answer. When consumers had both a positive pro-environment attitude and a strong innovativeness personality trait, they were much more likely to enact a series of pro-environment behaviors like recycling, turning out the lights, and buying green products (Englis and Phillips 2013). This finding has important implications for marketers who want to encourage purchase of environmentally friendly products. Specifically, marketers might find that an innovativeness-themed message such as "this product is new, original, and groundbreaking" might resonate particularly well with pro-environment consumers. Marketers might also want to emphasize innovativeness in the other parts of the marketing mix when reaching out to innovative consumers.

Triangulation of research happens when the findings from several different research techniques all lead to the same conclusion.

Multitrait approach (to personality) is where researchers are concerned with a number of personality traits taken together and how they combine to effect consumption.

The **multitrait approach** to personality suggests that several personality traits work together to have an impact on consumption. So, returning to the vegetarian example, the researcher would be interested in the effect of materialism in combination with other personality variables (such as shyness, conscientiousness, and openness) on eating decisions and behaviors. For both of these approaches to personality, researchers are trying to predict consumer behavior. However, because of its greater detail and complexity, the multitrait approach has generally been better at predicting behavior.

It is not surprising that personality traits are associated with a variety of behaviors, including media behaviors. One study, for example, examined the likelihood of an individual watching reality TV and that individual's personality traits. The researchers found that for younger individuals, those between fifteen and seventeen years old, the personality traits of materialism, entitlement, and narcissism were strongly related to watching reality TV shows. There was no such connection for eighteen- to twenty-one-year-olds (Opree and Kühne 2016). Critics might look at this result and question the direction of the effect. That is, are individuals with these personality traits drawn to reality TV or do the storylines and characters in the reality TV shows influence a viewer to develop these personality traits? Previous research indicates that personality traits remain constant over time, so we can feel safe in concluding that personality influences reality TV viewing. However, it is also possible that a small effect might move in the opposite direction such that heavy reality TV viewing could strengthen and reinforce existing personality traits.

Brand personality and traits

Brands can have humanlike personalities too. The Geico Gecko, with his inexplicable British accent, provides calm advice and projects an air of professionalism and competence in the insurance industry; the M&M's spokescandies are cute, clever, and fun; and the Pillsbury Doughboy is chubby, friendly, and quick with a laugh. In each of these examples, the brand mascot's traits mirror that of the brand. The **brand personality scale** identified five key brand personality traits of sincerity, excitement, competence, sophistication, and ruggedness. According to this scale, Hallmark cards are sincere, MTV is exciting, and *The Wall Street Journal* is competent (Aaker 1997). Over the years, researchers have used these dimensions to describe retail stores and products (Möller and Herm 2013). Consumers select the brands with personalities that reflect or enhance their own self-concepts. Some brands with sophisticated personalities (such Rolex or Prada) encourage consumer aspirations around luxury and glamor, while brands with rugged personalities (such as Jeep or Timberland) emphasize toughness and masculinity. The UK ad for the Jeep Renegade establishes a connection between the personality of the brand and that of the consumer (Photo 6.3). See Insights from Academia 6.1 for how a strong connection to a brand can insulate a consumer from pain.

Brand personality scale identified five key brand personality traits: sincerity, excitement, competence, sophistication, and ruggedness.

INSIGHTS FROM ACADEMIA 6.1

Brand-aid

Research in social psychology has found that when individuals have close personal relationships with other people, they are healthier, recover more quickly from health events, and even experience less pain. Can this same health benefit happen when consumers have relationships with brands? Yes! When consumers feel a particularly close relationship with a brand (*brand love*), the brand provides consumers with a feeling of social connectedness and actually helps insulate them from physical pain. While this line of research is still in its infancy, it does provide some ideas for marketers and healthcare providers. One approach could be to get patients to think about their brand love by offering them a chance to wear hospital gowns that are imprinted with the logo of their favorite sports team: "For your appendectomy, would you like the Eagles gown or the Seahawks gown?"

Reimann, M., S. Nuñez, and R. Castaño. 2017. "Brand-Aid." Journal of Consumer Research 44 (3): 673–91.

Sociological perspective on personality suggests that both internal and external factors impact how individuals view themselves.

A sociological perspective on personality

The **sociological perspective on personality** suggests that both internal and external factors impact how individuals view themselves (Heine 1971). With the sociological perspective, researchers often study conceptualizations of the self, which is a person's beliefs, feelings, and attitudes about his or her own identity. This perspective suggests that personality can change over time. The perspective of symbolic interactionism has played a big role in our understanding of the social perspective on personality.

Symbolic interactionism

The **symbolic interactionist perspective** says that relationships with other people play a large part in forming the self (Mead 1913) and that "the mind is the thinking part of the self" (Stets and Burke 2003, 130). An important part of the symbolic interactionist perspective is that it focuses on the small scale, like the interaction you have with a friend, rather than bigger interactions you may have with a large group of people. The interactions we have with other people exert an important role in how we think about the self and in the meanings we create (Ligas and Cotte 1999). There are a few things to remember about symbolic interactionism. First, there will always be variations in social consensus and the meanings that we construct. Say, for example, that you are one of those people who loves

● **Photo 6.3** *UK ad for the Jeep Renegade*

swimming in the ocean. You love jumping in the waves and putting on snorkeling gear to see all the cool things beneath the surface. Your friend, however, imagines only creepy, slithery things in the water and won't set foot near the ocean. In short, for the same stimulus, there will often be different interpretations. The second thing to remember is that meanings change over time because we are always talking to people, learning new things, and adapting our viewpoint. After sitting through a class on the environment and talking with other people, your friend becomes interested in the wonder of the ocean and is willing to consider going with you the next time you plan a trip. The third thing that is important to an understanding of symbolic interactionism is that these meanings impact behaviors. Going back to the example of your reluctant friend, the next time you're at the beach, she sports some snorkeling gear and dives in! Meanings impact behaviors.

Most individuals want to fit in with other people's expectations, but to understand those expectations, we need to first understand ourselves. The **self-concept** refers to how an individual thinks about and evaluates the self. It includes all of our thoughts, feelings, beliefs, and evaluations about who we are (Rosenberg 1979). An important part of the self-concept are beliefs about how the self is evaluated by others; individuals want to communicate the "correct" messages to others about the way they appear, so they often look to the beauty and fashion industries for inspiration. One example is Adidas, which promotes individuality. As a follow-up to the "All Originals" campaign by Adidas from 2011, the "Original Is Never Finished" campaign was launched in 2017 with a remix of the infamous "My Way" song from Frank Sinatra. The campaign builds on the idea of the importance of individuality by showing how you can express your individuality by wearing Adidas, but still connect with a wide variety of other people. The TV ad showed people from different walks of life, representing their passions, joy of life, creativity, and disdain for the ordinary. Basketball star Kareem Abdul-Jabbar and music artist Snoop Dogg also made appearances in the ad, reinforcing the theme of individuality.

Multiplicity of self

Consumer researchers have concluded that the self is dynamic and ever-changing (Shankar, Elliott, and Fitchett 2009). We know that the self comprises our beliefs, feelings, and evaluations, but it also includes knowledge of and feelings about the various roles we play in our lives. As we go through life, some roles are more prominent, depending on the context and how central that role is to the self. Your role as a student or part-time employee may be more central on a day-to-day basis than your role as a pizza-maker, which may only emerge on weekends or when you're home with your family. The concept of the **multiplicity of the self** shows us that different self-concepts motivate us to behave in different ways at different times and in different contexts. The important thing to remember is that the concept of the multiplicity of the self is not static; it changes and adapts over time. In addition, it straddles both the

Self-concept refers to the sum total of our thoughts, feelings, and imaginations about who we are.

Multiplicity of the self holds that different self-concepts motivate us to behave in different ways at different times and in different contexts.

psychological and the social realms of our lives, taking into account both the cognitive (what we know, what we believe, what we strive toward) and the social (what others expect, what society dictates). Table 6.2 illustrates the variety of conceptualizations of the self that researchers have used to understand this important concept.

Marketers use the perspective of the multiplicity of the self to more clearly understand consumer aspirations about who they want to be, as well as convictions about who they do not want to be. A consumer's perception of the ideal self will motivate the purchase of brands that may help to achieve that

Table 6.2 Various conceptualizations of the self

ASPECT OF SELF	DEFINITION	SAMPLE SUMMARY STATEMENT
Actual self	The core sense of self that is enduring and stable across situations; "the person that I believe I actually am"	"I'm honest and friendly."
Ideal self	The self we aspire to be, often just as important to how and what we consume as the actual self	"I would like to be more socially and environmentally aware."
Social self	Sometimes referred to as the "looking glass self," this is how consumers believe they are seen by significant others	"My friends think I'm funny and clumsy."
Ideal social self	How we would *like* to be seen by significant others; "the person that I would ideally like others to see me as being"	"I would like my friends to respect me and to be taken more seriously."
Situational or malleable self	Recognizes the self-concept as a dynamic entity, where different aspects of self are activated depending on the context	"I act one way when I'm with my parents and quite another when I'm with my friends."
Extended self	The idea that our possessions and belongings form such a close connection to us and our past that they come to represent us in some way; the extended self helps us to understand the connections that we feel toward items and brands that are special to us (Belk 1988)	"My new motorcycle says a lot about me."
Possible selves	Representations of a future self, which can be positive or negative (Cross and Markus 1991)	"I *see myself* owning a successful business one day; I *do not see myself* being homeless one day."
Negative selves	Refers to the person you are not and do not want to become (Banister and Hogg 2001)	"I am not buying this outfit; it will make me look like a druggie."

Source: Adapted, in part, from Szmigin and Piacentini (2015).

● **Photo 6.4** *Different selves are activated, depending on the situation*

Malleable self refers to the idea that people will act differently according to the situation, influenced by social roles, cues, and the need for self-presentation.

ideal self. Similarly, negative possible selves can motivate incentives for behavior, when, for example, you might study harder for the next exam because you want to avoid the negative possible self of becoming a college dropout.

The idea of the **malleable self** (Aaker 1999) acknowledges that individuals will switch between different aspects of the self, depending on the situation. The malleable self is influenced by social roles, cues, and the need for self-presentation. Take, for example, a common behavior like going out for lunch. Depending on the context, different selves will be activated, which will result in different behaviors. For a young dad, a visit to Pizza Hut for a child's birthday party reflects an actual self, enacting his "dad identity," whereas a trip to a more upscale restaurant where he may take some business clients may be reflective of a more ideal social self or a possible self (Photo 6.4). For each context, there are behaviors that are acceptable and those that are not socially acceptable. Insights from Academia 6.2 describes an instance of how possible selves can motivate behavior and Insights from the Field 6.1 examines the self in the virtual world.

 INSIGHTS FROM ACADEMIA 6.2

Better go now before it's too late

After college, as many young people make the transition to adulthood, they quickly realize that time is running out on their ability to see the world and do exciting things. Indeed, they see their slightly older friends and siblings being saddled with the responsibilities of work and family, and they easily imagine the lives of their own possible selves as filled with responsibilities and constraints. Because of this, middle-class young adults voraciously consume exploratory experiences like new restaurants, music concerts, activity groups, and foreign travel. Their goal is to experience something new, exciting, and challenging.

As one participant said about a trip to Asia, "I'm kinda done with Europe. I've been there many times and it doesn't feel like a challenge anymore. Asia feels like a challenge. I mean any place where you have to get inoculated against like crazy deadly diseases, that's the challenge."

Weinberger, M. F., J. R. Zavisca, and J. M. Silva. 2017. "Consuming for an Imagined Future: Middle-Class Consumer Lifestyle and Exploratory Experiences in the Transition to Adulthood." Journal of Consumer Research 44 (2): 332–60.

INSIGHTS FROM THE FIELD 6.1

The self in the virtual world

Social media is an important medium by which we construct the self. TikTok, Instagram, Twitter, and YouTube allow consumers to show off products and consumption-related activities with pictures and videos. Other people can literally watch consumption happen live, as the mukbang trend seems to indicate. *Mukbang* is a Korean term that roughly translates to "eat broadcast" and refers to the act of watching other people eat and talk about their food. One of the biggest mukbang celebrities has gained over 2.3 million subscribers by posting videos of herself eating various meals—she has also made millions of dollars by selling advertising on her site. What do viewers get out of this? The reasons are varied, but individuals who watch say they feel a social connection, less stress, and less loneliness (CBS 2019). The person doing the posting communicates information about his or her own self-identity (Hollenbeck and Kaikati 2012). However, what you see is not always real. Indeed, quite a bit of impression management is also taking place, with creative editing and multiple retakes.

Another way in which social media has impacted the self is in the changes that are happening in media consumption. The consumption of media today is nothing like that of your parents' generation. Indeed, consumers who watch TV today, for example, are completely different from the consumers of previous generations, who were passive recipients of information and entertainment. In the early twenty-first century, many viewers simply stream their shows. For those who do watch broadcast TV, many more utilize social media during advertising breaks and during the show itself. Viewers now turn to second screen conversations on Twitter and other social media to discuss the show with one another. They may comment about the characters and plot line and speculate about what might happen next. Because marketers know that consumers are doing this, they try to find ways to connect to viewers. A viewer watching *The Walking Dead* may turn to her phone to see the reaction of other fans to a surprise plot twist, for example. While she might miss an ad for Domino's Pizza that airs during the commercial break, she might notice when the Domino's Twitter account sends a message with #TWD (Lawler 2011). Brands hoping to connect with viewers at the heart of the conversation are able to deploy these kinds of tactics. The likelihood of their success will rest, in part, on how well the advertising message fits with the social self that is taking part in these conversations.

Questions

1. Check out the video from CBS News on the mukbang phenomenon (https://www.cbsnews.com/video/mukbang-watch-what-they-eat/) and think about the different conceptualizations of the self listed in Table 6.2. For both the mukbang star and the viewer, answer these questions: (a) Which selves are being activated? Explain. (b) How might activation of these selves influence other decisions or behaviors?

2. We learned in this insight that consumers use social media to express important aspects of the self. How might marketers utilize this important finding? Be specific.

Sources: Lawler (2011); Hollenbeck and Kaikati (2012).

The symbolic interactionist perspective concludes that individuals have many different selves and that to support those selves, a variety of products are required. Valued objects in a consumer's life, such as special mementos, clothing, or jewelry, as well as close attachments to sports teams or special vacation spots, are incorporated into the extended self and work to clarify the individual's self-concept. Our own consumer identity can be developed through the products and brands we consume to help us construct our own story of the self (Shankar, Elliott, and Fitchett 2009). As you get ready for a night out, you might use your special Dior shower gel, wear your Diesel jeans, and don your Jordans. Together, these brands help you to create the self you want to display to the world. It is easy to see how brands can become so wrapped up in an individual's identity can come to occupy a central part of that individual's self-concept.

The symbolic interactionist perspective is highly consistent with the view of the extended self, where individuals carefully select which products and brands to consume in order to construct their own identity (Ahuvia 2005; Belk 1988). This process of selection and careful construction is referred to as the narrative approach to identity and is consistent with consumer culture theory (e.g., Arnould and Thompson 2005). According to the consumer culture theory perspective, individuals are preoccupied with their own identities and work to improve and embellish that identity and personal narrative (see Insights from the Field 6.2).

Personality and self in marketing practice

Consumers often use products and consumption experiences to construct their own personalities and create (or reinforce) their various selves. For example, some consumers find it useful to construct their own identities by looking at other online identities, which are often linked to lifestyle and fashion. There are many examples of women fashion influencers, but men's fashion influencers attract large audiences too. One of the most influential is Robert Spangle, a former marine turned photographer and writer. His work has been published in *British GQ*, *Esquire UK*, *Vogue* online, *Men's Health Germany*, and *The Rake*. His keen eye for color and style, combined with extensive global travels, has given him the opportunity to capture a wide variety of colors, cuts, and fabrics on his subjects. His fifty thousand followers on Instagram are delighted too (Photo 6.6).

Marketing managers help consumers connect with their brand by developing narratives or stories about their brands, ones with which consumers can easily identify. The sports brand ASICS used a narrative approach to the self as the basis for its 2012 "Made of Sport" campaign, which depicted various elite athletes talking about their connection to the sport and motivation to continually push themselves. For example, one ad entitled, "I am made of sweat not swagger," featured Christophe Lemaitre, a French sprinter and the fastest man in Europe. Lemaitre talked about his deep dedication to running and what it takes to shave just a fraction of a second off his time. Another narrative featured Simon Wheatcroft, a British ultrarunner who runs distances of more than 26.2 miles. This ad is entitled "I am made of belief not barriers." To Wheatcroft, running allows him to explore his "physical and psychological limits" because he is blind (he runs with a guide). This campaign allows customers to see how elite athletes construct meaning from their sport and provides a bit of inspiration to consumers to do the same. It is interesting to note that the brand takes somewhat of a back seat in the narrative; the important part is the story and the athlete. See Photo 6.7 for an example of an ad from this campaign.

INSIGHTS FROM THE FIELD 6.2

Why don't more men study abroad?

Many college students dream about spending a semester abroad at some point during their academic careers. They dream about completely immersing themselves in a new culture, exploring a new city and environment, and meeting new people. Having an international experience has been linked to better grades, higher-paying jobs, and increased job satisfaction after graduation (Carotenuto 2015). Most students who study abroad are in the science, technology, engineering, and mathematics field of study (25.2 percent), followed by business (20.9 percent) and social science (17.1 percent). Where do these students go? Almost twice as many

● **Photo 6.5** *Students from the International Centre for Exploration & Education helped to rebuild a school after the 2015 earthquake in Nepal*

US students go to Europe (54.4 percent) as to the next two most popular destinations combined (Latin America and the Caribbean, 16.3 percent; and Asia, 11.1 percent). Unfortunately, although about three hundred thousand US students study abroad each year, only about 33.5 percent are men (the other 66.5 percent are women) (Institute of International Education 2017). While it is good news that so many women are getting to study abroad, why don't more men?

Compared to women, men seem to be drawn to shorter-term programs, are less likely to select a non-English-speaking destination, and are more interested in programs that directly connect to their studies at their home universities. Although there is much speculation about what would get more men to engage in an international experience, one technique that seems to work is to ask men what they want to *learn* when they go abroad rather than where they want to go (Carotenuto 2015). While there may be no simple answer as to why men are less likely to study abroad than women, one explanation could be that they may be less likely to perceive of an ideal self or a possible self in an international setting. Perhaps they don't "see" the benefits of going, so they don't see themselves there. However, by focusing on tangible benefits like what they might learn, as suggested (Carotenuto 2015), perhaps men can make a better connection between the skills they will learn during their international experience and the skills they may someday need in the workplace.

The International Centre for Exploration & Education is a small organization that helps university students step out of their comfort zones and experience the world (see https://www.explorationcentre.org). These noncredit programs are offered for "safer" destinations like Europe as well as more "challenging" destinations like Southeast Asia. The goal is to challenge students to "build your cross-cultural competencies, to gain real-world knowledge, and to become more flexible in order to live, work, and succeed in an increasingly globalized world" (International Centre for Exploration & Education 2019, Phillips 2017) (see Photo 6.5).

Questions

1. How might concepts of positive possible selves and negative possible selves be used to motivate more students, especially men, to have an international experience?
2. Take a symbolic interactionist perspective and develop a recommendation for how a small company like the International Centre for Exploration & Education could encourage more students to have international experiences.

Sources: Carotenuto (2015); Institute of International Education (2017); International Centre for Exploration & Education (2019); Phillips (2017).

● **Photo 6.6** *A shot from Robert Spangle's collection of global fashion*

Symbolic consumption

Symbolic consumption describes the meanings that are attached to products, as well as the process by which those meanings are transferred between the product, the consumer, and the broader society. As a process, symbolic consumption provides an important means by which consumers construct their own self-identities. We know that consumer products, services, and other experiences are imbued with symbolic meaning. Further, consumers may wish to communicate some of these meanings to others. For the process of symbolic consumption to work properly and meaning to be shared and transferred, the symbolic meanings must be widely recognized by the social group. The bottom line is that consumption symbols provide an important way of communicating with others in the world. It should be no surprise that different products represent different meanings. If the product is visible to others, such as a car, clothes, or shoes, it has a much better chance of communicating meaning to others. Figure 6.2 maps the relationships between the symbolic meaning of products/brands/stores, consumers' self-concepts, and related audiences (Grubb and Grathwohl 1967). The solid line represents the actual, tangible, intrinsic value the brand provides to the consumer who uses it. The dashed lines represent the intangible, extrinsic values and meanings.

The process itself is fairly simple. A consumer (Individual A) uses a brand in the hope that significant others, like friends, peers, and family (Audience B), will notice and that the positive meanings that Individual A associates with the brand are also widely held and understood by Audience B. When they do, those significant others transfer those symbolic meanings to Individual A. An example may help. To illustrate, consider a twelve-year-old boy who is an up-and-coming tennis star and whose favorite player is Swiss superstar Roger Federer (see Figure 6.3). Federer uses a Wilson Pro Staff RF 97 Autograph racquet, so our young tennis

● **Photo 6.7** *I am made of sweat not swagger*

hopeful also wants to use a Wilson racquet ("I can play tennis like Federer"), because (as indicated by the solid line) the racquet is among the best in the market. The young tennis hopeful also uses a Wilson racquet to enhance his status in the eyes of his friends and the other children taking lessons because these individuals know that using a Wilson racquet is a signal of high performance (all of these connections in meaning are represented by dashed lines). By using the Wilson racquet, the boy transfers the social meaning of the brand to himself and, in the process, achieves self-enhancement.

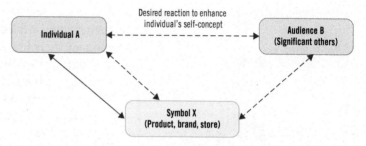

● **Figure 6.2** *Symbolic meaning of goods, consumer self-concepts, and related audience*

Source: adapted from Grubb and Grathwohl (1967: 25) and printed with permission from The American Marketing Association

The theory of **image congruency** proposes that consumers select products, brands, and retailers that correspond with their self-concept (Sirgy 1982). For example, what retailers do you feel especially comfortable (or uncomfortable) visiting: Cabela's, Barnes & Noble, Wegmans, Sephora? Your feelings of comfort have to do with congruency between your self-image and the image of the store. Specifically, **self-congruity** is the extent to which a product (or retail) image is consistent with a consumer's current self-image; ideal congruity occurs when the product image matches the ideal self-image (Ericksen and Sirgy 1992). Every product isn't for everyone, just like every retailer isn't for everyone. Marketers understand this. Because of this, marketers go to great efforts to make sure their brand and retail identities are as congruent as possible with the identities of their target market.

Symbolic consumption describes the meanings that are attached to products, as well as the process by which those meanings are transferred between the product, the consumer, and the broader society.

Image congruency proposes that consumers select products, brands, and retailers that correspond with their self-concept.

Self-congruity refers to the extent to which a product (or retail) image matches a consumer's self-image.

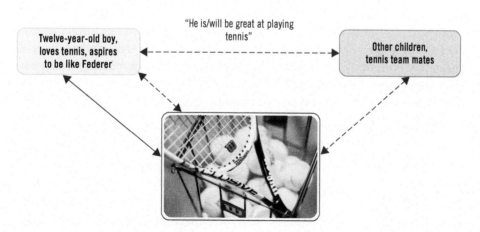

● **Figure 6.3** *Symbolic meanings move between brands, consumers, and others*

Source: RMC42/Shutterstock.com

● **Photo 6.8** *Burt's Bees products link the brand to customer values*

Consumer identity and corporate values

Increasingly, organizations are realizing that it is important to connect their brand and corporate values to consumer values. The outdoor clothing manufacturer Patagonia is honest and forthright about its corporate values and guiding principles. They have taken a very strong public stance on the issues of environmental preservation and social justice around the world. All this is backed by concrete changes and modifications to the organizational structure, new initiatives and partnerships, and specific goals and benchmarks. To top it off, Patagonia is incredibly transparent in all of its work. Simply look at Patagonia's Footprint Chronicles (https://www.patagonia.com/our-footprint/) to track the movement of different products as they make their way through the global supply chain. Consumers who purchase the Patagonia brand are able to connect their own values to those of the company. Burt's Bees, a company that sells organic and sustainably sourced skin care products and other items, is another company that links its brand values to consumer values. With its naturally-sourced ingredients, recyclable containers, and policy of no animal testing, consumers who purchase Burt's Bees products can rest assured that they are actualizing their own values of having a minimal impact on the natural world (see Photo 6.8).

Values are our desired end-states in life and preferred paths to achieving them; they constitute our purpose and goals in life. There are two main types of values that guide our behavior: **terminal values**, which represent our life goals, and **instrumental values**, which reflect the means, paths, and behavioral standards that are needed to fulfill our terminal values (see Table 6.3) (Rokeach and Ball-Rokeach 1989). We use our instrumental values to get to our terminal values. For example, enacting the instrumental value of ambition might lead to the terminal value of family security. It is important that marketers understand how consumers connect products to their own set of values. A model known as means–end chains and a research technique known as laddering can help researchers do this. First, a **means–end chain** is a series of connections that consumers make that link product attributes to a consumer's own closely held values. Means–end chains are made up of three basic levels: attributes, consequences, and values.

- **Attributes** are the actual features of the product or service, like the percentage of wool in your sweater or the return policy of a retail store.
- **Consequences** are the benefits that the attributes provide to consumers, like a warm, cozy sweater or confidence in purchasing a product from the store.
- **Values,** as stated previously, are a consumer's guiding principles or desired end-states in life, like comfort (the value for the 100 percent wool content) or independence (the value for the return policy).

Terminal values are our life goals and motivate our behavior.

Instrumental values are the means, paths, and behavioral standards by which we pursue our terminal values.

Means–end chains are a series of connections consumers make that link product attributes to their own closely held values.

Attributes are the characteristics or features of the product.

Consequences are the benefits that the product attributes provide to consumers.

Table 6.3 List of terminal and instrumental values

TERMINAL VALUES	INSTRUMENTAL VALUES
Family security	Honest
A world at peace	Responsible
Freedom	Ambitious
Self-respect	Forgiving
Happiness	Broadminded
Wisdom	Courageous
A sense of accomplishment	Helpful
A comfortable life	Loving
Salvation	Capable
True friendship	Clean
National security	Self-controlled
Equality	Independent
Inner harmony	Cheerful
Mature love	Polite
An exciting life	Intellectual
A world of beauty	Obedient
Pleasure	Logical
Social recognition	Imaginative

Source: Rokeach and Ball-Rokeach (1989).

In the previous example, the resulting means–end chain would look like this: 100 percent wool (attribute) → cozy (consequence) → comfort (value). For a researcher to find out how consumers link product attributes to values, they enact a research technique called **laddering**, which involves a series of questions that ask, "Why is *that* important to you?" In the end, the researcher can uncover a consumer's deeper connections to either instrumental or terminal values (Reynolds and Gutman 1988). Consider the example of the situation where a consumer is trying to decide whether to buy crunchy or smooth peanut butter (a product attribute). The researcher will start out with a question like, "The next time you purchase peanut butter, will you get crunchy or smooth?" Once the researcher finds out that the consumer prefers crunchy, the laddering starts. A good researcher will make sure to incorporate a research participant's responses

Values are a consumer's deep-rooted and enduring ideals and guiding principles.

Laddering is a research technique designed to uncover a consumer's means–end chains.

Researcher: why is it important to you that you eat something that tastes better?
Participant: I don't know, it just makes me happy

Researcher: why is it important to you to have crunchy peanut butter?
Participant: I just think it tastes better than the smooth

Researcher: the next time you purchase peanut butter, will you get crunchy or smooth?
Participant: Crunchy!

● **Figure 6.4** *Means-end chain and laddering questions*

Psychographic segmentation is based on building a picture of the consumer based on activities, interests, and opinions.

VALS™ uses a custom-designed survey to identify an individual's primary motivation (self-perception), the extent of resources available to realize their self-perception, five key demographics, and a proprietary algorithm to place individuals into one of eight predetermined consumer groups.

into each subsequent question so that, for example, if a participant responds that it "tastes better," in the next question, the researcher will focus on why it is important for it to taste better (see Figure 6.4 for an example of a means–end chain and laddering questions).

Psychographics

It makes sense that personality differences influence the types of products and brands purchased, and when we look at ads for products like cologne and cars, we can easily see links between characters or actors in the ads and the brands they represent. However, reviews of research show that personality can, at best, explain only about 10 percent of the variation in consumer behavior (see, for example, Kassarjian and Sheffet 1981; Foxall and Goldsmith 1988). Because of this, values and lifestyle segmentation strategies have been developed to provide a better understanding of how personality and values *work together* to impact a consumer's decisions and behaviors. These strategies break up the market into groups of consumers who are similar to one another based on their lifestyles and values. Segmentation helps marketers make more appropriate decisions regarding product, price, place, and promotion, all in an effort to more efficiently and effectively deliver the value proposition. Although there are several segmentation strategies that are in some ways related to lifestyle (geographic, behavioral, and demographic), the strategy that most closely connects values and lifestyles to products is psychographics.

Psychographic segmentation of the market builds a picture of the consumer based on activities, interests, and opinions. Remember that lifestyle and personality are different but closely related; personality refers to a consumer's internal characteristics, and lifestyle refers to external manifestations of how consumers live their lives. The advantage of lifestyle segmentation strategies like psychographics is that it can be done at a very general level (i.e., a population of people), at a product level (i.e., consumers who are really into healthy food), or by brand (i.e., loyal consumers of a particular brand of car).

VALS™ takes a slightly different approach to segmentation. Developed by Strategic Business Insights, Inc., VALS™ is designed to be used for a variety of marketing applications. VALS™ places US adults into segments based on psychological traits and demographics that are validated to correspond to consumer behavior. VALS™ uses a custom-designed survey to identify an individual's primary motivation (self-perception), the extent of resources available to realize their self-perception, five key demographics, and a proprietary algorithm to place individuals into one of eight predetermined consumer groups. The majority of consumers fall into one of three motivations: ideals, achievement, or self-expression. Resource measures include more than income and education—they can come from a variety of internal sources such as self-confidence, leadership ability, curiosity, vanity, and energy. A study of VALS™ consumer groups improves marketers' predictive ability of how different groups will most likely express themselves in the marketplace (Strategic Business Insights 2019). VALS™ reveals important insights that demographic segmentations cannot offer. For example, VALS™ shows why consumers who share similar demographic characteristics often demonstrate completely different consumption behaviors.

Going even further, combining information about an individual's VALS™ segment with information derived from batteries of other consumer-related questions such as attitudes, media behaviors, and product preferences, marketers can create robust target consumer profiles that include deep insights into a consumer's values, attitudes, lifestyles, and likely behaviors. When used in combination with these other consumer-related questions, the insights provided by VALS™ help marketers more effectively utilize their marketing dollars. Figure 6.5 provides an overview of characteristics for each of the eight VALS™ segments (Strategic Business Insights 2019).

Ideals			Achievement		Self-Expression		
Innovators	Thinkers	Believers	Achievers	Strivers	Experiencers	Makers	Survivors
Are confident enough to experiment	Plan, research consider before acting	Believe in right/ wrong for a good life	Have a me-first my-family-first attitude	Are the center of street culture	Want to stand out	Are distrustful of government	Are the quiet rank and file
Are information ready	Are the old guard	Want friendly communities	Are fully scheduled	Live in the moment	Want everything	Believe in sharp gender roles	Are cautious and risk averse
Are future oriented	Enjoy historical perspective	Not looking to change society	Are peer conscious	Wear their wealth	Are spontaneous	Protect what they think they own	Use television as a window to the world
Are receptive to new ideas and technologies	Have "ought" and "should" benchmarks for social conduct	Have no tolerance for ambiguity	Are anchors of the status quo	Desire to better their lives; have difficulty in doing so	Have a heightened sense of visual stimulation	Want to "work" on their world	Take comfort in routine and the familiar
Enjoy problem-solving challenges	Use technolgy in functional ways	Have strong me-too fashion attitudes	Believe money is the source of authority	Experience revolving employment	Introduce new sayings	Have strong outdoor interests; don't want to be walled in	Are loyal to products and brands
Are self-directed consumers	Are not influenced by what's hot	Want to belong	Are committed to family and job	Are looking for a fun time	See themselves as very sociable	Are not concerned with being fashionable	Are analog not digital
Are keenly aware of others' self-interests	Follow traditional intellectual pursuits	Trust traditional sources; don't question authority	Value tech that provides a productivity boost	Are impulsive	Are first in, first out of trend adoption	May appear to be anti-intellectual	Place emphasis on preservation

● **Figure 6.5** *Overview of characteristics of VALS™ segments*

Source: Strategic Business Insights (2019)

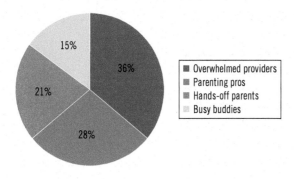

Other organizations, such as the Mintel Research Group, also utilize a combination of demographics and lifestyles to segment consumers into a wide variety of segments. For example, in a recent study of young families in the United States, Mintel identified four key segments (Mintel 2019):

• *Overwhelmed providers* (36 percent): This segment is generally fairly engaged in parenting, but struggle to balance family time with other obligations. Demographically, 55 percent are dads and 45 percent are moms. They are younger than the other segments and tend to live in urban areas.

• *Parenting pros* (28 percent): This segment is completely focused on their children. They have a positive outlook and are willing to take on more than their "fair share" of parenting duties. Demographically, this segment is made up of 69 percent women, has a below-median household income, and is slightly older than other segments.

• *Hands-off parents* (21 percent): This segment is not particularly engaged or worried in their role as parents. Demographically, there is an even split between men and women. These individuals are slightly older, are likely to live in the suburbs, and have an average household income.

• *Busy buddies* (15 percent): These individuals are highly engaged in parenting, but believe they have found a perfect work/life balance, so they are unwilling to spend even more time in parenting. From a demographic perspective, 45 percent are men and 55 percent are women, they are likely to be in the millennial age bracket, are the most likely to be employed, and are most likely to pay for child care.

Whether a researcher uses VALS™, Mintel (see Figure 6.6), or another segmentation system based on psychographics, the result is a more detailed depiction of the consumer. This, in turn, helps marketers to predict what they might do next. In the end, the goal is to predict what consumers will do so that managers can find more efficient and effective ways to deliver the value proposition. After a thorough discussion of how consumers construct their own personalities and selves, the next question is how these conceptualizations influence behaviors. The next section in this chapter investigates the concept of motivation.

Motivation is a drive that causes an individual to behave in a particular way. It is rooted in an individual's goals, desires, and wishes.

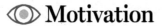 # Motivation

Motivation is a drive that causes an individual to behave in a particular way. It is rooted in an individual's goals, desires, and wishes. Why does one individual choose to take the public bus to school while another decides to drive?

spare
me the
guilt chip.

think popped!
never fried. never baked.

product of usa

p•pchips
original
potato chips

available at
Waitrose *Boots* Sainsbury's

thinking about food. Think about what happens when a consumer is contemplating indulging in a yummy desert; there are certainly both positive and negative consequences with such consumption! Marketers who know that their consumers will be experiencing approach–avoidance will often create messaging strategies that recognize the indulgence while suggesting that the consumer deserves it. Other marketers may create low-calorie options for indulgent products and promote them as a guilt-free option. See the ad for Pop Chips (Photo 6.10), which have fewer than one hundred calories per serving. See Insights from Academia 6.4 for another example of the approach–avoidance strategy.

Luckily for consumers, most consumer decision-making involves a choice between two or more fairly favorable alternatives. **Approach–approach conflict** occurs when an individual must select between two or more equally attractive alternatives. Have you ever been at a restaurant and found that there were at least two or three meals that you would like to try? Congratulations, you have experienced approach–approach conflict. Online clothing or home decorating retailers try to address this issue by offering easy return policies. Consumers can try out a few options at home and then return the items they don't like.

The last motivational conflict is **avoidance–avoidance conflict**. Here, every choice has a negative consequence. There is an old saying that you are between a rock and a hard place, meaning that both choices are fairly bad. Say, for example, that you just got offered a job with a fairly decent starting salary. However, you start looking at reviews of the company and find that they really treat their employees terribly. The work sounds incredibly boring and it is in a city far from home. You resolve to yourself that you will turn it down and keep looking. Then, the phone rings and the person who interviewed you says that

Approach–approach conflict occurs when an individual must select between two or more equally attractive alternatives.

Avoidance–avoidance conflict is when the choices available all have a negative consequence.

Do you have enough self-control to eat kale?

When individuals focus on having a healthy diet, they generally create strategies that fall into two categories: eating more foods like kale (an approach strategy) and eating fewer foods like cake (an avoidance strategy). The success of these approach and avoidance strategies, however, depends on the consumer's level of self-control. Consumers with low self-control tend to focus their attention and thoughts more on avoidance items they particularly like, while they also focus on approach items they particularly dislike ("But I love dessert and I just hate vegetables."). It is no surprise that these consumers are unlikely to be successful. By contrast, consumers with high self-control focus their thoughts on the opposite ("Cake makes me sick, but vegetables are yummy."). These high-self-control consumers have developed a different thought strategy that enables them to make healthier plans and choices. So, what are you having for dinner tonight?

David, M. E., and K. L. Haws. 2016. "Saying 'No' to Cake or 'Yes' to Kale: Approach and Avoidance Strategies in Pursuit of Health Goals." Psychology & Marketing 33 (8): 588–94.

Intrinsic need is an internal drive that all humans have, such as the need for food, water, and shelter, as well as emotional needs such as love, friendship, and acceptance.

the company would like to offer you an extra $5,000 signing bonus. Neither option in this avoidance–avoidance choice is good; you're between a rock and a hard place.

Maslow's hierarchy of needs

One of the most important and frequently discussed theories of motivation is **Maslow's hierarchy of needs** (Figure 6.7) (Maslow 1954). One of the most important contributions of this theory is that it differentiates between intrinsic and extrinsic needs, emphasizing the important role of intrinsic needs in human development. An **intrinsic need** is an internal drive that all humans have, such as the need for food, water, and shelter, as well as emotional needs such as love, friendship, and acceptance. By contrast, an **extrinsic need** is externally focused and is a drive toward some kind of external recognition, such as prestige or money. Extrinsic needs primarily come into play at the higher levels of the hierarchy. Determining whether an individual is behaving because of an intrinsic need or an extrinsic need can tell us a lot about that person's underlying motivations. Individuals who are intrinsically motivated perform the behavior because they really like it and enjoy it; they get some amount of satisfaction out of it. Conversely, individuals who are extrinsically

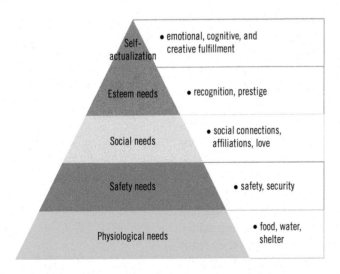

● **Figure 6.7** *Maslow's hierarchy of needs*
Source: adapted from Maslow (1954)

motivated perform the behavior because of the reward they are getting. Parents want their children to be intrinsically motivated to read; teachers want their students to be intrinsically motivated to explore a topic; and managers want their workers to be intrinsically motivated to do their best.

Maslow introduced the notion that individuals have a hierarchy of needs—the lower-level needs must be addressed before moving up to more abstract needs. That is, if you did not feel safe or if you were experiencing hunger, it would be almost impossible to move to a higher level of the hierarchy in an effort to achieve social, esteem, or self-actualization needs. The level of self-actualization is achieved after all the other needs are satisfied. Here, individuals try to live a life that is balanced and complete; they pursue activities that fulfill them emotionally and cognitively. In the developed world, most people have fulfilled their physiological and safety needs. In these areas of the world, marketers know that they can focus their efforts on promoting products and services that tap into the higher-level needs like social needs, esteem needs, and self-actualization. Thus, a clear understanding of the needs of the target market will point marketers in the right direction about how to develop product and communications strategies that will resonate best with those consumers.

Although Maslow's hierarchy seems quite logical, critics have identified some shortcomings of the model. First, the development of the model has been called into question. Indeed, it is simply a conceptual model that Maslow developed to explain his observations and is not based on actual data. Second, one important aspect of the model is that an individual must satisfy the needs at one level before moving up to the next. The model contends that it would not be possible to address social needs unless physiological needs were satisfied. However, this implies that extremely poor people are incapable of reaching higher levels of the hierarchy. This is simply not the case. Another problem is that the model does not account for the vast cultural differences in what might be motivating to an individual. History and current-day global news are full of instances where individuals give up their lives for a very important cause. These individuals are clearly skipping past their lower-level needs to achieve the level of self-actualization. A third and final criticism is that, over time, an individual's needs and the importance of those needs change.

One example of changing needs is the concept of safety. In many countries, people have a heightened sense of awareness because of attacks that might happen in public places, and individuals are aware of these safety issues as they carry out our daily activities. With many consumers experiencing a heightened sense of safety, appeals to safety are especially likely to resonate with individuals. Transit officials encourage safe driving and safe use of public transit; public health officials encourage individuals to use and dispose of their medicines safely; and municipal authorities encourage safe use of firecrackers and fireworks around Independence Day and the New Year. The global coronavirus pandemic caused many people to avoid crowded streets, recreation spots, shopping areas, and restaurants. Marketers frequently use

Maslow's hierarchy of needs is a model for understanding a person's motivations. It is based on the idea that there is an ordering of needs, from the most basic physical needs (physiological) to higher-level self-actualization needs. People satisfy their needs one level at a time, moving up toward self-actualization.

Extrinsic need is externally focused and is a drive toward some kind of external recognition, such as prestige or money.

● **Photo 6.11** *Home security systems are a $47 billion global industry*

safety as a messaging strategy. For evidence of the effectiveness of this messaging, simply look at the increase in the number of security-related products, including home security systems. Around the world, the global security market is estimated at $100 billion, with $47 billion of that in home security systems. In addition to better technology, connectivity, and integration with other devices, experts suggest that a heightened concern about security is driving the growth in this industry (Scalco 2017). A home security system can even increase the value of your home (see Photo 6.11).

See Insights from Academia 6.5 for an example of how researchers have used our understanding of intrinsic and extrinsic motivations to create different messaging strategies.

Motivation research

Motivation research is based on the premise that consumer decisions are based on both psychological and emotional factors. Sometimes, unconscious motives such as those discussed by Freud also exert an influence on consumer decision-making. Researchers taking a motivational approach will often rely on qualitative research techniques to generate their data. As we know, qualitative research depends heavily on a researcher's interpretation of a consumer's responses to understand the true desires and meanings behind a consumer's behavior. Motivation researchers utilizing some of these qualitative methods use a variety of techniques, but some of the more common are projective

INSIGHTS FROM ACADEMIA 6.5

Bring your bag or pay a tax!

Over the long term, intrinsic motivations will help consumers do their part to consume more responsibly and address the climate crisis. In the meantime, extrinsic motivations may be more effective in changing behaviors. Many cities and countries around the world have instituted a small fee for consumers who want plastic bags at retail stores. When consumers need to make a decision about whether to buy a plastic bag or bring a reusable bag, the way the retail store frames the choice matters. Specifically, messages can be framed as "avoiding a fee" (a gain) or as "paying a tax" (a loss). Strong evidence from previous research suggests that consumers have a preference for avoiding losses—they *really* don't like losing something, paying a penalty,

etc. In the case of which bag to use at the store, consumers who saw the "bring your bag and avoid a fee" advertisement (framed as a gain) were much less likely to bring their own bag to the store. By contrast, the "bring your own bag or pay a tax" message (framed as a loss) was much more helpful in encouraging shoppers to bring their own bags. Do you bring your own bags to the store?

Muralidharan, S., and K. Sheehan. 2016. "'Tax' and 'Fee' Message Frames as Inhibitors of Plastic Bag Usage among Shoppers: A Social Marketing Application of the Theory of Planned Behavior." Social Marketing Quarterly 22 (3): 200–217.

techniques, metaphor analysis, storytelling, word associations and sentence completion tasks, picture generation, and photo sorting (Kozinets 2010):

- *Projective techniques* ask consumers to use their personal experiences to interpret an ambiguous image (like an ink blot or a photo where it is not clear what is happening) by describing what the image means or by telling a story about it.

- *Metaphor analysis* asks consumers to select pictures from magazines or other sources that depict meanings behind a product, brand, company, or even "typical consumer" who buys that product.

- *Storytelling* involves consumers telling real-life stories about how they have used the product in their own lives.

- *Word association tasks* give participants one word at a time and then ask them to say the first word that comes to mind; *sentence completion tasks* ask participants to finish a sentence, such as, "When you see someone wearing Nike products, you know that. . ."

- *Picture generation techniques* ask consumers to make a drawing or doodle of, for example, a product, typical consumer, or company.

- *Photo sorting tasks* provide research participants with a pile of photographs that they need to sort into different piles. For example, the piles could represent the product you use today, the product you wish you could use, and the product that you would never use.

Employing qualitative research methods

● **Photo 6.12** *A collage is one type of qualitative research method*

Researchers use a variety of projective techniques in motivational research. One of the earliest techniques used was the thematic apperception test (TAT), which has often been utilized by clinical psychologists. Researchers using the TAT will give the research participant an ambiguous picture of, for example, two people talking to one another, and participants are asked to describe what is happening in the picture (Morgan and Murray 1935). Researchers are careful not to use any leading questions when they talk to research participants; their job is to encourage the participant to talk and connect the discussion to their own thoughts, experiences, and motivations. The TAT has been used for a wide variety of purposes, such as understanding patient motivations in carrying through with their doctor's recommendations, worker motivations in engaging in ethical behavior, and prisoner motivations

in getting a job and re-entering society. The TAT has also been used by advertising and consumer researchers, especially when researchers are in the early stages in a research project and are trying to fully understand a consumption phenomenon.

More recently, researchers have used several techniques in a single research project in an attempt to triangulate their findings. Earlier in this chapter, we found that triangulation occurred when researchers used several different research techniques to come to a convergence in their conclusions. Their goal is to understand a given consumer motivation from several perspectives, using several research techniques. One study, for example, attempted to find a way to better explain the phenomenon of *passionate consumption*, which the researchers describe as an object or a state of intense desire. Indeed, they suggest that desire is the next step after needs and wants: needs ➜ wants ➜ desires. It is characterized by stress and longing for the object. Think about those people who wait in line for the newest iPhone or Star Wars movie. Their thoughts and emotions are obsessed with the idea of fulfilling their desires and they often suspend other priorities to focus their efforts on obtaining these things. To understand the concept of passionate consumption more deeply, the researchers employed a variety of qualitative techniques, focusing on a few techniques in particular, such as collage building, construction of fairy tales, and drawings. The study was done with individuals who were living in three very different cultures: Denmark, Turkey, and the United States. In Photo 6.12, we see two collages that were created by US college students who expressed the concept of passion with images such as sweet deserts and foreign travel. Interestingly, the collages also reflected an underlying theme of guilt at stretching society's expectations about what was proper and acceptable behavior. These collages also included images of exercise and a woman with her hand up, as if she is trying to stop something. According to US social norms, individuals are supposed to be in control of their desires, thus the interesting juxtaposition of passion with guilt in the US representations (Belk, Ger, and Askegaard 2003). The researchers noted interesting differences between men and women, as well as across cultures.

Qualitative research methods help marketing managers and the creative people in advertising agencies develop deep insights about the most appropriate and effective ways to communicate important information about their brands so that those communications strategies align with consumer perceptions. When triangulation is used, the insights have the potential to be even more valuable.

Questions

1. Look at the qualitative research techniques that are discussed immediately before Insights from the Field 6.4. Select two methods and use them to describe your own conceptualization of the concept of *equity*. Describe your creations. Why did you select these two methods, as opposed to the others?

2. What are the benefits of using multiple methods to investigate the same concept? Are there any drawbacks to a multimethod approach?

Sources: Belk, Ger, and Askegaard (2003); Morgan and Murray (1935).

Based on careful interpretation of the results, marketers can understand what is important to consumers and how consumers might apply their own backgrounds, interpretations, biases, and desires to help them understand and behave in different situations. These findings can then help marketers find better ways to deliver the value proposition to consumers. Insights from the Field 6.4 provides more detail about qualitative research techniques and the importance of triangulation.

Some observers have criticized qualitative motivation research because of its reliance on interpretation rather than hard data, its sometimes off-the-wall techniques, and its sometimes outlandish explanations of consumer motivations. Some critics have also pointed out that, because the conclusions depend on the researcher's interpretation, different researchers will likely generate different conclusions. Motivation research also requires that researchers must be trained in qualitative techniques and data analysis (Donoghue 2000). Finally, research participants may feel uncomfortable about being asked to engage in some of these techniques, which calls into question the validity of the results (Steinman 2009).

Despite these criticisms, qualitative motivation research still provides a rich source of data that can then be organized to provide fascinating information about consumers' beliefs and motivations, some of which might not be apparent with other research methods. One benefit in particular is that participants are less likely to guess the underlying purpose of the research project, so they are less likely to respond in a way that they believe pleases the researcher (social desirability bias). Qualitatively based motivation research adds another tool to our arsenal of consumer research methods. It provides additional, contextually rich information about consumer behavior and decision-making. Often, the hypotheses developed using qualitative methods are later verified using quantitative methods (Steinman 2009). In all, insights from motivation research are useful for marketers because they reveal the deep-rooted motivations that drive behavior and thus enable organizations to form deeper connections with consumers.

◉ Summary

This chapter examined two fundamentally important topics in consumer behavior. One was the closely related topics of personality and the self. These concepts play a central role in a consumer's life and are strongly intertwined with one another. There are two distinct *perspectives on personality and self*: the psychological perspective and the sociological perspective. We discussed how these perspectives provided researchers with different definitions of the self, differing roles of the self-concept, and different implications for the theoretical and practical applications of personality and self. Insights from the Boardroom 6 described how most advertising to the mature market does a spectacularly bad job at portraying the typical older American. Indeed, self-perceptions of older Americans are far different from the way this population is often portrayed in ads.

Just as we have a multitrait approach to personality, we also have the *multiplicity of self*, which finds that there are many different dimensions of the self, including the actual, ideal, social, extended, situational, possible, and negative self. Each of these conceptualizations of the self performs certain functions for and serves to motivate the individual. In Insights from the Field 6.1, we learned about the self in the virtual world and the perplexing online trend of mukbang. Insights from Academia 6.2 highlighted the concept of a possible self that is burdened with a variety of home, work, and family responsibilities and found that many young people want to take advantage of travel and other experiences before life's responsibilities set in.

In connecting *personality to marketing practice*, it is important to appreciate that values act as guiding principles for behavior. We stressed the importance of understanding how consumers forge connections between product attributes and their values. These connections can be better understood by utilizing laddering to create means–end chains. Another important connection to marketing practice occurs when we recognize that an individual's personality can be represented as a set of characteristics, which can then be used to describe consumer segments. We emphasized the importance of using a combination of values and personality to create meaningful customer segments and introduced the widely used VALS™ model.

The other important topic we discussed was the concept of *motivation,* a drive that propels our behaviors, like our purchase and use of products and brands. Insights from the Field 6.3 explored how the outdoor clothing manufacturer Patagonia fulfills both functional and subjective needs for many consumers. We discussed motivational conflicts, introduced Maslow's hierarchy, and, finally, explored several qualitative **research** methods. In Insights from the Field 6.4, we found that a multimethod research can provide a clearer understanding of a given phenomenon.

KEY TERMS

approach–approach
conflict p. 225
approach–avoidance
conflict p. 224
archetype p. 201
attributes p. 216
avoidance–avoidance
conflict p. 225
brand personality scale p. 206
consequences p. 216
ego p. 201
extrinsic need p. 227
functional (or biogenic)
needs p. 221
hedonic p. 224
id p. 200
image congruency p. 215

instrumental values p. 216
intrinsic need p. 226
laddering p. 217
malleable self p. 210
Maslow's hierarchy of
needs p. 227
means–end chain p. 216
motivation p. 220
multiplicity of the self p. 208
multitrait approach p. 206
needs p. 221
personality p. 200
psychographic
segmentation p. 218
psychological perspective on
personality p. 200
self p. 200

self-concept p. 208
self-congruity p. 215
single-trait approach p. 203
sociological perspective on
personality p. 207
subjective (or psychogenic)
needs p. 221
superego p. 201
symbolic consumption p. 215
symbolic interactionist
perspective p. 207
terminal values p. 216
trait-based approach p. 202
triangulation p.205
values p. 216
VALS™ p. 218
wants p. 221

REVIEW QUESTIONS

1. How do the id, ego, and superego work together and work against one another to influence personality?
2. Using the two perspectives of personality, provide two definitions of yourself. Which perspective provides the most accurate

definition? Why? Which perspective provides the most useful definition? Why?

3. Using the model of symbolic consumption, pick an example of a product and describe how meaning is moved between the three elements. Why is this useful for marketers?

4. Describe the concept of means–end chains, how marketers uncover a consumer's means–end chains, and why they may be particularly useful to marketers.

5. What is the connection between consumer personality and consumer motivation?
6. Discuss the three motivational conflicts that a consumer might encounter and provide an example of each one.

DISCUSSION QUESTIONS

1. Refer again to Table 6.2 and select two of the conceptualizations of the self that are listed. For each one, describe in detail how a marketer might be able to utilize this concept to (a) create better products or services and (b) develop more meaningful messaging strategies.
2. Go to https://www.timberland.com/custom.html and design your own pair of Timberlands. What does your design say about your own personality and identity? How would you describe Timberland's brand personality?
3. The symbolic consumption process can occur with a product that has positive or negative associated meanings. In what ways might the concept of negative symbolic consumption be important for marketers? Pick an example of negative symbolic consumption from your own life and describe how it might fit into the diagram in Photo 6.9. What changes might

be made to the model to account for negative symbolic consumption?

4. Conduct an online search to find at least three examples of organizations that use a *combination* of personality and demographics to segment consumers. For each organization you identify: (a) describe the main target market segment, (b) explain how well the organization's products/services "fit" with the needs, wants, and desires of the segment, and (c) indicate how well the organization's messaging strategy "resonates" with the segment.
5. Conduct a means–end chain analysis with a friend or classmate using the laddering technique. Here are some questions you can use to get started: (a) When selecting a vacation spot, do you prefer a beach-type destination or a mountain-type destination? (b) When buying toothpaste, do you prefer the kind that whitens, the kind that fights cavities, or the kind that gives you fresh breath? Draw and label the resulting means–end chains.

For more information, quizzes, case studies, and other study tools, please visit us at
www.oup.com/he/phillips.

CASE STUDY 6

Insights into the changing Indian consumer

The lives of Indian consumers used to be bound by tradition and culture. However, with a booming economy and dramatic shifts in culture, there are many fascinating facets to the changing lives of Indian consumers. India has more than 1.35 billion citizens, a thriving economy, and a growing middle class—marketing and consumer researchers are looking for insights.

India is a vast, culturally diverse country with 1,500 dialects and many different faiths, histories, ethnicities, and cultural practices. India's economy varies dramatically across the country, with more educated and prosperous individuals generally living closer to urban centers like Mumbai, Delhi, and Bangalore and poorer individuals living on the outskirts of the cities or in rural areas. These differences are expressed in distinct differences in a variety of consumption practices involving personal care, food, fashion, and the home. Despite the country's recent economic growth, some Indians still struggle. First, the country is quite crowded—India is about one-third the size of the United States, but it has one billion *more* people. There are 455 people per square kilometer of land, compared to 36 people per square kilometer in the United States. Life expectancy in India is sixty-nine years, compared to seventy-nine years in the United States. Further, there are 87.3 mobile cellular subscriptions for every 100 people and 34.5 percent have Internet. Compare these figures to those in the United States, where there are 120.7 mobile subscriptions per 100 people and 75.2 percent have access to the Internet (World Bank 2018a, 2018b). Nonetheless, the bottom line is that this country of 1.35 billion is a stable democracy with plenty of educated, upwardly mobile consumers.

One issue that distinguishes India from any other country is the sheer size of its population of young people. There are 400 million people in India's millennial generation and 390 million in Gen Z (or iGen) (see Chapter 11). That means that there are more than *twice* the number of young people in India than the entire population of the United States; India has twice as many *young people* than the United States has *people*! How will all of these young people influence their country and the world? First, young people have become strong influencers for the purchase of tech-related products. Often, parents and other family members turn to them for advice and assistance. As mobile connectivity improves around the country, young Indians (and the people they influence) will rely more heavily on online sources for connectivity, information, entertainment, and shopping. Second, rather than seeking out luxury brands, young Indians are looking for brand names that offer both value and quality. Experts say that the biggest areas for growth will be restaurants, baby products, premium personal care products, scooters, sport utility vehicles, and jewelry. Finally, Indians are generally reluctant to engage in ostentatious displays of wealth, with one exception: weddings. With this large group of young people, there will be a dramatic increase in the number of weddings in the coming years. Parents spare little expense and will often save for years to pay for the wedding of a son or daughter. While the average US wedding costs about $30,000, the average Indian wedding costs about $75,000 and lasts for several days (Lu, Yiu, and Soman 2016). All of this will spur purchases of wedding-related products, products for a first home, and, later, products for a family.

The Boston Consulting Group is a global consulting firm that conducts research about a wide variety of different topics that are relevant to businesses. In a recent project, they collected and analyzed data on Indian consumption patterns. They generated these data from their own primary research efforts using surveys and in-depth interviews. They also pulled data from secondary sources about economic trends, spending patterns, and demographic shifts over the previous decade. Experts at the Boston Consulting Group compiled the data into information that could be useful for managers and then created four fascinating insights.

Data and information on the Indian consumer

From a demographic standpoint, experts predict that there will continue to be a growing affluence across the country. Importantly, a large proportion of Indians living in almost subsistence conditions are expected to move up to a higher standard of living by 2025. Figure 6.8 depicts the changes in income distribution that are expected to happen. For purposes of analysis, the household income breakdowns are as follows:

- *Elite*: more than $30,800 per year
- *Affluent*: $15,400–$30,800 per year
- *Aspirers*: $7,700–$15,400 per year

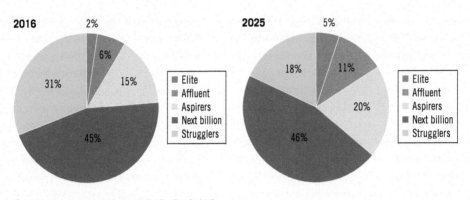

Figure 6.8 *Household income distribution in India*
Source: adapted in part, from Singhi, Jain, and Sanghi (2017)

- *Next billion*: $2,300–$7,700 per year
- *Strugglers*: less than $2,300 per year

If the economy in India continues to grow at its current pace, India will likely become the third largest economy in the world by 2025. There are three separate forces at work that will vitally change the structure of the society, in particular, the structure and nature of the nation's consumption patterns. First, Indians will become increasingly affluent by 2025. The proportion of individuals in the lowest income brackets will shrink as individuals move up the income scale. The top two income brackets, the elite and affluent, will be responsible for 40 percent of the country's spending, compared to 27 percent of its spending in 2016. A second force concerns continuing urbanization, as the population will continue to boom in smaller cities around the nation. Indeed, those cities with fewer than one million inhabitants will grow at the fastest rate. These cities will experience tremendous growth and will become major urban areas by 2025, as long as the cities can keep pace with improvements to infrastructure, housing, and transportation. Consumer spending is projected to be somewhat different in these emerging urban areas compared to that in more established urban centers like Mumbai, Delhi, and Bangalore. Consumers in fast-growing smaller urban areas will likely be very financially conservative in their outlook and will have a strong value-for-money orientation. Importantly, they will maintain their strong local cultural affinity. The third force at work is the shift in family structures. The traditional Indian household used to consist of an extended family where several

generations lived together; it was not uncommon to also have cousins and other family members living under the same roof. As 2025 approaches, family structures will become more nuclear—parents or a single person as the head of household, with or without children. This nuclear household structure will increase from 70 percent of households in 2016 to 74 percent by 2025. This shift in structure has important implications for consumer spending because nuclear households spend, on average, 20 to 30 percent more per capita than those living with an extended family (Singhi, Jain, and Sanghi 2017).

Insights about the Indian consumer

The Boston Consulting Group created four insights based on demographic data as well as on the three trends that were identified above. These insights are designed to help marketing managers across all industries.

Time compression is the pressure that the Indian consumer experiences when there are simply too many things to do in a given period of time. Because of decreased support from the extended family, a more fast-paced work environment, and time spent on social media, the Indian consumer is certainly feeling a time crunch. To adapt to time compression, Indians try to multitask and are adopting time-saving solutions like ready-to-eat and ready-to-cook meals. Many Indians are very interested in technologies that save time and convenience, and they are open to marketing communications that highlight these kinds of solutions (Singhi, Jain, and Sanghi 2017).

There is a *rising appeal of Indian goods* for the typical Indian consumer. Indian consumers are no longer looking abroad for their luxury or brand-name products. Instead, 60 percent are now willing to pay a bit of a price premium for products that carry the "Made in India" label. There has been a surge of interest in using natural ingredients for personal care and local flavors and spices in food. In the realm of fashion, Indian consumers are increasingly seeking locally woven and dyed fabrics, as well as local styles. For example, the traditional Indian bundi sleeveless jacket is starting to be worn by fashion-forward men all around the world, and Fab-India, a fashion brand that focuses exclusively on traditionally made and designed products, is one of the largest and most profitable retail apparel brands in the country (Singhi, Jain, and Sanghi 2017).

A third insight can be described as *the (almost) me, myself, and I Generation* and represents an increasing focus on the needs and aspirations of the self, combined with the demographic trend away from extended family households. The number of single adults has increased because, despite the intense pressure from families, young people are putting off marriage. For men, the average age of marriage is now 28 and for women it is 22.2. What do all of these single adults do? First, their spending habits are focused more on self-considerations like lifestyles than they are on functional considerations like the purchase of household products. Second, many young Indian adults spend their time building and interacting with their own social and virtual communities (Singhi, Jain, and Sanghi 2017).

Women taking their rightful place is the final insight that was derived from the research study. Young women are increasingly seeking new opportunities that a university education can provide. In fact, 20 percent of young women attend university, compared to 22 percent of young men. This, combined with changes in healthcare, an increasing societal awareness, and changes in electoral and representation laws, has placed women in a position to take leadership roles in business and government (Singhi, Jain, and Sanghi 2017). Educated women have greater economic independence, which gives them greater power in purchasing, familial, and consumption decisions. Messaging strategies that reflect this new reality and emphasize the unique needs and concerns of women will particularly resonate with young people.

India's economic strength has pulled millions of people out of poverty and subsistence living. For a vast number of Indians, consumption is no longer simply about needs; it is focused on wants and, in some cases, desires. The Boston Consulting Group research project started with the collection of data and information. It concluded with four key insights that can be utilized by marketers to better tap into this fascinating marketplace.

QUESTIONS

1. Consider the four insights about the Indian consumer and identify two separate products or services that would be well suited to address each one. How would a marketing manager for these products alter the communications strategy to appeal to each of these segments?

2. In what way would a marketing messaging strategy be different as consumers move from needs to wants to desires?

Sources: Lu, Yiu, and Soman (2016); Singhi, Jain, and Sanghi (2017); World Bank (2018a) and (2018b).

REFERENCES

Aaker, J. L. 1997. "Dimensions of Brand Personality." *Journal of Market Research* 34 (3): 347–56.

Aaker, J. L. 1999. "The Malleable Self: The Role of Self-Expression in Persuasion." *Journal of Marketing Research* 36 (1): 45–57.

Adams, J., and D. Nettle. 2009. "Time Perspective, Personality and Smoking, Body Mass, and Physical Activity: An Empirical Study." *British Journal of Health Psychology* 14 (1): 83–105.

Ahuvia, A. C. 2005. "Beyond the Extended Self: Loved Objects and Consumers' Identity Narratives." *Journal of Consumer Research* 32 (1): 171–84.

Arnould, E. J., and C. J. Thompson. 2005. "Consumer Culture Theory (CCT): Twenty Years of Research." *Journal of Consumer Research* 31 (4): 868–82.

Axelsson, M., E., Brink, J., Lundgren, and J. Lötvall. 2011. "The Influence of Personality Traits on Reported Adherence to Medication in Individuals with Chronic Disease: An Epidemiological Study in West Sweden." *PLOS One* 6 (3): e18241.

Banister, E. N., and M. K. Hogg. 2001. "Mapping the Negative Self: From 'So Not Me'. . . to 'Just Not Me.'" *Advances in Consumer Research* 28 (1): 242–48.

Belk, R. W. 1988. "Possessions and the Extended Self." *Journal of Consumer Research* 15 (2): 139–68.

Belk, R. W., G. Ger, and S. Askegaard. 2003. "The Fire of Desire: A Multisited Inquiry into Consumer Passion." *Journal of Consumer Research* 30 (3): 326–51.

Carotenuto, M. 2015. "Why Do More U.S. Women Study Abroad Than Men?" *Washington Post*, October 9, 2015. https://www.washingtonpost.com/news/answer-sheet/wp/2015/10/09/why-do-more-u-s-women-study-abroad-than-men/?utm_term=.98d53e5de26c.

CBS. 2019. "Muckbang: Watch What They Eat!" CBS NEWS. November 24, 2019. https://www.cbsnews.com/video/mukbang-watch-what-they-eat/.

Chouinard, Y. 2016. *Let My People Go Surfing: The Education of a Reluctant Businessman.* 2nd ed. New York: Penguin Books.

Cross, S., and H. Markus. 1991. "Possible Selves across the Life Span." *Human Development* 34 (4): 230–55.

Donoghue, S. 2000. "Projective Techniques in Consumer Research." *Journal of Family Ecology and Consumer Sciences* 28:47–53.

Englis, B., and D. M. Phillips. 2013. "Does Innovativeness Drive Environmentally Conscious Consumer Behavior?" *Psychology & Marketing* 30 (2): 160–72.

Ericksen, M. K., and M. J. Sirgy. 1992. "Employed Females Clothing Preference, Self-Image Congruence, and Career Anchorage." *Journal of Applied Social Psychology* 22 (5): 408–22.

Foxall, G. R., and R. Goldsmith. 1988. "Personality and Consumer Research: Another Look." *Journal of the Market Research Society* 30 (2): 111–25.

Freud, S. 1923. *The Ego and the Id.* London: Hogarth Press.

Goldsmith, R. E., and C. F. Hofacker. 1991. "Measuring Consumer Innovativeness." *Journal of the Academy of Marketing Science* 19 (3): 209–21.

Grubb, E., and H. Grathwohl. 1967. "Consumer Self-Concept, Symbolism and Market Behavior: A Theoretical Approach." *Journal of Marketing* 1 (4): 22–27.

Harris, E. G., and D. E. Fleming. 2005. "Assessing the Human Element in Service Personality Formation: Personality Congruency and the Five

Factor Model." *Journal of Services Marketing* 19 (4): 187–98.

Haws, K. L., W. O. Bearden, and G. Y. Nenkov. 2012. "Consumer Spending Self-Control Effectiveness and Outcome Elaboration Prompts." *Journal of the Academy of Marketing Science* 40 (5): 695–710.

Heine, P. J. 1971. *Personality in Social Theory.* Chicago: Alpine.

Hollenbeck, C. R., and A. M. Kaikati. 2012. "Consumers' Use of Brands to Reflect Their Actual and Ideal Selves on Facebook." *International Journal of Research in Marketing* 29 (4): 395–405.

Institute of International Education. 2017. "Profile of U.S. Study Abroad Students, 2004/05–2015/16." Open Doors Report on International Educational Exchange. Accessed December 5, 2017. https://www.iie.org/opendoors.

International Centre for Exploration & Education. 2019. "Explore the World with the International Centre for Exploration and Education." Accessed August 14, 2019. https://www.explorationcentre.org.

Jansson-Boyd, C. V. 2010. *Consumer Psychology.* Maidenhead, UK: Open University Press.

Kassarjian, H. H. 1971. "Personality and Consumer Behavior: A Review." *Journal of Marketing Research* 8 (4): 409–18.

Kassarjian, H. H., and M. J. Sheffet. 1981. "Personality and Consumer Behavior: An Update." In *Perspectives in Consumer Behavior*, edited by H. H. Kassarjian, 160–180. Glenview, IL: Foresman.

Kozinets, R. V. 2010. *Netnography: Doing Ethnographic Research Online.* London: Sage.

Kramer, T., and S.-O. Yoon. 2007. "Approach–Avoidance Motivation and the Use of Affect as Information." *Journal of Consumer Psychology* 17 (2): 128–38.

Lastovicka, J. L., L. A. Bettencourt, R. S. Hughner, and R. J. Kuntze. 1999. "Lifestyle of the Tight and Frugal: Theory and Measurement." *Journal of Consumer Research* 26 (1): 85–98.

Lawler, R. 2011. "SyncTweet Will Sync TV Ads with Your Twitter Stream." Gigaom. August 26, 2011. http://gigaom.com/2011/08/26/synctweet/.

Ligas, M., and J. Cotte. 1999. "The Process of Negotiating Brand Meaning: A Symbolic Interactionist Perspective." In *Advances in Consumer Research*, edited by E. J. Arnould and L. M. Scott,

26:609–14. Provo, UT: Association for Consumer Research.

Lu, J., A. Yiu, and A. Soman. 2016. "The Asian Consumer: India Consumer Close-up: Tapping the Spending Power of a Young, Connected Urban Mass." *Equity Research*, June 1.

Maslow, A. 1954. *Motivation and Personality.* New York: Harper.

McCrae, R. R., and P. T. Costa. 1990. *Personality in Adulthood.* New York: Guilford Press.

Mead, G. H. 1913. "The Social Self." *Journal of Philosophy, Psychology and Scientific Methods* 10 (14): 374–80.

Mintel. 2019. *Lifestyles of Young Families—US—January 2019.* London: Mintel.

Möller, J., and S. Herm. 2013. "Shaping Retail Brand Personality Perceptions by Bodily Experiences." *Journal of Retailing* 89 (4): 438–46.

Morgan, C. D., and H. A. Murray. 1935. "A Method for Investigating Fantasies: The Thematic Apperception Test." *Archives of Neurology and Psychiatry* 34 (2): 289–306.

Nace, T. 2017. "After 44 Years, Patagonia Released Its First Commercial & It's Not about Clothing." *Forbes*, August 24, 2017. https://www.forbes.com/sites/trevornace/2017/08/24/44-years-patagonia-released-first-commercial-clothing/#26a02dfa3c80.

Nielsen Company & BoomAgers. 2012. "Introducing Boomers: Marketing's Most Valuable Generation." White paper. Nielsen Company & BoomAgers, August 2012.

Opree, S. J., and R. Kühne. 2016. "Generation Me in the Spotlight: Linking Reality TV to Materialism, Entitlement, and Narcissism." *Mass Communication and Society* 19 (6): 800–819.

Phillips, J. 2017. Personal interview, December 5, 2017.

Reynolds, T. J., and J. Gutman. 1988. "Laddering Theory, Method, Analysis, and Interpretation." *Journal of Advertising Research* 28 (1): 11–31.

Richins, M. L., and S. Dawson. 1992. "A Consumer Values Orientation for Materialism and Its Measurement: Scale Development and Validation." *Journal of Consumer Research* 19:303–16.

Rokeach, M., and S. J. Ball-Rokeach. 1989. "Stability and Change in American Value Systems, 1968–1981." *American Psychologist* 44 (5): 775–84.

Rosenberg, M. 1979. *Conceiving the Self.* New York: Basic Books.

Ryan, A. 2017. Personal interview, May 5, 2017.

Scalco, D. 2017. "Why Home Security Systems Are on Track to Be a Multi-Billion-Dollar Market." Inc. January 26, 2017. https://www.inc.com/dan-scalco/why-home-security-systems-are-on-track-to-be-a-multi-billion-dollar-market.html.

Shankar, A., R. Elliott, and J. A. Fitchett. 2009. "Identity, Consumption and Narratives of Socialization." *Marketing Theory* 9 (1): 75–94.

Shimp, T. A., and S. Sharma. 1987. "Consumer Ethnocentrism: Construction and Validation of the CETSCALE." *Journal of Marketing Research* 24 (8): 280–89.

Singhi, A., N. Jain, and K. Sanghi. 2017. *The New Indian: The Many Facets of a Changing Consumer.* Boston: Boston Consulting Group.

Sirgy, M. J. 1982. "Self-Image/Product-Image Congruity and Advertising Strategy." In *Developments in Marketing Science*, edited by V. Kothari, 5:129–33. Marquette, MI: Academy of Marketing Science.

Steinman, R. B. 2009. "Projective Techniques in Consumer Research." *International Bulletin of Business Administration.* ISSN: 1451-243X Issue 5. 37–45.

Stets, J. E., and P. J. Burke. 2003. "A Sociological Approach to Self and Identity." In *Handbook of Self and Identity*, edited by M. Leary and J. Tangney, 128–52. New York: Guilford Press.

Strategic Business Insights. 2019. "US Framework and VALS™ Types." Accessed December 12, 2019. http://www.strategicbusinessinsights.com/vals/ustypes.shtml.

Szmigin, I., and M. Piacentini. 2015. *Consumer Behavior.* Oxford: Oxford University Press.

Weinberger, M. F., J. R. Zavisca, and J. M. Silva. 2017. "Consuming for an Imagined Future: Middle-Class Consumer Lifestyle and Exploratory Experiences in the Transition to Adulthood." *Journal of Consumer Research* 44 (2): 332–60.

Woodside, A. G. 2010. "Brand–Consumer Storytelling Theory and Research." *Psychology & Marketing* 27 (6): 531–40.

World Bank. 2018a. "The World Bank Country Profile: India." Accessed August 15, 2019. http://databank.worldbank.org/data/Views/Reports/ReportWidgetCustom.aspx?Report_Name=CountryProfile&Id=b450fd57&tbar=y&dd=y&inf=n&zm=n&country=IND.

World Bank. 2018b. "The World Bank Country Profile: United States." Accessed August 15, 2019. https://databank.worldbank.org/views/reports/reportwidget.aspx?Report_Name=CountryProfile&Id=b450fd57&tbar=y&dd=y&inf=n&zm=n&country=USA.

Zoepf, K. 2008. "Saudi Women Find an Unlikely Role Model: Oprah." *New York Times*, September 18, 2008. http://www.nytimes.com/2008/09/19/world/middleeast/19oprah.html?_r=0.

7 Attitudes and Behaviors

◉ Introduction

Think about your favorite football team. Obviously, you have a positive opinion about the team, but you also probably have attitudes about certain players, the coaches, the stadium, and other things that are related to your team. At the same time, you likely have attitudes about your least favorite team, its players, coach, etc. Experts in consumer behavior tell us that your attitudes about the team are composed of what you *know* about the team as well as what your *feelings* are about the team. For example, you know the team stats, the schedule, its history, and lots of other information. Your feelings about the team could be described as excitement, anticipation, and passion. Experts also tell us that your attitudes influence your behavior. You watch your favorite team play, sometimes even going to the games. You follow news about your team and pay attention to the draft. Indeed, consumer behavior, or in this case fan behavior, can be understood more precisely if we use attitudes to do so.

One of the most important jobs for marketers is encouraging consumers to have positive attitudes about their products, services, stores, and advertising. Consumer attitudes are one of the most widely used concepts in marketing because they take into account a consumer's feelings, thoughts, and behaviors. Attitudes are made up of what you think, what you feel, and what you do. Importantly, consumer attitudes influence their behaviors. In addition to influencing which products and brands consumers buy, attitudes also influence a variety of consumption-related behaviors, such as how they search for information, use the product or brand, and influence others, like friends, family, and even salespeople. The study of consumer attitudes and behavior is one of the most widely used concepts both within and outside marketing. Indeed, attitudes are used to study a wide variety of social behavior (such as engagement in an online community), civic behaviors (such as voting), health behaviors (such as getting a flu shot), and marketing behaviors (such as engaging in word-of-mouth communication). The focus of this chapter is on how attitudes are formed, how they influence consumer behavior, and how they can be changed (see Photo 7.1).

Photo 7.1 *Football fans have strong attitudes about their teams*

Attitude is a learned predisposition to respond in a consistently favorable or unfavorable manner in relation to some object.

Attitude object is the thing about which the attitude is held and can include brands, services, ideas, people, and behaviors.

What is an Attitude?

Simply stated, an attitude is your overall opinion or evaluation of something. To be precise, an **attitude** can be defined as "a learned predisposition to respond in a consistently favorable or unfavorable manner in relation to some object" (Fishbein and Ajzen 1975, 6). There are several important parts to this definition. First, attitudes are learned, often through experiences with our culture's educational system and social system, our friends and family, and our other interactions. Second, they have an evaluative dimension, which means that there is a favorable or unfavorable evaluation attached to the attitude. Third, an attitude has intensity—some attitudes are very strongly held while other attitudes are not as important to us and are weakly held. Finally, attitudes are fairly consistent and stable; they are generally compatible with our other attitudes and they do not tend to change much over time or across contexts (Oskamp and Schultz 2005).

From the perspective of marketers who are trying to predict consumer behavior, attitudes have an important link to behaviors. To determine more precisely which attitude will lead to which behavior, marketers need to specify the target object about which attitudes are being formed. This **attitude object** is the thing about which the attitude is held and can include a wide variety of people, places, ideas, objects, and behaviors (Herr and Fazio 1993). A consumer can simultaneously have attitudes about several related topics, such as holding an attitude about a behavior (e.g., skiing), an object (e.g., Head skis), or a person (e.g., Lindsey Vonn). Marketers often express these attitudes as A_{skiing}, $A_{Head\ skis}$, and $A_{Lindsey\ Vonn}$. Attitude theory predicts that, compared to people who have negative attitudes toward these attitude objects, if a person has a positive A_{skiing}, they will be more likely to go skiing; if they have a positive $A_{Head\ skis}$, they will be more likely to purchase Head skis; and if an individual has a positive $A_{Lindsey\ Vonn}$, they may be more likely to listen to her as a brand spokesperson.

Think about consumer attitudes toward marriage, for example, to see how the definition of attitudes applies to the concept of marriage. From an early age, individuals learn about and develop opinions about marriage through interactions with family, friends, and other consumers. These views are culturally determined and are reinforced through depictions in various media and marketplace offerings. As a young person, your family probably took you to a few weddings, and as you got older, you started forming

INSIGHTS FROM THE FIELD 7.1

Attitudes about consumer credit and debt

Around the world, consumer credit has increasingly become a reality for many consumers. One study examined several factors related to consumer debt, such as the number of debit and credit cards and the growth of cashless payments. This study found that the United States ranked fifth in the world behind Canada, Sweden, the United Kingdom, and France in being a "cashless economy." Consumers in the United States had, on average, three credit cards and one debit card, and 45 percent of their purchases were cashless transactions (Christie 2017). When we look at the deeply held cultural meanings that are attached to debt, we find that debt is sometimes thought to be necessary to acquire some *must have* items associated with an American middle-class lifestyle, including a house, a car, and a college education (Peñaloza and Barnhart 2011). Indeed, going into debt is acceptable when you're funding an education (79.1 percent say yes), buying a car (76.7 percent), or even covering living expenses (51.3 percent), but it is not all right to rely on debt to cover nonnecessities like a vacation (14.1 percent said yes) (Dow 2018). Another study of UK and Ireland students found a similar acceptance of debt as a normal part of life. On the positive side, students with more debt were more confident in their roles as consumers. However, these students were also less frugal in their spending habits (O'Loughlin and Szmigin 2006).

Research suggests that American consumers in general don't like to take on debt, but have become used to it and see it as a way to "live comfortably." Thirty-nine percent of Americans enjoy spending money more than they like saving it, but 61 percent enjoy saving money more than spending it. This is a big shift from the trend over the past few decades, where Americans liked to spend money as much as (sometimes more than) they liked to save it. In 2001, the numbers were 48 percent for those who liked

to spend and 48 percent for those who liked to save (Fleming 2016). We know that attitudes influence behaviors, and the behaviors of millennials toward debt is a nice illustration of this. These consumers are willing to change their behaviors to achieve their financial and personal goals. A very pressing goal for many millennials involves experiences like international travel, concerts, sporting events, and learning experiences such as classes in wine tasting, yoga, or languages. A full 55 percent of millennials are more willing to spend their money on experiences rather than "stuff" (compared to 45 percent of the overall population). And they are willing to change their behavior for it. For example, about 50 percent of millennials were willing to work harder and 42 percent were willing to look for a better-paying job to achieve their financial and personal goals (Mintel 2018).

Questions
Identify three people you know who are different ages and who come from different backgrounds.

1. Ask your research participants, "When is it definitely OK to take on debt?" and "When is it definitely not OK to take on debt?" How would you describe their attitudes toward debt? What are some differences and similarities in their responses?
2. We know that attitudes influence behaviors. Now, ask your research participants about their own behaviors. Have they ever tried to reduce their debt and increase their savings? Why did they do it and how did they do it? What conclusions can you draw about how different attitudes might lead to different behaviors?

Sources: Christie (2017); Dow (2018); Fleming (2016); Mintel (2018); Peñaloza and Barnhart (2011); Szmigin and O'Loughlin (2010).

your own opinions about marriage. Because of these experiences and inter-actions, you are likely to have developed a relatively stable attitude toward marriage. For example, it is better to get married early versus it is better to wait; it is better to live with someone before marriage versus it is not OK to live with someone; it is better to spend a lot of money to have a huge celebra-tion versus it is better to have a small, more personalized ceremony. These attitudes are likely to influence your behaviors regarding your own wedding someday! Insights from the Field 7.1 investigates another topic: consumer credit and debt.

◉ The Building Blocks of Attitudes

The tricomponent attitude model

Researchers have concluded that attitudes are made up of three main compo-nents: affect, behavior, and cognitions (Henderson and Hoque 2010). Often, this representation of attitudes is referred to as the ABC model of attitudes (for affect, behavior, and cognition).

The **affective component** concerns all of the emotional connections the consumer has with the attitude object; affect includes all of the positive and negative feelings or emotions related to the attitude object. These emo-tions could include a wide variety of feelings such as happy, excited, pas-sionate, content, scared, angry, or fearful. Think about your attitude toward Amazon. For the affective part of the attitude toward Amazon, you might feel relieved that you can actually get the product (because it is sold out everywhere else) and happy about the convenience of delivery to your home. At the same time, however, you might feel angry as you recall stories about how Amazon's rapid growth has pushed many small businesses to the brink (Altman 2015). All of these emotional reactions are a part of the affective component of an attitude.

The **behavioral component**, sometimes referred to as conation, refers to the actions or behaviors associated with the attitude object. Consumers can engage in a multitude of consumption-related behaviors, such as trying out a new can of Campbell's soup, putting on a seat belt, signing up for a customer loyalty program, or voting for a particular political candidate. Consumers can also have an *intention* to behave. A consumer may have an intention to stop smoking or to sign up for the product warranty. Behaviors and behavioral in-tentions both fall under the broad category of the behavioral component of attitudes; they both cover the *doing* aspect of the attitude.

The **cognitive component** of attitudes encompasses all of the be-liefs, knowledge, and thoughts the individual has about the attitude object. A consumer may believe that a particular pair of running shoes has good arch

Affective component (of attitudes) concerns all of the emotional connections the consumer has with the attitude object.

Behavioral component (of attitudes) refers to the action or behaviors associated with the attitude object.

Cognitive component (of attitudes) encompasses all of the beliefs, knowledge, and thoughts the individual has about the attitude object.

support or good traction in rainy conditions. These cognitions about a new pair of running shoes can come from our own memory (our own experience with the shoes) or from the external environment (we may have seen a recent ad about a new product attribute for the shoes). The ABC model not only helps us remember the components of attitudes, but also, most important, acknowledges that decision-making involves a consumer's heart (affect) and mind (cognition). Unfortunately, the ABC model does not provide specific guidance on how these elements are related to one another or how they combine to produce attitudes (Grimm 2005).

● **Photo 7.2** *American students in an Italian coffee shop*

An illustration will help make this clear. Every year, American university students travel around the world and experience diverse cultures. One of the most popular places to visit is Italy. In thinking about taking a trip to Italy, a student might consider a wide variety of beliefs and emotions before coming to a conclusion about a behavior (see Photo 7.2).

In analyzing this attitude object (A_{Italy}) using the tricomponent attitude model, each one of the ABC elements becomes apparent.

A. Affect—the consumer may feel a mix of emotions when considering Italy, from positive emotions like excited and thrilled to negative emotions like apprehension and fear.

B. Behavior—the consumer signs up for a study-abroad trip to Italy next semester.

C. Cognition—the consumer may create or access a set of knowledge and beliefs about Italy, based on memory (for example, the beautiful architecture and history, the amazing food and wine) and information from the environment (for example, a bunch of friends have been to Italy and they loved it). Consumers may utilize a great many beliefs about the attitude object (e.g., Italy), but only the most important beliefs will be influential in forming the attitude. **Salient beliefs** are the most important or relevant beliefs to the consumer.

Salient beliefs are those beliefs that are most important or relevant to consumers.

The three main components of attitudes—affect, behavior, and cognitions—are the building blocks of the more formal attitude theories, which we will explore later when we examine the three multiattribute models of attitudes. Check out Insights from Academia 7.1 to see when affective information might be more influential than cognitive information when forming an attitude.

INSIGHTS FROM ACADEMIA 7.1

Trust your gut

Sometimes consumers are faced with clear decisions—no to the five-alarm Grim Reaper hot sauce and yes to an extra scoop of chocolate ice cream. However, other decisions are less clear and there are definite trade-offs for each choice. Think about when you made the decision about which college to attend; there were probably many trade-offs. When uncertainty like this occurs, consumers are much more likely to rely on affective information ("How do I feel about it?") than on cognitive information ("What do I know about it?"). That is, when uncertainty exists, affective information is weighed more heavily in the formation of the attitude. Why does this happen? The authors suggest that uncertainty is a threat to the self and, therefore, consumers may be motivated to rely on inputs that are closer to the self, such as affect ("It just *feels* right"). Many people just trust their feelings. So, the next time there are a lot of trade-offs and you're not sure about a decision, ask yourself how you're feeling.

Faraji-Rad, A., and M. T. Pham. 2017. "Uncertainty Increases the Reliance on Affect in Decisions." Journal of Consumer Research *44 (1): 1–21.*

Hierarchy of effects

It is important to realize that the tricomponent/ABC model does not specify the exact interrelationship between three components or the weighting of each component. It does, however, describe a sequence of steps in the attitude formation process (Alexandris, Tsiotsou, and James 2012). This approach relies on establishing a starting point, which then tells us how the rest of the sequence will play out. The starting point can be either affect, behavior, or cognition (Beatty and Kahle 1988). This approach is referred to as the hierarchy of effects.

The high-involvement or standard learning hierarchy has cognition as a starting point and can be described as cognitions → affect → behavior. This hierarchy assumes that the consumer is highly engaged in a rational decision-making process. This hierarchy suggests that, for example, a consumer learns something about the product, feels positive about it, and then buys it. This hierarchy is most relevant when the decision involves a high-involvement purchase, such as a laptop or car. This hierarchy also suggests that the consumer carefully considers a variety of information that may sometimes be contradictory and then develops feelings for some of the brands. Finally, the consumer enacts a behavior (for example, takes a test drive, makes a purchase) based on those beliefs and feelings. In this hierarchy, cognitions drive the process of attitude formation.

The low-involvement hierarchy proposes the following sequence: cognitions → behavior → affect. Although this hierarchy also starts with cognitions, the difference is that the knowledge that is being generated or accessed is limited, perhaps because it is not essential for the decision. Often, cognitions are followed by behaviors quite quickly, which are then followed by the consumer's emotional response. Think about the process of buying a new pair of sunglasses. You will likely have some beliefs stored in memory about the brand of sunglasses you might like, some stores that have a good selection, and an approximate price range. However, you just might go to the store, try a few styles on, and buy a brand you had not previously considered. After you wear them a few times, you may start to really like them even more, especially if you find that they feel comfortable and give your eyes less stress when driving. The important point about this hierarchy is that it is particularly relevant for low-involvement and routine consumption contexts. In these contexts, consumers engage in very little external search for information and instead rely on their own knowledge and beliefs.

The behavioral hierarchy can be illustrated as follows: behavior → cognitions → affect. Here, the starting point is behavior, which then prompts the development of thoughts and beliefs, and finally the generation of feelings about the attitude object. On a whim, an out-of-town consumer may purchase a new baseball cap with the local team's logo sewn onto the front. The consumer may learn more about some of the key players and might even engage in conversations with others to learn more about the team (cognitions). Then, the consumer feels that not only is it fun to support the team, but also the cap fits nicely and looks good (affect).

The emotional hierarchy is represented by affect → behavior → cognitions. This hierarchy is experiential in nature and proposes that consumers who are engaged in this type of attitude formation are motivated by emotional triggers. Here, emotions are triggered first, followed by a behavior such as a purchase. After the behavior, the consumer may try to rationalize the behavior and generate a series of thoughts and beliefs. This hierarchy is used in the following example. Perhaps you are looking for a new bathing suit for an upcoming spring break trip. After trying on a few options, you may notice that one suit in particular makes you feel sporty, cool, and attractive when you wear it (affect). After purchasing it (behavior), you may start to generate some thoughts about it: Was the price right? Is the brand reliable and long-lasting? The four hierarchies are summarized in Table 7.1.

Table 7.1 Hierarchy of effects model of attitude formation

HIERARCHY AND SEQUENCE	MAIN EMPHASIS
High-involvement (standard learning) hierarchy: cognitions → affect → behavior	High involvement; consumer engages in extensive research to develop beliefs; emphasis on cognitive information processing
Low-involvement hierarchy: cognitions → behavior → affect	Consumer draws on limited knowledge; behavioral learning is important
Behavioral hierarchy: behavior → cognitions → affect	Consumer reacts to the consumption context; impulse-type buys
Emotional hierarchy: affect → behavior → cognitions	Consumer is concerned with the experiential aspects of the consumption context; hedonic consumption is important

Source: Adapted, in part, from Szmigin and Piacentini (2015).

INSIGHTS FROM THE FIELD 7.2

Parents to coaches: No way!

When a young person plays a sport as a child, that person is likely to be a lifelong fan of that sport. What happens when participation in a youth sport drops off precipitously? There are some challenges in store for the future of professional football because participation in youth football programs is dropping. Indeed, youth football league participation is down 14 percent from its peak in 2009. Any increases can be attributed to flag football and the greater number of girls who are playing flag and tackle football. This trend is particularly worrisome because this drop in participation is happening despite big increases in recruiting efforts (Cook 2016). Some experts suggest that the decrease is occurring because there are simply fewer children in that age group. The 2008–9 economic recession caused a dip in births across the United States, as many couples decided to hold off adding another child to the family. Because of this, there are now fewer children at the age where they would start participating in youth sports (Cook 2016). Other experts suggest that a large part of the drop is a result of increased parental concerns about head injuries and concussions.

There is certainly reason to be concerned. A growing body of research has found that the human brain engages in profound growth and development when a person is between the ages of eight and thirteen. When the brain is exposed to repeated impacts, cognitive development is disrupted and, later in life, problems are more likely to occur, such as decreased behavioral regulation and executive function, as well as increased apathy and depression (Belson 2017). Further, trust that the National Football League (NFL) will take measures to reduce head injuries has eroded. Only 33 percent of respondents in a nationwide survey said that they believe the NFL has taken meaningful action to reduce and prevent concussions, a figure that dropped from 41 percent in 2014 (Diamond and Beaton 2018). Parents have taken note of these disturbing news stories about concussions and are exerting influence on their children to shift to other, low-contact sports.

In 2018, 46 percent of parents (53 percent of mothers and 39 percent of fathers) said they would encourage their kids to play a sport other than football, up from 37 percent in 2014. Interest in the NFL is waning too—49 percent say they follow the NFL closely, down from 58 percent in 2014. Media executives suggest that the decline might be a result of overexposure of football, while league executives have pointed to a changing media landscape where fewer people watch live TV. For their part, the NFL defended its stature in the minds of Americans by pointing out that the NFL still had "33 of the top 50 most viewed shows in 2017" (Diamond and Beaton 2018).

Executives at the NFL have decided to not take these findings sitting down. They have responded to the drop in youth participation in recent years with an initiative called Heads Up Football, which is a coaching guide designed to promote safer tackling. This initiative has been utilized by more than 6,300 youth sports organizations around the country. The NFL has also spent $1 million on flag football programs and $2 million on a team of trainers who instruct gym teachers on safer football practices (Cook 2016). Will these efforts be enough to change attitudes and reverse the downward trend in interest and participation in youth football?

Questions

1. At a very basic level, attitudes are based on what we feel (affect) and what we think (beliefs). Create a list of at least five feelings and five thoughts that are relevant to a parent's attitudes about letting a child play youth football.
2. The research study discussed by Diamond and Beaton (2018) suggests that parents generally do not trust the NFL to do the right thing for the safety of their kids. Aside from what it is already doing, what could the NFL do to change those beliefs and demonstrate that they can be trusted?
3. Look at this situation from the perspective of a parent. Which hierarchy is most likely at play here when parents say no to their kids who want to play football? Discuss.

Sources: Belson (2017); Cook (2016); Diamond and Beaton (2018).

Marketers need to identify which hierarchy of effects is most relevant in different consumption contexts in order to plan more meaningful and impactful strategies. The clothing brand Free People is one example of a company that understands that its customers often operate under an emotional hierarchy. As such, the brand goes to great efforts to create an in-store environment that is truly experiential and multisensory, using scents, music, textures, and lighting. The goal is to encourage an emotional connection with the brand that will lead to a purchase behavior. Later, important beliefs will be generated (the brand is well made, it is fashionable, it is socially conscious). This strengthening of the brand meanings is a vital part of the Free People retailing strategy. The retailing strategy for utilitarian types of products like laptops would be very different and would likely focus on communicating product attributes in an attempt to influence beliefs about the product. In the end, knowing about the various hierarchies helps marketing managers create strategies to better meet the needs and expectations of consumers (see Insights from the Field 7.2).

◉ The Purpose and Role of Attitudes

As discussed earlier, attitude theory is an important tool for assessing evaluations and predicting behaviors across a wide variety of products and contexts (see Insights from Academia 7.2). Before we introduce the three main theories of attitudes, let's discuss the purpose of attitudes and the roles that attitudes play in consumer decision-making. First, a consumer's attitudes generally keep our thoughts and feelings in balance with one another. Second, attitudes perform a variety of functions for consumers.

Balance theory of attitudes

Humans have a psychological need to keep their feelings and thoughts fairly consistent with one another; this is true with products and consumption too. The **balance theory of attitudes** suggests that consumers seek balance between themselves, an attitude object, and some other important person or object (Lee, Lee, and Wu 2011). Consumers like to achieve an alignment between these three elements, so when the elements are unbalanced, consumers will adjust their perceptions to bring them back into balance (Dalakas and Levin 2005). For balance to occur, the three links, when multiplied together, must result in a positive outcome. That is, the links need to be either +/+/+ or +/−/−. Balance does not occur when we have a situation of −/−/− or −/+/+ (see Figure 7.1). Take the example of a consumer (P) who may have a positive impression of the new Star Wars movie (X). Our consumer thinks the acting is top notch, the storyline is captivating,

Balance theory of attitudes suggests that consumers seek balance between themselves, an attitude object, and some other important person or object.

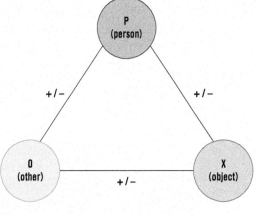

● **Figure 7.1** *The balance theory of attitudes*

and the special effects are spectacular! After talking to a friend, however, our consumer finds that the friend (O) really hated the movie! We have a situation of +/+/− and are therefore out of balance. The consumer likes the movie and likes the friend, but the friend does not like the movie. This situation can be brought back into balance in one of three ways. Our consumer can convince the friend that the Star Wars movie is really great after all (turning the − into a +), agree with the friend and conclude that the movie really wasn't so spectacular (turning the initial + into a −), or decide that the friend really wasn't all that great (hopefully not, but turning the + of the friendship into a −).

Balance theory can be applied to the tricomponent model of attitudes (affect, behavior, and cognitions). Consumers will experience a psychological drive to keep all three elements in balance with one another. When an imbalance occurs, consumers will experience discomfort and make adjustments so that balance is once again achieved (Woodside and Chebat 2001). For example, many consumers love to order popcorn and a soda when they go to the movies (behavior) because they enjoy the sweet taste of the drink and the crunchy, salty popcorn (affect). Some movie-goers even believe that the movie experience would not be complete without the soda and popcorn. Unfortunately, the salt, fat, and sugar are not at all healthy and such a diet could lead to health complications (cognitions). From a balance theory perspective, these three components are not in balance with each other and these soda and popcorn enthusiasts must adjust one or more of the linkages to re-establish balance. They could do one of three things to achieve balance. First, they could stop consuming soda and popcorn (behavior). Second, they could adjust their thoughts about the consumption of soda and popcorn by thinking that they only consume these items infrequently, so it won't impact their health (cognition). Finally, these consumers could try to change their emotional reactions to the soda and popcorn ("it's actually pretty gross") (affect). Any of these changes would bring the three elements back into balance. See Insights from Academia 7.2 for an example of balance theory in action.

Closely related to balance theory is the **theory of cognitive dissonance** (Festinger 1957). **Cognitive dissonance** is a state of being in which the individual has beliefs, attitudes, or behaviors that are out of balance. This imbalance results in a feeling of unease. In consumer behavior, cognitive dissonance is an important concept because it recognizes that individuals need consistency or consonance between their beliefs, attitudes, and behaviors. If you are a very strong supporter of animal rights, it would make you very uneasy to wear a fur jacket; if you love the Dallas Cowboys, it would make you feel quite uncomfortable to wear a Philadelphia Eagles jersey! Attitudes, beliefs, and behaviors must be in balance, and cognitive dissonance occurs when they are not. Dissonance sometimes occurs after the purchase of a product when, for example, a consumer experiences negative feelings (e.g., Oshikawa 1968). Maybe it was too expensive or maybe it doesn't have all the features the consumer really wanted. To reduce feelings of dissonance, consumers will change their beliefs, attitudes, or behaviors in an effort to achieve balance.

Theory of cognitive dissonance is based on the belief that people need consistency or consonance between their behavior and their attitudes.

Cognitive dissonance is the state of having inconsistent beliefs, attitudes, or behaviors, which results in a feeling of unease.

INSIGHTS FROM ACADEMIA 7.2

Advice to socially conscious companies: send stuff, not money

Customers put companies under substantial pressure to provide assistance to a variety of social and environmental causes. When an organization provides support for something like a natural disaster, such as an earthquake or a tornado (which is viewed as uncontrollable), consumers generally prefer to see contributions of supplies, equipment, and food rather than money. Why? From the consumer's perspective, these uncontrollable natural disasters are very emotionally upsetting and donations like supplies, equipment, and food are viewed as more effortful and emotional on the part of the organization—there is a match in the emotions associated with the event and the emotions of the nature of the response. Financial support, by contrast, is viewed as "throwing money at the problem." When an organization sends stuff, not money, to victims of natural disasters, consumers form more positive attitudes toward those companies. Since we know that consumer attitudes influence behaviors, organizations should be aware that mere support is not enough; it's the *type* of support that matters.

Hildebrand, D., Y. Demotta, S. Sen, and A. Valenzuela. 2017. "Consumer Responses to Corporate Social Responsibility (CSR) Contribution Type." Journal of Consumer Research *44 (4): 738–58.*

The functional theory of attitudes

Attitudes perform certain functions for us in our day-to-day lives (Katz 1960). The **functional theory of attitudes** is also referred to as a motivational theory of attitudes, since the purpose of these theories is to understand the motives and functions of attitude formation (Kardes 1993). Sometimes marketers want to change or strengthen consumer attitudes. According to the functional theory of attitudes, these attitude change attempts are more successful when they address the function that the attitude performs for the consumer. The four main functions that attitudes can perform are utilitarian, value-expressive, ego-defensive, and knowledge based (Russell-Bennett, Härtel, and Worthington 2013).

The first is the **utilitarian function**, which proposes that consumers seek maximum utility and value from their consumption (Grewal, Mehta, and Kardes 2004); consumers are striving to maximize rewards and minimize punishment. These consumers then go on to purchase a product because it performs a specific utilitarian function for the consumer. Flu medicine performs the function of shortening the time the consumer is sick with the flu; a reusable water bottle performs the function of allowing consumers to bring water along; and laundry detergent performs the utilitarian function of cleaning your clothes. When marketers clearly communicate that the product's attributes can effectively address consumer needs, consumers are likely to form more positive attitudes. The Tide detergent packaging highlights its use for high-efficiency laundry machines, as well as its clean breeze scent (Photo 7.3), two attributes that are likely important to consumers of this product.

Functional theory of attitudes seeks to identify and understand the motives and functions of attitude formation.

Utilitarian function (of attitudes) is based on the idea that consumers seek maximum utility and value from their consumption.

The second motivational function of attitudes is the **ego-defensive function**. Here, attitudes perform the function of defending or enhancing a consumer's self-image (Kardes 2001). When you go on a job interview, you dress and behave in a way that is probably a bit different from your regular, day-to-day routine. You might wear a suit, style your hair appropriately, and wear a nice watch. At a very basic level, the ego-defensive function of attitudes is concerned with protecting and enhancing our sense of self. When a consumer's ego is threatened and a product promises to remove that threat, the product is much more likely to be positively perceived. Many products that relate to health and beauty perform an ego-defensive function for consumers. Neutrogena's On-the-Spot acne treatment protects and enhances a consumer's self-image by helping to reduce the chances and severity of breakouts (see Photo 7.4).

Attitudes can also perform a **value-expressive function**, also referred to as the social identity function (Schossler 1998; Shavitt 1990). This function is concerned with the drive to project important aspects of the actual self (Grewal, Mehta, and Kardes 2004) and possible selves. The value-expressive function is characterized by consumers who use products and brands to express important aspects of the self. Most individuals want to be admired by others, and the value-expressive function of attitudes helps consumers communicate important aspects of their values to others. A young person may want to communicate values of independence and irreverence by getting a tattoo. Another consumer may choose to express values of wealth and good taste by buying and wearing luxury brands like Chanel. Still another consumer may want to express values of a just world and a sustainable planet by participating in a march or wearing a T-shirt in support of an environmental advocacy group like Greenpeace (see Photo 7.5).

The fourth and final function that is performed by attitudes is the **knowledge function**. This function is driven by the underlying human need to have an accurate, meaningful, stable, and organized view of the world (Kardes 1993). Attitudes that perform the knowledge function for consumers make it easier for consumers to evaluate any new information that a consumer encounters (Grewal, Mehta, and Kardes 2004).

● **Photo 7.3** *Attitudes toward laundry detergents like Tide perform a utilitarian function for consumers*

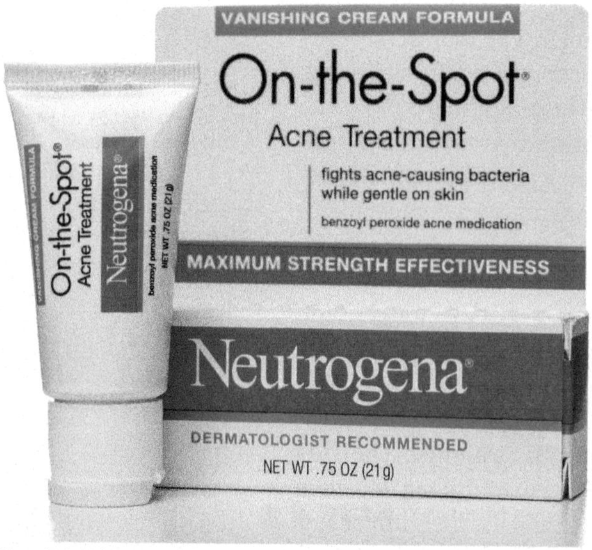

● **Photo 7.4** *Attitudes toward skin care products like Neutrogena perform an ego-defensive function for consumers*

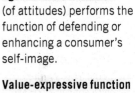

● **Photo 7.5** *Attitudes toward advocacy groups like Greenpeace perform a value-expressive function for consumers*

In essence, the knowledge function helps consumers organize and simplify new experiences. Because of that, the knowledge function of attitudes has been especially helpful for marketers to understand attitudes and predict behaviors toward brand extensions and diversifications. Take the example of a consumer who always travels with a MasterCard credit card. MasterCard protects the consumer's identity, is accepted all around the world, and provides cash back for purchases (see Photo 7.6). Knowing that this consumer is probably using this attitude to perform a knowledge function, we can predict that the consumer will have an easy time deciding how to pay for purchases when

Ego-defensive function (of attitudes) performs the function of defending or enhancing a consumer's self-image.

Value-expressive function (of attitudes) is concerned with the drive to express important aspects of the actual self and possible selves.

Knowledge function (of attitudes) relates to the human need to have an accurate, meaningful, stable, and organized view of the world.

● **Photo 7.6** *Attitudes toward services like MasterCard perform a knowledge function for consumers*

traveling (MasterCard!) and may be open to other MasterCard services such as insurance, travel services, and investments.

As discussed above, attitudes can perform four important functions for consumers—utilitarian, ego defensive, value expressive, and knowledge. In each of the examples we have discussed, the attitude performed a single function. Some products, however, can serve multiple functions for consumers (Shavitt 1989, 1990). In looking at all of the reasons why a consumer might buy a car, it is clear that cars are multifunctional products. Indeed, a car can perform a utilitarian function (such as safety and performance) as well as a value-expressive function (such as social status). Insights from the Field 7.3 describes how one retail store created two important insights about consumer needs and attitudes to develop a highly experiential retail environment.

 INSIGHTS FROM THE FIELD 7.3

Lowe's responds to attitudes toward home renovations

In any given week, 18 million people visit a Lowe's Home Improvement store. The company was founded in 1946 in North Carolina, currently employs 300,000 full-time and part-time associates, and has 2,200 stores in the United States, Canada, and Mexico. Lowe's posted $71.3 billion in sales in 2018, up from $68.6 million in 2017. The average customer buys $75.79 in merchandise per visit, and in 2018, there were 941 million customer transactions. Industry analysis found that the "professional market" accounted for 50 percent of all sales of US home improvement products, but only 20 to 25 percent of Lowe's sales. These professionals are contractors who work with homeowners on a variety of home improvement projects. In 2018, decision-makers at Lowe's announced a strategic priority to increase sales to the professional market (Lowe's 2018).

Marketing and consumer research experts at Lowe's quickly took up the challenge in trying to find ways to attract the professional market and made an important discovery. They found that they really needed to start with homeowners, not professionals. These homeowners needed to be able to more clearly picture what a home improvement project would look like in their own homes. Then, once homeowners knew what they wanted, they would make the final selections with the help of their contractors. In the end, the professionals would install the products that homeowners wanted. The next big question was how Lowe's could help

homeowners find the items they wanted for their new kitchen, bath, or other project (see Photo 7.7).

The consumer research and trend strategy team at Lowe's is located within the marketing department and, according to manager Jamie Slotterback, is responsible for identifying and tracking the trends that impact consumer behavior. Based on the team's extensive research findings, it developed the following insight: homeowners wanted to leave a majority of the creative and co-ordination decisions in a home renovation project to the professionals. Consumers were more than happy to make some of the smaller decisions, but were more satisfied if the majority of the decisions were made by the experts. The team also pulled another important insight from its research: there were four main "occasions" that brought homeowners to a home improvement store: (1) maintain, (2) replace, (3) refresh, and (4) remodel. The consumer research and trend strategy team found that a competitor, Home Depot, was dominating the maintain and replace market, those occasions where homeowners would come to the store for items that were simply designed to maintain or replace existing items in the house. These included things such as paint, caulking, and roofing materials to maintain the integrity of the house, as well as new lights, fixtures, and appliances to replace broken items (Slotterback 2019).

Importantly, the Lowe's team concluded that they would focus on the other two occasions: refresh and

● **Photo 7.7** *Lowe's Home Improvement stores are a familiar sight across America*

remodel. Here, homeowners would be looking for items to update and refresh their homes, such as a new waterfall shower or a new island for the kitchen. Homeowners may also be looking for a bigger, more complex remodeling project where they might need design help in determining which items to buy. Both of these occasions involved much more interaction with the store, more help, and more engagement. They would also likely result in significantly more revenue for the store (Slotterback 2019). Combining these two insights, the team concluded that homeowners wanted someone else to make the big decisions, especially with refresh and remodel decision. To put this conclusion into action, the team decided to launch the "coordinated collections" initiative. They hired Lara Lee, a well-known expert in creating customer experiences, and created in-store experiences so that consumers could see, feel, and touch several new kitchen and bathroom design concepts (Slotterback 2019). This coordinated collections initiative

has spilled into other areas of the store too, such as the lighting center and garden center. Homeowners can now visit these coordinated collections areas with their professional contractor to select the products they need for their refresh or remodel projects (see Photo 7.8).

● **Photo 7.8** *Consumers at Lowe's wanted to experience the products in a coordinated collection*

(continued)

From the perspective of the functional theory of attitudes, homeowners create attitudes that are likely to fulfill several motivational functions. For individuals who are looking to caulk a door or fix a broken handle on a cabinet, any attitudes formed by homeowners are likely to perform a *utilitarian function*. Some individuals who visit a Lowe's store are considering replacing a noisy refrigerator or a very outdated countertop, for example. To avoid any further embarrassment about these old items, they may create attitudes about new options. In this case, the attitude would be performing an *ego-defensive function* for the homeowners. Consider another situation where the homeowners may be hosting a big event at their home with lots of family and friends. If they decide to embark on a full kitchen remodel, they may form attitudes about a variety of items that will go into the new kitchen, many of which will perform a *value-expressive function* for the homeowners, highlighting their style and discriminating taste. Finally, the *knowledge function* of attitudes should be present across a few of these scenarios, as this function of attitudes builds on knowledge that the homeowners already have to make decisions about new brands, products, and alternatives easier.

Questions

1. We know that sometimes a single brand can fulfill a variety of attitude functions for a consumer. How could Lowe's efficiently communicate a single, meaningful message to consumers about the variety of different functions its products perform? Argue the case for a single unified message to consumers and then argue the case for different targeted messages.

2. Consider the following products: a trip to a museum, a highlighter pen, and a lawn care service. For each of these products, select at least two functions that an attitude might perform.

Sources: Lowe's (2018); Slotterback (2019).

The functional theory of attitudes provides important guidance for consumer researchers and marketers. The theory recognizes that attitudes perform a variety of functions for consumers in their day-to-day lives. Recognizing the function (or functions) that an attitude performs for a consumer is a critical step in helping marketers strengthen or change those attitudes. The theory suggests that attitudes change when they are no longer thought to perform their original function and consumers are thus motivated to change their attitudes. Take the example of a consumer of social media who relies on Instagram and Buzzfeed for news and information about the world. Initially, this "product" (the news) may have fulfilled the knowledge function for the consumer. However, eventually, our consumer may find that a more detailed and credible source is needed to make sense of the world and to have intelligent conversations with colleagues at work. Further, our consumer needs something more credible because he felt embarrassed getting news from these other sources. Our consumer then signs up for a digital subscription to the *New York Times*. This new "product" performs an important knowledge function as well as an ego-defensive function for the consumer. Marketers can sometimes help the process of getting consumers to change their attitudes by pointing out that a consumer's current product may no longer be the best option to perform a function for them.

◉ The Three Main Theories of Attitudes

Each of the three main theories of attitudes is referred to as a **multiattribute attitude model**, acknowledging that when consumers form attitudes, those attitudes are a combination of beliefs and evaluations about several different attributes, or features, of the product. Thus, at a very basic level, the attitude object is made up of a combination of impressions about product attributes and estimations about the importance of each attribute. Each multiattribute model has three elements:

- attributes—the characteristics or features of the attitude object (for example, the coffee is an AA Sumatra blend, with a fragrant aroma, somewhat nutty taste, full body, somewhat sweet, and served hot);
- beliefs—the consumer's knowledge about the extent to which the object has the attributes. Importantly, these beliefs could match with some, all, or none of the actual attributes of the product (for example, the consumer believes the coffee is somewhat nutty, sweet, and hot); and
- evaluations—the consumer's assessment of importance for each of these attributes (for example, when buying a cup of coffee, our consumer thinks it is very important that the coffee is full bodied, hot, and Fair Trade certified).

Think about attitudes toward Starbucks coffee ($A_{\text{Starbucks coffee}}$), we might find that this customer's attitudes are based on three primary attributes (nutty, sweet, and hot). Unfortunately, although Starbucks coffee does have some of the attributes the customer seeks, the customer simply is not aware that the coffee has them. This would be important information for a marketer to know so that communications strategies can be adjusted. We also find that the customer thinks it is very important (the evaluations) that coffee should be full bodied, hot, and Fair Trade certified. This is also important information for the managers at Starbucks and indicates that they might want to think about applying for Fair Trade certification, since it is an attribute that the coffee currently does not possess, but one that is quite important to customers. Multiattribute attitude models offer a way for marketers to unpack the elements of a consumer's overall attitude toward a product and use the information to predict how consumers might behave. By separating out the elements of an attitude, marketers can identify what is working or not working for consumers as they create attitudes. In addition, it provides marketers with important information about how they can adjust product and brand attributes, the product design, and communications strategies. Each of the three models will be described in the following section. The thing to remember for now is that this approach to attitudes allows marketers to quantify, or apply numbers to, the results. When the results are quantified, it makes it quite easy to compare attitudes across products, target markets, and time.

Multiattribute attitude models acknowledge that attitudes are a combination of beliefs and evaluations about several different attributes, or features, of a product.

The expectancy-value model

The origins of the expectancy-value model can be traced to the 1970s when a social psychologist named Martin Fishbein proposed the basic structure of attitudes. This model has been so influential over the years, it became the basis for other attitude models and is sometimes referred to as the Fishbein model. The **expectancy-value model** says that attitudes are based on two things: the beliefs that a product has a set of attributes and the evaluations of those attributes. For example, the consumer *believes* that the new coffee maker will be energy efficient, will deliver hot coffee, and will be easy to clean. The consumer *evaluates* these three attributes as not very important, very important, and somewhat important. Thus, this model proposes that a consumer has a set of beliefs and evaluations about products, which then combine to produce an attitude about that product (Fishbein and Ajzen 1975).

Expectancy-value model
says that attitudes are based on the belief that a product has a set of attributes and the evaluations of those attributes.

This model and the other two multiattribute models discussed in this section have been applied across a wide variety of social, cultural, political, and business contexts. For the sake of predicting what a consumer might do, Fishbein said that the attitude measured should be as specific as possible, so we should measure the attitude toward a behavior, rather than an object. For example, it is more precise to measure your attitude toward *buying* a Trek bicycle for your birthday this year, rather than just measuring the attitude toward Trek bicycles; it is more precise to measure the attitude toward *using* the new coffee maker in your new apartment than it is to simply measure the attitude toward the coffee maker.

Three key elements—attributes, beliefs, and evaluations—form the building blocks for each of the three multiattribute attitude models. The purpose of these multiattribute approaches is to quantitatively express the relationships between the model's components so that marketing managers can better predict what a consumer might do. To start, marketers will ask consumers to provide ratings for each of their salient beliefs. For example, extending our coffee maker example, the researcher might ask, "On a scale of 1 to 7, how likely is it that this new coffee maker is energy efficient?" This question would be asked for each of the product attributes, giving the researchers distinct ratings for each of the salient beliefs. Then, marketers will ask consumers to provide ratings for how important each attribute is to their decision. They would ask, for example, "When thinking about buying a coffee maker, on a scale of 1 to 7, how important is it that the coffee maker is energy efficient?" This will be done for each attribute, giving the researcher evaluation ratings for each attribute. To calculate attitudes, the researcher multiplies each belief by its evaluation and then adds up all of the belief × evaluation combinations. The result is an attitude toward an object, such as $A_{\text{Cuisinart coffee maker}}$ (see Case Study 7 for a detailed example of how marketers use this tool).

Taking a multiattribute approach to attitude measurement assumes that consumers can generally assign separate values to each belief and evaluation and then combine them to produce an attitude score. Consumer researchers don't claim that consumers actually have spreadsheets and formulas in their heads, but they do suggest that consumers can intuitively assess attributes and evaluations. Remember, although this model allows a focus on either A_{object} or $A_{behavior}$, because attitudes are likely to be different in different situations, it is recommended that researchers try to assess a consumer's attitude toward a specific behavior. To get an attitude toward a behavior, such as $A_{studying\ for\ my\ upcoming\ test}$, a researcher would ask slightly different questions to get the belief and evaluation scores. Once again, the researcher

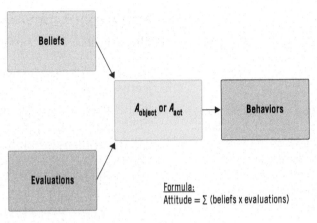

● **Figure 7.2** *The expectancy-value model of attitudes*

will start with a list of attributes. In this case, the attributes could be getting a good score, learning to really like the topic, and preparing myself better for my career. To get the belief scores for each attribute, a researcher might ask questions like, "On a scale of 1 to 7, how likely is it that if you study for your upcoming test, you will get a good score?" The researcher would do this for each of the attributes. Then, to get the evaluation scores, the researcher might ask, "On a scale of 1 to 7, how important is it to you that you get a good score?" Notice that when we're trying to assess the attitude toward the behavior, the questions are about *doing something* (Figure 7.2 shows how these elements are related).

The theory of reasoned action

This multiattribute model of attitudes builds on the expectancy-value approach discussed previously. The **theory of reasoned action (TRA)** has three important improvements over the previously discussed expectancy-value model. First, it focuses on attitudes toward a behavior, rather than an attitude that could be about a product or a behavior. In the expectancy-value model, $A_{behavior}$ or A_{act} was an option in the formula. In the TRA, A_{act} is a necessity. This shift in focus allows the TRA model to be more precise in its behavioral predictions. Second, the TRA acknowledges that social influences exert pressure on consumers as they make different decisions, so it adds an important variable called **subjective norms**, which are a consumer's assessment of how that behavior will be viewed by others. For example, some college students may really love Disney World, but they may be reluctant to suggest it as a spring break destination because of the anticipated negative reaction from their friends. The TRA model takes into account what the consumer thinks about how other people may react. Third, the TRA model more precisely focuses on behaviors in another important way. It adds a new variable called **behavioral intentions**, which represent a consumer's desire to enact a given behavior. The new components of this model of attitudes are related to one

Theory of reasoned action (TRA) is a multiattribute model of attitudes that says that behavioral intentions are determined by attitudes and subjective norms.

Subjective norms represent a person's perceptions of specific significant others' preferences as to whether the person should or should not engage in the behavior.

Behavioral intention is a consumer's desire to enact a given behavior.

another such that attitudes toward a behavior and subjective norms both independently influence behavioral intentions, which then influence actual behaviors (Ajzen and Fishbein 1980).

Here, it makes sense to spend more time discussing the concept of subjective norms, which represent an overall perception that other important individuals believe you should or should not perform the behavior. These significant others include, for example, your parents, siblings, friends, roommate, or boss. It is important to realize that the influence of these significant others will vary, depending on the context. Perhaps you are considering a new bike helmet. In this situation, the most relevant social influences may come from friends with whom you sometimes go biking or the salesperson at the bike shop. Different people in your life will exert influences on different purchases, so while your boss and coworkers may exert an important social influence on where you eat your lunch during the week, your friends and family are likely to exert more influence on where you eat your lunch on weekends and vacations.

Normative beliefs are the consumer's overall perception about relevant or important others' beliefs that the individual should or should not engage in a behavior.

Motivation to comply is the extent to which the individual feels driven to comply with or conform to the subjective preferences of these important people.

There are two components to subjective norms. First, we have **normative beliefs**, which are the consumer's perceptions about whether or not other people believe it is a good idea to engage in the behavior (Ajzen 2012). In our continuing example about running, a normative belief might be, "My teammates think I should wear Nikes when I go running." Remember, normative beliefs represent the consumer's *perception* about what others think, rather than a true and objective account of what they really think. The second component that makes up a subjective norm is the **motivation to comply**, which is the extent to which the individual feels driven to comply with or conform to the subjective preferences of these other people (Ajzen 2012). A consumer might feel driven to conform to what their teammates think by surmising, "It is important to me to go along with what my teammates think."

For a researcher to obtain the normative belief and motivation-to-comply scores, consumers would need to be asked a series of questions. First, to obtain the normative belief scores, a researcher would first need to identify the significant others who may exert an influence on our consumer's decision. In a situation in which a high school student is deciding which college to attend, the researcher may find that a student's parents, friends, and teachers would exert influence. Say our student is thinking about attending UCLA. To get the normative belief scores, a researcher might ask, "On a scale of 1 to 7, how much would your parents approve if you attended UCLA?" The researcher would then proceed to ask for the impressions our student has about the reactions from each significant other (friends and teachers). Next, to get the motivation-to-comply scores, a researcher would ask the consumer, "On a scale of 1 to 7, when you are picking a college, how important is it that you comply with what your parents say?" As before, the researcher will have a set of normative belief scores and motivation-to-comply scores. The subjective norm score is calculated by multiplying the normative belief and motivation-to-comply scores and then adding them together. Another benefit to using the TRA to study consumer attitudes is that the researcher can always assign weights to represent how the two components might be more or less important to the decision. For some decisions, attitudes may be more important, and for other decisions, subjective norms might be more influential. The TRA allows for those differences (see Figure 7.3).

The theory of planned behavior

The third multiattribute theory of attitudes is referred to as the **theory of planned behavior (TPB)** and is yet another advancement in consumer research theory and practice (see Figure 7.4). The purpose of the TPB is to provide an even deeper

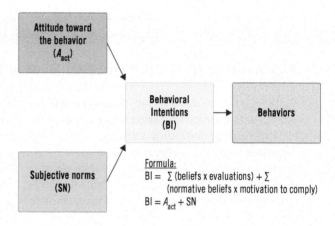

Figure 7.3 *The theory of reasoned action*

understanding of consumer perceptions and behaviors, but it adds one more variable to the mix: **perceived behavioral control**, which is the consumer's assessment of his or her own ability to successfully perform the behavior; it represents the confidence the consumer has in his or her own abilities and skills. Imagine that your significant other just surprised you with a day-long cooking class for your birthday and the two of you are scheduled to take the class next weekend! Perceived behavioral control would relate to how confident you feel in successfully following the instructor's directions in making a gourmet meal versus making a completely inedible mess. Perceived behavioral control takes into account a consumer's skills, abilities, knowledge, time, and opportunity. In extending our cooking class example, for a researcher to assess perceived behavioral control, consumers would be asked a series of questions like, "On a scale of 1 to 7, how easy or difficult would it be for you to successfully pass your cooking class?"

In the last step, the attitude, subjective norm, and perceived behavioral control scores are weighted, depending on their relative importance, and are then combined to provide the behavioral intentions. The TPB has been successfully used to predict a wide range of behaviors, including physical exercise (Ajzen and Driver 1992) and problem or addictive behaviors (Morojele and Stephenson 1992; Schlegl, Davernas, and Zanna 1992; Devries and Backbier 1994). It has also been used to predict consumption-related behaviors such as recycling (Boldero 1995) and gift buying (Netemeyer, Andrews, and Durvasula 1993). Insights from the Boardroom 7 describes how one ad agency utilizes attitudes to develop more impactful multicultural advertising.

Theory of planned behavior (TPB) is a multiattribute model of attitudes that says that behavioral intentions are determined by attitudes, subjective norms, and perceived behavioral control.

Perceived behavioral control is the consumer's assessment of his or her own ability to successfully perform the behavior.

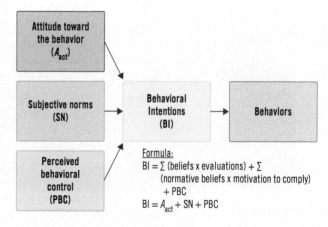

Figure 7.4 *The theory of planned behavior*

Do we live in a melting pot or a salad bowl?

Marta Insua has the distinct honor of having one of the best job titles around: chief creative officer. She works for Alma, an advertising agency based in Miami, Florida, and her answer to whether we live in a melting pot or a salad bowl is an emphatic, "Salad bowl!" Why? Think about it: Many years ago, when earlier generations of immigrants came to America, they became part of a big "melting pot." Many people coming from different places would not speak their native language at home (Italian, Polish, German) because they wanted to be seen as American. In many respects, they gave up their own heritage. Everyone who entered this big new country came together and became something completely new: an American. Although each individual person added his or her own "flavoring" to the mix, the result was one big, homogeneous pot. Today, the situation is much different. New immigrants don't have to renounce their identity. In fact, each individual component retains its identity, but most important, the whole is much more than the sum of the ingredients. Indeed, we live in a salad bowl. You can still identify each individual ingredient, but the whole salad tastes better with a lot of different things in it!

Insua has spent her career connecting attitudes, biculturalism, and insights. The specific area of expertise at Alma is biculturalism, specifically, individuals who identify themselves as both Latin American and American. Insua notes, "These people exist with a foot in each culture. The two cultures together provide more, not less." Basically, 1 + 1= 3 when you're talking about biculturalism. "You have to remember that these people are not 'either/or,' they are both!" says Insua (2017). Insua knows all about what it's like to keep the values and traditions of multiple cultures. "My family is originally from Spain, but we moved to Argentina and I grew up there as a child. Now, I'm living and working in South Florida," she says (2017). She started her career in advertising and worked her way up to media planner for DDB in Latin America, one of the biggest and most respected advertising agencies in the world. Later, she was recruited to the Miami office of DDB. Alma merged with DDB, but then the two agencies separated again a few years ago and Insua remained with Alma.

Because bicultural consumers strongly identify with two different cultures, it is challenging for marketers to know how to approach them. Being a bicultural consumer has some distinct advantages. Having different cultural perspectives makes a person more open to new ideas and to seeing a situation from multiple perspectives. Research has confirmed some distinct benefits for being bicultural. One recent study, for example, found that compared to individuals who identified with only a single culture, bicultural individuals demonstrate more fluency, flexibility, and novelty on a creative task. They produce more innovations at work, achieve more promotions, and have more positive reputations (Tadmor, Galinsky, and Maddux 2012). Insua says, "We were some of the first people to talk about this. It was an entirely new concept in the 1980s. Research says that you stay in touch with your culture, wherever you are. This is increasingly so today. It's a very special moment. Everything connects" (2017).

● *Marta Insua*

Understanding bicultural attitudes and associated insights is critical to creating meaningful marketing strategy. "We know that attitudes are the dispositional aspects of the person. Look deeper, however, and you can get their desires and motivations. We need to understand the depth of attitudes to understand their behavior. Attitudes are definitely predictors of intentions, which help us predict behaviors. But, attitudes aren't enough. You have to admit, attitudes are still a long distance away from behaviors," explains Insua (2017). Some things that are particularly important to bicultural customers are: (1) education and (2) advancement of family and children. Next, you have the problem with intentions. Insua says, "Yes, you can try to assess intentions, with qualitative or quantitative measures. But intentions still don't get you all the way to behaviors. Imagine this scenario, we've all been there, you bump into an old friend at the store or when you're out somewhere. You're so happy to see each other and you promise that you will be in touch and that you will get together for lunch some time. Of course, you have every intention of doing it, but guess what? Life gets in the way and it doesn't happen. That's the problem with intentions."

The solution? "We try to supplement all of this with deep insights," explains Insua (2017). Indeed, Insua was one of the early pioneers in the discipline of

HAVE SOUL

consumer insights, especially with bicultural consumers. Insua did this for DDB and then used the insights to develop media planning for them. She was responsible for training countless advertising executives and led several global forces, such as the worldwide brand planning group. Today, she is still focused on the "why" behind consumer decision-making. Insua says, "We are here to help clients better understand their customers. We need to have cultural understanding, but we also need to understand the nuance of what is happening. We need to emotionally resonate with them and move the emotional needle. This is invaluable. We help them understand and *act* on the insights."

In the end, just like a variety of tasty ingredients are blended to make a perfect salad, Insua blends her work with attitudes, biculturalisms, and insights to develop creative solutions for her clients.

Sources: Insua (2017); Tadmor, Galinsky, and Maddux (2012).

Compensatory and noncompensatory models

Decision rules are strategies that consumers use to help them make consumption choices. There are two types of decision rules: compensatory and noncompensatory. Each one of the multiattribute attitude models we discussed is compensatory. In a **compensatory model**, the components are combined in such a way that a low score on one component is compensated by a higher score on another. In forming an attitude, for example, all of the beliefs and evaluations are averaged to create an overall attitude; this allows for some "smoothing out" of the various beliefs. A consumer might think that the price for a given product is quite high, but also realizes that the product has excellent ratings and a generous return policy. Thus, the "negative" of the high price is compensated by the "positives" of the ratings and return policy.

Decision rules are strategies that consumers use to help them make consumption choices.

Compensatory models (in attitude theory) are made up of a number of components and are calculated in such a way that a low score on one component is compensated by a higher score on another.

Noncompensatory models of attitude formation describe the situation when one overriding component is dominant in the choice process.

Conjunctive decision rule is when a consumer chooses the brand that achieves the minimum level for each key evaluative attribute.

Lexicographic decision rule is when customers rank the product attributes by their importance, select the most important attribute, and then pick the brand that performs best on that attribute.

Elimination-by-aspects decision rule ranks evaluative aspects by importance and establishes a minimum cutoff point for each attribute.

There are some circumstances, however, when just one component may exert the most important influence on behaviors. Take the example of adopting a new pet from the shelter. We can look at it through the lens of the expectancy-value model. While you might have many positive beliefs about cats and dogs, your decision might be completely dependent on your belief that your apartment lease does not allow dogs. Because of this, you decide to welcome a cat into your home. We can also examine the situation through the lens of the TRA or TPB. Using the TPB, for example, you might have a very positive $A_{getting\ a\ cat}$ and very positive perceived behavioral control, but your roommate hates the idea of cats and you want continue to live peacefully with your roommate (subjective norm). This one, strong overriding component could shape your behavioral intentions and result in you deciding not to get a cat at all. These are examples of **noncompensatory models**, where one overriding component is dominant in the decision-making process.

There are several other noncompensatory decision rules that further simplify consumer decision-making. When customers use the **conjunctive decision rule**, they will choose the brand that achieves the minimum level for each key evaluative attribute. For example, if you are buying a used car, as long as it gets gas mileage better than twenty-five miles per gallon and it costs less than $15,000, it will be considered. Using the conjunctive rule, any brand that meets all the cutoff points will be considered. Using the **lexicographic decision rule**, customers rank the product attributes by their importance, select the most important attribute, and then pick the brand that scores highest on that attribute. For example, going back to our example of the car, if the most important consideration is gas mileage, our consumer would pick the car with the best gas mileage. If brands are tied on a particular attribute, consumers select the next most important attribute, and so on until a decision is made. The **elimination-by-aspects decision rule** ranks attributes by importance and sets a minimum acceptable cutoff point for each attribute. For the most important attribute, consumers will eliminate each brand that does not meet the minimum cutoff. Then, the second most important attribute is considered and any brands that do not meet the cutoff for that attribute are eliminated. The process continues until only one brand remains. Going back to our car example, perhaps our customer has a list of five cars that are currently under careful consideration. Any car that does not get at least twenty-five miles per gallon is eliminated, bringing the list down to four eligible cars. Next, any car that costs more than $15,000 is eliminated, bringing us down to three possible cars. This continues until only one option remains. For detailed examples of each of these rules, see Case Study 7.

Critique of multiattribute models of attitudes

Admittedly, these multiattribute models can be cumbersome and difficult for marketers to administer. Because of the large number of items to be measured, the surveys are lengthy and respondents experience fatigue. Also, generally speaking, these models are most useful in high-involvement consumption situations. Their predictive power is reduced when consumers have

INSIGHTS FROM ACADEMIA 7.3

Events are more enjoyable when you *wait* to post about them

Going to an event? Wait till later to post about it, because you will actually enjoy it more. Before going on a trip, many tourists create a behavioral intention to share the experience with their friends and family back home. Everyone does it. We take pictures and then post them to social media so everyone can see what we're doing. It turns out that tourists generally take pictures either for their own memories or for social media. If a tourist takes pictures for the sake of social media, they experience anxiety, become obsessed about how they look, and pay less attention to the actual experience. They are somewhat removed mentally and emotionally from the experience. Further, when this happens, tourists enjoy the experience less (their attitudes are more negative) and are less likely to recommend it to others (their behaviors are altered). #waittillyougethome

Barasch, A., G. Zauberman, and K. Diehl. 2018. "How the Intention to Share Can Undermine Enjoyment: Photo-Taking Goals and Evaluation of Experiences." Journal of Consumer Research 44 (6): 1220–37. https://doi.org/10.1093/jcr/ucx112.

only weak opinions and are only vaguely aware of the opinions of others. In recent years, multiattribute models have evolved even further, with the addition of additional variables such as emotions (Ajzen 2011) and additional connections between some of the variables (Ajzen 2005). For our purposes, however, the three primary multiattribute models of attitudes provide us with a solid understanding of how consumers construct attitudes, which then influence their behaviors. See Insights from Academia 7.3 for another example of the interplay between attitudes and behaviors.

Multiattribute attitude models have provided at least two important contributions to understanding consumer behavior. First, they have separated, defined, and simplified the key components that contribute to a consumer's behavioral intentions. We know how these elements are created in the consumers' minds and we know how these elements are related to one another. Second, these models can be diagnostic—we can use them to compare attitudes across products, customers, and even time. Importantly, this information can help marketers identify *how* an attitude can be changed.

Attitude And Behavior Change

We know that attitudes are learned. Because of this, they can also be changed. Whether it is changing a person's attitude about wearing a seat belt or a consumer's attitude about our product, there are at least three very specific tools that can be used to accomplish this change: changing the basic motivational function, altering the components of the multiattribute attitude model, or elaborating on the information in the communications message.

Changing the basic motivational function

Remember that there are four key functions that attitudes perform for consumers: utilitarian, value expressive, ego defensive, and knowledge (Katz 1960). This approach to attitude change starts with a clear understanding of the motivational needs driving the initial attitude formation. Then, a variety of communications techniques can be used to alter the function for the consumer. For example, many individuals have an attitude about the natural environment that is utilitarian. Consumers believe that the natural environment is there to provide benefits like food, water, materials, and recreation. What would happen if we would like to change this consumer's behavioral intentions about enacting some ecofriendly behaviors? We want people to turn off the tap when they brush their teeth, for example. If this consumer is steadfast in holding an attitude that is purely utilitarian, any change in behavioral intentions might be difficult. Why would this consumer want to enact an ecofriendly behavior when the environment is simply there to provide a utilitarian function? So, it might be wise to try to engage in an effort to get that consumer to view the natural environment in more value-expressive terms. A campaign could encourage the consumer to consider the aesthetic and spiritual beauty of the natural environment, not just its utilitarian benefits. After a time, if the consumer shifts the motivational function to a more value-expressive one, it might be easier to get the consumer to also shift important behavioral intentions (see Photo 7.9).

Altering components of the multiattribute model

Smart managers engage in brand-tracking research that examines consumer attitudes toward their brands as well as competitive brands. From this research, they can identify which product attributes are most important to consumers. Research can also reveal important information about social norms and perceived behavioral control. From this information, marketers can derive important insights about how they might be able to use attitude theory to change a consumer's attitudes. Indeed, the expectancy-value model, the TRA, and the TPB provide a clear roadmap to the possible ways in which a consumer's attitudes and behavioral intentions can be changed (see Table 7.2 and Insights from the Field 7.4).

Marketers can use these strategies to change behavioral intentions for their own customers as well as their competitors' customers. In the United Kingdom, EasyJet discount airline ran a campaign in which it attempted to change customer beliefs (b_i)

Photo 7.9 *Attitudes toward the environment can fulfill a value-expressive function*

Table 7.2 Strategies to change attitudes and behavioral intentions

CHANGE STRATEGY	EXPLANATION AND EXAMPLE
Change a belief (b_i)	Convince consumers that what they had previously thought about the product may be incorrect. *Microsoft has engaged in a variety of efforts to convince consumers that it has flexible and powerful graphics capabilities.*
Change an evaluation (e_i)	Change the degree to which consumers view the belief as important. *Microsoft can then try to convince consumers that graphics capabilities are extremely important in an operating system.*
Add a new belief (b_i) (and evaluation of that belief [e_i])	Add a new belief about the product that a consumer had not previously considered. When a new belief is added, a new evaluation will accompany it. *Dawn dishwashing liquid ran a series of ads about the fact that it is the number one most preferred cleanser that rescue workers use when they work to clean wildlife that has been exposed to oil spills. Many consumers place a lot of importance on a company's social responsibility efforts.*
Change a normative belief (NB_j)	Convince consumers to change their perceptions about what others think. *Tobacco Free Florida works to convince teenagers that their friends think smoking is definitely not cool.*
Change a motivation to comply (MC_j)	Change a consumer's motivation to go along with the wishes of an important person in his or her life. *Tobacco Free Florida also tries to reinforce and strengthen the already strong motivation of teenagers to comply with what their friends think.*
Add a new normative belief (NBj) (and motivation to comply with that belief [MC_j])	Add a new normative belief about the product that a consumer had not previously considered. A new motivation to comply will be added too. *In the United Kingdom, Virgin Trains ran the "Bound for Glory" campaign in which a young man was trying to impress his girlfriend's skeptical parents. For many people, it is important to respect the wishes of a significant other's parents.*
Change perceived behavioral control	Encourage consumers to purchase by noting, for example, the ease of ordering and checkout, obtaining financing, or product use. *For the on-the-go consumer, many retailers are offering "contactless checkout" with tap-and-go checkout lanes.*

Note: The i and j subscripts allow for each element to have multiple items, so if there are three separate beliefs, they would be designated as b_1, b_2, and b_3; if there are only two normative beliefs, they would be designated as NB_1 and NB_2.

for its Irish competitor, Ryanair. This campaign implied that Ryanair delivered passengers to secondary airports that were located several miles away from their actual destinations, which required those passengers to take long bus rides to get to their destination cities. This was not true. The two competitors have had a long history of attack ads against one another, but this one went a bit too far. The UK's Advertising Standards Authority agreed with

Attitudes toward safe driving

Attitude theories have been utilized to address a variety of social and cultural attitudes and behaviors. As with other attitude change strategies, the goal of these strategies is to influence and change behavior by modifying one of the primary building blocks of behavioral intentions: beliefs, evaluations, normative beliefs, motivations to comply, or perceived behavioral control. A few examples of attitude change efforts to encourage road safety are as follows:

- The "If you feel different, you drive different" campaign in the United States is sponsored by the US Department of Transportation and is designed to change beliefs and behavioral intentions about using drugs or alcohol before driving. The campaign says, "Driving either drunk or high is driving under the influence; impairment is impairment." Supported by national radio, TV, and digital ads, this campaign seeks to change the beliefs of some people who think that driving high is somehow not as big a problem as driving drunk. In the process, they hope to change behavioral intentions (National Highway Traffic Safety Administration 2019).
- In the state of New South Wales in Australia, an innovative multimedia campaign called "Stop it... or cop it" added a new belief by informing citizens that, at any time, any of the 16,500 police officers can enforce road rules like speeding, not wearing a seat belt, or using your phone while driving. So, rather than getting pulled over, citizens should simply "stop it" ("Stop It" 2019). The Centre for Road Safety has also launched a variety of campaigns focusing on changing normative beliefs and the motivation to comply with respect to drinking and driving, speeding, and a variety of other safety-related issues. For example, the "Driveway Safety—They're Counting on You" campaign is designed to encourage parents to be extra careful when backing out

of the driveway because "they're counting on you" ("Driveway Safety" 2019).
- Some of the hardest-hitting ads come from Ireland and Northern Ireland, which have engaged in a years-long campaign of brutally vivid depictions of the hazards of drunk, distracted, or otherwise unsafe driving. One ad, for example, shows an entire class of twenty-eight children on a field trip getting crushed by a speeding car. The message is that twenty-eight children have died in traffic accidents in Northern Ireland over the past four years. Although critics say that these depictions are too horrific and shocking, they have worked. According to experts, traffic fatalities have decreased since the introduction of these hard-hitting ads (Langan 2014). Although each ad has different goals, they primarily focus on the emotional components of attitude formation: evaluations and motivation to comply.

Questions

1. Using the TRA and the attitude question format we've presented, create some attitude survey questions of your own to track behavioral intentions toward road safety. Specifically, there should be four separate "sets" of questions: beliefs, evaluations, normative beliefs, and motivation to comply.
2. Binge drinking is a problem on college campuses across the country. Using the TPB, create at least two arguments or advertising messages that can be used to change behavioral intention for binge-drinking college students. In all, there should be at least ten messages in total: two each for beliefs, evaluations, normative beliefs, motivation to comply, and perceived behavioral control.

Sources: "Driveway Safety" (2019); Langan (2014); National Highway Traffic Safety Administration (2019); "Stop It" (2019).

Ryanair's complaints and banned EasyJet's campaign. Comparative advertising can sometimes be a dangerous strategy to pursue.

Elaborating on the information

Multiattribute attitude models give marketing managers specific insights about how to change consumer attitudes and behaviors. Another model that can help promote attitude change is the **elaboration likelihood model** (Petty and Cacioppo 1986), which describes a process by which consumers think about and mentally process communication messages. Consumers must have both the ability and the motivation to process (think about) the information presented in an advertising message. An important feature of this model is the **elaboration continuum**, which describes the depth of thought, or elaboration, that a consumer engages in when exposed to a communications message (Petty and Briñol 2012). This elaboration ranges from high, where the consumer engages in deep, critical thought, to low, where the consumer engages in only shallow and cursory thought. High elaboration and high involvement tend to go together; if you're purchasing a car or an overseas vacation, you will think about it a lot. When faced with an advertising message, you will systematically and critically engage with the information in the message (O'Keefe 2008). According to the elaboration likelihood model (Figure 7.5), individuals engaging in high elaboration will follow the central route to attitude change, while consumers engaging in low elaboration will follow the peripheral route to attitude change.

Central route processing occurs when a highly involved consumer pays attention to the information, carefully evaluates it, integrates it with existing knowledge, and develops an attitude based on logical reasoning. When highly involved consumers are motivated and able to pay attention to an advertising message, they take a logical, central route to attitude change. Consumers who use the central route for processing make greater use of product-related information (Rucker and Petty 2006). Maybelline UK used an ad for its new cream-whipped foundation product that provided detailed information about the product, how it was processed, and its distinct benefits over similar products. The ad encourages central route processing for consumers (see Photo 7.10).

Peripheral route processing is taken by consumers who have low levels of involvement. They pay attention to the surface characteristics of a communications message, such as attractive images, celebrities, or other eye-catching features of the ad. These consumers are unlikely to pay attention to the quality of the message, exert little effort in evaluating new information, rely more on their emotional reactions, and incorporate very little of their own knowledge into the process (Petty

Elaboration likelihood model describes a process by which consumers think about and process information. If they are highly involved, they use the central route to persuasion; if they have low involvement, they use the peripheral route to persuasion.

Elaboration continuum describes the amount of thought given to an advertising message/communication.

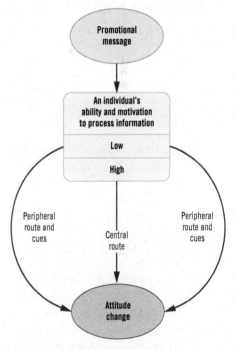

● **Figure 7.5** *The Elaboration Likelihood Model*

Source: from Petty, R.E. and Cacioppo, J.T. (1986), Communication and persuasion: central and peripheral routes to attitude change, New York: Springer-Verlag; reproduced from the original source with kind permission of Springer Science+Business Media.

● **Photo 7.10** *Maybelline ad encouraging a central route to persuasion*

● **Photo 7.11** *Evian ad encouraging a peripheral route to persuasion*

and Briñol 2012). Because marketers of low-involvement products know that many everyday purchases involve peripheral route processing, they construct ads that attract attention, but do little else. The ad for Evian water captures the attention of the viewer with a cute picture of a child wearing oversized clothes (see Photo 7.11). The campaign by the ad agency BETC in France is supposed to be fun and remind consumers of their inner child. It ran on print, digital, and social media platforms. Notice that the ad doesn't talk about the product attributes or give persuasive reasons for why consumers should buy it.

According to the elaboration likelihood model, regardless of the route to persuasion that is taken, attitude change occurs if the consumer has the ability and the motivation to process the information. For marketers, understanding which route to persuasion is taken by consumers is important because it provides important insights about attitude formation, strengthening, and change. First, however, marketers need to determine the likely level of involvement that a consumer has with the product. If marketers know that consumers have low levels of ability and motivation to process the ad (low involvement), they can construct their ads with famous celebrities or eye-catching images. Alternatively, if marketers know that consumers have high levels of ability and motivation to process the ad (high involvement), they can create ads with detailed information and strong arguments.

Summary

In one way or another, we spend a good part of our day either involved in consumption or thinking about consumption. Even cheering for your favorite football team or passionately arguing about Monday night's game is a consumption-related activity. This chapter presents a variety of approaches to understanding attitudes, an all-important tool for helping to understand and predict consumer behavior. In this chapter, we defined the *concept of attitudes* as used in marketing and found that attitudes are an important tool for marketers in helping to predict consumer behavior. As illustrated in Insights from the Field 7.1, consumer attitudes toward credit and debt help predict spending and saving behaviors. Next, we broke down the *various components* of attitudes, which, together, gave us a basic understanding of some of the foundational elements of our later attitude models. Insights from Academia 7.1 confirmed a long-held belief that many consumers have—sometimes it is important to "trust your gut" and listen to your feelings when making a decision. This again emphasizes the importance of paying attention to a consumer's heart and mind.

The *main theoretical approaches to attitudes* were presented, including the balance theory of attitudes, the functional theory of attitudes, and the multiattribute models of attitudes. The three multiattribute models of attitudes provided important insights into how attitudes and behavioral intentions are formed and how they might be changed. In that regard, Table 7.2 provided an important how-to guide for marketers who would like to drive attitude change. Insights from the Boardroom 7 provided a fascinating glimpse into how one ad agency has developed a depth of knowledge about attitudes within the Hispanic community, which it uses to construct ads that resonate with those consumers.

Our discussion of *compensatory and noncompensatory models* of consumer decision-making illuminated the various ways in which consumers combine and weigh important components in the decision-making process. Case Study 7 illustrates the decision rules that might be employed for a student thinking about going to graduate school to get a master's of business administration (MBA).

Finally, three important approaches to *attitude change* were also presented: changing the basic motivation function, altering components of the multiattribute models, and elaborating on the information. The elaboration likelihood model was presented as a method for understanding consumer processing of information as well as a guideline for advertisers in constructing persuasive ads.

The study of attitudes is critically important to understanding consumer behavior. Indeed, attitudes help researchers understand a wide variety of consumer behaviors and allow us to compare consumer perceptions across target markets, products, and time. Above all, a deep understanding of attitude formation and change provides marketing professionals with important insights about how to manage their brand portfolio in a dynamic and competitive marketplace.

KEY TERMS

affective component p. 244
attitude p. 242
attitude object p. 242
balance theory of attitudes p. 249
behavioral component p. 244
behavioral intentions p. 259
cognitive component p. 244
cognitive dissonance p. 250
compensatory models p. 263

conjunctive decision rule p. 264
decision rules p. 263
ego-defensive function p. 253
elaboration continuum p. 269
elaboration likelihood model p. 269
elimination-by-aspects decision rule p. 264
expectancy-value model p. 258
functional theory of attitudes p. 251

knowledge function p. 253
lexicographic decision rule p. 264
motivation to comply p. 260
multiattribute attitude model p. 257
noncompensatory models p. 264
normative beliefs p. 260
perceived behavioral control p. 261
salient beliefs p. 245

subjective norms
p. 259
theory of cognitive
dissonance p. 250

theory of planned
behavior (TPB) p. 261
theory of reasoned
action (TRA) p. 259

utilitarian function p. 251
value-expressive function
p. 253

REVIEW QUESTIONS

1. Define attitudes and discuss the ABC model of attitudes. What does it mean when we say that the ABC model has a problem because it does not specify the relationship between its three components?
2. What do marketers mean by the term *hierarchy of effects* when they are talking about attitudes? For each of the hierarchies, provide an example from your own life.
3. Describe balance theory and how marketing managers may find this theory useful.
4. In what way is cognitive dissonance theory similar to and different from balance theory?
5. What do we mean when we say that attitudes perform certain functions for consumers? How can an attitude perform multiple functions?
6. Describe the evolution of the three main multi-attribute attitude models. What are the benefits to using these models in consumer research?
7. How is attitude change different under the multiattribute attitude approach versus the elaboration likelihood approach?

DISCUSSION QUESTIONS

1. Think about all of the different kinds of restaurants that a consumer can visit. For each of the four categories of the functional theory of attitudes, identify and describe a restaurant. Can any of these restaurants perform multiple functions (refer again to the analysis of home renovations in Insights from the Field 7.3)? Discuss.
2. The TRA and the TPB are quite logical in their approach to understanding and predicting what consumers might do. What are some benefits of these approaches? What are some drawbacks?
3. Your local township has recently received a grant of $20,000 to develop a communications strategy to encourage military veterans to consider farming when they come home from service. Additional funds and low-interest loans are available to help them purchase land and equipment,

so that won't be a big obstacle. The problem, as your township supervisors see it, is in encouraging these men and women who have never farmed to start their own farms. Since you now know a lot about attitudes and attitude theory, what would you suggest they do to encourage more military service people to consider farming?
4. Visit the American Red Cross site at https://www.redcrossblood.org/donate-blood/how-to-donate/how-blood-donations-help/blood-needs-blood-supply.html and learn some facts about blood and blood donation. First, describe how (1) the functional theory of attitudes, (2) the theory of reasoned action, and (3) the elaboration likelihood model may be used to encourage a person to donate blood. Second, which of these three models is most useful or appropriate in suggesting ways to encourage blood donation? Discuss.

So, you're thinking about getting your MBA. . .*

Look into the future a few years and imagine that you are considering going to graduate school for your MBA. Imagine further that you have a set of decision rules that you would like to employ as you carefully consider the attributes of the graduate school. Because you have carefully studied this chapter, you are already familiar with both the compensatory and the noncompensatory decision rules (conjunctive, lexicographic, elimination by aspect). These models will be helpful as you carefully analyze this material and select the best graduate school for you.

While there are likely to be several key features or attributes of your new graduate school that are important, you are probably aware that the perfect school may not exist. It might not be in the perfect location, it might be too expensive, or it might have other drawbacks. Because of this, it is likely that you will have to carefully consider what is most important and even make compromises. Let's look at some attributes and their evaluations, and then let's see how different models and rules might be applied. In the end, we will see that these different models and rules result in very different attitudes and behavioral intentions.

Attributes, belief scores, and evaluation scores

Graduate schools have very different attributes that might be important to a potential graduate student (see Table 7.3 for hypothetical belief ratings). On a scale of 1 to 7, looking at *reasonable price*, graduate school 4 ranks best on this feature, since it has the highest score of 6. For *quality of the program*, schools 1 and 2 rate the highest (with scores of 6 and 5).

Obviously, not all of these attributes are equally important to you. Table 7.4 provides your evaluation for each attribute. For the sake of argument, you have said that *quality of the program* and *career placement assistance* are the most important attributes to you, and hence you have given them the highest evaluation scores (4 each on a scale of 1 to 5), while *average class size* is the least important feature (with a score of 1).

Table 7.3 Key attributes rated for each graduate school

ATTRIBUTES (*b*)	SCHOOL 1	SCHOOL 2	SCHOOL 3	SCHOOL 4
Reasonable price	4	5	3	6
Proximity to home	2	4	6	4
Average class size	2	3	4	4
Quality of the program	6	5	2	3
Reputation of the professors	4	3	4	1
Career placement assistance	6	5	5	4

Application of compensatory model

Remember that compensatory models include all of the most important (salient) attributes and evaluations. Further, a low score on one attribute can be compensated for by a high score on another attribute; the scores are averaged out. Using this approach to determine your attitude toward each graduate school, you would use the following calculation:

$$\text{Attitude} = \Sigma\,(b_i \times e_i),\ i = 1, \ldots, n$$

where

Σ = sum total
b_i = attribute ranking for each school
e_i = numerical evaluation rating for each attribute
n = total number of attributes

There are six attributes ($n = 6$), so there will be six b_i and e_i combinations. Look at Table 7.3 and 7.4 for all the scores that are needed to complete this calculation. To show how the calculations work, Table 7.5 provides the calculations for School 1. Calculate the attitude scores for the other graduate schools. Which school will likely be selected?

Application of noncompensatory models

Conjunctive decision rule

Would the outcome be any different if you used one of the noncompensatory models to select a graduate school for your MBA? Using the conjunctive decision rule, you would select a school based on whether it met a minimum cutoff for several key attributes. In our example, the cutoff point for reasonable price is 4, that for quality of program is 5, and the cutoff for all of the other attributes is 3. To show how the conjunctive decision rule works, Table 7.6 provides the findings for School 1. Using the attribute scores provided in Table 7.3, examine the cutoffs for the other schools (you do not need the evaluation scores at this time). Which school would be selected?

Table 7.4 Evaluation scores for each attribute

ATTRIBUTES (b_i)	EVALUATION SCORE (e_i)
Reasonable price	3
Proximity to home	2
Average class size	1
Quality of the program	4
Reputation of professors	1.5
Career placement assistance	4

Table 7.5 Attitude calculations based on the compensatory model

ATTRIBUTES (b_i)	SCHOOL 1	SCHOOL 2	SCHOOL 3	SCHOOL 4
Reasonable price	4 × 3 = 12			
Proximity to home	2 × 2 = 4			
Average class size	2 × 1 = 2			
Quality of program	6 × 4 = 24			
Reputation of professors	4 × 1.5 = 6			
Career placement assistance	6 × 4 = 24			
Total attitude score $\Sigma(b_i \times e_i)$	72			

Table 7.6 Calculations based on the noncompensatory model: conjunctive rule

ATTRIBUTES (b_j)	CUTOFF	SCHOOL 1	SCHOOL 2	SCHOOL 3	SCHOOL 4
Reasonable price	4	4 (yes)			
Proximity to home	3	2 (no)			
Average class size	3	2 (no)			
Quality of program	5	6 (yes)			
Reputation of professors	3	4 (yes)			
Career placement assistance	3	6 (yes)			
Meets all attribute cutoffs?		No			

Lexicographic decision rule

Another noncompensatory rule is the *lexicographic decision rule*. Here, you would rank the attributes by their importance and then choose the school that performs best on the attribute most important to you (these are obtained from the e_i scores). In the event of a tie between two options, you will look to the next most important attribute, and so on. Using Table 7.7, examine the rankings column where quality of program is most important and average class size is least important. Which school would be selected using this rule?

Elimination-by-aspects decision rule

The last noncompensatory model is the elimination-by-aspects decision rule, where a combination of rankings and cutoffs is used. The process starts with the most important attribute, quality of program. Any brand that does not meet the minimum cutoff for that attribute is eliminated. The remaining brands are then evaluated on the next most important attribute, and so on, until one brand remains. Using the data provided in Table 7.7 again, which school would be selected based on the elimination-by-aspects decision rule?

Table 7.7 Ranking and cutoff points

ATTRIBUTES (b_j)	RANKING	CUTOFF POINTS
Quality of program	1	5
Career placement assistance	2	3
Reasonable price	3	4
Proximity to home	4	3
Reputation of professors	5	3
Average class size	6	3

* *The author wishes to acknowledge Szmigin and Piacentini (2015) for providing a rough outline on which the present case study was developed.*

QUESTIONS

1. Which school was selected for each of the four methods? Why did each of these methods provide different results? Generally speaking, how can marketers use this information to develop useful insights?

2. Based on your findings, what marketing recommendations do you have for colleges and universities? For students as they are considering different graduate school options?

3. The multiattribute approach in this case only included calculations for the expectancy-value model, not the TRA or TPB. How might the decision about your MBA change if you had also included assessments for subjective norms and perceived behavioral control?

REFERENCES

Ajzen, I. 2005. *Attitudes, Personality and Behavior*. Maidenhead, UK: Open University Press.

Ajzen, I. 2011. "The Theory of Planned Behavior: Reactions and Reflections." *Psychology & Health* 26 (9): 1113–27.

Ajzen, I. 2012. "Theory of Planned Behavior." In *Handbook of Theories of Social Psychology*, edited by P. A. M. Van Lange, A. W. Kruglanski, and E. T. Higgins, 1:438–59. London: Sage.

Ajzen, I., and B. L. Driver. 1992. "Application of the Theory of Planned Behavior to Leisure Choice." *Journal of Leisure Research* 24 (3): 207–24.

Ajzen, I., and M. Fishbein. 1980. *Understanding Attitudes and Predicting Social Behavior*. Englewood Cliffs, NJ: Prentice Hall.

Alexandris, K., R. Tsiotsou, and J. James. 2012. "Testing a Hierarchy of Effects Model of Sponsorship Effectiveness." *Journal of Sport Management* 26 (5): 363–78.

Altman, I. 2015. "Is Amazon Killing Small Businesses?" *Forbes*, October 27, 2015. https://www.forbes.com/sites/ianaltman/2015/10/27/what-amazon-is-doing-to-small-businesses/#2b2e5ca652d4.

Beatty, S. E., and L. R. Kahle. 1988. "Alternative Hierarchies of the Attitude–Behavior Relationship: The Impact of Brand Commitment and Habit." *Journal of the Academy of Marketing Science* 16 (2): 1–10.

Belson, K. 2017. "Playing Tackle Football before 12 Is Tied to Brain Problems Later." *New York Times*, September 19, 2017. https://www.nytimes.com/2017/09/19/sports/football/tackle-football-brain-youth.html.

Boldero, J. 1995. "The Prediction of Household Recycling of Newspapers—The Role of Attitudes, Intentions and Situational Factors." *Journal of Applied Psychology* 25 (5): 440–62.

Christie, S. 2017. "The 10 Most Cashless Countries in the World—Where Does the UK Rank?" *Telegraph*, October 10, 2017. http://www.telegraph.co.uk/money/future-of-money/10-cashless-countries-world-does-uk-rank/.

Cook, B. 2016. "Youth Football Participation Trends Signal Whether NFL's Ratings Slip Will Be Long-Term." *Forbes*, November 28, 2016. https://www.forbes.com/sites/bobcook/2016/11/28/youth-football-participation-trends-signal-whether-nfls-ratings-slip-will-be-long-term/#27a8beb62da2.

"Driveway Safety—They're Counting on You." 2019. Centre for Road Safety, Transport for NSW. Accessed August 15, 2019. https://roadsafety.transport.nsw.gov.au/campaigns/theyre-counting-on-you/driveway-safety.html.

Dalakas, V., and A. M. Levin. 2005. "The Balance Theory Domino: How Sponsorships May Elicit Negative Consumer Attitudes." *Advances in Consumer Research* 32:91–97.

Devries, H., and E. Backbier. 1994. "Self-Efficacy as an Important Determinant of Quitting among Pregnant Women Who Smoke: The Phi Pattern." *Preventive Medicine* 23 (2): 27–37.

Diamond, J., and A. Beaton. 2018. "Ahead of Super Bowl, Poll Shows NFL Is Losing Its Core Audience." *Wall Street Journal*, February 2, 2018. https://www.wsj.com/articles/the-nfl-is-losing-its-core-audience-a-wsj-nbc-news-poll-finds-1517569200.

Dow, J. P. 2018. "Attitudes towards Credit after the Great Recession." *Applied Economics Letters* 25 (4): 254–57.

Festinger, L. 1957. *A Theory of Cognitive Dissonance*. Stanford, CA: Stanford University Press.

Fishbein, M., and I. Ajzen. 1975. *Belief, Attitude, Intention and Behavior*. Reading, MA: Addison–Wesley.

Fleming, J. H. 2016. "Americans Are Buried under a Mountain of Debt." *Gallup Business Journal* [serial online], March 3, 2016, 1. https://news.gallup.com/businessjournal/189713/americans-buried-mountain-debt.aspx.

Grewal, R., R. Mehta, and F. R. Kardes. 2004. "The Timing of Repeat Purchases of Consumer Durable Goods: The Role of Functional Bases of Consumer Attitudes." *Journal of Marketing Research* 41 (1): 101–15.

Grimm, P. E. 2005. "'Ab Components' Impact on Brand Preference." *Journal of Business Research* 58 (4): 508–17.

Henderson, S., and S. F. Hoque. 2010. "The Ethnicity Impact on Attitudes toward Country of Origin for Products with Different Involvement Levels." *Journal of International Consumer Marketing* 22 (3): 271–91.

Herr, P. M., and R. H. Fazio. 1993. "The Attitude-to-Behavior Process: Implications." In *Advertising Exposure, Memory and Choice*, edited by A. Mitchell, 119–40. Hillsdale, NJ: Erlbaum.

Insua, M. 2017. Personal interview, August 16, 2017.

Kardes, F. R. 1993. "Consumer Inference: Determinants, Consequences and Implications for Advertising." In *Advertising Exposure, Memory and Choice*, edited by A. Mitchell, 163–93. Hillsdale, NJ: Erlbaum.

Kardes. F. R. 2001. *Consumer Behavior and Managerial Decision Making*. 2nd ed. Upper Saddle River, NJ: Prentice Hall.

Katz, D. 1960. "The Functional Approach to the Study of Attitudes." *Public Opinion Quarterly* 24:163–204.

Langan, S. 2014. "Ireland's History of Graphic Safe Driving Ads—Do they Work?" *IrishCentral*. June 26, 2014. https://www.irishcentral.com/culture/irelands-history-of-graphic-safe-driving-ads-do-they-work-videos.

Lee, H. M., C. C. Lee, and C. C. Wu. 2011. "Brand Image Strategy Affects Brand Equity after M&A." *European Journal of Marketing* 45 (7/8): 1091–111.

Lowe's. 2018. *Lowe's: Focusing on Retail Fundamentals. Annual Report 2018*. Mooresville, NC: Lowe's. https://lowes.gcs-web.com/static-files/7e8ff02d-ca35-4eae-9a4e-843ff3858c33.

Mintel. 2018. "Consumers and the Economic Outlook—US—January 2018."

Morojele, N. K., and G. M. Stephenson. 1992. "The Minnesota Model in the Treatment of Addictions: A Social Psychological Assessment of Changes in Beliefs and Attributions." *Journal of Community and Applied Social Psychology* 2 (1): 25–41.

National Highway Traffic Safety Administration. 2019. "U.S. Department of Transportation Launches New Ad Campaign to Stop Impaired Driving." US Department of Transportation. August 14, 2019. https://www.nhtsa.gov/press-releases/us-department-transportation-launches-new-ad-campaign-stop-impaired-driving.

Netemeyer, R. G., J. C. Andrews, and S. Durvasula. 1993. "A Comparison of Three Behavioral Intentions Models: The Case of Valentine's Day Gift Giving." *Advances in Consumer Research* 20 (1): 135–41.

O'Keefe, D. J. 2008. "The Elaboration Likelihood Model." In *International Encyclopaedia of Communication*, edited by W. Donsbach, 4:1475–80. Boston: Blackwell.

O'Loughlin, D., and I. Szmigin. 2006. "'I'll Always Be in Debt': Irish and UK Student Behavior in a Credit Led Environment." *Journal of Consumer Marketing* 23 (6): 335–43.

Oshikawa, S. 1968. "A Theory of Cognitive Dissonance and Experimental Research." *Journal of Marketing Research* 5 (4): 429–30.

Oskamp, S., and W. Schultz. 2005. *Attitudes and Opinions*. Hillsdale, NJ: Erlbaum.

Peñaloza, L., and M. Barnhart. 2011. "Living U.S. Capitalism: The Normalization of Credit/Debt." *Journal of Consumer Research* 38 (4): 743–62.

Petty, R. E., and P. Briñol. 2012. "The Elaboration Likelihood Model." In *Handbook of Theories of Social Psychology*, edited by P. A. M. Van Lange, A. W. Kruglanski, and E. T. Higgins, 1:224–45. London: Sage.

Petty, R. E., and J. T. Cacioppo. 1986. *Communication and Persuasion: Central and Peripheral Routes to Attitude Change*. New York: Springer-Verlag.

Rucker, D. D., and R. E. Petty. 2006. "Increasing the Effectiveness of Communications to Consumers: Recommendations Based on Elaboration Likelihood and Attitude Certainty Perspectives." *Journal of Public Policy and Marketing* 25 (1): 39–52.

Russell-Bennett, R., C. E. Härtel, and S. Worthington. 2013. "Exploring a Functional Approach to Attitudinal Brand Loyalty." *Australasian Marketing Journal* 21 (1): 43–51.

Schlegl, R. P., J. R. Davernas, and M. P. Zanna. 1992. "Problem Drinking: A Problem for the Theory of Reasoned Action." *Journal of Applied Social Psychology* 22 (5): 358–85.

Schossler, A. 1998. "Applying the Functional Theory of Attitudes to Understanding the Influence of Store Atmosphere on Store Inferences." *Journal of Consumer Psychology* 7 (4): 345–69.

Shavitt, S. 1989. "Operationalizing Functional Theories of Attitude." In *Attitude Structure and Function*, edited by A. R. Pratkanis, S. J. Breckler, and A. G. Greenwald, 311–38. Hillsdale, NJ: Erlbaum.

Shavitt, S. 1990. "The Role of Attitude Objects in Attitude Functions." *Journal of Experimental Social Psychology* 26: 124–48.

Slotterback, J. 2019. Personal interview, August 1, 2019.

"Stop It or Cop It." 2019. Centre for Road Safety, Transport for NSW. Accessed August 15, 2019. https://roadsafety.transport.nsw.gov.au/campaigns/enhancedpolice.html.

Szmigin, I., and D. O'Loughlin. 2010. "Students and the Consumer Credit Market: Towards a Social Policy Agenda." *Social Policy and Administration* 44 (5): 598–619.

Szmigin, I., and M. Piacentini. 2015. *Consumer Behavior*. Oxford: Oxford University Press.

Tadmor, C. T., A. D. Galinsky, and W. W. Maddux. 2012. "Getting the Most out of Living Abroad: Biculturalism and Integrative Complexity as Key Drivers of Creative and Professional Success." *Journal of Personality and Social Psychology* 103 (3): 520–42.

Woodside, A. G., and J. C. Chebat. 2001. "Updating Heider's Balance Theory in Consumer Behavior: A Jewish Couple Buys a German Car and Additional Buying-Consuming Transformation Stories." *Psychology & Marketing* 18 (5): 475–95.

Decision-Making and Involvement

⊚ Introduction

Your umbrella is broken and they're calling for rain today. What do you do? You could buy a new umbrella, wear your rain jacket, or just take your chances. Has this ever happened to you? Our day-to-day lives are filled with a wide variety of decisions that need to be made and many of those decisions are related to consumption. When you are at the store, how carefully do you consider the product attributes? Do you read the product label? Have you ever intended to buy one brand, but ended up purchasing another? How much are you influenced by advertising?

This chapter focuses on the consumer decision-making process. It is concerned with questions about how we decide to purchase or not purchase a product, the things we think about and feel when making those decisions, and how we evaluate the whole decision process once it's done. Sometimes consumers are quite rational when making consumption choices, and sometimes they take shortcuts. Sometimes consumers are highly involved in the decision-making process, and sometimes they behave out of habit. For marketing managers, all of these issues are important in understanding consumer behavior, predicting behavior, and creating marketing strategies that give brands the best chance of satisfying consumer needs and wants.

⊚ Consumer Decision-Making

Consumers make a multitude of decisions every day. Some of these decisions are important and have long-lasting consequences (such as choosing which graduate school to attend), while many decisions are trivial (such as which flavor of ice cream to get). Sometimes, our decisions are automatic and occur with little notice, such as when we reach for the mustard instead of the ketchup for our hot dog. In consumer research, the decision-making process starts with the assumption that the consumer is attempting to solve a problem or achieve a desired goal. Our consumer may want to learn to play tennis or get a promotion at work. These kinds of problems or goals are fairly

Having read this chapter, you will be able to:

1. Explain consumer *decision-making* in low- and high-involvement situations.

2. Describe several ways in which consumer *involvement* can be increased.

3. Differentiate what happens at each *stage of the consumer decision-making process*.

4. Describe *shopping behavior*, as well as personal and social consumer shopping motivations.

5. Identify the problems that consumers have with choice and the strategies used to deal with choice situations, such as *satisficing and maximizing decisions*, and the use of *heuristics, anchoring, and framing*.

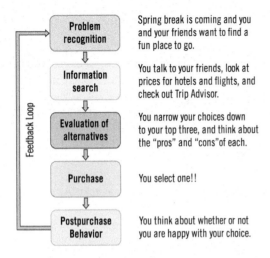

Figure 8.1 *The five-step consumer decision-making process*

Problem recognition occurs when a consumer realizes that there is a difference between what is actually happening and what ideally could happen. It is the start of the consumer decision-making process.

complex and likely involve a set of several decisions regarding choices and actions to successfully achieve them. Alternatively, our consumer may simply feel cold and damp after being caught in the rain, and would like to remedy the situation. These kinds of problems involve simpler solutions and relatively straightforward decision-making. As we will see in this chapter, there are significant differences in how the decision-making process occurs depending on the nature of the problem, the context of the decision, and the level of involvement consumers have with the decision. Individual characteristics of the consumer also influence the decision-making process.

The five-step model of consumer decision-making has been widely used to describe the process by which consumers make a decision. It has at least two important benefits. First, the model can be used in a variety of contexts and buying situations. It has been used to describe the steps through which consumers proceed when making decisions about tangible products, services, ideas, and even political candidates. Further, it has been applied to business-to-business situations, where the "consumer" is making a decision about, for example, a new copy machine for the office, new raw materials for the factory, or a new service provider or partner. The consumer decision-making model thus has wide applicability. The second benefit of the model is that it provides clear guidelines to marketers in how to approach consumers as they proceed through the model. So, because marketers know that consumers proceed through the model in a predictable way, marketers can then try to facilitate or influence the process at each of these steps. If marketers know, for example, that consumers are likely to search for information after they recognize they have a problem, marketers will want to ensure that information is easily accessible and understandable for consumers when they go looking for it.

Problem recognition

Problem recognition occurs when a consumer realizes that there is a difference between what is actually happening and what ideally could happen. In our introductory example in this chapter, our unlucky consumer is *actually* about to get soaked in the rain, but would *ideally* like to be warm and dry. This difference between the actual and ideal initiates the whole consumer decision-making process. Problem recognition may be triggered by internal factors such as hunger or thirst (the actual), which may lead to strategies to curb those feelings (the ideal). Problem recognition may also be triggered by external factors. As another example, perhaps you just received an invitation to your friend's upcoming birthday party and you realize that you have not yet gotten him a gift (the actual). This realization will launch an effort to find a good birthday present (the ideal).

Information search

Information search is the process by which we identify and gather appropriate data to help us make our choice. Before we start, we must be clear about two things. First, in Chapter 6, we discussed the difference between *wants* (the things that we would like to have) and *needs* (the things that are necessary for life). When we examine and use the five-step consumer decision-making process, we are referring to wants, not needs. Second, we also need to distinguish between an *internal search* for information, which comes from our own memories and experiences, and an *external search* for information, which comes from everywhere else. In Chapter 5, we talked about how information is stored in and retrieved from memory. This process of storage and retrieval is critical to understanding how consumers access product-related memories. Consumers can remember previous experiences with a product, comments from friends about a product, and ads they have seen about the product. An external search for information happens when, for example, consumers ask friends, check out online information, and visit a store to see a product in person. Sometimes information search is easy and straightforward. In the case of a simple consumption decision, such as what to do about an umbrella, we may already know from previous experience the location of a nearby shop (internal search), and any external search is mostly at the point of purchase in terms of choosing what color and price we prefer.

Let's examine the case of a more involved consumption decision. We would certainly retrieve any product-related memories with an internal search for information. External search can occur in many ways. Consumers can ask friends and family, as well as read a variety of print and online reviews. At this point, consumers are likely to be gathering data that are fairly broad in nature. For example, when thinking about getting a new car, a consumer may check ratings from sources such as J. D. Power and Associates and may look at a variety of brands, as well as size, function, and pricing options. At this stage, when dealing with a high-involvement decision like a car, the consumer is trying to narrow the possibilities and frame the decision so that it is less overwhelming.

Sometimes, consumers engage in **ongoing information search**, with no particular purchase decision in mind. When this happens, the data that we find are stored in memory for later use. A quick word about ongoing information search: Such ongoing search occurs without any specific or immediate need (Bloch, Sherrell, and Ridgway 1986). That is, ongoing search does not serve any immediate functional purpose; consumers often simply enjoy browsing online, checking out shops, and comparing different brands. The benefit of ongoing search is that product information is stored in memory and can be tapped for later use. The five classes of information need are functional, hedonic, symbolic, innovation, and aesthetic (Vogt and Fesenmaier 1998).

- *Functional information needs* are fulfilled when a consumer is educated about the product's utility, attributes, and applications. These needs are fulfilled by acquiring knowledge from direct experiences, from observing the experiences of others, and through other sources such as advertising.

Information search is the process by which we identify and gather appropriate information to aid our choice in a decision-making situation.

Ongoing information search occurs independent of a specific, immediate purchase problem.

- *Hedonic information needs* are fulfilled when consumers experience pleasure and fulfillment when they acquire new information. It is sometimes interesting, fun, and enjoyable to find out new things about new products!

- *Symbolic information needs* are fulfilled when information is shared with others to communicate the consumer's social position. Some consumers are experts, for example, at fashion or electronics. These consumers gather information to solidify their social positions.

- *Innovation information needs* are fulfilled when consumers acquire information that is new or different. These consumers are on a quest to find groundbreaking innovations.

- *Aesthetic information needs* are fulfilled when information is used as a stimulus to creative thinking, beauty, and appreciation.

All of the previous examples involve intentional, deliberate search that can tap into both internal and external sources for the information. Although much searching will be deliberate like this, as mentioned previously, the acquisition of some information is unintentional and not deliberate. Here, consumers often receive incidental information through talking to people, noticing advertisements, or simply observing the behavior of other consumers. Because of all the complex processes that can occur during this stage of the consumer decision-making process, marketers must consider carefully when, where, and how often consumers come in contact with information (see Insights from Academia 8.1).

 INSIGHTS FROM ACADEMIA 8.1

Do you think you're easily persuaded by advertising?

If you're like most consumers, you probably think that you are not easily persuaded by a slick advertisement promoting a product you don't need. You are confident in your ability to identify information that is useful and you would never admit that advertising prompted you to buy something you didn't need. Like most consumers, you would be wrong. It turns out that information that is presented in ads impacts consumers even when they specifically work to make sure that it does not. In an effect that is similar to classical conditioning, all it takes for an advertiser to get positive evaluations is to insert some pleasant pictures in an ad (e.g., the Coca-Cola polar bears). If marketers want consumers to feel negatively about something, they just need to insert some unpleasant imagery (e.g., cockroaches). These effects on evaluations happen even when the information has nothing to do with the product, when consumers are aware that the ad is attempting to persuade them, and when consumers specifically work to make sure to not let this happen. So, as much as we hate to admit it, advertising does indeed influence us.

Hütter, M., and S. Sweldens. 2017. "Dissociating Controllable and Uncontrollable Stimuli on Attitudes and Consumption." Journal of Consumer Research 45 (2): 320–49. https://doi.org/10.1093/jcr/ucx124.

Evaluation of alternatives

As we move away from the information search stage and into the evaluation-of-alternatives stage, consumers now should have a list of brands that are likely to solve their problem. Now we can place the results of the information search into categories (Narayana and Markin 1975; Crittenden, Scott, and Moriarty 1987):

- The **evoked set** includes a broad set of possible brands that first come to mind when the consumer is faced with a choice.
- The **consideration set** is the subset of brands from the evoked set that the consumer might consider buying.
- The **inept set** are those brands that the consumer has rejected from consideration, because of a negative previous experience or other negative information. They are not under consideration at all.
- The **inert set** includes brands in the product category that the consumer has neither a positive nor a negative opinion about; they're simply not thought about.

An example of these categorizations can be seen when a consumer is considering purchasing a perfume for his or her mother's birthday. The inept set might include brands the consumer knows about but would not consider buying, in this case, Katy Perry's Killer Queen. Definitely not for Mom. The customer may also be generally aware of certain brands such as Shalimar or White Shoulders but simply doesn't know enough about them to think about them much (inert set). Inevitably, brands that are familiar are likely to be in a consumer's evoked set, perhaps Chanel No. 5, Lancôme, and Elizabeth Arden. Perhaps because Chanel No. 5 seems a bit "more mature," our consumer keeps Lancôme and Elizabeth Arden in the consideration set. Knowing about the contents of a consumer's evoked set, consideration set, inept set, and inert set helps marketers tremendously. First, it reinforces the need to ensure that consumers are familiar with their brands and that they are readily available in memory. It reinforces the need for a company to craft well-designed marketing communications and distribution strategies. Second, it tells marketers important information about how consumers view the product compared to the competition. Importantly, which brands do they actively consider when proceeding through each step of the consumer decision-making process? Insights from the Field 8.1 illustrates an alternative model that marketing managers may use to understand consumer decision-making: consumer decision journeys.

When they are in the evaluation stage of the consumer decision-making process, consumers may use **evaluative criteria**, which are the conditions or benchmarks that are used to compare the alternative offerings to help make a choice. These evaluative criteria are based on a consumer's beliefs, attitudes, and intentions. For example, our consumer could have a set of salient beliefs about the quality of the ingredients of the perfume or the pleasantness of the

Evoked set includes a broad set of possible brands that first come to mind when the consumer is faced with a choice.

Consideration set is the subset of brands from the evoked set that the consumer might actually consider buying.

Inept set are those brands that the consumer has rejected from consideration because of a negative previous experience or other negative information. They are not under consideration at all.

Inert set includes brands in the product category that the consumer has neither a positive nor a negative opinion about; they're simply not even thought about.

Evaluative criteria are the conditions or benchmarks that are used to compare the alternative offerings to help make a choice.

Consumer decision journeys

Another way to look at consumer choice is through a model called the *consumer decision journey*. In contrast to our five-step consumer decision-making model, this approach offers a different way of understanding what consumers do as they go about making decisions. This approach suggests that consumers start with a somewhat large number of brands, which gradually decrease as consumers move toward their final choice. This model of consumer decision-making was created by McKinsey & Company, a global management consulting firm. Drawing on purchase decision data from almost twenty thousand consumers across five industries and three continents, the results suggest that rather than being a linear process, some consumers are engaged in a more circular journey with four key points where a brand may or may not be considered (see Figure 8.2):

1. The consumer creates an initial consideration set based on existing brand perceptions and recent touchpoints (i.e., advertisements, conversations with friends, product experiences).

2. As the consumer evaluates products and creates evaluative criteria, the consumer brings new brands in for consideration while dropping other brands. This part of the process is quite elaborate and deliberate for the consumer.

3. One brand is selected and the purchase is made.

4. The consumer assesses the purchase, which will inform the next decision journey.

Creators of the model suggest that because media is increasingly fragmented and there are often too many choices, a consumer's initial consideration set typically contains very few brands. No matter. Brands are added as consumers move through the loop again and again. The researchers at McKinsey also suggest that during the active evaluation phase (Step 2), two-thirds of the communication about the product or brand is customer generated versus one-third that is company generated. This reinforces the need to have information that is available to consumers when they want it, in an easily understandable format. In the end, the consumer decision journey offers an interesting

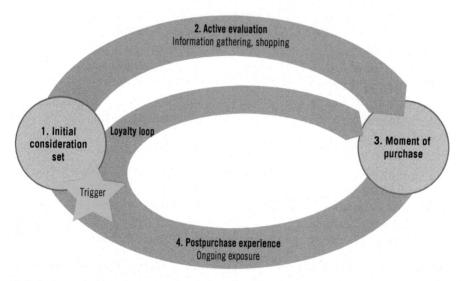

● **Figure 8.2** *The consumer decision journey*

Source: McKinsey Quarterly, June 2009, www.mckinsey.com/insights/mckinsey_quarterly McKinsey & Company. Reprinted by permission

insight into the consumer decision-making process and reinforces the point that, as with many models we discuss here, there is room for flexibility in how we apply and interpret the models.

Questions

1. Look at the consumer decision journey and the five-step consumer decision-making process.

What are some key differences between these two models? What are some similarities?

2. Think about one high-involvement purchase you made recently: which college to attend. Was your decision-making process more like the customer decision journey or the consumer decision-making process? How so? Be specific.

Source: Court et al. (2009).

● **Photo 8.1** *Consumers can rely on advertising imagery and messaging to help in evaluating some products like perfume and skincare products*

smell. Our consumer could also have attitudes about the brand name and the retail store where it will be purchased. So, our consumer's evaluative criteria will be based on scent, the brand name, and the retail store (see Photo 8.1). By the end of the evaluation-of-alternatives stage, the goal for the consumer should be to have a mental list (or even a real list) of pros and cons for the choices as well as a general sense of how the brands stack up in relation to one another.

Choice

The next step in the consumer decision-making process is to make a choice about which product will be the best option. Often, consumers use **decision criteria**, or rules for making the decision, to help them make the final choice among a set of alternatives that are all fairly good. At this point in the decision-making process, consumers have become familiar with the attributes of the product and how it might solve their problem, so they probably have a

Decision criteria are rules for making a final purchase decision.

good idea about how to make the best decision. If a consumer is an expert in the product category, a set of decision criteria might already exist. A consumer who is an avid photographer will know which kinds of camera lenses are best. If a consumer is a novice in the category, however, that consumer may construct decision criteria during the decision-making process (Bettman and Sujan 1987). For example, the consumer might ask a friend who is a professional photographer or consult photography blogs. Going back to our example of finding a perfume for Mom's birthday, our consumer could determine that the decision criteria are a perfume that is under $100 and one that has a well-known brand name. After much consideration, the consumer may decide to buy the Lancôme perfume.

Postpurchase behavior

Just because a consumer has made a choice does not mean that there will be follow-through and an actual purchase. Many contextual factors may get in the way, from something unexpected in the purchase environment (your choice is sold out), to new information about the product (perhaps there was a product recall), to something in the consumer's own personal life (bad weather, loss of a job). Assume for now, however, that a purchase has been made. Ideally, marketing managers want their customers to be happy with their purchase. However, there may be other outcomes of purchase too. After consumers are done consuming a product, they may make a judgment about whether they are satisfied or not satisfied with the experience. They may perform a variety of other postpurchase behaviors, such as doing more research, telling others about the experience, or even complaining. Finally, consumers may find a variety of ways to dispose of the product. If so motivated, a consumer might even engage in several postpurchase behaviors. The important thing to remember with postpurchase behavior is that what happens at this stage of the consumer decision-making process feeds back again to the beginning of the process for the next time a consumer is faced with problem recognition (see Figure 8.1 again).

Satisfaction and attribution assessments

The first category of postpurchase reactions revolves around an assessment of whether the consumption experience was satisfactory. The **disconfirmation paradigm** describes the difference between a consumer's prepurchase expectations of the product's performance and the actual postpurchase experience. The difference between the two will dictate satisfaction or dissatisfaction for the customer. When a product performs *better* than expected, customers are satisfied. When the product performs *worse* than expected, customers are dissatisfied. See Insights from the Field 8.2 for an interesting glimpse at how liberals and conservatives react differently when they become dissatisfied with an organization.

In addition to making a simple determination as to whether they were satisfied, consumers may look for reasons to explain the outcome of their choice

Disconfirmation paradigm is the difference between a consumer's prepurchase expectations of the product's performance and the actual postpurchase experience.

decision. Essentially, why did this happen? **Attribution theory** describes how consumers attempt to find a reason for an outcome (Weiner 2010). Take the example of a customer who just bought a new pair of skis. Our customer takes the new skis out for a day on the slopes and is quite dissatisfied. Perhaps the new skis are too advanced for our skier; perhaps the skis are not made well; perhaps the weather conditions were poor and therefore any pair of skis would have had trouble. Consumers are more likely to search for a possible attribution when they are dissatisfied with the consumption experience There are two key points about how attribution connects to consumer decision-making:

1. Attributions can be either internal or external. Thus, a consumer can view the outcome as something that happened because of his or her own knowledge and expertise (an internal attribution) or as resulting from outside forces that are relatively uncontrollable, like the weather (external attribution) (Weiner 2010). Thus, on some occasions, we may blame ourselves for the outcome, such as, "I'll never get the hang of this new operating system" (an internal attribution). On other occasions, we may make an external attribution to the product, such as, "The interface is not intuitive."

2. Consumers can also make attributions to stable or unstable causes. An attribution to a stable cause means that the outcome is unlikely to change, regardless of greater effort or even better luck. Conversely, an attribution to an unstable cause indicates that the outcome could indeed change over time, with better luck or with more effort (Weiner 2010). Consumers may, for example, be more likely to make attributions to unstable causes when they deal with service-based businesses where the experience can vary, such as banks or airlines. This can also happen when the nature of the product means that the quality could vary, such as with a bakery. With attribution to unstable causes, consumers assume that the bad outcome could be the result of a variety of unstable factors and may try again to see if the outcome improves. However, mass-produced products are more likely to lead to stable attributions; consumers assume that the bad outcome is the result of constant, unchangeable forces. If you purchase a new brand of ice cream and don't like the taste, you are unlikely to buy the brand again because you will assume that it will always taste the same.

Knowing how consumers make attributions provides important insights to marketers. Marketers must be aware of the likely type of attribution their products will be subject to and ensure that they respond appropriately. Mass-produced consumer packaged goods need strict quality control so that they meet consumers' preferences, and service businesses often use *mystery shoppers* to ensure that they are consistently providing the appropriate level of service. As much as possible, marketers want to avoid making a customer dissatisfied.

INSIGHTS FROM THE FIELD 8.2

To boycott or not to boycott: it depends on your politics

Unfortunately, there are many instances in which consumers become angry at an organization for some reason, whether it is because of a political stand they have taken or because of some other news or scandal. For example, customers boycotted oil giant BP after the 2010 oil spill in the Gulf of Mexico and Chick-Fil-A for making donations to groups that take an anti–lesbian, gay, bisexual, transgender, and queer position. How can we predict which consumers will become outraged and take such actions? In large part, it depends on the customer's political ideology. In the United States, 32.7 percent of respondents who self-identified as liberals bought a product for a political reason and 45.5 percent boycotted a product for a political reason. Compare these numbers to individuals who self-identified as conservatives, where 19.8 purchased a product for a political reason and 29.2 percent boycotted a

product for a political reason. The same general results hold for Europe. In each of fifteen countries examined, individuals who were on the political left were much more likely to boycott a company compared to those on the political right (Jost, Langer, and Singh 2017) (see Figure 8.3).

Why does this happen? There is still no consensus, but a growing body of research indicates that liberals seem to be strongly influenced by perceived injustices, such as unfair treatment of workers, animal cruelty, and environmental degradation. These left-leaning consumers use their consumer purchases to register their displeasure and, hopefully, promote change in a broken system (Jost, Langer, and Singh 2017).

If customers are wary of a boycott, how can they let a company know about their displeasure? One of the most popular and seemingly successful ways of

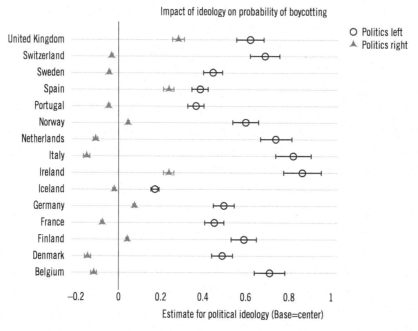

Figure 8.3

Political ideology is strongly related to boycotting behavior

Source: Jost, Langer, and Singh (2017)

complaining is using social media. Most companies have dedicated Twitter accounts for customer feedback that are monitored continuously. In a recent J. D. Power survey of more than twenty-three thousand online US shoppers, 67 percent reported that they have used social media to lodge a complaint (Bortz 2017). Because the complaint is public, companies are often shamed into doing the right thing. To make effective use of social media for complaining, however, one expert recommends the following (Bortz 2017):

1. Pick the right platform—if a company has a Twitter account dedicated to customer feedback (like @AskAmex or @NikeSupport), use it.
2. Speak the lingo—if you use hashtags effectively, you are more likely to be noticed by the company.
3. Provide the details—describe exactly what happened and provide a picture, if possible.
4. Time it right—if you post your complaint outside normal business hours, you are more likely to be noticed.

5. Take the conversation private—after a company contacts you about a resolution to your problem, take the discussion offline.

In the end, it is important to be patient and try again if you don't get satisfaction the first time. Although just 15 percent of messages on social media ever receive a response, social media can still sometimes be more effective than other approaches (Bortz 2017).

Questions
1. Have you ever boycotted a company? Why or why not? If you're angry with a company, what do you do? Why? Is your method effective? Discuss.
2. Some companies encourage consumer complaints because they see it as an opportunity to effectively resolve a problem for a customer. What benefits could a company get from encouraging its customers to complain?

Sources: Bortz (2017); Jost, Langer, and Singh (2017).

Once a consumer has formed an expectation that an upcoming consumption experience will likely be satisfactory or unsatisfactory, that expectation can become fixed and difficult to change. For many years, the car company Škoda was believed to be unreliable and cheap when their cars were produced in the former Eastern bloc country of Czechoslovakia. In 2000, following the fall of the Berlin Wall, Volkswagen acquired Škoda and developed an ambitious advertising campaign that addressed its previous image head-on. The company aimed to convince people that the quality and reliability of Škoda had improved significantly. This was accomplished using humor: individuals were shown test driving the car, but when they found out the car was a Škoda, they shied away from it. Using the tagline, "It's a Škoda. Which, for some, is still a problem," the campaign attempted to change strongly held expectations. By 2016, Škoda ranked highest in vehicle dependability in the United Kingdom (J. D. Power 2016), and by 2019, it had approximately $17.5 billion in sales (MarketLine 2019).

Disposal of goods
With environmental concerns often at the forefront of the news and of utmost concern for many consumers, marketers are becoming increasingly concerned with how their customers dispose of products. When consumers purchase a product, a growing number are starting to think about when or how they

are going to dispose of it. Consumers dispose of products in a variety of ways, including:

1. giving the item to friends and family;
2. giving it freely through specialized sites such as Freecycle (www .freecycle.org);
3. donating it to charity;
4. disposing in the trash;
5. recycling;
6. swapping the item for something of similar value;
7. exchanging for another item; or
8. selling the item through yard sales, flea markets, private advertisements, or auctions.

The environmental impacts of consumption and waste are becoming a pressing concern as the world population grows, more people around the world are living a consumer lifestyle, landfill space is becoming limited, and natural resources are becoming stretched thin. Marketers, local governments, nonprofits, and other organizations are finding creative ways to help consumers properly recycle and dispose of their products and other waste (Photo 8.2).

Plastic is one of the biggest problems in the waste stream. Although plastic is easy to use in product packaging and consumer products, when it is not recycled, it can cause some profound dangers to wildlife and humans. First, plastic is made from petroleum, so it must be drilled, refined, and processed to be used. This is a dirty and dangerous process. Further, petroleum is a fossil fuel and releases carbon dioxide when burned, one of the main gasses causing global climate change. Second, once plastic is used in a product or packaging, it is not likely to be recycled. According to the US Environmental Protection Agency, only 12.9 percent of plastic is recycled in the United States (Environmental Protection Agency 2016). The rest is incinerated, ends up in landfills, or makes its way out into the world's oceans, where it causes damage to marine birds, fish, and mammals. Increasingly, however, companies, consumers, and municipalities are becoming more aware of these issues and are taking steps to reduce plastic usage. Northern Ireland is among a growing number of places that have added a tax on plastic shopping bags, resulting in a 90 percent reduction in plastic bag consumption and far less litter (Harrison 2013).

Other postpurchase behaviors

After proceeding through the consumer decision-making process, consumers may also engage in a variety of other postpurchase behaviors. One of the first things consumers should do is register the product, make decisions about payment plans, and sign

● **Photo 8.2** *Colorful bins and signage help customers figure out how to dispose of their products and other waste*

INSIGHTS FROM ACADEMIA 8.2

Really? I don't remember that!

Why would consumers purchase a product when they know that product was produced in an unethical or environmentally harmful way? Many consumers claim that they simply forget. This *willfully ignorant memory effect* happens because when consumers are faced with negative information about a product they like, they feel ethically obligated to do something about it. They might reason, "Sure, it's a great-looking shirt, but I won't buy it because child labor was involved." However, by willfully forgetting, the consumer can purchase the shirt and not feel guilty.

Consumers believe that it is more morally acceptable to forget negative ethical information ("I just forgot!") than it is to remember negative ethical information but ignore it ("Too bad about the children, I really like that shirt!").

Reczek, R. W., J. R. Irwin, D. M. Zane, and K. R. Ehrich. 2018. "That's Not How I Remember It: Willfully Ignorant Memory for Ethical Product Attribute Information." Journal of Consumer Research 45 (1): 185–207. https:// doi.org/10.1093/jcr/ucx120.

up for any product warranties. In addition, consumers may decide to become more involved with the product and the rest of the consumption community by signing up with a users' group, posting to social media about it, or finding other ways to meet with and connect to other like-minded consumers. Still another postpurchase behavior may be for a consumer to buy other products that "go along" with the purchase that was just made. For example, a customer who just purchased a new car may buy a variety of accessories for the car.

The important thing to remember in this phase of the consumer decision-making process is that the process itself does not end here. Indeed, all the thoughts and feelings that are generated as a result of the five-step consumer decision-making process are stored in memory, waiting for the next problem recognition event to occur (see Insights from Academia 8.2).

Involvement and Consumer Decision-Making

Do all consumers proceed through the five-step consumer decision-making process in the same way? Certainly not. As we have discussed, **involvement** is the perceived relevance of a purchase to the consumer. Much of what happens with the consumer decision-making process depends on involvement. With high-involvement decisions, a consumer proceeds through the deliberate five-step consumer decision-making process. This can be referred to as extended problem solving, because, as you should remember, it all begins with problem recognition. With a low-involvement decision, consumers may skip a step or two. They could also speed though a few steps. If this is the case, consumers

Involvement is the perceived relevance of a purchase to the consumer.

may engage in what experts refer to as habitual decision-making. These low-involvement consumers are less motivated to engage in extensive information search or to rigorously evaluate product alternatives. In low-involvement decisions like this, consumers may use simple evaluative criteria or decision rules (as discussed in Chapter 7). The important thing to remember is that the five-step consumer decision-making process allows for this flexibility. Sometimes consumers can move very quickly through the steps, sometimes consumers can repeat steps, and sometimes consumers can skip steps all together.

Learning

Another important point about high- and low-involvement decision-making is that with high-involvement decisions, consumers are in an active state of learning, as outlined in Table 8.1. **Active learning** involves deliberate and extensive acquisition of knowledge before purchase (Erdem et al. 2005). Here we want to learn more about the brands we are considering because the purchase decision is important to us. Although problem recognition occurs in a low-involvement decision just as it does with high-involvement decisions, in the evaluation of alternatives stage of the process, a low-involvement consumer is likely to use beliefs that have been acquired from passive learning. **Passive learning** is the acquisition of knowledge without active learning. Consumer researchers found that passive learning happens quite often with individuals. When individuals watch broadcast TV, for example, they are exposed to a variety of ads. It takes very little effort to watch these ads; the messages are received in a passive, unengaged state and are stored for later use. Consumers don't need to really remember much about the product, except that it is recognized the next time they do their shopping. Simple recognition of the brand could result in a purchase. Once the consumer has tried the brand, according to the hierarchy of effects model (Chapter 7), affect and cognitions will follow. Passive learning assumes that there is very little counterarguing or resistance to the message (Krugman and Hartley 1970). In contrast, because active learning is exciting and engaging, marketing messages are likely to prompt greater resistance and more counterarguments (see Figure 8.4 and Insights from Academia 8.3).

The choice context

Depending on the choice context, involvement can also impact what happens during the consumer decision-making process. Consider one scenario in which the consumer has a low level of involvement and believes that there are very few differences between brands. Even though, objectively, there may indeed be very real differences, the consumer simply doesn't have the motivation or interest in finding out. In a low-involvement/few-choices context like this, a

Active learning involves the deliberate and extensive acquisition of knowledge before purchase.

Passive learning is the acquisition of knowledge without active learning.

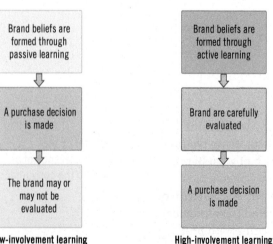

Low-involvement learning   High-involvement learning

Figure 8.4 *Learning in low and high involvement decision-making*

INSIGHTS FROM ACADEMIA 8.3

Tell me a story!

Because involvement is so important to consumer decision-making, it makes sense that some marketers try to utilize advertisements to increase a consumer's involvement. One way they do this is by using narratives in advertisements. Narratives are mini stories about the brand or about a consumer who has used the brand and result in more positive attitudes toward the ad (A_{ad}) and the brand (A_{brand}). In what way are narratives in ads persuasive? These stories make the consumer feel more emotionally involved in the ad, experience more positive emotions, believe the ad to be more credible, and believe the brand will help to fulfill certain consumption goals. So, when a marketer wants to encourage greater involvement, it makes sense to tell a story!

Kim, E., S. Ratneshwar, and E. Thorson. 2017. "Why Narrative Ads Work: An Integrated Process Explanation." Journal of Advertising 46 (2): 283–96.

consumer may have very little interest in the choices that are available. This could result in the consumer getting stuck in inertia, where the same brand is purchased again and again. Although this might *look* like brand loyalty, the consumer is simply purchasing the product out of habit and not because of a preference for the brand. A simple price promotion by a competing brand may find the consumer switching brands. Similarly, low-involvement consumers may be just as likely to randomly chose any brand within their price range or the brand with the most appealing packaging or promotion.

Suppose our low-involvement consumer perceives several differences in the choice context. Perhaps there are different flavors, sizes, colors, patterns, etc. If this is the case, consumers might be motivated to engage in variety-seeking and try different brands. Variety-seeking often occurs with low-involvement products such as soft drinks and snacks. Variety-seeking behavior opens up an important opportunity for marketers to introduce new flavors or other options because consumers are prepared to try new things and the cost of disappointment is low. It is also likely that a consumer may simply make a random choice or experiment with something completely new (see Table 8.1).

Consider the opposite context, in which a consumer has a high level of involvement. One scenario could be that our consumer might see few differences between brands. This decision may even include an element of risk, which, if things go bad, will prompt the consumer to engage in dissonance reduction strategies (see Chapter 7). Consumers in this context will likely engage in an extended search and look for reassurance that they have made the right choice after purchase.

If, however, high-involvement consumers find themselves in a choice context where there are significant differences among brands, quite a different set of processes may occur. Here, consumers will likely engage in purposeful and active decision-making to ensure that they make the best decision. Consumers are likely to carefully proceed through the five-step consumer decision-making

Table 8.1 Differences in decision-making with high- and low-involvement purchases

THE CHOICE CONTEXT	LOW INVOLVEMENT (LOW PRICE, LOW RISK)	HIGH INVOLVEMENT (HIGH PRICE, HIGH RISK)
There are few differences among brands	• Inertia (the appearance of loyalty) • Random choice	• Complex decision-making and dissonance reduction
There are significant differences among brands	• Variety-seeking • Random choice • Experimentation	• Complex decision-making • Brand loyalty

Source: Adapted, in part, from Szmigin and Piacentini (2015).

Brand loyalty is the preference for purchasing one brand over another.

process and to develop actual **brand loyalty**, or a preference for purchasing one brand over another. Ideally, marketing managers would like consumers to buy their favorite brand because those consumers believe the brand offers greater value than what the competition can offer. In one study of brand loyalty, 77 percent of US consumers purchased the same brands on a regular basis. This 77 percent can be broken down into two subsets of consumers: 37 percent who are *true blue* loyalists and will purchase their favorite brand, even if another brand is more convenient or cheaper, and 40 percent who are *repeat purchasers* and purchase the brand out of habit or because it is convenient (DeMers 2017).

Other forms of involvement

Involvement does not remain constant—it varies over time and circumstances. Even with the same product, consumers will demonstrate varying levels of involvement because of differences in their personality, socioeconomic and demographic factors, and previous experiences. Involvement can also vary, depending on the context and the product's relevance (Antil 1984). Consumer researchers have identified several types of involvement:

Product involvement is the perceived personal relevance of the product based on needs, values, or interest.

Message-response involvement reflects the consumer's interest in marketing communications.

Enduring involvement is the preexisting relationship between the customer and the product.

- **Product involvement** is the perceived personal relevance of the product, based on needs, values, or interest (Zaichkowsky 1985, 1986). An avid baseball fan is going to be very involved in the playoffs and World Series.
- **Message-response involvement** reflects the consumer's interest in marketing communications (Batra and Ray 1983). Some people enjoy ads and look forward to seeing them. One report found that millennials prefer Super Bowl ads over the game itself (Spies-Gans 2016).
- **Enduring involvement** is the preexisting relationship between the consumer and the product (Houston and Rothschild 1978). Even after moving away, people will be interested in hearing anything about the news, music, sports, or other happenings from their hometown.

- **Ego involvement** occurs when consumers perceive products or brands as relevant to their personal interests (Foxall 1993). A consumer may have saved for a long time to get an expensive watch or a new car, so the item means a lot to them.

- **Situational involvement** depends on some particular event or time in our lives. You may not be particularly interested in the workings of microwave ovens, but when yours breaks, you will be highly involved until you purchase a new one.

Personal and contextual factors influence a consumer's level of involvement. Another contextual element that can increase involvement are advertisements. Ad agencies can create arresting and compelling ads that can sometimes influence a consumer's level of involvement. Check out Insights from the Field 8.3 to see how advertisers try to increase involvement by using emotion in their ads.

Increasing customer involvement

Higher levels of customer involvement often work to a marketer's advantage, so marketers frequently create strategies to increase customer involvement. This can be achieved in several ways.

Link the brand to hedonic needs. In 2014, Häagen Dazs ran a series of advertisements that directly associated the act of eating ice cream with sex. Häagen Dazs still associates its ice cream with hedonistic pleasures, as in a recent print advertisement claiming that "attraction can't be faked" and "neither can our strawberries" (see Photo 8.3).

Ego involvement occurs when consumers perceive products or brands as relevant to their personal interests.

Situational involvement is involvement with a product class or brand dependent on some other event or time in our lives.

● **Photo 8.3** *Increasing involvement through hedonism*

Using emotions to increase involvement

In 2019, Xfinity ran an ad entitled "A Holiday Reunion." It featured the lovable extraterrestrial E. T., coming back to Earth after thirty-seven years and finding his friend Elliott, who had grown up and now had a family of his own. They spend a few days together where they watch some holiday movies, check out virtual reality technology, and eat a lot of sweets (with Reese's Pieces, of course). The actor who played the original young boy, Elliott, plays him again and there are many nods to the original Stephen Spielberg film, including a nighttime flying bike ride. As E. T. takes off in his spaceship and says goodbye, the final message in the four-minute ad is, "Reconnect for the holidays." Xfinity's decision to go with such a long, emotional ad was a gamble, but the company decided to do so because it wanted to convey a message of friendship and love, especially at a time of discord in the United States (see Photo 8.4). The effect was simple and straightforward—it made viewers smile and some even shed a few tears (Andrew 2019).

A very different approach was used by Budweiser during the 2017 Super Bowl. The ad portrayed the harrowing journey of a young German immigrant (Busch) coming to the United States in the mid-1800s and making his way to St. Louis, Missouri, where he eventually meets another immigrant (Anheuser), and they decide that they will brew beer together (Anheuser–Busch). The sixty-second ad is shot in a dramatic fashion with emotional music and exciting close calls for our hero. Watching the ad feels like you're watching a mini movie. It ends with the tag line, "When nothing stops your dream, this is the beer we drink." The ad was seen by 188 million people when it aired in February 2017 (Monllos 2017) and countless others saw it later on social media. The ad was designed to reclaim some of the lost market share that Budweiser has ceded in recent years to smaller craft brewers. To do this, managers knew that they needed to try to tug at consumers' heartstrings to increase emotional involvement in the story and the brand. Every shot in the ad was carefully

● **Photo 8.4** *E. T. came home for a holiday visit in Xfinity's 2019 ad*

considered and scripted. For example, the production team decided to primarily use close-up shots of the hero, rather than wide-angle shots that would show sweeping landscapes. Their belief was that the story was about Busch and his against-all-odds journey, "so hopefully that comes through. It's also a technique to make it feel more immersive and experiential and more like classic storytelling," said Chris Sargent, the director. The production, design, and creative experts also made sure that the content was shot in such a way that it could easily be viewed on digital formats and shared on social media. According to Budweiser's own research, 82 percent of people who watch the Super Bowl also use another screen throughout the game and 80 percent of any ad-related searches happen on mobile devices (Monllos 2017).

Questions

1. Look at two advertisements on YouTube that use an emotional appeal. What types of emotions are they trying to evoke? Be specific (e.g., fear, happiness, contentment, excitement). How do these ads motivate greater consumer involvement? What kind of involvement do you think consumers may experience as a result of watching the ads?

2. Identify several production techniques that advertisers use to help consumers experience an emotional connection to the product. To what extent do you think the ads succeed in accomplishing their goal of increasing involvement? Defend your answer.

Sources: Andrew (2019); Monllos (2017).

Use distinctive or novel ways of communicating your product. A pint of Guinness beer looks like no other beer. It has a distinctive dark color and a thick white head, it is poured differently than other beers, and it comes in a distinctive glass. It is easy to differentiate Guinness from the competition and make the thirsty consumer appreciate it even more (Photo 8.5).

Use celebrities. If celebrities are admired, they can help increase involvement with a brand. Actress Kristen Stewart has been the face of the luxury brand Chanel since 2013 and has recently helped advertise its new fragrance, Gabrielle (see Photo 8.6). Stewart is admired for her versatility as an actress as well as her portrayals of strong female characters. Finding the "right" celebrity endorser is no easy task, as we find out in Insights from the Field 8.4.

Tell a story. As mentioned previously, storytelling can be very effective in increasing customer involvement, especially when there is enough time to present a compelling narrative, such as in a movie theater or online. Insights from the Field 8.3 offers two particularly effective examples of storytelling for brands Xfinity and Anheuser–Busch. Marketing practitioners recommend that effective storytelling should: (1) share a relatable journey—it should be about common struggles or experiences; (2) offer value in every piece of content—don't waste your customer's time with meaningless fluff; and (3) include a call to action for your

● **Photo 8.5** *Compared to other beers, Guinness is distinctive*

Identifying the right celebrity endorser is no easy task

American movie stars and celebrities have been used to advertise a wide variety of brands, and many have enjoyed exceptional popularity and appeal in global markets. In Japan, approximately 70 percent of commercials feature a celebrity, and throughout Asia, many brand managers rely on Hollywood stars to endorse their products. In South Korea, Drew Barrymore advertises Baskin Robbins ice cream; Angelina Jolie works as an endorser for the world's oldest cosmetic company, Japan's Shiseido; Leonardo DiCaprio endorses OPPO, the Chinese mobile company; and basketball star Kobe Bryant endorsed Mercedes in the Chinese market. Outside of Asia, Sylvester Stallone is the face of Russian Ice vodka; George Clooney worked for DNB Norwegian bank; and Jennifer Aniston endorsed the Netherlands' most famous beer, Heineken (S. Jones 2018). These national and global brands use globally well-known and popular celebrities to appeal to local consumers.

Global brand managers also rely on local talent to try to appeal to local markets. In Taiwan, for example, successful celebrity, fashion influencer, and singer Dee Hsu is a well-known and loved personality. Hsu was the voice of Dory, the forgetful blue tang fish, in the Chinese adaptation of Disney's *Finding Dory* and frequently graces the cover of top fashion magazines such as *Elle* and *Vogue*. Because of her expertise and influence, many of the top fashion houses in the world, such as Gucci, Saint Laurent, and Van Cleef & Arpels have used Dee Hsu as a celebrity spokesperson to appeal to the lucrative Taiwanese market (Chiun 2018).

Finding the best celebrity endorser is more complicated than simply selecting a famous or attractive person to represent the brand. Indeed, there should be a match between the brand and the person who endorses it. The beauty match-up hypothesis suggests that simple good looks are not enough for celebrity endorser success and that it is the *type* of beauty that really matters, especially for decisions about fashion. Six beauty types were identified—classic beauty/feminine, cute, sensual/exotic, girl next door, sex kitten, and trendy. Fashion editors confirmed that some fashion models were ideally suited to represent some brands, while other models were ideally suited to endorse other brands. For example, the sex-kitten look fit well with *Cosmopolitan* magazine, and the classic beauty/feminine look was a good fit with fashion brand Chanel (Solomon, Ashmore, and Longo 1992). Extending these findings, there should also be a match between what consumers know about an endorser and what they know about the brand. It would ridiculous, for example, to have LeBron James endorse car insurance—there is not much of a match in what he does and the attributes of the product. However, it might make sense for him to endorse sports equipment, pain medication (he very likely has his share of muscle and joint pain), or financial services (let's face it, James is one of the best paid players in the National Basketball Association). One study found that celebrity endorsers who were both believable *and* attractive helped in creating more positive attitudes for the ad and the brand (Van der Veen and Song 2013).

Social media is an ideal platform for some celebrity endorsers who want to expand their own "brand," and few are more skilled at this than Kim Kardashian, who makes more money from mobile platforms than she does with any of her other endeavors. She has spent years endorsing other brands and reportedly makes $300,000 for each sponsored post on Instagram. An icon of social media, she made $45.5 million in 2017 with her reality TV show, cosmetics brand, and other endorsements. However, Kardashian has also recently placed greater emphasis on herself as a brand. With more than 184 million cross-platform followers, she can easily connect to her fans. Two of Kardashian's biggest social media activities are her $2.99 *Kimoji* app, which gives users a host of emojis based on the star, and a mobile game called *Kim Kardashian: Hollywood*, which itself made $200 million in just three short years (Robehmed 2017).

Finding the right celebrity is not easy. However, whether the celebrity is global or local, there should be a match between the celebrity and the product. In addition, marketers know that social media is an indispensable tool in strengthening the celebrity effect by forging even stronger connections between consumers and celebrities, as well as between consumers and brands.

Questions

1. Describe at least two advantages and two disadvantages of using local (instead of globally well-known) celebrities to increase consumer involvement.

2. In which part(s) of the five-step consumer decision-making process could a celebrity endorser be effectively utilized? Discuss.

Sources: Chiun (2018); S. Jones (2018); Solomon, Ashmore, and Longo (1992); Van der Veen and Song (2013).

GABRIELLE

CHANEL

THE NEW FRAGRANCE

● **Photo 8.6** *Kristen Stewart is a celebrity endorser for Chanel*

audience—this should be a genuine call to engage, such as an invitation to post a picture or share their own story (DaCosta 2018).

Build a relationship. Sometimes this is easier said than done. However, if the company is a customer-centric organization, all it takes is a little time and attention. Toyota does a particularly good job at trying to build relationships with its customers and does so across a variety of platforms. Salespeople check on recent buyers by calling and texting them to see how things are going and even send hand-written thank you notes. The corporation also sends video links to new buyers that highlight new features of the car, such as the cruise control system or advanced safety features. Further, consumers are invited to join affinity groups and attend events with other people who have recently purchased a Toyota. In the end, the goal is to forge connections so that the next time a consumer or a family member needs to purchase a new car, Toyota will be in the consideration set. See Insights from the Boardroom 8 for an inside look at how one hockey franchise builds relationships with its fans.

There is no such thing as a casual hockey fan

● *Cindy Stutman*

Meet Cindy Stutman, senior vice president of business operations for the Flyers, Philadelphia's National Hockey League (NHL) team. Stutman knows that there are a lot of crazy sports fans out there. Sure, people love other sports, like baseball and football, but there is something different about hockey fans. Hockey fans have a depth of love and passion for their sport that is unparalleled in other sports. Stutman has been working in sports marketing for almost twenty years, has conducted countless research projects, and has witnessed the extent to which hockey fans proclaim their love of the game.

Fans of other sports attend games for a variety of reasons and, while there, they check their phones, engage in conversations, and sometimes only keep one eye on the game. By contrast, hockey fans are *all in*. They "are *into* it, across the board, screaming and chanting and stomping and going nuts, essentially for 2½ hours straight . . . they love their sport in a way few people love anything" (Leitch 2013). Where are these

fans? According to one study, the top three NHL teams with the most passionate fans are: (1) the Pittsburgh Penguins, (2) the Boston Bruins, and (3) the Chicago Blackhawks (Settimi 2019). What makes hockey fans so passionate about the game is the deep level of involvement with every aspect of the sport. However, it seems to come down to three main things—fans are involved in the traditions, the players, and the entire atmosphere of the game. Taken together with the fact that hockey is more relatable than other sports, it allows fans to become more involved.

Over time, once you get to know hockey, you become attached to its traditions, such as hat tricks (where fans throw hats onto the ice when a player scores three goals in a row), and special traditions that belong to certain teams, such as Detroit Redwings fans throwing octopuses on the ice (originally meant to symbolize the number of wins [eight] needed to clinch the title). In Philadelphia, it is widely believed that Kate Smith's rendition of "God Bless America" gives the Flyers an extra bit of luck. "When she sings it, it's a feeling you just can't describe," says Stutman. Traditions surrounding the Stanley Cup are also revered. Everyone who has ever won the NHL championship has had their name engraved on the cup. The cup even has a handler who accompanies it wherever it goes. "Every player on the winning team gets to do what they want for a day. They take it different places for photo ops, it's the player's choice" (Stutman 2017).

The players are another dimension that help develop a strong level of involvement with hockey. According to Stutman (2017), "They're regular hard-working guys. It doesn't matter if you're blue or white collar, you can identify with that." Fans have a stronger attachment to the players in general. They like to see what the guys are doing with the Stanley Cup and just generally talk with other fans about the players, stats, trades, and other things. Just like your family knows all about you, fans want to know all about the team and the players. Stutman explained that the Flyers organization tries to connect season ticket holders and others with the players as often as possible with autograph sessions, meet and greets, etc. She elaborated, "Hockey is a hard-working sport and Philly is a hard-working city. There is a natural tie between the team, the sport, and the city" (2017). This strong connection may be "partially due to the fact that it feels like a familial relationship with the team. Mr. Ed Snider was the owner and founder—he was with us for 49 years." Hockey simply represents "a different kind of comradery than other sports" (Stutman 2017).

Finally, a third dimension of involvement is the atmosphere of the game. Stutman (2017) notes, "On any given night of the week, a majority of our ticket holders have been with us for 10+ years. We have a group of season ticket holders that have been with us since the beginning. They're in their 51st year! Think about it. A season ticket holder gets 44 games per year. Imagine the time, money, and emotional investment that people who have been with us for so many years have made." She says, "The fans know all of the people who sit in their area and all of the people that work here—the people at the concession stands, ticketing, security."

Stutman has had some unusual experiences with hockey fans, including quite a few requests to sprinkle a person's ashes on the ice. Stutman (2017) reasons, "We can't do that. We explain that when the Zamboni comes around, we don't want the ashes to be scooped up in the slush. We want to be respectful." Management always tries to engage the fans, but they pay particular attention to the fans who just live and breathe hockey: "That's our core base. We're as loyal to them as they are to us," explains Stutman. Management tries to give longtime season ticket holders added value to their experience, like access to meet the players, interaction with front office management at town hall–style meetings, a chance to sit on the bench during warmup, or the opportunity to ride the Zamboni during intermission. As Stutman says, "We're in the business of making memories for people."

Compared to fans of other sports, hockey fans are just different. They really don't care if you're not just as passionate because it doesn't matter. What matters is hockey. "There is no such thing as a casual hockey fan. Hockey is all there is, and hockey is all that matters" (Leitch 2013).

Get the consumer to participate. When Doritos wanted to increase its market share with the male sports market, it created a campaign entitled "Crash the Super Bowl," in which it invited everyday consumers, not professionals, to create ads for Doritos. Amateur advertisers responded with a host of mind-blowing, creative ads that they submitted to the Doritos website. The top entries were selected by a panel of judges and then customers got to vote on their favorite ads, which then appeared during the Super Bowl. This ten-year campaign, which ran until 2016, is largely credited with taking Doritos from a $1.54 billion to a $2.2 billion brand. What's next? Get ready for "Legion of the

Bold," in which five thousand creative fans of the brand pitch and submit ideas via Vine videos, banner ads, creative briefs, etc. (Schultz 2016). This new campaign means that each and every day, Doritos gives these creative consumers a chance to strengthen their involvement with the brand.

Shopping Behavior

Market mavens are active information-seeking consumers or smart shoppers, and they like to provide information to others on a broad variety of goods, services, and marketplace characteristics.

Because shopping is a part of everyday life, consumer researchers have studied shopping behavior extensively. For most consumers, there is a difference between *going shopping*, which is a pleasurable activity done with a friend or partner, and *doing the shopping*, which is often a chore (Bowlby 1997). Since the early 1950s, marketers have tried to understand the motivations and behaviors involved in shopping and have even segmented consumers by their shopping behaviors (cf. Stone 1954; Ganesh, Reynolds, and Luckett 2007). Some consumers are very involved with the shopping experience and are known as **market mavens** (Feick and Price 1987). These consumers actively seek information, are very knowledgeable, and like to share their expertise with others on a broad variety of products, attributes, services, and other marketplace characteristics (Slama and Williams 1990). It is important for marketers to identify market mavens because they are key influencers in their social circles. See Insights from Academia 8.4 for another insight about consumer shopping behavior.

INSIGHTS FROM ACADEMIA 8.4

Is it possible to be both fashionable and sustainable?

Because of increasingly dire reports about climate change, many consumers feel a need to be sustainable in their day-to-day lives. At the same time, many consumers also have a desire to purchase attractive, fashionable products. The result of these two consumer perceptions leads to imbalance. Traditional advertising and mass media approaches have had a difficult time convincing consumers that they can be both fashionable *and* sustainable. What is an ecofashion brand to do? One option is to offer "staged personalized experiences" for consumers. These hands-on shopping experiences allow consumers to learn about and become more accepting of adopting a sustainable fashion product. Consumers can visit stores, look at labels, talk to salespeople, and try the products. Retailers can also offer selections of their products in pop-up shops where consumers have a greater chance of seeing them. When consumers participate in these shopping experiences, attitudes and intentions toward ecofashion products become more positive. So yes, you can be fashionable and sustainable!

Han, J., Y. Seo, and E. Ko. 2017. "Staging Luxury Experiences for Understanding Sustainable Fashion Consumption: A Balance Theory Application." Journal of Business Research 74:162–67.

Shopping motivations

Knowing why and how consumers shop provides insights to marketers about how to optimize the shopping experience. Consumer researchers have found that consumers have both personal and social motivations when they shop (e.g., Tauber 1972).

Personal motives for shopping

Role playing. Shopping is related to certain roles a consumer has in society, such as caregiver (e.g., shopping for food) or social influencer (e.g., shopping to learn about the latest fashions). Online shopping also allows consumers to maintain important social roles by providing time-strapped consumers the convenience to shop when they are able (Parsons 2002).

Diversion. Shopping can be a recreational and pleasurable activity too. Immersive shopping experiences and online sites allow consumers to divert their attention away from their everyday tasks and "get away" for a while.

Self-gratification. Consumers sometimes go shopping to compensate for other problems or victories in their lives, for example, by buying themselves a "reward."

Learning about new trends. Browsing both online and brick-and-mortar shops allows consumers to stay current with new styles, trends, and innovations.

Physical activity. Some people go shopping to get physical exercise. In shopping malls in Doha, Qatar, for example, where the temperatures can reach 100°F for six months every year, mall managers actively encourage shoppers to visit the mall to exercise and to escape the heat (Nordland 2013).

Sensory stimulation. Shopping malls and shopping districts in cities and towns around the world offer a variety of sensory stimuli that hit each of the five senses. Online and mobile shopping are increasingly adding sensory stimulation to their experiences too.

Social motives for shopping

Social experiences. Some consumers shop so that they can socialize with others. For example, a customer might chat with the pharmacist while picking up prescriptions, ask questions of the farmer at the Saturday farmer's market, and exchange pleasantries with the other customers in the waiting room while getting the car's oil changed. Social experiences do not have to occur in person; they also extend to uploading, sharing, commenting on, and liking posts on social media.

Communicating with others who have similar interests. Sometimes stores can be a place where a customer can strike up a conversation with other customers and staff. Knowledgeable staff may be hired because of their expertise so that they can share their expertise with customers. This is especially likely with specialty stores like photography stores, gaming shops, or antique stores. Online communities bring consumers together too. In fact, they can increase customer satisfaction, strengthen commitment, and enhance positive word of mouth (Royo-Vela and Casamassima 2010).

Peer group attraction. Sometimes, customers may want to visit a particular online or brick-and-mortar store because they associate it with an aspirational group. You might find out that your very fashionable friend or your favorite celebrity shops there, so you want to check it out too.

Status and authority. Some high-end stores have staff that are particularly attentive and make customers feel special. Nordstrom is legendary for the extreme steps its sales staff will go to to make a customer happy, such as driving to a customer's house to remove a security tag because it was not removed at the store or accepting returns that were clearly not purchased from Nordstrom. At Nordstrom, online and in-store customer service are seamless.

Pleasure of bargaining. Some customers simply love the chance to haggle or negotiate for a bargain either online or in-person. In some places like flea markets and yard sales, bargaining for a better deal is expected. Bargaining is also more frequently accepted in different parts of the world (see Photo 8.7).

Regardless of the motivation, shopping still costs money and some consumers are very concerned about finding the most reasonable prices for items (see Insights from the Field 8.5).

Blended shopping

It is somewhat rare today for a consumer to make a high-involvement purchase without first going online to check out product features, ratings, and prices. Blended shopping occurs when consumers rely on both online and hands-on experiences as they proceed through the five-step consumer decision-making

● **Photo 8.7** *Street market in Agra, India*

Who are the bargain shoppers? You might be surprised.

Consumers who once would have been embarrassed to be seen in discount stores now view shopping at discount retailers as smart and savvy; some might even brag to their friends about the great bargains they get. Indeed, 59 percent of Americans say they search for bargains because of the thrill of finding a great deal; 31 percent do it because they want to pay off personal debt. Where do these consumers go to find a bargain? Surprisingly, even though there are plenty of discount stores available, most budget shoppers go to mass-market retailers like Costco or Walmart (56 percent), grocery stores

● **Photo 8.8** *Many high-income customers are driven to find a great bargain*

where they likely purchase store-brand products rather than name brands (52 percent), and Amazon (25 percent) (Mintel 2017).

Surprisingly, compared to low-income customers, high-income customers are more likely to search for bargains and hit discount stores. For Americans making more than $100,000 per year, 21 percent report that they visit online discount sites, compared to 12 percent of all shoppers. In addition, 74 percent check prices on Amazon before they shop (compared to 60 percent of all shoppers) and, once they're in the store, 39 percent check out their mobile devices to locate the best price (compared to 26 percent of all shoppers). Not surprisingly, high-income customers are loathe to pay extra for shipping; 80 percent refuse to pay extra for two-day shipping from Amazon (C. Jones 2018) (see Photo 8.8).

Even icons in the world of retail have responded to this trend for bargain prices. At the same time that many iconic department stores have been closing, others have tried to reinvent themselves and provide retail options that appeal to the budget-minded shopper. Macy's has invested heavily in its new discount retail concept, Macy's Backstage, while Saks Fifth Avenue

has done the same with Saks Off Fifth. Both retailing giants have opened their discount stores in space that was formally occupied by the same department stores. One retailing expert summed it up by saying, "A lot of retailers need to shrink their store base, and that is tied to everything that's happened with digital and changing shopping patterns" (Maheshwari 2017). The trend away from department stores is undeniable; consumers shop differently in the twenty-first century and, unfortunately, some retailers are struggling to adapt.

Questions
1. What personal and social shopping motivations might be at work when a consumer visits a discount store or online site?
2. Refer to the five-step consumer decision-making model and describe the step-by-step process a consumer might go through when deciding where to shop for something to wear for a formal event, such as a prom or a winter ball.

Sources: C. Jones (2018); Maheshwari (2017); Mintel (2017).

process. They might, for example, check out prices and ratings online and then go to a nearby store to see the product in person. For a high-involvement purchase, they might want to touch, hold, or try on the product. Then, once the consumer is certain that it is the best product, he or she can go home, find the best price online, and have it delivered. There are many ways in which the shopping experience can be blended. This back and forth between online and in-store experiences is happening more often and is making the job of the retailer more and more difficult. Some retailers have responded by offering special experiences for their customers, such as virtual mirrors that can allow consumers to see what different outfits will look like without having to go to the dressing room. In the end, marketers must find the ideal blend of online and in-store experiences that work best for their particular customers.

Impulse purchasing

Impulse purchases occur when a purchase is made because of a sudden powerful urge to buy a product with little regard to the consequences.

Most of us have made an **impulse purchase,** which is an unplanned purchase that has been made because of a sudden, powerful urge to buy the product with little regard to the consequences (Rook 1987). Normally, there are very few consequences to buying a low-value item, such as a candy bar or a T-shirt. However, sometimes we can purchase items on impulse that do have consequences—it was too much money, it was not the right style, etc. Some shopping environments increase our likelihood to impulse purchase. Upscale food retailers like Whole Foods often have free samples of mouth-watering foods as you make your way around the store. It is almost impossible to resist putting some of those items in your shopping cart! Impulse purchases can often be the result of emotional reactions, rather than rational reasoning (Thompson, Locander, and Pollio 1990). There are four types of impulse purchases (Bayley and Nancarrow 1998):

1. Accelerator impulse—consumers purchase numerous items at a time and stockpile them in anticipation of some future need. Sales promotions that offer "buy one get one" deals are especially attractive to this type of impulse purchaser.

2. Compensatory impulse—consumers purchase items as a reward for themselves for a success or as a "pick me up" for a failure. Kit Kat encourages consumers to "give me a break" and "break me off a piece of that Kit Kat bar," while L'Oréal says that consumers should buy their products "because we are all worth it" (see Photo 8.9).

3. Breakthrough impulse—consumers suddenly make a purchase to resolve a long-held conflict or desire. Finally, now is the time. The purchase might help a consumer deal with a particular issue or problem, like finally signing up for some graduate-level classes or booking that long-anticipated flight to Europe.

4. Blind impulse—the purchase of a product is not easily explained and can even be considered dysfunctional. Consumers can be overwhelmed

BECAUSE WE ARE ALL WORTH IT.

● **Photo 8.9** *L'Oreal encourages compensatory impulse purchases with its slogan, "Because we are all worth it"*

by the product attributes, the sales context, or the marketing of the product. They do not consider any cost or functional implications; they just "have to have it."

◉ When Choosing Is a Problem

Most consumers living in the developed world have a vast array of products and brands from which to choose. A simple trip to a pharmacy will reveal hundreds of choices for products to be taken for a cold or the flu. There seems to be an almost endless set of choices to be made for even the simplest products (Schwartz 2005). Is having so many choices a good thing? Some experts and consumer advocates contend that greater amounts of choice lead to confusion and discomfort. While consumers do benefit from some variety in the choices that are available to them, sometimes too many options can lead to choice overload and consumers become indifferent to additional choices that are added (Sharma and Nair 2017). How many alternatives is optimal? Like most things in marketing, it depends. The important thing to remember is that marketers must first look at the characteristics of their target market and then determine when additional choice provides benefits to those consumers and when it may result in difficulties such as confusion or choice overload. The following sections discuss issues related to consumer choice. While reading about these issues, remember that purchase choice is the fourth step in the five-step consumer decision-making process.

Satisficing and maximizing

Although it might seem like a good idea for a marketer to have many options for consumers to evaluate, just the opposite is true. Researchers have found that consumers are often overwhelmed by too many choices. Surprisingly, when there are *fewer* options, they make *more* purchases (Iyengar and Lepper 1999, 2000). This section discusses two strategies consumers use when there many options to consider: satisficing and maximizing.

We've all been there. It's time to do the laundry and you realize that you're out of laundry detergent. Time to buy some more detergent. Do you buy the one designed for cold-water washing? The one that promises to whiten your whites? The one that protects your colors? Which scent do you choose? Do you want powder, liquid, or pods? For many consumers, a "good enough" decision will suffice. Traditional economic models assume that consumers have access to all of the information regarding the costs and benefits of their choices. However, information itself takes time, effort, and money to acquire (Schwartz et al. 2002). Therefore, it is rational to make a good enough decision, rather than the best decision, because the time, effort, and money to make the best decision may simply not be worth it. This is called **satisficing** (Simon 1956).

Satisficing is an important strategy for consumers because consumers are limited by a number of factors, such as time, their own cognitive limitations, and the complexity of the context. A satisficer will often choose a brand based on simple decision criteria, such as price. Over time, satisficers often find other brands that meet their decision criteria and switch to those brands. Marketers use their own primary research as well as secondary research data from sources like Information Resources, Inc., and Nielsen to generate insights about purchases. They then use these insights to identify which products to keep in production, which products to phase out, and how many choices are optimal for their consumers.

Maximizers are quite different from satisficers. They tend to carefully consider all the alternatives and purchase the brand with the best combination of features and benefits. Maximizers often have a difficult time making a choice. First, these consumers often question whether they have identified all of the available alternatives. If they have not been able to evaluate all of the alternatives, maximizers will often doubt their decision, feel unhappy with their choice, and experience regret (Schwartz et al. 2002). Second, maximizers may have a difficult time finding the objectively best option in a crowded field of competing brands, all with very favorable attributes. Further, even if they do select a very good option, they may not feel satisfied with their choice because of the high standards they have set for themselves (Schwartz et al. 2002). There are certainly situations where being a maximizer is the best approach. Think about laser eye surgery, for example. Most individuals will want an eye surgery center that is better than "good enough."

Satisficing occurs when a consumer buys a product that is "good enough," rather than the best decision.

Maximizers are consumers who carefully consider all the alternatives and purchase the brand with the best combination of features and benefits.

Heuristics

Heuristics are another way in which consumers settle on a final choice decision. They are methods that simplify decision-making that are based on past experiences. Think of a heuristic as a mental shortcut. On the positive side, heuristics have the benefit of helping us make quick decisions. They are helpful in situations where there are many choices, when there are few differences between brands, and when the consumer is faced with a low-involvement choice. Consumers use heuristics because they're easy—they require less time and effort (Shah and Oppenheimer 2008). On the negative side, sometimes heuristics can lead us to make less than optimal decisions (Tversky and Kahneman 1974). There are many different types of heuristics, but we will examine those that are of particular interest to consumer researchers. Heuristics comprise four broad categories: prediction, persuasion, choice, and compliance (Jansson-Boyd 2010):

- Consumers use **prediction heuristics** to predict a future outcome. Two important types of prediction heuristics are the availability and representativeness heuristics.

  - The **availability heuristic** refers to a situation where consumers judge the likelihood or frequency of something happening based on how easy it is to remember similar events. If a consumer's memory is especially vivid, if the memory is very recent, or it is important, it will be more "available" in memory and more likely to influence the decision. Therefore, if you just saw a vivid news report of an accident at a county fair close to your home, you may be reluctant to attend the fair this weekend.

  - The **representativeness heuristic** occurs when consumers judge something based on how similar it is to some stereotypical case. Say, for example, that the first time you decide to visit a sushi restaurant, you spend the rest of the night sick with an awful stomachache. Using the representativeness heuristic, you will probably conclude that all sushi restaurants are terrible and you never want to go again. An extension of this occurs when store brands copy the package design and color of name-brand products in the hopes that the similar look will encourage consumers to conclude that the products are also similar.

- Consumers use **persuasion heuristics** to challenge or change their attitudes, which may then change their decisions.

  - One persuasion heuristic is the **consensus rule,** whereby a majority opinion is used for guidance (Chaiken, Liberman, and Eagly 1989), such as when an advertisement proclaims that a majority of consumers prefer a particular brand.

  - Another is the **expertise rule**, whereby consumers rely on the advice of an expert, such as when an ad depicts a financial planner giving

Heuristics are methods to simplify decision-making that are based on past experiences. They are often referred to as mental shortcuts or rules of thumb.

Prediction heuristics are used when the consumer is trying to predict a future outcome. The two types of prediction heuristics are the availability heuristic and the representativeness heuristic.

Availability heuristic refers to a situation where people judge the likelihood or frequency of something happening based on how easy it is to remember similar events.

Representativeness heuristic occurs when consumers judge something based on how similar it is to some stereotypical case.

Persuasion heuristics are used by consumers to challenge or change their opinions.

Consensus rule is a persuasion heuristic whereby a majority opinion is used for guidance.

Expertise rule is a persuasion heuristic whereby consumers rely on the advice of an expert.

● **Photo 8.10** *Example of consensus rule and expertise rule*

Choice heuristics is a process that allows people to reduce the number of attributes to be considered for possible alternative choices.

Compliance heuristics narrow down a consumer's choice to those involved with complying with a request.

Scarcity is a compliance heuristic that is based on the notion that consumers will respond when they perceive that a product is rare or scarce.

Reciprocity is a compliance heuristic that involves the return of a favor.

investment advice (Ratneshwar and Chaiken 1991). Photo 8.10 depicts a US advertisement from the 1930s that uses both the consensus rule and the expertise rule.

- **Choice heuristics** assist consumers by reducing the number of attributes to be considered; they are "rules" that help to make decisions easier. Choice heuristics (or decision rules) are oriented toward reducing cognitive effort. Consumers often use the *conjunctive decision rule*, the *lexicographic decision rule*, and the *elimination-by-aspects rule* (see Chapter 7).

- **Compliance heuristics** narrow down a consumer's choice to those involved with complying with a request.

  - One compliance heuristic, **scarcity** (Brannon and Brock 2001), is based on the notion that consumers will respond when they perceive that a product is rare or scarce. They will "comply" with messages such as, "Limited time offer!" by making an immediate purchase.

  - Another compliance heuristic, **reciprocity** (Langer 1989), involves the return of a favor, so if a salesperson at the beauty counter helps a customer apply makeup, the customer may comply with any request to make a purchase.

Anchoring and framing

The third broad category of choice problems involves helping consumers find a "starting point" for their choice. **Anchoring** helps consumers start the choice process by helping them focus on one product attribute (that is, unfortunately, sometimes arbitrary). An example might help. A consumer may visit a store and believe that a jacket priced at $200 is a bargain if all the other jackets are priced at over $300. If, however, this same consumer were to investigate other stores and see similar jackets for $100, the $200 jacket might not seem like such a bargain. The initial price of the jacket was arbitrary; it depended on the store that was visited first. However, once the price becomes anchored in the consumer's mind, it influences what price the consumer was willing to pay (Ariely 2008).

   Framing describes how a consumer makes a decision within different contexts; it is the perspective from which the consumer considers the decision (Tversky and Kahneman 1986). Think about it like this. If you have ever gone snorkeling or scuba diving, you know that the underwater world is filled with beautiful structures and marine life. You don't get to see any of this, however, from the surface. Perspective *matters*. By framing the decision differently, marketers influence consumers to alter their choices. Imagine that you and your friends want to get away to Florida for spring break. You might search a variety of sites like Travelocity or Priceline to get a cheap flight. On one site, you find a great deal: a $500 ticket! Now, you need to decide how to pay. You find that you have two options: either pay direct by credit card and get a $20 discount or get the ticket for $480 ticket but pay an extra $20 surcharge if you use PayPal. These options are basically the same, but they are framed differently and, as we have seen earlier in this text, since consumers like the idea of getting bargains, they will likely be drawn to the first option. Framing is used to influence a consumer's decision-making in many contexts, especially food labeling. For example, marketers know that labeling a food product 75 percent fat free is viewed much more favorably than saying the product has a 25 percent fat content. Knowing about how framing works can also help marketers craft more effective messages. Marketers know, for example, that expert consumers already have decision criteria; they have experience in the product category and know exactly how to make the best decision. Novice consumers, however, rarely have well-developed decision criteria. When this is the case, marketers can help novices create decision criteria by framing the choice for them (Bettman and Sujan 1987). Insights like these and many others described in this book are part of what makes marketing such a dynamic and fascinating field of study.

Consumers enact a variety of strategies to help them make more efficient and optimal choices as they balance the costs of greater search and deliberation against the benefits of a better-quality choice. As consumers, we should also be aware of our own decision-making tendencies and shortcuts that might get in the way of us making the best decision possible. As marketers, it is important to know how and when consumers use these strategies and shortcuts in order to assist in creating insights about developing better products and more effective communications strategies.

Anchoring helps consumers start the choice process by helping them focus on one product attribute (which is, unfortunately, sometimes arbitrary).

Framing describes how a consumer makes a decision within different contexts; it is the perspective from which the consumer considers the decision.

◉ Summary

Understanding *decision-making* and *involvement* is the basis for the development of important insights about a variety of product development and marketing communications strategies. We examined the *five-step consumer decision-making process*, drawing on a range of examples to illustrate the steps that a consumer proceeds through to make a decision. In Insights from the Field 8.1, we introduced the concept of the consumer decision journey to show how companies might benefit from thinking about decision-making as more of a circular journey than a linear process. To show how a decision can proceed through the decision-making process and to illustrate how a decision can depend on many factors, Case Study 8 examined the decision-making processes associated with buying Method products.

We also examined the complexity of consumer involvement and provided a range of examples to illustrate these complexities. Organizations generally work to increase the involvement consumers have with their brand and several strategies were presented. For example, Insights from the Field 8.3 took a deeper look into how emotion could be used to create enduring involvement with the brand. In particular, it looked at how Xfinity and Anheuser–Busch were able to use creative advertising executions to tug at the emotional heartstrings of consumers. Insights from the Boardroom 8 also focused on involvement by describing how one expert has found that there is no such thing as a casual hockey fan.

Shopping behavior was examined next. We discussed a variety of personal and social shopping motivations, as well as blended shopping and impulse purchasing. An in-depth look at the behaviors and characteristic of bargain shoppers was the focus of Insights from the Field 8.5.

Decision-making may be deliberate and thoughtful, as discussed previously, or it may be somewhat impulsive, as discussed in the section that explored what happens when choosing is a problem. Research indicates that having many choices can be detrimental for consumers. When that is the case, consumers are content to settle for a "good enough" solution, known as *satisficing*. In other situations, consumers may need to ensure that they are getting the objectively best option. In such cases, we are *maximizing* our choices. Consumers also tend to take shortcuts to decision-making to save time and effort. It makes sense that consumers do this, because if they carefully considered each and every piece of information and proceeded carefully through each step in the consumer decision-making process for each decision, their lives would grind to a halt because there would be no time to do anything else. Therefore, shortcuts like *heuristics*, *anchoring*, and *framing* help consumers navigate their way much more efficiently.

KEY TERMS

active learning p. 292
anchoring p. 311
attribution theory p. 287
availability heuristic p. 309
brand loyalty p. 294
choice heuristics p. 310
compliance heuristics p. 310
consensus rule p. 309
consideration set p. 283
decision criteria p. 285
disconfirmation paradigm p. 286
ego involvement p. 295

enduring involvement p. 294
evaluative criteria p. 283
evoked set p. 283
expertise rule p. 309
framing p. 311
heuristics p. 309
impulse purchase p. 306
inept set p. 283
inert set p. 283
information search p. 281
involvement p. 291
market mavens p. 302
maximizer p. 308

message-response involvement p. 294
ongoing information search p. 281
passive learning p. 292
persuasion heuristics p. 309
prediction heuristics p. 309
problem recognition p. 280
product involvement p. 294
reciprocity p. 310
representativeness heuristic p. 309
satisficing p. 308
scarcity p. 310
situational involvement p. 295

REVIEW QUESTIONS

1. What do we mean when we say that consumers proceed through the same five-step consumer decision-making process, regardless of whether they are making low- or high-involvement decisions? What *does* change in the process when a consumer makes a high- versus a low-involvement decision?

2. Explain the difference between enduring involvement and situational involvement.

3. What is the difference between evaluative criteria and decision criteria? Give at least two examples of each.

4. Which methods would you recommend for increasing involvement with a new hairstyling product? Defend your recommendation.

5. Identify and describe at least three personal and three social motivations for shopping.

6. Describe the different types of impulse purchasing and provide an example of each one.

7. What are the key differences between a maximizer and a satisficer? Identify a situation where it would be better to be a maximizer and one where it would be better to be a satisficer.

8. Explain the differences between heuristics, framing, and anchoring.

DISCUSSION QUESTIONS

1. Use the five-step consumer decision-making model to describe how you might proceed through the process for:
   a. a low-involvement purchase—tea or coffee, and
   b. a high-involvement purchase—a new winter coat.

   Describe in detail how these two processes differ. For the two decisions, how might a marketer influence what happens at each of these steps? Be creative!

2. Think of two or three brands that you regularly buy. Consider the type of involvement you have with them—are you a repeat purchaser or a true blue loyal consumer? Why? Why does this difference matter to marketers? Under what circumstances might you buy a different brand in the same product category? What influences your different choice of brand?

3. Imagine for a moment that you are a bit down on your luck—perhaps you have just graduated and have not yet gotten a job (we hope this doesn't happen!). What strategies would you use when shopping to keep costs down? How might your personal and social motivations for shopping change? Be specific.

4. Describe an impulse purchase that you recently made. How did you feel when you bought it and how did you feel afterward? Into which category of impulse purchasing does it fall? Was it a low- or high-value item? Did you keep it or return it? Were you pleased that you made the purchase?

5. Describe situations where a consumer might use an availability heuristic, a representativeness heuristic, and a compliance heuristic. For each of these situations, how might this particular heuristic help a consumer by reducing time and effort?

For more information, quizzes, case studies, and other study tools, please visit us at **www.oup.com/he/phillips**.

CASE STUDY 8

High-involvement soap? Really?

It might sound ridiculous, but it's true. By connecting to important life events like a marriage or the birth of a new baby, Method Products has attempted to increase involvement with its line of ecofriendly soaps, detergents, and other products. Using a fully integrated marketing campaign, including social media, managers at Method have tried to do what no other soap company has ever accomplished.

In 2013, Method Products was competing in an incredibly tough, mature market: soap. Industry giant Procter & Gamble (P&G) dominated everything that happened in the market. That is, until Method stepped in. Founded in 2001 by two roommates who wanted to make earth-friendly cleaning products in beautiful packaging, Method Products established a foothold in a very competitive arena where sales volume and costs mattered. Method focused on soaps, detergents, and a variety of other cleaning products. Their slogan was "People against dirty." Their products were made from plant-based material (rather than harmful chemicals) and their attractive packaging was 100 percent postconsumer recycled plastic. The soap dispensers, for example, were beautiful tear-shaped bottles in a variety of colors, which were a welcome addition to bathroom or kitchen counters for style-conscious consumers. For a small company like Method, entering the competitive soap market was incredibly tough. First, retailers often demand expensive *slotting fees* before they will even carry the product on their shelves. For companies like P&G, this was no problem, but for Method these fees almost made it impossible to get their product in front of consumers. Second, big players like P&G could easily achieve the volume of production needed to keep their prices low and margins high. Method's production, by contrast, was done in smaller batches that made it impossible to achieve the big cost savings that P&G could enjoy. Finally, consumers often purchased products like soap based on price, so prices at retail needed to be kept low.

How could Method Products help overcome some of these issues at retail and encourage consumers to try their products? They went straight to the consumer. An important insight occurred when researchers at Method found that consumers are willing to switch brands when they undergo important life events, such as a wedding or the birth of a child. The chief marketing officer said, "We find that people who love Method discover us at a point of inflection." So, in 2013, Method launched an ad campaign to help consumers feel more involved in their purchases of soap by connecting the soap to these important life inflections. A series of four thirty-second ads were created that followed the romance of a couple as they met, moved in together, and had a baby. The ad with the baby, for example, showed the baby flinging a meatball and hitting his dad. Luckily, the couple had some Method laundry detergent to take care of the mess! The campaign premiered in movie theaters and also included TV, Facebook, and geographically targeted online ads. Estimates were that the campaign cost $6.2 million (Newman 2014).

Method's next campaign built on the message that its products could clean up any mess you could throw at it. The ads were mini dramas in which big messes were no problem with Method products. One ad had a woman take a leaf blower and send a birthday cake, candles included, all over the room; another depicted a woman throwing fruit through a huge, industrial-sized fan, which sprayed bits of pulverized fruit all over the room. The taglines were "Fear no mess" and "Method: Clean ingredients for dirty play." The execution of the ads was quite artistic—they depicted the action in slow motion, set to beautiful music. The $12 million effort never made it to traditional broadcast TV, but instead appeared on connected TVs, YouTube,

Facebook, Instagram, Pinterest, and the Viggle app. Promotional materials also appeared in stores and in surprising out-of-home locations to catch the attention of consumers (Neff 2016). Method products are now offered at national retailers like Target, Walmart, Jet.com, Staples, and Bed Bath & Beyond. The company has enjoyed success in recent years, and in 2013 it was acquired by Ecover, a Belgian company that became the largest ecofriendly soap and cleaning company in the world with the acquisition (Dye 2017). Ecover and Method were then both acquired by S. C. Johnson in 2017. Officials at S. C. Johnson were anxious to bring in well-known and trusted ecofriendly brands to appeal to a younger audience seeking "natural" and "organic" products (Dye 2017). Although it is now under a new corporate umbrella, the Method Products brand remains. These acquisitions have allowed for important synergies that have helped lower production and distribution costs. They have also allowed Method to tap into much bigger marketing budgets to help increase involvement with consumers.

QUESTIONS

1. Is it really possible for consumers to be highly involved in soap, as managers at Method Products hoped? How could this be accomplished?

2. Do you think the consumer decision-making process or the consumer decision journey is more appropriate in describing what happens when a consumer purchases a Method product? Defend your decision.

3. How could heuristics come into play during this decision-making process?

4. Carefully describe some key evaluative criteria and decision criteria in making a purchase such as this.

5. In what way do you think that Method's social media efforts might help or hinder the job of trying to get consumers to be more involved? Use some of the theories and principles we discussed in this chapter to defend your answer.

Sources: Dye (2017); Neff (2016); Newman (2014).

REFERENCES

Andrew, S. 2019. "Phone Home! E.T. Reunites with Elliott and Viewers in a Thanksgiving TV ad." CNN. November 28, 2019.https://www.cnn.com/2019/11/28/entertainment/et-thanksgiving-commercial-trnd/index.html.

Antil, J. H. 1984. "Conceptualization and Operationalization of Involvement." In *Advances in Consumer Research, edited by* T. C. Kinnear, 11:203–9. Provo, UT: Association for Consumer Research.

Ariely, D. 2008. *Predictably Irrational: The Hidden Forces That Shape Our Decisions.* London: Harper Collins.

Batra, R., and M. L. Ray. 1983. "Operationalizing Involvement as Depth and Quality of Cognitive Responses." In *Advances in Consumer Research*, edited by A. Tybout and R. Bagozzi, 10:309–13. Ann Arbor, MI: Association for Consumer Research.

Bayley, G., and C. Nancarrow. 1998. "Impulse Purchasing: A Qualitative Exploration of the Phenomenon." *Qualitative Market Research* 1 (2): 99–114.

Bettman, J. R., and M. Sujan. 1987. "Effects of Framing on Evaluation of Comparable and Noncomparable Alternatives by Expert and Novice Consumers." *Journal of Consumer Research* 14 (2): 141–54.

Bloch, P. H., D. L. Sherrell, and N. Ridgway. 1986. "Consumer Search: An Extended Framework." *Journal of Consumer Research* 13 (1): 119–26.

Bortz, D. 2017. "5 Social Media Hacks for Better Customer Service." *Time*, February 16, 2017. http://time.com/money/4672443/social-media-hacks-customer-service/.

Bowlby, R. 1997. "Supermarket Futures." In *The Shopping Experience*, edited by P. Falk and C. Campbell, 92–110. London: Sage.

Brannon, L. A., and T. C. Brock. 2001. "Norms against Voting for Coerced Reform." *Journal of Personality and Social Psychology* 64:347–55.

Chaiken, S., A. Liberman, and A. H. Eagly. 1989. "Heuristic and Systematic Processing within and beyond the Persuasion Context." In *Unintended Thought*, edited by J. S. Uleman and J. A. Barg, 215–52. New York: Guilford Press.

Chiun, A. 2018. "All the Reasons Why Fashion Loves Dee Hsu." E! December 30, 2018. https://www.eonline.com/ap/news/1000255/all-the-reasons-why-fashion-loves-dee-hsu.

Court, D., D. Elzinga, S. Mulder, and O. Vetvick. 2009. "The Consumer Decision Journey." *McKinsey Quarterly.* June 1, 2009. https://www.mckinsey.com/business-functions/marketing-and-sales/our-insights/the-consumer-decision-journey.

Crittenden, V., C. A. Scott, and R. T. Moriarty. 1987. "The Role of Prior

Product Experience in Organizational Buying Behavior." *Advances in Consumer Research* 14 (1): 387–91.

DaCosta, C. 2018. "Three Simple Steps to Crafting a Captivating Brand Story." *Forbes*, February 27, 2018. https://www.forbes.com/sites/celinnedacosta/2018/02/27/3-simple-steps-to-crafting-a-captivating-brand-story/#54a11db17b7d.

DeMers, J. 2020. "Is the Concept of Brand Loyalty Dying?" *Medium*, May 11. Accessed September 13, 2020. https://medium.com/swlh/is-the-concept-of-brand-loyalty-dying-c172aee287a6.

Dye, J. 2017. "SC Johnson Scoops Up Method, Ecover Product Brands." *Financial Times*, September 14, 2017. https://www.ft.com/content/258928f1-cf88-348c-9cc3-cc90ca4aca09.

Environmental Protection Agency. 2016. *Advancing Sustainable Materials Management: 2014 Fact Sheet*. November, EPA530-R-17-01. Washington, DC: US Environmental Protection Agency, Office of Land and Emergency Management (5306P).

Erdem, T., M. P. Keane, T. SabriÖncü, and J. Strebel. 2005. "Learning about Computers: An Analysis of Information Search and Technology Choice." *Quantitative Marketing and Economics* 3 (3): 207–47.

Feick, L., and L. Price. 1987. "The Market Maven: A Diffuser of Marketplace Information." *Journal of Marketing* 51 (1): 83–97.

Foxall, G. R. 1993. "The Influence of Cognitive Style on Consumers' Variety Seeking among Food Innovations." *British Food Journal* 95 (9): 32–36.

Ganesh, J., K. Reynolds, and M. Luckett. 2007. "Retail Patronage Behavior and Shopper Typologies: A Replication and Extension Using a Multi-format, Multi-method Approach." *Journal of the Academy of Marketing Science* 35 (3): 369–81.

Harrison, S. 2013. "Northern Ireland Bag Levy Could Reduce Litter." *BBC News*, April 8, 2013. http://www.bbc.co.uk/news/uk-northern-ireland-22037034.

Houston, M. J., and M. L. Rothschild. 1978. "Conceptual and Methodological Perspectives on Involvement." In *Research Frontiers in Marketing: Dialogues and Directions, 1978 Educators' Proceedings*, edited by

S. Jain, 184–87. Chicago: American Marketing Association.

Iyengar, S. S., and M. R. Lepper. 1999. "Rethinking the Value of Choice: A Cultural Perspective on Intrinsic Motivation." *Journal of Personality and Social Psychology* 76:349–66.

Iyengar, S. S., and M. R. Lepper. 2000. "When Choice Is Demotivating." *Journal of Personality and Social Psychology* 79:995–1006.

Jansson-Boyd, C. V. 2010. *Consumer Psychology*. Maidenhead, UK: Open University Press.

J. D. Power. 2016. "Skoda Ranks Highest in Vehicle Dependability in the UK for a Second Consecutive Year." Press release. July 13, 2016. http://www.jdpower.com/press-releases/jd-power-2016-uk-vehicle-dependability-study.

Jones, C. 2018. "Higher-Income Shoppers Hunt for Bargains More Than Most." *USA Today*, January 15, 2018. https://www.usatoday.com/story/money/2018/01/15/higher-income-shoppers-hunt-bargains-more-than-most/1028643001/.

Jones, S. 2018. "How Hollywood Celebrities Are Used for Global Endorsements." Hollywood Branded. July 2, 2018. https://blog.hollywoodbranded.com/how-hollywood-celebrities-are-used-for-global-endorsements.

Jost, J. T., M. Langer, and V. Singh. 2017. "The Politics of Buying, Boycotting, Complaining, and Disputing: An Extension of the Research Program by Jung, Garbarino, Briley, and Wynhausen." *Journal of Consumer Research* 44 (3): 503–10.

Krugman, H. E., and E. L. Hartley. 1970. "Passive Learning from Television." *Public Opinion Quarterly* 342:184–19.

Langer, E. J. 1989. *Mindfulness*. Reading, MA: Addison–Wesley.

Leitch, W. 2013. "The Greatest Fans in the World." Sports on Earth. Accessed December 10, 2017. http://www.sportsonearth.com/article/41810720/.

Maheshwari, S. 2017. "Department Stores, Once Anchors at Malls, Become Millstones." *The New York Times*, January 6, 2017, A1–B4.

MarketLine. 2019. "Company Report Generator." Accessed August 16, 2019. https://b2b-marketline-com.ezproxy.sju.edu/CompanyAnalyzer/Default.aspx.

Mintel. 2017. *The Budget Shopper—US—November 2017*. London: Mintel.

Monllos, K. 2017. "How Budweiser Created an Epic Immigrant Story to Reclaim the Super Bowl Spotlight." *Adweek*, January 29, 2017. http://www.adweek.com/brand-marketing/how-budweiser-created-an-epic-immigrant-story-to-reclaim-the-super-bowl-spotlight/.

Narayana, C. L., and R. J. Markin. 1975. "Consumer Behavior and Product Performance: An Alternative Conceptualization." *Journal of Marketing* 39 (4): 1–6.

Neff, J. 2016. "See the Spots: Method Makes a Pretty Mess to Back Its Products." *AdAge*, April 29, 2016. http://adage.com/article/cmo-strategy/spots-method-makes-a-pretty-mess-back-cleaners/303796/.

Newman, A. A. 2014. "With a French Accent, a Soap Brand Tells a Tale of Well-Scrubbed Lovers." *New York Times*, Late edition (East Coast), March 21, 2014, B4.

Nordland, R. 2013. "Too Hot to Exercise (and Who Really Wants To?)." *New York Times*, July 7, 2013. http://www.nytimes.com/2013/07/08/world/middleeast/in-qatar-too-hot-to-exercise-and-who-really-wants-to.html?_r=0.

Parsons, A. G. 2002. "Non-functional Motives for Online Shoppers: Why We Click." *Journal of Consumer Marketing* 19 (5): 380–92.

Ratneshwar, S., and S. Chaiken. 1991. "Recognition Is Used as One Cue among Others in Judgement and Decision Making." *Journal of Experimental Psychology: Learning, Memory and Cognition* 32:150–62.

Robehmed, N. 2017. "How Kim Kardashian West Bounced Back to $45.5 Million—and a New Cosmetics Company." *Forbes*, June 13, 2017. https://www.forbes.com/sites/natalierobehmed/2017/06/13/how-kim-kardashian-west-bounced-back-to-45-5-million-and-a-new-cosmetics-company/#43c9fef58f59.

Rook, D. 1987. "The Buying Impulse." *Journal of Consumer Research* 14 (2): 189–99.

Royo-Vela, M., and P. Casamassima. 2010. "The Influence of Belonging to Virtual Brand Communities on Consumers' Affective Commitment, Satisfaction and Word-of-Mouth Advertising: The Zara Case." *Online Information Review* 35 (4): 517–42.

Schultz, E. J. 2016. "How "Crash the Super Bowl" Changed Advertising."

AdAge, January 4, 2016. http://adage.com/article/special-report-super-bowl/crash-super-bowl-changed-advertising/301966/.

Schwartz, B. 2005. *The Paradox of Choice: Why More Is Less*. New York: HarperCollins.

Schwartz, B., A. Ward, J. Monterosso, S. Lyubomirsky, K. White, and D. R. Lehman. 2002. "Maximizing versus Satisficing: Happiness Is a Matter of Choice." *Journal of Personality and Social Psychology* 83 (5): 1178–97.

Settimi, C. 2019. "The NHL's Best Fans of 2019." Forbes, SportsMoney Section. December 13. Accessed September 13, 2020. https://www.forbes.com/stories/the-nhls-best-fans-of-2019/#12.

Shah, A. K., and D. M. Oppenheimer. 2008. "Heuristics Made Easy: An Effort-Reduction Framework." *Psychological Bulletin* 134 (2): 207–22.

Sharma, A., and S. K. Nair. 2017. "Switching Behavior as a Function of Number of Options: How Much Is Too Much for Consumer Choice Decisions?" *Journal of Consumer Behavior* 16:e153–60. https://doi.org/10.1002/cb.1670.

Simon, H. A. 1956. "Rational Choice and the Structure of the Environment." *Psychological Review* 63:129–38.

Slama, M., and T. Williams. 1990. "Generalization of the Market Maven's Information Provision Tendency across Product Categories." *Advances in Consumer Research* 17:48–52.

Solomon, M. R., R. D. Ashmore, and L. C. Longo. 1992. "The Beauty Match-Up Hypothesis: Congruence between Types of Beauty and Product Images in Advertising." *Journal of Advertising* 21 (4): 23–34.

Spies-Gans, J. 2016. "Millennials Are Watching the Super Bowl for the Commercials, Not the Game." *Huffington Post*, February 4, 2016. https://www.huffpost.com/entry/you-gov-super-bowl-commercials-game_n_56b105d3e4b0a1b96203f436.

Stone, G. 1954. "City Shoppers and Urban Identification." *American Journal of Sociology* 60 (1): 36–45.

Stutman, C. 2017. Personal interview, December 6, 2017.

Szmigin, I., and M. Piacentini. 2015. *Consumer Behavior*. Oxford: Oxford University Press.

Tauber, E. M. 1972. "Why Do People Shop?" *Journal of Marketing* 36 (4): 46–49.

Thompson, C. J., W. B. Locander, and H. R. Pollio. 1990. "The Lived Meaning of Free Choice: An Existential-Phenomenological Description of Everyday Consumer Experiences of Contemporary Married Women." *Journal of Consumer Research* 17 (3): 346–61.

Tversky, A., and D. Kahneman. 1974. "Judgement under Uncertainty: Heuristics and Biases." *Science* 185 (4157): 1124–31.

Tversky, A., and D. Kahneman. 1986. "Rational Choice and the Framing of Decisions." *Journal of Business* 59 (4): S251–78.

Van der Veen, R., and H. Song. 2013. "Impact of the Perceived Image of Celebrity Endorsers on Tourists' Intentions to Visit." *Journal of Travel Research* 53 (2): 211–24.

Vogt, C. A., and D. R. Fesenmaier. 1998. "Expanding the Functional Informational Search Model." *Annals of Tourism Research* 25 (3): 551–78.

Weiner, B. 2010. "The Development of an Attribution-Based Theory of Motivation: A History of Ideas." *Educational Psychologist* 45 (1): 28–36.

Zaichkowsky, J. L. 1985. "Measuring the Involvement Construct." *Journal of Consumer Research* 12:341–52.

Zaichkowsky, J. L. 1986. "Conceptualizing Involvement." *Journal of Advertising* 15 (2): 4–14.

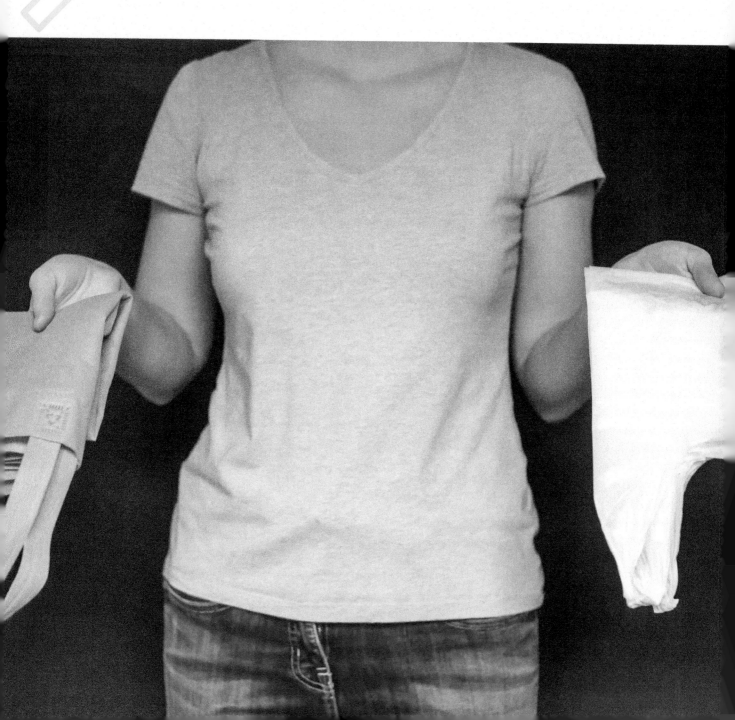

⊙ Introduction

As we have seen throughout this book, it is critically important to understand the underlying mechanisms of consumer behavior. We have examined a variety of models and topics to help us explain *why* consumers do what they do. In focusing our efforts on these underlying motivations, our goal is to better predict what consumers might do next. How will they react to our new ad campaign? How will they navigate our new website? How will they react to our new in-store promotion? Answers to these kinds of questions can be provided by a thoughtful analysis of *consumer behavior*.

This chapter takes a slightly different approach and focuses on actual buyer behaviors because this information can provide important insights too. Much of the research on *buyer behavior* comes from observing and measuring what consumers do. Researchers who focus on buyer behavior will examine scanner data from retail stores, click-through and search data from web analytics, and even observational data from watching how consumers walk around a retail store examining labels and comparing prices. Sometimes, consumer panels are created with hundreds or thousands of consumers to provide data on several topics. While none of these data can provide definitive answers about *why* consumers do what they do, marketers can develop insights from behaviors and draw some important conclusions about the *why* of consumer behavior. By analyzing patterns of buyer behavior, we can provide some very interesting insights into how consumers will behave in a variety of circumstances and how they will react to a variety of stimuli. The first half of this chapter is focused on tracking buyer behaviors and the second half is focused on how a marketer can use that information to influence consumer behaviors.

⊙ Tracking Buyer Behavior

In looking at your grocery cart each week, what percentage of the products are new brands that you have never used before? Most likely, the vast majority of the products and brands in your cart are ones

LEARNING OBJECTIVES

After you read this chapter, you will be able to:

1. Differentiate between *purchase frequency*, *market penetration*, and *market share*.

2. Explain how consumer panel data is gathered and how it can reveal information about *purchase frequency, the nature of the market*, and *explaining why consumers buy*.

3. Describe the key conceptual and outcome differences between *purchase loyalty* and *attitudinal loyalty*.

4. Describe how marketers influence behavior by *segmenting the brand, differentiating the brand, making the brand distinctive, encouraging greater engagement with the brand*, and *fostering relationships with the brand*.

5. Identify and distinguish the different *types of relationships* consumers have with brands.

6. Describe tactics marketers use to *facilitate stronger, more meaningful relationships* with consumers.

you *have* used before. We probably stop at the same gas station and the same coffee shop and get our hair cut at the same barber or salon. For most products and services, we purchase brands with which we are familiar. Depending on how often we need to replace our products or renew our services, we demonstrate predictable purchase patterns.

When marketing managers want to examine repeat purchasing patterns, they often use consumer panel data. Some consumer panels ask customers to record their purchases by scanning their grocery receipts or swiping a card, either at the store or when they get home. Other panels are simply a collection of consumers who answer a variety of questions on a range of topics over a period of time, such as leisure activities, use of different media, or other consumption-related behaviors. Although consumer panels are often very different from one another, they do have a few things in common. First, the behavioral data are often combined with attitudinal and demographic information so that researchers can pull out subsets of research subjects and compare their responses. They might find, for example, that women aged eighteen to twenty-five are much more likely to recycle than any other subsample of consumers. Second, panels are typically large, representative samples of the overall population. That is, the panel should have the same proportion of ethnicities, ages, income brackets, etc., as the target market or even the overall population. If a consumer panel was constructed for the United States, 18 percent of the participants should be Hispanic, 12.5 percent should be Black, and 5.6 percent should be Asian (Krogstad 2017). The third characteristic of consumer panels is that the research participants are often compensated for their time and effort. Participants often receive cash, discounts, or gift cards as compensation.

The primary goal of consumer panels is to identify purchasing patterns. Indeed, consumer panels can provide important information to marketing managers, such as details about repeat purchases over time, purchase frequency, the nature of the market, and maybe even explanations of why consumers buy.

Panel data

Panel data can provide a lot of fascinating information to researchers about the characteristics of their consumers, their attitudes toward a variety of issues, and their behaviors. This is especially true if data from the same panel are gathered at regular intervals over time. In one study with 4,077 panel participants, a wide variety of questions was asked in order to answer several research questions. Then, each question was deeply probed with multiple items. For example, the researchers asked eighteen separate questions about gender identity, fifteen about attitudes toward the environment, fifteen about the tendency to think innovatively, thirty-seven about lifestyle activities, and eighteen about pro-environmental behaviors. Why so many questions for each variable? The technique of having a variety of questions for each variable provides a fuller, more comprehensive, and more nuanced depiction of the phenomenon of interest. Table 9.1 depicts a small sampling of two categories of questions from this

Table 9.1 A sample of panel data questions

DEMOGRAPHIC QUESTIONS
1. Gender
2. Year you were born
3. Household income
4. Marital status
5. Number of people living in household
6. Number of people under the age of eighteen living in household
7. Occupation
8. Highest level of education competed
9. Ethnicity
10. Area of residence: urban, suburban, or rural
11. The state in which you live

FASHION OPINION LEADERSHIP: using a 1–5 scale, where 1 is strongly disagree and 5 is strongly agree, indicate whether you agree or disagree with each of the following statements.
1. I often influence people's opinions about new fashion products.
2. When they choose new fashion products, other people do not turn to me for advice (this question is reverse scored).
3. I often persuade other people to buy new fashion products that I like.
4. People I know pick fashion products based on what I have told them.
5. Other people rarely come to me for advice about choosing new fashion products (reverse scored).
6. My opinion on new fashion products seems not to count with other people (reverse scored).

study: demographics and fashion opinion leadership (Englis and Phillips 2013). It is important to realize that this panel provided data not just on what consumers do, but also on what they think and feel. Many other panels that are derived from scanner data, for example, only provide data on behaviors. Consumer panels differ in their depth and breadth of questions, but all are designed to help reveal patterns and relationships between variables.

Purchase frequency

The frequency with which a product is purchased is also important for marketing managers. Very often, consumers will purchase two or more packages of the same brand at a time. **Purchase frequency** is the average number of times a consumer purchases the product in a given period. When purchasing cereal, you might buy just one box at a time, but when you buy yogurt, you might throw several containers into your basket to eat throughout the week. Marketers are quite interested in two additional variables that can be derived from panel data:

Purchase frequency is the average number of times consumers purchase a brand in a given period.

1. **Market penetration**—the proportion of customers who buy an item in a given period. Market penetration is often expressed as a percentage: for example, 25 percent of the target market has tried our product in the first year while 75 percent has not; we therefore have 25 percent market penetration.

Market penetration is the proportion of people who buy an item in a given period.

Market share is the proportion of the total sales for one brand versus the other brands in the market.

2. **Market share**—the proportion of the total sales for one brand versus all brands in the market. This figure is usually based on sales dollars, rather than sales volume. This is also expressed as a percentage: for example, Coca-Cola has 45 percent global market share in the soft drink industry. That is, 45 percent of all the money spent on soft drinks around the world is spent on Coke-branded products.

A brand may have impressive market share because it is bought very often by a few customers or because it has many infrequent customers. Data like these provide important insights for marketing managers because they indicate how the customer base is structured: that is, many buyers who buy infrequently, fewer buyers who buy the brand frequently, or a combination of both. This, in turn, will have important implications for how the organization interacts with customers as well as how it delivers the value proposition with a variety of product, price, place, and promotion strategies that are relevant to the target market.

It is interesting to note that, across many brands and product categories in a given market, although the penetration of brands may differ widely, the average purchase frequency of any brand tends to be similar. This is an important finding in terms of understanding how buyer behavior affects the market and calls into question some assumptions about what brand loyalty really means. To illustrate the importance of the difference between market penetration, market share, and purchase frequency, refer to the example of pizza companies in the United States. The top eight pizza companies are listed in Table 9.2 (Pizza Today 2018).

Brand loyalty is the preference for purchasing one brand over another.

We can see that the top eight players in the US pizza market account for 84 percent of the market share, while a number of small brands collectively hold 16 percent of the market. We can see that the top two brands, Pizza Hut and Domino's, control thirty-seven percent of the market. The overall market penetration for pizza is 71, indicating that 71 percent of American households purchase pizza in a given year. Further, each brand has a different penetration (e.g., 20 percent for Pizza Hut). If you add the percentages for each brand, you will see that it sums to more than 100, because many customers purchase more than one brand of pizza. The purchase frequency is simply the number of times on average the brand was purchased in one year. American consumers purchase pizza 5.6 times per year, but purchase Pizza Hut pizza 3.6 times per year.

We can draw some conclusions by examining Table 9.2:

1. Although market shares for pizza differ significantly, the average purchase frequencies do not. Consequently, one important insight is that, regardless of the market share of the brand, it needs to reach the average purchase frequency of about 2.5 to be in the top tier of brands.

2. As market share declines, average purchase frequencies also decrease. This relationship between market share and purchase frequency is called **double jeopardy,** a phenomenon whereby brands with smaller

Double jeopardy is where brands with smaller market share have fewer buyers and those fewer buyers buy the brand less often.

Table 9.2 Penetration and purchase frequency for the US pizza market

BRAND	MARKET SHARE (%)	MARKET PENETRATION (%)	ANNUAL PURCHASE FREQUENCY (PER BUYER)
Any pizza	100	71	5.6
Pizza Hut	19	20	3.6
Domino's	18	17	3.4
Papa John's	11	17	2.7
Little Caesars	10	18	2.5
Papa Murphy's	8	15	2.3
California Pizza Kitchen	7	13	2.2
Sbarro	6	10	2.0
Marco's Pizza	5	9	1.7
Other brands	16	21	1.1
Average for top eight	10.5	14.9	2.6

Note: The numbers in Table 9.2 are for comparison purposes only.

market share have fewer buyers who buy the brand less often. Brand managers need to be concerned when they are faced with this situation. Because of double jeopardy, the more customers you have, the more likely they will be to repeat buy, so being big really does make a difference. The concept of double jeopardy implies that increasing market share will lower defection rates for consumers, which makes defection particularly troublesome for smaller companies (Sharp 2010) (see Insights from Academia 9.1).

3. Discrepancies in the data can usually be easily spotted by tracking market share, market penetration, and purchase frequency over time. Often, if a discrepancy arises, it can be explained by looking at the broader context of the business and its customers. Little Caesars, for example, has recently dropped a few spots in the rankings because of a recent reorganization that shifted marketing dollars away from some of their strategic priorities.

The nature of the market

It is important to note that the markets we are considering are well established rather than new. An important feature of these markets is that they do not change much. This is known as a **near-stationary (static) market,**

Near-stationary (static) markets are established, mature markets that appear stable over a period of several months or a year.

INSIGHTS FROM ACADEMIA 9.1

When should apps be free?

The concept of double jeopardy says that there is a two-fold penalty for brands that have low market share—they have fewer buyers and those buyers purchase less frequently. How does a marketer of mobile apps build market share? One thing to consider in trying to get quicker and wider acceptance of an app is whether it should be free. First, if an app is already linked to a brand (e.g., Google Maps is connected to Google), the app can attract more users and achieve a stronger brand image if it is offered for free. Second, if an app is branded independently (e.g., Angry Birds), it will actually attract more users and obtain a more positive brand image if it is offered for a price. Thus, to overcome the concept of double jeopardy, a small organization with no associated online or offline brand should launch a *paid* app to have the best chance of grabbing a significant share of the market. Let's hope the marketers for Angry Birds don't read this!

Stocchi, L., C. Guerini, and N. Michaelidou. 2017. "When Are Apps Worth Paying For? How Marketers Can Analyze the Market Performance of Mobile Apps." Journal of Advertising Research 57 (3): 260–71.

Nonstationary (dynamic) markets are markets in which the forces change quickly and dramatically.

Variety-seeking consumers are very interested in trying different brands and product attributes.

Habit-persistent consumers are those who make decisions based on their previous purchases.

which is an established mature market that appears stable over a period of several months or years. An example might be basic household or clothing items that everyone has, including everyday items like socks, a garden hose, and coffee mugs. There is not much thought or involvement in the purchase of these items, in part because styles and features change very little from year to year. By contrast, a **nonstationary (dynamic) market** is one in which the forces change quickly and dramatically. Changing tastes, shifting priorities, or the introduction of innovative technology could accelerate these changes in the market. Think about cars, entertainment systems, and clothing that you might wear on a date. An analysis of behavioral data can tell us whether the market is static or dynamic.

Another important dimension to the nature of markets is *how* consumers make decisions within the market. **Variety-seeking consumers** are very interested in trying different brands and product attributes. They have a desire for new tastes and experiences. For example, these consumers are likely eager to try out different restaurants and different dishes at those restaurants. **Habit-persistent consumers**, by contrast, are those who make decisions based on their previous purchases. The preferences that consumers have for certain brands and product attributes are reinforced over time. For example, if you really like Wilson tennis rackets (like Serena Williams), you will develop stronger preferences for the brand each time you use it and will likely buy another the next time you need one. The vast majority of consumers are habit persistent (Erdem 1996). To marketers, this is important information that provides insights into how to communicate with consumers. Behavioral data can help marketers understand the nature of the market as well as the nature of their consumers, as can be seen in Insights from Academia 9.2.

Organic consumers, please step forward!

How can marketers identify consumers who consistently purchase organic products? The answer is that it depends on how long the consumer has been purchasing organic products. Panel data from 8,704 Danish consumers were examined to learn what organic products consumers purchased and to identify any behavioral or purchasing patterns. First, consumers who started to buy organic products continued to buy organic over time; they rarely went back to traditional foods. Second, for many consumers, the *entry point*, or first organic purchase, was milk. Third, over time, consumers of organic milk broadened their organic choices to enter a second stage of purchasing, with products like fresh vegetables, fruits, baking products, and eggs. One insight from these findings is that consumers who purchase organic products are not a stand-alone market segment. Instead, several sub-segments can be identified, including: (1) infrequent and narrow purchasers, (2) entry-point consumers, (3) second-stage consumers, and (4) frequent and broad purchasers. What kind of consumer are you?

Juhl, H. J., M. H. J. Fenger, and J. Thogersen. 2017. "Will the Consistent Organic Food Consumer Step Forward? An Empirical Analysis." Journal of Consumer Research 44 (3): 519–35.

Marketers also need to understand the rates at which consumers decide to leave a brand for good. Thus, consumer panel data that provide information about the rates of defection also provide critical information for marketing managers. Some product categories, such as automobiles, have high rates of consumer repeat purchases. In Thailand, Toyota, for example, enjoys a 56 percent repeat purchase rate, while Mitsubishi achieves only 29 percent (see Table 9.3). The market share, market penetration, and repeat purchasing patterns provided in Table 9.3 are very similar to those in North America and Europe (Colombo, Ehrenberg, and Sabavala 2000; Bennett 2005). Other industries are even more fortunate. For example, defection rates from service industries are generally quite a bit lower, at around 3–5 percent (Sharp 2010).

Check out Insights from Academia 9.3 to see how some unscrupulous marketers use what they know about buyer behavior to alter consumer perceptions and behaviors.

Explaining why consumers buy

We know from Chapter 8 that when a marketer increases the number of choices available for consumers to consider, consumers may actually react negatively. Although it is sometimes beneficial to have a greater number of choices, studies have shown that more options often leads to less optimal choices and lower levels of happiness (Schwartz 2005).

What is a consumer to do when faced with all of these choices? We know that, from the customer's perspective, the relative importance of most everyday purchases is low—toothpaste and suntan lotion are not high-involvement purchases. Because of this, consumers may exhibit a variety of behaviors such

INSIGHTS FROM ACADEMIA 9.3

Copycat brands damage national brands

Imitation is the sincerest form of flattery. —Oscar Wilde
Don't believe it. Copycat brands are those that imitate the color, shape, brand name, or look of a national brand. Simply take a stroll down the aisle of cold medications the next time you're at the store; there are an inordinate number of similar-looking packages and brands. What happens, however, when the copycat is an out-of-category product, such as hand lotion? Surprisingly, the results for the national brand are even worse. Consider the example of the chocolate spread, Nutella. Copycat Lutella tried to compete in the new product category of chocolate bars. Nutella does not have any products in the chocolate bar category. However, the Lutella brand chocolate bar (copycat, out-of-category)

received higher evaluations and higher willingness to buy than it did in the chocolate spread category. Further, there was a backlash reaction *against* Nutella! Why? The authors concluded that consumers in the out-of-category market (here, chocolate bar consumers) did not have clear standards of evaluation for this new market entrant, so decided to give it the benefit of the doubt. These findings have important implications for trademark and copyright infringements.

Van Horen, F., and R. Pieters. 2017. "Out-of-Category Brand Imitation: Product Categorization Determines Copycat Evaluation." Journal of Consumer Research 44 (4): 816–32.

Table 9.3 Repeat Purchasing in the Thai Car Market

BRAND	MARKET SHARE (%)	MARKET PENETRATION (%)	REPEAT PURCHASE (%)
Toyota	46	61	56
Other	24	32	47
Honda	10	18	31
Nissan	8	15	33
BMW	7	9	30
Mitsubishi	5	10	29
Average	17	24	38

Source: Bennett and Graham (2010); Szmigin and Piacentini (2015).

as inertia, randomly choosing brands, or even engaging in variety-seeking behavior. Most consumers purchase products out of habit, and unless there is a strong reason to switch, they will not do so. However, by examining consumer panel data, researchers can see what prompts a consumer to stay with a brand or switch brands. Researchers can determine, for example, if a consumer switches because of a price discount, the entry of a new brand on the market, or a new advertising campaign. Earlier in this text, we learned that brand loyalty is the preference for purchasing one brand over another. Unfortunately, consumer panel data cannot provide detailed insights into what motivates consumer behavior. Consumer panel data can only describe what consumers do, not why they do it. Marketers can, however, draw conclusions based on their behavior. For example, a marketer can see if a price discount prompts additional purchases, if a new advertising campaign gets consumers to visit the website, or if a new package design results in more frequent purchases. Thus, by examining buyer behavior, researchers can infer what might be the underlying motivation for that behavior (see Photo 9.1).

● **Photo 9.1** *Modern consumers are faced with a dizzying array of choices*

What does repeat purchasing tell us about brand loyalty? Not much (cf. Brown 1953; Sharp 2010). Many consumers purchase from a repertoire or collection of different brands, and each one will be perfectly acceptable. Earlier in this text, we referred to this concept as a consumer's consideration set. For example, if you are facing an afternoon slump in energy, you might be equally happy with a Snickers bar, a Twix, or a Milky Way. This is your consideration set—the three brands you would actually consider buying. By thinking about brand loyalty as loyalty to a repertoire of brands, marketing managers have a variety of strategic options at their disposal. For example, marketers might try to increase brand satisfaction to ensure the brand stays in the consumer's repertoire. Another strategic move would be for a marketing manager to focus more attention on retaining customers than on acquiring new ones. This is because, as in the chocolate bar example, acquiring more customers also helps the competition, since customers may only have a one in three chance of buying your brand.

One important implication of behavioral research is for marketing managers to understand the nature of loyalty among their customers. The goal of the 100 percent loyal customer is not only unlikely, but also not necessarily worthwhile because of how much these customers actually buy. When a company moves to a higher market share, for example, from 60 to 70 to 80 percent, the last customers who join and become customers of the brand will likely be light users of the category who purchase fewer items than other customers. This is especially true of smaller brands in the category (remember the double jeopardy effect) (Ehrenberg, Uncles, and Goodhardt 2004). In the end, the cost of attracting these customers will likely outweigh any additional profit that is gained from them. Therefore, from a strategic standpoint, it makes little sense for a marketer to try to attain 100 percent brand loyalty.

● **Photo 9.2** *Starbucks has an intensive distribution strategy to reach its customers*

Another implication of this research is the importance of a broad distribution strategy for the brand. Growing a brand's distribution into a previously unrepresented area is an important strategy because it reaches potential buyers who have not been able to gain access to the brand. Not only are light or nonbuyers given access to the brand, but also heavy buyers have improved availability. This is a strategy that many retailers, like Starbucks, often pursue. In addition to stand-alone Starbucks stores, Starbucks kiosks and Starbucks make-at-home coffee products are available in a variety of places where customers can easily find them. There are more than thirty thousand Starbucks stores in eighty markets around the world (Starbucks Company Profile 2020). This distribution strategy increases the opportunity for consumers to buy from Starbucks as they go about their daily lives (see Photo 9.2).

It is important to distinguish between two types of brand loyalty: purchase loyalty and attitudinal loyalty. **Purchase loyalty** involves the repeated, often habitual, purchase of a brand. In a related vein, **attitudinal loyalty** involves a liking or a commitment to the brand that is often based on some perceived value obtained from consumption of the brand (Chaudhuri and Holbrook 2001). Purchase loyalty and attitudinal loyalty are, not surprisingly, correlated with one another—if you have positive attitudes toward a brand, you are going to be likely to buy it. While behavioral data (like consumer panel data) can provide information about purchase loyalty, managers can only make inferences about attitudinal loyalty from this kind of data. For example, if there is a price increase for the brand and sales remain steady, managers may conclude that consumers exhibit some amount of attitudinal loyalty toward the brand. Why is it important to distinguish between these types of brand loyalty? Purchase loyalty exerts a positive influence on market share. When a given consumer purchases more frequently (purchase loyalty), market share will increase. This is especially true when many consumers are making more frequent purchases. This is no surprise. However, attitudinal loyalty exerts a positive influence on a brand's price. Consumers who have higher attitudinal loyalty will pay a higher price for the product (Chaudhuri and Holbrook 2001). This relationship is summarized in Figure 9.1. See Insights from the Field 9.1 for a description of how consumer panels have been used to explain green consumption.

Consumers obviously have different motivations and reasons for the choices they make. Our consumer behavior models

Purchase loyalty involves the repeated, often habitual, purchase of a brand.

Attitudinal loyalty involves a liking or a commitment to the brand that is often based on some perceived value obtained from consumption of the brand.

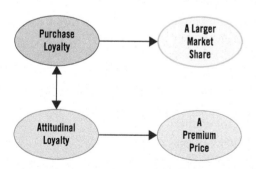

● **Figure 9.1** *Market effects of purchase loyalty and attitudinal loyalty*

only go part way in predicting what an individual consumer will actually do. That is, behavioral data can certainly provide insights about what they might do (such as those discussed in Insights from the Field 9.1), but at the end of the day, consumers have free will, distractions, and other goals in their day-to-day lives. One thing we do know, however, is that customers do have some general behavioral tendencies. For example, consumers who are light users of a brand may buy from a wide repertoire of brands. These consumers do not buy much within the product category, but when they do, they buy a variety of brands. Surprisingly, consumers who are heavy users also tend to buy relatively few brands. However, when they buy, they buy a lot. We know, for example, from consumer panel data from the United Kingdom, that just 4 percent of consumers who buy Coca-Cola products are responsible for 25 percent of Coke's sales volume in that country (Sharp 2010). Rather than just focusing on the heavy users, however, marketing managers must pay careful attention to both kinds of consumers—light and heavy.

A marketing manager for Coca-Cola might want to attract light users in an attempt to get them to purchase more each week. This strategy is reasonable because there are many light users, and getting each one to make a small uptick in purchase volume could result in huge increases in sales. Marketing managers also want to attract heavy users. The rationale for this strategy is that these people already really enjoy the brand and don't need to be convinced that Coca-Cola is a great product. However, we must also consider whether such an effort would be beneficial because these consumers may have already reached saturation point. How much Coca-Cola can a person drink? Figuring out what to do is a challenge for marketers, but these differences between a company's heavy and light buyers can be further understood by examining the Pareto principle, the law of buyer moderation, and the duplication of purchases principle.

The Pareto Principle

Sometimes called the 80/20 principle, the **Pareto principle** suggests that about 80 percent of a company's sales come from 20 percent of its customers. In practice, this ratio changes from industry to industry and from product to product—it could be 70/30 or 60/40—but the core principle is the same. That is, a relatively small percentage of customers is responsible for a large proportion of a company's sales. In the United States, the average ratio for consumer packaged goods is 73/27. Cigarettes have the highest ratio, at 89/11 (followed by light beer, low-calorie soft drinks, and wine), while laundry detergents have among the lowest, at 64/36. Within a given product category, brands have different ratios too. For example, market leaders Coca-Cola and Pepsi have 79/21 and 80/20, respectively. However, 7UP has 71/29 and A&W has 70/30 (Kim, Singh, and Winer 2017). What can a marketing manager do with these findings? First, managers working with a very high ratio must be very careful to ensure that the very loyal, but few, customers are kept satisfied with a consistently high-quality product. Each of these customers is responsible for a large

Pareto principle suggests that about 80 percent of a company's sales come from 20 percent of its customers (also called the 80/20 principle).

Using consumer panels to explain green consumption

While many consumer research panels are unable to provide deep insights into the *why* of consumer behavior, some panels are given a variety of questions that relate to their underlying motivations. When panels are designed to elicit this kind of data from panel participants, panels can indeed be used to provide insights into both the *what* and the *why* of consumer behavior.

Marketers and public policy experts have worked hard to find ways to explain the green consumer, someone who has a strong pro-environment attitude and expresses that attitude by enacting a set of green behaviors. Because of the increasing threat that global climate change presents, understanding the green consumer is an important step in transitioning to a more sustainable economy. In one study, a consumer panel of over 1,400 American consumers was constructed to find out what green consumers do and what they think. Thus, the focus was on both green behaviors and green attitudes (Englis and Phillips 2013) (see Chapter 7 for a refresher on attitudes).

The first set of questions focused on the behavioral patterns of green consumers. The most common green behaviors for Americans were switching off lights when leaving a room (82 percent), using lower-temperature washes in the washing machine (61 percent), and giving or receiving hand-me-downs (58 percent). Americans were not very likely to engage in the following kinds of behaviors: using public transportation, carpooling, or investing in socially responsible companies (only about 10 percent of panel participants engaged in these kinds of behaviors). Information like this is important because it allows marketers to better understand the vast array of green behaviors that consumers consider and enact. It further gives marketers detailed information about what behaviors are most likely to be enacted and provides clues as to how to influence green behaviors. Encouraging consumers to switch off lights might not result in a big increase in behaviors because 82 percent of consumers are doing it anyway. However, encouraging carpooling or the use of public transit might be a big

stretch for consumers. American consumers are well known for their love of cars, and these new behaviors may be too far outside their comfort zone at this time. Instead, it might be possible for marketers to successfully encourage consumers to purchase more green cleaning products (about 22 percent of the population already does this) (Englis and Phillips 2013).

Actual insights occur, however, when researchers dive a little deeper and try to discover why consumers perform these behaviors. When a research finding or discovery can be framed so that it is useful to marketing managers, they have uncovered an insight. This study constructed a panel designed to do just that. Among their other findings, researchers uncovered a fascinating pattern to the findings. Consumers who were more innovative in their way of thinking—they were willing to try new things and consider unique concepts—were much more likely than other consumers to take a green attitude and do something about it. That is, compared to other individuals who might have green attitudes but not do much about it, consumers with an innovative mindset were much more consistent in having green attitudes *and* green behaviors (Englis and Phillips 2013). This insight sparks many possibilities for marketing managers. First, marketers may want to target innovative consumers for their messaging. Innovative consumers are willing to try new things, some of which are outside their normal comfort zone. Thus, marketers may target people who are willing to take risks, who are not too brand loyal, and who like to engage in variety-seeking. A second way marketers may use this insight is by altering their core advertising message to be more innovation focused. For example, an advertiser could use messaging that discusses "challenging the status quo" or "pushing boundaries." An advertiser might want to use words such as *new, unique, creative,* and *innovative* (see Figure 9.2).

Consumer panels are incredibly useful in telling marketers what consumers do. Carefully constructed panels may even be able to help marketers develop important insights into why consumers behave as they do.

Figure 9.2 *Closing the Green Attitude/Behavior Gap*

Questions

1. As we learned in Chapter 7's discussion of attitudes, a consumer's attitude is supposed to lead to behavior that is consistent with that attitude.

Unfortunately, this is not always the case with green attitudes and behaviors. Refer to Chapter 7 and discuss why green attitudes might not always lead to green behavior.

2. Can a consumer who has an innovative mindset be brand loyal? Use the material in this chapter to defend your argument.

Source: Englis and Phillips (2013).

proportion of sales, and although marketing managers never like to lose a customer, they *really* don't want to lose one of *these* customers. Further, marketing managers may want to enact a strategy to convert some light customers to heavier users. For marketing managers who are dealing with lower ratios, a joint strategy may be better: keep the heavy users satisfied and attract new customers to the brand (Kim, Singh, and Winer 2017).

The law of buyer moderation

Over time, consumers don't generally continue to be either heavy users or light users of a product or brand. The **law of buyer moderation** suggests that, over time, light buyers tend to become heavier and heavier buyers tend to become lighter (Anschuetz 2002; Sharp 2010).

> **Law of buyer moderation** is the tendency for light buyers to become heavier and heavier buyers to become lighter.

Changes in a household's buying patterns can arise for all sorts of reasons—changes in the family's financial situation, family members moving in or out of the house, the overall economy, or even the weather. When the global coronavirus pandemic hit in 2020, household purchasing patterns were radically altered. While the reasons are manifold, smart marketers are in tune with the complexities of their target market, the industry, and the competition. This underscores the importance of understanding all kinds of customers, even noncustomers. Thus, while individual light consumers or nonconsumers within a mass market might deliver less profit for the brand, over time, they do deliver a large number of units sold, contributing significantly to revenue and profit. Later, these light consumers and nonconsumers might also turn into heavy users. Importantly, marketers must not assume that buying patterns that occurred in one year will be replicated the following year.

The duplication of purchases principle

As we have seen, for a variety of reasons, consumers often buy several brands within a given product category. Because consumers may have several favorite brands that form their consideration set, one brand's customers are another brand's customers too. Indeed, in most cases, a brand will share its customers with others in that category. In a given period, for example, at least 65 percent of UK consumers of Diet Coke, Fanta, and Pepsi also bought regular Coca-Cola (Sharp 2010). The **duplication of purchases principle** is the extent to which brands in a given category share their customers with other brands in that category (Sharp 2010). Since Coca-Cola and Pepsi are the two biggest brands in the category, all other brands compete with them. However, that does not necessarily mean that they share a lot of the same customers; sometimes the biggest brands in the category share customers and sometimes they do not. In the ice cream market, for example, Ben & Jerry's and Häagen Dazs share about twice the number of customers with each other as they do with other brands in the market (Sharp 2010). Findings like these suggest that marketers should exercise caution about concluding that their brand appeals to a customer segment that is unique and distinct from that of the competition. Instead, it is very likely that the brand appeals to several segments that have some similarities. Marketers can analyze panel data or scanner data to identify patterns of duplicated purchases. This information can be used by marketing managers to identify whether they have a particularly close competitor.

Influencing Consumer Behavior

Consumer panel data can be tremendously important in helping to develop a better understanding about what consumers do. After all, marketers must predict what consumers will do in a variety of situations. Now that we have a basic understanding of what consumers may do, marketers can use that information to help develop better strategies. The following section will discuss a variety of decisions that a marketer may need to make: segmenting customers, differentiating the brand, making the brand distinctive, encouraging greater engagement with the brand, and fostering relationships with the brand.

Segmenting customers

As we saw in the previous discussion, an analysis of heavy and light buyers can provide numerous insights into how marketers should segment the market. One way to segment the market based on behavior is by *purchase frequency*—for example, light users, medium users, or heavy users. Wawa, a convenience store chain on the east coast of the United States, segments its coffee market into light users (those who purchase one to four cups of coffee per month) and heavy users (those who purchase between thirty and sixty cups of coffee per month). This segmentation strategy helps decision-makers at Wawa create strategies to encourage light users to increase their purchases and heavy users to maintain their level of purchases.

Another way to segment the market based on behaviors is by *product use*—how is the product utilized by the customer? Take the example of shoes. One consumer may purchase a new pair of Nike shoes for working out; another customer might purchase the same shoes because they go with a certain outfit. Thus, one product may be used in different ways by different consumers. Segmenting by product use can be beneficial in creating better-targeted communications strategies toward these different segments. If one segment is interested in buying the Nikes for working out, the marketer would want to use messaging that talks about the functionality of the shoe. For a segment that would be interested in Nike as a fashion choice, a message focusing on style would be more warranted.

Marketers may sometimes find that their segments may not always match up with how consumers actually use products. Behavioral data also help managers better clarify and refine their segmentation categories. Going back to the example of shoes, many segmentation strategies divide consumers into those who are seeking athletic, casual, work, or dress shoes. What happens, however, when consumers defy the segmentation categories that marketers have created for them (see Photo 9.3)? Consumer panel data can help marketers create more precise segments that are more flexible and overlapping. These new segments acknowledge that consumers will purchase multiple brands, use products for different purposes, and have different levels of purchase and attitudinal loyalty. In the end, once marketers create better segmentation strategies, they will then be able to create better product, price, distribution, and promotional strategies (see Insights from the Field 9.2). Behavioral data are not only useful for decisions about the final marketing mix, however. Sometimes, these data can provide direction to the management team about appropriate responses to a crisis situation (see Insights from the Field 9.3).

Differentiation means that, from the consumer's standpoint, the brand must stand out as being different in some way from the competition.

Differentiating the brand

When buying a brand, to what extent does a consumer have to feel that there is something particularly different about it? If you were choosing between brands of ice cream, for example, does the ice cream brand need to be very different from the other brands for you to choose it? Perhaps it has special ingredients or unique flavors? Behavioral data can help marketers better understand how they might differentiate a brand for consumers. Aldi, for example, is a food retailer that does not stock national brands and was considered by 67 percent of consumers "different" from other supermarkets. Similarly, Subway, the sandwich-based fast-food brand, was viewed by 50 percent of consumers as different from competitors McDonald's, Domino's, and KFC (Romaniuk, Sharp, and Ehrenberg 2007). **Differentiation** means that, from the

● **Photo 9.3** *Consumers can sometimes defy the segmentation categories that marketers have created*

Do consumers buy more soup in the winter?

In the United States, consumers buy turkeys at Thanksgiving and hotdogs for Independence Day. In Italy, people eat panettone cakes at Christmas, and in Australia they throw meat—very often lamb—on the barbecue to celebrate the New Year. These items are seasonal purchases and their sales are generally highest at certain times of the year. For other kinds of products, the story is different. Even for near-stationary (or static) markets, where one would expect consistent levels of sales over the year, the time of year and the implementation of sales promotions will affect monthly sales. So, do consumers buy more soup in the winter? Some do; most do not. You might think that sales for soup would go up during the winter, and you would be right. Partially. An analysis of behavioral data found that the soup category has two distinct market segments. That is, while evidence shows that more soup is purchased in the winter than in the summer, this effect is driven by the behaviors of two segments of consumers within the soup market. The first segment purchases soup at a steady rate all year round; colder weather doesn't prompt them to purchase more soup. The second segment, however, purchases a lot of soup in the winter and very little in the summer (Wellan and Ehrenberg 1990). This finding was surprising to onlookers because the traditional view of this segment was simply that

consumers purchased soup year-round, but increased their purchases during the cold-weather season. Insights like these help marketing managers make decisions about when to advertise and how to deal with the off-season sales declines (Ehrenberg, Uncles, and Goodhardt 2004). By engaging in this type of behavioral analysis, managers can identify different market segments, better define and clarify those segments, and then develop appropriate marketing strategies.

Questions

1. Imagine that you are the marketing manager for another cold-weather product: hot chocolate. Further, imagine that you have two customer segments just like the ones described above. Create a marketing communications message to promote purchase loyalty for each of the two segments. Do the same to promote attitudinal loyalty for each segment.

2. How might marketers utilize their understanding of variety-seeking and habit-persistent consumers to build market share in a static market like soup? How would this change for a dynamic market?

Sources: Wellan and Ehrenberg (1990); Ehrenberg, Uncles, and Goodhardt (2004).

consumer's standpoint, the brand must stand out as being different in some way from the competition. Otherwise, there is little reason to buy one brand over another.

Some brands have done a fantastic job at differentiating themselves from their competitors. One such brand is Lush, the soap and makeup brand that offers a completely new retail experience to browse and shop for their ethically sourced products. Balls and cakes of soap are piled high in wooden displays and on antique-looking tables and trays. The sales staff is friendly and very accommodating in providing free samples. Indeed, the stores have a very warm and comforting feel to them. Buying soap from Lush is a different buying experience than buying soap anywhere else. Another brand that has successfully differentiated itself from the competition is T-Mobile. Let's face it, a lot of companies offer cellular services. T-Mobile is different, however, because it appeals to hip, young people who don't want to be tied down to a long-term plan with limits on data and roaming. T-Mobile also offers an easy way for consumers to get out of their existing cellular contracts so that they can switch to T-Mobile. Being a customer of T-Mobile is a different experience than being a customer of another cellular company (see Photo 9.4).

Marketers sometimes attempt to achieve differentiation by price, but this is sometimes difficult because, within a competitive set, prices of brands will be fairly similar. Marketers often use price-related promotions in the hope that they will appeal to potential customers of the brand, but their long-term impact on sales is questionable. One study that examined 150 promotions in Britain, Germany, Japan, and the United States found that there were no sales increases following the promotion and very few new buyers. In addition, repeat buying did not increase following the promotion. In the end, price promotions primarily encourage existing consumers to stock up on the product (Ehrenberg, Hammond, and Goodhardt 1994).

Experts suggest that differentiation is important for achieving a long-term strategic competitive advantage in the marketplace (cf. Porter 1985). Differentiating the brand could occur in two ways. First, the brand should perform better than the competition on an attribute that is important to consumers. Perhaps it has a better user interface (Apple), has superior customer service (Zappos), or has an excellent record of safety (BMW). As long as the brand performs better on these attributes and communicates this advantage to customers, it has a good chance of becoming differentiated in the minds of consumers. Unfortunately, one drawback to the differentiation strategy is that it can usually be easily copied, especially in service businesses, so the organization must be ready to consistently outperform the competition on this attribute. A second way that differentiation can occur is by connecting consumer

● **Photo 9.4** *T-Mobile is perceived as being different from its competitors*

CEOs behaving badly: Does it change consumer attitudes and behaviors?

In the summer of 2018, managers at pizza giant Papa John's, the world's fourth largest pizza chain, were hoping for something to help their months-long record of stagnant and slumping sales (Papa John's is the third largest pizza company in the United States [Pizza Today 2018]). Stock prices were down 30 percent and same-store sales were down 5.3 percent. Why the big drop? Experts attributed the move away from Papa John's to two main things. First, there was increased competition from delivery services such as Grubhub, which offered home delivery from a wide variety of restaurants. Suddenly, pizza wasn't just one of a few foods that offered home delivery. Second, Papa John's received praise from several white supremist groups when its founder and chief executive officer (CEO) John Schnatter blamed players in the NFL and their protests for racial justice for a slump in pizza sales (Papa John's is a sponsor of the NFL). Papa John's quickly responded that it did not want support from such groups, but not before the company was roasted on social media and by late-night comedians. In May 2018, things got much worse. In a conference call with the company's ad agency, Schnatter used an offensive racial slur ("the n-word"). During the call, Schnatter complained that Colonel Sanders was able to use the word and not get into any public relations trouble. In July 2018, when the news broke about the meeting, there was immediate backlash from customers and others. In the age of increased awareness of the need for racial and social justice, these kinds of behaviors are simply not tolerated. Several consumer groups boycotted the brand, Major League Baseball canceled a planned promotion with the company, a local gym removed its Papa John's sign from the building, and the ad agency announced it was ending its relationship with the company. Stock prices immediately dropped by 5 percent when the news hit and, within twenty-four hours, Schnatter resigned (Hsu 2018).

Were customers shifting away from Papa John's because of a change in attitudes or were they just trying out other brands in their repertoire? The answer is unclear. Papa John's main competitors are Pizza Hut, Domino's, and Little Caesars (Photo 9.5). Papa John's was already experiencing a long slump in sales, which indicates that customers were moving to other alternatives, including other food delivery options or other pizza options. There is some indication, however, that the attitudes for some consumers did change. First, a series of blogs, hashtags, and Facebook pages were created to encourage consumers to boycott the company. Many of the postings complained about the poor quality of the pizza and many were simply upset with the company and the CEO. Second, the market share for Domino's pizza increased at the same time Papa John's decreased, indicating that consumers were indeed shifting to Domino's and away from Papa John's (CNBC 2018). So, it seems probable that attitudes changed as well as behaviors.

● **Photo 9.5** *For many consumers, Domino's, Pizza Hut, Little Caesars, and Papa John's make up a repertoire of brands.*

The Papa John's example is an extreme example of how consumers could be outraged about the behavior of a company and its CEO and then exhibit that displeasure by changing their attitudes about the company and their purchase behaviors. What is abundantly clear in this case is that stakeholders were concerned enough about the public backlash that they pushed senior-level executives to make the bold, decisive move to ask for Schnatter's resignation. Not all scenarios are as clear-cut. Indeed, we know that attitudes can influence behaviors and behaviors can influence attitudes. In the Papa John's case, it is possible that consumers changed their attitudes first and then changed their behaviors—they did not like the behaviors of the company or perhaps they did not like the pizza—and then changed their behaviors and purchased another brand. It is also possible that consumers changed their behavior and then their attitudes—they shifted away from Papa John's and then justified that move by altering their opinions about the quality of the product and/or the behavior of the company. Once again, a careful observation of behavioral data and an understanding of the context in which it occurs is essential to drawing accurate conclusions about what is motivating consumers.

In examining patterns of buyer behavior over time, marketers will inevitably find that even highly loyal buyers of a brand will try other brands from time to time. Why does this happen? Remember that consumer behavior is the outcome of many years of experience; the underlying brand beliefs and evaluations that form the building blocks of attitudes stay fairly constant over time (Ehrenberg, Uncles, and Goodhardt 2004). Because of this, a consumer's past behavior is often the best predictor of his or her future behavior. It would be a mistake to conclude that consumers have drastically different attitudes toward different brands. Instead, it is far more likely that, within a given product category, a consumer's attitude about one brand is not that different from that of another brand (Barwise and Ehrenberg 1985). This suggests that when faced with a case in which a CEO is behaving badly, customers may express their displeasure by substituting another brand from their repertoire. In the case of Papa John's, these consumers were not willing to give up pizza, but they *were* willing buy it from a different company.

Questions

1. The case of a CEO behaving badly is not new. Find another example of a CEO's actions landing him or her in trouble. How did consumers react? Were consumer attitudes or behaviors changed in any way? How? Discuss.
2. We know that a consumer's attitudes are built from a set of attribute beliefs and evaluations (see Chapter 7 for a refresher). When faced with a scandal like the one at Papa John's, how could the marketing team work to influence and improve consumer attitudes by altering their beliefs and evaluations? Be specific.

Sources: Barwise and Ehrenberg (1985); CNBC (2018); Ehrenberg, Uncles, and Goodhardt (2004); Hsu (2018).

values to the organization's values. Hopefully, the organization will have a clear and compelling set of values by which it operates. If these values are in line with what the customer believes and holds dear, the customer might also perceive an important point of differentiation. Take the example of Southwest Airlines, the company that stands out from its competitors for treating its passengers with courtesy and dignity. To back up that set of values, it will take a passenger's first *two* checked bags for free. Their "Transfarency" campaign famously claimed that "we don't dream up ways we can trick you into paying more" (Chew 2015). Meaningful differentiation communicates the values and purpose of the company—it's not just about *what* the company does, but also about *why* the company does what it does (Breindel 2017).

Making the brand distinctive

Distinctive brands have unique colors, logos, tag lines, or celebrities that are associated with the brand.

A brand should also be **distinctive** so that customers are able to spot it and recognize it. A brand that is distinctive has unique colors, logos, tag lines, or celebrities that are associated with the brand. Critical for the marketer is that the customer identifies the brand and that this activates or reinforces the customer's memory of the brand, thus making it easier to choose. Coca-Cola has at least two very distinctive elements to its brand. The first is the curvy-shaped bottle. The second is the white Coca-Cola script that appears on its packaging and marketing materials. Regardless of where you see it, it is immediately recognizable as a Coca-Cola product (see Photo 9.6).

Similarly, anyone who has traveled to New York City will recognize its distinctive "I Love New York" branding campaign (see Photo 9.7). To succeed in distinctiveness, the brand must be unique; it cannot be mistaken for any other brand. It also must be everywhere so that when consumers see it, they will retrieve the memories and emotions that they identify and connect with the brand. This inevitably means a lot of investment in communicating to the consumer over time. The "I Love New York" campaign was launched in 1977 when the New York State Department of Commerce decided it need a public relations campaign to improve the city's poor image. Today, the more than fifty-nine million tourists who visit New York each year can find the logo on anything. In fact, it would be difficult to find an object that does not have the logo emblazoned on it! The key to the success of the campaign is

that it has transcended the simple message of affection and love for a city. It also evokes strong emotions and the spirit of New York (Klara 2017).

A small note of caution is warranted here with respect to differentiation and distinctiveness. For most purchase situations, it is quite difficult to have product attributes that are very different or distinct from that of the competition. Indeed, as discussed earlier, products in a given repertoire (or consideration set) are generally not that different or distinct in performance, attributes, or price. Regardless, it is still necessary for marketers to advertise their brand so that consumers are reminded of it and it stays in their consideration set. What *is* necessary is that the brand is remembered. Perhaps counterintuitively, the job may be easier for brands that are closer to and therefore more substitutable by other brands. Why? Because advertising might be more effective at shifting small behaviors than at influencing bigger behaviors. For example, a consumer might switch from Frosted Flakes to Cheerios, but will probably not make the bigger switch to eggs or breakfast bars. Therefore, at least in the short term, advertising might be more effective in nudging behavior than impacting more extreme behavioral change (Ehrenberg, Barnard, and Scriven 1997). With regard to differentiation and distinctiveness, what matters is that, over time, consumers connect meaning with that brand, such that a particular message, product attribute, or product package can trigger the same memories and emotions as the brand itself.

Gamification is a method that uses a variety of gaming tactics to increase consumer engagement.

Encouraging greater engagement with the brand

Did you know that your attention span is about the same as that of a goldfish? Yes, Canadian researchers have found that the typical person has an attention span of only about eight seconds. A goldfish, by the way, has a nine-second attention span (McSpadden 2015). Given this fact, it is incredibly difficult for a marketer to not only attract a consumer's attention, but also keep it. Although there are many ways to engage consumers in the brand, one relatively new and fun strategy that marketers have used is **gamification**, which utilizes gaming tactics like "competition, rewards, status, achievement, socialization, and learning" (Boykiv 2015). Schools, hospitals, and a host of other organizations and companies are encouraging consumers to interact with their brands on a more consistent basis as well as on a deeper level. Reminders are sent periodically to users if they haven't played the game in a while, and when they do play, they often end up playing for a few minutes at a time. If a game can encourage a customer to interact with and play with a brand for a few minutes, the marketer has succeeded in connecting more closely with that consumer. Consider the example of Pez, the maker of Pez candies and Pez dispensers, which was founded in 1927 in Austria. Today, Pez is in more than eighty countries around the world (Pez – the Company 2020). Customers can download the free Pez app and play a variety of games to earn points. New games are unlocked by scanning codes on candy packages. The games are designed for kids as well as adults; the point is to connect new interactive technology with the traditional values of the brand. The game also seeks to connect people across locations and generations (see Photos 9.8 and 9.9).

● **Photo 9.8** *Pez eight-pack fruit candy with keys to unlock games*

● **Photo 9.9** *Pez has a highly interactive game designed to engage customers*

This chapter is about understanding, tracking, and predicting behaviors, and games allow marketers to do just that. Games encourage consumers to engage in a variety of behaviors such as reading about the brand, watching video content, earning points or badges, and connecting with other like-minded consumers. Personalized interactions are designed to appeal to a consumer's vanity, and interactions that remember and adapt as the customer plays the game add excitement and challenge to the game. In addition to the increase in engagement, there are many other more tangible benefits for the company. First, marketers have the chance to gather more data about the customer—data such as what they swipe through, what they tap on, and what topics they spend some more time with. Second, marketers have the opportunity to introduce new product options, explore brand extensions, and test new product concepts. In addition, the greater engagement created by the game provides the opportunity to cross-sell items to consumers who may have never considered such options. Third, games can encourage visits to brick-and-mortar stores because some games provide special rewards that are only redeemable at an actual location. This increases foot traffic and also increases the opportunity for additional sales. Gaming works particularly well with millennials, who like to play games and are quite tech-savvy. Regardless of a customer's age, however, a game offers an interesting value proposition to the user—invest your time and attention and in return you will have your interest sparked, have some fun, and have a chance to earn rewards or prizes. See Insights from the Boardroom 9 for a discussion of how engagement has been increased for fans of the Denver Broncos!

Fostering relationships with the brand

As seen in Insights from the Boardroom 9, a careful examination of patterns of behavior can provide insights about how managers might encourage deeper relationships with the brand. Branding strategies are designed to keep consumers loyal to the brand. This is often backed by creative advertising that reminds them about new and different brands. Ample evidence suggests that consumer behaviors are largely low involvement and a function of habit, dependent on what brands are familiar and readily available (Sharp 2010). In addition, there is plenty of evidence to show that brand image impacts a consumer's choice of brand, but even the leading brand in a market with strong brand images will, for most consumers, be just one brand in their repertoire. Therefore, media strategies need to maximize reach and keep reminding customers of their presence (Sharp et al. 2012).

Some consumers do form stronger connections with brands and, even though they purchase other brands, they experience strong feelings toward their favorite brands. Some consumers even like to connect with other like-minded consumers over their shared affection for their brand (Schau and Muniz 2002; Casaló, Flavián, and Guinalíua 2008). Indeed, many consumers are passionate about brands that are dear to them. The most often cited examples are Apple (Muniz and Schau 2005) and Harley-Davidson (Schouten and McAlexander 1995).

As we discussed earlier in this chapter, brand loyalty can be described as either purchase loyalty (where consumers habitually purchase the brand) or attitudinal loyalty (where consumers have a positive attitude toward the brand). A brand relationship is somewhat different from both concepts. A **brand relationship** occurs when a deeper level of connection is forged between the self and the brand, such that the connection grows and develops in a way that is similar to a personal relationship. Consumers develop deep feelings of affection, liking, and even love for the brand (Fournier and Yao 1997). Brand relationships can be described in a variety of ways, but one way is to distinguish them as falling into the following categories: brand affinity, brand love, and brand addiction.

Brand relationship occurs when a deeper level of connection is forged between the self and the brand, such that the relation grows and develops in a way that is similar to a personal relationship.

Brand Affinity

Brand affinity occurs when there is a strong emotional tie between the brand and the consumer. Consumers don't just buy Apple products because of a rational assessment about the performance of the product; they buy the products because they genuinely like the brand and feel a connection to the product, the brand, and the company. From a relationship standpoint, we could say that this would be the *friendship* phase of a relationship. The consumer likes spending time with and interacting with the brand.

Brand affinity occurs when there is a strong emotional tie between the brand and the consumer.

From an ethical standpoint, marketers must walk a fine line between attracting consumers to their brand and being responsible corporate citizens. Take the example of marketers who work with products like sugar-based cereals and fast food. With childhood obesity on the rise, marketers must be careful. Concerns raised by parents about strong-arm advertising tactics are understandable, especially when ads stretch the limits in how they depict product appearance and performance. One study using consumer panel data found that the more an advertiser spends on traditional advertising, such as TV and print, the greater the degree of brand affinity for children. The top five brands most popular among children were McDonald's, Coca-Cola, Oreo, M&M's, and Pringles. Perhaps not coincidentally, these are also the brands that spend the most on advertising to children (Kim, Williams, and Wilcox 2016).

Brand love

Going one step further, **brand love** describes a passionate emotional attachment to a particular brand (Carroll and Ahuvia 2006). Just like the love you might feel for your partner, with brand love, you think about this brand, you prefer this brand over all others, and you enjoy the time you spend with the brand. When a person experiences brand love, there are two distinct marketing-related benefits. First, the consumer has higher levels of both purchase loyalty and attitudinal loyalty. They always prefer their brand and will

Brand love is stronger than brand affinity and describes a passionate emotional attachment to a particular brand.

Marketing for the Denver Broncos: easiest job in the National Football League?

● *Dennis Moore*

Some jobs are easy. When your job is to fill a stadium with throngs of happy fans and you have had decades of sellout games, your job is pretty easy. That's what a lot of people think. But they're wrong. Meet Dennis Moore, the senior vice president of sales and marketing for the Denver Broncos. Moore has worked in professional sports for more than twenty years and has been with the Broncos for more than fifteen years. Although he is in a position that many NFL franchises would envy, Moore keeps busy finding ways to deepen relationships with fans and soon-to-be fans. It all starts with a careful analysis of patterns of behavior.

The NFL itself does a lot of the heavy lifting with the marketing of its franchises. Over the preseason and regular season, the Broncos brand is seen in homes all around the country on twenty separate occasions each fall. That leaves the teams substantial leverage to create and implement their own marketing strategies. "The Broncos are widely regarded as one of the great brands in sports and the NFL," claims Moore, who utilizes a wide variety of research techniques to find out what

Broncos fans think and do. "Across the Rocky Mountain Region, the Broncos are the #1 team. This is across a variety of measures including Facebook likes, etc. We're the #1 liked team in our geographic area." According to their research firm, a "fan" is "someone who has watched, attended, or listened to one of your games in the last 12 months. In Colorado, that figure is 75%! That's the highest of any other team—we control a lot of the mindshare of this market," says Moore (2018).

These positive results come with a downside. Unfortunately, not everyone who is a fan can attend a game because the games are always sold out—home games have been sold out since the 1970s—and even when fans can get access to tickets, the price is often prohibitive. Moore observes, "The difference between marketing for sports and marketing for a consumer product is that a very small percentage of our fans will ever be able to attend a game. Think about it, on an annual basis, we can welcome 750,000 fans to our park. Compare that to baseball where they can have 3 million people attend their home games on an annual basis." Even though 750,000 seats in a season might seem like a lot of "product," there is simply not enough to meet the demand.

So, what can marketing managers do when a big proportion of consumers can't actually consume the product, as in the case of the Denver Broncos? Moore believes the key is to market the Broncos as more of a lifestyle brand and build relationships with fans. "We see our role in marketing as more of a content and social media brand. We curate and distribute all of our content; all of that is done by us in-house. That's how we directly form relationships with our fan base. It's much less about a purchase. We don't have inventory to sell. Our perspective is how do we connect fans to the brand in an authentic way? That engagement is a huge part of what we do," observes Moore.

The first step is building the brand's identity. "We want to be a first-class brand—the Mercedes Benz or the BMW of the NFL. We want to do everything in a first-class manner, and we want to be transparent," notes Moore. The positioning of the Broncos as a *luxury brand* is different from how other brands position themselves. "The Ravens, for example, are very different—they're very tough with more of a hard-working, blue-collar appeal. We, on the other hand, want to be about family, first-class, community," observed Moore (2018). The second step is building initiatives to strengthen relationships. Moore is currently working on two big initiatives. The first is multicultural marketing, which is especially important in a market like Colorado, where more than 21 percent of the population is Latinx. The second is youth marketing, to get more kids excited about the Broncos.

- *Multicultural marketing.* "The Hispanic/Latinx community is growing all the time—by 2050, population estimates predict that one in three Americans will be Latinx. We see this as our life-blood over time so the brand needs to be accessible and engaging," notes Moore (2018). Within this initiative, there are two important priorities. Priority number one is accessibility. All the games and content must be accessible in English and in Spanish, in an effort to engage all fans, regardless of language preference. Priority number 2 is that there must be events and access to the brand with the Hispanic community. "We have a bilingual staff. Many of our people are from or have ties to those cultures and have a deep cultural understanding of what it means to be Hispanic/Latinx. We have events where we invite families to come to the stadium, meet the players, and cheer. It's all in Spanish. We have some ratings information and attendance numbers and it's growing all the time," said Moore (2018).
- *Targeting the youth market.* For the youth market, the priority is to engage kids early and turn them into lifelong Broncos fans. An NFL survey shows that avid fans first become fans in elementary school or earlier. This has been a challenge recently. It is well known that if you grew up playing football, you'll be a fan of the NFL. "This also works with kids who play flag football or are into gaming, like Madden Player—66% of 6–11 year olds list gaming as their main source of entertainment. A problem recently for us is that participation in youth football is down; parents are less inclined

to let their kids play," said Moore. Another issue is that "Denver is the #1 fastest growing city in the country which means that fewer and fewer people are actually *from* Colorado and fewer kids are 'born' Broncos fans." So, how can Moore and his team engage these kids and turn them into lifelong Broncos fans? It all starts in the beginning, so to speak. Every baby who is born at any hospital in Broncos Country is offered a special birth certificate and a beanie with the team colors. Later, "Orange Fridays" happen at school, where the kids are encouraged to wear Broncos colors. The team has an affinity club for kids, a magazine, events, giveaways, and interactive online games. The Broncos recently partnered with the local dairy council in a "Fuel Up to Play 60" initiative where kids are encouraged to eat healthy, drink milk, and get active for sixty minutes each day. "Data on this program says that kids are much more engaged with the players and brand when they are encouraged using this approach compared to when they are encouraged by their pediatrician to do the same thing," reported Moore (2018).

In building stronger relationships, the Broncos "want to be authentic and first-class. We don't do traditional marketing. Three quarters of the people around here are already fans and we're already top of mind. We want to create authentic experiences to engage them and we believe this is far better than traditional media approaches or models," said Moore. What is the return on investment on all of these initiatives? "Sure, we have numbers on the attendance at our different events. But for us, the return on investment is that one person who says that because of us, they got up off the couch and did something. That's our payback!"

even forego a purchase if their own brand is not available. Second, the consumer will engage in positive word of mouth; they will speak out about and recommend the brand to others (Carroll and Ahuvia 2006).

The love that some people have for the Harry Potter franchise is undeniable. J. K. Rowling's series of books about a young wizard fighting off the forces of evil with his friends at his back has captured the imaginations and hearts of millions of fans around the world. The Wizarding World of Harry Potter opened in Orlando, Florida, in 2010 and, because of its success, two more theme parks were soon opened in Los Angeles, California, and Osaka, Japan. One economist estimated that the Harry Potter franchise is worth $5.24 billion to the UK economy. More than 450 million copies of the book in seventy-nine languages have been sold. Interest continues to remain strong; ten wands are purchased every minute and three costumes are purchased every hour on eBay. In total, eBay racked up $3.3 million worth of Harry Potter–related items in 2016 (Cox 2017). It is not unusual for consumers to make brands a permanent part of their lives and even their bodies. One particularly passionate fan spent two years planning the details of a full-sleeve Harry Potter tattoo. He felt a personal connection to the story of Harry, who had to overcome hardships, and he shared a deep connection to the values of the story, such as honesty, loyalty, and honor. This fan carefully selected each image, its placement, and a tattoo artist who was also an ardent fan. He believed that the selection of the artist was especially important to ensure that the tattoo was done carefully and with the utmost respect to the characters and the story (see Photo 9.10).

● **Photo 9.10** *Harry Potter tattoos*

Brand addiction

A somewhat new concept to marketing and consumer research, brand addiction describes still another type of relationship that a consumer can forge with a brand. With **brand addiction**, there is a mental and behavioral preoccupation with the brand, the consumer experiences almost uncontrollable urges to possess any new product from the brand, and once the brand is acquired, the consumer experiences positive emotions (Cui, Mrad, and Hogg 2018). Brand addiction is distinguished from other addictions to drugs or alcohol, because there is no chemical dependency. However, they are similar in that there are very strong mental and emotional drives that can only be satisfied by acquisition of the brand. A consumer would be addicted to a brand if, for example, that person was impatient to get the brand, followed the news about the brand, and allocated a certain amount of money each month to purchasing his or her favorite brand (Mrad and Cui 2017). Although marketers want consumers to form close relationships with their brands and maybe even feel like they can't do without the brand, no responsible marketer would be in favor of consumers taking this connection too far. Indeed, there is sometimes a "dark side" to consumer behavior when a consumer becomes addicted to behaviors such as gambling, plastic surgery, exercise, video games, or hoarding. Responsible consumer researchers want to know the triggers for these addictive behaviors so that they can help these consumers break the cycle of addiction and get on to the road to recovery.

See Insights from the Field 9.4 to learn about shopper marketing and to see how some retailers are trying to forge closer relationships with millennials.

Brand addiction is an unhealthy mental and behavioral preoccupation with the brand in which the consumer experiences almost uncontrollable urges to possess any new product from the brand, and once the brand is acquired, the consumer experiences positive emotions.

Shopper marketing is a research perspective that focuses on what consumers do by examining purchase data, observing how consumers interact with a product, and analyzing consumer panel data.

INSIGHTS FROM THE FIELD 9.4

This is not your mother's retail store

The concept of shopper marketing is gaining headway for many marketers in the early twenty-first century. Indeed, in today's fast-paced world where consumers change their minds and behaviors quickly, there is sometimes very little time to find out why consumers do what they do. Rather than focusing on the *why*, researchers who focus on **shopper marketing** examine what consumers do by looking at purchase data, observing how consumers interact with a product, and analyzing consumer panel data. Researchers have found that the shopping experience has changed dramatically since your parents' days. The stimulus for many changes to the retail environment comes from millennial consumers, who are tech-savvy, impatient to get the product,

and looking for a deal. A few statistics should be cause for concern for any retail manager (Stanley 2016):

- Over the next decade, millennial consumers are expected to spend $65 billion on consumer packaged goods.
- A full 72 percent of Americans are alarmed about how much information retailers have about them.

Taken together, there is enormous economic potential in meeting the needs of young, tech-savvy customers, but the data that can be used to help meet those needs must be used carefully and safeguarded by retailers. Experts predict that these forces will combine in the next decade and will push the issue of convenience to

(continued)

the forefront for many young, tech-savvy consumers. In the retail environment, that means technology needs to be thoroughly integrated into the entire retail experience. Here are four notable insights that researchers have identified to help retailers provide twenty-first century consumers the convenience they seek.

1. *Digitally enable your customers*—it should be no surprise that customers want easy search, check-out, and payment options on their mobile devices. When the entire experience is highly interactive and personalized, consumers will appreciate the convenience of the experience even more (Deloitte 2020).

2. *Revisit your product strategy*—realize that customers will not tolerate "out of stock" or "on back-order" situations when they are buying products at retail. After all, if the store doesn't have the item, they can easily get it online from another vendor. On the flip side, carrying a lot of inventory can be very costly for a retailer, so better data collection and prediction software is needed to find that perfect balance of readily accessible stock and very little overstock (Deloitte 2020).

3. *Up your game in brick-and-mortar*—stores are more than just stores in the twenty-first century. Although digital shopping is grabbing a bigger share of the consumer wallet, stores are still an indispensable part of delivering products to consumers. Importantly, retail allows consumers to explore and discover new offerings in a way that is still difficult to achieve in the digital environment. In addition, retail offers opportunities for a firm to further demonstrate its values through immersive displays and knowledgeable salespeople. Outdoor retailers REI and Cabella's are great examples of this. Finally, real-time technology offers the chance for salespeople to be empowered to meet the needs of consumers. The retail environment can thus provide convenience to the consumer by providing a place to explore, learn about, and interact with products (Deloitte 2020).

4. *Deliver on your promise via the supply chain*—retailers can ensure that they offer convenience to consumers by using a variety of GPS-synched and networked technologies. This allows retailers to ensure quick delivery and fulfillment with a variety of innovations. One innovation is real-time, flexible inventory and delivery software which enhances delivery accuracy. Another innovation is the establishment of several small closely-located urban distribution centers. In contrast to massive distribution centers that are often located hours away in rural areas, these smaller networked distribution centers ensure quick and convenient delivery (Deloitte 2020).

Questions

1. Shopper marketing focuses on the *what*, not the *why*, of consumer behavior. What are some benefits to this approach? What are some limitations?

2. How might a consumer develop a relationship with a retail store? Do you have a relationship with a retail store? How might technology be used to forge a stronger connection between a customer and a retail store? Discuss.

Sources: Deloitte (2020); Stanley (2016)

In the previous section, we discussed three categories of relationships that a consumer might forge with a brand. In the following paragraphs, we will discuss ways in which a marketer can attempt to facilitate connections and build stronger, more meaningful relationships with the brand. Behavioral data can often be combined with other data on a consumer's attitudes, beliefs, and feelings. Remember that we are treating a brand relationship as if it is similar to a personal relationship. The goal is for customers to like to spend time with the product and interact with the product because they enjoy it and receive benefits for doing so.

1. *Establish a learning relationship with the customer.* Just as two people learn more about one another as their relationship progresses, it is important for a marketer to learn about the customer, especially if that individual has been a customer for some time. Marketers can invite customers to share their stories, test a new version of the product, or preview a new ad campaign. Because these customers are already well versed in the product and its attributes, they will be able to provide insights that may have never been considered by the marketing team. Importantly, a marketer should be sure to incorporate that advice into changes in the product or delivery of the product. Consumers want to see that the company listened to them and incorporated some of their suggestions. When one Tesla customer tweeted about a problem with the car's software, CEO Elon Musk replied—within thirty minutes—that the issue would be addressed in the car's next software update (Joyce 2018).

2. *Engage them, engage them, engage them.* Each touchpoint should be a chance to further engage the customer (each time a customer comes in contact with the brand or its message is called a touchpoint). A smart marketer will be sure to offer chances to further engage with each and every touchpoint. For example, a customer could be asked to answer three short questions at the end of a service encounter or redirected to see an extended version of a new TV ad campaign. Although a marketer will need to walk a fine line between irritating customers and engaging them, each customer touchpoint is an opportunity for further engagement.

3. *Remember your customers.* There are few things more frustrating than trying to speak with a live person when you're making a call to a company's customer service line. The frustration can hit critical levels if the customer has to explain the problem multiple times to multiple people. Marketers can demonstrate their respect for a customer's time by carefully listening and recording what happened each time contact is made. Technology allows marketers to easily access caller ID information and instantly pull that customer's records before a call is even picked up. The concept of remembering customers extends beyond service encounters. Retailers are now using apps and GPS technology to identify customers when they enter their stores and pull up their complete purchase history with the brand.

4. *Treat them like the individuals they are.* Customers don't just want to be recognized and remembered; they want to be acknowledged and treated like individuals. Marketers have vast amounts of data on previous purchases and can draw conclusions about these customers, such as family size, age of family members, and likely income levels. Using behavioral data to create finely targeted promotions not only acknowledges that each individual is unique, but also makes it more likely that the promotion will resonate with that customer.

5. *Never, ever, sell customer data.* The data the marketer collects about customers comprise an incredibly rich resource that took significant

time, money, and effort to obtain. The data provided to the company were provided voluntarily and customers may feel that a breach of trust has occurred if they find out their data have been sold. Further, the data an organization has gathered on its customers can be an incredible source of competitive advantage that should not be seen by competitors. If used correctly, the data will provide deep insights into what motivates customers and what makes them tick. These data should be protected and utilized to help develop stronger relationships with the most valuable person in the organization: the customer.

Check out Insights from the Field 9.5 to see how one Swiss retailer used data to help solve an especially perplexing problem about pricing and organic food.

INSIGHTS FROM THE FIELD 9.5

When higher prices lead to higher sales

It seems illogical that higher prices will lead to higher levels of sales, but that's what happened when Swiss retailer Migros (pronounced "me-gro") expanded its line of ecofriendly products. Migros has a wide variety of retail and commercial operations, including home improvement stores, garden centers, electronics stores, household goods, clothing stores, hotels, amusement parks, and learning centers. The biggest part of its business, however, is the large number of grocery stores it runs throughout the country. Migros is the largest retailer in Switzerland and the largest private employer in Switzerland, and the company enjoys an extremely high level of positive attitudes and goodwill among the population. Rather than having contracts with wholesalers and other "middlemen," the company deals directly with manufacturers and is therefore able to keep prices low for its 2.2 million customers (Dun & Bradstreet 2020, Phillips 2013). Consumers really like Migros.

The question about what to do about ecofriendly products and their pricing began with a series of customer complaints. Consumers were asking for more ecofriendly options at the grocery store, such as organic, genetically modified organism–free, and sustainably sourced choices. Migros, like a good corporate citizen, responded to these customer requests and expanded its line of ecofriendly options, but sales soon plummeted. In trying to determine why consumers were not purchasing the ecofriendly options they had asked for, researchers constructed a 3,600-person consumer panel and asked these consumers to respond to a series of questions.

What the researchers found was quite interesting because it showed that consumers seemed to base their purchase decisions on the information that was available at the point of purchase. First, when consumers were given minimal information (just the price and origin of the product), consumers made their purchase decisions based on price. Just 22 percent of customers purchased the ecofriendly product. Because many ecofriendly products are more expensive to produce than traditionally raised products, they are generally a little more expensive for consumers. Therefore, this first finding was not surprising. Next, when the retailer offered detailed information on the ecofriendly product at the point of purchase (such as that it had not been sprayed with pesticides and was free of genetically modified organisms), consumers learned that there was a rationale for the product's higher price and many agreed that the benefits were worth it. Thus, when consumers read the in-store signage describing the benefits of the ecofriendly options, sales surged, with a full 77 percent of customers purchasing the ecofriendly product. The conclusion was that offering extra information provided consumers with a justification for the higher price of ecofriendly products.

Questions

1. Have you ever had the intention to buy something (either online or at the store) but then purchased something else because of what you experienced in the immediate purchase environment? Describe at least two examples of when you purchased something different from what you intended in both the online environment and the retail environment. For each example, describe how marketing tactics may have been used to alter your behavior.

2. In the Migros example, when consumers changed their behaviors and purchased the ecofriendly products, do you think their attitudes also changed? Discuss in detail.

3. Consumers clearly have a brand affinity and maybe even a brand love for Migros. What could a retail company like Migros do to strengthen that relationship bond?

Source: Meise et al. (2014).

👁 Summary

This chapter was organized into two sections: tracking buying behavior and influencing consumer behavior. Its focus was a bit of a departure from the chapters in this book that focus on the underlying mechanisms that drive behavior. Instead, this chapter started at the end point, so to speak, and attempted to assess behaviors first. Data and information about buyer behavior then allowed us to peel back the layers on some fascinating consumption motivations and recommend several strategic steps a marketer could take. *Repeat buying* habits and the implications for *brand loyalty* were examined. We also introduced the concepts of *purchase frequency*, *market penetration*, and *market share*. We concluded that market penetration and market share were two of the most important indicators of performance for a brand. Bigger brands have greater numbers of customers who purchase more often; smaller brands have fewer customers who purchase less often. This double jeopardy effect makes it particularly hard for smaller brands to succeed in the marketplace.

Throughout the chapter, we provided numerous examples from *consumer panel data* to illustrate the importance of using these data to track buyer behaviors. In doing so, we found that the data can provide critical information about *purchase frequency*, *the nature of the market*, and *explaining why consumers buy*. We also identified three separate principles or laws that can help to explain general tendencies and patterns of behavior: the Pareto principle, the law of buyer motivation, and the duplication of purchases principle.

We found that there are different *types of brand loyalty, purchase loyalty* and *attitudinal loyalty*, each of which has different implications for marketers. Specifically, purchase loyalty results in higher market share, while attitudinal loyalty allows a marketer to charge a higher price for the product. *Light and heavy buyers of the brand* were found to have their own distinct patterns of behavior and these purchase patterns likely change over time.

In the second half of the chapter, we focused our analysis on how marketers could take some of the information they obtained from behavioral data to develop strategies to influence consumer behavior. Detailed discussions ensued about *segmenting the brand*, *differentiating the brand*, *making the brand distinctive*, *encouraging greater engagement with the brand*, and *fostering relationships with the brand*. Insights from the Boardroom 9 discussed how the Denver Broncos fostered deeper relationships with its brand by segmenting the market and creating customized strategies designed to meet the needs of two important segments.

In discussing the *types of relationships* consumers could have with a brand, we found that three types could be described: brand affinity, brand love, and brand addiction. We acknowledged that although a marketing manager will often try to foster stronger relationships between the brand and consumers, sometimes a line can be crossed where that relationship is harmful (brand addiction), and responsible marketers will do what they can to curb such occurrences. Finally, to wrap up the section on influencing consumer behaviors, several methods were discussed that may help a marketer *facilitate stronger, more meaningful relationships* with consumers. The case of Migros in Insights from the Field 9.5 was used to illustrate the importance of using behavioral data, engaging with customers, and finding ways to implement their suggestions.

In the end, the tracking of buyer behavior is a fascinating exercise. It sometimes provides surprises, as in the case of Migros, where sales of eco-friendly products jumped when the prices remained high but more point-of-purchase information was provided. Buyer behavior data can sometimes give marketers information they don't want to hear, such as that heavy buyers generally buy less over time (the law of buyer moderation) or that buyers often split their loyalty among a repertoire of brands (the duplication of purchases principle). Tracking behavioral data also allows marketers to develop insights into what motivates consumers to do what they do—when this happens, marketers can develop creative strategies to influence consumer behaviors.

KEY TERMS

attitudinal loyalty p. 328
brand addiction p. 345
brand affinity p. 341
brand love p. 341
brand relationship p. 341
differentiation p. 333
distinctive brands p. 338
double jeopardy p. 322
duplication of purchases principle p. 332

gamification p. 339
habit-persistent consumers p. 324
law of buyer moderation p. 331
market penetration p. 321
market share p. 322
near-stationary (static) market p. 324

nonstationary (dynamic) market p. 324
Pareto principle p. 329
purchase frequency p. 321
purchase loyalty p. 328
shopper marketing p. 345
variety-seeking consumers p. 324

REVIEW QUESTIONS

1. Provide at least one recommendation you could give to managers of small brands and one recommendation you could provide to managers of large brands to help them avoid the problem of double jeopardy.

2. Explain the Pareto principle, the law of buyer moderation, and the duplication of purchases principle. What do each of these tell us about heavy and light users of a brand?

3. What kinds of information can we get from a careful understanding of *what* consumers do? What kinds of information can we get from understanding *why* they do what they do? Why are both important?
4. Describe the differences between purchase loyalty and attitudinal loyalty. In Figure 9.1, why is there a double-headed arrow connecting purchase loyalty and attitudinal loyalty?
5. Describe the difference between brand differentiation and distinctiveness. In what way do they influence consumer behavior?
6. Why might a company want to avoid 100 percent market share as a goal?

DISCUSSION QUESTIONS

1. Why is the focus of the first half of the chapter on *buyer behavior*, but the focus of the second half of the chapter is on *consumer behavior*?
2. As we found in Insights from the Field 9.3, CEOs sometimes make the news for behaving badly. However, some CEOs make the news for the good things they do. Find an example of such a situation and discuss it. To what extent did the CEO's actions impact the behaviors and/or attitudes of the company's customers?
3. Why do you think that the vast majority of customers are habit-persistent consumers rather than variety-seeking customers? Imagine that you are the marketing manager for a high-involvement product. How might you communicate differently with your habit-persistent consumers versus your variety-seeking customers? How might these communication strategies change for a low-involvement product?
4. For consumers who purchase from a repertoire of brands, how might it be possible to increase purchase loyalty? How might it be possible to increase attitudinal loyalty? Which is preferable? Why?
5. Although there are numerous ways in which a marketer can increase engagement with a brand, one particularly interesting and fun way is with gamification. Describe a brand-based game with which you are very familiar. What are the various ways in which it attempts to engage you in the brand? Have your behaviors changed? Have your attitudes changed? Discuss.

For more information, quizzes, case studies, and other study tools, please visit us at **www.oup.com/he/phillips**.

CASE STUDY 9

Shopping in China is different than you think

At 1.39 billion people (World Bank 2018a), China makes up almost 19 percent of the world's population. Put another way, almost one of every five people on the planet is Chinese. Consumer behavior is sometimes difficult to predict. With the added complexities of a slowing economy, global trade disputes, a growing middle class, and a greater desire for luxury brands, predicting what the Chinese consumer will do is especially difficult.

One widely held notion about China is that with so many consumers entering the middle class, there is a pent-up demand for branded products, especially Western products. These new consumers now have the funds to purchase the brands they have been wanting to have, but could not afford. This notion is only partially correct. A recent study by the consulting company Bain & Company found that branded products generally have a high level of market penetration in Chinese households. A vast majority of fast-moving consumer goods (FMCG) have found their way into the lives and homes of Chinese consumers. In addition, Chinese consumers have a fondness for their own domestic brands as well as some foreign brands. When further dissected, these two key behavioral tendencies indicate that the Chinese marketplace simultaneously operates at two speeds: fast and slow.

The investigation into the Chinese market started when the consulting firm Bain & Company examined China's top twenty-six consumer goods categories, which accounted for more than 80 percent of the FMCG in the country. The research combined behavioral data from two panels of consumers. The first was a panel of forty thousand households in urban China that used barcode scanners to track their FMCG purchases for at-home consumption. The second was a panel of four thousand individual urban consumers who utilized smartphones to track food and beverage purchases for consumption outside the home (Lannes et al. 2017). Together, the information from the two panels provided rich insights into how shopping in China is quite different from some widely held expectations.

Important behavioral trends

Market penetration for most categories was quite high, with most brands (81 percent) being found in urban Chinese households. Although some experts might applaud this number, it is also concerning to some marketers because it indicates that market penetration may have hit a plateau. Looking at the context gives further clues as to why this might be the case. One reason is that most brands are already available via mass distribution, so if consumers wanted the brand, they could easily get it (Lannes et al. 2017). Another reason is that Chinese consumers have fairly easy access to the Internet, and with it, a host of

product-related information, reviews, and marketing. For every 100 people in China, there are 104 cellular subscriptions (World Bank 2018a), compared to 121 in the United States (World Bank 2018b), indicating that the reluctance for Chinese consumers to buy is not a result of their lack of knowledge about the products. It simply might be that the remaining 19 percent of the market might not ever be interested in these products.

Another behavioral trend is that many consumers seem to prefer "healthy and high priced" over "less healthy and low priced" options. First, products that are perceived as less healthy (such as candy) have lower levels of penetration than healthier alternatives (such as packaged water). Further, Chinese consumers are willing to pay more for these higher-quality and healthier products. In the personal care category, sales growth increased by 10.5 percent, and in the home care category, sales growth increased by 3.5 percent. For luxury brands in the personal care category, this is especially true—consumers are willing to pay for healthy, high-quality products that they apply to their bodies (Lannes et al. 2017).

Key insight: two-speed growth in the marketplace

The trend toward high levels of market penetration for many brands and a shift toward higher-priced, healthier alternatives leads to a key insight about China's mature and complex marketplace: China's marketplace simultaneously operates at two speeds, fast and slow. While some sectors are accelerating at a fast pace, other sectors are slowing down and contracting. Additional behavioral data were able to provide further details about this two-speed phenomenon. In fact, the two-speed effect seemed to occur across product categories, in distribution, in pricing, and in the competition between local and foreign brands.

Across-product categories

First, the two-speed effect showed up clearly in a variety of FMCG product categories. One trend that was fueling the two-speed effect was that fewer Chinese consumers were cooking and consuming their meals at home. Instead, they were dining out, using food delivery options, and eating on the go. Thus, food and beverage for home consumption is considered slow, while food and beverage for out-of-home consumption is considered fast. Food delivery grew by 44 percent and out-of-home dining increased by 10 percent over the previous few years. By contrast, in the category of food and beverage that is consumed at home, sales were up by a mere 0.1 percent, making it one of China's most extreme slow-growth sectors. Personal care and home care are two other sectors of the marketplace in which there was fast growth. Indeed, sales in the categories of personal care and home care were up by 8.6 percent, making it one of China's most impressive high-growth sectors. Consumers significantly increased their spending on a variety of these products, including makeup, facial tissue, and fabric detergent (Lannes et al. 2017). Thus, although Chinese consumers are less inclined to eat at home, they do want to take care of themselves and their homes.

In distribution

Second, China also displays a two-speed effect with some trends in its distribution channels. Sales at hypermarkets, supermarkets, and minimarkets decreased by 2 percent (making it slow), while sales at convenience stores increased by more than 7 percent (making it relatively fast). Online shopping increased by 52 percent over the previous year and now represents 7 percent of all FMCG sales (making it very fast). The most frequently purchased products online were skin care products, shampoo, diapers, and cookies. In the past, marketers may have been persuaded to add retail locations to increase penetration and market share. Today, however, tech-savvy Chinese consumers prefer to acquire products online (Lannes et al. 2017).

In pricing

Third, the two-speed effect was evident in the difference between brands that appeal to the high-end consumer and brands that appeal to the mass market. Premium segments were fast; mass segments were slow. For premium segments, Chinese consumers seemed to be willing to pay for healthier products, for luxury products, and for products that would help them improve their lifestyles. The case of instant noodles, a supposed staple in the Chinese diet, is particularly interesting. While penetration and sales for instant packaged noodles declined, these same measures increased for premium-priced noodles that were viewed as better-quality and healthier options. Similarly, sales of packaged water increased dramatically because it

was viewed as a healthier and better-quality option than tap water (Lannes et al. 2017). Sales of branded luxury goods are another case in which Chinese consumers seem to be willing, and maybe even eager, to spend money. Although they are not FMCG products, sales of Swiss watches have jumped 30 percent and sales of luxury cars have increased 18 percent in the past few years. As long as housing values (usually a Chinese person's most significant financial investment) steadily improve, this trend is expected to continue (Wong 2018).

In the competition between foreign and domestic brands

Finally, the two-speed effect was apparent in how Chinese consumers were buying local versus foreign brands. Compared to foreign brands, local brands seemed to be growing in share and penetration. Indeed, of twenty-six categories examined, foreign brands saw increases in only four categories and decreases in eighteen categories. Local brands were preferred for personal care items, while foreign brands were preferred in food and beverage items. The products with the most significant shift from foreign to domestic brands are makeup, conditioner, shampoo, and toothbrushes. A few foreign branded products are making headway against domestic brands: chewing gum, fabric softener, noodles, and beer. Why are local brands seemingly better able to meet the needs of their consumers? For the most part, local brands have an advantage because they have a single-country focus and are quick to react to and meet the changing needs of consumers (Lannes et al. 2017) (see Photo 9.11).

This key insight about the two-speed nature of the market is important because it provides guidance for marketers who want to enter and expand into the Chinese market. Marketers must adjust their view of China as a "single, high-velocity environment" and instead create strategies that suit the needs of each market. For fast-paced product categories, marketing managers should create strategies to facilitate growth. They should take advantage of the economic trends and consumer excitement for their products. For slow-speed product categories, marketing managers will want to create strategies that are designed to manage expenses and slow the decline (Lannes et al. 2017).

Sources: Lannes et al. (2017); World Bank (2018a, 2018b); Wong (2018).

● **Photo 9.11** *Consumption in China is simultaneously fast and slow*

QUESTIONS

1. Behavioral data provide important information to marketers, but it is also important to consider the context in which this behavior occurs. Why?

2. In what way could (a) a US marketer and (b) a Chinese marketer attempt to create stronger, more meaningful relationships with Chinese consumers?

3. If a marketer is seeking to characterize the Chinese consumer's consumption patterns, how useful are the traditional measures of market penetration and market share? How about purchase loyalty and attitudinal loyalty?

4. Imagine that you are a marketing manager for a big, foreign-based FMCG brand that is entering China for the first time. What would you need to be especially cautious about? How would your answer change if you were the marketing manager of a small foreign brand?

REFERENCES

Anschuetz, N. 2002. "Why a Brand's Most Valuable Customer Is the Next One It Adds." *Journal of Advertising Research* January/February:15–21.

Barwise, P. T., and A. S. C. Ehrenberg. 1985. "Consumer Beliefs and Brand Usage." *Journal of the Market Research Society* 27:81–93.

Bennett, D. 2005. *What Car Will They Buy Next?* Report 19. Adelaide, Australia: Ehrenberg–Bass Institute for Marketing Science.

Bennett, D., and C. Graham. 2010. "Is Loyalty Driving Growth for the Brand in Front? A Two-Purchase Analysis of Car Category Dynamics in Thailand." *Journal of Strategic Marketing* 18 (7): 573–85.

Boykiv, Y. 2015. "Gamify Your Brand to Increase Customer Engagement." Inc. May 11, 2015. https://www.inc.com/yuriy-boykiv/gamify-your-brand-to-increase-customer-engagement.html.

Breindel, H. 2017. "How to Differentiate Your Brand in a Sea of Me-Too Competitors." *Forbes*, August 25, 2017. https://www.forbes.com/sites/forbesagencycouncil/2017/08/25/how-to-differentiate-your-brand-in-a-sea-of-me-too-competitors/#79875bcc5d1e.

Brown, G. H. 1953. "Brand Loyalty—Fact or Fiction?" *Advertising Age* 43:251–58.

Carroll, B. A., and A. C. Ahuvia. 2006. "Some Antecedents and Outcomes of Brand Love." *Marketing Letters* 17 (2): 79–89.

Casaló, L. V., C. Flavián, and M. Guinalíua. 2008. "Promoting Consumer's Participation in Virtual Brand Communities: A New Paradigm in Branding Strategy." *Journal of Marketing Communication* 14 (1): 19–36.

Chaudhuri, A., and M. B. Holbrook. 2001. "The Chain of Effects from Brand Trust and Brand Affect to Brand Performance: The Role of Brand Loyalty." *Journal of Marketing* 65 (2): 81–93.

Chew, J. 2015. "Southwest's New Ad Mocks Other Airlines' Fees." *Fortune*, October 8, 2015. http://fortune.com/2015/10/08/southwest-ad-fees/.

CNBC. 2018. "Cramer: Pizza Execs Say Papa John's Is 'Falling Apart.'" CNBC. July 12, 2018. https://www.cnbc.com/video/2018/07/12/cramer-pizza-execs-say-papa-johns-is-falling-apart.html.

Colombo, R., A. S. C. Ehrenberg, and D. Sabavala. 2000. "Diversity in Analyzing Brand-Switching Tables: The Car Challenge." *Canadian Journal of Marketing Research* 19:22–36.

Cox, J. 2017. "Harry Potter Is the UK's Most Successful Businessman—and J. K. Rowling Knows It." *The Independent*, June 26, 2017. https://www.independent.co.uk/voices/harry-potter-reveal-j-k-rowling-british-economy-most-successful-businessman-a7808841.html.

Cui, C. C., M. Mrad, and M. K. Hogg. 2018. "Brand Addiction: Exploring the Concept and Its Definition through an Experiential Lens." *Journal of Business Research* 87 (June): 118–27.

Deloitte. 2020. *2020 Retail Industry Outlook: Convenience as a Promise.* Deloitte Development, LLC. Accessed September 14, 2020. https://www2.deloitte.com/content/dam/Deloitte/us/

Documents/consumer-business/us-retail-industry-outlook-2020-final-100720.pdf.

Dun & Bradstreet. 2020. Migros-Genossenschafts-Bund. Company Profile. Accessed September 14, 2020. https://www.dnb.com/business-directory/company-profiles.migros-genossenschafts-bund.8e7921678522fb196c08aff6dc2fdf7f.html

Ehrenberg, A., N. Barnard, and J. Scriven. 1997. "Differentiation or Salience." *Journal of Advertising Research* 37 (6): 7–14.

Ehrenberg, A. S. C., K. Hammond, and G. J. Goodhardt. 1994. "The After-Effects of Price Related Consumer Promotions." *Journal of Advertising Research* 34 (4): 11–21.

Ehrenberg, A. S. C., M. D. Uncles, and G. J. Goodhardt. 2004. "Understanding Brand Performance Measures: Using Dirichlet Benchmarks." *Journal of Business Research* 57 (12): 1307–25.

Englis, B. G., and D. M. Phillips. 2013. "Does Innovativeness Drive Environmentally Conscious Consumer Behavior?" *Psychology & Marketing* 30 (2): 160–72.

Erdem, T. 1996. "A Dynamic Analysis of Market Structure Based on Panel Data." *Marketing Science* 15 (4): 359–78.

Fournier, S., and J. L. Yao. 1997. "Reviving Brand Loyalty: A Reconceptualization within the Framework of Consumer–Brand Relationships." *International Journal of Research in Marketing* 14 (5): 451–72.

Hsu, T. 2018. "Racial Slur Leads to Papa John's Founder Quitting Chairman Post." *New York Times*, July 11, 2018. https://www.nytimes.com/2018/07/11/business/papa-johns-racial-slur.html.

Joyce, G. 2018. "Five Times Customers Asked for Change and Brands Actually Delivered It." Brandwatch. July 12, 2018. https://www.brandwatch.com/blog/5-times-customer-change/.

Kim, B. J., V. Singh, and R. S. Winer. 2017. "The Pareto Rule for Frequently Purchased Packaged Goods: An Empirical Generalization." *Marketing Letters* 28 (4): 491–507.

Kim, K. K., J. D. Williams, and G. B. Wilcox. 2016. "'Kid Tested, Mother Approved': The Relationship between Advertising Expenditures and 'Most-Loved' Brands." *International Journal of Advertising* 35 (1): 42–60.

Klara, R. 2017. "How the 'I Heart NY' Logo Transcended Marketing and Endures 4 Decades after Debut: It Still Represents the Spirit of the City." *AdWeek*, September 10, 2017. https://www.adweek.com/brand-marketing/how-the-i-heart-ny-logo-twice-transcended-marketing-and-endures-4-decades-after-its-debut/.

Krogstad, J. M. 2017. "US Hispanic Population Growth Has Leveled Off." Pew Research Center. August 3, 2017. http://www.pewresearch.org/fact-tank/2017/08/03/u-s-hispanic-population-growth-has-leveled-off/.

Lannes, B., J. Ding, M. Kou, and J. Yu. 2017. "China's Two-Speed Growth: In and Out of the Home." Bain & Company. June 29, 2017. http://www.bain.com/publications/articles/china-shopper-report-2017-chinas-two-speed-growth-in-and-out-of-the-home.aspx.

McSpadden, K. 2015. "You Now Have a Shorter Attention Span Than a Goldfish." *Time*, May 14, 2015. http://time.com/3858309/attention-spans-goldfish/.

Meise, J. N., T. Rudolph, P. Kenning, and D. M. Phillips. 2014. "Feed them Facts: Value Perceptions and Consumer Use of Sustainability-Related Product Information." *Journal of Retailing and Consumer Services* 21:510–19.

Moore, D. 2018. Personal interview, January 19, 2018.

Mrad, M., and C. C. Cui. 2017. "Brand Addiction: Conceptualization and Scale Development." *European Journal of Marketing* 51 (11/12): 1938–60.

Muniz, A. M., Jr., and H. J. Schau. 2005. "Religiosity in the Abandoned Apple Newton Brand Community." *Journal of Consumer Research* 31:737–47.

Pez – the Company. 2020. Pez International. Accessed September 14, 2020. https://int.pez.com/en/Company/PEZ-the-company.

Phillips, D. M. 2013. "Advice from the front lines of sustainability: Take the stairs, there is no elevator." *Journal of Applied Management and Entrepreneurship.* 18 (2), 103-115.

Pizza Today. 2018. "2018 Top 100 Pizza Companies." November 1, 2018. https://www.pizzatoday.com/pizzeria-rankings/2018-top-100-pizza-companies/.

Porter, M. E. 1985. *Competitive Advantage: Creating and Sustaining Superior Performance.* New York: Free Press.

Romaniuk, J., B. Sharp, and A. S. C. Ehrenberg. 2007. "Evidence Concerning the Importance of Perceived Brand Differentiation." *Australasian Marketing Journal* 15:42–54.

Schau, H. J., and A. M. Muniz, Jr. 2002. "Brand Communities and Personal Identities: Negotiations in Cyberspace." *Advances in Consumer Research* 29:344–49.

Schouten, J., and J. H. McAlexander. 1995. "Subcultures of Consumption: An Ethnography of the New Bikers." *Journal of Consumer Research* 22 (3): 43–61.

Schwartz, B. 2005. *The Paradox of Choice: Why More Is Less.* New York: HarperCollins.

Sharp, B. 2010. *How Brands Grow.* Oxford: Oxford University Press.

Sharp, B., M. Wright, J. L. Dawes, C.Driesener, L. Meyer-Waarden, L. Stocchi, and P. Stern. 2012. "It's a Dirichlet World: Modeling Individuals' Loyalties Reveals How Brands Compete, Grow and Decline." *Journal of Advertising Research* 52 (2): 1–10.

Stanley, T. L. 2016. "5 Trends That Are Radically Reshaping Shopper Marketing." *AdWeek*, June 19, 2016. https://www.adweek.com/brand-marketing/5-trends-are-radically-re-shaping-shopper-marketing-171960/.

Starbucks Company Profile. 2020.. Starbucks, Inc. Accessed September 14, 2020. https://www.starbucks.com/about-us/company-information/starbucks-company-profile.

Szmigin, I., and M. Piacentini. 2015. *Consumer Behavior.* Oxford: Oxford University Press.

Wellan, D. M., and A. S. C. Ehrenberg. 1990. "A Case of Seasonal Segmentation." *Market Research Society* 30 (1): 35–44.

Wong, J. 2018. "What Will Keep the Chinese Consumer Strong? Chinese Shoppers Are Splurging Again. What Will Keep Them Going?" *Wall Street Journal (Online)*, February 22, 2018.

World Bank. 2018a. "Country Profile: China." Accessed August 17, 2019. https://databank.worldbank.org/views/reports/reportwidget.aspx?Report_Name=CountryProfile&Id=b450fd57&tbar=y&dd=y&inf=n&zm=n&country=CHN.

World Bank. 2018b. "Country Profile: United States." Accessed August 17, 2019. https://databank.worldbank.org/views/reports/reportwidget.aspx?Report_Name=CountryProfile&Id=b450fd57&tbar=y&dd=y&inf=n&zm=n&country=USA.

10 Social Structures and Processes

⊙ Introduction

Think about some of your favorite memories. Perhaps these memories include events like special holiday dinners with family, a weekend trip with someone special, or just a fun night hanging out with friends. Perhaps some of your best stories and some of your favorite pictures include some of these kinds of events. For the most part, we don't consume in isolation and we do not make consumption decisions in isolation either. The people we are with, those whom we know, those we have feelings toward, and the groups with which we identify all influence a variety of consumption processes, decisions, and behaviors. Thus, much of our consumption, and even some of our favorite memories, revolve around and are influenced by other people.

Because other people exert such an important influence on our consumption processes, decisions, and behaviors, marketers know that they need to understand the intricacies of these influences. That way, marketers can develop strategies to more efficiently and effectively deliver the organization's value proposition. An important focus of this chapter is the various social structures that exist. Each culture has a set of formal and informal social structures that influence an individual's value system, education, and goals. In addition, this chapter will focus on the processes by which these social structures exert their influence on consumer behavior. Throughout the discussion of structures and processes, implications for how marketing managers use their insights will also be interwoven.

⊙ Reference Groups

As we have discussed, consumption often takes place in a public setting. When this happens, other consumers can see those products and will often come to a conclusion about the consumer's beliefs, attitudes, and behaviors. For example, the Mexican restaurant chain Chipotle cooks up fresh and delicious food with natural ingredients. The company is quite clear about operating according to a strong set of values, which include caring for the planet, the local community, customers, and employees. It does this by enacting a series of initiatives, such as purchasing fresh ingredients from local farmers, insisting on humane treatment of animals, treating their employees and customers like

LEARNING OBJECTIVES

Having read this chapter, you will be able to:

1. **Define the reference group concept** and describe the types of reference groups.

2. Describe the **processes of reference group influence**, making sure to include the mechanisms of group influence as well as the importance of conformity.

3. Explain the **importance of social power** and how influence and information flow within groups, as well as between groups and individuals.

4. Describe how the **family** exerts influence on consumption decisions and behaviors.

5. Discuss the **concept of social class** and the process by which it impacts consumer behavior.

● **Photo 10.1** *Chipotle promotes a natural, local, and healthy food system*

Social power is the degree of influence an individual or organization has among peers and within society as a whole.

Reference groups are sets of individuals that other individuals use as a basis for comparison and guidance when forming their beliefs, attitudes, and behaviors.

Contactual or associative groups are generally close membership groups with which we interact regularly (we are in contact with them) and with which we associate.

Disclaimant group is a group to which we currently belong or to which we belonged in the past, but to which we no longer want to belong.

Aspirational groups are composed of individuals with whom the consumer can identify or admire (often from afar) and to whom they aspire to be like in some way.

family, and advocating more broadly for a more natural and healthy food system (Photo 10.1). If we see a consumer enjoying a visit at Chipotle, we may conclude that this person is also committed to these same values.

Reference groups are a type of social structure made up of individuals that other individuals use as a basis for comparison and guidance when forming their beliefs, attitudes, and behaviors. Individuals use reference groups as a benchmark to evaluate their own situations (Hyman 1942). The reference group can be either real or imaginary, as long as the group is relevant to an "individual's evaluations, aspirations or behavior" (Park and Lessig 1977, 102).

Types of reference groups

Reference groups vary across two dimensions: member/nonmember status and group attractiveness (see Table 10.1). **Contactual or associative groups**

Table 10.1 Reference group membership

MEMBERSHIP

		MEMBER	NONMEMBER
ATTRACTIVENESS	POSITIVE	Contactual or associative	Aspirational
	NEGATIVE	Disclaimant	Avoidance or dissociative

Source: Adapted, in part, from Assael (1998) and Szmigin and Piacentini (2015).

are generally close membership groups with which we interact regularly; we are in contact with them. This closeness may be because of the ties of family, friends, classmates, neighbors, coworkers, etc. Advertising for Lavazza coffee is particularly effective at stressing the importance of contactual groups. Founded in Turin, Italy, in 1895, Lavazza has a proud tradition of excellent coffees and blends. The company is still run by the Lavazza family and its advertising campaigns often stress the importance of enjoying a cup of coffee surrounded by friends and family. For example, the "Born Social in 1895" campaign was launched in 2017 and highlighted the social aspects of coffee consumption. As the original founder Luigi Lavazza said, "Coffee isn't just something to drink, it's not just a coffee, it's a way for us to get together." The advertisements always depict Lavazza as an important part of the group itself (see Photo 10.2) ("Born Social" 2019).

A **disclaimant group** is a group to which we currently belong or to which we belonged in the past, but to which we no longer want to belong. An individual may be part of a social group, but over time starts to feel disconnected because of shifting interests or priorities (Photo 10.3). Disclaimant groups may be transitional groups from our past that we would like to put behind us (e.g., school friends going on different paths) or groups that are stigmatized in some way by society (e.g., we may belong to a weight-loss group but prefer that our friends not know). The important thing is that, although we are members of the group, we are trying to avoid the group and move on.

Aspirational groups are composed of individuals with whom the consumer can identify or admire (often from afar) and whom they aspire to be like in some way. An aspirational group can be represented by a single person we aspire to be like. We may respect these people for their skills (such as Olympic athletes) or for

● **Photo 10.2** *Lavazza advertisement promoting the importance of coffee in strengthening social connections*

● **Photo 10.3** *Disclaimant groups, reflecting shifting interests among friends*

● **Photo 10.4** *Steampunk man*

Dissociative or avoidance groups are groups we have negative feelings toward and with whom we do not wish to be associated.

Formal groups are reference groups that have a highly-defined structure, a set of rules, a hierarchy for membership where some people are designated leaders, and a set of clear goals.

their style, glamour, or lifestyle (such as famous actors). We may even try to emulate them through the consumption of certain products or brands. When American Meghan Markle became engaged to the United Kingdom's Prince Harry, admirers on both sides of the Atlantic tried to get their hands on some of Markle's fashion picks, such as the white coat from her engagement picture, which was from Line the Label. The coat was quickly renamed the Meghan Coat after Markle wore it for the official engagement photo. Interested fans can keep up on her "effortless casual chic style" by checking out the Meghan's Mirror style site (meghansmirror.com).

Dissociative or avoidance groups are groups we have negative feelings toward and with whom we do not wish to be associated. We have never been members of these groups, nor do we want to be. An example of a dissociative group could be a motorcycle gang. Much of this is culturally dependent. For example, alt-right groups in Germany are dissociative groups because not only are they often violent, but also they have adopted Nazi imagery and values; the Pachuco groups in Mexico who see themselves as "classy gangsters" with a unique style of dress, hair, and tattoos are also dissociative groups. The steampunk movement, which emerged in England and spread through Europe and North America, is certainly not violent or criminal, but could also be a dissociative group for some individuals. Members who belong to a steampunk group appreciate science fiction and technology, but also espouse a liking for Victorian style. They also have a unique style of dress, art, and literature (see Photo 10.4). The identification of a dissociative group depends in large part on individual perceptions; what may be a dissociative group for some people may be an aspirational group for other people.

Experts also classify reference groups by their level of formality. A **formal group** has a highly defined structure, a set of rules, a hierarchy for membership where some people are designated leaders, and a set of clear goals. Examples include sororities, fraternities, businesses, organizations, sport groups, and places of worship. There are certain ways to behave, dress, and consume when you are in a formal group. When someone does not conform, there are certainly social and institutional pressures and processes to bring that person back into line. Imagine wearing a T-shirt and flip-flops to the office. You would quickly be notified that you need to change into something more appropriate. Thus, although many companies have *casual Fridays*, the formal group exerts power to communicate and enforce appropriate behaviors.

An **informal group** is formed by individuals who share a common set of interests or goals. These individuals are drawn together over a mutual interest (such as gaming or music), common values (e.g., a political action group), or friendship. It is often possible to find informal groups within a formal group. Most large organizations (formal groups) have several informal groups, such as a baseball team, a hiking club, or a volunteer group. Marketers who attempt to gain access to formal groups will have a difficult time because most formal groups are reluctant to share information about their members. Marketers also have a difficult time accessing informal groups because of their transient nature. To overcome these obstacles, some marketers have created and managed their own informal groups to facilitate connections and information sharing between consumers. Movie studios, for instance, regularly provide ways for fans to further engage with the movies or actors.

Informal groups are reference groups formed by individuals who share a common set of interests or goals.

Reference group influence

Now that we know about the main types of reference groups, let's turn to the process by which these groups can exert an influence on consumers. In the following sections, we will see that even if a consumer is not directly in the presence of a reference group, that group will still push the consumer toward some types of decisions and behaviors and away from other types of decisions and behaviors.

Mechanisms of reference group influence

Individuals can be directly influenced by a reference group through direct contact with its members or indirectly influenced by simply observing the behavior of the group (Leigh 1989). Reference groups can influence which products or brands are purchased, when they are purchased, and how they are consumed. The three main mechanisms of reference group influence are informational, utilitarian, and value expressive (Park and Lessig 1977) (see Table 10.2).

Understanding reference group influence is another part of what makes the job of a marketer challenging. Take the example of Gucci and its relationship with the hip-hop community. For a while, the brand itself was a darling of the hip-hop community and was featured in numerous videos and songs. Some artists even started to say, "What's Gucci?" as a way to say, "What's up?" Initially, hip-hop artists signed lucrative endorsement deals with Gucci, sales increased, and everyone seemed happy. Then, in 2019, Gucci landed itself in a huge amount of hot water when it introduced what they called the wool balaclava sweater, but what critics have called the blackface sweater. At first glance, the black turtleneck sweater looks fairly normal and, like most turtlenecks, it can be unrolled and pulled up over the bottom half of the face. However, inexplicably, when this is done, the unfolded fabric has a cutout over

Table 10.2 Reference group influence

TYPE OF INFLUENCE	DEFINITION	EXAMPLE
Informational	Individuals utilize the reference group to get information from influencers or experts, which then alters their own behaviors.	Consumers might purchase the same equipment as a celebrity chef or might check out sites like TalkToChef, which provides live, two-way video conversations with real chefs to give advice and fix mishaps in the kitchen (see talktochef.com).
Utilitarian	Individuals conform their behaviors to group norms to attain a reward from or avoid a punishment by the reference group.	Much of this influence occurs through socialization with our family and friends. To get admiration and praise at the next holiday family get-together, a consumer might take extra care to prepare and serve some of the family's favorite food items.
Value expressive	Individuals use the reference group to enhance their self-image, build their self-concept, or improve their self-esteem.	Consumers want to be like others whom they admire or respect, so they often adopt a brand that is linked with an attractive celebrity or well-respected social or political leader. Wearing an Omega watch definitely says something about the discriminating taste of the wearer (see Photo 10.5).

the mouth and exaggerated big red lips that allow the wearers to wear black-face wherever they go. The reaction was swift and severe. Although Gucci apologized and removed the sweater from all stores, hip-hop stars dropped the brand, brand endorsers condemned it, and social media from all sectors was enraged and encouraged boycotts (Peters 2019). The Gucci blackface fiasco is a great example of a brand that was happy to take advantage of the increased attention and sales that came from its brand's association to well-known and revered hip-hop artists (an important aspirational reference group). However, in its exuberance, Gucci forgot to collect data, distill information, and create insights about this reference group.

Public versus private consumption

Depending on whether the consumption is private versus public, reference groups exert differential influence on behavior. Think about your choice of laundry detergent. How many people know what detergent you use? Probably not too many; it's a private consumption experience.

● **Photo 10.5** *George Clooney is an admired and respected actor as well as an activist for human rights*

The influence of reference groups also varies by whether the consumption experience is considered a luxury or a necessity. For most people in developed countries, a refrigerator and a microwave oven are necessities for the kitchen; an espresso machine might be a luxury. Refer to Figure 10.1 to see how reference groups influence these private/public and necessity/luxury purchases (Bearden and Etzel 1982).

Development of conformity

Membership in a reference group results in some degree of conformity among its members. **Conformity** can be defined as the adoption of a group's beliefs, attitudes, and behaviors in an effort to comply with the group. If your friends all want to go to a climate march on Saturday afternoon, but you would rather watch a football game, you may conform to the group's decision to main-

	Public	
Product / **Brand**	*Weak reference group influence on product choice*	*Strong reference group influence on product choice*
Strong reference group influence on brand choice	**Public necessities** Because it is a necessity, (e.g., car, suit, phone), the influence for the product will be **weak**. But, because it will be seen by others, influence for the brand will be **strong**.	**Public luxuries** Because it is a luxury (e.g., yacht, vacation home), the influence for the product should be **strong**. And, Because it is seen by others, the influence for the brand will also be **strong**.
Weak reference group influence on brand choice	**Private necessities** This product is owned and consumed out of public view (e.g., mattress, washing machine). Because it is a necessity, the product influence is **weak**. Because it is not seen by others, the influence for the brand is also **weak**.	**Private luxuries** This product is consumed in private, but also conveys important meaning about the consumer (e.g., expensive cologne or perfume). Because this is a luxury item, the influence of the product is **strong**; because the product is consumed in private, the influence for the brand is **weak**.

(left margin: Necessity; right margin: Luxury; bottom: Private)

Figure 10.1 *Model of reference group influence on consumption*
Source: Adapted from Bearden and Etzel (1982)

tain the friendship. In Photo 10.6, Bulova announces its new collaboration with Manchester United. The not-so-subtle message is, if you like Manchester United, you should buy a Bulova watch. Within the private realm of relationships, conformity can be very important, as we can see in Insights from Academia 10.1. In the more public realm of popular culture and news, there is great social pressure to respond to big events (Earls 2009) by, for example, marching in an event, wearing a ribbon of support, changing your profile picture, or posting about it. Thus, reference groups also influence behavior, depending on the amount of pressure a consumer feels to conform. There are five main types of conformity: compliance, identification, internalization, normative social influence, and informational social influence (see the work of Asch 1955; Mann 1969; and Sherif 1936).

- **Compliance** refers to publicly changing behavior to fit in with the group but privately disagreeing. The motivation here is to get a reward or avoid punishment. For example, you might go to a political rally with your new roommate, but privately dislike the candidate.

- **Identification** occurs when individuals like or admire an individual or group, so they try to be like that individual or group. For example, you might wear the jersey of your favorite football player.

- **Internalization** is the most complete form of conformity. It involves both an attitudinal and a behavioral change in favor of the group, for example, you whole-heartedly and enthusiastically become a vegetarian!

Conformity is the adoption of a group's beliefs, attitudes, and behaviors in an effort to comply with the group.

Compliance is a form of conformity and refers to publicly changing behavior to fit in with the group, but privately disagreeing.

Identification is a form of conformity and occurs when individuals like or admire an individual or group, so they try to be like that individual or group.

Internalization is a form of conformity and involves both an attitudinal and a behavioral change in favor of the group.

EXCITING
TIMES AHEAD!
WE ARE THRILLED TO BE A PART OF IT

BULOVA

THE OFFICIAL TIMEKEEPER OF MANCHESTER UNITED

● **Photo 10.6** *Bulova advertisement using conformity to encourage consumption*

Normative social influence is a form of conformity when you feel pressure to go along with people around you to fit into the group.

- **Normative social influence** occurs when you feel pressure to go along with people around you in order to fit into the group. Here, the motivation is to fit in and not be rejected by the group. Unlike compliance, there are no punishments or rewards. For example, even though you like wine, all of your friends like beer, so you drink beer when you're with them.

- **Informational social influence** happens when you rely on the expertise or knowledge of other people to help with a decision. For example, after moving to a new city, you might ask your new friends to recommend a dentist.

Of course, not everyone will conform to perceived or actual pressure from a reference group. Perhaps individuals have a preference for independent decision-making, maybe they reject the group's norms, or it simply may be possible that the consumer has a strong difference of opinion. Consumers may also resist when the group is exerting too much pressure and is attempting to limit independent choice. When this happens, consumers will very likely reassert their freedom of choice, a process known as **reactance** (Venkatesan 1966). If an individual feels that the freedom to make a choice is limited, reactance can be a powerful force. What happens when consumers are more socially isolated and not as likely to be influenced by these kinds of group dynamics? One research study found that some consumers will compensate for the weak ties they have with others and try to forge stronger ties to products (see Insights from Academia 10.2).

 INSIGHTS FROM ACADEMIA 10.1

Are you a Coke person or a Pepsi person?

The answer to this question could be critical, especially if you want to date someone! Let's face it, a lot of consumption happens when we are in the presence of others. When you meet someone new and strike up a friendship or dating relationship, you will quickly start to learn about that other person's consumption choices and preferred brands. The researchers in this study used a variety of quantitative and qualitative methods to investigate how real-life couples influence one another. When individuals in a relationship have similar preferences for brands, such as Apple versus Samsung, Ford versus Toyota, or even a low-involvement product like Coke versus Pepsi, they have fewer conflicts and higher levels of life satisfaction. On the flip side, when two people have different preferences ("I like Apple, but you like Samsung"), there are more conflicts in the relationship and reduced life satisfaction. So, the next time you're out on the dating scene, after getting the person's name and number, be sure to ask the Coke versus Pepsi question too!

Brick, D. J., G. M. Fitzsimons, T. L. Chartrand, and G. J. Fitzsimons. 2018. "Coke vs. Pepsi: Brand Compatibility, Relationship Power, and Life Satisfaction." Journal of Consumer Research 44 (5): 991–1014.

INSIGHTS FROM ACADEMIA 10.2

Does your product have a face?

Humans need social interaction. If, for whatever reason, social interaction is lacking, individuals try to compensate for that loss. Sometimes, they compensate by forming a connection to important products in their lives. When the product is *anthropomorphic*, or has characteristics of a person, it is much easier to form a connection to the product. So, when consumers have very little meaningful social interaction, they can make up for that exclusion by interacting with a product that is anthropomorphic. Photo 10.7 shows the three products that were used in this experimental study.

Participants who viewed the anthropomorphic version described it as "happy" and "smiling"; participants who viewed the other two versions viewed the product as simply a "vacuum" and "useful." In the end, feelings of social exclusion were significantly lessened for those consumers who viewed the humanlike version of the product.

Mourey, J. A., J. G. Olson, and C. Yoon. 2017. "Products as Pals: Engaging with Anthropomorphic Products Mitigates the Effects of Social Exclusion." Journal of Consumer Research 44 (2): 414–431.

Anthropomorphic   Non-anthropomorphic   Non-anthropomorphic, Positive

● **Photo 10.7** *Three versions of a product; one is anthropomorphic*

◉ Social Power and Reference Groups

As we have discussed, reference groups exert influence on individuals because individuals are motivated to comply with the group. Reference groups also exert influence because of the power they hold and exert. The social power that reference groups and individuals use is potential influence—it is not always used, but the threat or possibility of its use is often enough for others to change their behavior. The six bases of social power are coercive, reward, legitimacy, expert, reference, and informational (see the work of French 1956; Raven 1993; and French and Raven 1959).

Informational social influence is a form of conformity and occurs when individuals rely on the expertise or knowledge of other people to help with a decision.

Reactance occurs when consumers perceive that their decision-making freedom is limited, so they reassert their freedom.

Reward power occurs when a person or group has the ability to provide benefits for conforming to the group norms.

Coercive power is the opposite of reward power and occurs when conformity to the group happens because of the threat of punishment.

Legitimate power rests with someone who has a particular position of authority in a particular context.

Expert power comes from a group or individual because of special experience, skills, or expertise. Doctors, scientists, and professors have expert power.

Referent power stems from an admiration of the qualities of another person or group and results in the individual trying imitate those qualities by copying the behavior.

Informational power is based on logical argument and knowledge someone may have acquired from experience or know-how.

Opinion leaders (or influencers) are individuals who, compared to others, exert more influence on the decisions of other individuals.

- **Reward power** occurs when a person or group has the ability to provide benefits for conforming to the group norms. For example, your coach could give the team the afternoon off from practice if it makes a big win or achieves a certain goal during practice.

- **Coercive power** is the opposite of reward power and occurs when conformity to the group happens because of the threat of punishment. Similarly, your coach could also threaten to make the team stay late or do extra drills if it underperforms.

- **Legitimate power** rests with someone who has a particular position of authority in a particular context. Your boss, for example, has legitimate power to influence your behavior.

- **Expert power** comes from a group or individual because of special experience, skills, or expertise. Doctors, scientists, and professors have expert power.

- **Referent power** stems from an admiration of the qualities of another person or group and results in the individual trying imitate those qualities by copying the behavior. Consumers often try to emulate the behaviors of celebrities or sports stars, for example.

- **Informational power** is based on logical argument and knowledge someone may have acquired from experience or know-how. Informational power comes from having knowledge, facts, or inside information that others want to know. For example, a tech-savvy friend could help you set up a new website for your band or a graduate student could help walk you through your calculus homework.

It is important to note here that some of these sources of power can sometimes overlap one another. Indeed, your boss could have legitimate power, reward power, coercive power, and informational power. Similarly, your family could exert reward power, coercive power, and, hopefully, referent power.

◉ Opinion Leaders and Opinion Seekers

Opinion leaders are individuals who, compared to other individuals, exert more influence on the decisions of other individuals (Rogers and Cartano 1962). Researchers have known for a long time that the media has little direct impact on most individuals. Instead, information and influence typically flow from the media to a group of influencers to individuals. This is called the **two-step flow of communication** (e.g., Lazarsfeld, Berelson, and Gaudet 1944; Katz and Lazarsfeld 1955). The same pattern of influence occurs in marketing. A group of influencers pay attention to new reports and information coming from companies and brands and then pass that information to their

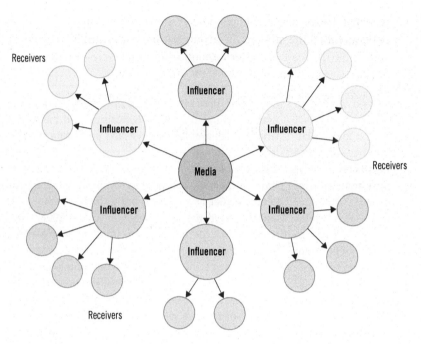

● **Figure 10.2** *Two-step flow of communication*

followers. In the early twenty-first century, we know that social media has accelerated this relationship even further. Indeed, social media influencers regularly post, tweet, and snap to their followers about a wide variety of topics, ranging from social and cultural issues, to marketing, to political issues (see Figure 10.2). This two-step flow of communication is especially apparent with consumer tribes, the focus of Insights from the Field 10.1.

Opinion leaders are well connected, knowledgeable, and persuasive in their social groups, so they have a disproportionate influence on a product's success in the marketplace. *The law of the few* suggests that as a product is introduced to a new market, opinion leaders accelerate the process of mass-market acceptance. There are three categories of opinion leaders: connectors, market mavens, and salespeople (Gladwell 2001).

- **Connectors** are individuals with a large and diverse network of friends and associates; they like to bring people together.

- **Market mavens** possess information and pass it along to others. They are often experts within their field or have inside knowledge about a topic. As discussed in a previous chapter, market mavens have a high level of involvement in the marketplace and with brands (Feick and Price 1987).

- **Salespeople** are artful at persuasion and are often charismatic. They do not resort to strong-arm tactics to influence others. Instead, their influence is subtle.

Two-step flow of communication is a model that says that influence flows from the media to opinion leaders, who then pass on information to the broader public.

Connectors are individuals with a large circle of friends and associates, many of whom are from other subcultures.

Market mavens are active information-seeking consumers or smart shoppers, and they like to provide information to others on a broad variety of goods, services, and marketplace characteristics.

Salespeople (relating to opinion leaders) are artful at persuasion and are often charismatic. They do not resort to strong-arm tactics to influence others. Instead, their influence is subtle.

Social media tribes

Are you really into *Game of Thrones* and looking to hang out with other fans? Are you hoping to connect with other hip-hop music lovers and talk about the latest songs? Do you want to meet other people whose ancestors emigrated from the same village in Italy? For any given interest, there are likely thousands of online groups that you can join to connect with other like-minded people. In addition, most of these groups will have at least one person (and maybe a few people) who leads the groups. The act of connecting with other people who have similar interests is not new. What *is* new is the ease with which we can make these connections so that we can collaborate and communicate with other like-minded people all around the world. These groups of people have been called *tribes* because they represent a group that often has a purpose or a goal in mind (Godin 2008). Whether it is an affinity tribe, where people connect with other like-minded individuals, or a purpose-driven tribe, where people try to achieve a political or social goal, tribes on social media have become commonplace. Tribes lead and connect people and their ideas. Indeed, tribes can change our world (Godin 2008).

Traditionally, we have belonged to tribes at work, with our friends and family, and with other social groups that are important to us. Today, social media allows us to have tribes everywhere. Tribes give people who are on the fringes—socially and geographically—a chance and a vehicle to connect with people who are just like them. People can share their opinions and ideas with a multitude of others who have similar interests. One of the most powerful things about tribes is that no one can force someone to become a member of a tribe; people connect because they want to connect (Godin 2008).

For social movements, tribes can be especially useful because when there is a group of people who care about the same issue, sometimes all they need is some direction and leadership. This is the strategy that was used by Al Gore when he established the Climate Reality Project. Rather than doing it himself, Gore realized

that it was more efficient (and potentially more effective) to have a corps of individuals around the world who could deliver informative talks on climate change (see www.climaterealityproject.org). Movements like this work because individuals need to feel connected; some of them are yearning to do something and just need a leader or a voice to bring them together and point them in the right direction (Godin 2008). The Bombas sock company is an example of an organization that has a strong social mission and clear leadership that is determined to do the right thing. Because socks are one of the most frequently requested items in homeless shelters, Bombas has agreed that for every pair of socks it sells, it will donate one pair to a person in need (see www.bombas.com). Customers become loyal to Bombas because of the comfortable, high-quality product, as well as the company's social mission. Once they become loyal, Bombas can rely on its tribe of customers to spread the story to other like-minded individuals.

Tribes are not just important for social movements. They can also be influential for for-profit organizations. Zappos is an example of an organization that found a passionate online following of shoe lovers. Although lower prices can definitely be found elsewhere, Zappos has become legendary for its customer service, including sending pizza to customers who tweet about being hungry. Importantly, Zappos allows for other shoe enthusiasts to talk with one another and with Zappos customer service representatives. Once again, the result is a tribe of individuals who are passionate about the service and would not think of shopping anywhere else (see www.zappos.com). In addition, these loyal customers spread the story of Zappos far and wide across their own social networks.

There can certainly be some pitfalls for those who ignore group norms and try to become "insta-famous" social media icons. In early 2018, an Irish social media influencer asked a Dublin hotel for a free night's stay in exchange for positive reviews and comments to her social media followers. The hotel owner responded with a series of scathing comments and, in a short amount of time, the whole thing blew up into a controversy with thousands of comments supporting both the social media influencer and the hotel owner. The controversy became referred to as #BloggerGate (AJStream 2018). Admittedly, it is quite common for social media influencers to be paid for their posts. Ozzymanreviews, with 1.8 million followers, is operated by an Australian man who posts about a variety of products and receives between $1,200 and $2,000 for each sponsored post on Instagram. Theambitionista, with 475,000 followers, focuses on fashion-related topics and gets between $1,000 and $1,800 per post (AJStream 2018).

What makes for a successful connection between a corporation and a social media influencer? First, there must be transparency so that followers will know when the influencer genuinely likes something and when he or she is being paid for positive reviews. Buying likes and shares doesn't work because savvy followers can easily find out and "out you" to the rest of the group. Although one report claims that 93 percent of top celebrity Instagram ads are not properly disclosed, transparency is critical in maintaining trust with a group of followers. Influencers walk a fine line between being aspirational, but also relatable. When influencers have formal collaborations or agreements with brands, they are perceived as not as relatable, and that hurts their credibility (AJStream 2018).

A second ingredient needed for success is a match between the brand and the celebrity's background and expertise. This issue was a big reason why the Irish social media influencer mentioned previously experienced so much backlash. As someone who was mainly concerned with pop culture and fashion, there was very little connection between her area of expertise and a luxury hotel. Indeed, many who criticized her suggested that she just wanted a free hotel for Valentine's Day. When there is a match between the brand and the influencer, the content will resonate with followers. When social media influencers put themselves in the public eye to make a living, they can sometimes be held to unrealistic standards. However, if they remember to be transparent with their followers and only post about issues with which they already have some degree of expertise, there will be fewer chances for difficulties (AJStream 2018).

In the not-so-distant past, marketing relied quite heavily on mass-market advertising. Today, marketing is about engaging with tribes. Indeed, in today's *attention economy*, social media tribes can make or break a brand (Godin 2008).

Questions

1. Think about your own social media activity. Who do you follow and who follows you? What do you get out of this activity with these tribes?
2. Have you ever purchased a brand that was promoted by an influencer on social media? Why or why not?
3. Thinking about some of the social media influencers you follow, to what extent (1) are they transparent and (2) do they promote brands that are a match to their own experience/expertise? Discuss.

Sources: AJStream (2018); Godin (2008).

On the receiving end of the communication process, we have **opinion seekers**, who are people who search for information and advice to assist in their decision-making. In looking back at the consumer problem-solving or decision-making processes, opinion-seeking is a form of external information search.

In this discussion, we use the terms opinion leaders and **influencers** interchangeably. In examining the influence across a network, it is important to consider the *who*, the *what*, and the *how*. First, it is important to consider the kind of people who are doing the influencing. Celebrities such as Oprah

Opinion seekers are people who search for information and advice to assist in their decision-making.

Influencers (or opinion leaders) are individuals who, compared to others, exert more influence on the decisions of other individuals.

Winfrey can recommend a previously unknown book, which then becomes a bestseller. This influence has more to do with Oprah's celebrity power through the mass media than with the actual message or how it is communicated. In this case, the *who* is more important than the *what* or the *how* (Watts 2007). Second, another thing to consider in examining influence is *what* the message is actually about. If it is a message that is important to many people or a message with which many people can identify, the message will spread across a network quickly. In March 2018, news reports revealed that a Russian-linked research firm harvested information from eighty-seven million Facebook users to target them with a variety of political messages. Facebook lost $80 billion in market value immediately after the news broke and then responded by making it much easier for users to use and enable their privacy settings (Valinsky 2018). For their part, users responded with the #DeleteFacebook hashtag, which was used and shared tens of thousands of times. Although it is difficult to tell how many people left Facebook because of the controversy, some very popular influencers encouraged their followers to delete their profiles (Hsu 2018).

Third, we need to consider *how* the message is communicated. You don't have to be a celebrity to use the power of mass communication to dramatically influence public opinion. A notable example is musician Dave Carroll's YouTube video "United Airlines breaks guitars" (see: https://www.youtube.com/watch?v=5YGc4zOqozo). Carroll produced this funny video with a catchy song to express his frustration with the airline after it allegedly damaged his guitar and provided poor customer service and follow-up. At the time of this writing, his video had more than twenty million views and his song had become a bestseller on iTunes in Canada. Does this mean that anyone can influence the market if they have the right message? Maybe. It certainly struck a chord with many passengers who have been frustrated by the airlines' lack of care, but above all, the video was a highly effective communications tool because of the catchy tune and the "Ugh, I've been there!" scenes.

Opinion leaders and information flow

Some experts have suggested that social influence may be more complex than the two-step flow of communication might have us believe. They have suggested that information flow in social media succeeds because of "a critical mass of easily influenced individuals influencing other easy-to-influence people" (Watts and Dodds 2007, 454). In addition, influence can flow back and forth between leaders and seekers. Finally, there could be multiple steps as the influence moves through high-level opinion leaders, to low-level opinion leaders, to the follower.

Executives at Timberland experienced the power of this process when its iconic boot was picked up as a fashion accessory for hip-hop fans. It started when artists like Tupac and Kanye West were seen wearing the shoes, and Notorious B.I.G. didn't just wear the shoes—he rapped about them. Once this happened, fans everywhere had to have a pair. Although this had been happening since the 1990s, it wasn't until the early 2000s that the marketing team at Timberland started to take notice. They were initially surprised by this new group of dedicated customers, because their original target market was a group of men in blue-collar jobs like construction, who needed to keep their feet safe and protected in harsh environments (see Photo 10.8 for an ad aimed at Timberland's original target market). Soon, however, managers at Timberland embraced the idea of a new target market and, among other innovations, created a website where customers could design their own "Timbs" with custom stitching, colors, and images to suit their own tastes. It is likely that the success of Timberland with this new target market was helped in large part by influencers who then passed along the information to their own networks.

Expert influencers

Expert influencers are people who have high levels of knowledge or experience in a particular context. Examples include a doctor who can influence individuals about health-related issues or a chef who can exert influence about flavors, ingredients, and methods of cooking. Expert influencers like these people have

Photo 10.8 *Timberland ad from about 2015*

power to influence the marketplace, primarily because other people make assumptions about the expert. One research study found that when an expert uses strong negative language, including all capital letters, emoticons, and exclamation points, the "helpfulness" of the review increases and the attitude toward the product decreases. In contrast, when a novice does the same in a review, there are no changes in the perceived helpfulness of the review or in attitudes toward the product (Folse et al. 2016). Clearly, we take expert opinions seriously.

Trendsetters and coolhunters

Trendsetters are a special kind of influencer; they start popular movements in music, fashion, food, drinks, and entertainment. These agenda-setters are of particular interest to marketers because where these "cool" people lead, others will follow. Certainly, what is cool for one group of consumers may not be cool for another. However, we can define *cool* as knowledge or expertise in what is considered trendy or fashionable (Nancarrow and Nancarrow 2007). *Coolhunters* follow trendsetters in an effort to also become cool. In an effort to quickly identify emerging trends, consumer and marketing researchers have developed research methods to track and engage trendsetters. These research methods are primarily qualitative in nature and include ethnographies and shop-alongs. During a shop-along, for example, a researcher accompanies a consumer throughout an entire shopping trip, observing every detail of the shopping experience. From a marketing perspective, there are some challenges with trendsetting and coolhunting. First, these qualitative research

Trendsetters are a special kind of influencer; they start popular movements in music, fashion, food, drinks, and entertainment.

techniques rely on interpretation, which sometimes makes it difficult for marketers to accurately identify a trend and creatively turn it into a consumer product. Second, not all trends have mass-market appeal. Finally, and perhaps most important, once a new trend achieves mass-market acceptance, it is no longer cool.

◉ Word of Mouth Influence

The two-step flow of communication relies on both formal communication from a media source and informal communication from influencers (Katz and Lazarsfeld 1955; Rogers 1962). **Word of mouth** (**WOM**) is an informal communication, either positive or negative, about products, attributes, retailers, or consumption experiences. Consumers naturally share information with one another about a variety of consumption-related experiences and impressions. Word of mouth influence happens both in face-to-face contexts and in electronic contexts (referred to as eWOM).

Word of mouth (WOM) is an informal communication, either positive or negative, about products, attributes, retailers, or consumption experiences.

Getting to know the power of word of mouth

Word of mouth can be a powerful tool for marketers, if used correctly. To successfully deploy a WOM effort, we must first distinguish between WOM that is self-generated versus WOM that is company generated. Second, we must understand how to spur WOM activity among consumers.

Endogenous versus exogenous

There are two different kinds of WOM communication, and one— **endogenous WOM**—is clearly preferred by marketers, especially when it is positive. Endogenous WOM springs up naturally when consumers, as a part of a normal conversation, share consumption-related information. On the flip side, **exogenous WOM** generally requires more effort on the part of the marketer. This type of WOM only occurs because of a firm's marketing efforts; the organization does something that is interesting, exciting, and worth talking about. Endogenous and exogenous WOM often work synergistically with one another, as depicted in Insights from the Field 10.2. Firms must be very careful when attempting to generate exogenous WOM because consumers may imagine ulterior motives for the firm. If this happens, consumers may be less willing to engage in positive WOM and may even engage in negative WOM (Verlegh et al. 2004).

Endogenous word of mouth springs up naturally when consumers, as a part of a normal conversation, share consumption-related information.

Exogenous word of mouth only occurs because of a firm's marketing efforts; the organization does something that is interesting, exciting, and worth talking about.

The Word of Mouth Marketing Association has a code of ethics and standards of conduct as a requirement for membership of the association. Although the understanding is that industry members "do the right thing" by engaging in responsible self-regulatory efforts, most of the code is built on laws that are already in place at the US Federal Trade Commission. There are

Have you seen their sushi bar? Word of mouth at Wegmans

Word of mouth is a powerful source of influence and marketers try to encourage positive WOM among consumers about their brands. Given the opportunity, marketers would prefer to encourage endogenous WOM, because it is generally considered the most authentic form of brand communication. This type of communication is perceived as more genuine because it is the consumer, not the company, who is saying positive things about the brand. Many examples exist of once-obscure singers and other artists becoming famous through the power of WOM and social media. Shortly after a twelve-year-old Justin Bieber posted a video of himself singing a song from a local competition in 2008, he started to gain a following on YouTube. Soon, he posted more videos of himself singing and playing the guitar and became an online sensation. By the ripe old age of thirteen, he had signed his first record contract with Usher. Shawn Mendes started out uploading his music to Vine and soon gained a loyal and passionate following. Adding his songs to iTunes helped tremendously in getting the world to know about and like his music. In 2015, he got his first big break when he opened for Taylor Swift's "1989" World Tour (Kircher 2015).

Word of mouth influence has been employed across many contexts, and few have been as successful as the Rochester, New York–based food retailer Wegmans.

● **Photo 10.9** *Wegmans stores generate positive word of mouth*

(continued)

The family-run organization was founded in 1916 and is known for its wide variety of fresh produce, bakery items, meat, and fish. It also has a variety of freshly prepared items and meals, including a hot food bar, pizza, sandwiches, and a sushi bar. Importantly, visiting a Wegmans store is an experience in itself and it is easy to get lost in the displays of tasty temptations and load up your shopping cart. Sales associates are easy to find, extremely friendly, and always smiling (see Photo 10.9). Even though it is only a regional retailer, Wegmans consistently outperforms the competition on indicators such as corporate reputation, workplace environment, customer satisfaction, and ethics ("Company Overview" 2020). What makes Wegmans employees so happy? Wegmans invests heavily in employee development programs and scholarships, and it has a very favorable benefits package. Many of the company's mid- and upper-level managers have been with the organization for decades, with many who started working at Wegmans when they first graduated from high school or college. In addition, employees appreciate working for a company that has high standards and ethics. Wegmans invests heavily in its local communities and sources many of its items from local farmers and producers (Danziger 2018). All of these factors motivate increased endogenous and exogenous WOM about Wegmans.

Endogenous word of mouth— endogenous WOM is clearly working in Wegmans' favor—researchers have found that 90 percent of conversations about Wegmans are positive and only 6 percent are negative. Consumers particularly like the quality of the products and shopping experience; there is always something innovative and exciting to catch the eye of the customer. This positive WOM definitely translates into customer loyalty; even though it is only a regional player, Wegmans is America's favorite grocery store (Danziger 2018).

Exogenous word of mouth—Wegmans is also successful at generating exogeneous WOM because of the company's values and its initiatives. Wegmans made nationwide headlines a few years ago when it named Colleen Wegman the president and CEO of the organization, a fourth-generation family member and the first woman to take over the helm of the company. This news made significant waves throughout the entire food industry. Buzz has also been created because of the organization's various initiatives, some of them stemming from Colleen Wegman's position as the chair of United Way's board of directors. She has given frequent interviews and speeches, as well as commencement addresses. Wegmans also engages in frequent community service projects and donations to food banks (Clausen 2017). Consumers appreciate these newsworthy stories and use WOM to talk to one another about them.

Questions

1. Find at least three examples of endogenous WOM and three examples of exogenous WOM. What are some similarities and differences between the two types?

2. How easy is it to detect exogenous WOM? Are there any clues or signals that consumers can use to differentiate between endogenous and exogenous WOM?

3. What do we mean when we say that endogenous and exogenous WOM work synergistically with one another?

Sources: Clausen (2017); "Company Overview" (2020); Danzinger (2018); Kircher (2015); Wilson, Giebelhausen, and Brady (2017).

three key guidelines regarding testimonials and WOM endorsements of products (Word of Mouth Marketing Association 2014, 3–4):

- There must be disclosure of any "material connections" for both paid and unpaid relationships that might not reasonably be expected by the audience.

- Endorsements must reflect the honest opinions, findings, beliefs, or experience of the endorser.

- To limit their potential liability, marketers should provide guidance and training to all individuals involved. Marketers should monitor all activities and take steps to stop any activities that are deemed deceptive.

Initiating word of mouth

How do companies accomplish these kinds of results? Sometimes it just happens organically, as in the case of Wegmans. They have a superior retail experience, top-notch products, and an active set of social responsibility initiatives. Sometimes, organizations need to hire outside help with WOM. Ripple Street is a WOM marketing firm that brings people together to hang out and talk about their favorite brands. For its biggest clients, Ripple Street will recruit one thousand fans, who in turn invite their friends to a brand-focused party. The fee for this service is $100,000. To be invited to the event, these fans and friends need to have large social networks and be active in posting pictures and comments to those networks. An executive at Ripple Street commented, "We find the biggest fans and get them to work for the brands that they love . . . all the videos and pictures and blog comments they create are there for [the client] to use and show as evidence of how much people love the [brand]" (O'Malley 2005). Ripple Street also organizes smaller parties and in 2018 added a variety of new services and applications that bridge online, offline, and in-store consumer experiences. Ripple Street has over one million registered users and its recent clients include such well-known global giants as Mattel, Dr. Pepper, Snapple, and Nickelodeon (Raitt 2018).

Word of mouth is often initiated with *product seeding*, which allows consumers to experience the product and then naturally start talking about it (Samson 2010). Whom do marketers like to target with WOM campaigns? Research indicates that, rather than target the most loyal customers, it is best to target less loyal customers who are communicating with acquaintances, not friends. Why? When less loyal customers communicate with acquaintances about the merits of a brand, conversations are generated that would never have happened on their own. Obviously, friends talk to one another on a regular basis. Exogenous WOM efforts, however, might get acquaintances to talk with one another about the brand, when they would not have done so otherwise. When exogenous WOM occurs with these customers, short-term sales increase (Godes and Mayzlin 2009; Samson 2010).

It seems logical that most marketing managers would want to encourage positive WOM. After all, you want people to always say positive things about your brand, right? Not so fast. Negative WOM has some distinct benefits too. Specifically, for those consumers who feel a close personal connection to the brand, negative WOM by others can encourage these consumers to increase their intentions to buy the product. Why? These consumers feel defensive about the brand and do not appreciate the negative attacks against a brand they love and to which they feel connected. In essence, an attack against the brand is an attack against the self (Wilson, Giebelhausen, and Brady 2017).

The world is flat

According to *New York Times* columnist Thomas Friedman, technology has made it much easier for people all around the world to connect, communicate, and collaborate. Technology has thus resulted in a "flattening" of distinctions between technology "haves" and "have nots" and means that individuals around the world can have access to the world's libraries, music, news, and trends (Friedman 2009). With regard to communication about brands, eWOM has the opportunity to reach large numbers of people around the world. Consumers search for information and advice that is offered by companies and other consumers. A full 82 percent of US adults report that, at least sometimes, they read online ratings or reviews before buying a new product for the first time. How often a consumer looks at online reviews depends on the customer's age. While 53 percent of consumers under thirty years old read online reviews, only 34 percent of people ages fifty to sixty-four do so. Americans are somewhat skeptical of the information they get from these reviews, with 48 percent saying that it is often hard to tell if an online review is truthful and unbiased. Not surprisingly, the more a consumer uses online reviews, the more likely that consumer will be to report that reviews are trustworthy; 65 percent of consumers who always or often read reviews say that they are generally accurate (Smith and Anderson 2016).

When marketers use eWOM, they have the ability to influence people on a global scale. We know that individuals tend to trust others who are similar to themselves (Eccleston and Griser 2008), so even if they live in different parts of the world and have completely different lives, if they have a similar interest, they have something in common. One example of a site that offers information and advice in a narrowly focused area is TripAdvisor, where consumers share their restaurant, hotel, and travel experiences with other travelers. TripAdvisor even provides its top restaurants and hotels with stickers to put on their front windows and doors to reinforce the connection to the positive reviews they have received. TripAdvisor also actively encourages customer feedback to assist other consumers in making decisions. After travel is completed, users are sent a request to fill out an evaluation of their experience. Two additional dimensions of WOM are crowdsourcing and social media platforms.

Crowdsourcing and user-generated content

Have you ever heard the expression two heads are better than one? The idea is that when two or more people work on a problem, it is easier to come up with a solution. Further, the solution itself is often better! The online environment provides a forum where people can share and explore a wide variety of ideas and innovations. **Crowdsourcing** happens when a company or organization takes a task or a problem that normally would be performed by employees and

Crowdsourcing happens when a company or organization takes a task or a problem that normally would be performed by employees and gives it to a group of people to solve.

gives it to a group of people to solve (Howe 2006). Here, people can develop creative solutions to problems by seeing the problem from different perspectives, bringing greater diversity of expertise to the problem, and building on one another's ideas (Boudreau and Lakhani 2013; Earls 2009; Surowiecki 2004). Wikipedia is a form of crowdsourcing, as is Waze, the GPS and traffic app that provides users real-time information from other drivers.

One concern with crowdsourcing is that not only are participants not paid for their creative output, but also any output becomes the property of the company. Some critics claim that this represents a form of Internet exploitation (Postigo 2003). Others have argued that the company provides a forum that allows large numbers of people, who would not otherwise do so, see the creative output of their work (Brabham 2008). One example of crowdsourcing is the Steam Workshop company, which invites gamers to create content for games. They can create modifications for existing games, as well as simulations, characters, and other tools for gamers to use. Participants can play and discuss games, and they often work together with other developers in a variety of workshop spaces. Some participants can even earn money by selling their works. Another example is Shutterstock and iStock, which sell royalty-free photography. Clients purchase credits to buy images and photographers receive 20 percent of the purchase price every time their image is downloaded. Thus, creators benefit because they make money and get exposure for their work, and consumers benefit because they receive cheaper and better solutions (Earls 2009).

Although there is inevitably some loss of control over the process, organizations that crowdsource reap important benefits too. One obvious benefit is that crowdsourcing offers a diversity of opinions and approaches that are often far better than a company's in-house expertise. Another benefit is that the project can be scaled so that a vast number of people can work on the solution to get the job done more quickly and efficiently than a company's in-house team. A third, and less obvious, benefit is that members of the "crowd" simply have different motivations. While regular employees are normally extrinsically motivated by incentives such as bonuses and promotions, members of a crowd are more intrinsically motivated. They love the challenge and enjoy the process of solving a particularly difficult project or problem (Boudreau and Lakhani 2013).

The role of social media

Much user-generated content has arisen through the growth of social media, which allows users to create content and share it among friends and acquaintances. The number of people who are now using social media is staggering. However, not surprisingly, the use of social media differs by demographic in the United States. Indeed, if we compare younger to older demographics, we find some striking differences. For the eighteen- to twenty-four-year-old demographic in the United States, 94 percent use YouTube, 78 percent use Snapchat, 71 percent use Instagram, and 45 percent use Twitter (see

Table 10.3 Percentages of usage of social media vehicles

	FACEBOOK	YOUTUBE	INSTAGRAM	SNAPCHAT	LINKEDIN	TWITTER
Men	62	75	30	23	25	23
Women	74	72	39	31	25	24
Ages eighteen to twenty-four	80	94	71	78	25	45
Ages fifty to sixty-four	65	68	21	10	24	19
Education: some college	71	74	36	31	22	25
Education: college+	77	85	42	26	50	32
Total	68	73	35	27	25	24

Source: Smith and Anderson (2018).

Table 10.3). These differences represent complex problems for advertisers who must communicate with different target markets. The traditional formula of advertising on network TV no longer works as it did in your parents' generation. Just as it would not make sense to communicate with someone fifty to sixty-four years old via Snapchat, it doesn't make sense to communicate with someone eighteen to twenty-four years old using LinkedIn. Instead, advertisers need to speak with different target markets on their own terms using their social media vehicle of choice. In the case of younger audiences, advertisers might be well advised to use multiple platforms (Smith and Anderson 2018).

◉ The Family

Do you buy the same brand of pasta and sauce as your family? How about soap and laundry detergent? As young people grow up and start making their own purchase decisions, they make a variety of decisions about which brands they will buy. Many consumers buy the same brands they had at home when they were growing up. That's one reason why the influence of family on decision-making is so fascinating. Because of the frequency and intensity of interactions between family members, especially when the children are young, families are especially important in terms of consumer socialization. The family is a reference group that exerts an especially strong influence on an individual's consumption decisions and behaviors. Just like other reference groups, the family structure accomplishes this by exerting **informational**, **utilitarian**, and **value-expressive influence**, with the informational influence playing a particularly strong role with young adult consumers (Shim 1996; Bravo, Fraj, and Martínez 2006) (see Photo 10.10).

Family decision-making can be complex, with the adults and children all exerting influence on one another (Shoham and Dalakas 2005). For example, research into family choices about vacation destinations has found that different family members have different roles and power in the decision process. Although children are generally active participants in decision-making, parents act as gatekeepers by filtering out any choices they believe to be inappropriate (Wu, Holmes, and Tribe 2010). Fashion and clothing purchases are another example of influence in families. While much influence is from parent to child, an interesting trend seems to be taking place in that sometimes influence flows from child to parent when children help their parents decide what is fashionable or trendy (Boden 2006).

● **Photo 10.10** *Example of the family unit in an advertisement for Nestlé*

Family structure and roles

Some people may argue that there is no longer a strict definition of a "traditional" family in the United States; families are becoming increasingly diverse in a variety of ways. Regardless of the composition of the family, decision-making in the family is a joint (rather than individual) process, and family members occupy different buying roles depending on the nature of the product or service being consumed. Typically, parents are the decision-makers and ultimate purchasers, but other family members also fulfill important roles, such as initiating purchases, influencing the purchasing process, and consuming the product. Insights from the Boardroom 10 provides an in-depth description of decision-making in Hispanic families that are new to the United States.

With ever-faster advancements in technology and social media, family decision-making has changed dramatically from that of previous generations. Thus, the **reciprocal view of family decision-making and consumer socialization** offers a more holistic and realistic perspective about what happens in many modern families. This reciprocal view recognizes that there is a significant amount of influence that flows back and forth between parents and children. This view of family decision-making has three main components (Ekström, Tansujah, and Foxman 1987), each representing a type of influence between parents and children:

- First is **parental yielding**, where a parent is influenced by a child's request and "surrenders" the decision-making authority. This often occurs when, for example, a parent says, "Fine, you can have that candy bar!" while in the checkout lane at the grocery store.

Information refers to data that have already been organized and analyzed.

Utilitarian function (of attitudes) is based on the idea that consumers seek maximum utility and value from their consumption.

Reciprocal view of family decision-making and consumer socialization recognizes that there is a significant amount of influence that flows back and forth between parents and children.

Parental yielding is when a parental decision-maker is influenced by a child's request and "surrenders" the decision-making authority.

- Second, children employ a range of tactics such as informing, persuasion, and reasoning strategies to exert their influence within family decision-making.

Reverse socialization is where parents acquire consumer skills from their children.

- Third, **reverse socialization** often occurs, which is when parents acquire consumer skills from their children. This is evident in the areas of technology, fashion, celebrity/popular culture, environmental issues, and ethical issues.

INSIGHTS FROM THE BOARDROOM 10

It's not the destination, it's the journey.
—Ralph Waldo Emerson

● Andrew Speyer

This quote not only represents Andrew Speyer and the impressive trajectory of his career, but also represents a key insight he's discovered in his work with the Hispanic market. After graduating from the University of Miami with a degree in English and Latin American studies, he landed his first job at advertising powerhouse Crispin Porter Bogusky in Miami, where he worked on the antitobacco "Truth Campaign." Launched in 2000, this campaign has been credited with lowering the US teen smoking rate from 23 percent to 8 percent (Beer 2015). To Speyer, this is still the most impactful work he

has ever done; it's the one campaign he brings up and talks about most often. Over the years, he has worked at a number of other agencies, always honing his skills in marketing to Hispanics and, over that time, he has worked with such nationally well-known brands as American Airlines, P&G, S. C. Johnson, VW, BMW, Citibank, Chase Bank, MTV, and Verizon. Today, he is a regional marketing director for Airbnb. His diverse work experiences, as well as his own background, have made Speyer one of the foremost experts in the Hispanic market. Perhaps one of the most important insights Speyer has developed over his years of doing research is that the Hispanic market is much more *process oriented* than *outcome oriented*.

One project illustrates the importance of that insight quite well. While working with a well-known cleaning product that promises to do the hard work for you, Speyer saw firsthand the importance of *process* over *outcome* with the Hispanic market. On the surface, this product seems to have a lot of positive benefits; who wouldn't be interested? The Hispanic market, that's who. Speyer and his team discovered that "the idea that the person cleaning the house does not have to work hard was not appealing. In the general market, the benefits to the product were outcome based—what mattered is that the house was clean and it was done with little effort. In the Hispanic market, effort and process count *a lot*. In fact, the outcome is less important than the process that got you there," shared Speyer (2017). He elaborated, "For many Hispanics, especially those recently arrived or the ones who are not as acculturated, women have a self-definition as mother, caretaker, homemaker, provider, and nurturer much more so than the general market." It simply would go against her own self-definition if she didn't put a lot of work and effort into these things. It's an expression of her love for her family and she feels good about herself when she does this.

Another example is from work he did on a brand of frozen food. The frozen food segment was created at the end of World War II, when women began to work outside the home and earn college degrees in greater numbers. This was an era of money, innovation, and a whole different set of demands on the household. One product that was introduced at this time was a whole frozen lasagna that could be popped into the oven for an easy and tasty dinner. The product itself was developed at a time when families still sat down and had dinner together. Right away, Speyer and his team found that there were two big trends that were working against this product for today's consumers. First, for the general market, although families like the convenience of a frozen meal that is easy to make, many families simply don't sit down together for dinner any longer. For the Hispanic market, although they still embrace the idea of sitting down with the family for a meal, the thought of having a frozen dinner doesn't resonate because it wasn't made by hand. For Hispanics, the *process* of assembling a meal by hand is incredibly important and they would have a hard time accepting a frozen dinner that required no preparation. So, for both markets, the current product was not relevant. Instead, Speyer and his team recommend single-serve lasagna in a variety of flavors.

What do Hispanics find surprising about American culture? Two big things stand out. The first is "how readily Americans simply throw things away because the Hispanic culture is one that fixes things. Hispanics know how to use tools and fix things. Also, the

consumption cycle that Americans are expected to reach is very elevated" (Speyer 2017). Many Americans are on a very fast-paced cycle of buy–use–throw away. Another surprise is that, unlike their general market counterparts who move out and get an apartment of their own, "younger Hispanics tend to move back home after college and live with their families well into adulthood. They have a lot of money because they're young professionals and don't have a lot of expenses, so many of them go out and buy a BMW or Lexus, which are certainly symbols of affluence and quality. It is no accident that South Florida, where the population of Hispanics in some areas is greater than 50% (Klas 2016), sells more BMW and Lexus cars than anywhere else in the country" (Speyer 2017).

With the fifty million Hispanics living in the United States growing to an estimated one hundred million by 2050 (Chappell 2015), this group of consumers is hard to ignore. Here are a few more observations about consumer behavior:

- Even if Hispanics don't need to speak Spanish, they prefer to do so.
- Many have very little connection to established mainstream or broadcast media.
- For bigger purchases, many consumers make decisions jointly with their families.
- Even for bigger purchases, many avoid financing deals and instead prefer to use cash (Speyer 2017).

Speyer concludes with two notes of caution when dealing with the Hispanic market. First, he cautions that although these conclusions are "gross generalizations" (2017) and don't apply to every consumer and every situation, they do apply more often than not. Second, the Hispanic market isn't one monolithic group. Hispanics come from different parts of the world and have very different value systems, cultures, and norms—a marketer certainly can't treat them all alike. So, if you're interested in embarking on a "journey" into the Hispanic market, remember the importance of process over outcome!

Sources: Beer (2015); Chappell (2015); Klas (2016); Speyer (2017).

Children and advertising

Companies are recognizing the importance of understanding children and are using the full range of media available to communicate with children and parents to encourage buy-in and engagement. See Insights from the Field 10.3 for an example of a campaign stressing the parent–child relationship. As another example, LEGO has been positioned as a lifestyle brand for children, with brand extensions in the form of clothing, movies, and video games designed to deepen this connection with the brand. Some critics claim that "big business is grooming our children for profit" by unethically targeting ads and product placements to them, as well as using them to act as influencers within their own social groups (Nairn and Mayo 2009).

 INSIGHTS FROM THE FIELD 10.3

Every time you go away . . .

In 2016, Heathrow Airport in London partnered with creative ad agency Havas London to create a campaign encouraging people to use Heathrow for their travel needs. Marketing managers for Heathrow wanted to position Heathrow as the global leader in bringing people together. By doing this, they hoped to increase year-over-year bookings of tickets as well as sales at their airport retail shops. Heathrow is one of the world's biggest airports, facilitating the travel of seventy-five million passengers per year. The execution of the ad relied heavily on images of families coming together and enjoying their time together. The ads depicted two adorable teddy bears, Doris and Edward Bair, who travel and come home to see their kids and grandkids. In the end, it became one of the most well-loved campaigns in the United Kingdom (Dowen 2017).

After conducting its research, the ad agency and the Heathrow marketing team realized that they needed to capture the hearts and minds of consumers, as well as encourage them to spend some emotional time with the brand. A key insight was that in order to position Heathrow as a global leader in bringing people together, the campaign needed to shine a light on the passengers. Whether families were seeking to connect or individuals were traveling for business, these passengers shared a common experience. In effect, these strangers shared more than they realized. The marketing and agency team then settled on three key subgoals (Dowen 2017):

1. Communicate the importance of Heathrow to an individual's travel plans—everyone has a story, regardless of where they're traveling or the purpose of the travel.
2. Tap into a "higher purpose" that resonates with the target market.
3. Use Steps 1 and 2 to remind people that Heathrow is the best airport for connections.

The campaign was launched in 2016 and was supported by online, print, and outdoor advertising (Dowen 2017). In the 2018 "Coming Home for Christmas" ad, the story continues with Doris and Edward Bair, who have now retired to Florida from the United Kingdom. Even though life in Florida is beautiful, with relaxing days spent at the pool, the Bairs are feeling quite sad this holiday season after they FaceTime with the kids and grandkids back in the United Kingdom. So, they decide to pack up their bags and fly home to surprise the family. On the way, they enjoy a pleasant flight and, before they leave the airport, they do a little Christmas shopping. The last scene of this mini drama shows them in a heart-warming reunion beside the Christmas tree that is likely to bring a tear to the viewer's eye. The imagery and execution are incredibly effective, as confirmed by an independent research study, which found that the ad trounced the competition in creating the highest

● **Photo 10.11** *Family exerts a strong influence on decision-making and behavior*

overall positive engagement for the holiday season (Oakes 2018) (check out the ad here: https://www.you-tube.com/watch?v=s5TkTj7Lqec) (see Photo 10.11).

This Insight from the Field illustrates not only the importance of the family in decision-making and behavior, but also the importance of creating insights in the development of strategy and execution.

Questions

1. Identify two or three other ad campaigns that depict a family relationship. What is the nature of the relationship? Do you think that the family context is suitable for this product? Why or why not?

2. Look at recent advertising for some other luxury brands. How do they convey the value of the product? How do some of the other concepts in this chapter (e.g., WOM, opinion leaders) help us shed light on the communications strategies used in these ads?

Sources: Dowen (2017); Oakes (2018).

These criticisms do have some validity. Across a number of studies, several strong and consistent results have found that advertising has a negative effect on children and adolescents. Overall, children who are exposed to more advertising are more likely to be materialistic and to have conflicts with their parents. For food marketing, the more children see food-related ads, they more likely they are to be obese. Another consistent finding is that the more they are exposed to alcohol-related advertising, the more likely they are to use alcohol early and to drink greater quantities of alcohol (see Lapierre et al. 2017). There is a plethora of research on the various effects of advertising on children, but most have come to the conclusion that there are more negative effects than positive effects. Marketers are starting to recognize that parents increasingly want to stop these negative effects. For example, because social media depends on advertisers for revenue, many of the social media giants have made big changes to their platforms in an attempt to keep parents happy and keep advertisers buying ads. For example, in 2018, after a series of inappropriate and offensive YouTube videos were posted by users, resulting in the loss of $750 million in advertising revenue for the site, the company hired thousands of software programmers to identify and remove inappropriate video clips from the site (Bergen and Shaw 2018).

Sociocultural trends and the family

If researchers can be certain about one thing about the modern-day family, it is that there is no clear definition of it. Both small and seismic shifts in the sociocultural landscape have resulted in many researchers giving up on the notion of finding an actual definition of "the family." For example, in Asia, the Middle East, and South America, several generations of a family often live under one roof or close together. Marriage rates are lowest in the Americas, Europe, and Australia, with couples preferring to live together (see Insights from Academia 10.3). Fertility rates vary widely around the world too. In East Asia and Europe, for example, fertility rates are so low (about 2.1 children per woman) that they are just enough to replace, but not increase the population. Compare this to an average of 5.5 children per woman in Nigeria (World Bank Data 2018a). The following sections will highlight four key sociocultural trends that impact the decision-making and consumption habits of American families.

 INSIGHTS FROM ACADEMIA 10.3

Should we order pizza or Thai tonight?

For many couples, it is quite common to go out to eat, order take-out, or cook and eat a meal together. Not surprisingly, couples exert a lot of influence on one another's food choices. What *is* surprising is who influences whom . . . and when. Researchers used a survey and three experiments to investigate how relationship status impacted food choice. They found that when the relationship is still in its formational stages, women are more likely to be influenced by the food choices of their partners. They will likely select a healthy meal if their partner does so; they will also select an unhealthy meal if the partner does so. From her perspective, at the beginning stages of a relationship, the woman's motivation is relationship formation and she wants to appear agreeable to the potential partner. Things change, however, once the relationship is more firmly established. When this happens, men are more likely to be influenced by the food choices of their partners. At this point, a man's motivation is to maintain the relationship, so he attempts to be more agreeable in his decisions and behaviors. Thus, he will be more likely to be influenced by his partner's healthy (or unhealthy) food choices. Now you know what your grandpa means when he says, "Happy wife, happy life!"

Hasford, J., B. Kidwell, and V. Lopez-Kidwell. 2018. "Happy Wife, Happy Life: Food Choices in Romantic Relationships." Journal of Consumer Research 44 (6): 1238–56.

A more multicultural America

There is sometimes confusion about the terminology used to describe the cultural background of an individual. First, a **bicultural** individual is someone who can identify with two distinct cultures. These cultures can be different races, ethnicities, religions, or nationalities. Perhaps a person has a Polish mother and an Indian father. Someone else could have one parent who is Jewish and another who is Christian. By having a foot in each culture, these consumers often adhere to important attitudes and customs of each culture. Similarly, a **multicultural** individual is someone who can relate to or identify with more than two cultures. When this occurs, individuals have several sets of cultural knowledge, customs, and behaviors with which they can identify and celebrate.

Families and countries can also be made up of different cultures. When we talk about a multicultural America, we are acknowledging that the country is becoming much more diverse in a variety of ways. The three biggest segments are African American, Asian American, and Hispanic. By 2044, the majority of the US population will be individuals from these cultural backgrounds. They already make up the fastest growing segment of the population in the United States and are responsible for 92 percent of the recent growth in population in the United States. Together, they make up 38 percent of the population and add 2.3 million people to their numbers every year. The growth in bicultural and multicultural individuals is also increasing, at an annual rate of about 14 percent (Nielsen 2015). Their influence on the overall American culture has been profound. Simply look at the number of diverse media channels, music choices, fashion trends, advertising, products, and food choices that are now available to all Americans. Just as Americans are becoming more diverse, America is also becoming more culturally diverse.

More single-parent households

Another trend that is impacting American life is the rise in single-parent households. In the United States, 31 percent of children live with just one parent, while 65 percent live with both parents (the remainder live with other people, such as grandparents). Compare this to some of the United States' biggest trading partners: the percentage of children living with one parent is 14 percent in India, 16 percent in Germany, 19 percent in Canada, 20 percent in Mexico, and 33 percent in the United Kingdom (World Family Map 2019). Of the families that are run by a single parent, 85 percent live with the mother and 15 percent live with the father (Mintel 2018). Society's views are changing too. In the United States, for example, 70 percent of women agree that one parent can bring up a child just as well as two parents together (DePaulo 2017).

This has implications on consumption-related behaviors. For example, compared to children who live with two-parent or blended families, children who live with a single parent are more involved in the family's consumption-related decision-making and behaviors (Tinson, Nancarrow, and Brace 2008).

Bicultural individuals can identify with two distinct cultures.

Multicultural individuals can relate to or identify with more than two cultures.

Another implication is that children raised in a single-parent household have fewer resources. While a full 19 percent of single-parent families have trouble making ends meet, only 6 percent of families with married parents report these financial troubles (Pew Research Center 2015). Single-parent families often need to make sacrifices, such as cutting back on discretionary spending or delaying big purchases.

Older first-time parents

In the United States, the average age of first-time mothers increased to 26.3 in 2014. Compare this to 24.9 in 2000 and 21.4 in 1970. Overall, births to women over the age of 35 are increasing and births to younger women have been decreasing (Mintel 2018). Why is this happening? Many professional women want to be established in their careers before they decide to start a family; having both a career and children is no easy task. Also, many women have decided that they want to accomplish specific goals before having a child, like financial goals (such as paying off student loans) or personal goals (such as traveling the world). The result is that individuals are older when they start families. Once children do arrive on the scene, older first-time parents generally spend more money on their children because they are further along in their careers and thus have more savings and income. More money means that parents can provide a higher living standard for the child (Kincaid 2015). They feel compelled to indulge the child and spare little expense.

One fascinating trend related to older parents is the shift in the parent–child distance. Whereas older generations had more of a hierarchical distance between parents and children, today's children and parents say they feel a very close connection to one another. This close connection can lead to similar tastes and preferences, for example, in a variety of consumption activities. Parents and children may like similar music, fashion, food, and entertainment. Harry Potter books and movies, for example, are enjoyed by people of all ages. It is not surprising then, that some experts have noticed that these older parents may sometimes even regard their children as an extension of themselves, a mini-me, so to speak. Marketers have picked up on this trend—some of the world's top fashion designers also have children's lines, such as Lilly Pulitzer, Marc Jacobs, and Oscar de la Renta (Feder 2015).

Lower birth rates

In the United States, women have, on average, 1.8 children over their lifetimes. South Africans have 2.4, Indians have 2.3, Mexicans have 2.2, Chinese have 1.6, and Canadians have 1.5 (World Bank Data 2019b, 2019c, 2019d, 2019e, 2019f, 2019g). Lower birth rates mean that children grow up with fewer siblings, which means that these children may have a harder time developing important skills like standing up for themselves, negotiating with others, and appreciating differences in others. Compared to children who grow up with many brothers and sisters, children in smaller families simply don't have the daily practice of dealing with an annoying sister or brother, especially when that child has to share a room, toys, and/or bathroom. Lower birth rates also mean that parents can allocate more resources, including time and money, per child. The child with fewer or no siblings doesn't have to deal with a parent who is forced to make a choice about who to pick up after practice or who has to use an older sibling's old sports equipment.

Children who grow up with no siblings are often referred to as *only children* and there is a common stereotype that these children are more selfish and more sensitive to criticism. The counterargument is that spoiling a child is more of a parenting problem, and the addition of another child or two to the mix is unlikely to fix that problem. A recent study, however, may shed some light on this issue. It utilized brain imaging technology and found that the brain structures of children with siblings are different from the brain structures of children who grow up without siblings. Indeed, brain scans revealed that only children had lower levels of "agreeableness" but higher levels of "flexibility and creativity" than their counterparts who had siblings. That is, the brain structures for agreeableness were less developed, but the structures for flexibility and creativity were more developed for only children (Yang et al. 2017). Before marketers take this finding too seriously, there are many reasons why the structure of the brain can be altered, and until there are more studies that confirm the findings, this research should be interpreted with caution.

◉ Social Class and Consumption

Another social structure that exerts an impact on consumption behaviors and processes is social class. **Social class** divides groups of people based on a composite measure of income, occupation, and education. There are two important points that need to be made with regard to social class. First, within a given social status level, members are linked to one another on the basis of wealth and power (Weber 1978). Therefore, an individual's social class signals distinction and social position to others. Second, it is important to emphasize that social class is not just about income; it is about a combination of income, occupation, and education. In the United States, there are six broad social classes, and each one encompasses a set of consumption behaviors that is very clear to members of that class. Although there are several methods for sorting individuals into social class groups, Table 10.4 presents one classification that provides some guidance for marketers and other decision-makers.

Admittedly, it is sometimes difficult to talk about social class in the United States. Most people like to believe in the American Dream: if you

Social class is a classification system that divides groups of people based on a composite measure of income, occupation, and education.

Table 10.4 Social class in America

Capitalist class (the top 1 percent)	Generally divided into two categories. The first is *old money*, individuals who have inherited their money or receive it from investments (think the Rockefellers or the Vanderbilts). The second is *new money*, or self-made millionaires and billionaires, like Bill Gates and Oprah Winfrey. Their money comes from hard work, talent, and even some luck. They are often referred to as *nouveaux riche* ("newly rich").
Upper middle class (about 15 percent of the population)	Individuals in this class are often referred to as *white-collar* professionals and have professional careers, such as doctors, professors, upper-level managers, and lawyers. These individuals generally have a college degree as well as one or more graduate-level degrees.
Lower middle class (about 34 percent of the population)	These individuals usually have a high school education and may have attended some college or had technical training. They are generally lower-level managers, supervisors, or craftspeople.
Working class (about 30 percent of the population)	These individuals are often referred to as *blue-collar* workers because they often wear a uniform to work. They most likely have finished high school. Their jobs are as police officers, electricians, carpenters, and mechanics, for example.
Working poor (about 15 percent of the population)	These individuals are laborers who receive very low pay for unskilled work. Sometimes they are seasonal or temporary workers; they hold jobs such as low-paid salesclerks or gardeners and receive hourly pay instead of salaries. They may or may not have a high school education. Sometimes, they work two or more part-time jobs and very few of these individuals have healthcare or retirement benefits from their employers. Their jobs are often at risk of being outsourced.
Underclass (about 5 percent of the population)	There is a fine line between individuals in this class and the working poor class because all it takes for someone to drop down to the underclass is a health crisis or an outsourced job. Individuals in this class live a very difficult existence and are more likely to experience shorter life expectancies and health problems than the other social classes. Many rely on public assistance.

Source: D. L. Gilbert (2015).

are smart and you work hard enough, it is possible to be successful. The idea is that individuals who work hard enough can pull themselves up and achieve anything they desire. However, it is sometimes quite hard to make such a move because a person's education and occupation make it difficult to achieve big advancements in income (see Photo 10.12). Indeed, a person in the bottom two social classes has only a 9 percent chance of making it to the top two social classes. The United States has one of the "tallest" social class structures in the developed world; there are huge differences between the people at the top and the people at the bottom. Because of this, critics argue that rather than looking at how easy it is to move up or down the social class ladder, it is more informative to compare how well your family is doing compared to previous generations (N. Gilbert 2017). In other words, to tell how you and your family are doing, ask how much access, opportunity, and resources your family has compared to that of your parents and grandparents.

● **Photo 10.12** *Education exerts a big impact on social class*

Social class classification systems, such as those depicted in Table 10.4, tend to focus on the types and amounts of resources available to its members. There are three types of resources (Bourdieu 1984):

- *Economic capital* describes the amount of financial resources to which the individual has access.

- *Social capital* concerns the important connections in an individual's network.

- *Cultural capital* is knowledge and behavior that comes from an individual's upbringing and education in a particular social class. Knowing which fork to use or which wine to order at a fancy restaurant would be part of the cultural capital for someone in the capitalist class or upper middle class, whereas knowing how to change a tire might be part of the cultural capital for someone in the working class.

If we view consumer behavior through the lens of these three types of capital, we can see that an individual's tastes are an indicator of social class. Individuals need to possess the "right kinds" of capital to successfully navigate the terrain of their own social class. Picture someone, perhaps a police officer, who just won the lottery. Even though this person has economic capital, this lucky new millionaire will have a hard time fitting in with other individuals in the *newly rich* social class because of a lack of social and cultural capital. Similarly, imagine an unlucky individual who has the social and cultural capital of the upper middle class, but suddenly has the economic capital of the working poor. This person would also have a difficult time fitting in. Research on social class, types of capital, and status has provided a rich source of insights for consumer researchers (e.g., Moisio, Arnould, and Gentry 2013; Piacentini and Mailer 2004; Üstüner and Holt 2010).

We know that consumers at the lower end of the social class structure have a difficult time accessing certain resources and therefore are more likely to be at a disadvantage in the marketplace. Consumer researchers have examined the coping mechanisms for people living with severe resource constraints (e.g., Baker, Gentry, and Rittenburg 2005; Hamilton and Catterall 2005; Piacentini, Hibbert, and Hogg 2013) and have found, for example, that those living with few resources are more likely to use cash, are less likely to use bank accounts and credit cards, and seldom qualify for discounts (e.g., through credit or debit payment options). In addition, those with few resources may not have access to Wi-Fi and the Internet, which can make it difficult to make price comparisons or get free shipping, for example. Despite some challenges in reaching these customers, marketers must ensure that consumers with fewer resources are not unfairly disadvantaged in the marketplace.

Studying social structures and processes adds to our depth of understanding of consumer behavior. It reinforces the complex nature of consumer behavior and emphasizes the fact that no consumer makes a decision in isolation. Indeed, often with very little awareness of its occurrence, a myriad of external structures and processes shape the consumer's existence.

◉ Summary

This chapter explored the role of social structures and processes on consumer decision-making and behavior and, in so doing, introduced several insights that are relevant for marketing managers.

Reference groups were introduced and we found that reference groups exerted different influences on consumer decision-making and behavior. To illustrate this point, we introduced a wide range of examples from contemporary consumer culture, such as the Steampunk movement and TalkToChef, an interactive forum offering expert advice on cooking. We also found that organizations can sometimes end up in a lot of hot water when they do not pay careful attention to important reference groups, as happened with Gucci's blackface sweater.

Processes of reference group influence were introduced and we paid particular attention to informational, utilitarian, and value-expressive mechanisms of influence. Figure 10.1 helped differentiate four different kinds of consumption experiences (public necessities, public luxuries, private necessities, and private luxuries) and the types of reference group influence most relevant for each one. We also examined the types of conformity and the use of power in social relationships. In Insights from Academia 10.1, we described how relationship partners can impact our choice of something as simple as a Coke or Pepsi and how similarity in brand choices can even lead to better life satisfaction.

Moving on, we looked at the different types of *social power* that is exerted between groups and individuals. Smart marketers are keenly aware of the important role that reference groups play in a customer's life and how they influence and share product-related information. The two-step flow of communication provided a useful model to explain the relationships between opinion leaders and opinion seekers. Insights from the Field 10.2 examined endogenous and exogenous WOM communications about Wegmans, the highly successful regional grocery store. We found that tribes facilitate many social connections and communication processes and concluded that marketers must find ways to leverage the influence of opinion leaders, while also being careful not to violate the norms of social media communication.

Next, we discussed the influence of *the family* on consumer behavior, paying particular attention to key trends that influence American family life. Further, we found that the family can be an important reference group and concepts related to family can be effectively utilized by marketers, as demonstrated in the Heathrow Airport example. Finally, the concept of *social class* was presented and we concluded that income, occupation, and education provided a much more comprehensive depiction of social class than income alone. We introduced one way to classify individuals into broad social classes and emphasized the importance of access to resources as a way to communicate one's social class and live within it. As always, knowing how this process works can provide valuable insights to marketers as they create products and communicate information about the value proposition. Case Study 10 pulls together concepts of reference group influence and social media as it takes an in-depth look at "The Facts Now Campaign," an effort to encourage teens in Florida to not use tobacco.

KEY TERMS

aspirational groups p. 358
bicultural p. 385
coercive power p. 366
compliance p. 363
conformity p. 363
connectors p. 367
contactual or associative group p. 358
crowdsourcing p. 376
disclaimant group p. 358

dissociative or avoidance groups p. 360
endogenous word of mouth p. 372
exogenous word of mouth p. 372
expert power p. 366
formal group p. 360
identification p. 363
influencers p. 369
informal group p. 361

informational group influence p. 362
informational power p. 366
informational social influence p. 365
internalization p. 363
legitimate power p. 366
market mavens p. 367
multicultural p. 385
normative social influence p. 364

REVIEW QUESTIONS

1. List the four main types of reference groups and provide at least two examples of each one. What is the difference between informal and formal groups?
2. Describe the three main mechanisms of reference group influence. Provide at least two examples of each mechanism that might come into play when you are shopping for party supplies.
3. Why is conformity so important to social structures and processes? What are the five types of conformity?
4. How are opinion leaders different from influencers? In what way do opinion leaders impact information flow and influence within their networks?
5. Are families or tribes a more relevant concept for marketers today? Support your answer with arguments from the chapter.
6. Is the concept of social class an outdated notion in America today? Why or why not?

DISCUSSION QUESTIONS

1. Look at Figure 10.1 and create your own matrix with products and brands you use. Fill in at least two to three products in each of the four squares of the matrix. In what way would this matrix look different for your parents? What about for someone in a different social class?
2. Select two different kinds of conformity. For each one, identify a situation where an individual's consumption behavior might be altered. Discuss a variety of ways in which a marketing manager could use this information.
3. Do a quick Internet search and find a crowdsourcing site. Describe it. What benefits is the site owner getting? What benefits does the consumer or participant receive? In your opinion, is this cheap labor for the site owner or a creative outlet for the participant? Support your answer.
4. Under what circumstances could a company benefit from negative WOM? If a company does experience negative WOM, what should it do in the short term? What about the long term?
5. There are at least four important trends impacting the American family. Select one and create a set of insights that marketers can use to better connect with their target audience. For example, lower fertility rates mean smaller families. One insight could be that big-box retailers like Costco need to provide smaller package sizes for smaller families. Be creative!
6. Why is the topic of social class so uncomfortable for some Americans? Rather than relying just on income, why is it important to understand social class as a compilation of income, occupation, and education? How does this impact the insights that marketers create?

CASE STUDY 10

Tobacco Is The Only Product That, If Used Correctly, Will Kill You

The tobacco industry knows this, and it also knows that it needs to recruit 1,300 new consumers every day to replace consumers who die from tobacco-related diseases. Armed with staggeringly high budgets and some of the best creative marketing minds in the industry, Big Tobacco's message is clear: using tobacco is sexy and fun. All of the stop smoking and tobacco free campaigns are clearly outgunned. "The Facts Now Campaign" in Florida is an exception. It utilized social networks, cultural literacy, and social media to connect with teenagers on their own terms. Importantly, the campaign relied on teenagers to do a lot of the work for them by spreading the message and influencing their own social networks. In the end, "The Facts Now Campaign" was a true success story.*

The tobacco industry outspends antitobacco messaging by a margin of eighteen to one. In Florida alone, it spends $500 million per year. Big Tobacco needs to attract a youth audience because, once teenagers get hooked, they will be lifelong consumers. The ads are sexy, sleek, and especially appealing to youth audiences. By contrast, most antitobacco ads just present the clear, often boring, facts about how tobacco is bad for your health. The problem is, young people already know that. Sure, everyone knows that tobacco kills. Eventually. However, this future is so far off that the teen brain has a hard time comprehending it. So why do they use tobacco? Their friends. "The threat of tobacco doesn't scare them" nearly "as much as social alienation." Also, they believe they're too strong to become addicted. "Big Tobacco knows this and exploits this naivete" (Tobacco Free Florida 2016).

Enter Tobacco Free Florida, an effort by the Florida Department of Health, which launched "The Facts Now Campaign," designed to convince young people that what they do *now* affects them *now*. Two insights from preliminary research helped in designing the campaign. First, teenagers want to have the facts so that they can make their own decisions. In other words, they don't want to be told what to do. Second, teenagers need to be presented with information about what tobacco can do to them now, not at some distant time in the future. Critical to the overall effort was portraying a David versus Goliath message. That is, the execution focused on how corporate giants were using unfair and unethical messages like "mind tricks" to push young people to use their products (see Photos 10.13–10.16).

Central to "The Facts Now Campaign" was the development of a "dynamic, interactive, modular-based website hosted by Tumblr." One distinctive thing about the website was that the content (gifs, memes, videos, and interactive games) was sharable. It presented the facts in small, easy-to-consume pieces, just the way teenagers like it. To drive traffic to the website, the campaign "leveraged media in all of the places Florida teenagers like to spend time, like Buzzfeed, Pandora, Spotify, and good ol' TV"

● **Photo 10.13** *The "Skull Candy" mobile messaging for iPhone*

Photo 10.14 *The "Brain Wax" image used in print, mobile, and social media*

Photo 10.15 *The "Mind Trick" image used in print, mobile, and social media*

Photo 10.16 *The "US without Florida" image used in print, mobile, and social media*

(Tobacco Free Florida 2016). The campaign even had a presence and handed out information and swag at several music festivals and Supercon, a comic book and science fiction convention, which regularly brings fifty thousand fans to its four-day event. All these efforts were designed to push teenagers to the website, where they could access more sharable information. The campaign's objectives and outcomes are listed in Table 10.5.

Using a budget of only $3.8 million, "The Facts Now Campaign" posted some very impressive results, with brand awareness and engagement exceeding all original expectations (see Table 10.5). In addition, one of the audio ads won a Clio Award, the highest honor in advertising (listen to it here: https://clios.com/health/winner/audio-technique/tobacco-free-florida/the-facts-now-horse-race-14502). Importantly, using the power of social media and social networks, teens supported and encouraged one another to make the right choice to either not try tobacco or quit the habit. Tobacco Free Florida claims that Florida has the lowest rate of teen smoking in a generation. Indeed, the teen smoking rate dropped from 10.6 percent in 2006 to 3 percent in 2016 (Tobacco Free Florida 2016). "The Facts Now Campaign" is truly a David versus Goliath success story.

QUESTIONS

Find out more about "The Facts Now Campaign" by checking out the YouTube video here: https://www.youtube.com/watch?v=d9rlic6Ol38.

1. Which types of reference group influences are at work here—informational, utilitarian, and/or value expressive? Discuss. For the reference group influence(s) that you selected, how would that influence be altered if a teenager consumes tobacco products in private versus in public?

2. There are six types of power that can be exerted in a reference group. For each one, create an antitobacco message that would be impactful to an audience (be sure to identify your audience for each message).

3. There are three types of opinion leaders—connectors, market mavens, and salespeople. Discuss how each of these leaders may behave differently within his or her own social network when passing along information from "The Facts Now Campaign." Is one type of leader more effective than the others? Why?

*Special thanks go to Marta Insua at the Alma Advertising Agency in Cocoanut Grove, Florida. Much of the information for this case was derived from a case study that was submitted to the 2016 Effie Awards of North America. That case study was developed for "The Facts Now Campaign," a youth prevention campaign with the Florida Department of Health's Tobacco Free Florida campaign.

Source: Tobacco Free Florida (2016).

Table 10.5 Objectives and Results of "The Facts Now Campaign"

OBJECTIVES	RESULTS
Objective 1: achieve 8 percent brand awareness of "The Facts Now Campaign" among Florida teens	Result 1: "The Facts Now Campaign" achieved 11.2 percent brand awareness
Objective 2: achieve increased engagement on four social media platforms: Tumblr: 60,000 website visits and 90,000 engagements Facebook: 3,000 likes and 10,000 engagements Twitter: 3,000 followers and 3,000 retweets YouTube: 300,000 views	Results 2: engagement[1] on all four social media platforms was achieved: Tumblr: 542,120 website visits and 152,000 earned engagements Facebook: 11,903 likes, 14,058 engagements, 720,259 earned engagements Twitter: 6,526 followers, 9,414 retweets, 2.9 million engagements YouTube: more than 5 million views

[1]*Engagement is often measured in the number of shares; earned engagements is a measure of the overall conversation that involves your brand and is measured by the total number of mentions, shares, retweets, etc.*

Source: "The Facts Now Campaign."

REFERENCES

AJStream. 2018. "Is There a Dark Side to Social Media Influencers?" *Aljazeera.* January 31, 2018. http://stream.aljazeera.com/story/201801311930-0025583.

Asch, S. E. 1955. "Opinions and Social Pressure." *Scientific American* 193 (5): 31–35.

Assael, H. 1998. *Consumer Behavior and Marketing Action.* 6th ed. Mason, OH: South-Western College Publishing.

Baker, S. M., J. W. Gentry, and T. L. Rittenburg. 2005. "Building Understanding of the Domain of Consumer Vulnerability." *Journal of Macromarketing* 25 (2): 128–39.

Bearden, W. O., and M. J. Etzel. 1982. "Reference Group Influence on Product and Brand Purchase Decisions." *Journal of Consumer Research* 9:332–41.

Beer, J. 2015. "How the Truth Campaign Plans to End Youth Smoking Once and for All." FastCompany. August 13, 2015. https://www.fastcompany.com/3049629/ how-the-truth-campaign-plans-to-end-youth-smoking-once-and-for-all.

Bergen, M., and L. Shaw. 2018. "YouTube Tries to Think of the Children." *Bloomberg Businessweek*, January 29, 2018, issue 4556, 21–22.

Boden, S. 2006. "'Another Day, Another Demand': How Parents and Children Negotiate Consumption Matters." *Sociological Research Online* 11 (2). http://www.socresonline.org.uk/11/2/boden.html.

"Born Social in 1895." 2019. Lavazza. Accessed January 10, 2020. https://www.lavazza.us/en_US/mondo-lavazza/pubblicita.html.

Boudreau, K. J., and K. R. Lakhani. 2013. "Using the Crowd as Innovation Partner." *Harvard Business Review*, April. https://hbr.org/2013/04/using-the-crowd-as-an-innovation-partner.

Bourdieu, P. 1984. *Distinction: A Social Critique of the Judgement of Taste.* Translated by R. Nice. London: Routledge.

Brabham, D. C. 2008. "Crowdsourcing as a Model for Problem Solving." *International Journal of Research into New Media Technologies* 14 (1): 75–90.

Bravo, R., E. Fraj, and E. Martínez. 2006. "Differences and Similarities in Measuring Family Influences on Young Adult Consumers: An Integrative Analysis." *European Advances in Consumer Research* 7:104–11.

Chappell, L. 2015. "Sales to Hispanics Outpacing the Market: Latinos Have Their Own Style of Shopping, Media Habits, Vehicle Preferences." *Automotive News*, May 18, 2015. http://www.autonews.com/article/20150518/RETAIL01/305189994/sales-to-hispanics-outpacing-the-market.

Clausen, T. 2017. "Colleen Wegman Named President, CEO of Wegmans." *Democrat & Chronicle*, March 29, 2017. https://www.democratandchronicle.com/story/money/business/2017/03/29/collee-wegman-named-president-ceo-wegmans/99784274/.

"Company Overview." 2020. Wegmans. Accessed September 16, 2020. https://www.wegmans.com/about-us/company-overview/.

Danziger, P. N. 2018. "Why Wegmans Food Markets Gets the Love of Customers." *Forbes*, March 3, 2018. https://www.forbes.com/sites/

pamdanziger/2018/03/03/why-wegmans-food-markets-gets-the-love-of-customers/#563b11d24ce5.

DePaulo, B. 2017. "One Parent Can Do Just as Good a Job as Two, Women Say." *Psychology Today*, August 9, 2017. https://www.psychologytoday.com/us/blog/living-single/201708/one-parent-can-do-just-good-job-two-women-say.

Dowen, C. "How Bears Took Heathrow on a Journey." *Campaign* December: 80–82.

Earls, M. 2009. *Herd: How to Change Mass Behavior by Harnessing Our True Nature.* Chichester, UK: Wiley.

Eccleston, D., and L. Griser. 2008. "How Does Web 2.0 Stretch Traditional Influencing Patterns?" *International Journal of Market Research* 50 (5): 575–90.

Ekström, K. M., P. S. Tansuhaj, and E. R. Foxman. 1987. "Children's Influence in Family Decisions and Consumer Socialization: A Reciprocal View." *Advances in Consumer Research* 14 (1): 283–87.

Feder, B. 2015. "13 Designers with an Equally Cool Kids Line." Brit + Co. April 21, 2015. https://www.brit.co/kids-fashion-designers/.

Feick, L. F., and L. L. Price. 1987. "The Market Maven: A Diffuser of Marketplace Information." *Journal of Marketing* 51:83–97.

Folse, J. A. G., M. Porter, M. B. Godbole, and K. E. Reynolds. 2016. "The Effects of Negatively Valenced Emotional Expressions in Online Reviews on the Reviewer, the Review, and the Product." *Psychology & Marketing* 33 (9): 747–60.

French, J. R. P. 1956. "A Formal Theory of Social Power." *Psychological Review* 63:181–94.

French, J. R. P., and B. Raven. 1959. "The Basis of Social Power." In *Studies in Social Power*, edited by D. Cartwright. Ann Arbor, MI: Institute for Social Research.

Friedman, T. 2009. *Hot, Flat, and Crowded: Why We Need a Green Revolution—And How it Can Renew America. Release 2.0: Updated and Expanded.* New York: Picador/Farrar, Straus, and Giroux.

Gilbert, D. L. 2015. *The American Class Structure in the Age of Growing Inequality.* 9th ed. Los Angeles: Sage.

Gilbert, N. 2017. "Prosperity, Not Upward Mobility, Is What Matters." *Atlantic*, January 5, 2017. https://www.theatlantic.

com/business/archive/2017/01/prosperity-upward-mobility/511925/.

Gladwell, M. 2001. *The Tipping Point.* London: Abacus.

Godes, D., and D. Mayzlin. 2009. "Firm-Created Word-Of-Mouth Communication: Evidence from a Field Test." *Marketing Science* 28 (4): 721–39.

Godin, S. 2008. *Tribes: We Need You to Lead Us.* London: Penguin Books.

Hamilton, K. L., and M. Catterall. 2005. "Towards a Better Understanding of the Low Income Consumer." *Advances in Consumer Research* 32 (1): 627–32.

Howe, J. 2006. "Crowdsourcing: A Definition." June 2, 2006. http://crowdsourcing.typepad.com/cs/2006/06/crowdsourcing_a.html.

Hsu, T. 2018. "For Many Facebook Users, a 'Last Straw' That Led Them to Quit." *New York Times*, Technology, March 21, 2018. https://www.nytimes.com/2018/03/21/technology/users-abandon-facebook.html.

Hyman, H. 1942. "The Psychology of Status." *Archives of Psychology* 269:1–95.

Katz, E., and P. Lazarsfeld. 1955. *Personal Influence.* New York: Free Press.

Kincaid, E. 2015. "Why Having Kids Later Is a Really Big Deal." *Business Insider*, June 30, 2015. http://www.businessinsider.com/why-delaying-parenthood-and-having-kids-later-is-a-big-deal-2015-6.

Kircher, M. M. 2015. "9 Major Stars Who Got Their Start on YouTube, Vine, and Even MySpace." *Business Insider*, August 25, 2015. https://www.businessinsider.com/9-major-stars-who-were-discovered-online-2015-8.

Klas, M. E. 2016. "Hispanic Growth in Florida: Will It Determine the Election?" *Miami Herald*, July 2, 2016. http://www.miamiherald.com/news/politics-government/state-politics/article87250257.html.

Lapierre, M. A., F. Fleming-Milici, E. Rozendaal, A. R. McAlister, and J. Castonguay. 2017. "The Effect of Advertising on Children and Adolescents." *Pediatrics* 140 (s2): s152–56.

Lazarsfeld, P., B. R. Berelson, and H. Gaudet. 1944. *The People's Choice.* New York: Duell, Sloan and Pearce.

Leigh, J. H. 1989. "An Extension of the Bourne Typology of Reference Group Influence on Product-Related Decisions." *Journal of Business and Psychology* 4 (1): 65–85.

Mann, L. 1969. *Social Psychology.* New York: Wiley.

Mintel. 2018. "Kids as Influencers—US." Mintel Group. February.

Moisio, R., E. J. Arnould, and J. Gentry. 2013. "Productive Consumption in the Class-Mediated Construction of Domestic Masculinity: Do-It-Yourself (DIY) Home Improvement in Men's Identity Work." *Journal of Consumer Research* 40 (2): 298–316.

Nairn, A., and E. Mayo. 2009. *Consumer Kids.* London: Constable & Robertson.

Nancarrow, C., and P. Nancarrow. 2007. "Hunting for Cool Tribes." In *Consumer Tribes*, edited by B. Cova, R. V. Kozinets, and A. Shankar, 129–143. Oxford: Butterworth–Heinemann.

Nielsen. 2015. "The Multicultural Edge: Rising Super Consumers." Nielsen Company. March 18, 2015. https://www.nielsen.com/wp-content/uploads/sites/3/2019/04/the-multicultural-edge-rising-super-consumers-march-2015.pdf.

O'Malley, G. 2005. "NBC Goes Viral in Effort to Win with 'Biggest Loser.'" MediaPost. September 8, 2005. http://www.mediapost.com/publications/article/33866/nbc-goes-viral-in-effort-to-win-with-biggest-lose.html.

Oakes, O. 2018. "Heathrow Tops List of 'Most Engaging' Festive Ads, Face-Reading Study Finds." Campaign. November 26, 2018. https://www.campaignlive.co.uk/article/heathrow-tops-list-most-engaging-festive-ads-face-reading-study-finds/1519444.

Park, C. W., and V. P. Lessig. 1977. "Students and Housewives: Differences in Susceptibility to Reference Group Influence." *Journal of Consumer Research* 4 (2): 102–10.

Peters, M. 2019. "T. I., Soulja Boy, Waka Flocka Flame & More Boycott Gucci Over Blackface Sweater." *Billboard*, February 9, 2019. https://www.billboard.com/articles/columns/hip-hop/8497459/ti-soulja-boy-waka-flocka-flame-more-boycott-gucci-over-blackface-sweater.

Pew Research Center. 2015. "Parenting in America: Satisfaction, Time, and Support." December 17, 2015. http://www.pewsocialtrends.org/2015/12/17/2-satisfaction-time-and-support/.

Piacentini, M. G., S. A. Hibbert, and M. K. Hogg. 2013. "Consumer Resource Integration Amongst Vulnerable Consumers: Care Leavers in Transition to Independent Living." *Journal of*

Marketing Management 30 (1/2): 201–19.

Piacentini, M. G., and G. Mailer. 2004. "Symbolic Consumption in Teenagers' Clothing Choices." *Journal of Consumer Behavior Theory and Practice* 3 (3): 251–62.

Postigo, H. 2003. "From Pong to Planet Quake: Post-industrial Transition from Leisure to Work." *Communication and Society* 6 (4): 593–607.

Raitt, M. 2018. "Influencer Marketing Pioneer House Party Moves to Ripple Street: Platform Rebrands and Expands Suite of Offerings and Services." Global Newswire. May 7, 2018. https://www.globenewswire.com/news-release/2018/05/07/1497653/0/en/Influencer-Marketing-Pioneer-House-Party-Moves-to-Ripple-Street.html.

Raven, B. H. 1993. "The Bases of Power: Origins and Recent Developments." *Journal of Social Issues* 49 (4): 227–51.

Rogers, E. 1962. *Diffusion of Innovations*. New York: Free Press.

Rogers, E. M., and D. G. Cartano. 1962. "Methods of Measuring Opinion Leadership." *Public Opinion Quarterly* 26 (3): 435–41.

Samson, A. 2010. "Product Usage and Firm-Generated Word of Mouth: Some Results from FMCG Product Trials." *International Journal of Market Research* 52 (4): 459–82.

Sherif, M. 1936. *The Psychology of Social Norms*. New York: Harper.

Shim, S. Y. 1996. "Adolescent Consumer Decision-Making Styles: The Socialization Perspective." *Psychology & Marketing* 13 (6): 547–69.

Shoham, A., and V. Dalakas. 2005. "He Said, She Said . . . They Said: Parents' and Children's Assessment of Children's Influence on Family Consumption Decisions." *Journal of Consumer Marketing* 22 (3): 152–60.

Szmigin, I., and M. Piacentini. 2015. *Consumer Behavior*. Oxford: Oxford University Press.

Smith, A., and M. Anderson. 2016. "Online Shopping and e-Commerce: Online Reviews." Pew Research Center. December 19, 2016. http://www.pewinternet.org/2016/12/19/online-reviews/.

Smith, A., and M. Anderson. 2018. "Social Media Use in 2018." Pew Research Center. March 1, 2018. http://www.pewinternet.org/2018/03/01/social-media-use-in-2018/.

Speyer, A. 2017. Personal interview, August 11, 2017.

Surowiecki, J. 2004. *The Wisdom of Crowds: Why the Many Are Smarter Than the Few*. New York: Anchor.

Tinson, J., C. Nancarrow, and I. Brace. 2008. "Purchase Decision Making and the Increasing Significance of Family Types." *Journal of Consumer Marketing* 25 (1): 45–56.

Tobacco Free Florida. 2016. "2016 Effie Awards North America Entry." Entry ID 441491. Category: David vs. Goliath.

Venkatesan, M. 1966. "Experimental Study of Consumer Behavior Conformity and Independence." *Journal of Marketing Research* 3 (4): 384–87.

Üstüner, T., and D. B. Holt. 2010. "Toward a Theory of Status Consumption in Less Industrialized Countries." *Journal of Consumer Research* 37 (1): 37–56.

Valinsky, J. 2018. "Facebook Is Making Its Privacy Settings Easier to Find." CNNTech. March 28, 2018. http://money.cnn.com/2018/03/28/technology/new-facebook-privacy-settings/index.html.

Verlegh, P. W. J., C. Verderk, M. A. Tuk, and A. Smidts. 2004. "Customers or Sellers? The Role of Persuasion Knowledge in Customer Referral." *Advances in Consumer Research* 31:304–5.

Watts, D. J. 2007. "Challenging the Influentials Hypothesis." *Word of Mouth Marketing Association* 3:201–11.

Watts, D. J., and P. S. Dodds. 2007. "Influentials, Networks, and Public Opinion Formation." *Journal of Consumer Research* 36:441–57.

Weber, M. 1978. *Economy and Society*. Berkeley: University of California Press.

Wilson, A. E., M. D. Giebelhausen, and M. K. Brady. 2017. "Negative Word of Mouth Can Be a Positive for Consumers Connected to the Brand." *Journal of the Academy of Marketing Science* 45:534–47.

Word of Mouth Marketing Association. 2014. "WOMMA Ethics Committee White Paper: Ethical Word of Mouth Marketing Disclosure Best Practices in Today's Regulatory Environment." January 13, 2014. https://www.slideshare.net/WOMMAChicago/womma-ethics-committee-white-paper-2014.

World Bank Data. 2018a. "Country Profile: Nigeria." World Bank. Accessed August 18, 2019. https://databank.worldbank.org/views/reports/reportwidget.aspx?Report_Name=CountryProfile&Id=b450fd57&tbar=y&dd=y&inf=n&zm=n&country=NGA.

World Bank Data. 2018b. "Country Profile: United States." World Bank. Accessed August 18, 2019. https://databank.worldbank.org/views/reports/reportwidget.aspx?Report_Name=CountryProfile&Id=b450fd57&tbar=y&dd=y&inf=n&zm=n&country=USA.

World Bank Data. 2018c. "Country Profile: South Africa." World Bank. Accessed August 18, 2019. https://databank.worldbank.org/views/reports/reportwidget.aspx?Report_Name=CountryProfile&Id=b450fd57&tbar=y&dd=y&inf=n&zm=n&country=ZAF.

World Bank Data. 2018d. "Country Profile: India." World Bank. Accessed August 18, 2019. https://databank.worldbank.org/views/reports/reportwidget.aspx?Report_Name=CountryProfile&Id=b450fd57&tbar=y&dd=y&inf=n&zm=n&country=IND.

World Bank Data. 2018e. "Country Profile: Mexico." World Bank. Accessed August 18, 2019. https://databank.worldbank.org/views/reports/reportwidget.aspx?Report_Name=CountryProfile&Id=b450fd57&tbar=y&dd=y&inf=n&zm=n&country=MEX.

World Bank Data. 2018f. "Country Profile: China." World Bank. Accessed August 18, 2019. https://databank.worldbank.org/views/reports/reportwidget.aspx?Report_Name=CountryProfile&Id=b450fd57&tbar=y&dd=y&inf=n&zm=n&country=CHN.

World Bank Data. 2018g. "Country Profile: Canada." World Bank. Accessed August 18, 2019. https://databank.worldbank.org/views/reports/reportwidget.aspx?Report_Name=CountryProfile&Id=b450fd57&tbar=y&dd=y&inf=n&zm=n&country=CAN.

World Family Map. 2019. *World Family Map: Mapping Family Change and Child Well-Being Outcomes*. Charlottesville, VA: Institute for Family Studies and Wheatley Institution. https://ifstudies.org/ifs-admin/resources/reports/worldfamilymap-2019-051819final.pdf.

Wu, K., K. Holmes, and J. Tribe. 2010. "'Where Do You Want to Go Today?' An Analysis of Family Group Decisions to Visit Museums." *Journal of Marketing Management* 26 (7/8): 706–26.

Yang, J., X. Hou, D. Wei, K. Wang, Y. Li, and J. Qiu. 2017. "Only-Child and Non-Only-Child Exhibit Differences in Creativity and Agreeableness: Evidence from Behavioral and Anatomical Structure Studies." *Brain Imaging and Behavior* 11, no. 2 (April): 493–502.

11 Culture

◉ Introduction

Have you ever met someone from a different culture? Perhaps you were traveling abroad or perhaps you met an exchange student, a tourist, or even a new neighbor from a culture other than your own. You may have been surprised by some of the differences in how that person looked at the world compared to how you look at the world. Maybe there were even certain behaviors that puzzled you. Culture is one of the most important external influences on behavior. Culture is composed of the shared understandings, meanings, and customs that together act as a "blueprint" to guide behavior. Importantly, culture helps individuals effectively navigate their own culture and other cultures by letting them know what is appropriate and acceptable. Certain characteristics of culture are stable over time and across contexts, while others are more flexible and adaptable to the needs of the situation. The study of culture is fascinating; it helps us distinguish one group of people from other groups of people, offers insights into what it means to be a member of a given culture, and identifies potential pitfalls in reaching out to different cultures.

Cultural influences also apply to consumer decision-making and behavior in a myriad of ways, from everyday mundane decisions to celebrated special events like holidays, weddings, and the birth of a baby. In this chapter, we focus on understanding culture and its relevance and impact on marketing practice. We will present some basic cultural concepts and then discuss how culture is communicated and reinforced through myths and rituals. We will examine different ways that we can understand culture and we will look at some subcultures in detail. Because culture and subculture are always changing, marketing managers face an especially challenging and exciting time in successfully using cultural insights to inform their work.

LEARNING OBJECTIVES

After reading the chapter, you will be able to:

1. **Define culture** and discuss the various characteristics of culture.

2. Describe and differentiate between the three **elements of the cultural system**.

3. Describe the purpose of **cultural myths and rituals**.

4. Demonstrate an understanding of how **cultures are classified** and describe the value of these classifications.

5. Discuss important characteristics of **subcultures** that are based on demographic characteristics and subcultures that are based on consumption communities.

👁 What Is Culture?

Culture is the sum total of learned ideas, beliefs, values, knowledge, and customs that together regulate the behavior of members of a particular society.

Culture is the total of all learned ideas, beliefs, values, knowledge, and customs that regulate the behavior of members of a particular society. Think about culture as the character or the personality of a society. In the following sections, we will see that culture is something that is learned and we will discover that all cultures have several important characteristics.

Culture is learned

Culture is learned through the process of socialization. Socialization concerns all of the social interactions, observations, and active processing of information about the values, norms, and practices of the culture. By engaging in the active process of socialization, an individual forms impressions and understandings about the culture. This socialization, or social learning, occurs through one of two processes: enculturation or acculturation.

Enculturation concerns the process by which individuals learn about their own culture.

Enculturation concerns the process by which individuals learn about their own culture. A wide variety of cultural practices and values are picked up by children simply by watching their parents, family members, and teachers. Food preferences provide a good demonstration of the process of enculturation. As children observe the adults in their lives, they begin to copy many of their dietary choices. These choices are then reinforced through social rewards such as praise. Often, when a young person returns home from college for their first break or holiday visit, older members of the family will prepare traditional foods for the student's homecoming as a special treat. Another example of enculturation in action comes from Australia, Ireland, and England, where individuals like to spread Vegemite on their toast in the morning. This popular addition to toast is made from fermented yeast and has a slightly bitter taste. Individuals who grew up outside these countries have a hard time understanding the appeal of Vegemite, but the Australians, Irish, and English swear by it. Children learn important information about their culture, such as taste, through the process of enculturation, which includes habituation and repeated exposure (refer again to our discussion on instrumental learning in Chapter 5).

Acculturation describes the process by which an individual learns about a new culture; it concerns the movement of meaning and the adaptation to new cultural contexts.

The second way in which cultural learning occurs is through **acculturation,** which describes the process by which an individual learns about a new culture; it concerns the movement of meaning and the adaptation to new cultural contexts. **Consumer acculturation** can be understood as the process of movement, translation, and adaptation of a consumer from one cultural environment to another. Consumer research has found that there are four main outcomes of consumer acculturation (Penaloza 1994). Although the study was originally done on Mexican immigrants to the United States, this framework can be applied to any person moving to a new culture. It is important to note that these categories are not mutually exclusive; they can overlap over time and across circumstances:

Consumer acculturation is the process of movement, translation, and adaptation of a consumer from one cultural environment to another cultural environment.

- *Assimilation*: Consumers entering the new culture abandon their own culture in favor of the new culture. For example, younger people might jump in and embrace the popular fashion and music of US culture.

- *Maintenance*: Aspects of both cultures are maintained. On weekends, perhaps Sunday dinners and religious practices are maintained, but during the week, more assimilation into the broader culture occurs.

- *Resistance*: Consumers prefer aspects of their own culture and reject aspects of the new culture. For example, traditional male and female roles are maintained from the old culture, despite more progressive changes to these roles in the new culture.

- *Segregation*: New immigrants separate themselves from some aspects of the new consumer culture, such as when they exclusively shop at certain stores or live in certain neighborhoods.

Some of our biggest societal institutions, such as family, school, and church, facilitate enculturation and acculturation. Take the case of a cup of tea and how perceptions of it have changed because of a variety of factors, including our more fast-paced lives and working schedules. The British people are well known for their love of tea. Even in the former British colonies, like India, Australia, and New Zealand, a visitor can find a wide variety of teas at any café, restaurant, or bar (see Photo 11.1). However, recent trends seem to indicate that as younger people develop different tastes, interest in the "most British thing there is" may be waning. Indeed, tea consumption in the United Kingdom has dropped by 63 percent since the 1970s. By contrast, coffee consumption has tripled. Why is this happening? Experts point to several factors, including the perceived boring nature of tea, the time it takes to brew a cup or pot of tea, and the all-important greater caffeine content of coffee (Ferdman 2016).

Global consumer culture (GCC) is a connection (via shared beliefs, ideas, behaviors, etc.) with other people around the world based on the brands and products that they enjoy.

With the rise of social media and increased connections to people, trends, and innovations around the world, there has been an increased interest in a **global consumer culture** (GCC), which is a connection (via shared beliefs, ideas, behaviors, etc.) with other people around the world based on the brands and products they enjoy. Since the beginning of the earliest global trade routes, consumers have been enjoying and even celebrating countless global products. What is different now is that technology has made it very easy to connect and share ideas with other consumers around the world (see Insights from Academia 11.1). Consumers are more likely to adopt a GCC if they experience one or more of the following (Cleveland and Laroche 2007):

1. have exposure to global and foreign mass media;
2. have exposure to and use the English language;
3. have exposure to the marketing activities of multinational corporations;
4. have social interactions through traveling;
5. are more cosmopolitan in their outlook;
6. are open to and desire to emulate a GCC; and
7. can self-identify with the GCC.

● **Photo 11.1** *The British love of tea may be fading*

Consumers caught in the middle

Although there is certainly a rise in the number of consumers who embrace the global consumer culture (GCC), the process itself is not as simple as just accepting or not accepting it. Most consumers experience a tension in which they are pulled toward consumption that expresses their own national identity while also being pulled toward consumption that is more in line with a GCC. How does this consumer negotiate the conflict of being caught in the middle? Research shows that the pull of national identity is stronger for local and national products, such as food and clothing. However, the pull of GCC is stronger for electronics and luxuries. The implications for marketers entering a new culture are clear. If the product is culturally bound,

such as clothing and food, changes should be made to fit the local tastes and customs. An example is the Maharaja Mac by McDonald's in India, made with vegetarian patties rather than beef to appeal to the mostly vegetarian nation. Alternatively, if the product is not culturally bound, such as an iPhone, no significant changes are needed. Consumers in the target market are likely to accept a GCC perspective and appreciate these products just the way they are.

Sobol, K., M. Cleveland, and M. Laroche. 2018. "Globalization, National Identity, Biculturalism, and Consumer Behavior: A Longitudinal Study of Dutch Consumers." Journal of Business Research *82:340–53.*

The basic characteristics of culture

A given culture is composed of a set of distinct beliefs, values, knowledge, and customs. **Beliefs** are the thoughts an individual has about some object, idea, or person (see Chapter 7). **Values** are deep-rooted and enduring ideals and guiding principles. Values are long-lasting and transcend most situations; they guide and shape behavior across a variety of contexts. In Chapter 6, we noted that some values such as freedom, equality, and happiness were strongly held for many people. An example of values can be found in how people treat their pets. In many Western countries, the family pet is seen as an important member of the family. People for the Ethical Treatment of Animals engages in a variety of campaigns that try to tap into this value, such as that depicted in Photo 11.2. We wouldn't wear the fur from our dog, so why would we wear fur from another animal? The study of culture helps us understand why.

Knowledge refers to familiarity with people or things, which can include understandings, facts, information, and descriptions gained through experience and education. Knowledge about a culture's distinct beliefs, values, knowledge, and customs is referred to as cultural knowledge. Individuals in a particular culture, for example, generally have a good amount of knowledge about dating and romantic relationships in that culture. This cultural knowledge is not easily transferrable to another culture.

Beliefs are the thoughts an individual has about some object, idea, or person.

Values are a consumer's deep-rooted and enduring ideals and guiding principles.

Knowledge refers to familiarity with people or things, which can include understanding, facts, information, and descriptions gained through experience and education.

Norms are informal societal rules that govern behavior, such as the set of behaviors you enact when you go to a restaurant (sit down, look at a menu, etc.) or when you stand in line for something. For example, some cultures have a fairly strict set of cultural norms around queuing, or standing in line. In Switzerland, for example, individuals queue in a very orderly fashion and wait their turn. If someone tries to cut in line, a Swiss person will likely let them know about it. Loudly. In China, queuing is not a strong cultural norm. Instead, people often jostle for a spot in line and cut the line. However, since it is a cultural norm in China, people rarely get upset. It is just the way things are done there. **Customs** are the norms of behavior that have been passed from generation to generation. They're long-standing ways of behaving; your parents and your grandparents did it, so you do it. For example, most Americans have turkey and pumpkin pie at Thanksgiving. With both norms and customs, the focus is more on behavior; both serve to control basic behavior within a culture around the core facets of life, such as the division of labor within the home or the celebration of rites of passage, such as marriage or the birth of a baby.

Mores ("more-ayz") are a particular type of custom and have a strong moral overtone. Mores often involve a taboo or forbidden behavior, and violation of mores is met with strong censure from other members of a society. Some cultures strongly condemn people living together before they are married; in other cultures it is perfectly acceptable. **Conventions** are another specific form of custom and relate to the norms for the conduct of everyday life. They are often subtle and not always easy for people outside a culture to learn. They may include conventions around how to behave at a dinner party or the "correct" way to dress within a specific cultural group. In Ireland, "going to the pub" is a common cultural activity and is viewed as a quintessential part of Irish culture. Conventions might include routines for buying drinks, buying a round for your friends, and etiquette around buying a drink for the bartender. This knowledge of cultural conventions is important for marketers, especially in terms of showing consumers how products might fit into already-established consumption patterns.

It is probably clear by now that culture influences the way we behave. For the most part, consumers want to fit into and be accepted by their

Photo 11.2 *"You Wouldn't Wear Your Dog" Campaign by People for the Ethical Treatment of Animals*

Norms are a set of informal rules that society imposes to guide individual behavior.

Customs are the norms of behavior that have been passed from generation to generation.

Mores are a particular type of custom and have a strong moral overtone.

Conventions are a specific form of custom and relate to the norms for the conduct of everyday life.

culture. How do people know what is or is not acceptable behavior? Culture is communicated to members of society through a common language and commonly shared symbols. To see how strongly some of these meanings are communicated and reinforced, imagine the comments and strange looks your family would receive if it decided to have fish instead of turkey on Thanksgiving. Some family members would likely be terribly disappointed and the event might even go down in family history as "the Thanksgiving that wasn't." Marketers know about the importance of cultural meaning and often depict and reinforce desired modes of behavior and expectations.

◉ Making Sense of Culture: Myths and Rituals

In addition to the building blocks of culture just discussed, it is important for cultures to have stories and practices that help provide a collective sense of its values and what is important to the culture. Two key aspects of this are myths and rituals.

Myths are stories that convey meaning

Myth is a story that contains symbolic elements that express the shared emotions and ideals of a culture.

A **myth** is a story that contains symbolic elements that express the shared emotions and ideals of a culture. Myths are traditional stories about our cultural heroes or even supernatural beings and often feature a conflict, such as good versus evil (Woodside, Sood, and Miller 2008). The tale of George Washington chopping down a cherry tree and then admitting to the deed by saying "I cannot tell a lie" reinforces the cultural value of honesty. Myths serve the function of emphasizing how things in a culture are interconnected; they maintain social order by authorizing a social code. Importantly, myths provide psychological models for individual behavior and identity. Myths are often used in a nostalgic way in advertising, encouraging consumers to look back in time and remember the good old days (which often involves reimagining the past). The candy company Werther's Original frequently uses myths in its advertising when, for example, it depicts images of a child visiting an old-fashioned candy store and getting a special piece of candy from the shop owner himself (see Photo 11.3).

Archetypes are the stable characters that capture basic ideas, feelings, fantasies, and visions that seem constant and frequently re-emerge across times and places.

Archetypes are the stable characters that capture basic ideas, feelings, fantasies, and visions that seem constant and frequently re-emerge across times and places. In the tale about George Washington and the cherry tree, George Washington is the archetype of an honest son who tells his father the truth, even though he knows he will be punished. Effectively, cultural myths and archetypes depict cultural ideals and provide us with guidelines for behavior (see Insights from the Field 11.1).

● **Photo 11.3** *Use of a nostalgic myth in advertising*

● **Photo 11.3** *Use of a nostalgic myth in advertising*

 INSIGHTS FROM THE FIELD 11.1

Archetypes and myths at the gym

Stories are a way of communicating and are very powerful in people's lives. Because of this, marketing managers strive to create brand myths, or stories, to produce powerful emotional connections with consumers. These archetypes and myths must be culturally relevant to be believed and accepted as meaningful by consumers. Two gyms have used the "typical gym" archetype in completely different ways to reinforce their brand identities. Many individuals who think about going to the gym for the first time find it very intimidating. Everyone there seems to know how to operate the machines and everyone seems to have a perfect body (see Photo 11.4 and notice the "Train till you puke" T-shirt). The typical gym archetype is someone who is completely obsessed with bodybuilding or working out and likely spends hours each day at the gym. A key part of this archetype is that these people behave in an unkind or even judgmental way toward less fitness-obsessed individuals.

● **Photo 11.4** *Example of a gym archetype*

(continued)

One company that has leveraged this gym archetype is Planet Fitness, which has used the idea of *gymtimidation* in their advertising and has harnessed both the gym archetype and myths to promote its brand. According to executives at the company, 80 percent of people in the market "aren't really comfortable with the gym experience" (Stein 2016). This insight resulted in a campaign that directly addresses the archetype with the tag line, "The world judges, we don't—At Planet Fitness, be free." In addition to carefully placed TV spots, the campaign also was supported by social media, print, outdoor (e.g., billboards), and radio advertising. The ads themselves depict a series of uncomfortable situations in which people are "judged" by others, such as a job applicant who is criticized for her outfit, a woman who is laughed at when she asks a handsome man to dinner, and a helpful man who has mace sprayed in his face by an old woman. The ad ends with the message that although the world might judge you, we at Planet Fitness will not. All the communications are reinforced with the iconic thumbs-up logo signifying "you're ok" the way you are (Olenski 2016).

The campaign by Planet Fitness has connected itself with some high-profile cultural events, like the 2017 New Year's Rockin' Eve, where the company set up a stage in Times Square with a band (Stein 2016) and an Olympics-themed series of ads that celebrated the 2018 Winter Olympics. For Planet Fitness, the brand identity it wishes to promote is one of friendly acceptance in which the consumer can simply "be free," no questions asked.

Another organization that has utilized the typical gym archetype as a point of contrast to communicate its message is SoulCycle. In contrast to the image of the solitary individual working out on a piece of equipment or with some weights, SoulCycle clients pay a premium price of forty dollars for the almost transcendent experience that occurs in each forty-five-minute workout. Some claim that the experience is life-altering. The group workouts are done in candlelit rooms with loud, high-energy music. The group moves together to shouts of encouragement from the instructors. Together, the group achieves goals that it could not achieve alone. "We laugh, we cry, we grow—and we do it together, as a community" ("Our Values" 2019).

SoulCycle has achieved an almost cultlike following, in part because individuals really feel that they matter to the other members in the group. The instructors are instrumental to this feeling of connection to the brand. The shared experience of sweating it out on a bike, combined with an inspirational instructor urging you on, forges a strong bond. However, this connection is about more than just an inspirational instructor. The instructors are active on social media, and even when they're not leading a class, they're connecting and sharing with their followers who, in turn, are connecting and sharing with one another. Still another factor that is instrumental to the connection is the set of stories that the founders, instructors, and clients share with one another. Some of these stories achieve almost mythlike status, like the young woman who experienced the death of her father on her sixteenth birthday, suffered ten years of despair and destructive behavior, and then turned her life around and was able to "love herself again" at twenty-six after she started going to SoulCycle (Clifford 2016).

Both Planet Fitness and SoulCycle started with messaging that was designed as a reaction to the typical gym archetype. The gyms went in different directions with their messaging strategies, but both relied strongly on connecting with their community of customers.

Questions

1. Think of at least three cultural archetypes with which you are familiar and discuss how they (or their opposites) are reflected in advertising, retailing, and digital media.
2. A central part of the Harry Potter series revolves around the four main houses at Hogwarts School. Students belong to one of four houses: those from Hufflepuff are friendly, those from Ravenclaw are smart, those from Gryffindor are brave, and those from Slytherin are trouble-makers. For each of these archetypes, discuss how you might develop a social media campaign encouraging members to visit a new Harry Potter themed restaurant in town.

Sources: Clifford (2016); Olenski (2016); Stein (2016).

Rituals are behaviors that reinforce and move meaning

Rituals are very important in the transfer of meaning within cultures. The term **ritual** refers to a symbolic and expressive activity, often involving a series of behaviors that are repeated over time (Rook 1985). There are many rituals in our lives. Some can be viewed as quite mundane, such as getting dressed in the morning, whereas other rituals are considered sacred and relate to broad cultural or religious values. For example, in the traditional villages of Fiji, outside visitors need to follow a complex ritual with prescribed behaviors before they will be permitted to stay in the village. First, the visitor will be asked to sit in a community building and present the village elders with the gift of a yaqona plant, which is used to make the traditional kava drink. The village elders will then ask the visitor to explain the purpose of the visit and, after conferring, will make a big bowl of kava and welcome the visitor to stay in the village. To complete the ritual, everyone must have at least one drink of kava from a coconut shell (see Photo 11.5). Before we talk about how rituals help move meaning, let's first talk about the different types of rituals that specifically relate to consumer behavior.

Ritual refers to a symbolic and expressive activity, often comprising multiple behaviors that occur in a fixed sequence and are repeated over time.

● **Photo 11.5** *To visit a traditional Fijian village, a complex ritual must first be performed*

Grooming rituals are those private behaviors that consumers undertake to aid the transition from the private to the public self (and back again).

Possession rituals are the rituals associated with transforming mass-produced products from the marketplace to the home or workplace.

Exchange rituals involve transferring items, such as gifts, between two people.

Self-gifts are a specific example of gift giving, where consumers purchase self-gifts as a way of regulating their own behavior.

Holiday rituals refer to the rituals associated with both vacations (tourism holidays) and culturally bound holiday seasons.

Rites of passage rituals are those rituals that mark a change in a person's social status.

Divestment rituals involve those actions related to removing meaning from a product.

Grooming rituals are those private behaviors consumers undertake to aid the transition from the private to public self (and back again). Rituals associated with getting ready for a night out (showering, fixing hair, choosing an outfit) prepare consumers as they move from their private space to more public and social spaces (McCracken 1986).

Possession rituals are the rituals associated with transforming mass-produced products into more personal products for the home or workplace. For example, after purchasing a new car, many consumers personalize it by adding accessories such as seat covers, steering wheel covers, or new sound systems (McCracken 1986).

Exchange rituals involve transferring items, such as gifts, between two people. These rituals may be extensive, including obtaining/finding gifts as well as giving/receiving gifts. Although gifts have economic value, they also have symbolic value, which emphasizes the social connections between people.

Self-gifts happen when consumers purchase gifts they intend to keep, as a way of regulating their own behavior. We may buy a gift as a reward for some success or as a way to cheer ourselves up if we are having a bad day (McCracken 1986).

Holiday rituals are the rituals associated with both vacations (called *holidays* in some counties) and culturally bound holiday seasons (such as Christmas, Passover, and Eid). Holidays involve important rituals and represent a suspension of our everyday lives as we perform specific ritualistic behaviors, such as religious services, special meals, and gathering of family. Many film studios schedule major film releases to coincide with the holiday seasons, tapping into family rituals around holidays and movie-going (as well as time off from work and school).

Rites of passage rituals are the rituals that mark a change in a person's social status. Examples of such changes might include a child's first day at school, getting married, becoming a parent, and even getting divorced. In the United States, a baby shower is a way of welcoming a new baby into the family and of marking the beginning of a new chapter in a couple's life. However, baby showers are not popular in other cultures such as Germany, where they are considered bad luck. In general, life transitions are a time of uncertainty and individuals rely on familiar products and brands to support them through these transitions (see Insights from Academia 11.2).

Divestment rituals involve those actions related to removing meaning from a product. This happens in two ways. First, before an individual can fully enjoy a previously used product, any special touches or features from the previous owner are cleaned up or washed away. New homeowners will often repaint the walls and replace the curtains that the previous owner left behind. Second, before an individual gives a product away

INSIGHTS FROM ACADEMIA 11.2

Is graffiti really just a rite of passage?

One type of graffiti, *tagging*, is typically a name or a mark that is painted on a wall, highway, or other object. Just like more elaborate graffiti that depicts pictures or other images, tagging is illegal and often scorned by authorities (see Photo 11.6). However, tagging is a ritual that marks a rite of passage for individuals in marginalized communities. Young people express their individuality, creativity, and arrival into adulthood by tagging something. When they do so, they build self-esteem,

relieve stress, and establish their identity within the group. They even employ artifacts, scripts, roles, and audiences during and after the tagging. The next time you see graffiti, maybe you will appreciate the rituals that were involved in its design and placement!

Brown, G. H., L. M. Brunelle, and V. Malhotra. 2017. "Tagging: Deviant Behavior or Adolescent Rites of Passage?" Culture & Psychology 23 (4): 487–501.

● **Photo 11.6** *Tagging can be seen as a rite of passage*

or disposes of it, meaning will be removed. For example, a consumer who would like to sell his or her car will first remove any personal items (McCracken 1986).

Elements of the ritual

There are many elements that are common to rituals. As with other aspects of culture, these elements are not formally written anywhere, but are learned through immersion in the culture (Rook 1985). First there are

Ritual artifacts are the objects and products that accompany or are consumed in a ritual setting.

Ritual script guides the use of the ritual artifacts—which artifacts to use, by whom, the sequence of use, and the types of comments that accompany the ritual.

Ritual performance roles are the roles performed by people involved in the ritual as they perform according to a "script."

Ritual audience is the group that witnesses or participates in the ritual in some way beyond those involved in the particular performance roles.

ritual artifacts, which are the objects and products that accompany or are consumed in a ritual setting. These artifacts often communicate specific symbolic messages understood by ritual participants. At Rosh Hashanah, the Jewish New Year, you will see a number of objects, such as a ram's horn, candles, and sweet delicacies. There is also a **ritual script** that guides the use of the ritual artifacts—which artifacts to use, by whom, the sequence of use, and the types of comments that accompany the ritual. **Ritual performance roles** are the roles performed by people involved in the ritual as they perform according to "script." That is, certain individuals, like the rabbi, must enact certain behaviors. Finally, there is a **ritual audience**, which is the group that witnesses or participates in the ritual in some way beyond those involved in the particular performance roles.

The Japanese tea ceremony is a ritual that can be analyzed according to these elements. The ritual artifacts include the tea, the teapot, the crockery, and other tools. With its strong Buddhist influence, the traditional tea ceremony is steeped with meaning. The script includes the very complex set of actions the host must perform to prepare the tea, including how the teapot is held, how the hot water is poured, and how the teacup is eventually presented to the guest. In terms of performance roles, the host who is preparing the tea and the appreciative recipient of the tea each enact a series of roles. Finally, the audience refers to any other guests or observers who are present during the ceremony. Taking part in these rituals helps to reinforce a culture's important meanings (see Photo 11.7).

● **Photo 11.7** *Japanese tea ceremony*

The cultural production system

Earlier in this chapter, we said that rituals help move meaning. What does that mean, exactly? Who decides what meanings are transferred to which products? Although many researchers have described the process, a Canadian researcher named Grant McCracken provided in-depth descriptions of how cultural meaning moves from the wider cultural environment to individual consumers (e.g., McCracken 1986). McCracken's work has influenced countless researchers, many of whom conduct research in marketing. According to one study, the cultural production system works in three basic steps, with three types of participants (see Venkatesh and Meamber 2006) (see Figure 11.1):

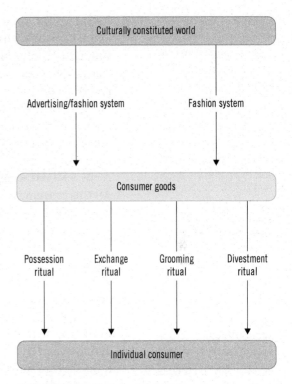

Figure 11.1 *Movement of cultural meaning*

Source: McCracken (1986). Printed with permission from University of Chicago Press.

- First, our shared meanings and culture connect meaning to specific objects, such as products. *Cultural producers* like artists, musicians, and designers create these objects.

- Second, advertising and the fashion system help to connect the meanings in the objects to consumers. *Cultural intermediaries* like marketers and organizations utilize creative advertising to accomplish this movement of meaning.

- Third, once *consumers* use the products through rituals, those meanings are connected to the self.

Many products and brands regularly languish in obscurity until they are picked up and used by celebrities or advertised heavily. There are numerous examples of fashion trends that were introduced by a cultural icon and then picked up by the masses using this three-step process. An early example was the Beatles and their iconic tousled hairstyles of the 1960s. Teenage boys all around the world wanted to emulate the irreverent, unkept look and started asking their barbers to do the job. Soon, teenagers were causing their parents major anxiety by sporting these hairstyles. Sunglasses are another example of a product that can be picked up and adopted by consumers after they see them being used by celebrities. Luckily, sunglasses are a more affordable way for some consumers to take part in the process of moving meaning from the culturally constituted world, to the world of consumer goods, and eventually to themselves. Take the example of some of Hollywood's A-list celebrities like Brad Pitt or Leonardo DiCaprio (see Photo 11.8). Top designers often create one-of-a-kind designs for an individual celebrity. Celebrities then are photographed wearing the designs, social media lights up, and the product moves from the culturally constituted world to the domain of consumer goods. The sunglasses worn by

Leonardo DiCaprio were originally inspired by silver screen legend Cary Grant and if consumers want to get the same sunglasses, they can purchase a pair by Garrett Leight at Bloomingdale's for $340. Other manufacturers also offer less expensive versions of this consumer good. Once a product makes it into the realm of consumer consciousness and becomes a consumer good, like the sunglasses, consumers incorporate them into their own lives via rituals. Insights from Academia 11.3 illustrates how the branding of the British royal family can also be viewed from the perspective of the cultural production system.

The cultural system

All this movement of meaning occurs within a broader cultural system, which is composed of three main elements: ecology, social structure, and ideology. **Cultural ecology** refers to the physical geography of a place and the way individuals and the cultural system have adapted to that environment. The physical characteristics, resources, and weather of a particular area will exert a strong influence on culture because, among other things, it influences the products we buy, the food we eat, and how we spend our leisure time.

Another element is **social structure**, which is an established set of structures that dictate the patterns by which individuals interact with one another and live their lives. It includes how individuals are supposed to behave and the tasks they are supposed to perform in a variety of situations. Often, this applies to domestic life, where different gender roles and parent–child relations are played out. However, a social structure also influences interactions in politics, work,

Cultural ecology refers to the physical geography of a place and the way individuals and the cultural system have adapted to that environment.

Social structure tells us about the way that orderly social life is maintained in a culture.

● **Photo 11.8.** *Brad Pitt and Leonardo DiCaprio sporting sunglasses at the Cannes Film Festival*

INSIGHTS FROM ACADEMIA 11.3

The branding of the queen

Despite its declining economic and political influence, the British royal family functions, in many respects, as a brand. There seems to be a strong desire for many consumers to fully immerse themselves in anything related to the royal family. There is a particular fascination with Cinderella love stories, such as when Prince William married Kate Middleton. Much to the surprise of many onlookers, there is a particular fascination with the royal family in the American Midwest! Indeed, there is a strong following, fueled by social media, of the fashion and lifestyle choices made by royals. When Princess Charlotte was born in 2015, estimates were that there was a $5 billion bump in global sales of look-alike items such as her swaddling blankets and tiny cardigan sweaters. When Princes William and Harry took a gap year before their university studies, millions of other young people did too. What do consumers get from this consumption of the British royal family brand? We know that brands represent a set of promises that consumers receive as a result of consumption. So, when consumers adopt the "royalty brand"—through rituals—they feel a small but very real connection to that same elegant, globe-trotting, royal mystique.

Otnes, C. C., and P. Maclaran. 2018. "Royalty: Marketplace Icons." Consumption Markets & Culture 21 (1): 65–75.

and social situations. Social structures are often reflected and reinforced in advertisements. For example, the Virgin Atlantic ad in Photo 11.9 targeted a British audience that was weary of the cold, dreary weather in the United Kingdom and encouraged them to visit the United States. One dimension of social structure is depicted and reinforced here—when a couple is in a car, the man typically drives and the woman typically sits in the passenger seat. Remember that social structures set out patterns of behavior between people. In addition, stereotypes about cultural ecology come into play here too; it is easy to see that the British couple is embracing what they may believe to be a carefree and independent American moment with the top down, an open road, and sleeves rolled up.

The third element of the cultural system is **cultural ideology**, which are the beliefs, values, principles, and worldview held by members of the culture. It is important to remember that none of the three elements of culture is static; indeed, they shift and change over time. Some cultures undergo more sudden changes. Taiwan, for example, is in the midst of an important cultural shift. China claims sovereignty over the island, but large groups of Taiwanese citizens, often led by young people, are demanding more independence and self-determination. This sunshine movement has staged mass protests, changed the prevailing mindset of many people, and helped to elect politicians who are sympathetic to their cause (Ho 2018).

Together, myths and rituals communicate and reinforce important cultural meanings. It is easy to see that the movement of meaning is a complex and dynamic process, which is precisely why consumer researchers are interested in exploring and understanding it.

Cultural ideology reflects the mental characteristics of a group of people, building on the assumption that members of a society possess the same worldview, ethos, ideas, and principles.

● **Photo 11.9** *Virgin Atlantic ad that depicts both cultural ecology and social structure*

◉ Classification of Cultures

To provide a deeper understanding of culture and consumers, marketers have devised several methods by which we can classify cultures. A discussion of the two most popular forms of classification are provided in the following section.

Individualism and collectivism

Over the years, many consumer researchers have described the various elements and characteristics of culture. One of the more enduring methods of differentiating cultures is to examine them according to whether they are more individualistic or collectivistic (Triandis 1995). Although in reality, very few cultures fall neatly into one or the other dimension, the individualistic–collectivistic distinction does provide some insights into individual behavior in different cultures. In **individualistic cultures**, such as the United States, the United Kingdom, and Australia, an individual's behavior is mainly determined by personal motivations and goals. Although these goals may overlap with collectivistic goals, individual goals are dominant. In Australia, legislation on recycling allows individuals to collect a deposit for each drink container they return to a recycling center. This incentive encourages people to recycle because they receive an individual benefit (money), which works for

Individualistic cultures emphasize an individual's personal motivations and goals.

this individualistic society. Incidentally, there is also a clear societal and community benefit from this behavior—a clean environment.

Collectivist cultures, by contrast, are concerned about collective well-being, and individuals will often put the well-being of the group over their own personal well-being. Collectivist cultures can be found in places like Portugal, Venezuela, and many Asian countries (de Mooij and Hofstede 2002; Bu, Kim, and Son 2013). Marketers know that there are benefits to reflecting appropriate cultural values in their ads. Any marketer wishing to target consumers in China, for example, would need to be keenly aware of its strong collectivistic culture. An ad campaign may want to emphasize "we" instead of "me" messaging; imply approval from others, such as family or friends; and appeal to broader goals that might benefit the entire community.

The differences between individualists and collectivists have been studied extensively. On the one hand, in a work setting, individualists are more likely to generate ideas, be confident in those ideas, and disagree with the group. On the other hand, collectivists are more likely to generate better-quality ideas and are less likely to disagree with the group (Saad, Cleveland, and Ho 2015). Results and insights from studies like this have broad implications for marketing managers.

Multidimensional view of cultural values

Another classification system was developed by the Dutch sociologist Geert Hofstede, who proposed that cultures could be identified according to how important six key values were to the culture. Hofstede's contention was that, regardless of culture, several core societal values can be used to describe them. After studying a group of IBM employees for several years, Hofstede developed a multidimensional classification system for culture (Hofstede 1984, 2001). Hofstede proposed six key dimensions of culture: individualism–collectivism, masculinity–femininity, power distance, uncertainty avoidance, long-term orientation, and indulgence. Note that Hofstede's framework includes the individualism–collectivism dimension just discussed, as well as five additional dimensions.

The **individualism–collectivism** dimension assesses the extent to which individual goals are balanced against collective or group goals. High **individualism** is characterized by a focus on the self, with little regard to interpersonal connection or collective responsibility. One example of individualism in advertising can be seen with the cosmetics and skin care giant L'Oréal, which coined the phrase, "Because I'm worth it." L'Oréal has used this phrase in its advertising since 1973. It celebrates a woman's self-confidence and style. High **collectivism**, by contrast, is characterized by strong group cohesion and little emphasis on individual needs or wants. The "Incredible India" campaign has been running since 2002 to encourage tourists to visit this historically and culturally rich country that has a strongly collectivistic culture (see Photo 11.10).

The **masculinity–femininity** dimension assesses the extent to which a culture is more action oriented, assertive, and analytical (**masculine**) or more sympathetic, understanding, and compassionate (**feminine**) in its overall outlook and behavior (de Mooij and Hofstede 2002). Sweden, for example, is

Collectivist cultures are characterized by a focus on collective well-being.

Individualism–collectivism is one of the key dimensions of culture, as defined by Hofstede.

Individualism is characterized by a focus on the self, with little regard to interpersonal connection or collective responsibility.

Collectivism is characterized by strong group cohesion and little emphasis on individual needs or wants.

Masculinity–femininity is one of the key dimensions of culture, as defined by Hofstede.

Masculine is a cultural motivation that is more action oriented, assertive, and analytical.

Feminine refers to one of the key dimensions of culture that is more sympathetic, understanding, and compassionate.

often seen as a more feminine culture, while Russia and Slovakia are more masculine cultures (Sidle 2009). It is important to note that most cultures display a mix of both masculine and feminine traits.

Power distance (PD) is another one of the cultural dimensions proposed by Hofstede. It describes how differences in power influence interpersonal relationships. In cultures with high PD, a big difference exists between individuals who have and exert power and those that do not. These cultures tend to have a steep hierarchical structure. High PD would exist, for example, at the office when your boss makes a decision without consultation and all of the subordinates are expected to obey the decision without question. In low-PD cultures, individuals are more likely to share power and a flatter structure of relations exists. Malaysia and the Philippines score high on PD (Sweetman 2012), whereas Denmark, Sweden, and Norway demonstrate low PD (Sweetman 2012).

Uncertainty avoidance (UA) is the extent to which a cultural group is tolerant of uncertainty, ambiguity, and risk. A big part of UA is the level of anxiety experienced by members when faced with uncertain or unknown situations. High-UA cultures tend to avoid ambiguous situations.

Power distance (PD) is one of the cultural dimensions proposed by Hofstede. It describes how differences in power influence interpersonal relationships.

Uncertainty avoidance (UA) is the extent to which a cultural group is tolerant of uncertainty, ambiguity, and risk.

● **Photo 11.10** *The long-running "Incredible India" campaign encourages tourists to visit this collectivistic culture*

Japan, Germany, and France have fairly high UA and take steps to reduce ambiguity and risk by enacting complex rules, laws, and regulations to protect their citizens (Aguinis, Joo, and Gottfredson 2012). Low-UA cultures, by contrast, are more open to risk and a lack of structure. The United States, China, and the United Kingdom score relatively low on UA, indicating that they enjoy a bit of risk, novelty, and ambiguity (Aguinis, Joo, and Gottfredson 2012).

Long-term orientation concerns a culture's time orientation and the extent to which it is concerned about the future as well as the past. Cultures with a long-term orientation appreciate how the present-day situation fits into an overall bigger context of events. Individuals in these cultures demonstrate thriftiness and perseverance in order to achieve a long-term goal. They also revere their past. China has a very strong long-term orientation. By contrast, cultures without a long-term orientation, like the United States, are more often concerned with enjoying the here and now; they are less likely to be concerned about the future and they will be unlikely to consult the past. Instead, these individuals focus on achieving quick results.

Indulgence is the last of Hofstede's dimensions. It represents the tendency for a society to be open to the gratification of basic and natural human motivations to have fun and enjoy life, such as the people of Australia. The opposite of indulgence is restraint, where individuals hold back their desire to have fun and enjoy life. Many communist and former communist countries fall into this category (Hofstede, Hofstede, and Minkov 2010).

Long-term orientation concerns a culture's time orientation and the extent to which it is concerned about the future as well as the past.

Indulgence represents the tendency for a society to be open to the gratification of basic and natural human motivations to have fun and enjoy life.

Critiques of Hofstede

Although his work represented a breakthrough in our understanding of culture, Hofstede's work has not been without criticism (cf. McSweeney 2002; Baskerville 2003; Fang 2010). These criticisms revolve around two main issues. The first set of criticisms involves how Hofstede conducted his original study and the people he interviewed (only IBM). Essentially, these dimensions were developed in a Western corporate cultural setting at one point in time, and it is likely that different dimensions would emerge if he had worked in other cultural settings at different times.

The second set of criticisms involve Hofstede's assumptions about culture. His cultural dimensions assume that national identity is the same as cultural identity and therefore ignores the variations within the culture and across subcultures. Although Hofstede's six dimensions are helpful in seeing broad cultural differences, it would be wrong to assume that everyone in a certain culture adheres to that culture's broad set of values. In the end, although they have been criticized over the years, these dimensions have been widely used by policy makers, organizational decision-makers, and marketers because they provide a broad understanding of a culture's values and associated behaviors. For marketing managers, they are especially helpful in understanding the best way to communicate culturally relevant messages (see Insights from the Field 11.2).

Cultural innovations are opportunities for marketers

Cultural innovations are distinct shifts in the way individuals in the culture think about the world and their roles within it. Simply looking at the predominant view of female beauty provides an example of how these shifts occur. Since the 1990s, the ideal image of female beauty has gone from waif-thin to more curvy and realistic in terms of what women actually look like. The "Real Beauty" campaign by Dove leveraged this cultural innovation by depicting "real" women in its ads. The campaign has been running since 2004 and has received a plethora of awards and praise by critics. Cultural innovations, in which cultural values evolve and change, occur frequently. In the United States, we see greater acceptance of different gender identities and nontraditional families. In marketing, as recently as 2010, depicting images that reflected these kinds of cultural innovations would have seemed unthinkable. By 2020, however, it became quite common to see ads reflecting these new cultural realities. The important point is that cultural innovations happen all the time and smart marketers can leverage the opportunities presented by these shifts (Holt and Cameron 2012).

Coca-Cola has been at the forefront of attempting to portray itself as a culturally sensitive organization—its products are for everyone, anytime, and anywhere. However, the company has waded into territory that many other consumer products firms would find somewhat risky. In an attempt to ride the cultural innovation of a more inclusive multicultural society—and perhaps even to push it along a bit—it aired a sixty-second ad during the 2014 Super Bowl in which individuals of all shapes, sizes, colors, and ethnicities sang the song "America the Beautiful" as stunning imagery of some of America's most beautiful scenery was displayed. Regular consumers are also shown in a variety of activities. The song starts out in English and then switches to some other languages, including Arabic and Hindi. Significantly, the ad includes two individuals who are often negatively stereotyped: Muslims and Arabs (see the ad here: https://www.youtube.com/watch?v=RiMMpFcy-HU).

At the time, reactions to the ad were either strongly positive or strongly negative. Those who were more politically conservative were angry, but those who were politically progressive really liked the ad (Hoewe and Hatemi 2017). Despite this controversy, executives at Coke decided to air the ad again in 2017 as a statement against the country's divisive political climate. Not surprisingly, the ad received a host of negative feedback again, as well as threats of a boycott. Similarly, it was also showered with praise as being forward-thinking and inclusive (O'Reilly 2017).

Marketing managers at Coke created another ad in 2018 that showed support for individuals who were observing the holy month of Ramadan. During this time in the Muslim calendar, individuals are required to fast from dawn until dusk every day. According to one spokesperson at Coca-Cola, the ad was designed to show "friendship, kindness, solidarity, and inclusiveness with the millions of Muslims around the world who fast from sunup to sunset during the month of Ramadan." The ad ends with an important message of inclusion, "What unites us is bigger than what divides us" (Tan 2018) (check out the ad here: https://www.adsoftheworld.com/media/film/cocacola_sunset).

Are executives at Coke trying to break down barriers and create more understanding of different cultures or are they simply trying to sell more product? Coca-Cola's attempt to support the cultural innovation of a multicultural America is a somewhat risky move because of its potential to alienate a portion of its customer base. However, executives at Coke seem committed to their approach. Two of the world's top ad agencies were engaged in developing these ads. The imagery and music are beautiful, as are the messages of understanding and inclusion. Both of these ads generated a lot of discussion, as well as shares and comments on social media. Further, although some people complained, a large group of consumers greatly appreciated the positive messages of acceptance and inclusion from one of America's most well-known and powerful companies.

Questions

1. What do you think? Are executives at Coke trying to break down barriers and create more understanding of different cultures or are they simply trying to sell more product? Support your answer with evidence from the chapter.

2. One persistent cultural stereotype is that Canadians are nice. Look at the Canadian Broadcasting Company archives for a story about the "I am Canadian" campaign (http://www.cbc.ca/archives/entry/i-am-canadian-by-molson) and try to find some more recent ads from this campaign. In what way could using such a stereotype be beneficial to a marketer? In what ways should marketers be cautious about using this approach?

3. In thinking about the examples we have discussed (Dove, Coke, and Molson), are marketers *facilitating* a cultural innovation or are they simply *reflecting* a cultural innovation? Support your answer.

Sources: Holt and Cameron (2012); Hoewe and Hatemi (2017); Tan (2018).

Culture and Consumption

Our study of culture has so far examined the content of culture, the movement of cultural meaning, and cultural classifications. Marketers and advertisers create insights from this vast collection of research and use them to create relevant and often inspiring communications strategies. In this section, after exploring an example of culture and consumption (see Insights from the Field 11.3), we will examine the difference between sacred and profane consumption, which helps marketers understand how important a consumption experience is to a consumer.

A critical part to understanding the impact of culture on consumption relies on how important the consumption experience is to the consumer. Essentially, how central is this consumption experience to the consumer's self-concept? In the following sections, we will first introduce the concept of sacred versus profane consumption. Then, we will explore the topic more thoroughly with a discussion of sacralization and desacralization.

Sacred and profane consumption

Within the realm of consumer research, experts refer to **sacred consumption** to describe those consumption activities that are set apart from everyday consumption activities and are treated with some degree of respect or awe. It is important to remember that sacred consumption is not necessarily associated with religion. In addition to tangible objects, the concept of sacred consumption can also apply to places, people, and events. For example, marketers in the tourism industry encourage tourists to engage in once-in-a lifetime experiences by visiting places that are deemed so special that they are sacred in the minds of consumers. These places could include, for example, the pristine tropical island of Bali, the Taj Mahal in India, or the ancient mountain town of Machu Picchu in Peru. Certain people can also have sacred status,

Sacred consumption describes those consumption activities that are set apart from everyday consumption activities and are treated with some degree of respect or awe.

Thought about growing a beard?

Culture has long had an influence on fashion, and one of the most obvious fashion statements sits right on the face of most males: facial hair. The full beard has made a bit of a comeback in the United States, with some people paying an extraordinary amount of money for grooming products and some even going so far as to pay thousands of dollars for facial hair transplants to achieve a face full of thick hair. It is less likely you will find someone with a full beard in parts of Asia and Africa. The cultural meaning and importance of facial hair have changed over the years, but today a clean-shaven face "has come to signify a virtuous and sociable man, whereas the beard marks someone as self-reliant and unconventional" (Oldstone-Moore 2015).

No-shave November is a cultural movement that is designed to raise awareness about cancer and everything a patient loses when dealing with this terrible disease, including his or her hair. The effort is supported by a website where participants can buy T-shirts and print flyers to hang on the wall and inform coworkers why they're so hairy. An active social media campaign also spreads the message even further. The idea is that men are supposed to donate the money they would normally spend on shaving products to a variety of cancer organizations ("What Is No-Shave November?" 2019). The organization has been credited with raising millions of dollars for a wide variety of cancer research organizations.

For those men who are still reluctant to try growing a beard or simply can't grow a good-looking beard, don't worry. Experts have predicted that we may have reached a "peak beard" moment in this trend because as beards become more common, they become less interesting, unique, and innovative (Janif, Brooks, and Dixson 2014) (see Photo 11.11).

Questions

1. In Chapter 10, we introduced the concepts of bicultural and multicultural individuals. How might

● **Photo 11.11** *No-shave November has raised millions for cancer research*

a marketer create a culturally informed campaign for an individual who adheres to more than one culture?

2. In the previous section of this chapter, we discussed a variety of rituals that helped consumers move meaning from the realm of consumer goods to the self. For each of the following foreign products, describe how a marketer of this product could encourage the use of one or more rituals by someone living in the United States: Vegemite spread for bread (from Australia), a French press for coffee (from France), and a meal at a new Nepalese restaurant in town.

Sources: Janif, Brooks, and Dixson (2014); Oldstone-Moore (2015); "What Is No-Shave November?" (2019).

---

especially when they are idolized and set apart from others, such as Nelson Mandela or Kobe Bryant. Events may also be perceived as sacred by consumers. For example, sports fans will happily travel long distances to support their teams, endure hardships of cold and rain, and even sing songs and chants for their team (Belk, Wallendorf, and Sherry 1989). In contrast, the term **profane consumption** is used to capture those consumer objects and events that are more "everyday" in nature; they do not share the "specialness" of sacred consumption (Belk, Wallendorf, and Sherry 1989). Important insights about new product development, distribution, pricing, and communication can be derived from examining the differences between sacred and profane consumption.

Profane consumption is the term used to capture those consumer objects and events that are more "everyday" in nature; they do not share the "specialness" of sacred consumption.

Sacralization and desacralization

How does a consumption experience become sacred or profane in the minds of consumers? **Sacralization** happens when we attach sacred meaning to profane consumption so that everyday products, people, places, and events are elevated and have a distinctiveness and specialness in the eyes of consumers. Although this is often a challenge for marketers, we know that marketers attempt use a variety of tactics, such as using memorabilia associated with special places or experiences (e.g., a T-shirt from your favorite band's farewell concert or whiskey from your trip to Ireland). In many ways, people who are collectors of different objects—antiques, military items, coins, political artifacts—often imbue these objects with sacred qualities.

Sacralization happens when we attach sacred meaning to profane consumption so that everyday products, people, places, and events are elevated and have a distinctiveness and specialness in the eyes of consumers.

Desacralization happens when a sacred item, person, place, or experience is no longer special and is downgraded to the realm of "everyday" in the minds

● **Photo 11.12** *The Day of the Dead has become desacralized*

Desacralization happens when a sacred item, person, place, or experience is no longer special and is downgraded to the realm of "everyday" in the minds of consumers.

of consumers. In Mexico, for example, the Day of the Dead is celebrated as a way to commemorate family members and others who have died. People erect small altars, pray, decorate gravesites, and eat special food. This tradition used to be quite solemn and can be traced back to the culture of the ancient Aztecs. In recent decades, however, the Day of the Dead has become a time for partying, parades, and other forms of celebration. Revelers from the three-day event even have their choice of souvenirs to bring home (see Photo 11.12); for many, the day has lost its sacred status and has simply become an excuse to party. The important thing to remember is how critical it is for a marketer to understand a culture's language, symbols, and values (see Insights from the Field 11.4 on language).

INSIGHTS FROM THE FIELD 11.4

Lost in translation

Language is an important part of culture, but words often have meanings that are not so obvious from literal translations. In fact, culture influences how words are interpreted. There are numerous examples of marketing communication blunders resulting from a lack of understanding of wider cultural contexts.

- From Ireland: "The future's bright . . . the future's Orange" is the tag line of the telecommunications company Orange. However, the tag line had to be changed for the Northern Ireland market because of the long-standing historical clashes between the Protestants (who used the orange color) and the Catholics (who used green). The implication of the message was that "the future is bright, the future is Protestant," which was not well received by the Irish Catholic population (Tooher 1996).
- From the Arabic world: when Nike decorated its shoes with the stylized word "air" that looked like a flame, many Muslims around the world saw the symbol and realized that it looked a lot like the word Allah. It was viewed as incredibly disrespectful and many likened it to placing the name Jesus on a pair of shoes. Nike recalled the shoes and apologized (Murphy 1997).

- From China: When Pampers entered the Chinese market, the package included an image of a stork carrying a baby, which is quite common in Western cultures. Chinese consumers, however, were perplexed by the image because in China, babies are brought by giant floating peaches, not storks (Brooks 2013).
- From Belgium: When Ford Motor Company entered the market in Belgium, it wanted to convey the idea that its cars were well manufactured and beautiful. It used the tag line, "Every car has a high-quality body," which, when translated into Belgian, became "Every car has a high-quality corpse" (Brooks 2013).

Questions
1. How can companies avoid these blunders? What specific suggestions do you have for how such errors may be avoided?
2. Find at least two other examples of advertisements for brands that are attempting to target a *new* audience. First, briefly describe the new cultural environment that is being targeted. Second, use McCracken's six dimensions to analyze how successful the ads might be in resonating with the new audience.

Sources: Brooks (2013); Murphy (1997); Tooher (1996).

◉ Subcultures

Within each culture, there are subcultures. A **subculture** is a smaller, cohesive group of people that share similar values, beliefs, tastes, and behavioral patterns. Subcultures are important to marketing because they often capture meaningful links and connections between groups in society. In marketing, the term subculture is widely used to refer to any subgroup of consumption. Marketers are particularly interested in subcultures that are based on demographic characteristics or consumption communities.

Subcultures based on demographic characteristics

Although many different demographic subcultures exist, we will focus on three of the most important ones for marketing: age, ethnicity/race, and gender/gender identity.

Age-based subcultures

Marketers use age-based subcultures in a variety of different ways. One way that marketers are able to use them is by classifying individuals according to the age they are right now. For example, most individuals who are eighteen now are likely graduating from high school and many are considering college. Each year, as young people turn eighteen, they are likely to be faced with similar consumption-related decisions as they take their next steps into the future. People in their thirties right now are probably starting families, while people in their fifties are probably sending their kids off to college and becoming empty nesters. The tween subculture (young people between eight and twelve years old) is especially interesting to marketers because people in this age group are consumers in training. A key characteristic of this group is that they are beginning to make independent purchases, but still need advice from time to time. When thinking about advice and guidance, 87 percent look up to their parents, followed by teachers (62 percent) and YouTube stars (42 percent). Many also report that they have a very close relationship with their parents (85 percent) (Mintel 2018a). Capturing the tween market could prove quite lucrative for brands because these consumers may become lifelong consumers.

A second way that age-based subcultures can be used is by key stages or milestones in a person's life (single, married with no children, young family, etc.). The assumption is that individuals in these groups have different consumption goals and consume different types of products and services. That is, regardless of whether an individual is an older parent or a younger parent, he or she will have similar consumption goals and purchase similar products when a baby enters the picture.

A third use of age-based subcultures is based on an individual's generation. The idea is that people who are of the same generation have similar life experiences, values, worldviews, and tastes in things like music, entertainment, and other products. They listened to the same bands, watched the same

Table 11.1 Key generational subcultures

The *Generation Z*, also known as the i*Generation*: This group includes anyone born between 1995 and 2007 and is named for the strong influence of technology in their lives. This group makes up about 17 percent of the US population (Mintel 2018b).

- This group is likely to delay getting married and starting a family until their late twenties or early thirties. They have always had easy access to smart technology, as well as an infinite amount of information and entertainment at their fingertips (Mintel 2018b).
- Gen Zs are also the most ethnically diverse generation the United States has seen and they appreciate diversity in marketing communications (Mintel 2018b).
- Very soon, these individuals will start to make some big consumption-related decisions, such as further education, a first car, and/or a first apartment (filled with stuff).

Millennials (or *Generation Y*): Born between 1977 and 1994, they make up about 24.5 percent of the US population (Mintel 2017).

- Millennials break from traditions of older generations by being much more likely to live with roommates or a partner than with a spouse (Mintel 2017).
- The majority of older millennials are now parents, despite some who have an aversion to "adulting" (Mintel 2017).
- Unlike previous generations, millennials participate heavily in the sharing economy and are frequent users of services like Airbnb and Uber (Mintel 2017).

Generation X: This is a relatively small group, comprising just 15 percent of the US population. Individuals in this generation were born between 1965 and 1976 (Mintel 2016a).

- Generation X individuals describe themselves as responsible, realistic, and compassionate, which is in stark contrast to how others describe them: slackers, cynical, and forgotten (Mintel 2016a).
- This generation is in the middle of their peak earning and spending years, but they are also experiencing a financial tug-of-war because they are trying to pay off debts while saving for retirement (Mintel 2016a).
- This generation also broke many of the earlier "traditional" ideas of family; women and men share more chores around the home and many were raised by two working (sometimes divorced) parents, so they have a strong bent toward independence (Mintel 2016a).

Baby boomers: Born between 1946 and 1964, this group comprises 23 percent of the US population (Mintel 2016b).

- These individuals were born after the end of World War II, which was a time marked by optimism and economic security. However, these individuals came of age during the social and political upheaval of the 1960s.
- Boomers were responsible for many of the economic successes, as well as the social and cultural advancements over the past few decades.
- This subculture is massive in size and therefore exerts significant power in the marketplace. They are also characterized by high levels of income and savings, spending power, political power, and leisure time (Mintel 2016b).

shows, and were of a similar age during major world events, like 9/11, for example (see Table 11.1 for more detail).

Marketers have found it quite informative to use a consumer's generational subculture. However, we must express a note of caution here. Global marketing experts cannot assume that generations are comparable across the world. It would be a vast oversimplification to assume that millennials in Japan, for example, are the same as millennials in the United States, the United Kingdom, Argentina, or anywhere else.

Ethnic and racial subcultures

Before we begin, we must understand the difference between ethnicity and race. **Race** refers to the color of a person's skin and other physical features, while **ethnicity** refers to a variety of cultural factors, such as nationality, ancestry, shared customs, and language. A person's race is easy for others to see, while a person's ethnicity is not. Thus, although someone might have Asian racial characteristics, it would be a mistake to say, for example, that a South Korean and a Vietnamese person share the same ethnicity. Researchers have argued that race acts as a symbol for others to interpret and, in many cases, make assumptions about. It is no surprise to anyone living in our society today that people make judgments and assumptions about others based on their race (Khanna 2011). Researchers have struggled with creating easy-to-understand distinctions between the concepts of race and ethnicity, as well as between different races and different ethnicities. In the end, there are no clear-cut rules and there are many areas of overlap (Frey 2015).

The three biggest racial subcultures in the United States are Hispanic, Black, and Asian (see Frey 2015). Experts predict that by 2044, the United States will be a majority minority nation. That is, there will be more non-White people than White people. The United States is currently undergoing a transformative demographic shift that will eventually result in America being a multiracial nation. As White birth rates continue to decline, the number of White immigrants decreases, and the White population ages, experts suggest that an increasingly diverse, educated, and connected group of young people is necessary to fuel America's economic growth throughout the twenty-first century. This demographic shift means that there will also be shifts in political and economic power as more individuals become educated, succeed, and take positions of power in business, science, and government (Frey 2015). Check out Insights from the Boardroom 11 to find out more about ethnic subcultures and advertising.

The Hispanic population comprises 18.3 percent of the population (US Census Bureau 2019) and is growing at a rate of 2.0 percent per year, a significant decrease from a peak of 4.2 percent in 2001. The Hispanic population is not evenly dispersed across the United States; 54 percent of Hispanics live in just three states: California, Texas, and Florida (Krogstad 2017). The Black population makes up 13.4 percent of the population and is growing at 0.9 percent, and the Asian population comprises 5.9 percent of the population but is growing at the rate of 3.0 percent per year, mainly because of immigration (Krogstad 2017; US Census Bureau 2019). There have always been individuals who have come from multiracial backgrounds but, for whatever reason, have identified as being from a single race. Given a choice, 2.7 percent of the US population does not identify with a single race and instead identifies with two or more races (Krogstad 2017; US Census Bureau 2019). In the next few

Race refers to the color of a person's skin and other physical features.

Ethnicity refers to a variety of cultural factors such as nationality, ancestry, shared customs, and language.

INSIGHTS FROM THE BOARDROOM 11

Any road will get you there if you're not sure where you're going

● *A. Bruce Crawley*

"There is absolutely no question that US consumer markets, in virtually every product or service category, are becoming increasingly diverse, creating substantially more challenges for traditional marketing communications firms," says A. Bruce Crawley (2017). Crawley is the president and CEO of Millennium 3 Management (M3M), which specializes in marketing communications, social media management, and strategic communications consulting. M3M targets mainstream and diverse audiences and has worked with a variety of global brands such as Limited Brands, Major League Baseball, Marriott, McDonald's, Pepsi, and Spectacor.

According to Crawley, "the worst mistake brands make in outreach to Black audiences, for example, is to underestimate the need to do appropriate cultural and behavioral research" (2017). As a result, some of those communications efforts are particularly offensive, because they make liberal use of racial and cultural stereotypes. As an example, he mentions a recent TV spot for a fast-food company (he declined to say which one) in which a Black actor is shown demonstrating exaggerated, undignified bodily movements and culturally demeaning facial expressions. "You can't pull that actor out of that spot and substitute into it a person of European descent. The concept of those kinds of demeaning behaviors is simply not transferable across racial categories, and audiences, Black, White or otherwise, simply would not accept them as a valid representation of White consumers. Such approaches are increasingly offensive and don't help brands to sell goods or services" (2017).

Crawley has had an instinct for effective marketing and communications since his earliest days when, as a young child, he stood on the streets of Philadelphia and sold double-handled shopping bags to passersby. Crawley was the first person in his family to attend college. "I picked 'accounting' because it was the first choice, alphabetically, on the list of available majors and I learned that there was no science requirement over the four-year program. I wasn't absolutely sure at that point what accountants did in their professional lives, but I was convinced, even then, that I did not want to be a scientist!" Once enrolled, he found accounting classes "boring" and, by the time he got to his sophomore year in college, he had started asking his professors, "OK, so when do we learn about how to persuade people to make decisions and to actually sell products?" (2017). His accounting professor suggested he change his major to marketing and the rest is history.

After many successful years in industry, Crawley realized he could make a greater impact by opening his own marketing communications firm. He brought a great deal of mainstream marketing and communications expertise to his new venture, but always the entrepreneur, he also decided to focus on niche communications to diverse consumer markets. He observed, for example, that although African Americans comprise 13.4 percent of the US population (US Census Bureau 2019) and spend approximately $1.2 trillion annually, the Black experience was rarely being adequately portrayed in mainstream advertising. These data, Crawley believes, create a strong argument for why it is especially important for marketers to do substantial, in-depth research prior to approaching

African American and other diverse consumer markets to ensure that their paid media investments don't underperform or backfire completely.

Such research, when effectively done, often leads "to the discovery of opportunities that are substantially different than those that exist among general market consumers" (Crawley 2017). Indeed, Black consumers "overindex" on a variety of products, such as in personal care categories, like hair and skin care products, as well as in food categories, such as pork, poultry, seafood, and leafy greens (Nielsen 2016).

Research also reveals that Black millennial consumers are particularly interesting. Indeed, they are technology trailblazers and, importantly, they are strongly influential in their peer groups. Specifically, compared to other audiences, they are much more likely to be among the first of their friends and colleagues to try new products (25 percent more likely), they often take the opportunity to discuss their tech knowledge with others (20 percent more likely), and they want others to say "wow" when they see their electronics (31 percent more likely) (Nielsen 2016). With respect to the influence of advertising, Black millennials report that celebrity endorsements are important (47 percent more important than the general population) and they are also very much influenced by "what's hot and what's not" (29 percent more than the general population) (Nielsen 2016).

When brands reach out to M3M to target mainstream or Black audiences, Crawley says his advice is always the same. As he's fond of saying, "Any road will get you there if you're not sure where you're going." He wants his clients to be comfortable, therefore, with their understanding of the desired outcomes for any

proposed campaign, regardless of the race, gender, or culture of the targeted audience. Crawley believes that successful targeting to the Black audience rests on three key factors:

- The communication itself is respectful, just like communications to other mainstream consumer segments;
- The research-facilitated messaging is precisely executed; and
- The selection of TV, print, social media, etc., for the message includes a combination of mainstream and ethnic-specific channels.

At M3M, strategy and a clear understanding of desired outcomes, as opposed to industry peer recognition, always drive the process. In the end, Crawley hopes to enhance his clients' success by helping them utilize research to better connect with the country's increasingly diverse consumer segments, across all racial and ethnic classifications.

decades, this trend will most certainly accelerate (Frey 2015). What happens when someone defines him- or herself as biracial or multiracial? How do these people perceive themselves and how are they perceived by others? People who have a mixed Black–White heritage, for example, may appear Black to the larger culture, but may also identify with the customs and practices of a White ethnicity (Italian, Irish, etc.). A lot of research has been conducted about how people negotiate the line between two races. The main point, however, is that our definitions of race and ethnicity are fluid and depend substantially on an individual's choice in the matter (Khanna 2011).

From a marketing standpoint, much of the research on race and ethnicity has focused on the depiction of individuals of different racial backgrounds in advertising (cf. Williams, Lee, and Henderson 2008) and the different treatment that customers receive based on their race (cf. Harkness 2016). Toyota made headlines in 2017 when it advertised its Camry to three ethnicities (Black, Hispanic, and Asian) using three sets of cultural values and cues. Indeed, it even hired three ad agencies to help develop meaningful content that would resonate with its audiences. Instead of using cultural stereotypes, which happens far too often, these ad executions were careful to highlight core values for each target audience (Maheshwari 2017). In looking at social media today, very few platforms ask for a user's ethnicity. However, they don't need to ask. Many social network platforms like Facebook, LinkedIn, and Twitter are able to distill a user's ethnicity by examining likes, status updates, and other activity. In this way, marketers are able to find ways to target racial and ethnic subcultures for online advertising (Carmichael 2011).

Subcultures based on gender and gender identity

Gender refers to the biological reality of a person—male or female—as well as that individual's own psychological perceptions about his or her gender (Fischer and Arnold 1994; Palan 2001). **Gender identity** refers to how an individual perceives him- or herself within the broader social context. That is, gender identity is the bundle of cognitions and emotions associated with how the individual perceives his or her own roles and rules for behavior within the society (Caterall and Maclaran 2002; Palan 2001). In Western societies, boys are socialized to be more competitive, independent, and aggressive, whereas girls are socialized to be more sympathetic and cooperative (Cramphorn 2011).

One stream of research in the area of gender identity focuses on how individuals perceive themselves along two dimensions: the feminine dimension, which examines how "gentle, warm, and compassionate" a person is, and the masculine dimension, which examines how "aggressive, dominant, and forceful" a person is (Bem 1974; Spence 1993). It is important to note that women are not necessarily feminine and men are not necessarily masculine. Also, a feminine person is not the opposite of a masculine person and vice versa. Indeed, there are two dimensions of gender identity (feminine and masculine), and a person can be high or low on each of these dimensions (see Figure 11.2).

Gender refers to the biological reality of a person—male or female.

Gender identity refers to how an individual perceives themselves, their roles, and rules for behavior within the broader social context.

Bem's model assumes that a person's gender identity is fairly stable over time and context. **Non–gender binary**, however, is a self-definition for some individuals that does not fit neatly into any of the previous models of gender or gender identity. For these individuals, their identity can shift over time and in different contexts. Non–gender binary individuals avoid the simple, discrete definitions of gender and gender identity. Instead, they prefer a fluid definition whereby they can be feminine, masculine, both, or neither.

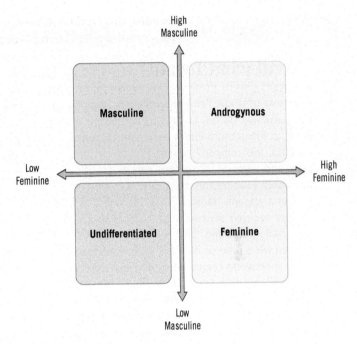

● **Figure 11.2** *Bem's Model of Gender Identity*
Source: based on Bem (1974)

The concept of gender identity is important to marketers because it allows them to create insights into how they can construct advertising messages that will ideally resonate with particular groups. As with race and ethnicity, much of this depends on an individual's own definitions of identity. Some marketers have success with breaking preexisting expectations, as with Under Armour's "I will what I want" campaign (see Insights from the Field 11.5).

Intersectionality occurs when multiple identities exist at the same time, as in the case, for example, of a Black female or a gay baby boomer. For a Black female, picture a traffic intersection where the north/south road is race and the east/west road is gender. Each "road" has its own set of assumptions, guidelines, and norms of behavior. Intersectionality happens when these two identities come together at a crossroads. The broader culture understands *Black* people and *female* people, but *Black female* is less well understood. Because the media, our educational system, church groups, and other social institutions reinforce meanings associated with each identity, it is sometimes difficult to simultaneously negotiate several identities at once (Crenshaw 1989). Understanding the concept of intersectionality and the different realities that individuals live is critical to providing meaningful insights to marketers as our culture becomes increasingly diverse.

Non–gender binary is a self-definition for some individuals that rejects the simple, discrete definitions of gender and gender identity. Instead, they prefer a fluid definition whereby they can be feminine, masculine, both, or neither.

Intersectionality is a cultural definition whereby multiple identities exist at the same time.

Subcultures based on consumption communities

The modern concept of community has been built on research insights from sociology and anthropology. In marketing, our understanding of communities has evolved from subcultures of consumption (Schouten and McAlexander 1995) to brand communities (Muniz and O'Guinn 2001) and consumer tribes (Cova and Cova 2002). Like other subcultures we have discussed, these subcultures share similar values, beliefs, tastes, and behavioral patterns.

"I will what I want"

The story of Under Armour's growth is inspiring. The company was started in 1996 by entrepreneur Kevin Plank in his grandmother's basement (Schultz 2014). By 2013, the company posted $2.3 billion in global sales and years of 20 percent annual growth. However, only $500 million of its sales was coming from women's apparel (Murray 2016). Marketers at Under Armour focused on two main insights to create an expectation-breaking new campaign. First, young women were tired of the "You go girl" message that many sportswear companies had used—the message was overused (Schultz 2014). Second, young women are heavy users of social media and share images and messages that they find inspiring. A full 93 percent of women ages eighteen to thirty-four share or upload content to social media and 46 percent click on ads on social media (Mintel 2018c).

These two insights led to a completely new approach for women's sportswear. The goal of the "I will what I want" campaign was to celebrate young women "who had the physical and mental strength to tune out the external pressures and turn inward and chart their own course" (Schultz 2014). Under Armour wanted to depict the power of mental, emotional, and physical strength. One ad featuring Misty Copeland, a Black ballet dancer who broke all stereotypes, was especially inspiring. The ad depicted close-up shots of her muscular legs and body as she danced to a voice-over that told her all of the things that were wrong with her body: her feet were wrong, her limbs were wrong, and her whole body was wrong for ballet. Copeland was able to overcome the adversity of countless rejections to become the first African American principal dancer

with the American Ballet Theatre. The audience knew her story and the ad resonated with them. It received four million views on YouTube and viewers who went to the website spent an average of four minutes there. Overall, the campaign resulted in five billion (yes, billion!) media impressions globally and $35 million in earned media. The real proof was a 28 percent jump in women's sales and a 42 percent increase in traffic to the website. This campaign catapulted Under Armour to the number two spot in the sportswear industry, ahead of Adidas and behind Nike (Murray 2016).

Marketing managers at Under Armour leveraged important insights about the target market and its use of social media, as well as an important message and arresting images of strength in the face of adversity. In the end, it was a winning combination.

Questions

1. Previously, we discussed the importance of constructing messages that resonate with a target market. Now, we're talking about how advertising can be effective when it defies expectations. Which of these approaches is correct? Support your answer with evidence from this chapter.

2. Some product categories, such as tobacco and alcohol, require particular care with regard to targeting specific cultures and subcultures. Find some examples of advertisements for products like alcohol or tobacco that have targeted a specific culture or subculture and discuss the extent to which you think the ad is appropriate.

Sources: Mintel (2018b); Murray (2016); Schultz (2014).

Subcultures of consumption

Subculture of consumption is defined as a group of consumers connected through a shared consumption activity.

A **subculture of consumption** is a group of consumers who have a "shared commitment to a particular product class, brand, or consumption activity" (Schouten and McAlexander 1995, 43). These subcultures of consumption have two important characteristics. First, there is an identifiable ethos and value system that brings its members together. They stand for something;

they have an identity and a set of core values that guide their decision-making and behavior. Second, a subculture's members express their shared values via the relationships they have with certain brands. The Harley–Davidson community is a classic example of a subculture of consumption. People who own Harleys are *really* into their Harleys and like to celebrate freedom and the open road. They connect with one another in a variety of forums, attend rallies, purchase products, and enjoy spending time together talking about their shared love of Harley–Davidson bikes.

Brand communities

Brand community is the second type of consumption community. It focuses on the strong relationships that consumers have with one another around a brand. Thus, a **brand community** "is a specialized, non–geographically bound community, based on a structured set of social relations among admirers of a brand" (Muniz and O'Guinn 2001, 412). For members of a brand community, the *community* is more important than the *brand*. Researchers have identified three key characteristics that make a brand community unique:

Brand community refers to a non–geographically bound community that is connected through brand admiration, with a structured set of social relations.

- Consciousness of kind is the recognizable connection that consumers have, both with each other in the brand community and with the brand. For Apple enthusiasts, the brand ethos and values of innovation and independence are accepted and shared between members of this subculture of consumption.

- Rituals and traditions, such as shared brand consumption experiences, reproduce and transmit meaning within and beyond the subculture. Members also engage in rituals such as storytelling to create and reinforce important shared meanings. Coca-Cola, for example, has a rich history and consumers who are devoted Coke drinkers like to engage in rituals and traditions associated with the brand.

- Moral responsibility *to the brand* is one more characteristic of a brand community that makes it unique. Here, members express an obligation or responsibility to the community, its members, and the brand. There is often an "us versus them" mentality.

An interesting twist on brand communities is the antibrand community. There have been many high-profile examples of consumers who have actively opposed brands or companies because of their wrongdoing. As with brand communities that bring people together in a positive way about the brand, antibrand communities also share a commitment to express their anger and frustration with a particular brand (Hollenbeck and Zinkhan 2010). The I Hate Walmart Facebook page has forty-one thousand followers and is liked by forty-two thousand people. Two other higher-profile examples are United Airlines (#BoycottUnited and #BoycottUnitedAirlines) and Volkswagen (#ihatevw). Members of these antibrand communities share stories, pictures, and memes as a way to engage in consumer activism against the brand.

Consumer tribes consist of a group of consumers, emotionally connected by similar consumption values and usage, who utilize a brand as the link to create a community and express identity.

Consumer tribes

Consumer tribes are the last type of consumption community. **Consumer tribes** consist of a group of consumers who are committed to one another more around the consumption experience than around the actual brand. They are connected by similar consumption patterns and values and use the tribe to express their identity, but the brand itself is more of a secondary consideration (Cova 1997). Just like subcultures of consumption and brand communities, members of a consumer tribe are connected to one another through a shared passion for a particular consumer behavior or brand. However, consumption tribes are more flexible in that they recognize that its members may belong to several tribes at the same time. Consumers express different dimensions of their self-identity when they have membership in multiple consumer tribes.

Unlike subcultures of consumption and brand communities, a consumer tribe does not exert a strong influence on the lives of consumers and members generally do not feel a strong moral obligation to the tribe. Tribes are distinct from other ways of thinking about consumption communities in that they place less emphasis on the specific product or service, but instead focus on consumer-to-consumer relationships. Tribes can emerge as a result of an appreciation for certain consumption-related behaviors (e.g., mountain climbers, roller coaster enthusiasts), brands (e.g., Subaru), or popular cultural trends (e.g., the growing enthusiasm for anything with cannabidiol (CBD)). Case Study 11 presents the story of Free People and its connection to two important subcultures: millennials and consumer tribes.

Subcultures based on consumption communities are often further influenced by the various subcultural dynamics of age, ethnicity, and gender that were discussed earlier in this chapter. It is important to note that much of the discussion here focuses on American and Western subcultures. However, regardless of where a subculture exists, they both *reflect* and *influence* major societal, demographic, behavioral, and consumption-related trends.

◉ Summary

When you learn something from people, or from a culture, you accept it as a gift, and it is your lifelong commitment to preserve it and build on it.
—Yo-Yo Ma (world-renowned cellist)

This examination and discussion of *culture* has centered on the content of culture as well as the ways in which culture influences some of the most important decisions and events in our lives. In our investigation of the *elements of the cultural system*, we explored the ways in which ecology, social structure, and ideology all influence the content of a culture and investigated how individuals learn about culture. In advertising, cultural elements are often depicted, and sometimes cultural stereotypes are utilized to either reinforce or challenge strongly held perceptions. In discussing the concept of cultural archetypes, we highlighted a fascinating example of how two brands successfully utilized the typical gym archetype in Insights from the Field 11.1.

The section on *classification of cultures* presented several dimensions that researchers and marketers could use to describe a culture's values, beliefs, and behavioral patterns. We took a closer look at Hofstede's six dimensions of cultural classification and even acknowledged two important flaws in Hofstede's model. To illustrate the importance of the study of culture, Insights from the Field 11.2 focused on Coca-Cola's release of two ads that promoted the idea of greater cultural understanding and inclusion.

After describing some of the important dimensions of cultural *content*, the discussion shifted to the *process* of culture. Specifically, we described the nature of *cultural myths and rituals*. We found that consumption rituals were the vehicle by which cultural meaning is moved from the broader cultural environment to the consumer. During this discussion, several examples from around the world were highlighted.

The discussion of the content and process of culture provided a firm foundation on which we then were able to create insights that would be relevant to *marketing communications*. In our ensuing discussion of sacred and profane consumption, we presented an interesting study on the branding of the Royal Family in Insights from Academia 11.3 and the no-shave November movement in Insights from the Field 11.3.

Finally, the concept of *subcultural groups* was presented, with particular emphasis on subcultures based on demographic characteristics and subcultures based on consumption communities. Insights from the Field 11.5 explored the Under Armour campaign with Misty Copeland and how it broke with expectations on how to talk with women about sports and performance. Similarly, Insights from the Boardroom 11 discussed some of the missteps marketers often make in targeting Black audiences.

Although the study of culture in consumer behavior is fascinating, one of the reasons it is especially challenging is that the cultural landscape continues to shift quite dramatically. The Black Lives Matter movement and the global Coronavirus pandemic both launched dramatic shifts in public perceptions and our shared cultural understandings. Looking toward the future, marketers can rest assured that there will be no shortage of new trends and insights to use in their work.

KEY TERMS

acculturation p. 400
archetypes p. 404
beliefs p. 402
brand community p. 431
collectivism p. 415
collectivist cultures p. 415

consumer acculturation p. 400
consumer tribes p. 432
conventions p. 403
cultural ecology p. 412
cultural ideology p. 413
culture p. 400

customs p. 403
desacralization p. 422
divestment rituals p. 408
enculturation p. 400
ethnicity p. 425
exchange rituals p. 408

REVIEW QUESTIONS

1. How do marketers define culture?
2. What are the two ways in which an individual learns about a particular culture? In what ways do these learning processes differ?
3. Define the following characteristics of culture: beliefs, values, knowledge, norms, customs, and mores.
4. Carefully describe Hofstede's six dimensions of culture. Discuss the two important criticisms of Hofstede's model.
5. What are myths? How do they help us understand culture? Give examples of at least three myths from your culture or subculture.

6. What is the purpose of a ritual? For each of the six rituals that are relevant to consumer behavior, provide two examples from your own life.
7. What is the global consumer culture and why is it relevant to marketers?
8. What is the difference between culture and subculture? In what way are subcultures based on demographic characteristics and subcultures based on consumption communities different from one another?
9. How is intersectionality different from bicultural or multicultural identification (as discussed in Chapter 10)?

DISCUSSION QUESTIONS

1. Refer again to the material on subcultures based on demographic characteristics. Construct an argument for why it makes sense for marketing researchers and managers to utilize subcultures based on demographic characteristics, as well as an argument for why it does not make sense.
2. Select a subculture that is different from your own (we discussed three in this chapter, but there are many others). Analyze that culture according to Hofstede's multidimensional view of cultural values.

3. Find at least two advertisements that make use of myths and two that make use of archetypes in the brand narrative. For each ad, (a) carefully describe the myth or archetype. (b) To what extent does the myth or archetype have universal appeal? (c) To what extent are these myths or archetypes dependent on cultural or social context?
4. What important rituals in your own life or culture include consumption as a key part of the ritual? In what ways could a marketing manager utilize rituals to influence consumer behavior in a service setting?

5. Social marketing works to encourage individuals to engage in behaviors that positively influence the environment or society. How could marketing managers utilize rituals to influence this kind of consumer behavior?
6. Choose an easily identifiable group of consumers (e.g., ski enthusiasts, country music

fans) and analyze it in terms of the three main perspectives on subcultures based on consumption communities: subcultures of consumption, brand community, and consumer tribes. Which perspective is most useful for developing insights for marketers? Discuss.

For more information, quizzes, case studies, and other study tools, please visit us at www.oup.com/he/phillips.

CASE STUDY 11

Cultural And Subcultural Influences At Free People

The story of Free People illustrates several ways in which cultural and subcultural forces influence the creation and growth of an organization. Free People was originally founded during the massive cultural upheavals of the early 1970s when the Vietnam War, the civil rights movement, and the environmental movement were reshaping the country's cultural landscape. Free People grew and prospered by offering products and a value system that resonated with the subculture of the eighteen- to thirty-year-old group and consumer tribes. As it entered the 2010s, Free People committed a costly blunder when it engaged in cultural appropriation, but by 2020, it had righted itself and announced a new venture.

WHERE IT ALL STARTED

The Free People retail chain was first started in 1970 amid very humble beginnings on the first floor of a tiny one-hundred-year-old brownstone house on the edge of the University of Pennsylvania campus in West Philadelphia. Disillusioned by the Vietnam War, Judy Wicks and Richard Hayne rented the building with every last dollar they had and filled it with clothing and home decor that they had purchased wholesale, along with a variety of secondhand items, salvaged items, and records. The newly married couple had no money, no savings, and no ability to qualify for a business loan. Hayne hand-painted the sign that hung outside the store and the couple scoured the Chinatown section of the city on trash days to find wooden crates to use for shelving inside. They were in their early twenties, just back from a volunteer trip to Alaska, and disillusioned by the abuses of big corporations and government. The modern environmental

movement was just starting to gain steam and Wicks and Hayne wanted to target a young group of adults with their edgy, hippie-styled clothing and home furnishings. Free People was meant to appeal to individuals who wanted to have an artistic, free-thinking, and independent lifestyle. The store itself was also supposed to be free from a single style or trend. Importantly, the new store's values supported freedom from the dominance of corporate control over the media, economy, and government. The name Free People was aptly chosen (Wicks 2013).

Over the years, the company expanded considerably and, along with Anthropologie, came under the corporate umbrella of Urban Outfitters. By 2019, Richard Hayne was the president and CEO of Urban Outfitters and the conglomerate had a combined market valuation of $2 billion (Wu 2019). Free People had 137 stores across the United States and continued to offer an eclectic mix of merchandise that can be described as bohemian or boho-chic. Around that time, Urban Outfitters and Anthropologie suffered financial difficulties, with sales decreasing by 5 and 3 percent, respectively (Wilson 2019). Analysts suggested that the company needed to reduce its retail footprint, because about half of its sales were online, where there is often deep discounting. The United States has six times the amount of retail space per capita as Japan and Europe, and Hayne agreed that the firm simply had too many stores (Turner and Banjo 2017). During the same period of retail downturn, sales at Free People increased 6 percent (Wilson 2019) and it experienced overall steady growth, outpacing the other two divisions. In 2017, Free People posted net sales of $872.9 million and was responsible for about 20 percent of Urban Outfitter's revenue (Rupp 2017).

CULTURE AND FREE PEOPLE

Each item in a Free People store is a part of the story—of the brand and of the customer. The success of Free People can certainly be attributed to its strong corporate culture and brand equity. The company was built on a foundation of strong values that empowered people and encouraged freedom of thought, expression, and lifestyle. Another reason for its success is its ability to deliver a unique shopping experience and products that resonate with important elements of the eighteen- to thirty-year-old subculture and consumer tribes.

Viewing Free People through the lens of the eighteen- to thirty-year-old subculture

The brand is aggressively and unapologetically targeted to individuals in the eighteen- to thirty-year-old subculture. These individuals are striking out on their own for the first time and some of the older individuals are getting apartments and even getting married. This is a time of tremendous change where young people leave their homes and make independent decisions for the first time. Importantly, for these young people this period represents a break from their parents. The styles that Free People offers could be described as "stuff your parents wouldn't want you to wear." Much of it is stressed, shredded, too loose or too tight, and deliberately dissolute looking. The important thing, however, is that the young person buying and wearing these styles is demonstrating a rebellion against the past. Free People clothing encompasses the look of the eighteen- to thirty-year-old subculture.

Viewing Free People through the lens of consumer tribes

Consumer tribes are characterized by a combined set of values, beliefs, and behaviors that often revolve around a brand or a consumption behavior. Consumer tribes recognize that individuals can express a strong connection to several brands at once; what matters is that the members of the tribe all share a common cause, vision, or value system. For the consumer tribe that frequents Free People stores, members often have an irreverent and broody vision of the future. Toxic political discourse, climate change, and corruption in the highest levels of business and government have caused these individuals to have a gloomy and pessimistic outlook. These individuals are fiercely independent. At the same time, they have strong connections to their own social networks and are willing to devote significant time and effort to a greater cause. In the early 2020s, Free People promoted a style that combined several different looks at one time (see Photo 11.13). For individuals in this consumer tribe, this style can be seen as a metaphor for the changing and often conflicting times in which we live. Wearing this style not only incorporates these meanings into the self, but also communicates this message to others.

A CULTURAL MISSTEP

In the early 2010s, several fashion houses introduced Navajo-inspired designs into their collections. The designs included muted earth-tone colors and geometric designs, as well as other symbols that are distinctive of Navajo culture, such as howling coyotes and squash blossoms. Accessories included chunky silver and turquoise jewelry. At the time, the style became a nationwide trend, with designers from California to New York offering their own interpretations of the designs to their own collections. The reaction from the Navajo Nation was decidedly negative. They accused the designers of cultural appropriation—stealing the important symbols of the Navajo culture and using them for their own purposes. Several designers responded by removing the offensive items, but Free People and Urban Outfitters kept the items in their stores. When additional items such as underwear and liquor flasks started showing up with Navajo designs in these stores, the Navajo Nation became enraged. The items, such as

● **Photo 11.13** *Free People can be viewed through the lens of the eighteen- to thirty-year-old subculture or the lens of consumer tribes*

"Navajo hipster panties" and the "Navajo print flask," were seen as "derogatory and scandalous," and the Navajo Nation argued that it hurt their fame and reputation. In 2012, the Navajo Nation filed a lawsuit to stop Urban Outfitters and its affiliates from "misappropriating the Navajo trademark and name" and in 2016 the lawsuit was settled for an undisclosed sum (Trebay 2012; Woolf 2016).

WHAT'S NEXT?

To expand its' reach, all three brands—Urban Outfitters, Free People, and Anthropologie—jumped into the rent-and-wear market in 2020. The total value of the clothing rental market was estimated to grow from $1.3 billion in 2019 to $2.5 billion by 2023. The firm's new service is called Nuuly, and for $88 per month, customers get to select six items from more than a thousand styles and brands, including professional clothes for the office and weekend looks. Once a customer receives her package of clothes, she can wear them as many times as she wants and can even purchase any items she likes. At the end of the one-month rental period, customers pack up the box with any unwanted items and send them back. A few days later, the package for the next month arrives. The value of the service, including the items, shipping, and dry-cleaning, is estimated to be $800 per month. The company hoped to have fifty thousand subscribers by the end of 2020, which would result in $50 million in annual revenue. Importantly, because of the continued steady growth of Free People compared to the other two brands, it was expected to take a bigger share of subscribers. From the company's perspective, the rental service solves the problem that many young and engaged consumers have: updated fashion versus sustainable lifestyle (Silverman 2019).

Free People has interwoven important cultural concepts into its story from the start. Except for one important misstep, throughout its history the company has prospered because it has stayed close to its original founding principles that celebrated freedom of thought, expression, and lifestyle. Cultural insights have informed the company's design concepts, connections with consumers, and its newest initiative.

QUESTIONS

1. When Free People was first founded in the 1970s, the founders took many cues from the social and cultural upheaval of the time and incorporated them into the founding principles of the company. In effect, the store is a reflection of the culture of the time. Identify another company that was founded during a different period. In what way is that company a reflection of the culture of its time?

2. Examine the Free People case from the perspective of consumption myths and rituals. First, which myths might be particularly relevant for Free People and its customers? Describe them in detail. Second, describe the process by which meaning moves from consumer goods to individual consumers. Which rituals would be most likely to be utilized by consumers of Free People?

Sources: Rupp (2017); Silverman (2019); Trebay (2012); Turner and Banjo (2017); Wicks (2013); Wilson (2019); Woolf (2016); Wu (2019).

REFERENCES

Aguinis, H., H. Joo, and R. K. Gottfredson. 2012. "Performance Management Universals: Think Globally and Act Locally." *Business Horizons* 55 (4): 385–92.

Baskerville, R. F. 2003. "Hofstede Never Studied Culture." *Accounting, Organizations and Society* 28 (1): 1–14.

Belk, R. W., M. Wallendorf, and J. F. Sherry Jr. 1989. "The Sacred and the Profane in Consumer Behavior: Theodicy on the Odyssey." *Journal of Consumer Research* 16 (1): 1–38.

Bem, S. L. 1974. "The Measurement of Psychological Androgyny." *Journal of Consulting and Clinical Psychology* 42:155–62.

Brooks, C. 2013. "Lost in Translation: 8 International Marketing Fails." Business News Daily. October 7, 2013. https://www.businessnewsdaily.com/5241-international-marketing-fails.html.

Bu, K., D. Kim, and J. Son. 2013. "Is the Culture–Emotion Fit Always Important? Self-Regulatory Emotions in Ethnic Food Consumption." *Journal of Business Research* 66 (8): 983–88.

Carmichael, M. 2011. "Where Does Multicultural Targeting Fit in a Diverse World?" *Advertising Age* 82, no. 22 (May 30): 1.

Caterall, M., and P. Maclaran. 2002. "Gender Perspectives in Consumer Behaviour: An Overview and Future Directions." *The Marketing Review* 2:405–25.

Cleveland, M., and M. Laroche. 2007. "Acculturation to the Global Consumer Culture: Scale Development and Research Paradigm." *Journal of Business Research* 60 (3): 249–60.

Clifford, C. 2016. "4 Ways SoulCycle Built a Cult-like Following—and You Can Too." CNBC. October 7, 2016. https://www.cnbc.com/2016/10/07/4-ways-soulcycle-built-a-cult-following-and-you-can-too.html.

Cova, B. 1997. "Community and Consumption: Towards a Definition of the 'Linking Value' of Product or Services." *European Journal of Marketing* 31 (3/4): 297–316.

Cova, B., and V. Cova. 2002. "Tribal Marketing: The Tribalisation of Society and Its Impact on the Conduct of Marketing." *European Journal of Marketing* 36:1–27.

Cramphorn, M. F. 2011. "Gender Effects in Advertising." *International Journal of Marketing Research* 53 (2): 147–70.

Crawley, B. 2017. Personal interview, April 12, 2017.

Crenshaw, K. W. 1989. "Demarginalizing the Intersection of Race and Sex: A Black Feminist Critique of Antidiscrimination Doctrine, Feminist Theory, and Antiracist Politics." *University of Chicago Legal Forum* 1989:139–67.

de Mooij, M., and G. Hofstede. 2002. "Convergence and Divergence in Consumer Behavior: Implications for International Retailing." *Journal of Retailing* 78 (1): 61–69.

Fang, T. 2010. "Asian Management Research Needs More Self-Confidence: Reflection on Hofstede (2007) and Beyond." *Asia Pacific Journal of Management* 27 (1): 155–70.

Ferdman, R. A. 2016. "The Slow Death of the Most British Thing There Is." *Washington Post*, May 4, 2016. https://www.washingtonpost.com/news/wonk/wp/2016/05/04/why-the-british-are-drinking-coffee-instead-of-tea/?noredirect=on&utm_term=.bf401f58924a.

Fischer, E., and S. J. Arnold. 1994. "Sex, Gender Identity, Gender Role Attitudes, and Consumer Behavior." *Psychology & Marketing* 11 (2): 163–82.

Frey, W. H. 2015. *Diversity Explosion: How New Racial Demographics Are Remaking America*. Washington, DC: Brookings Institution.

Harkness, S. 2016. "Discrimination in Lending Markets." *Social Psychology Quarterly* 79 (1): 81–93.

Ho, M-S. 2018. "The Activist Legacy of Taiwan's Sunflower Movement." *The Carnegie Endowment for International Peace*. August 2, 2018. https://carnegieendowment.org/2018/08/02/activist-legacy-of-taiwan-s-sunflower-movement-pub-76966.

Hoewe, J., and P. K. Hatemi. 2017. "Brand Loyalty Is Influenced by the Activation of Political Orientations." *Media Psychology* 20: 428–49. https://doi.org/10.1080/15213269.2016.1202839.

Hofstede, G. 1984. *Culture's Consequences: International Differences in Work-Related Values*. Abridged ed. London: Sage.

Hofstede, G. H. 2001. *Culture's Consequences: Comparing Values, Behaviors, Institutions and Organizations across Nations*. 2nd ed. London: Sage.

Hofstede, G., G. J. Hofstede, and M. Minkov. 2010. *Cultures and Organizations: Software of the Mind*. New York: McGraw–Hill.

Hollenbeck, C. R., and G. M. Zinkhan. 2010. "Anti-Brand Communities, Negotiation of Brand Meaning, and the Learning Process: The Case of Wal-Mart." *Consumption, Markets & Culture* 13 (3): 325–45.

Holt, D., and D. Cameron 2012. *Cultural Strategy*. Oxford: Oxford University Press.

Janif, Z. J., R. C. Brooks, and B. J. Dixson. 2014. "Negative Frequency-Dependent Preferences and Variation in Male Facial Hair." *Biology Letters* 10 (4). https://doi.org/10.1098/rsbl.2013.0958.

Khanna, N. 2011. "Ethnicity and Race as 'Symbolic': The Use of Ethnic and Racial Symbols in Asserting a Biracial Identity." *Journal of Ethnic and Racial Studies* 34 (6): 1049–67.

Krogstad, J. M. 2017. "US Hispanic Population Growth Has Leveled Off." Pew Research Center. August 3, 2017. http://www.pewresearch.org/fact-tank/2017/08/03/u-s-hispanic-population-growth-has-leveled-off/.

Maheshwari, S. 2017. "Four Cultures, Four Car Ads." *The New York Times*, October 13, 2017. Vol. 167, no. 57749, B1–B5.

McCracken, G. 1986. "Culture and Consumption: A Theoretical Account of the Structure and Movement of the Cultural Meaning of Consumer Goods." *Journal of Consumer Research* 13 (1): 71–84.

McSweeney, B. 2002. "Hofstede's Model of National Cultural Differences and Their Consequences: A Triumph of Faith, a Failure of Analysis." *Human Relations* 55 (1): 89–118.

Mintel. 2016a. "Marketing to Generation X—US." Mintel Group. June 2016.

Mintel. 2016b. "Marketing to Baby Boomers—US." Mintel Group. July 2016.

Mintel. 2017. Marketing to Millennials—US." Mintel Group. June 2017.

Mintel. 2018a. "Marketing to Kids and Tweens—US." Mintel Group. March 2018.

Mintel. 2018b. "Marketing to the iGeneration—US." Mintel Group. May 2018.

Mintel. 2018c. "Social Media Trends—US." Mintel Group. April 2018.

Muniz, A. M., Jr., and T. C. O'Guinn. 2001. "Brand Community." *Journal of Consumer Research* 27 (4): 412–32.

Murphy, C. 1997. "Nike Pulls Shoes that Irked Muslims." *The Washington Post.* June 25. Accessed September 19, 2020. https://www.washingtonpost .com/archive/business/1997/06/25/ nike-pulls-shoes-that-irked-muslims/ b02211fb-c120-4780-9ce4-4c01225c8e92/

Murray, M. R. 2016. "Under Armour's Viral Campaign for the Female Market Proved a Winning Strategy." *Washington Post*, July 16, 2016. https:// www.washingtonpost.com/business/ under-armours-viral-campaign-for-the-female-market-proved-a-winning-strategy/2016/07/15/73c50602-42f d-11e6-88d0-6adee48be8bc_story. html?utm_term=.1500b3b3c728.

Nielsen. 2016. "Young, Connected, and Black: African-American Millennials Are Driving Social Change and Leading Digital Advancement." 2016 Report by The Nielsen Company, LLC., a part of the Diverse Intelligence Series. R. K. *Roussell* and K. Mancini, managing editors.

Oldstone-Moore, C. 2015. *Of Beards and Men: The Revealing History of Facial Hair.* Chicago: University of Chicago Press.

Olenski, S. 2016. "Exclusive: Planet Fitness to Launch New Global Campaign on New Year's Eve." *Forbes*, December 30, 2016. https://www.forbes .com/sites/steveolenski/2016/12/30/ exclusive-planet-fitness-to-launch-new-global-campaign-on-new-years-eve/2/#24242ad9586f.

O'Reilly, L. 2017. "Coke's 'America the Beautiful' Pre-game Super Bowl Ad was Just as Divisive the Last Time it Aired." *Business Insider*, February 5, 2017. https://www.businessinsider.com/coke-pre-game-america-the-beautiful-super-bowl-ad-has-aired-before-2017-2.

"Our Values." 2019. SoulCycle. August 9, 2019. https://www.soul-cycle.com/ community/inside/ourvalues/3153/.

Palan, K. M. 2001. "Gender Identity in Consumer Behavior Research: A Literature Review and Research Agenda." *Academy of Marketing Science Review* 2001 (10): 1–24.

Penaloza, L. 1994. "Atravesando Fronteras/Border Crossings: A Critical Ethnographic Exploration of the Consumer Acculturation of Mexican Immigrants." *Journal of Consumer Research* 21 (1): 32–54.

Rook, D. W. 1985. "The Ritual Dimension of Consumer Behavior." *Journal of Consumer Research* 12 (3): 251–64.

Rupp, L. 2017. "Urban Outfitters Inc. Reports a Better Quarter Than Expected." *The Philadelphia Inquirer*, August 16, 2017, WEB, P-com, 00.

Saad, G., M. Cleveland, and L. Ho. 2015. "Individualism–Collectivism and the Quantity versus Quality Dimensions of Individual and Group Creative Performance." *Journal of Business Research* 68:578–86.

Schouten, J., and J. H. McAlexander 1995. "Subcultures of Consumption: An Ethnography of the New Bikers." *Journal of Consumer Research* 22 (3): 43–61.

Schultz, E. J. 2014. "Ad Age's 2014 Market of the Year: Under Armour." *AdAge*, December 8, 2014. http://adage.com/article/news/ marketer-year-armour/296088/.

Sidle, S. D. 2009. "Building a Committed Global Workforce: Does What Employees Want Depend on Culture?" *Academy of Management Perspectives* 23 (1): 79–80.

Silverman, E. 2019. "Urban Outfitters Starts a Rent-a-Wear Service: For $88 Subscription, a Rotating Line of Clothing." *The Philadelphia Inquirer*, July 31, 2019, A7.

Spence, J. T. 1993. "Gender-Related Traits and Gender Ideology: Evidence for a Multifactorial Theory." *Journal of Personality and Social Psychology* 64 (4): 624–35.

Stein, L. 2016. "Planet Fitness Expands Judgement Free Mantra beyond Gym." *AdAge*, December 29, 2016. http:// adage.com/article/cmo-strategy/planet-fitness-campaign-expands-judgement-free-mantra/307308/.

Sweetman, K. 2012. "In Asia, Power Get in the Way." *Harvard Business Review*, April 10, 2012. https://hbr.org/2012/04/ in-asia-power-gets-in-the-way.

Tan, J. 2018. "Coca-Cola Shows Support for Muslim Consumers with Uplifting Ramadan Ad." Marketing. August 6, 2018. https://www.marketing-interactive. com/coca-cola-shows-support-for-muslim-consumers-with-uplifting-ramadan-ad/.

Tooher, P. 1996. "The Future's Not So Bright as Orange Gets the Red Light in Ulster." *Independent*, July 13, 1996. http://www.independent.co.uk/news/ the-futures-not-so-bright-as-orange-gets-the-red-light-in-ulster-1328424. html.

Trebay, G. 2012. "An Uneasy Cultural Exchange." *New York Times*, Late edition (East Coast), March 15, 2012, E1.

Triandis, H. C. 1995. *Individualism and Collectivism.* Boulder, CO: Westview Press.

Turner, N., and S. Banjo. 2017. "Urban Outfitters Tumbles as CEO Warns Retail Bubble Has Burst." *The Philadelphia Inquirer*, March 9, 2017, A11.

US Census Bureau. 2019. QuickFacts: People: Race and Hispanic Origin. Accessed August 19, 2019. https://www .census.gov/quickfacts/fact/table/US/ PST045218.

Venkatesh, A., and L. A. Meamber. 2006. "Arts and Aesthetics: Marketing and Cultural Production." *Marketing Theory* 6 (1): 11–39. https://doi.org/ 10.1177/1470593106061261.

"What Is No-Shave November?" **2019.** No-Shave November. Accessed August 18, 2019. https://www.no-shave.org.

Wicks, J. 2013. *Good Morning Beautiful Business: The Unexpected Journey of an Activist Entrepreneur and Local Economy Pioneer.* White River Junction, VT: Chelsea Green.

Williams, J. D., W. Lee, and G. R. Henderson. 2008. "Diversity Issues in Consumer Psychology." In *Handbook of Consumer Psychology*, edited by Curtis P. Haugtvedt, Paul M. Herr, and Frank R. Kardes, 877–912. London: Taylor & Francis Group/Erlbaum.

Wilson, M. 2019. "Urban Outfitters in Mixed Q2; Free People Continues to Shine." Chain Store Age. August 20, 2019. https://chainstoreage.com/ finance-0/urban-outfitters-in-mixed-q2-free-people-continues-to-shines.

Woodside, A. G., S. Sood, and K. E. Miller. 2008. "When Consumers and Brands Talk: Storytelling Theory and Research in Psychology and Marketing." *Psychology & Marketing* 25 (2): 97–145.

Woolf, N. 2016. "Urban Outfitters Settles with Navajo Nation after Illegally Using Tribe's Name." *The Guardian*, November 18, 2016. https://www.the-guardian.com/us-news/2016/nov/18/ urban-outfitters-navajo-nation-settle-ment.

Wu, J. 2019. "Urban Outfitters CEO Calls Second-Quarter Earnings Not One of Its 'Finest' as Profit Slides 35%." CNBC. August 20, 2019. https://www .cnbc.com/2019/08/20/urban-outfit-ters-reports-q2-2019-earnings.html.

12 Ethics and Social Responsibility

◉ Introduction

Imagine that you just enjoyed a wonderful meal at a restaurant, paid the bill, and discovered that you got an extra twenty dollars back in change. Would you return the money? What if you knew the waiter would have to pay the money back to the restaurant himself? What if the waiter was your friend? The focus of this chapter is ethics and social responsibility, both from the perspective of the consumer and from that of the marketer. In this chapter, we introduce two frameworks for making an ethical decision, utilitarianism and the common good. Both frameworks can help an individual and a marketing team when they are facing an ethical dilemma by providing guidelines by which a decision can be judged. Marketing occupies a unique position in an organization because it is the key interface between the organization and the rest of the world. Because of this, marketing has a unique obligation to pay particular attention to the ethical issues consumers face as well as the ethical implications of the organization's own actions.

The utilitarianism and common good frameworks provide a foundation on which we will next introduce the consumer connection—a careful examination of that special consumer–organization connection in which ethical issues sometimes arise. We examine several trends that can be categorized as trends that *raise* ethical questions or dilemmas and trends that are *a reaction to* ethical questions or dilemmas. In examining these two sets of trends, it is fascinating to see how consumers are often simultaneously pulled in one direction by their own needs and desires and in another direction by the tactics that are employed by marketers. The chapter concludes with a brief examination of corporate social responsibility (CSR), which can be used to help businesses operate ethically. Importantly, our discussion examines the expectations consumers have regarding the ethical behavior of organizations. It is no surprise that consumers often alter their own behavior based on their perceptions about the ethical behavior of organizations by buying different brands, telling other consumers, and posting about it on social media. The knowledge of consumer behavior that we have developed thus far provides us with a richer understanding of ethics and social responsibility, which we will use as we proceed through the chapter.

LEARNING OBJECTIVES

After reading this chapter you will be able to:

1. Describe *utilitarianism* and the *common good*, key differences between them, and ways in which the common good has benefited marketing.

2. Explain why we focus our discussion on *ethics* and not on morals.

3. Describe why the field of marketing has a *unique obligation* to understand ethics.

4. Discuss the concept of *consumer misbehavior*, and describe several acquisition-related misbehaviors and consumption-related misbehaviors.

5. Identify several trends that *raise ethical concerns* about our modern consumer lifestyle and several trends that are a *reaction to ethical concerns and dilemmas*.

6. Describe the purpose of *corporate social responsibility (CSR)* and the concept of *shared value*.

◉ Ethical Frameworks

How do marketing decision-makers and consumers decide what is right or wrong? How can they judge whether a company is engaging in ethical behavior? Further, how can we assess the ethics of someone else who is separated from us by culture, geography, or maybe even time? **Ethics** describe a set of standards by which we can judge behaviors and ourselves. It can be an important decision-making tool. Ethics describe basic principles for how individuals should treat one another with fairness, honesty, and integrity. Ethics and morality are not the same thing. On the one hand, **morality** can be thought of as a state of virtue and is often connected to strongly held religious beliefs. Ethics, on the other hand, can be viewed as a set of standards and reasons for acting in a moral way. It is important to realize that ethics don't necessarily give us the right answer to a problem. Instead, ethics provide a framework by which we can clarify issues and perhaps even come up with several good answers. At the heart of ethics is a concern for others. Two key ethical frameworks that are particularly useful for understanding marketing and the behavior of consumers are utilitarianism and the common good.

Utilitarianism

One framework for understanding ethics is **utilitarianism**, which holds that the choice leading to the greatest good for the greatest number of people is the most ethical one. Consider the example of a small lakefront community that wants to create a recreation area for local residents where people can hike, picnic, and enjoy a variety of water activities. The problem is that a big part of the lakefront is currently owned by one resident who has no intention of selling the property to the local community for a park. Using utilitarianism, the community government should take the property away from the single resident so that all the other residents could enjoy the new lakefront park. Sure, one resident would be very unhappy, but the result would be the greatest good for the greatest number of people. Utilitarianism is the most reason-based approach for determining right from wrong and is used to help make many business decisions ("Utilitarianism" 2017). Marketers frequently make utilitarian decisions based on predictions about higher sales, greater market share, or higher product adoption rates.

Utilitarianism has two distinct disadvantages. First, because it is difficult to predict the future, it is difficult to say with certainty whether a decision will be good or bad. For example, perhaps projections about sales figures or product adoption rates are incorrect. Second, utilitarianism has a difficult time accounting for human rights and social justice. Our lakefront homeowner's rights will certainly be trampled in the scenario just mentioned. Consider another scenario that is common in the pharmaceutical business. What happens when a pharmaceutical company finds that one ingredient for a new lifesaving drug comes from a remote area of the Amazon rainforest? Harvesting the ingredient will mean that an indigenous tribe will be displaced and the

Ethics describe a set of standards by which we can judge behaviors and ourselves.

Morality can be thought of as a state of virtue and is often connected to strongly held religious beliefs.

Utilitarianism is an ethical framework that holds that the choice leading to the greatest good for the greatest number of people is the most ethical one.

environment will be harmed. However, the drug will likely save and improve the lives of thousands of people around the world. Utilitarianism would say that, since the risk is only a small village full of natives compared with thousands of lives, the most ethical choice would be to harvest the new ingredient for the drug. However, what about the rights of the indigenous people and their land? Many people would argue that the move from the big pharmaceutical company is neither an ethical nor a moral decision. Couldn't the ingredient be found elsewhere? How about finding a synthetic version of the ingredient? Issues like social justice, human rights, and the environment have little room under utilitarianism, so it does have limitations as a decision-making tool.

The common good

The philosophical concept of the common good starts with the observation that all people exist in a society with relationships to one another. The idea is that the members of this group have certain common interests and common resources. Working together to achieve these common interests and to protect these common resources is the most efficient way to ensure that everyone has equal representation, access to resources, and benefits. In a modern democracy, members share police and fire protection, public roads and transportation, a national defense, public schools, and a judiciary system that makes sure there is fair treatment of all individuals. These democracies also provide benefits to their citizens, such as parks, libraries, and museums, as well as clean air and clean water. Few people would want to advocate for each individual member in a society to take care of all these things on their own; few individuals would want to build and maintain a section of road right outside their home, for example. Instead, it is simply more efficient if these resources are shared and taken care of collectively. The common good gives us a framework for understanding how individuals can make decisions and behave. Rather than waging a narrow debate about the economic cost of a new sports stadium, for example, the discussion could be expanded to consider whether the new stadium will serve the common good for the community. This expanded debate allows for a variety of viewpoints and, importantly, allows for noneconomic benefits to be considered.

Rather than everyone looking out for their own individual, short-term needs, the **common good** allows for a common set of beliefs and general agreement about what is right and wrong. Here, the most ethical choice is the one that provides the most benefits to the group. This includes economic and noneconomic benefits. For the common good to work, there must be a respect for and an adherence to truth, honesty, and integrity. Without a common set of ethical standards, there would be no stable civilization, because individuals would look out for their own interests and there would be no civility. Consider the analogy of a traffic intersection. Without a set of standards for behavior, there would be complete bedlam. People would look out for their own self-interests, at the expense of others. Indeed, there is a great opportunity for many people to be hurt when other people look out just for themselves. These

Common good is an ethical framework that allows for a common set of beliefs and general agreement about what is right and wrong. Here, the most ethical choice is the one that provides the most benefits to the group.

people tend to be the socially and economically disadvantaged members of a society. Further, a system where everyone looks out for their own self-interests would set up an environment in which there would be unequal enforcement of rules, corruption, and bribery (Reich 2018).

Consider another analogy: a soccer game. The players and fans all have a common understanding of the rules and how the game is played. When everyone follows the rules, the most talented team usually wins. The teams are happy (especially the winning team) and the fans are happy. What would happen if, instead of cooperating, the players followed their own rules or played to maximize their own self-benefits? The game would be chaos and no one would be satisfied with the outcome. The same is true with a group of people living in a society—there needs to be some common set of standards and rules that everyone follows. It is important to understand that the common good should be viewed not as a static goal, but as more of a moving target, whose meanings change over time and place. Also, the common good is about inclusion. It is not about giving up freedoms and liberties; it is about having an obligation to one another and working together to achieve common goals. Finally, it is not about charity and handouts; it is about giving everyone in the society an equal chance to succeed (Reich 2018).

The tragedy of the commons

Following the general principle of the common good works quite well when there are many resources and a small number of people who would like to use those resources. Think of a big park with plenty of acreage and very few visitors. Going to the park is a pleasant experience because visitors will see grand vistas and enjoy the solitude and peace of the park. However, when the park is small and there are many visitors, roads get clogged, trash builds up, and a visit to the park is more likely to leave the visitor with a headache than a calm, peaceful feeling. The real irony here is that when individuals behave in their own *individual* self-interest, the value of the resource for *everyone* is diminished. Going back to our example of the park, imagine what would happen if visitors had no consideration for the others who were also visiting the park. Perhaps they left their trash everywhere and parked their cars in the grass instead of in the parking lots. Perhaps they even did some particularly egregious things, like cutting down trees or dumping waste in rivers and streams. Maybe these people had fun (they maximized their own self-interest), but these actions made it worse for others visiting the park. The value of the experience and the enjoyment for everyone else would be greatly diminished. The **tragedy of the commons** predicts that when individuals attempt to maximize their own self-interest in using a common resource like the park, the value of that resource is reduced for everyone (cf. Basurto and Ostrom 2009; Ostrom 1999).

Luckily, the common good can still prevail and we can return to a situation where everyone can enjoy the park. First, an outside formal entity such as the government can establish a set of rules and regulations for use of the

Tragedy of the commons is a problem that exists with the common good framework of ethical decision-making. It predicts that when individuals attempt to maximize their self-interest in using a common resource like a park, the value of that resource is reduced for everyone.

public resource. These rules and regulations would need to be very clear and should spell out penalties for violations. Second, if formal regulations like this are not feasible or possible, groups could self-organize to regulate their own behavior. Scouting groups, hiking groups, school groups, etc., could cooperate and establish rules for the use and maintenance of the park. The groups would need to create a detailed set of rules as well as penalties for violations. With these agreements in place, everyone who would like to utilize the resource can do so and, importantly, the value of the resource is preserved for everyone and the common good is maintained (Basurto and Ostrom 2009; Ostrom 1999).

● **Photo 12.1** *Difficult choices*

Ethical frameworks like the common good and utilitarianism help individuals set out important parameters that will hopefully lead to better decisions (see Photo 12.1). Insights from Academia 12.1 describes an ethical dilemma in the travel industry.

INSIGHTS FROM ACADEMIA 12.1

Why do some consumers find an experience exciting and fun, while others find it ethically wrong?

Over one million people each year take part in slum tourism, making a visit to some of the poorest and most desperate corners of the world (Shepard 2016). Take the example of tourism in India's slums or Brazil's favelas. Proponents say that it brings in tourism dollars and raises awareness. Critics argue that it is humiliating and degrading to the people who live there. As one individual who grew up in a Kenyan slum said, "They get photos, we lose a piece of our dignity." What determines a consumer's reactions to this and other "morally ambiguous" consumption experiences? The answer seems to lie in how likely consumers are to identify with the local population. If consumers feel close to and can identify with the locals, they are much less likely to be interested in such a trip; if they do not feel a connection to the locals, they are much more likely to be interested in the trip. Having a better understanding of when consumers are more or less likely to face ethical dilemmas will help researchers better predict how they might react in a variety of situations.

Von Schuckmann, J., L. S. G. Barros, R. S. Dias, and E. B. Andrade. 2018. "From Slum Tourism to Smiley Selfies: The Role of Social Identity Strength in the Consumption of Morally Ambiguous Experiences." Journal of Consumer Psychology *28 (2): 192–210.*

Marketing and the common good

The common good has been used as a way to understand and evaluate the complex interactions that occur between marketing and diverse groups of consumers, all with differing needs and motivations (Dann and Dann 2016; Fremeaux and Grant 2017; Murphy and Sherry 2014). Marketing itself has already demonstrated that it has helped to improve the common good. How has this happened? To start, the formal definition of marketing from the American Marketing Association says that marketing is about creating value for a variety of stakeholders: "Marketing is the activity, set of institutions, and processes for creating, communicating, delivering, and exchanging offerings that have value for customers, clients, partners, and society at large" ("Definitions of Marketing" 2019). The definition acknowledges that there is an interconnected nature to these stakeholders and that they work together (through marketing) for their mutual benefit.

Over its long history, the process and function of marketing have benefited from using the common good framework for ethical decision-making in at least three specific ways. First, it has established complex, global systems to bring products from the far reaches of the planet to consumers located in other parts of the planet. These complex distribution, inventory, sorting, warehousing, and processing systems not only move ingredients and product components efficiently and effectively around the world, but also employ people around the world and raise their standards of living. Second, marketing has increased the quality of life for billions of people, including marketers and consumers. From a marketer's perspective, marketing is a fascinating, dynamic field that provides endless opportunities for analysis, creativity, and strategy. Many individuals who work in marketing find that the work is challenging, but also personally satisfying. From a consumer's perspective, marketing provides access to products that make their lives more efficient, safer, and more enjoyable. Simply look at the items in a typical middle-class kitchen to see how preparing a meal is safer and easier today than it was in your grandparents' day (Wilkie and Moore 1999). Among other things, packaging, labeling, and refrigeration systems make foods safer; equipment like microwaves and coffee makers make preparation easier. Third, the field of marketing research has expanded to include areas that specifically investigate the impact of marketing on society. Some topics that are actively being investigated and considered are marketing ethics, social marketing, and public policy (see Wilkie and Moore 2012; Davis, Ozanne, and Hill 2016). The findings of these research studies provide important data, information, and insights for individuals such as marketers and policy makers to improve the lives of others (Stewart 2015).

In the field of marketing, it is critically important to consider a variety of perspectives when making a decision. The two ethical frameworks, utilitarianism and the common good, provide decision-makers with standards by which they can, hopefully, come to more ethical decisions. The common good framework has been particularly useful in marketing and consumer research, especially in recent years as more marketers and researchers acknowledge that their decisions have broader implications that go beyond the economic

INSIGHTS FROM THE FIELD 12.1

Ubuntu

You cannot be human on your own. We speak, walk, and think by imitating other human beings. We are human only through relations. We are made for complementarity.

—*Archbishop Desmond Tutu, South African civil rights leader*

The philosophical concept of Ubuntu ("oo-boon-too") can trace its origins to South Africa. It refers to an interconnected humanness in all of us; the well-being of the entire group is dependent on the well-being of every other member in the community. If one person is suffering, the entire group suffers. The philosophy of Ubuntu has gathered a following of dedicated individuals who see it as a solution to the often utilitarian-focused Western economic models.

South Africa has endured decades of civil strife, political corruption, and discrimination. Because of this, many people living there have experienced intense physical and psychological trauma. The philosophy of Ubuntu has provided a way for citizens of South Africa to start the long road to recovery and resilience. Ubuntu offers a more person-centered approach to promoting resilience in even the most desperate communities. For example, small businesses that utilize local materials and local labor are becoming more and more popular, as are local financing organizations that offer small business loans to start-ups and entrepreneurs. Rather than using the services and products of multinational firms, there is a preference for small, local firms (Sarra and Berman 2017). Today, the philosophy of Ubuntu has inspired followers from around the world, who use it as a guide by which they live their lives. Ubuntu even has numerous interest groups around the world and there

is a political party in South Africa that ascribes to the philosophy of Ubuntu.

Connecting Ubuntu to marketing, we can see that sustainable consumption, the slow food movement, and culturally rich travel experiences would all be consistent with the philosophy of Ubuntu. Let's take a closer look at the slow food movement in the United States. Tired of consuming processed food from global food companies, a key part of this grass-roots movement is a dedication to eating food that is locally sourced and minimally processed. Adherents to the movement not only believe that food is better tasting and healthier when it comes from local farms, but also know that the profits from their purchases go straight to the local community. There are also tremendous environmental benefits when food is delivered locally, rather than being shipped from hundreds of miles away. In the United States alone, there are more than 150 chapters and six thousand members of the slow food movement (About Slow Food USA 2018). Ubuntu's recognition of the importance of *the other* is gaining traction with a lot of consumers as they become discouraged with the current economic system and look for ways to form deeper connections within their communities.

Questions

1. Select another trend that is discussed in the section "The Consumer Connection" in this chapter. Describe the extent to which the trend might be consistent with the philosophy of Ubuntu.
2. In Chapter 6, we discussed the concept of the self. In what ways is Ubuntu consistent with and/or not consistent with the concept of the self?

Sources: Sarra and Berman (2017); About Slow Food USA(2018).

considerations of a decision. Insights from the Field 12.1 discusses the philosophical concept of Ubuntu, which is a guiding life philosophy in some parts of the world and is starting to gain some traction in the United States, and Insights from Academia 12.2 discusses consumer activism against companies behaving badly.

INSIGHTS FROM ACADEMIA 12.2

Brands that lie, cheat, and steal . . . and the consumers who punish them for it

There are some very unethical marketers out there. Some use questionable tactics to persuade disadvantaged groups to use their products, some raise the price of life-saving pharmaceuticals, and some cover up harmful product ingredients or side effects. When consumers view a company's or a brand's actions to be harmful, they are more likely to act unethically themselves by lying, cheating, or stealing from the company. Even when consumers themselves are not direct victims of the harm, some feel compelled to "even the score" by striking back at the offending company. Further, when consumers do enact these kinds of retribution behaviors against the company, they do not experience feelings of guilt.

Rotman, J. D., M. Khamitov, and S. Connors. 2017. "Lie, Cheat, and Steal: How Harmful Brands Motivate Consumers to Act Unethically." Journal of Consumer Psychology 28 (2): 353–61.

👁 The Consumer Connection

Much of contemporary consumer culture is motivated by abundance and excess. Advertising messages frequently focus on self-development and enhancement. In support of this quest for continuous improvement, marketers make these kinds of products and brands easily available. Simply look at the fashion industry, the home improvement industry, or the beauty and health-care industries to see how marketers provide products to consumers to satisfy their desires to have better clothes, better homes, and better bodies. The following section presents a variety of consumer trends that either *raise* ethical questions or dilemmas or are *a reaction to* ethical questions or dilemmas.

Trends that raise ethical questions or dilemmas

One of our underlying principles in this book has been that marketers generate data and information to create insights that help predict how consumers will behave. We approach this from the assumption that consumers behave according to clearly established social norms. However, some consumers behave in ways that are definitely not what we would expect—some consumers behave in deviant and dysfunctional ways (Daunt and Harris 2012). Some dysfunctional behaviors occur within the marketplace context and are linked to the acquisition of products and services. Examples include materialism, compulsive buying, in-store abuse of staff, or theft. Other dysfunctional behaviors can be linked to product misuse, such as hoarding, gambling, or the addictive consumption of food, drugs, or alcohol. **Consumer misbehavior** describes behaviors that violate generally accepted consumption rules and "disrupt the consumption order." These types of behaviors represent the dark side

Consumer misbehavior is a behavioral act by a consumer that violates generally accepted consumption rules and disrupts the consumption order.

of consumer behavior. As we discussed in Chapter 11, social norms tend to be formed and reinforced through a culture's customs, rules, laws, and values. The main distinguishing feature of consumer misbehavior is that it falls outside the culturally accepted norms of exchange and consumption (Fullerton and Punj 2004; L. C. Harris and Reynolds 2003; Moschis and Cox 1989). Importantly, the deviant nature of consumer misbehavior also assumes that consumers already know the "accepted" norms of the encounter. A consumer in a new culture who makes a mistake (such as refusing the offer of a cup of tea in a rug shop in Pakistan) can certainly not be considered to be engaging in misbehavior; this person is simply a hapless tourist.

Unfortunately, misbehaviors are a pervasive part of everyday customer behavior (Fullerton and Punj 2004). These misbehaviors are often deliberate, but can also occur when a customer has little control over the situation, lacks knowledge, or lacks experience about appropriate roles and responsibilities. Social media can sometimes provide a check on consumer misbehavior. One example happened in 2018 when a drunk and disorderly tourist aggressively taunted a bison at Yellowstone National Park. This is not only profoundly unsafe, but also illegal. After the video was captured and shared on social media, the man was identified, arrested, and charged with harassing wildlife (McCarthy and Jacobo 2018). Marketers can reduce the incidence of consumer misbehavior by providing clear guidance and information about how to behave. The day after Thanksgiving in the United States is called Black Friday and it is one of the biggest shopping days of the year. Black Friday is becoming a global phenomenon, and every year, consumers are injured and some even die as they attempt to get some of the great bargains advertised by retailers (see Photo 12.2 for a typical scene of Black Friday mayhem). Marketing

● **Photo 12.2** *Black Friday in São Paolo, Brazil*

managers and other top-level decision-makers must not only carefully assess their own roles in fueling and perpetuating consumer misbehavior, but also find ways to direct consumers toward proper behaviors.

An important aspect of the dark side of consumer behavior involves the disruption for other consumers, for the environment, and for society at large. Therefore, it is important when considering the darker aspects of consumption to question the broader ramifications of marketing practices, as well as the broader negative consequences associated with excess in contemporary consumer culture. As populations around the world increase and climate change starts to have even more severe effects, individuals are likely to face resource shortages and other constraints that will likely lead to a reassessment of both individual and social attitudes about consumption. Several consumer trends raise ethical issues and have been debated by marketers, public policy experts, and consumer advocates. These trends can be categorized as falling into two primary categories: trends that concern the acquisition of products and those that concern the consumption of products. First, we will spend some time discussing trends that concern the *acquisition of products*. In doing so, we will discuss materialism, compulsive buying, and theft.

Materialism

Materialism is a value that places a strong emphasis on material goods as a way in which consumers can reach important life goals (Richins and Chaplin 2015). Individuals who are materialistic will judge their own self-worth and that of others according to the material objects they own, will believe that acquiring new products will result in happiness, and will have product acquisition as a central part of their lives (Richins and Dawson 1992). Ask any foreigner about his or her perceptions of Americans and you will likely hear some not-so-flattering things about how Americans are materialistic and wasteful and live in an overly consumer-oriented society. As difficult as it is to hear, some of these criticisms may be warranted. Consider the following (Muniz 2014):

Materialism is a value that places a strong emphasis on material goods as a way in which consumers can reach important life goals.

- Americans waste $443 billion in energy every year by not turning out lights, using appliances inefficiently, or using heating and cooling systems inefficiently.
- Americans who buy their coffee every day spend $1,092 on average per year.
- Americans waste $2 billion per year in unused gift cards.
- Each American throws away approximately $529 per year in wasted food.
- The average American household carries more than $15,000 in credit card debt.
- On average, Americans die with $62,000 in debt.

Compared to previous generations, Americans are much more affluent, eat out at restaurants much more frequently, have bigger houses filled with more stuff, and own more cars. You would think that Americans would be also be happier;

however, they are not. Americans are not any more emotionally or psychologically well-off in the early twenty-first century than in previous generations. Importantly, compared to people who are not materialistic, individuals who are more materialistic are actually *worse* off. Indeed, numerous research studies indicate that the least materialistic people have the highest levels of life satisfaction (cf. DeAngelis 2004). Why does this happen? There are several reasons. First, individuals who actively pursue material goods spend less time on activities that can lead to greater happiness, such as spending time with family and friends or pursing self-actualizing activities like art or music. Second, individuals who focus on material possessions are more oriented toward externalized rewards, rather than internalized rewards. This difference in focus means that they get satisfaction from external objects, rather than from their own state of mind or emotional well-being. Third, materialistic individuals sometimes place too much weight on how much they believe the acquisition of material goods will improve their lives, thus setting themselves up for inevitable disappointment (DeAngelis 2004) (see Insights from Academia 12.3).

INSIGHTS FROM ACADEMIA 12.3

Mom, if you love me, you'll buy this for me!

Sometimes, parents provide material rewards to their children, such as a special toy or sporting equipment for good grades, passing their driver's license test, or doing chores around the house. Other times, the rewards are social or emotional, such as spending extra time together or engaging in an activity together. You can't blame the parents. They want to reinforce good behaviors and express their love for their children. Parents should, however, be careful when deciding which kind of rewards to give. In a study that utilized consumer panel data and surveys, researchers investigated the kinds of rewards that parents gave their children and how materialistic those children were when they grew up. Compared to parents who provided social or emotional rewards, parents who provided material rewards had children who were much more likely to be materialistic when they grew up (see Photo 12.3).

Richins, M. L., and L. N. Chaplin. 2015. "Material Parenting: How the Use of Goods in Parenting Fosters Materialism in the Next Generation." Journal of Consumer Research 41 (6): 1333–57.

● **Photo 12.3** *A little girl begs her mom for a toy*

● **Photo 12.4** *Shopping can turn into compulsive buying*

Compulsive buying

Another form of acquisition-related misbehavior is **compulsive buying**, which occurs when buyers have a strong, often uncontrolled preoccupation with shopping and purchasing. The result is that the consumer experiences significant negative consequences, such as financial difficulties, anxiety, depression, and broken relationships. Compulsive buyers are driven by the experience of shopping and purchasing, as well as the rush of positive emotions that come with it. Experts suggest that compulsive buying affects between 3 and 6 percent of the US population (Koran et al. 2006; Rose and Segrist 2012). Many causes have been suggested, ranging from psychological reasons (such as low self-esteem, a negative mood, a coping mechanism, or fantasy fulfilment) to socially oriented causes (including dissatisfaction with self-identity, materialism, or a need to exercise power and control) (O'Guinn and Faber 1989; Elliott, Eccles, and Gournay 1996; Dittmar 2005). Contemporary consumer culture often makes the situation even worse for compulsive buyers; these consumers with low self-esteem or self-worth are particularly vulnerable. Responsible marketers work to eliminate any negative consequences that their messages might encourage (see Photo 12.4).

Compulsive buying is an unusual obsession with shopping such that it significantly affects the life of the person afflicted.

Theft

Another problem for marketers and society is consumer theft, another acquisition-related misbehavior. When discussing theft, it is important to appreciate the wide spectrum of potentially dishonest consumer behaviors. For example, very few people give a second thought to taking a pen from the bank, eating a few grapes at the grocery store, or taking more than one after-dinner mint at a restaurant (one for now, one for later). Few consumers believe these behaviors are dishonest, since the items are so insignificant. At the other end of the dishonesty spectrum are shoplifters who plan and organize acts of theft. In this section, the focus is on these more significant behaviors where thieves (acting on their own or in a gang) leave the store with products that have not been purchased. Although shoplifting is a criminal behavior and hence primarily within the domain of criminologists and law enforcement officials, it also falls into the realm of consumer behavior (Fullerton and Punj 1997).

Consumer theft refers to stealing as a way to acquire consumer objects.

    Consumer theft refers to stealing as a way of acquiring consumer objects; it impacts all consumers. Because this problem represents a significant cost for companies, businesses must have strategies for handling consumer theft (Photo 12.5). With annual losses topping $13 billion in the United States, consumer theft is costly for businesses as well as consumers. Indeed, because businesses recover their lost revenue by charging other consumers higher prices, *all* consumers pay the price for shoplifting. Estimates suggest that one of every eleven Americans has shoplifted something. Research shows that shoplifting is more common among those who have a higher education and income, suggesting that financial considerations are not motivating these people. The most frequently stolen items in the US? Designer handbags, high-end vacuums, and high-end mixers (Rainey and Hobbs 2013).

The most popular items to steal are also generally in high demand by consumers, are small in size, and are easy to sell or pass on to someone else. The average amount per theft is $800 (Reilly 2017) and, surprisingly, cheese is the most popular item across the world to steal (Barkham 2012). Other factors also influence whether an item is shoplifted. First, some unique characteristics of the product can determine the likelihood of it being stolen. The CRAVED model tells us that the most popular items for consumer theft are those that are concealable, removable, available, valued, enjoyed, and disposable (Barkham 2012). Other product-related characteristics include those that may be embarrassing (e.g., a pregnancy test) or illegal (e.g., cigarettes or alcohol for people who are underage). Second, environmental factors can impact whether an item is stolen. These factors can include the way that products are displayed to make them look enticing, as well as the ease with which thieves can steal products or switch tags. Environmental factors are under the direct control of marketers, so they must pay particular attention to these issues. A third factor that influences whether a product is shoplifted revolves around the actual consumer. Consumers who harbor negative attitudes toward the store or big corporations may believe that the company deserves it and can absorb the cost. In a related vein, some shoplifters may simply not believe that theft is morally wrong (see Figure 12.1).

Retailers need to walk a fine line between making their products enticing and available, but also discouraging consumer theft. Many retailers make access to expensive products difficult, often by locking them away (e.g., perfume and jewelry), by keeping them behind a counter, or by using security tags. Marketers must also enact strong measures to protect the online security of the organization and its customers. Customer data, financial and sales data, and product-related data must be protected against hackers and others looking to steal this valuable information. While these

● **Photo 12.5** *Consumer theft is a big problem for retailers*

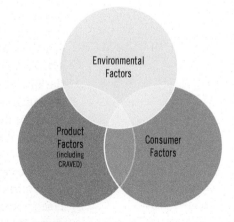

● **Figure 12.1** *Factors influencing whether a product is shoplifted*

retail and online security strategies may not be convenient for customers, they are needed to reduce opportunities for theft. Unfortunately, the cost of theft must be covered and honest consumers often suffer in the long run by paying higher prices.

The second category of consumer misbehavior trends revolves around the consumption of products. In our discussion of *consumption-related misbehaviors*, we primarily focus on those behaviors that pose health and wellness problems for consumers. We will focus on three significant problematic areas: obesity, gambling, and excessive use of alcohol.

Obesity

The global obesity epidemic is far-reaching, impacting individuals in nearly every part of the world. Obesity is measured by body mass index (BMI), which takes into account a person's height and weight. Body mass index can be determined by dividing a person's weight in kilograms by the square of that person's height in meters. Thus, $BMI = weight \ (in \ kilograms)/height^2 \ (in \ meters)$. Someone is overweight if his or her BMI is greater than or equal to twenty-five, while someone is **obese** if his or her BMI is greater than or equal to thirty.

> **Obese** individuals have a body mass index greater than or equal to thirty.

Obesity levels around the world have more than tripled since 1975. Approximately 39 percent of adults are overweight (39 percent of men and 40 percent of women) and 13 percent of adults are obese (11 percent of men and 15 percent of women). The problem of obesity is not just an issue for adults. For children between five and nineteen years old, the rate of being overweight jumped from just 4 percent in 1975 to over 18 percent by 2016. Further, 1 percent of children were obese in 1975, while approximately 7 percent were obese by 2016 (6 percent of girls and 8 percent of boys). Why is this happening? Individuals are increasingly eating high-calorie and high-fat foods while at the same time reducing their level of physical activity. Our work, choices of transportation, and suburban lifestyles mean that, compared to previous generations, we are much more sedentary. We are simply not burning calories as fast as we are consuming them (World Health Organization 2018).

According to the US Centers for Disease Control and Prevention, the picture in the United States is much worse: approximately 40 percent of the US population is obese, with 35.7 percent of adults aged twenty to thirty-nine and 42.8 percent of adults aged forty to fifty-nine falling in the obese range of the BMI. Women are more likely to be obese than men, and Hispanics (47.0 percent), Blacks (46.8 percent), and Whites (37.9 percent) are more likely to be obese than Asians (12.7 percent). American children are much more likely than their global counterparts to be obese: 13.9 percent of children two to five years old, 18.4 percent of children six to eleven years old, and 20.6 percent of children twelve to nineteen years old are obese (Hales et al. 2017).

There are very real consequences to being overweight and obese. Healthcare professionals have seen dramatic increases in cardiovascular diseases, like heart disease and stroke, diabetes, musculoskeletal disorders, and some cancers. The health implications for children are even more dire. These children are more likely to experience breathing difficulties and to have bone fractures, hypertension, early signs of cardiovascular disease, insulin resistance, and psychological effects. When they become adults, they are more likely to be obese, to be disabled, and to suffer premature death (World Health Organization 2018). In low- and middle-income countries around the world, the consequences of being overweight and obese paint a similarly grim picture. Already burdened with a prevalence of infectious diseases and undernutrition, overweight and obese individuals in low- and middle-income areas are less healthy and thus less capable of fighting off infectious diseases. Further, children who are born in these countries are especially vulnerable because they likely have not had adequate prenatal or early childhood nutrition (World Health Organization 2018). In Western economies, people living on low incomes are more vulnerable to becoming obese because they have more limited access to healthy, fresh produce; a greater reliance on cheap, processed foods; and greater exposure to marketing for unhealthy foods.

Public policy makers and marketing decision-makers have attempted to address the issue of *food desert* areas, typically located in inner cities, where there are few full-service grocery stores that offer a selection of fresh, healthy foods. Because local consumers have few healthy options, they resort to less healthy alternatives for themselves and their families. Compared to living in a food desert, living near fast-food restaurants can be even worse for your health. Research shows that living in an area where there is a high density of fast food and unhealthy food choices (a food swamp) is much more likely to lead to obesity than living in an area where there are few full-service grocery stores (a food desert) (Cooksey-Stowers, Schwartz, and Brownell 2017). It is important for decision-makers, public policy makers, and consumers alike to be aware of such findings so that they can identify the factors that lead to obesity and develop appropriate solutions to this problem.

Gambling disorder

At one time or another, most people have purchased a lottery ticket, played a slot machine, or played a game of chance. Lottery ticket sales have increased every year since the first state lottery was introduced in 1965, even though the chances of winning are miniscule: 1 in 175 million. You might be surprised to learn the average American loses almost $400 per year to gambling and a sizable proportion of gamblers (more than a quarter) report health problems, financial difficulties, and a range of negative emotions, such as guilt (Muniz 2014). **Gambling disorder** is a consumption-related misbehavior that involves repeated and problematic gambling. People who suffer from gambling disorder experience a high similar to the high that comes from using alcohol or drugs. As such, individuals who have this disorder crave gambling, just like someone would crave alcohol or drugs. Individuals who have a gambling disorder often have problems at work, stress in their personal relationships, financial problems, and legal problems. In 2013, the American Psychiatric Association officially classified gambling disorder as a mental disorder

Gambling disorder happens when someone engages in repeated and problematic gambling. People who are suffering from gambling disorder experience a "high" that is similar to one that comes from alcohol or drugs.

involving a problem with impulse control. They noted that individuals can become addicted to it, just like they can become addicted to drugs or alcohol (Jabr 2013).

Experts estimate that in the United States alone, twenty million people have an unhealthy relationship with gambling to the extent that it causes problems with their home and work lives; two million people are addicted to gambling. Today, individuals do not even need to leave their homes to gamble. All they need is Wi-Fi and a phone. Surprisingly, the process of becoming addicted to gambling is very similar to the process of becoming addicted to drugs or alcohol. First, when individuals place a bet, they experience a high. Second, the body becomes used to this feeling, so bigger and bigger bets must be placed to achieve a high. This is similar to when an individual begins to become addicted to other substances. He or she develops a tolerance for the substance and needs bigger doses to achieve a high. After a while, the brain of an individual with a gambling disorder will undergo a variety of physical changes, including changes in blood flow and electrical activity. These changes make it extremely difficult for people to stop gambling on their own. Indeed, individuals who have a gambling disorder even experience withdrawal symptoms when they stop gambling: feeling shaky, nauseous, and physically ill (Jabr 2013).

Excessive alcohol consumption

Excessive alcohol consumption is another major global problem. Around the world, 3.3 million deaths per year (5.9 percent of all deaths) can be attributed to alcohol consumption. A further 5.1 percent of the global burden of disease can be traced to excessive alcohol consumption. Excessive alcohol consumption can lead to a greater likelihood of cancers, cardiovascular diseases, diabetes, gastrointestinal diseases, and injuries. Breaking the numbers down, about 16 percent of drinkers aged fifteen and over engage in episodes of heavy drinking. Generally speaking, the more economically prosperous a country, the more people consume alcohol. There is very little gender equality when it comes to drinking alcohol; 7.6 percent of all male deaths and 4.0 percent of all female deaths are connected to the consumption of alcohol. However, although a man is more likely to die as the result of alcohol consumption, a woman is more likely to get sick from alcohol consumption because her body is more strongly affected by alcohol (females generally have a smaller liver capacity and lower body weight). When looking at the global patterns of alcohol consumption, we can see some striking differences (see Table 12.1). Because there are some people in each region who do not drink, the amount of alcohol consumed per person is different than the amount of alcohol consumed per drinker. Southeast Asia demonstrates one of the most striking differences, perhaps because the people who do drink seem to drink a lot, more than six gallons of the equivalent of pure alcohol per drinker per year (World Health Organization, 2014).

It is clear that excessive alcohol consumption inflicts a considerable personal and financial burden on the world. Because of this, the World Health Organization has worked to create a global strategy designed to reduce these

Table 12.1 Global differences in alcohol consumption

WORLD HEALTH ORGANIZATION REGION	TOTAL ALCOHOL CONSUMPTION PER CAPITA (AMONG ALL CITIZENS)*	TOTAL ALCOHOL CONSUMPTION PER CAPITA (AMONG DRINKERS ONLY)*
Africa	1.58	5.15
The Americas	2.23	3.59
Eastern Mediterranean region	0.18	2.99
Europe	2.88	4.44
Southeast Asia region	0.90	6.10
Western Pacific region	1.80	3.96
World	1.64	4.54

Gallons of the equivalent of pure alcohol that are consumed.

Source: Derived from World Health Organization (2014).

risks and harms. By 2025, it hopes to achieve a 10 percent relative reduction in excessive alcohol consumption (World Health Organization 2014). The realization of the harms associated with excessive alcohol consumption has prompted many countries around the world to institute their own educational programs, restrictions on when and how alcohol can be sold or served, and limitations on marketing. A sizable majority (60.4 percent) of the countries in the study reported some restrictions on alcohol advertising, including 10.1 percent that had a complete ban on alcohol advertising. The variety of restrictions included measures such as bans on product placement on television, bans on beer company sponsorships at sporting events, and bans on beer sales promotions (World Health Organization 2014).

Experts from a wide range of disciplines, including public health, criminology, psychology, and social marketing, have worked to better understand the drivers of excessive alcohol consumption, especially in young people. These young consumers drink alcohol for a variety of reasons, such as socialization (Griffin et al. 2009; Smith and Foxcroft 2009; Szmigin et al. 2008) and acting gender roles (Measham 2002; Abel and Plumridge 2004). The alcoholic beverage industry often facilitates the excessive use of alcohol with the use of aggressive price promotions and point-of-sale materials. One need look no further than spring break to see how marketing often encourages excessive alcohol consumption in young people. (See Insights from the Field 12.2 to learn about how the actions of one man started a global movement.)

There are many more consumption-related misbehaviors, but we have examined three in some detail: obesity, gambling, and excessive alcohol consumption. It is important to make the distinction between consumer

The Free Hugs Project

In response to the April 2013 bombing at the Boston Marathon, Ken Nwadike Jr. started the Free Hugs Project. Nwadike had become increasingly disillusioned by a growing recognition that, even in an age of increasing social connectivity via the Internet, many people continue to feel isolated and alone. Anger and hatred, sometimes fueled by dishonest politicians and unscrupulous businesses, were dividing America.

For Nwadike, the problem of isolation was very relevant. As a young teenager, Nwadike and his family were homeless and faced the daily uncertainty of not knowing where their next meal would come from or whether they would have a safe place to sleep. As a release from the stress, Nwadike started to run and eventually earned a college scholarship for his running abilities. The tipping point happened, however, when terrorists set off bombs at the Boston Marathon, killing three people and injuring several hundred others. A sport that Nwadike loved and an event that brought people together were suddenly torn apart, literally, because of hatred. At the following year's race, Nwadike decided to hold a simple "Free Hugs" poster and offer passersby a simple hug. The effect was surprising. People ran to him, took selfies, and even broke out into tears. The message was simple: peace, unity, and positivity. The Free Hugs Project has garnered global attention, with "Free Hugs" being offered in many cities around the world. Nwadike's videos on Facebook and YouTube have received hundreds of millions of views worldwide ("Free Hugs Campaign" 2018).

The Free Hugs Project has not been without problems. When Nwadike visited Charlottesville, North Carolina, in 2016 after protests turned violent between neo-Nazi groups and protesters, he was caught between protesters and the police. Although the police appreciated his calming influence, protesters on both sides were suspicious of his motives and shouted angry comments at him (Kurtz and Amatruda 2016).

Nwadike has become a frequent motivational speaker at businesses, colleges, and civic events. He has also made numerous appearances on news programs around the country and around the world.

Why does the Free Hugs Project connect so well with some people? One reason may be related to a discussion we had in Chapter 4 on touch perception. Some consumers are high-need-for-touch consumers. They derive important product-related information from the sense of touch and are more likely to form trust for the product (and maybe even the retailer). There is a strong evolutionary need for individuals to touch and be touched. We discussed one research study that determined that if a waitress briefly touches a customer on the shoulder or arm, she will get more tips. The Free Hugs Project builds on this need for touch as well as a need for personal connection. Although it is doubtful that Nwadike skillfully crafted his movement to fit into well-established psychological concepts and marketing strategies, he was fortunate enough to find a message that really resonates with people: "We're all human beings and that's what matters . . . my primary focus is to push more love and create more peace and unity in the world" ("Free Hugs Campaign" 2018) (see Photo 12.6). A little hug can do big things!

● **Photo 12.6** *The Free Hugs Project promotes global peace and understanding*

Questions

1. The Free Hugs Project has been successful, in part, because it taps into an individual's need for touch and social connection. Review some of the concepts we discussed in other parts of this textbook. What other consumer behavior principles or models could help explain the success of the Free Hugs Project?

2. Organizers at the Free Hugs Project use their own marketing strategies to raise awareness and get the word out about their efforts, encourage people to attend events, and even purchase merchandise. One of the most well-known and frequently used models in consumer behavior is the five-step consumer decision-making model.

Describe in detail how a consumer might proceed through each step of the model as he or she is either contemplating attending a Free Hugs event or purchasing Free Hugs merchandise.

Sources: Kurtz and Amatruda (2016); "Free Hugs Campaign" (2018).

misbehaviors and addiction. Consumer misbehaviors are actions that violate the culturally accepted norms of exchange and consumption. There are two types of consumer misbehavior: acquisition-related misbehaviors and consumption-related misbehaviors. **Addiction** can be defined as consumption-related misbehaviors in which the individual: (1) has a low degree of self-control, (2) spends a great amount of time and frequency engaging in the behavior, (3) has low levels of enjoyment (because the behavior is driven by need), and (4) results in a high likelihood of harmful consequences (Martin et al. 2013). Marketing can sometimes facilitate these addictive behaviors. Simply look at how easy it is to overeat in the United States. There is a plethora of high-fat, high-sodium foods that are relatively inexpensive and easy to buy or prepare at home. Restaurants have huge portion sizes and numerous chain restaurants offer all-you-can-eat specials. If a person has a food addiction, it is especially hard to live in America.

Addiction occurs when an individual: (1) has a low degree of self-control, (2) spends a great amount of time and frequency engaging in the behavior, (3) has low levels of enjoyment (because the behavior is driven by need), and (4) results in a high likelihood of harmful consequences.

Unfortunately, marketing cues can sometimes facilitate misbehavior and addiction. Ads that depict the sound of beer being poured into a glass or a nightclub scene could trigger cravings in some addicted consumers. Responsible marketers, therefore, must be particularly careful about their marketing communications strategies. In the gambling industry, for example, marketers remind gamblers to limit their gaming and seek help if they think they need it. Casinos have frequent signage and information about help if gamblers think they may be addicted. They also encourage addicted gamblers to remove themselves from mailings or other promotional offerings and to block online gambling sites. The line that a marketer must walk is quite thin, because marketers want to encourage consumers to enjoy their product, but they do not want addicted consumers to be additionally burdened or harmed (Martin et al. 2013).

Trends that are a reaction to ethical questions or dilemmas

The trends that are discussed in the following section generally describe groups of consumers who have decided that there is something distinctly wrong or perhaps unethical about the modern consumer culture. After reading the previous section, it is easy to see why some consumers are frustrated.

Some consumers have reacted to their misgivings and have created communities around alternative ways of viewing consumption and alternative ways of consuming. Some individuals are particularly concerned about the environmental impacts of their consumption and want to do what they can to help the situation. Three trends that are a reaction to ethical questions or dilemmas are mindful consumption, sustainable consumption, and voluntary simplicity.

Mindful consumption

Many commentators argue that contemporary consumer culture cannot be maintained for long. There are many reasons for this assessment, including the threat of climate change, an ever-increasing global population, environmental degradation, and civil strife around the world. More and more, consumers are becoming mindful of their own consumption activities. **Mindful consumption** is a recognition that there are consequences to a consumer's consumption choices. Consumers then alter their consumption behaviors in an attempt to have fewer negative impacts on their own lives as well as the lives of others. Following the world financial crisis of 2008–9 and the devastating earthquake and tsunami of 2011, which killed nearly twenty thousand people, many Japanese people reassessed their consumption habits and adopted a more mindful consumption perspective. The *danshari* movement is one trend in which consumers are living a more minimalist lifestyle. The word *danshari* is derived from the Japanese word for throwing away and letting go. Some experts estimate that thousands of people adhere to this minimalist lifestyle trend, which has its roots in Zen Buddhism. The trend for mindful consumption has spread around the world. With fewer material possessions cluttering their lives, many individuals are able to spend more time and money on other pursuits, such as travel and spending time with friends and family (Lim 2016). Indeed, many books, television programs, and online resources are focused on helping individuals reduce consumption levels, identify low-cost alternatives, and live a life of more mindful consumption.

Sustainable consumption

The trend toward sustainable consumption is also beginning to become more widespread. **Sustainable consumption** starts with a recognition that our consumption choices impact one another and the planet. These impacts are not only localized, but also can stretch across long distances and across time. Indeed, the choices consumers make today will certainly impact future generations. Sustainable consumption differs from mindful consumption in two important respects. First, sustainable consumption is directed toward the issue of sustainability and a clear consideration of how a consumer's choices have consequences for other individuals and the environment. Consumers aren't just mindful of the impacts; they focus on impacts that specifically concern the environment and society. The second difference is that sustainable consumption doesn't just encourage a consideration of the sustainable consequences of a given consumption choice—sustainable consumption encourages *action*.

Mindful consumption is a recognition that there are consequences to a consumer's consumption choices. Consumers then alter their consumption behaviors in an attempt to have fewer negative impacts on their own lives as well as the lives of others.

Sustainable consumption starts with a recognition that our consumption choices impact one another and the planet. It encourages sustainable actions.

Consumers are certainly interested in not only thinking about sustainability, but also demonstrating their concerns with the products they buy (Black and Cherrier 2010). In a multinational study by the consumer products giant Unilever (the parent company to such well-known brands as Dove and Ben & Jerry's), one-third of consumers said they purchased brands based on their environmental impact and 21 percent said they would actively choose brands if companies clearly listed their sustainability credentials on the product packaging. The results were not consistent across countries. While only 53 percent of UK shoppers said they felt better when they purchased products that were sustainably produced, 78 percent of US shoppers, 85 percent of Brazilian and Turkish shoppers, and 88 percent of Indian shoppers said they felt better. At Unilever, the brands that have integrated sustainability into their product and purpose grew 30 percent faster than the brands that did not (Unilever 2017). See Insights from Academia 12.4 for one surprising finding about the use of colors in communicating a sustainable message.

This increased awareness of the issues around more sustainable living, including activities such as composting and recycling, are now becoming increasingly encouraged by governments around the world. Increasingly, countries are imposing bans on plastic shopping bags, excess packaging, and drinking straws. China caused a big jolt in the recycling world when, tired of being the world's garbage dump, it stopped accepting shipments of plastic on January 1, 2018. Until then, about half the world's recycled paper, metal, and plastic was processed in China. Before the ban, the United States sent 13.2 million tons of paper and 1.42 million tons of plastic each year to China to be recycled, making recycling the sixth largest American export to China (de Freytas-Tamura 2018). Check out Insights from the Field 12.3 to find out

 INSIGHTS FROM ACADEMIA 12.4

Blue is greener than green

The purpose of this study was to determine how color influences a consumer's ethical judgments. The researchers used a series of experiments to determine which colors were perceived to be the most ecofriendly. The shade of blue used in the Walmart logo was judged as the most ecofriendly, whereas the shade of red used in the Target logo was viewed as the least ecofriendly. Surprisingly, the color green was viewed as only somewhat ecofriendly. These views of the ecofriendliness of the company even carry over into perceptions of the company's ethical business practices. Specifically, consumers who viewed a logo with an ecofriendly color were much more willing to view the actions of the company as being ethical. On the flip side, consumers who viewed a logo with a non-ecofriendly color were much more likely to view the actions of the company as being unethical. So, if you want to be viewed as ecofriendly and ethical, change your logo to blue!

Sundar, A., and J. J. Kellaris. 2017. "How Logo Colors Influence Shoppers' Judgments of Retailer Ethicality: The Mediating Role of Perceived Eco-friendliness." Journal of Business Ethics 146 (3): 685–701.

Do you recycle in the shower?

Few people think about recycling when they're in the shower. The marketing and sustainability teams at Johnson & Johnson (J&J) wanted to change that. Although many consumers participate in curbside recycling, most of the materials that end up in the recycling bin are from bottles, containers, and cans that originate in the kitchen. The problem is that most of J&J's products are found in the bathroom. So, despite even the best efforts to make J&J's operations and consumer products more sustainable, those efforts were falling short if a sizable proportion of consumers did not follow through and place their empty bottles of shampoo, conditioner, body wash, etc., in a recycling bin. Two other factors seemed to add to the reluctance of many consumers to recycle items from their bathrooms. First, consumers seem to have less knowledge about what kinds of bathroom items can and cannot be recycled. This confusion is reinforced by advertising images that typically only show kitchen products like soda cans and plastic bottles being thrown into recycling bins. Second, many consumers have recycling containers or bins that are located in or around the kitchen; very few have them in the bathroom (Sustainable Lifestyles Frontier Group 2015).

Further research at J&J revealed that consumers might be open to the idea of recycling more in the bathroom. First, "60% of moms confessed they wish they remembered to recycle more. But they also said they would be more likely to recycle in the bathroom if they had a bin there to help them remember." Another piece of the research found that 75 percent of moms thought that showing their kids how to recycle was a "teachable moment" (Mazzoni 2017). Finally, if consumers were shown specific details about how to recycle, there was a 48 percent lift in intentions to recycle and a 31 percent lift in perceptions that J&J was an environmentally responsible company (Sustainable Lifestyles Frontier Group 2015). Because of these insights, the "Care to recycle" campaign was born.

Launched on April 9, 2017, to coincide with Earth Day, the ingenious thing about the "Care to recycle" campaign is that it touched all three parts of the attitude model: affect, cognition, and behavior (see Chapter 7 for a review of attitudes). Building on the teachable moment trigger, the target for the effort was mothers. Johnson & Johnson wanted a simple solution that was easy to understand, made consumers feel good, and could easily motivate behavior. Consumers received free recycling bins for each qualifying purchase on CVS.com and an educational campaign instructed consumers about what can be recycled. This was also supported by an app that allowed customers to donate one dollar to a conservation nonprofit for every uploaded "recycling selfie" (Mazzoni 2017). As for behaviors, J&J wanted to encourage two distinct actions: the purchase of more J&J products with sustainable benefits and the recycling of more J&J containers. Thus, the final creative execution provided elements to help motivate each of the three key elements of the attitude model (see Table 12.2).

Table 12.2 Summary of key executional components of the "Care to recycle" campaign

COGNITIVE MOTIVATOR	AFFECTIVE MOTIVATOR	BEHAVIORAL MOTIVATOR
• Increase knowledge with easy-to-understand recycling guide	• Bond with your children in a teachable moment	• Put your bottle in the recycling bin • Intend to buy more Johnson & Johnson products

As with any research effort and promotional execution, the same basic principles of marketing still must be carefully followed. Asking the right research questions, generating data and information, creating insights, and developing relevant marketing campaigns all help marketers to better engage with customers. At the end of the day, the most important consideration is whether the effort is able to increase the value proposition to the customer.

Questions

1. At the beginning of this chapter, we discussed two ethical frameworks that can be used to help guide ethical decision-making. Suppose you are a consumer who needs to be convinced that you need to recycle. Discuss recycling from a utilitarian viewpoint and from a common good viewpoint.

For each viewpoint, be sure to answer these questions: What is important to you as a consumer? What benefits as a consumer do you receive from recycling?

2. Building on your answer to Question 1, imagine that you are a marketing manager who is creating a messaging strategy for encouraging consumers to recycle. First, create an advertising message that would resonate with a consumer who is approaching recycling from a utilitarian viewpoint. Second, create a different advertising message that would resonate with a consumer who is approaching recycling from a common good viewpoint.

Sources: Mazzoni (2017); Sustainable Lifestyles Frontier Group (2015).

about how Johnson & Johnson has addressed the issue of plastic and helped consumers live more sustainably.

Other sustainability-related behaviors reflect an increase in self-reliance among consumers, with more people moving from consumption to production (Burch 2012). The increasing prevalence of community gardens gives individuals (especially those living in cities) the opportunity to grow their own fruits and vegetables, while also meeting and socializing with neighbors (see Photo 12.7). Flea markets, community yard sales, and online auction sites such as eBay and Facebook Marketplace have meant that consumers can sell their unwanted possessions to others instead of throwing them away. There are also numerous websites (such as freecycle.org) dedicated solely to giving away unwanted items for free, thus reducing waste that could otherwise end up in landfills. Finally, numerous sites now exist where individuals can barter services and goods with their neighbors. For example, a homebound older person may barter some fresh-baked cookies for a ride to the grocery store. When consumers put their minds to it, they can come up with some very creative ideas for engaging in more sustainable consumption (see Insights from the Field 12.4).

● **Photo 12.7** *Buying local is one way to engage in sustainable consumption*

Picture a warmer future

Research suggests that individuals spend much of their time planning for and anticipating the future. Indeed, consumers think about the future three times as often as they think about the past (Seligman and Tierney 2017). This focus on the future is definitely beneficial for individuals. Many of the socially constructed elements of our culture—our educational system, our businesses, and our laws—exist because individuals can anticipate what others will do in the future. We make sacrifices today because of bigger payoffs tomorrow. Students work hard in college because they know that there will be great benefits in the future. In addition to these tangible benefits, for most individuals, thinking about the future results in higher levels of happiness and lower levels of stress. This is because individuals are also generally optimistic; they are more likely to imagine positive outcomes as opposed to negative ones (Seligman and Tierney 2017). Although thinking about the future is common, many people still have a hard time imagining a future where the planet is warmer and seas are higher (Hajer and Wytske 2018). Why do individuals have a hard time imagining a warmer future? A combination of four key factors are at work here (Treuer 2018):

- Most people try to avoid uncertainty, and the near-term as well as the long-term impacts of climate change are definitely uncertain.
- Individuals do not see direct cause-and-effect relationships; actions and their impacts are separated. For example, driving a few extra miles in your car will release more carbon dioxide, but there will be no immediate, visible impact for anyone to observe.
- Individuals in general are likely to seek information that confirms their preexisting opinions on climate change and are quite unlikely to seek information that disconfirms those opinions. Thus, climate skeptics are unlikely to be motivated to become more informed on the topic.
- As we learned earlier when discussing processing heuristics (Chapter 8), individuals are likely to favor information that is more available and representative. Since most individuals have not experienced high levels of water in the streets or in their homes, for example, it is hard for them to imagine such a future.

This difficulty in imagining a warmer future means that many individuals and policy makers are reluctant to make changes now that will avoid the worst impacts of climate change in the future. However, climate experts have issued numerous warnings that planetary warming must be kept to just 2 degrees Celsius (or 3.6 degrees Fahrenheit); otherwise, catastrophic effects will occur around the planet (Intergovernmental Panel on Climate Change 2018). Even with this "best case scenario of just a 2-degree Celsius rise in temperature, sea levels in places like New Orleans, New York, and Miami are expected to rise by six feet. Across the world, coastal areas will be regularly flooded, buildings will be lost, farmland will be ruined, and people will have to retreat inland (Intergovernmental Panel on Climate Change 2018). Because government officials, scientific organizations, and environmental advocacy groups know that individuals have a difficult time imagining these events, they are starting to provide tools for helping people imagine what this might look like (Drollette 2019). The Union of Concerned Scientists, for example, has an interactive tool where individuals can enter zip codes to see which areas will be inundated with sea-level rise (see https://ucsusa.maps.arcgis.com/apps/MapJournal/index.html?appid=b53e9dd7a85a444884 66e1a38de87601) and NASA has a time-lapse tool that depicts changes in sea levels, temperatures, carbon dioxide, and Arctic ice coverage over time (see https://climate.nasa.gov/interactives/climate-time-machine) (National Aeronautics and Space Administration 2019).

Questions

1. Use the concept of possible selves (Chapter 6) to help explain why many individuals have a hard time imagining a future in which the worst effects of climate change have happened.

2. Does being a climate skeptic rise to the level of being a consumer misbehavior? Why or why not?
3. Imagine that you are trying to convince your climate-skeptic friend that the time is now for action on climate change. Construct two strong arguments—one based on utilitarianism and one

based on a common good perspective—for why it makes sense to take immediate action.

Sources: Drollette (2019); Hajer and Wytske (2018); Intergovernmental Panel on Climate Change (2018); National Aeronautics and Space Administration (2019); Seligman and Tierney (2017); Treuer (2018).

Voluntary simplicity

In the search for a simpler way of living, the emergence of the voluntary simplicity movement in the 1970s provided one route for consumers to opt out of some of the demands of consumer and marketplace cultures. **Voluntary simplicity** refers to a lifestyle choice where individuals opt to limit material consumption and free up resources, such as time and money, which they believe will raise the quality of their life (Huneke 2005). Voluntary simplicity can stretch across a wide spectrum and variety of practices and values, ranging from consumers who fully embrace the ideas around reducing consumption (driven by ethical concerns to own and use fewer goods) to those consumers who simply "refine" their consumption toward ethical standards (e.g., buying Fair Trade coffee in their supermarket), enabling them to continue to have similar levels of consumption, but to consume differently and in line with their ethical concerns (Shaw and Newholm 2002). Some individuals are "highly committed simplifiers" and others are "less committed simplifiers" who change their behavior, but not in highly disruptive ways (Huneke 2005).

One example of a highly committed simplifier is Colin Beavan, the subject of a 2009 documentary film called *No Impact Man*. To raise awareness about the environmental costs of modern Western lifestyles, the film follows Beavan and his family for one year as they attempted to have zero impact on the environment. They gave up a variety of everyday conveniences such as riding elevators, walking through automatic doors (because they require electricity), and using any fossil fuel–based transportation. This was especially difficult because they lived on the ninth floor of a New York City apartment building. They ate all organic, locally produced food. They also gave up what some would consider essential items, such as electricity, heat, and coffee. In an effort to not use any paper products, the family even gave up toilet paper. In the end, Beavan, his wife, and their two-year-old child spent a lot of quality time together as they endured the struggles of the project (Scott 2009). In the years since the project, Beavan has turned on the electricity again, but still uses his bike, buys local food, and walks up to his apartment. Does Beavan use toilet paper now? He refuses to say (E. A. Harris 2012).

The Amish community is a special case of a group of individuals who have decided to turn their backs on modern life and live a more simple, peaceful, and

Voluntary simplicity refers to a lifestyle choice where individuals opt to limit material consumption and free up resources, such as time and money, which they believe will raise the quality of their life.

● **Photo 12.8** *Amish buggies are a frequent sight on roads in rural areas of Pennsylvania, Ohio, and Indiana*

spiritual life. The Amish can trace their origins to sixteenth-century Switzerland and the Protestant Reformation. Many of them moved to North America between 1730 and 1850 in search of religious freedom and economic opportunity. Amish people are Christian and have a shared set of values, including humility, pacifism, and separation from the broader culture. At approximately three hundred thousand strong, the Amish can be found in many parts of the United States and Canada, but these communities are particularly prevalent in rural areas in Pennsylvania, Ohio, and Indiana. Religion plays a big role in their daily lives and directs how they interact with others within the Amish community as well as outside the community. They follow a very strict set of rules about their clothing, their relationships, and their occupations. Their days are spent working on the farm or around the house, in trades like carpentry or metal working, or in small shops. Their lives have very few of the trappings of modern life: no electricity, no cars, and no phones. Smoking, drinking, and caffeine are not allowed (see Photo 12.8) (Kraybill 2014; "Amish in America" 2012).

The first section in this chapter discussed two frameworks for ethical decision-making and the next section discussed several topics that were designed to highlight the consumer connection to ethical decision-making. We discussed acquisition-related and consumption-related consumer misbehaviors. In addition, we discussed a few positive actions that consumers have taken to change their consumption habits as a reaction to their perceptions of the modern consumer lifestyle. Given the increasing emphasis of ethical frameworks as well as several consumer connection trends, it is not surprising that marketers are starting to pay attention. The following section of this chapter will discuss how marketers have altered their own practices in response to some of these ethical issues (see Insights from the Boardroom 12).

◉ Corporate Social Responsibility

Because of many of the problems that are starting to become apparent in modern consumer life, there has been a call for corporations to respond. Many have done so. The management teams at these organizations recognize that their corporations need to operate within a society by becoming an integral part of the particular neighborhood, culture, and society in which they

INSIGHTS FROM THE BOARDROOM 12

Vanilla gets no respect

● *Bill Simon*

You have to feel sorry for vanilla. On the one hand, it is the most popular flavor in the world and appears in baked goods, ice cream, and a host of other products. Vanilla is everywhere. On the other hand, vanilla is the second most expensive spice in the world, at about $200 per pound for vanilla beans (Elhence 2017), and few people appreciate the long, arduous, and danger-ous process involved in the production of vanilla. Im-portantly, not many people appreciate how sustainable production of vanilla can alter the course for seventy thousand small farmers, save lives, and help a nation. One person who does appreciate the importance of va-nilla is Bill Simon, vice president of sales (US Consumer Products Division) at McCormick & Company.

McCormick produces flavors and spices from around the world and sells its products to other food producers as well as to consumers. Founded in 1889, McCormick has long had a commitment to the glob-al sourcing of its ingredients. Today, with more than

$5.3 billion in annual sales, McCormick works closely with suppliers around the globe to bring the ingredi-ents together for its three thousand individual con-sumer products ("McCormick" 2019). Vanilla is one of McCormick's most complicated products.

Approximately 80 percent of the world's supply of vanilla comes from Madagascar and some of its sur-rounding islands. The process of making vanilla is very long and difficult. First, the vanilla plant takes three years to reach full maturity and produce vanilla beans. The plant itself is a member of the orchid family and farmers must hand pollinate each flower for it to be able to produce the bean. This pollination must be done within a short window of just a few hours; otherwise, the pollination is ineffective ("The Power of Partnership" 2018). The harvesting, drying, curing, and conditioning comprise another long process and can take as long as fourteen additional months ("Vanilla" 2014). Second, be-cause the crop is so valuable, there is ample opportunity for theft, corruption, and violence. There is a "great deal of political and civil strife and many of the people who live there find it hard just dealing with their own daily living requirements. Some farmers and other people have traditionally been taken advantage of by aggrega-tors and middlemen. Some of these criminal actors have also used buying and selling vanilla as a way to launder money," said Simon (2018). Because of corruption and criminal activity, farmers often became entrapped in a cycle of debt, back-breaking work, and child labor. The International Labor Organization estimated that twenty thousand children regularly worked in Madagascar's vanilla industry (Lind 2016). Finally, Madagascar has seen a massive amount of deforestation as individuals cut down forests to plant more vanilla plants. This has led to poor water quality, lost habitat, and lost species throughout the region (Watts 2018).

When news of the plight of vanilla farmers, chil-dren, and the environment started to become pub-lic, Bill Simon began to hear about it. "Consumers wanted to know what we were doing. At McCormick, we have taken a lot of time and care—sometimes 30

(continued)

years—making these connections and carefully establishing these procedures. McCormick has a long history of community engagement. This has led to a corporate culture that is now formalized within our Purpose-Led-Performance (PLP) agenda and that positions us well to respond to issues like these that are important to our customers and consumers," noted Simon (2018).

In 2017, under its purpose-led-performance sustainability agenda, McCormick accelerated its program to tackle these issues and secure a long-term sustainable supply of vanilla. The company leveraged its existing long-term relationships with several nongovernmental organizations and suppliers to set up a series of cooperatives. Farmers—and often entire villages of farmers—now safely sell their vanilla beans to the cooperative, which, in turn, provides them with a higher price and more stable income than they could get from the typical middlemen. According to Simon, "We have boots on the ground in Madagascar" (2018). Not only do these cooperatives allow for better prices for the farmers, but also they now have access to training, financing, technical assistance, and sharing of resources. "We have three main goals regarding our efforts with vanilla. First, we need to make sure there is a long-term sustainable supply of vanilla; second, we need to ensure that the quality is consistent; and third, we are committed to improving the livelihoods of our farmers and strengthening the communities where they live," noted Simon (2018).

One of the key components of the cooperative arrangement is to have full vertical integration all the way down to the cooperative and the farmers. "We can then trace the vanilla as it moves from the farmer all the way through the supply chain to the consumer which is

very unique to McCormick" (Simon 2018). Traceability is critically important to making sure the process not only works correctly, but also is ethical and sustainable. It allows for McCormick to say, for example, that the vanilla beans that arrived at the US facility can be traced back, step by step, through the entire supply chain to a specific cooperative or farmer. If something is wrong with the quality of the beans, McCormick has the ability to remove those beans from processing and address the issue immediately.

Simon acknowledged that consumer concerns and preferences played a vital role in McCormick's decision to do something about vanilla and eventually move forward with supporting the cooperatives in Madagascar. Consumers raised concerns about the human and environmental impacts of vanilla, and McCormick responded through its boots-on-the-ground purpose-led-performance agenda. Now that the cooperatives are functioning, the next step, Simon said, is to "get the word out to them about what we're doing, to let consumers know they can continue to buy McCormick vanilla with confidence. Vanilla is such a valuable crop and most people have no idea what goes on behind the scenes." Simon noted, "It makes you proud to work for a company that cares and has so many people involved to make this change and do the right thing" (2018). Maybe now vanilla will get the respect it deserves!

reside. **Corporate social responsibility** (CSR) is a business approach that takes into account the needs of stakeholders and works to achieve economic, social, and environmental success. Importantly, this framework must be long-term and sustainable (Pontrefract 2017). When it's done right, the corporate social responsibility philosophy should permeate all parts of the organization so that everyone in the corporation behaves ethically and responsibly in all of their interactions with one another and important stakeholders, especially customers. Specific CSR initiatives can include partnering with nonprofit

Corporate social responsibility (CSR) is a set of standards and procedures for running a business that takes into account the needs of stakeholders and works to achieve economic, social, and environmental success.

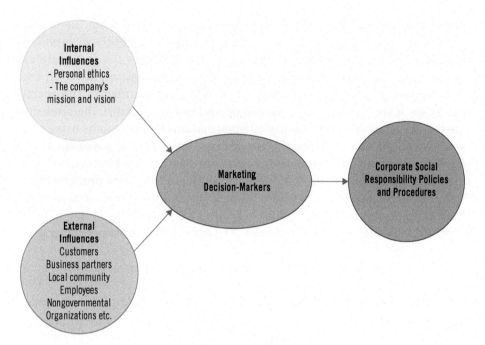

● **Figure 12.2** *Influences on decision-makers and corporate social responsibility*

organizations, creating products that are healthier, offering easy-to-understand nutritional information, or even organizing a day for employees to clean up a nearby park. There is no one-size-fits-all framework for a company to engage in CSR. It is important to realize that the push for CSR comes from internal as well as external sources. Internally, decision-makers themselves have seen that there are big benefits to operating in a socially responsible way. A company is more innovative, competitive, and efficient in its operations, so it makes perfect sense for upper-level managers to do what they can to operate under a CSR umbrella. Internally, marketing decision-makers and other employees are also likely to be influenced by personal sets of ethical standards as well as by the company's mission statement and vision. Externally, numerous stakeholders such as customers, the government, business partners, and nongovernmental organizations might exert an influence on a marketing decision-maker (see Figure 12.2).

It is not surprising that many people think that a choice must be made between doing what's right for the business and doing what's right for the broader environment and community. For decades, businesses, business schools, economists, and politicians have told us this. Luckily, many experts, including those from businesses, business schools, economists, and, yes, even politicians, are starting to realize that this is a choice that we don't have to make. In fact, it is a false choice. The good news is that businesses do well when the environment and community do well. The really good news is that sometimes businesses are ideally suited for addressing some of society's most pressing social and environmental problems. Traditionally, nongovernmental organizations and the government were tasked with doing what they could to address these sorts of issues. But the impact of these efforts was limited by how much the nongovernmental organizations could raise in donations or how much the government could raise in taxes. Businesses, however, are not limited by these kinds of constraints. When environmental and social issues are at the center of the business operation—for example, the products are made from locally sourced ingredients, manufacturing is done using 100 percent renewable energy, or the service is delivered using a diverse labor force—every unit that is produced or every service that is performed is doing good. Further, as long as the organization continues to make a profit on each sale, it can continue to do these good things for the environment and society. As long as the organization is making a profit from each sale, it can keep expanding its operations, selling more, and making a difference (Porter and Kramer 2011).

Shared value is a concept in which an organization creates economic value for itself and its investors, while also creating social and environmental value.

The concept of **shared value** is one in which an organization creates economic value for itself and its investors, while also creating social and environmental value. Shared value is about addressing a social or environmental issue with a business model, and it is a new way of thinking about the purpose for a business's existence. Shared value does not say that an organization must make more charitable donations to a variety of causes. Instead, a shared value conceptualization of business says that a business can meet consumer needs and wants in a socially and environmentally responsible way, while also making a profit (Porter and Kramer 2011). The following sections briefly highlight the ethics of two very different organizations and discuss the concerns of consumers.

Shared value = economic value + social & environmental value

Using versus not using corporate social responsibility to guide corporate behavior

One company with a consistently good reputation for CSR is the LEGO Group. In 2017, it received a number one ranking for having the best reputation on a global CSR survey ("LEGO Group" 2017). The LEGO Group was the first toy company in the world to join the United Nations Global Compact, the world's largest CSR initiative. What other things led to such a high ranking for LEGO? Importantly, it has a strong CSR statement and has partnered with the World Wildlife Foundation to develop its initiatives, such as setting ambitious goals for reducing carbon dioxide and sustainable sourcing of raw materials ("Environmental Leadership" 2019):

> *The LEGO Group is committed to making a positive impact on the world our children will inherit.*

LEGO backs up this statement with initiatives that are tracked and reported. Among other things, LEGO is consistently transparent in providing information to a variety of stakeholder groups on its activities, initiatives, and progress ("Environmental Leadership" 2019). Clearly, LEGO doesn't just talk about ethics and CSR: everything is backed by actions.

Despite a strong push from various stakeholders, there are still organizations that have committed fairly severe ethical lapses of judgment. One company with an exceedingly bad reputation is Volkswagen (VW) (Bond 2017; Matussek and Behrmann 2018), which made global news in 2015 when it was discovered that it installed software in its cars that was able to cheat US emissions testing equipment. Volkswagen customers thought they were driving fuel-efficient and ecofriendly cars, but soon found out that they were duped by the car company. If that wasn't enough to shake up management's commitment to more ethical behavior, a few years later, two additional scandals rocked VW. One scandal involved the efforts by VW to stop the publication of a report from the World Health Organization that found that diesel emissions caused cancer. Another scandal erupted when it was discovered that VW (as well as Daimler and BMW) had paid for research projects that exposed both monkeys and humans to toxic diesel fumes to examine the negative health consequences associated with breathing diesel exhaust (Connolly 2018; Cremer 2018). In the wake of this research scandal, a top manager was suspended while the rest of the upper-level management team committed to more ethical standards in their operations (Cremer 2018). Although VW supports a variety of environmental and social projects around the world, it remains to be seen if they will find ways to more holistically incorporate ethical decision-making into all levels of their operations.

Do customers really care?

It is now time to circle back to our main concern in this textbook—the consumer—and discuss the expectations consumers have regarding the ethical behavior of organizations.

When asked how they would feel about a company that supports social or environmental issues, a full 92 percent of Americans said they would have a more positive image of the company, 87 percent would be more likely to trust the company, and 88 percent would be more loyal to the company (Cone Communications 2017). When making purchase decisions, 70 percent say that they consider the company's ethics. Which consumers are most likely to be influenced by a company's ethics? Individuals who are aged eighteen to thirty-four and make more than $75,000 per year (86 percent say they are influenced by a company's ethical record). The issues that consumers are most concerned about are employee treatment (48 percent are concerned), where the products are made (34 percent), and the environmental friendliness of the company (33 percent) (Mintel 2015). Which companies do consumers believe to be especially ethical or unethical? See Table 12.3.

Consumers not only have views about the ethics of a company, but also are willing to enact certain behaviors. When a company is not ethical, 35 percent are willing to tell others about it, 30 percent are willing to stop

Table 12.3 The most ethical and most unethical companies

MOST ETHICAL COMPANIES	MOST UNETHICAL COMPANIES
Chick-fil-A*	Walmart*
Starbucks*	McDonald's*
Panera Bread	Chick-fil-A*
Google	Monsanto
Walmart*	Bank of America
Trader Joe's	British Petroleum
McDonald's*	Exxon Mobil

*These companies were viewed by consumers as being among the most ethical and the most unethical.

Source: Derived from Mintel (2015).

buying the product even if it is more affordable, 27 percent are willing to stop buying the product even if the product is high quality, and 24 percent are willing to stop buying even if they have to go out of their way to do so (Mintel 2015). These numbers provide strong evidence for the importance of a firm doing the right thing. As one of the organization's most important stakeholders, customers are very willing to take a stand for organizations to behave ethically. In the end, consumers want to know not only what a company stands for but also what a company *stands up* for (Cone Communications 2017).

This chapter starts to answer the question, Where do we go from here? It illuminates two frameworks for ethical decision-making for both consumers and marketing decision-makers. The chapter also discusses consumer-focused trends that raise ethical issues and dilemmas, as well as trends that are a reaction to ethical issues and dilemmas. Corporate social responsibility was introduced as a way to illustrate the important steps that businesses were taking to be more aware of and responsive to ethical issues. Importantly, throughout the chapter, connections were drawn to some of the core consumer behavior concepts we discussed in earlier chapters. In this way, we build on the consumer behavior knowledge that has already been established to better understand ethics and social responsibility. In the end, an examination of ethics provides a way for marketers and consumers to identify a "true North" as they traverse the often-complex world of consumer behavior.

◉ Summary

The purpose of this chapter was to investigate the issue of ethics and social responsibility. Although there are several frameworks for understanding ethical decision-making, two that are particularly relevant are *utilitarianism* and the *common good*. We discussed a variety of scenarios that illustrated the differences between these two approaches and stressed the importance of examining *ethics*, rather than morals, in our approach. Although the field of marketing had benefited from both approaches, there seems to be a particularly strong synergy with the common good approach. We also discussed reasons why the field of marketing has a *unique obligation* to understand ethics. In introducing the concept of Ubuntu, an ethical framework originating in South Africa, we reinforced the notion that ethical frameworks from vastly different cultural traditions seem to have more similarities than differences with one another.

The consumer connection was then forged with a discussion of two key trends, the first of which *raises ethical issues and dilemmas*. This rather detailed discussion included a broad discussion of *consumer misbehavior* and then broke that misbehavior down into two distinct categories: acquisition-related issues and consumption-related issues. We discussed a variety of examples in this section of the chapter, including a research insight about the role of parental behavior in promoting materialism in their children. As an introduction to the second key trend that focused on *reactions to ethical issues and dilemmas*, we introduced the Free Hugs Project, created as a reaction to the Boston Marathon bombing and a recognition that there were many lonely and isolated people who just needed to forge a social connection. Although there are many actions individuals can take, we discussed three: mindful consumption, sustainable consumption, and voluntary simplicity.

Finally, we discussed *corporate social responsibility* and the concept of *shared value*. As organizations feel internal and external pressure to make their own operations more ethical, CSR will become standard operating procedure.

KEY TERMS

addiction p. 459	ethics p. 442	sustainable consumption p. 460
common good p. 443	gambling disorder p. 455	tragedy of the commons p. 444
compulsive buying p. 452	materialism p. 450	utilitarianism p. 442
consumer misbehavior p. 448	mindful consumption p. 460	voluntary simplicity p. 465
consumer theft p. 452	morality p. 442	
corporate social responsibility (CSR) p. 468	obese p. 454	
	shared value p. 470	

REVIEW QUESTIONS

1. Discuss the two main frameworks for ethical decision-making. What is the difference between the two?
2. In what way does the field of marketing have a unique obligation to understand and adhere to principles of ethical decision-making?
3. Why do we focus our discussion on ethics and not morals in this chapter?
4. Describe the three factors that influence whether a product is stolen.
5. How does excessive consumption differ from addiction? Why is gambling disorder considered an addiction?
6. What are some key differences between mindful consumption, sustainable consumption, and voluntary simplicity?
7. Why are companies starting to implement CSR statements and programs? What are the benefits of this approach?

DISCUSSION QUESTIONS

1. In what ways is the philosophy of Ubuntu different from and in what ways is it similar to the common good?
2. We've all been there. We all have that one stubborn relative at Thanksgiving or at our summer barbecue who seems stuck in the 1950s. Construct an argument to convince your Uncle Pete that modern businesses need to operate according to the common good.
3. In what ways does the tragedy of the commons make it particularly difficult for individuals to share resources and work together toward common goals? What can be done to fix this problem?
4. Describe three ways in which marketing has benefited from using the common good framework for ethical decision-making.
5. Do you think there is any merit to the criticism that Americans are materialistic? Why or why not?
6. If you decided to reduce your consumption, how would you do it? In what ways would your beliefs, evaluations, attitudes, and behaviors change (hint: review Chapter 7)?
7. Have you ever altered your own behaviors when you found out about a company behaving unethically? What did you do? What prompted you to do it? Discuss in detail. If you haven't done this, why not?

For more information, quizzes, case studies, and other study tools, please visit us at
www.oup.com/he/phillips.

CASE STUDY 12

Eliminating The Idea Of Waste

TerraCycle's mission is to eliminate the idea of waste. In the process of fulfilling this mission, TerraCycle has introduced a variety of fascinating products and engaged consumers in the issue of sustainability by making them active participants in the process.

Once called the "coolest little start-up in America" (Burlingham 2006), TerraCycle turned worm poop into a multi-million-dollar business. That's right, worm poop. It all started when Tom Szaky was a freshman at Princeton and needed to find a better way to "fertilize some plants" he had growing in his dorm room. He got the brilliant idea of going to the dumpster behind the cafeteria, scooping up some food waste, and feeding it to a bunch of worms. The worms happily devoured the food and, doing what worms do, created a lot of waste of their own. Szaky then gathered up this nutrient-rich fertilizer, fed it to his plants, and voila! A business idea was born. Others soon got word of the miraculous properties of the fertilizer, and after hundreds of phone calls to sales managers, Szaky started selling the fertilizer to Home Depot and Walmart (Phillips and Phillips 2016).

Then, Szaky found himself wondering: What if TerraCycle tried to eliminate the *idea* of waste? With this mission guiding them, the people in the research and development lab worked long hours to find endlessly fascinating ways to repurpose and recycle even the most difficult to recycle items. TerraCycle's product line soon expanded to include recycling programs for a variety of hard-to-recycle products like juice pouches, cigarette butts, toothbrushes, chewing gum, and flip-flops. Juice pouches, for instance, are incredibly difficult to recycle because they have layers of plastic, foil, and paper that are fused together. Despite the difficulties in recycling this product, as well as many others, TerraCycle found creative ways to make sure these items did not end up in the landfill (Phillips and Phillips 2016).

In Chapter 9, we discussed innovative ways in which organizations could create greater engagement with their customers. TerraCycle has also worked to engage its customers, a group of very dedicated, sustainably minded individuals who are well aware of the consequences of their consumption choices and want to take action. In a 2017 study by the Boston communications firm Cone, an astounding 87 percent of Americans said they would purchase a product from a company if that company advocated for an issue they cared about. Indeed, consumers want to see that the values of the companies with which they are associated align with their own values. A majority of consumers seem to be willing to reward those companies that are doing the

right thing. A full 89 percent of Americans said that, given two brands with similar price and quality, they would switch to the brand that is associated with a good cause (Cone Communications 2017). These are precisely the kinds of consumers in TerraCycle's target market.

TerraCycle has worked to engage consumers in three distinct ways. First, the company offered a wide variety of recycled and upcycled consumer products that were available online, as well as in big-box retail outlets such as Staples, Walmart, Home Depot, Lowe's, and Target. Consumers could browse the aisles and find a variety of products such as gardening products (like stepping stones or lawn chairs made from recycled plastic), the worm poop fertilizers (for roses, African violets, etc.), and office supplies (file trays, pencil holders, etc.) made from upcycled and recycled products and packaging collected through its recycling programs. The back-to-school season was a particularly busy time of year for TerraCycle. Parents and their kids could find a variety of backpacks, tote bags, duffle bags, umbrellas, and pencil cases for sale (see Photo 12.9 for an example). Thus, TerraCycle was able to help consumers meet their own sustainability goals and make a social statement with a wide variety of upcycled and recycled products.

The second way in which TerraCycle engaged its customers was by working closely with several consumer packaged goods companies like Unilever and Procter & Gamble to make their operations more sustainable and thus demonstrate their environmental commitment to their own customers. These companies were starting to feel pressure from their own consumers, who wanted them to offer more sustainable choices. In response, these companies partnered with TerraCycle to help them make their supply chain and products more

● **Photo 12.9** *Tote bag made from a US Mail pouch*

● **Photo 12.10** *Playground made from 100 percent recycled toothbrushes, toothpaste tubes, and floss containers*

green. One example is Procter & Gamble's shampoo product, Head & Shoulders. TerraCycle worked with the company to produce the first fully recyclable shampoo bottle made with 25 percent beach plastic, plastic that has been recovered from the shores of rivers and oceans (Szaky 2017). The bottle was introduced to consumers in the summer of 2017 through the retailer Carrefour in France on World Oceans Day. Although the bottle was more expensive to produce than the bottle made from traditional plastic, production specialists at Procter & Gamble expected the prices to drop once production expanded (Sherman and Young 2017).

The third and main way in which TerraCycle engaged consumers was through its recycling collection programs. By 2019, close to 203 million individuals in twenty-one countries collected a variety of products in their own communities ("TerraCycle's Global Impact" 2019). Schools, organizations, businesses, and individuals simply registered online to start collecting whatever items they wanted. For example, a school group may want to collect dried-up pens and whiteboard markers; a soccer club may want to collect discarded juice pouches. Once the group had a large enough pile of items, the collection leader (the teacher or coach) simply went online, downloaded a postage-paid sticker, packaged up a box, and shipped it to TerraCycle headquarters in Trenton, New Jersey. In return for their efforts, collectors received a check in the mail amounting to a few cents per item. Many groups relied on these

checks as a significant part of their annual fundraising efforts (Phillips and Phillips 2016). In 2018, TerraCycle collaborated with Colgate to encourage schools to send in their old toothpaste tubes, floss containers, toothbrushes, and packaging—the school that sent in the most material would win a new playground, which would be constructed with these recycled materials (see Photo 12.10). By 2019, TerraCycle and its partners had donated close to $45 million dollars to schools and charities ("TerraCycle's Global Impact" 2019).

By 2017, TerraCycle was making $24 million in revenue per year, with just under $1 million in profits (Sherman and Young 2017). TerraCycle seemed to be at the nexus of three converging trends in the marketplace: the desire of consumers to be more green, the desire of consumers to be engaged in the process of sustainability, and the desire of consumer packaged goods companies to respond to the sustainability needs of their own consumers. By finding ways for consumers to be engaged in the process of sustainability, TerraCycle created a group of consumers who not only talked about how important sustainability was to them, but also demonstrated their passion by becoming actively engaged in the process.

QUESTIONS

1. This case study focuses on how one small company was able to actively engage customers in the process of sustainability. What are some benefits to encouraging consumer engagement?

2. What do we mean when we say that businesses are faced with a "false choice" when they contemplate doing what is right by the environment versus doing what is right economically? In what way does the concept of shared value shed some light on this choice?

3. Over the next few years, TerraCycle hopes to grow and sell more products. Isn't this goal in direct conflict with the concepts of mindful consumption, sustainable consumption, and voluntary simplicity? Discuss.

Sources: Burlingham (2006); Phillips and Phillips (2016); Sherman and Young (2017); Szaky (2017); "TerraCycle's Global Impact" (2019).

REFERENCES

Abel, G. M., and E. W. Plumridge. 2004. "Network 'Norms' or 'Styles' of 'Drunken Deportment'?" *Health Education Research Theory and Practice* 19 (5): 492–500.

"Amish in America." 2012. Public Broadcasting Service. Accessed February 21, 2019. https://www.pbs.org/wgbh/americanexperience/features/amish-in-america/.

Barkham, P. 2012. "Why Is Cheese the Most Shoplifted Food Item in the World?" *Guardian*, January 10, 2012. http://www.guardian.co.uk/lifeandstyle/shortcuts/2012/jan/10/cheese-most-shoplifted-food-item.

Basurto, X., and E. Ostrom. 2009. "Beyond the Tragedy of the Commons." *Economics and Policy of Energy and the Environment* 52 (1): 35–60.

Black, I. R., and H. Cherrier. 2010. "Anti-consumption as Part of Living a Sustainable Lifestyle: Daily Practices, Contextual Motivations and Subjective Values." *Journal of Consumer Behavior* 9 (6): 437–53.

Bond, D. 2017. "VW Joins List of Corporate Misfires with Poor Handling of Crisis." *Financial Times*, January 12, 2017. https://www.ft.com/content/3185935e-d8be-11e6-944b-e7eb37a6aa8e.

Burch, M. A. 2012. "Educating for Simple Living." Simplicity Institute. Accessed June 8, 2013. http://simplicitycollective.com/wp-content/uploads/2012/08/EducatingforSimpleLivingSimplicityInstitute1.pdf.

Burlingham, B. 2016. "The Coolest Little Start-Up in America." Inc. July 1, 2016. https://www.inc.com/magazine/20060701/coolest-startup.html.

Cone Communications. 2017. *2017 Cone Communications CSR Study.* Boston: Cone Communications.

Connolly, K. 2018. "VW Suspends Media Chief Amid Scandal over Fume Tests on Monkeys." *Guardian*, January 30, 2018. https://www.theguardian.com/business/2018/jan/30/vw-suspends-media-chief-monkey-exhaust-tests-diesel-emissions.

Cooksey-Stowers, K., M. B. Schwartz, and K. D. Brownell. 2017. "Food Swamps Predict Obesity Rates Better Than Food Deserts in the United States." *International Journal of Environmental Research and Public Health* 14 (11): 1366–86.

Cremer, A. 2018. "VW Pledges Rules to Ensure Moral and Ethical Behavior after Latest Reputational Damage." *Reuters*, Business News, February 23, 2018. https://www.reuters.com/article/us-volkswagen-emissions-compliance/vw-pledges-rules-to-ensure-moral-and-ethical-behavior-after-latest-reputational-damage-idUSKCN1G72KJ.

Dann, S., and S. Dann. 2016. "Exploring Catholic Social Teaching in a Social Marketing Context." *Journal of Macromarketing* 36 (4): 412–24.

Daunt, K. L., and L. C. Harris. 2012. "Exploring the Forms of Dysfunctional Customer Behavior: A Study of Differences in Servicescape and Customer Disaffection with Service." *Journal of Marketing Management* 28 (1/2): 129–53.

Davis, B., J. L. Ozanne, and R. P. Hill. 2016. "The Transformative Consumer Research Movement." *Journal of Public Policy & Marketing* 35 (2): 159–69.

DeAngelis, T. 2004. "Consumerism and Its Discontents." *Monitor on Psychology* 35 (6): 52.

"Definitions of Marketing." 2019. American Marketing Association. Accessed August 20, 2019. https://www.ama.org/the-definition-of-marketing/.

De Freytas-Tamura, K. 2018. "Plastics Pile Up as China Refuses to Take the West's Recycling." *New York Times*, January 11, 2018. https://www.nytimes.com/2018/01/11/world/china-recyclables-ban.html.

Dittmar, H. 2005. "Compulsive Buying—A Growing Concern? An Examination of Gender, Age, and Endorsement of Materialistic Values as Predictors." *British Journal of Psychology* 96 (4): 467–91.

Drollette, D. 2019. "Hard Numbers Help Visualize Climate Change. And It's Not Pretty." *Bulletin of the Atomic Scientist*, February 8, 2019. https://thebulletin.org/2019/02/hard-numbers-help-visualize-climate-change-and-its-not-pretty/.

Elhence, P. 2017. "7 of the World's Most Expensive Spices." *Luxury Insider*, May 19, 2017. http://www.luxury-insider.com/dining/guide-most-expensive-spices.

Elliott, R., S. Eccles, and K. Gournay. 1996. "Revenge, Existential Choice, and Addictive Consumption." *Psychology & Marketing* 13 (8): 753–68.

"Environmental Leadership." 2019. LEGO Corporation. Accessed August 20, 2019. https://www.lego.com/en-us/aboutus/responsibility/environmental-leadership.

"Free Hugs Campaign—Ken Nwadike, Jr. Bio." 2019. Free Hugs Project. Accessed August 20, 2019. https://freehugsproject.com/about-free-hugs-campaign/.

Fremeaux, S., and M. Grant. 2017. "The Common Good of the Firm and Human Management: Conscious Capitalism and Economy of Communion." *Journal of Business Ethics* 145 (4): 701–9.

Fullerton, R. A., and G. Punj. 1997. "What Is Consumer Misbehavior?" *Advances in Consumer Research* 24:336–39.

Fullerton, R. A., and G. Punj. 2004. "Repercussions of Promoting an Ideology of Consumption: Consumer Misbehavior." *Journal of Business Research* 57 (11): 1239–49.

Griffin, C., A. Bengry-Howell, C. Hackley, W. Mistral, and I. Szmigin. 2009. "'Every Time I Do It I Absolutely Annihilate Myself': Loss of (Self-)Consciousness and Loss of Memory in Young People's Drinking Narratives." *Sociology* 43 (3): 457–76.

Hajer, M., and V. Wytske. 2018. "Imagining the Post-fossil City: Why Is It So Difficult to Think of New Possible Worlds?" *Territory, Politics, Governance* 7 (2): 122–34. https://doi.org/10.1080/21622671.2018.1510339.

Hales, C. M., M. D. Carroll, C. D. Fryar, and C. L. Ogden. 2017. *Prevalence of Obesity among Adults and Youth: United States, 2015–2016. NCHS Data Brief, No. 288.* Washington, DC: US Department of Health and Human Services, *Centers for Disease Control and Prevention, National Center for Health Statistics.*

Harris, E. A. 2012. "An Environmental Crusader's Newest Goal: Congress." *The New York Times*, May 15, 2012, A25.

Harris, L. C., and K. L. Reynolds. 2003. "The Consequences of Dysfunctional Customer Behavior." *Journal of Service Research* 6 (2): 144–61.

Huneke, M. E. 2005. "The Face of the Un-consumer: An Empirical Examination of the Practice of Voluntary Simplicity in the United States." *Psychology & Marketing* 22 (7): 527–50.

Intergovernmental Panel on Climate Change. 2018. *Summary for Policymakers of IPCC Special Report on Global Warming of 1.5°C Approved by Governments.* Geneva: Intergovernmental Panel on Climate Change.

Jabr, F. 2013. "How the Brain Gets Addicted to Gambling." *Scientific American*, November 1, 2013. https://www.scientificamerican.com/article/how-the-brain-gets-addicted-to-gambling/.

Koran, L. M., R. J. Faber, E. Aboujaoude, M. D. Large, and R. T. Serpe. 2006. "Estimated Prevalence of Compulsive Buying Behavior in the United States." *American Journal of Psychiatry* 163:1806–12.

Kraybill, D. B. 2014. "Opting Out: How the Amish Have Survived in America." *Commonweal*, March 7, 2014, 13–15.

Kurtz, J., and T. Amatruda. 2016. "Activist Hands out 'Free Hugs' amid Violent Protests in Charlotte." CNN. September 23, 2016. https://www.cnn.com/2016/09/22/us/ken-nwadike-free-hugs-poppy-harlow-cnn-newsroom/index.html.

"LEGO Group Ranked Number 1 on 2017 Global CSR RepTrak 100." 2017. LEGO Corporation. Press release. September 14, 2017. https://www.lego.com/en-sg/aboutus/news-room/2017/september/lego-group-csr-reptrak100.

Lim, M. 2016. "Less Is More as Japan Minimalist Movement Grows." *Reuters*, Lifestyle Section, June 19, 2016. https://www.reuters.com/article/us-japan-minimalism/less-is-more-as-japanese-minimalist-movement-grows-idUSKCN0Z50VP.

Lind, P. K. 2016. "Madagascar's 152 Million Pound Vanilla Industry Soured by Child Labor and Poverty." *Guardian*, December 8, 2016. https://www.theguardian.com/global-development/2016/dec/08/madagascar-152m-vanilla-industry-soured-child-labour-poverty.

Martin, I. M., M. A. Kamins, D. M. Pirouz, S. W. Davis, K. L. Haws, A. M. Mirabito, S. Mukherjee, J. M. Rapp, and A. Grover. 2013. "On the Road to Addiction: The Facilitative and Preventive Roles of Marketing Cues." *Journal of Business Research* 66 (8): 1219–26.

Matussek, K., and E. Behrmann. 2018. "VW Can't Escape the Diesel Scandal Fallout." *Bloomberg Business*, September 12, 2018. https://www.bloomberg.com/news/articles/2018-09-12/vw-can-t-escape-the-diesel-scandal-fallout.

Mazzoni, M. 2017. "These Consumer Engagement Campaigns Prove Companies Still Care." Triple Pundit. March 31, 2017. http://www.triplepundit.com/2017/03/consumer-engagement-2017/.

McCarthy, K., and J. Jacobo. 2018. "Man Arrested after Going Head-to-Head with Bison at Yellowstone National." ABC News. August 3, 2018. https://abcnews.go.com/GMA/Living/man-head-head-bison-yellowstone-prompting-warnings-national/story?id=57010279.

"McCormick—A Global Leader in Flavor." 2019. McCormick. Accessed August 20, 2019. https://ir.mccormick.com/.

Measham, F. 2002. "'Doing Gender'—'Doing Drugs': Conceptualising the Gendering of Drugs Cultures." *Contemporary Drug Problems* 29 (2): 335–73.

Mintel. 2015. *The Ethical Consumer—US—July 2015*. Mintel Group. July 2015.

Moschis, G. P., and D. Cox. 1989. "Deviant Consumer Behavior." *Advances in Consumer Research* 16 (1): 732–37.

Muniz, K. 2014. "20 Ways Americans Are Blowing Their Money." *USA Today*, March 24, 2014. https://www.usatoday.com/story/money/personalfinance/2014/03/24/20-ways-we-blow-our-money/6826633/.

Murphy, P. E., and J. F. Sherry Jr. 2014. *Marketing and the Common Good: Essays from Notre Dame on Societal Impact*. Abingdon, Oxon, Canada: Routledge.

National Aeronautics and Space Administration. 2019. "The Climate Time Machine." Accessed February 20, 2019. https://climate.nasa.gov/interactives/climate-time-machine.

O'Guinn, T. C., and R. J. Faber. 1989. "Compulsive Buying: A Phenomenological Exploration." *Journal of Consumer Research* 16 (2): 147–57.

Ostrom, E. 1999. "Coping with Tragedies of the Commons." *Annual Review of Political Science* 2 (1): 493–535.

Phillips, D. M., and J. K. Phillips. 2016. "Sustainable Growth at TerraCycle: Should Manufacturing Be Moved?" Case #9B16A010. London, Ontario, Canada: Ivey.

Pontrefract, D. 2017. "Stop Confusing CSR with Purpose." *Forbes*, November 18, 2017. https://www.forbes.com/sites/danpontefract/2017/11/18/stop-confusing-csr-with-purpose/#3b3e78da3190.

Porter, M. E., and M. R. Kramer. 2011. "Creating Shared Value." *Harvard Business Review* January–February:62–77.

"The Power of Partnership—NCBA CLUSA and McCormick Work to Support Vanilla Farmers." 2018. McCormick Spice. Video production. Accessed July 30, 2018. https://www.youtube.com/watch?v=TnhFoqrHfRO.

Rainey, C., and A. Hobbs. 2013. "Been Caught Stealing." *New York Magazine*, December 6, 2013. http://nymag.com/news/intelligencer/topic/shoplifting-2013-12/.

Reich, R. 2018. *The Common Good*. New York: Knopf.

Reilly, K. 2017. "Shoplifting and Other Fraud Cost Retailers Nearly $50 Billion Last Year." *Money*, June 22, 2017. https://money.com/shoplifting-fraud-retail-survey/.

Richins, M., and L. N. Chaplin. 2015. "Material Parenting; How the Use of Goods in Parenting Fosters Materialism in the Next Generation." *Journal of Consumer Research* 41 (6): 1333–57.

Richins, M. L., and S. Dawson. 1992. "A Consumer Values Orientation for Materialism and Its Measurement: Scale Development and Validation." *Journal of Consumer Research* 19 (3): 303–16.

Rose, P., and D. J. Segrist. 2012. "Difficulty Identifying Feelings, Distress Tolerance and Compulsive Buying: Analyzing the Associations to Inform Therapeutic Strategies." *International Journal of Mental Health and Addiction* 10:927–35.

Sarra, J., and K. Berman. 2017. "Ubuntu as a Tool for Resilience: Arts, Microbusiness, and Social Justice in South Africa." *Conflict Resolution Quarterly* 34 (4): 455–90.

Scott, A. O. 2009. "Portrait of a Marriage: Eco-geeks Unplugged." *New York Times*, September 11, 2009, C8.

Seligman, M. E. P., and J. Tierney. 2017. "We Aren't Built to Live in the Moment." *New York Times*, May 19, 2017. https://www.nytimes.com/2017/05/19/opinion/sunday/why-the-future-is-always-on-your-mind.html.

Shaw, D., and T. Newholm. 2002. "Voluntary Simplicity and the Ethics of Consumption." *Psychology & Marketing* 19 (2): 167–85.

Shepard, W. 2016. "Slum Tourism: How It Began, the Impact It Has, and Why

It Became So Popular." *Forbes*, July 16, 2016. https://www.forbes.com/sites/wadeshepard/2016/07/16/slum-tourism-how-it-began-the-impact-it-has-and-why-its-become-so-popular/.

Sherman, S., and E. Young. 2017. "This Guy Makes Money off Your Cigarette Butts and Flip-Flops." *Bloomberg*, November 27, 2017. https://www.bloomberg.com/news/features/2017-11-27/terracycle-makes-money-off-your-recycled-cigarette-butts-and-flip-flops.

Simon, B. 2018. Personal interview, July 27, 2018.

About Slow Food USA. 2018. Accessed August 7, 2018. https://slowfoodusa.org/about/

Smith, L., and D. Foxcroft. 2009. "Drinking in the UK: An Exploration of Trends." Joseph Rowntree Foundation Report. May 6, 2009. http://www.jrf.org.uk/publications/drinking-in-the-uk.

Stewart, D. W. 2015. "Why Marketers Should Study Public Policy." *Journal of Public Policy & Marketing* 34 (1): 1–3.

Sustainable Lifestyles Frontier Group. 2015. *Big Brands, Big Impact: A Marketer's Guide to Behavior Change.* New York: Futerra and Business for Social Responsibility.

Szaky, T. 2017. "We Helped Create the World's First Recyclable Shampoo Bottle Made with Beach Plastic—Here's Why." Weforum. January 27, 2017. https://www.weforum.org/agenda/2017/01/creating-the-world-s-first-recyclable-shampoo-bottle-made-with-beach-plastic/.

Szmigin, I., C. Griffin, C. Hackley, A. Bengry-Howell, L. Weale, and C. Hackley. 2008. "Reframing 'Binge Drinking' as Calculated Hedonism, Empirical Evidence from the UK." *International Journal of Drug Policy* 19 (5): 359–66.

"TerraCycle's Global Impact." 2019. TerraCycle. Accessed August 20, 2019. https://www.terracycle.com/en-US/.

Treuer, G. A. 2018. "The Psychology of Miami's Struggle to Adapt to Sea-Level Rise." *Bulletin of the Atomic Scientists* 74 (3): 155–59.

Unilever. 2017. "Report Shows a Third of Consumers Prefer Sustainable Brands." Press release, May 1, 2017. https://www.unilever.com/news/press-releases/2017/report-shows-a-third-of-consumers-prefer-sustainable-brands.html.

"Utilitarianism." 2017. McCombs School of Business. Accessed July 13, 2018.

https://ethicsunwrapped.utexas.edu/glossary/utilitarianism.

"Vanilla: The Journey from Source to Table." 2014. McCormick Spice. Video production. December 11, 2014. https://www.youtube.com/watch?v=VQl-oHeII6w.

Watts, J. 2018. "Madagascar's Vanilla Wars: Prized Spice Drives Death and Deforestation." *Guardian*, March 31, 2018. https://www.theguardian.com/environment/2018/mar/31/madagascars-vanilla-wars-prized-spice-drives-death-and-deforestation.

Wilkie, W. L., and E. S. Moore. 1999. "Marketing's Contributions to Society." *Journal of Marketing* 63 (4): 198–218.

Wilkie, W. L., and E. S. Moore. 2012. "Expanding Our Understanding of Marketing in Society." *Journal of the Academy of Marketing Science* 40 (1): 53–73.

World Health Organization. 2014. *Global Status Report on Alcohol and Health, 2014.* Geneva: World Health Organization.

World Health Organization. 2018. "Obesity and Overweight." Fact Sheet, February 16, 2018. https://www.who.int/en/news-room/fact-sheets/detail/obesity-and-overweight.

13 What's Trending in Consumer Behavior

⊙ Introduction

Researchers and marketers can examine consumer behavior from a variety of perspectives, from those that are very socially and culturally oriented to those that are based on cognitive, rational models. What each perspective has in common, however, is that they all rest on the solid foundation of established research in fields such as psychology, economics, sociology, political science, ethics, and anthropology. It is on this strong foundation of research theories and models that we were able to build a variety of insights—from the boardroom, from academia, and from the field—to demonstrate the importance and complexity of consumption in the modern world. With our wide variety of examples of organizations and consumption contexts, we have reinforced this complexity. Indeed, it should be quite clear that consumer behavior is a dynamic, exciting, and rewarding field of study.

In this second chapter in the "Where Do We Go from Here?" section of the textbook, we explore three key areas of significant change and complexity. The first is the domain of advancements in consumer research that allow researchers to have more accurate and timely assessments of what is happening in the hearts and minds of consumers. Here, in an effort to improve consumer well-being, we also examine consumer behavior through the lens of transformative consumer research. Remember, one of the main objectives of consumer research is to predict what consumers will do, so better research means better predictions. The second trend concerns the consumer and provides an in-depth discussion about the empowered consumer, the sharing economy, the frugal consumer, concerns about privacy, the sustainable consumer, and authentic consumption experiences. The last trend is in the domain of technology. This theme of technology is visited repeatedly throughout the chapter, and we examine it specifically in terms of the consumer–technology interface and thus discuss how consumers negotiate their consumption roles with the opportunities and challenges that technology provides. Three issues—consumer research trends, consumer trends, and technological trends—all provide fertile ground for new insights as we seek to understand what is in store for the consumer of the future.

LEARNING OBJECTIVES

After reading this chapter you will be able to:

1. Describe the **key trends in consumer research** that help us better understand what is going on in the hearts and minds of consumers.

2. Discuss the six key **consumer trends** that have significantly altered the lives of consumers in modern society.

3. Identify and describe several **technological trends** and their relevance for consumer behavior.

◉ Trends in Consumer Research

In their quest to better understand what is going on in the hearts and minds of consumers, researchers seek new methods and technologies. We highlight three new advancements in consumer research that have spurred considerable interest from researchers: the use of new technologies, continuous data collection, and an expansion of research focus.

Use of new technologies

In traditional consumer research methodologies, consumers are asked questions about their beliefs, emotions, and preferences. Unfortunately, this methodological setup is fraught with problems. We have seen earlier in this text that consumers often make decisions that are quick and convenient, rather than rational. In some cases, consumers themselves may not know why they chose a particular product or brand. One problem with asking direct questions is that consumers often lack the ability to be introspective enough to describe why they behave in a certain way. Further, there is often no connection between consumer attitudes and behaviors. Another problem is that respondents often give answers that reflect favorably on themselves. For example, there are far more consumers who report that they have healthy eating habits than there are consumers who *actually* have healthy eating habits. Another drawback to direct questioning is that, in an attempt to be helpful, respondents often try to give responses that they think the researcher wants to hear. Still another problem is that consumers are often asked to describe events from the past, such as consumption experiences or advertisements they have seen. As we learned in our discussion of memory, consumers often have difficulty recalling previous behaviors, thoughts, experiences, and emotions (Bagozzi 1991).

Neuromarketing is a branch of research that uses scientific methods involving the functioning of the brain to understand and predict consumer behavior (Lee, Broderick, and Chamberlain 2007). Neuromarketing utilizes brain-imaging technology such as electroencephalography (EEG) and functional magnetic resonance imaging to identify changes in blood flow and electrical activity in different parts of the brain (we introduced these research techniques in Insights from the Boardroom 5). Neuromarketing helps researchers examine brain activity, which helps them draw conclusions about memory, emotions, and decision-making. All of this occurs without the active participation of the consumer (Morin 2011). Importantly, neuroimaging reveals information about the decisions the brain is making before they are filtered through any social, cultural, or other filters.

Electroencephalographic research methods start with the placement of numerous electrodes on a person's scalp. An EEG provides real-time information about electrical activity, not blood flow in the brain. EEGs have been applied in numerous research studies over the years to provide greater insight into consumer brain functioning. One of the more interesting studies came out of Australia. Public health officials and nonprofit organizations there were

Neuromarketing is a branch of research that uses scientific methods involving the functioning of the brain to understand and predict consumer behavior.

concerned about how to effectively spend public money on a variety of public service announcements and appeals. With limited tax dollars and donations to spend, these groups wanted to be sure they created advertising appeals that resulted in the biggest changes in behavior and increases in donations. So, the researchers examined a variety of appeals from some of the most well-known nonprofits, including UNICEF, the United Nations, and the Clinton Foundation, to help them determine which type of appeal was most effective. Research participants watched a series of ads and filled out a survey about their liking for the ads. Although the initial survey results identified several ads that were equally effective, the EEG identified one that was clearly superior: ManUp, which was designed to combat the problem of male suicide (see https://www.youtube.com/results?search_query=man+up+campaign+austra lia). It had a series of close-up shots of a baby, boys, and men with sad music and a voice-over asking, "Why do we tell boys to stop crying, to harden up, to grow a pair? Well f*ck that. If you feel down, speak up. Because silence can kill." It used a strong emotional appeal and was action oriented, asking viewers to speak up and share their pain. This insight was invaluable in helping to craft additional appeals throughout Australia (Harris, Ciorciari, and Gountas 2019) (see Photo 13.1).

A complex relationship exists between the brain and our social environment, cultural context, and preferences—neuromarketing can help researchers understand these relationships. Consider what happened during the infamous Pepsi Challenge of 1975. At that time, Pepsi launched a blind taste test in shopping malls around the United States as part of a promotional campaign directly attacking its chief competitor, Coca-Cola. Shoppers were given two unmarked cups, one containing Pepsi and the other containing Coca-Cola. They were invited to taste both and select the one they preferred. Then, the identity of the brands was revealed to the participants. The results showed a strong preference for the taste of Pepsi (McClure et al. 2004). In retrospect, one of the problems with the Pepsi Challenge was that while it may have tested consumers' *taste* preference, it did not test their *brand* preference. In a follow-up experiment using neuromarketing methods, participants' brains were scanned to reveal neural responses to the taste of the drinks and to the brand images. When there was no brand information, that is, the participants did not know whether they were drinking Pepsi or Coke, there was little difference in their neural responses. However, when those who described themselves as preferring Coke were told that the drink they were tasting

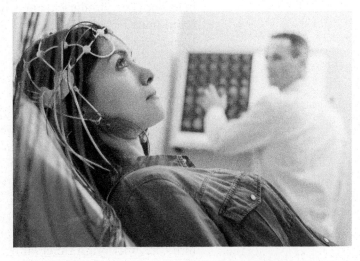

● **Photo 13.1** *Young woman getting ready to start a neuroimaging research study*

was Coke, there was significant activity in key areas of the brain (McClure et al. 2004). A possible explanation is that the brand effectively has a life of its own in the minds of consumers. Thus, an important insight is that "preference" is built on much more than taste (Ariely and Berns 2010).

Research like this indicates that it is virtually impossible to find a purely objective response to brands. Consumers do not experience a brand purely in terms of its physical characteristics because their brains also bring up memories associated with the consumption experience, including associated beliefs, imagery, and emotions. For example, what impact would knowledge of the price of a product have on evaluations of that product? Is there really something to that old saying, you get what you pay for? In one study, neural responses were measured when research participants sipped wine. When participants were told that the wine was expensive, certain parts of the brain became activated; when they were told the wine was inexpensive, those same parts of the brain were not activated. In this study, there was a strong correlation between their neural responses and their self-reported preferences. In the end, participants preferred the "expensive" wine even though it was actually the same as the "inexpensive" one (Plassmann et al. 2008) (see Photo 13.2).

Marketers have found that neuromarketing is a useful tool for accessing a consumer's hidden desires and preferences. For example, marketers might show participants pictures of new product designs or advertising executions and then measure the brain activity of the participants to see which is preferred. Various foods have been tested using functional magnetic resonance

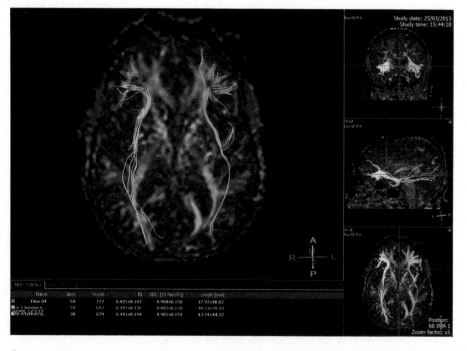

● **Photo 13.2** *Neuroimaging can help researchers understand consumer preferences*

INSIGHTS FROM ACADEMIA 13.1

So, you're thinking about a Pepsi? Yeah, we already knew that.

Just as people have personalities, brands have personalities, too, which can fall along a variety of dimensions: excitement, competence, sincerity, ruggedness, and sophistication. Google, for example, is high in excitement; Campbell's is high in sincerity; and Harley–Davidson is high in ruggedness. Because consumers use these dimensions to make assessments about people, it is easy for them to make assessments about brands using these same dimensions. Researchers can now look at brain scans and determine some very interesting information about these assessments of brand personalities. First, researchers must locate the *what*

of brain activity—how much neural activity is taking place. Second, they need to assess the *where*—exactly where in the brain the activity is taking place. The *what* and *where* correspond to personality traits. Therefore, by looking at a consumer's brain scan to see what and where activity is taking place, marketers can predict which brands consumers are thinking about.

Chen, Y., L. D. Nelson, and M. Hsu. 2015. "From 'Where' to 'What': Distributed Representations of Brand Associations in the Human Brain." Journal of Marketing Research *52 (4): 453–66.*

imaging technology, and different perceptions of taste, smell, texture, and even sound have been mapped onto areas of the brain to identify their contribution to the overall experience (see Small et al. 2001). Product development teams use insights from these neuromarketing techniques to design more appealing food products. However, a great deal of caution must be used here, too—some unscrupulous companies could use data from neuromarketing to create foods that are so carefully linked to neural responses that individuals overeat (Ariely and Berns 2010). Although researchers have not yet been able to find a "buy button" in a consumer's brain, neuromarketing has significant promise as a useful tool to assist marketers in product design, the development of advertising, brand image, pricing, and store layout (Hubert and Kenning 2008) (see Insights from Academia 13.1).

Another innovation in consumer research is **automated text analysis**, the systematic interpretation of large amounts of textual data into meaningful patterns and themes. Because of the vast amounts of consumer comments, blogs, feedback, message boards, and social networks, this technology has allowed marketers to free themselves from the burdensome task of reading and responding to every piece of text that is uploaded or submitted. Automated text analysis uses complex grammatical and linguistic formulas to pull meaning from what is written. Importantly, automated text analysis can identify patterns and themes that might not be obvious to the human reader. Take the example of product reviews on Amazon.com. Sometimes, a single product can have hundreds of reviews and a marketer may be left somewhat bewildered by comments that are too vague, seem to contradict one another, or otherwise provide little direction to the marketer as to why the product may be underperforming. Automated text analysis, however, relies on linguistic structure and theory to provide marketers

Automated text analysis is the systematic interpretation of large amounts of textual data into meaningful patterns and themes.

Search engine optimization is a tool used by consumer researchers that focuses on what consumers do when they conduct a search on Google, for example. It utilizes key words, phrases, links, apps, etc., to deliver higher rankings on the search engine results page.

with insights about attention, decision-making, attitude formation, cultural characteristics, and social interactions (Humphreys and Wang 2018).

Search engine optimization is another tool that consumer researchers use; it focuses on what consumers do when they conduct a search on Google, for example. To increase their place in the rankings of online search results, marketers will insert key words, phrases, and links so that their website rises to the top of the list when an individual conducts a search. The idea is that the best way to find new customers is to make sure they can find you. Higher rankings on a Google results page can ensure that. According to one estimate, 92 percent of people will not go beyond the first page of results. In addition, it is important to be near the top of the results; the first five results receive 68 percent of clicks, while the remaining five results on the page get a mere 4 percent of clicks (Shelton 2017). How do marketers know which words, phrases, and links to insert on their websites so that they will result in the highest rankings? Marketers examine a variety of tools, such as Google Analytics and Google AdWords, to find clues about what consumers are thinking when they're conducting a search. Search engine optimization has evolved somewhat over the years, in part because so many searches are now happening with mobile devices. Search engine optimization algorithms can incorporate a company's apps, regular updates and feeds, videos, and up-to-the minute product and pricing information. Further, some app developers have allowed Google access to the inner workings of the app so that Google can "find them" more easily during searches (Barr 2016) (see Insights from the Boardroom 13).

Continuous data collection

Your phone, smart TV, and computer are tracking you! Another trend in consumer research is the constant collection and integration of data by marketers. New technology that is supposed to make our lives easier and more convenient is also making it easier for marketers to track our daily habits. Indeed, every time a consumer clicks on an ad, changes a channel, visits a store, or buys a product, those behaviors are being recorded. The top five TV brands that are sold in the United States—Samsung, LG, Sony, Vizio, and any TCL brand running the Roku platform—all have built-in technology that allows tracking of preferences and viewing habits (Graham 2018). This technology sends back minute-by-minute reports on a consumer's viewing habits and preferences. Manufacturers of these TVs say that this collection of data allows them to be more precise in their programming recommendations and advertising. Thus, you are more likely to be offered recommendations for programs and products that you already like. Data collection is facilitated by GPS technology, voice recognition, and facial recognition programs. All this technology is supported by powerful computing software that can integrate the data as well as crunch millions of pieces of data in seconds (Graham 2018).

GPS technology not only helps wayward travelers get directions, but also can track where consumers are and therefore allow marketers to gather substantial data about a consumer's behaviors. Not only can marketers use these data to understand where consumers go and when, but also they can combine the data with demographic information that consumers provide to them to predict when consumers of different ages, ethnicities, or lifestyles visit different shops, restaurants, or other attractions. Indeed, an important advancement in data collection is that data from many sources can be combined and integrated. For example, marketers can use these data to offer carefully targeted pricing discounts and other incentives, such as sending a coupon to consumers who are within a certain proximity to encourage more visits during low-traffic hours. There are countless opportunities for marketers. Take another example of a chore that few consumers enjoy: bringing the car in for an oil change. A marketer at a "quick lube" garage could find out, for example, that 40 percent of their consumers visit the grocery store on a Friday evening after work. A particularly savvy marketer could offer special discounts to those consumers for Friday night oil changes: "Get your oil changed while you're shopping!" This offer could be backed up by a convenient shuttle service between the garage and the grocery store. An offer like this solves an important problem for consumers with both convenience and a price discount.

Voice recognition software is vital to a variety of data collection methods and is especially relevant with artificial intelligence (AI)–enabled home assistant devices. Home assistants like Alexa and Siri have introduced profound changes in American life. No longer do we need to run downstairs to check if the front door is locked before bed. Instead, we just need to say, "Alexa, lock the doors." No more do you have to remember the name of that movie your friend told you was funny; just ask, "Siri, what was the name of Bradley Cooper's last movie?" and you will get the answer. As voice command and AI home assistants have started to gain a real foothold on American life, experts say that the ubiquitous TV remote is on its way out. Once again, as technology allows for efficiency in our lives, the technology also allows marketers to collect data on us (Kitchen 2018). It would not be out of the question for you to be talking at home about how you would love some pizza for dinner, only to have Alexa pick up the conversation and relay that data to Domino's. In response, your smart TV might then air an ad for Domino's and your phone could get pinged with a coupon.

Facial recognition software is another technology that allows for vast amounts of consumer data to be collected and integrated with other data. Facial recognition is now being used to unlock phones and other devices. It is also being utilized by retail stores. Cameras in the parking lots capture license plate numbers and cameras in the stores themselves capture a person's face, as well as information about that person's gender, age, and race. A consumer's movements throughout the store are also tracked, such that a marketer will know that you visit the store on average six times per month and you spend on average of ten minutes in the health and wellness aisle before heading to the junk food aisle. These data can be combined with credit card information, which would allow the retailer to know what your normal basket of purchases looks like and provide incentives to encourage you to try new brands or visit the store more frequently (Graham 2018).

Baking "optimization" into a customer's search experience

● *Ryan Wall*

Talking to Ryan Wall about search engine market research and search experience optimization is almost like attempting to take a deep, cleansing breath of fresh air when your face is being blasted by the force of a jet engine taking off. Wall delivers a rapid-fire explanation of the importance of search as a consumer research tool for understanding consumer need states. He is passionate about what he does, and by the time he is done with his explanation, you are too. Ryan Wall is the chief strategy officer for Idea Evolver, a fast-growing tech company that helps companies optimize a customer's search experience.

Idea Evolver works with some of the most well-known brands in the United States to help brand managers gain a better understanding of their customers and understand how best to intercept them online across devices and offline. By examining natural language searches and results, Idea Evolver develops a set of key insights into how consumers search for products and services, the attributes they are looking for, and how they view a brand's reputation. According to Wall, "We help companies better understand their customers so that they can better design their products,

content strategies, and messaging." The important thing is that "it's not about looking at the optimization after the fact, it's about baking optimization into it from the beginning" (Wall 2017).

For example, Idea Evolver worked on one project for Oikos Greek yogurt. Their spokesperson was John Stamos and, for the most part, everything was going well, with Oikos having about 50 percent of the market share (Watrous 2016). However, according to Wall (2017), "Once we looked at the searches that customers were doing regarding Greek yogurt, we found that John Stamos was really not that great of a fit. Sure, he was a good-looking Greek guy, but that was it. There was nothing else resonating with the core audience that was really looking for this product." Specifically, Wall and his team found that consumers were searching for protein, nutrition, and benefits information. These insights reinforced the thinking of the management team to refocus their efforts and sign a new spokesperson, Cam Newton, who at the time was the quarterback for the Carolina Panthers. Newton helped launch the new Oikos Triple Zero yogurt—zero added sugar, zero artificial sweeteners, and zero fat. In addition, Oikos strongly promoted the fact that the product had fifteen grams of protein (which was much more than regular yogurt, but about the same as other brands of Greek yogurt). Unlike other yogurts, which were positioned to female audiences as a weight-loss tool or a meal substitute, the Oikos Triple Zero yogurt was promoted primarily to men as a "protein snack" and is now the official yogurt of the NFL. The brand was hailed by the food industry as being the number three most successful new food product launch of 2015, making $108 million in a very competitive market (BNP Media 2016). Decision-makers at Oikos were thrilled with the results. Triple Zero "has been growing very fast and recapturing or reigniting growth," said company president Emmanuel Faber (Watrous 2016).

Idea Evolver completed another project recently with Sabra, the company that makes hummus. Wall explained, "We found that consumers were looking for a dessert hummus as well as for different flavors that were more popular than the ones on the shelf." Once these insights were presented to the brand management team at Sabra, "they were very interested" (Wall 2017). Indeed, a quick search online shows a surprising variety of recipes for desserts using hummus as well as many sweet, dessert-flavored hummus recipes. Sabra's product development team is currently investigating a variety of new flavors.

Public Squash, a nonprofit that Wall and his colleagues established in 2015, utilized SEO data when it partnered with the New York City Parks Department to open the city's first outdoor squash court. "There are 2,009 handball courts around the city and they are significantly underutilized. We used our search engine market research to tell the story that four times the number of New Yorkers are interested in squash when compared to handball. On top of that, the dimensions of a handball court are almost identical to a squash court, reinforcing the plug-and-play opportunity. The sport wants to grow but it is stuck. By installing outdoor courts, we can meet the growing demand for squash courts and improve the visibility and accessibility of the game," explained Wall (2017). As a result, the city donated a handball court at Hamilton Fish Park, where the first New York City public outdoor squash court was installed in April 2018.

Wall believes it is important that "brands invest in insights in order to inform their business systems and how they communicate across all channels. It's not just how they communicate to the end consumer, it's how they communicate within the organization too" (2017). What's the next big thing in consumer insights? Wall predicts voice search and conversational interfaces. He notes, "We're going from type to touch to voice. It is already becoming the new way to communicate with devices and content." Overall, what keeps Wall and his team so passionate about what they do? "We've taken search to a whole new level. It's data to design. The data drives strategy, content, and product," he says.

Marketers collect data like these to help them better reach their customers (see, for example, Insights from the Field 13.1), but technology companies like Intel and Qualcomm collect data too, which they can then sell to third parties—these data are extremely valuable and advertisers will pay a lot of money for them. It is no surprise that some consumers are concerned about the tracking of their behaviors. One problem is that not only do marketers collect data through Internet-enabled devices, but also these devices allow hackers to potentially gain access to those devices and private information, such as passwords and credit card information. How could consumers stop the collection of their data? It is not easy. The only way for consumers to avoid this collection of data is for them to update their privacy settings, opt out of data collection, and always download the latest security software, safety measures that many consumers do not want to take the time to do (Graham 2018).

Expansion of research focus

The third trend in consumer research we will discuss is the shift in focus to a more holistic approach to understanding the role of marketing in society. **Transformative consumer research (TCR)** refers to a stream of research

Transformative consumer research (TCR) refers to a stream of research that focuses on benefiting consumer welfare and quality of life across the world.

INSIGHTS FROM THE FIELD 13.1

Netflix knows when a movie is too scary for you to finish

Back in the "olden days," that is, before 2007, Netflix mailed DVDs to customers, who then watched the movies and mailed them back. Although executives at Netflix said that they wanted to start streaming content before 2007, they realized that many households did not have fast enough Internet speeds to allow it. By 2017, Netflix had 117 million subscribers globally, many of whom were tuning in to its original content (BBC Newsbeat 2018). Until streaming services were fully operational, Netflix was limited in the data it could collect from its customers, and marketing managers primarily developed what few insights they could from the title of the movies and how long viewers kept them.

After 2007, all of that changed. Netflix was able to make recommendations to viewers almost instantly. After finishing an episode of a favorite series, the next episode would quickly begin. Their own research showed that, unless Netflix queued the next episode or made another recommendation, consumers lost interest in about sixty to ninety seconds. About 80 percent of the content consumers watched was influenced by recommendations from Netflix. When it comes to scary movies, the data that Netflix collected provided some important insights. Netflix collected data on what device was used to watch the movie, whether viewers watched the credits, and a host of other data, such as when portions of the show were rewatched, when (and for how long) the program was paused, how and what consumers searched, and what was watched immediately before and after a given program. In analyzing these data, decision-makers found that if a customer watched 70 percent of the movie and then switched it off, it was because the movie was too scary to finish. Of course, many people turn off

movies before they are finished, but this happens long before the 70 percent threshold. According to data from Netflix, the top three scariest movies were *Cabin Fever* (2016), *Carnage Park* (2016), and *Mexico Barbaro* (2014) (Marr 2018) (see Photo 13.3).

The insights that were provided also helped Netflix create its own content that had a fairly good chance of resonating with its audiences. The data thus helped in making decisions about directors, actors, and other creative executions. By using these insights to create content, Netflix had a success rate of 80 percent for its programming, compared to a mere 30 to 40 percent for programs on traditional TV (Marr 2018). An important consequence of Netflix's obsession with data collection and use of insights is that it set its service apart from the competition. Not only did Netflix managers know more about their customers than anyone else, but they also took that data and created a consistently enjoyable viewing experience for their customers. It is in this way that the use of data could be viewed as a competitive advantage for Netflix. There was little reason for a happy customer to try a different streaming

● **Photo 13.3** *Netflix user*

service. Netflix spent substantial effort, time, and money collecting data and creating insights. Perhaps because of this and its recognition about its own strategic competitive advantage that these data allowed, Netflix never sells its data. Unlike Facebook, which collects data from its users and then sells that data to advertisers, Netflix has recognized the importance of consumer data to its success and has fiercely protected it (Pressman and Lashinsky 2018).

Questions

1. Do you have different viewing habits when you're alone versus when you're with your family and friends? Why does this happen? Consult the material in Chapter 10 and discuss the ways in which social influences might impact a consumer's viewing habits.
2. Early in this textbook, we discussed the importance of creating a value proposition for consumers. In what way would Netflix's *use of data* and *protection of data* provide a unique value proposition for its customers?
3. The data that Netflix collected are behavioral data—all focused on a consumer's viewing patterns and habits. If Netflix wanted to obtain deeper insights into its consumers, what other sorts of data might be useful to gather? Be specific. What insights could these data provide that behavioral data can't provide?

Sources: BBC Newsbeat (2018); Marr (2018); Pressman and Lashinsky (2018).

that endeavors to benefit consumer welfare and quality of life across the world. A central tenet for TCR research is that *all* stakeholders need to be included in the research effort early in the process, as well as throughout the project. The TCR perspective is broad and has important implications for consumer welfare, such as food security and well-being (Block et al. 2011), addiction (Martin et al. 2013), poverty (Blocker et al. 2013), and risky consumption behavior among young people (Mason et al. 2013). What distinguishes TCR work from other areas of consumer research is that it emphasizes the dissemination and sharing of valuable insights (Mick et al. 2011) in an effort to alleviate and even solve some of the most pressing consumer welfare problems.

When using TCR to help address a consumer-related issue, relevant stakeholders are included in all aspects of research and implementation. Take the example of young people who engage in risky behaviors such as texting and driving, taking drugs, recklessly consuming alcohol, or engaging in risky sexual encounters. Why are young people so likely to engage in risky behaviors like this? This is an incredibly important question because risky behavior leads, among other things, to injuries, emergency room visits, and death for far too many young people. In fact, 40.6 percent of all deaths for young people (aged ten to twenty-four) are from unintentional injuries (Heron 2019). Neuromarketing techniques combined with a TCR approach can provide some useful answers and solutions to this problem. First, scans of adolescent brains reveal that certain areas of the brain are particularly sensitive to social rewards that come from their peer groups. Thus, compared to older people, young people really enjoy being admired or included in their social groups. Similarly, they are quite distressed when they are excluded from their social group. In addition, when young people know that others are watching, they are especially likely to engage in risky behavior (Mounts 2015). Given this evidence from neuromarketing, what can we do to curb risky behaviors? Transformative consumer research offers some guidance. Teachers, coaches, school nurses, and other key influencers should be encouraged to help identify signs of stress and problem behaviors; police officers and emergency medical technicians could be trained and equipped to deal with instances of alcohol and drug overdoses; and substance abuse professionals should also be included to add their own specialized expertise. This broadening role of consumer research beyond the narrow confines of understanding how and why consumers purchase incorporates stakeholder perspectives throughout the process. Importantly, it also helps identify consumption-related problems and improves consumers' lives in a holistic way.

Consumer Trends

It would be impossible to adequately cover all the trends that are happening in consumer behavior. However, six trends seem particularly relevant to consumer behavior in the future: the empowered consumer, the sharing economy, the frugal consumer, concerns about privacy, sustainable consumption, and authentic consumption experiences. Each of these trends has something in common. They all start with consumers who now have an increasing amount of power and influence compared to marketers. No longer are individuals passive consumers of products, services, and information that is provided to them by the marketing team. Instead, consumers find their own information and share it, make their own decisions, and expect to be heard. We will therefore start our discussion of consumer trends with the empowered consumer.

The empowered consumer

For several years, the power in the consumer–marketer relationship has been shifting away from the marketer and toward the consumer. Customers have become accustomed to sharing their input on a wide variety of products and services. Consumers can't escape requests for reviews the moment they leave an Airbnb vacation house or jump out of an Uber car. They spend time leaving feedback on TripAdvisor, Amazon, and Yelp. They also spend time looking up reviews that other customers have left. A staggering 91 percent of customers read online reviews and 84 percent trust online reviews as much as they trust their friends (Bloem 2017). One reason for this shift in power rests with rising consumer expectations. To start, consumers have high expectations for the performance of products and services; they should help make a consumer's life easier, more efficient, and more enjoyable. Further, consumers expect that the entire purchase process, from shopping to checkout to delivery, will be intuitive and seamless. The product itself should also work as intended and be intuitive to operate and install. Mobile apps that integrate the operation of the product with useful tips and performance monitoring are especially helpful. Further, technological advances mean that consumers now have seamless integration and continuous access to entertainment, weather reports, maps, email, and news (see Photo 13.4). Consumers therefore expect that any company or product information will also be provided seamlessly.

● **Photo 13.4** *The empowered, connected consumer*

Another important reason why consumers are becoming more empowered is that customers *know* that marketers are tracking them and trying to engage with them. This also gives customers more power in the customer–organization relationship. From the marketer's perspective, they know that when they create content for consumers, it must be relevant, engaging, and authentic (Hall 2017). Marketers also know that any interaction with consumers must take place on the customer's terms. For example, today's customers want to communicate with an organization through texting, message boards, and Twitter. Because of this, many brands now have Twitter accounts specifically designed for this, like @AmazonHelp, @AppleSupport, and @MicrosoftHelps. Importantly, there should be a live customer service representative there to respond appropriately to these messages. Further, if there is a problem, those customer service representatives will need to offer a solution to the problem. If this doesn't happen, the consequences for the company can be incredibly damaging. Consider the mountains of negative feedback that Uber received over a variety of questionable actions, including its too-slow responses to allegations of workplace hostility and the sexual harassment and assault of passengers by Uber drivers. Twenty employees were dismissed and the CEO eventually resigned (Levin 2017). Not only does the empowered consumer expect to be heard when he or she has a complaint, but also, with the help of social media, consumers are increasingly banding together to demand action from organizations (cf. Rosenbaum 2015).

The sharing economy

In some parts of the world, sharing is a part of everyday life. In Fiji, for example, items are typically shared with members of the entire village. People come together and buy one truck for everyone's use; food, tools, and supplies are also shared. If someone is sick or if a family has a new baby, others help. Villagers take joint responsibility and pride in their land, and everyone pitches in to keep the village tidy and clean. In the Western world, this sense of collective ownership and responsibility does not exist, but there are small areas in which the concept of sharing is starting to spread. It is important to note that the concept of sharing and borrowing is nothing new; in the past, people knew their neighbors so well, they often borrowed things from them. People borrowed books from libraries and movies from rental companies. **Sharing economy** is a term used to describe an economic system that is based not on the purchasing of products, but on the sharing of products.

Imagine yourself in a few years. You just got an important promotion and you want to celebrate your success with a trip to Europe! One of the things you could do there is rent a luxury car to drive around for a few days. At Elite Rent-a-Car in Switzerland, you can cruise the Alps with a Maserati, Alfa Romeo, or any number of other luxury vehicles. Other companies leveraging this trend toward access rather than ownership include Zipcar (car sharing), VRBO and Airbnb (vacation rentals), and even home improvement stores like Lowe's (tool and equipment rental). For the sharing economy to work, consumer perceptions of ownership must change as they consider what they can live without, as well as how they can find alternative ways of accessing products and services. For many of these consumers, buying the product or service is not nearly as important as the solution or the experience. That is, they don't need to *own* a car to get from Chicago to New York—they just want to get from Chicago to New York. The concept of sharing extends to the sharing of experiences via social media. Importantly, this sharing of products and the associated social media sharing both function as status symbols for consumers in the way that products have in previous generations (Malnight and Keys 2012). Posting your vacation photos is important because you are able to share the experience, but the number of likes is also critical. In this context, ownership is becoming less valued. Capital Bikeshare in Washington, DC, and nextbike in Berlin, Germany, are just a few of the many bikeshare programs in cities all around the world. Once registered with the service, your bike is remotely unlocked from its docking station; when you're done, you return the bike to any of the docking stations located around the city. You can even leave the bike at a different location and its GPS tracking system will tell the company where to pick it up. The pricing strategy is structured to encourage longer rental periods, such as twenty-four-hour, three-day, eight-day, and monthly rentals. Apart from removing the burden and responsibility of ownership, sharing services like this also reduce the fear of theft and the concern about safe parking (see Photo 13.5).

Renting and borrowing are beneficial for consumers for several reasons. First, it saves consumers money, while still giving them access to products. Renting for a few days can save up to 90 percent off the purchase price for a variety of items, such as clothing, shoes, and accessories. When renting a vacation house or a car for a longer time, the savings are even greater. Second, renting allows consumers to focus on the *outcome* or benefits of consumption, rather than the sometimes tedious steps that precede consumption. That is,

Sharing economy is a term used to describe an economic system that is based not on the purchasing of products, but on the sharing of products.

● **Photo 13.5** *Capital Bikeshare in Washington, DC*

renting fashion allows consumers to stay current with a variety of designer trends, rather than spending the time and effort to go shopping. Similarly, renting a bike allows consumers to focus on the enjoyment of using a bike to see a new city, rather than spending the time and effort to bring their own bike along on the trip. Third, renting saves space, which is a particular concern for young people and urban dwellers. It is sometimes much easier to rent items as needed than it is to jam-pack items that are rarely used into small apartments, closets, and garages. Finally, renting or borrowing is beneficial to the planet because items are being used and shared, which decreases the need for production and disposal of products (see Insights from the Field 13.2).

The frugal consumer

The 2008–9 global economic recession had lasting effects on consumer buying habits and decision-making. Consumers who are careful with their money and alter their behaviors because of monetary considerations are called **frugal consumers**. Some of these changes in purchasing are unexpected. For example, while some women may give up higher-priced items like designer clothes and shoes, cosmetic sales often increase during economic hard times because these products are viewed as an affordable indulgence. Indeed, sales of lipstick and nail polish often increase when consumers feel economically pinched, a phenomenon referred to as the *lipstick index* (Wolverson 2011).

Frugal consumers like to look for price deals and products that will add value to their lives. Individuals who are just graduating from college and starting their careers and families (Generation Z members and millennials)

Frugal consumers are careful with their money and alter their behaviors because of monetary considerations.

INSIGHTS FROM THE FIELD 13.2

Renting a Rolex

As consumer confidence in the sharing economy increases, more consumers with higher discretionary income are renting designer gowns, bags, jewelry, and luxury cars for short periods of time, anything from a few days to a month or more. Experts refer to this phenomenon as *borrowed luxury*.

Luxury rental companies are popping up all around the world to meet the demand of individuals who want to experience a small amount of luxury without the guilt, financial burden, hassle, and insurance costs that accompany actual luxury spending. Consumers can have their choice of many kinds of products, including designer dresses (Rent the Runway and Girl Meets Dress ["What Is GMD" 2019]); handbags (Bag Borrow or Steal ["Here's Why" 2019]), watches (Borrowed Time Watches), and luxury cars (Turo ["About Turo" 2020]) and Elite Rent ["Rent Luxury Cars" 2019]), with a fraction of the negative consequences. To cater to the needs of its clientele, the Borrowed Time Watches club, for example, offers luxury watch rentals for men, with different levels of membership reflecting the preferences and desires of its members, from "executive," for enthusiasts who want an all-year membership, to "basic," which suits the occasional wearer ("Reserve and Borrow" 2019). Rent the Runway, for example, allows individuals to browse a variety of top-name designer clothes and accessories for several occasions, such as weddings, work events, or vacations. The company will send the customer's size, plus a backup size. After the event, all a consumer needs to do is package the items up and send them back. Rent the Runway takes care of any repairs and dry cleaning so the items are ready for the next person to rent. The company even offers monthly subscription services ("One Subscription" 2019) (see Photo 13.6).

Savvy consumers are not only renting or borrowing a variety of luxury items, but also starting to see opportunities for themselves to make money. Not only are individual consumers renting out their own homes and vacation homes, but they are renting out access to their pools and other private spaces like home gyms

● **Photo 13.6** *Borrowed luxury*

and tennis courts. A host of companies have sprung up to help homeowners (who might live far away) easily navigate local township regulations regarding rentals, cleanings, and other logistics. Lease Killers, for example, will handle all the details of your Airbnb rental and, in return, take a 10 percent cut (McLaughlin 2016). Poshmark is an online portal that allows consumers to buy and sell slightly used fashion items to other members, and Etsy is an online marketplace that allows small or part-time business owners to open online stores where they sell hand-crafted or small-production-run items. Not to be outdone, big manufacturers are also helping customers make money in the borrowing/renting market. In 2018, General Motors launched an app allowing General Motors car owners to offer their cars for rent. The app promises that car owners will receive

60 percent of the revenue from each rental. For their part, managers at General Motors hope that getting their high-end luxury vehicles into the hands of more customers will trigger greater sales (Narayanan 2018). The entire sharing economy is a fascinating study in how the distinction between consumer and producer is becoming blurred.

Questions

1. In Chapter 8, we learned that customer satisfaction happens when product performance is greater than expectations. As we learned in this insight from the field, customers increasingly expect that their voices will be heard. What can a marketer do when customer expectations keep increasing like this? That is, how can marketers make sure performance always stays ahead of increasing expectations?

2. In Chapter 5, we learned about the different kinds of learning and discussed the theory of operant conditioning. Imagine that a marketing manager would like to encourage customers to check the company's website first, before making a call to the customer help line. How might marketing managers use concepts from operant conditioning to provide positive reinforcement, negative reinforcement, punishment, and extinction to encourage consumers to do this?

Sources: "Here's Why" (2019); McLaughlin (2016); Narayanan (2018); "One Subscription" (2019); "Rent Luxury Cars in Europe" (2019); "Reserve and Borrow" (2019); "What Is GMD?" (2019); "Who Are Dreamcar Hire?" (2019).

are more likely than other groups to be frugal because they may be facing student loan payments and/or depressed wages. It is hardly a surprise that these consumers feel an economic pinch. Compared to when their parents were their age, these individuals are earning $2,000 less income per year (adjusted for inflation). That's why smart budgeting makes sense (Jones 2016). When consumers do cut back, more expensive categories such as home remodeling projects and new cars tend to fare quite poorly because consumers are reluctant to take on new debt. Consumers are less likely to eat out and go to the movies, preferring instead to cook and watch TV and movies at home. Frugal consumers also use websites and apps that provide money-saving advice. Groupon, for example, provides its 49.3 million unique users deal-of-the-day promotions that are available only to registered users for twenty-four hours. By the end of 2017, 171 million people had downloaded Groupon's mobile app and 72 percent of its sales were completed through mobile devices (Statista 2018). In response to the needs of frugal consumers, the following trends have emerged (Jones 2016):

- *A rise in budget retail*: Stores such as Dollar Tree and 99 Cents Only stores have expanded their offerings and the number of their stores, and the Irish discount chain Primark was the fastest growing retailer in the United States in 2018.

- *Personalized promotions*: Organizations use data analytics to send targeted coupons and discounts to customers to encourage greater engagement with the brand and, of course, greater sales.

● **Photo 13.7** *The Dubai Aquarium*

- *Experiences are increasingly important*: By saving money on products, frugal consumers can then spend that money on experiences that allow them to connect with a culture, one another, or even a brand. The Dubai Aquarium at the Dubai Mall offers an extraordinary shopping experience that is more of a destination than a store. The aquarium has the longest Plexiglas tunnel in the world (see Photo 13.7).

Concerns about privacy

With the proliferation of news stories about data hacking and security breaches, it is no wonder that consumers are concerned about the privacy of their data. Living in a digital age means that marketers are constantly trying to understand consumer behaviors. As discussed in Chapter 9, much of the information comes from consumer panel data, like the data available from research firms Nielsen and IRI. This information is provided to these research firms with full knowledge that the data are gathered for research purposes. However, other less scrupulous organizations also harvest data from unknowing consumers. In 2018, a story broke that the personal data of 87 million Facebook users were harvested by a company that said it was conducting academic research. This was a lie. In fact, the data were being harvested by a company called Cambridge Analytica, an organization that gathers and then sells data for political purposes. Personal data included not only pictures and general information that users posted on Facebook, but also, for some users, their phone numbers, addresses, and emails. In the furor that followed, additional privacy features were added, numerous Facebook pages were disabled, and CEO Mark Zuckerberg was called to testify before Congress. Facebook also launched an advertising campaign to help win back the trust of its users. In the end, although it lost 2.8 million users, it retained 1 billion active daily users (Steimer 2018).

It is important to note that there is a distinct difference between data that are gathered from legitimate marketing-related efforts and data that are gathered by organizations like Cambridge Analytica. First, with legitimate marketing research, customers are fully aware that their data are being gathered and they provide their consent for this to happen. Each time a customer obtains a customer loyalty card or downloads an app, he or she must agree to the company's statement about data and privacy. For more elaborate research efforts where a consumer is a part of a panel or focus group, for example, these research participants are required to complete elaborate consent forms that specify how the data will be gathered and used.

These participants are free to discontinue their participation at any time and are also often compensated for their efforts. Disreputable firms, however, do not let individuals know they are gathering data, do not tell them how the data are used, and do not compensate them for their data. Second, the reason for the collection of data differs between legitimate firms and other firms. Most marketers want to do their best to provide products that meet and even exceed the expectations of their consumers. They want to create compelling advertising that resonates with consumers. They also want to be keenly aware of consumer needs, wants, and trends so that they can pre-

● **Photo 13.8** *Despite the data breach, Facebook lost very few users*

dict what kinds of offerings consumers might like in the future. Marketing research helps marketers accomplish these goals. Disreputable firms often have dubious reasons for collecting data. In the case of Facebook and Cambridge Analytica, individuals were targeted with dishonest messaging and ads. In the end, marketers have been entrusted by their customers with important, personal data and it is their responsibility to keep that data safe (see Photo 13.8).

In 2018, the General Data Protection Regulation (GDPR) went into full effect in the European Union (EU). The GDPR is a set of regulations that applies to any non-EU company that collects and processes data collected from EU residents. These strict guidelines specify how, when, and where a company can collect, distribute, and use customer data. Organizations doing business in the EU must provide an option to "opt in" to any type of system that might collect customer data (which is quite different than the "opt out" option typically available to US consumers). The US standard for privacy is built on the assumption that consumers should have no expectation of privacy and that their data will be collected—customers must specifically notify the company that they do not want that to happen by opting out. That is just the start. The GDPR also requires that any companies doing business in the EU hire a data security specialist, update their security systems, update their data access policies, and provide individuals access to their own data that have been collected (Gillett 2018). The GDPR is quite strict and many organizations have struggled to meet its requirements. However, passage and implementation of the GDPR also proved that when they need to, organizations can indeed be much more careful about the security of customer data. See Insights from Academia 13.2 for more information about the targeting of messages and Insights from the Field 13.3 for an inside look at how one company uses technology such as AI to create the perfect-tasting beer.

INSIGHTS FROM THE ACADEMIA 13.2

That's *so* me!

Have you ever searched for something online and then received ads for those same kinds of products? This is called behavioral targeting—targeting an ad based on the search behavior of a consumer. It happens to everyone, but what do consumers think of this strategy? Using a series of four experiments, researchers found that upon receiving a targeted ad, consumers believe that marketers have made inferences about them. Further, in the consumer's mind, the ads function as an "implied social label." That is, if a consumer does a search for hiking boots and then receives a series of ads for rugged outerwear and equipment, that consumer will start to see himself or herself as a rugged outdoors kind of individual and will even form stronger intentions to purchase the products. Although research in this area is still relatively new, it does suggest that targeted ads could play a role in our own self-definition.

Summers, C. A., R. W. Smith, and R. W. Reczek. 2016. "An Audience of One: Behaviorally Targeted Ads as Implied Social Labels." Journal of Consumer Research *43 (1): 156–78.*

Sustainable consumption

Sustainable consumption is another important trend. Because more consumers are starting to consider the environmental and social implications of their consumption choices, they are engaging in sustainable consumption. For the record, **sustainable development and operations** "meet the needs of the present without compromising the ability of future generations to meet their own needs" (United Nations 1987). This is an important definition for businesses that need to make decisions about their own operations, and it is an important definition for public policy makers who need to make decisions about economic and land development. For consumers, the definition is also useful. When people engage in sustainable consumption, they recognize that their consumption choices impact other people as well as the planet. These consumers then alter their consumptions choices accordingly. Thus, consumers consider their own needs in the present, but also try to be aware of the ability of future generations to meet their needs.

In 2017, Nespresso, one of the world's biggest producers of coffee and coffee-related products, launched its "The choices we make" campaign to highlight its sustainability efforts in Columbia and throughout the world. With Nespresso's help, coffee farmers have implemented better planting, harvesting, and processing methods that not only produce better quality coffee, but also save farmers time and money. Although it has been operating under strict sustainability standards since 2003, Nespresso decided it was time to launch the new campaign because their consumers were concerned about—and making purchasing decisions about—sustainability. Nespresso wanted to reassure its customers about the sustainable initiatives that it had already

Sustainable development and operations "meet the needs of the present without compromising the ability of future generations to meet their own needs" (United Nations 1987).

launched (Sustainable Brands 2017). In turn, Nespresso hoped that consumers would conclude that purchasing a Nespresso product would help them reach their own sustainability goals.

Sustainable consumption covers a wide variety of activities, such as activities around the home (turning off the lights, recycling), choices of sustainable food and drink (locally sourced or organic foods), sustainable transportation (public transportation or walking), and sustainable fashion (consignment shopping). Most of these sustainable consumers will have a deeply embedded set of values that is based on reverence for the planet and obligation to other living beings. Because every consumer is different, how consumers enact those values will also be different. Some might donate money to organizations like Greenpeace or the World Wildlife Fund, others might change their purchasing habits or lifestyles, and still others may decide to voice their concerns directly to organizations in an effort to enact change. Regardless of how it is done, sustainable consumption is here to stay.

Authentic consumption experiences

With the prevalence of news stories about Internet scams, corrupt politicians, and lying business leaders, it is no surprise that consumers have a great appreciation for authenticity. This is especially true with marketing, where unscrupulous marketers sometimes stretch the truth about product performance, are reluctant to follow through on guarantees or warranties, and misrepresent their own good deeds. PepsiCo committed a big authenticity fumble in 2017 with its advertisement featuring model Kendall Jenner and a street protest. In the ad, Jenner is being photographed in a fashion shoot and sees a protest across the street. It is not clear what the protest is about, but she walks to where the action is taking place and hands a can of Pepsi to one of the police officers, which immediately calms everyone down and resolves the situation. Pepsi received intense backlash from a variety of groups, many of whom suggested that the ad was completely contrived and inauthentic. Importantly, it made light of individuals who put themselves in physical danger to protest important issues such as police brutality, immigration, or the environment. In response to the outrage, Pepsi pulled the ad and issued an apology: "Pepsi was trying to project a global message of unity, peace, and understanding. Clearly, we missed the mark, and we apologize" (Smith 2017) (see Insights from the Field 13.3).

The importance of authenticity cannot be overstated. It is inevitable that, at some point in a brand's life, there will be a stumble or two. However, if the brand is open, honest, and transparent, consumers will be willing to give the brand a second chance. A marketer's only solution is to ensure that any messaging about the brand is genuine and that it aligns with the company's values. When brands communicate that they are not authentic (as in the case of Pepsi's fiasco), consumers will be watching closely for another misstatement or questionable move. Honesty is always the best policy (Deibert 2017).

INSIGHTS FROM THE FIELD 13.3

Thinking outside the bottle[*]

Some people like lagers, some like pale ales, some like stouts. Some consumers like added flavorings, some like seasonal brews, and some like the traditional flavors. How can a brewery decide what kinds of beer to brew when consumer tastes are so variable? Since 2017, the Carlsberg Group has created a two-pronged approach to helping each customer find the perfect beer. First, it employs artificial intelligence (AI) to help each individual consumer find that beer. Next, it engages consumers with creative storytelling.

Founded in 1847, the Carlsberg Group is the world's fourth-largest brewery by sales. The Carlsberg Laboratory, headquartered in Copenhagen, Denmark, works on the science of brewing and recently partnered with Microsoft Corporation to launch a new multi-million-dollar research project entitled *The Beer Fingerprinting Project* (Microsoft Reporter 2017). Microsoft provided a host of AI tools, including machine learning, a digital Cloud platform, and chatbots. These AI tools allowed Carlsberg's team of scientists to develop innovative, individualized beers for its consumers (Mullan 2018).

Carlsberg's laboratory is a busy place. It creates one thousand different beer samples daily, enough for every person in Pittsburgh to have four samples per year. Further, beer is a complex mixture of over six hundred ingredients, many of which exist in minute amounts, but combine to give each beer its distinctive taste and aroma (Microsoft Reporter 2017). With such a high volume of samples and the complicated mixture of ingredients, it's difficult to manage the data and identify insights. Currently, the typical development time for a new beer is between eight and twenty-four months. By integrating AI, the development time can be cut by 30 percent (Milne 2017). How? Rather than relying on human perception, AI sensors speed up the development process by allowing brewers to accurately identify and quantify these beer flavor constituents. *The Beer Fingerprinting Project* uses a series of high-tech sensors to accurately gauge the delicate nuances and aromas in each beer sample, which are then mapped

to create a unique "flavor fingerprint" (Microsoft Reporter 2017). Distinct cultural preferences can also be accommodated. Chinese customers, for example, generally enjoy the tastes of rice, sorghum, and melon in their beer ("Beer around the World" 2018). By matching tastes and aromas with cultural preferences, Carlsberg can maximize its AI data to find every drinker the perfect beer.

Then, Carlsberg further utilizes AI to engage customers with conversations about beer. Using a series of linguistic formulas, chatbots are able to have a conversation with customers and provide recommendations based on ingredient preferences, taste preferences, and previous Carlsberg experiences. For example, a consumer who prefers a malty beer that is rich in character with fruit and caramel flavors may be recommended the Elephant Beer, whereas another consumer who prefers lighter, more carbonated beers may receive a recommendation for one of the Pilsners.

Brand storytelling is also a key part of Carlsberg's strategy because it taps into the imagination and emotions of consumers. During a recent renovation project at Carlsberg, workers found a bottle of beer in a forgotten beer cellar dating back more than a hundred years. Carlsberg's head brewmaster was able to recreate the historic lager from the old yeast in the bottle (Gannon 2016). In describing the story of finding and recreating the century-old beer, Carlsberg sparked further curiosity and engagement with consumers.

Global companies like Carlsberg have found success by integrating new technologies such as AI with tried-and-true methods like storytelling to satisfy their customers and strengthen engagement with them. In this way, Carlsberg is "thinking outside the bottle."

Questions

1. Boutique craft breweries are becoming increasingly popular. How can global breweries such as Carlsberg maintain an authentic local experience while also appealing to a larger market?

[*] This Insight from the Field was developed and written by Caitlyn R. Phillips.

2. The decision to buy and consume a particular beer or wine depends on much more than just taste. Discuss in detail how the different mechanisms of reference group influence (Chapter 10) can impact these buying and consuming decisions.

3. In what ways might reference group power (Chapter 10) help to discourage an individual from excessive alcohol consumption?

Sources: "Beer around the World" (2018); Gannon (2016); Microsoft Reporter (2017); Milne (2017); Mullan (2018).

One company that has a solid reputation for authenticity is Love Your Melon, a small start-up that originated from a great idea that two friends had while taking a class in entrepreneurship at the University of St. Thomas in Minnesota in 2012. The sophomores created a business plan to produce and sell stylish, well-made knit hats and beanies in the United States and donate 50 percent of their profits to nonprofit organizations and research institutions working to find a cure for pediatric cancer. Neither student had a personal connection to the issue of pediatric cancer, but they were driven by the desire to have the biggest impact they could on a vulnerable population. Pediatric cancer impacts about 45,000 children per year in the United States and one-third of these children will lose their battle against this deadly disease. Because of extensive treatments, many patients lose their hair and therefore get cold easily. Also, the loss of a child's hair says to the world, "I have cancer," which also exacts an emotional toll on the children. "Our professors didn't think that our model would work. They didn't think that we could sell 200 hats in a whole semester," said one of the cofounders. They sold that amount in two days (Taylor 2016)! By 2019, the company had launched its first TV ad campaign and had donated 175,000 hats to children and more than $6.2 million to organizations such as Alex's Lemonade Stand and St. Jude's Children's Research Hospital (Riddle and Hengel 2019). The company has no interest in selling out to one of the bigger fashion brands that might be able to help them scale their operations and expand their distribution; what matters is being a part of something meaningful (Taylor 2016). The story of Love Your Melon is compelling and authentic (see Photo 13.9). Check out Insights from Academia 13.3 to learn more about another kind of authenticity: terroir.

● **Photo 13.9** *Love Your Melon*

INSIGHTS FROM ACADEMIA 13.3

New England barbecue? No thanks!

At times, production of a product can only happen in very specific places. For example, champagne can only be produced in the Champagne region of France. By law, if it is made anywhere else, it is called sparkling wine. Other products simply are better or more authentic when they come from a specific location. Clam chowder is best when it is from New England, and nothing beats Texas barbecue. This connection to a specific place is called *terroir* and it describes the unique sociocultural, historical, and geographical qualities that make some products special when they come from a specific place. In addition, when considering agricultural products, different locations will result in very different tastes because of differences in the soil and climate. Researchers examined a variety of laws, reports, and other economic data and found that there is a distinct location–product synergy; there is extra value to *those products* that are produced *at that location*. Consumers appreciate the product more and are willing to pay more to obtain it. So, next time you're in New England, skip the barbecue and order the clam chowder.

Charters, S., N. Spielmann, and B. J. Babin. 2017. "The Nature and Value of Terroir Products." European Journal of Marketing *51 (4): 748–71.*

Technological Trends

Is technology the answer to all our problems or is it destructive and harmful to humankind? This debate between "technology as damnation" and "technology as salvation" has raged for centuries (Giesler 2012) and became especially heated during the Industrial Revolution, when workers staged work slowdowns and strikes to protest the use of machinery that was making their jobs obsolete. Like it or not, however, technology is here to stay. The **Internet of things** is a term used to describe the vast collection of wireless-enabled devices that collect data and share that data with one another, with companies, and with other interested parties. Home assistant devices, appliances, phones, and wearable technology are able to combine and sync data among themselves and then store that data to provide greater portability and access. The protesters of the Industrial Revolution would have never been able to imagine how connected modern lives have become.

Internet of things is a term used to describe the vast collection of wireless-enabled devices that collect data and share that data with one another, with consumers, and with others.

Because technology and environments change at an incredible pace, monitoring global consumer trends is vitally important for marketers. To meet this need and to identify technological trends as they emerge, a multitude of organizations specialize in identifying global consumer trends and business ideas. As the future unfolds, there is likely to be an even greater increase in demand for products, apps, and services that fit the needs of empowered consumers. Many allow consumers to track their own health, nutrition, and lifestyles. This trend is referred to as the **quantified self** (Wolf 2010) and is based on the idea that tracking metrics empower individuals to engage in self-improvement.

Quantified self refers to the idea that tracking metrics can lead to self-improvement in some way.

Examples include the Fitbit, which tracks a user's daily activity, calorie intake, sleep patterns, heart rate, and calories burned. The Apple Watch communicates wirelessly with other devices and includes a camera, a compass, a phone, Internet capabilities, and GPS navigation (see Photo 13.10). Newer models of wearable devices monitor other health-related indicators to predict, for example, anxiety attacks, diabetic shock, heart attacks, and stroke.

Technology has also made inroads into healthcare with a variety of apps that are being used by doctors and patients to improve health outcomes. Doctors can easily enter a list of symptoms into a variety of platforms and receive a diagnosis

● **Photo 13.10** *Syncing a Fitbit to other devices*

for their patients. They can also receive up-to-date medical files on patients and suggestions on which drugs to prescribe, and they can conduct virtual medical exams with patients who are in remote locations. In some remote locations like the Australian Outback, for example, the nearest hospital can be a hundred miles away (or more), so a small force of flying doctors, the Royal Flying Doctor Service, has been crisscrossing the most remote areas of Australia and providing care for Australians for more than ninety years (Royal Flying Doctor Service 2018). Now, technology allows doctors to meet with patients remotely. For consumers, the Medisafe app reminds patients to take their prescribed medicines on time and is free for iOS and Android users. The Runkeeper app not only keeps track of your runs, but also uses gaming tactics to give runners habit-forming cues and rewards to encourage them to keep running and stay engaged. Numerous apps help consumers count calories, track activity, eat healthier meals, and make better lifestyle choices. Importantly, many of these apps put more control over consumers' health into their own hands, thus appealing to the more empowered consumer.

Another technological trend is the more frequent and varied application of **radiofrequency identification (RFID) technology**. The RFID technology relies on small electronic tags that are attached to products. From a marketer's standpoint, RFID can help track inventory in warehouses and stores; it allows retailers, for example, to know in real time how well different products are selling in their stores. Sensors placed in the floor of warehouses, for example, can track and direct the movement of materials and vehicles within the building. From the customer's perspective, RFID makes purchase and consumption experiences more efficient and seamless. RFID wristbands are even worn by concert goers and guests at theme parks. For example, Disney theme parks all around the world utilize RFID wristbands called "MagicBands" as an all-in-one device that allows easy access around the parks. Wearers can get

Radiofrequency identification (RFID) technology relies on small electronic tags that are attached to products. It can be used to track inventory and help consumers make consumption experiences more efficient and seamless.

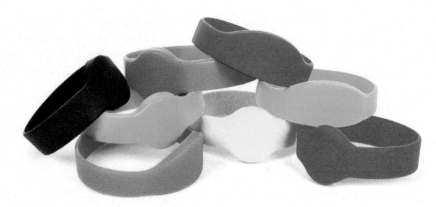

● **Photo 13.11** *Radiofrequency identification (RFID) wristbands have a multitude of uses*

easy and quick access to experiences, purchase souvenirs, eat at restaurants, and gain entry into their Disney property hotel rooms. Professional Disney photographers around the park capture dozens of pictures of guests and their families during their visit, which are tracked on the MagicBand. Then, when the trip is over, they can get access to all of their memorable Disney pictures (see Photo 13.11).

Quick response (QR) codes are optical, machine-readable barcodes that record and store information related to items.

Marketing activities and campaigns are sometimes facilitated by the use of **quick response (QR) codes**, which are optical, machine-readable barcodes that record and store information related to items (Dean 2013). A QR code is scanned by a QR reader on a Smartphone or tablet to connect to web content. These QR codes can be placed on practically anything, including packaging, advertisements, airline or train tickets, or products—anywhere consumers can scan the codes. Quick response codes are often used to provide detailed information about products. Grocery stores frequently provide QR codes that allow customers to check food safety information, including information on allergens, food recalls, calories, and even instructions for preparation at home. The codes are particularly effective in situations that can provide consumers with real-time updates, such as information about train and bus schedules, restaurant specials, or airline updates (see Photo 13.12).

● **Photo 13.12** *Quick response (QR) code and reader*

The trend toward the quantified self and the explosion in social media sharing are driven by technological advancements, facilitated by consumers who have a desire to share their life experiences on social media. These tools change a consumer's sense of self in the world, allowing consumers to access objective data that can lead to self-improvement, introspection, and discovery. In addition, these technological tools alter the ways in which consumers interact with one another and with organizations. For marketers, they offer opportunities to develop greater connectivity and conversations with consumers (see Insights from the Field 13.4 and Insights from Academia 13.4).

With the proliferation of data, consumer behaviors are often reduced to a spreadsheet full of numbers. How can a marketer take all these thousands of lines of data and distill them into insights that describe real human tendencies and truths? The answer is simple. Marketers must constantly find ways to obsess about consumers—they must understand that their job is not just about getting customers. It is also about keeping them and engaging them in a conversation about how the brand can make their lives better, easier, happier, or more efficient. This constantly changing dynamic is what makes the study of consumer behavior and marketing so rewarding.

Telepresence is a sensation that is very close to the actual experience and often happens when a consumer uses virtual reality technology.

INSIGHTS FROM THE FIELD 13.4

Enhancing visitor engagement with social media

In the past few years, museums and other cultural venues have increased visitor engagement with a variety of social media strategies. Some of their efforts are just about as creative and groundbreaking as the world-renowned artwork that they house. New York's Metropolitan Museum of Art ("The Met") opened in 1870 and is home to some of the world's most significant works of art. Today, it welcomes 7.4 million visitors per year (Press Release 2019) and has recently committed to a comprehensive and integrated social media effort to encourage greater engagement with the museum and its collections. The team uses Facebook, Instagram, Twitter, and Pinterest to connect visitors and others around the world to the museum and its collections. Success is measured by audience engagement and education of the public. For example, during the Met's blockbuster Harry Potter exhibition, the museum had a series of parallel social media efforts that put many of the items in historical context. The bezoar stone which Harry used to save Ron, for example, is real and the Met has one of these rare stones in a gold filigree case. One social media post gave a brief background on the item and pointed out its location in the collection. The team also is careful to use different platforms, depending on the demographic characteristics of the target audience. For example, because most of its users are slightly older (in their forties and older), Facebook was used to communicate with people about the museum's history of rock and roll exhibit called "Play it Loud." People could take a live Facebook tour of the exhibit and even get a preview of the collection before it was officially opened to the public (Cascone 2020) (see Photo 13.13).

Other museums are utilizing social media to initiate a dialogue with visitors and expand accessibility to their collections. The Virginia Living Museum, for example, used social media to generate a list of names for a two-year-old turtle it was rehabilitating before it was released into the wild. The winning name? Gingersnap (Web Staff 2018). The Tate Museum in London used the popular gaming platform *Minecraft* in connection with a number of key works of art to allow users to more deeply explore the worlds of the painting and time period. What happens when

(continued)

● **Photo 13.13** *New York's Metropolitan Museum of Art*

you can't visit a museum, but you want to experience it anyway? Take a virtual tour of a museum, or better yet, take a virtual tour of the actual place (Roddy 2014). *Assassin's Creed: Origins* allows players to take a "Discovery Tour" and enjoy a free virtual tour around ancient Egypt to experience its culture and learn more about its history. Dubbed an educational virtual museum tour, the program has received numerous accolades for its realism and educational value (Ore 2017). Another app that engages art lovers is Google's Arts & Culture app. Simply download the app, take a selfie, and the app will utilize facial recognition technology to identify famous (and not-so-famous) paintings around the world that contain people with similar faces. You might just find your likeness in a seventeenth-century Italian painting (Haselton 2018)! These efforts are designed to encourage greater consumer-to-consumer interactions, more meaningful engagement between museums and visitors, and, of course, more foot traffic.

Questions

1. Identify and discuss other examples of museums that have creatively used social media. What was the museum's overall goal in using this social media initiative? How effective do you think it was? What improvements could be made?

2. Check out this video introduction of the Discovery Tour initiative from *Assassin's Creed: Origins*: https://www.youtube.com/watch?v=_yMDdQKfv70. Museum marketers hope that such an immersive experience into the world of ancient Egypt might encourage more interest in Egypt and thus more visits to museums that have big Egyptology collections. Others might argue that the experience satisfies any curiosity a consumer might have and might actually depress museum visits. What do you think? Support your position with arguments from our text.

3. Be creative and develop an idea for an interactive activity using social media for museums or art galleries that are seeking to increase engagement. Be sure to discuss your target market and what goals you would like to achieve with the activity.

Sources: Haselton (2018); Ore (2017); Roddy (2014); Web Staff (2018).

INSIGHTS FROM ACADEMIA 13.4

It was almost like I was there!

When consumers use virtual reality (VR) to visit a store, try out a new product, or even explore a new city, they experience **telepresence**, a sensation that is very close to the actual experience. Thus, the VR experience is about as close to a real experience as a consumer can get. The important thing about VR is that it allows the viewer to interact with the store, product, etc., by making decisions about what to explore and view. This dimension of VR is quite different from watching a video, for example, where no interaction is possible. In a series of three experimental studies, the researchers found that when consumers use VR to interact with the brand, they are more likely to experience telepresence. When that happens, they have much more positive attitudes toward the brand (see Photo 13.14).

Spielmann, N., and A. Mantonakis. 2018. "In Virtuo: How User-Driven Interactivity in Virtual Tours Leads

● **Photo 13.14** *Customer using virtual reality (VR) technology and perhaps experiencing telepresence*

to Attitude Change." Journal of Business Research *88* (July): 255–64.

Summary

Although it would be impossible to describe all the trends that will likely impact consumers in the future, we identified several categories of trends that are likely to be particularly important as the twenty-first century continues to unfold: trends in consumer research, consumer trends, and technological trends. Together, they help marketing decision-makers answer the important question, Where do we go from here?

First, we discussed some of the *trends in consumer research*, including new technologies, continuous data collection, and an expansion of our research focus to be more inclusive and holistic. Neuromarketing techniques are a particularly interesting tool that can be used to distinguish between what consumers *say* they want and what they *really* want. Insights from the Boardroom 13 highlighted how marketers use techniques from search engine optimization and search experience optimization to reveal important thought processes that consumers undertake as they are searching for information online. Companies can then use those insights to create better products (Sabra's new dessert-flavored hummus) and better advertising executions (Cam Newton as the new spokesperson for Oikos).

Next, we highlighted a variety of *consumer trends* that are influencing the way consumers behave and make decisions. First, the *empowered consumer* expects that marketers will listen and respond to their problems. The move toward a *sharing economy* means that traditional understandings of ownership are shifting and *frugal consumers* are much more savvy with their hard-earned money. Technology brings *concerns about privacy* to the forefront and Case Study 13 highlighted some privacy concerns that arise when individuals utilize DNA testing services. We have discussed the issue of sustainability several times throughout this text, and *sustainable consumers*, who think about and act on their concerns for the environment and society, represent a growing coalition of individuals with which companies must reckon. Finally, we discussed the consumer quest for *authentic consumption experiences*. It is important to recognize that none of these consumer trends exists in isolation. Indeed, a frugal consumer can also be an empowered, sustainable consumer who participates in the shared economy and is concerned about privacy and authenticity.

Finally, taking what we discussed about consumer research and consumer trends, we presented several *technological trends* that marketers have utilized, such as RFID technology and QR codes. In Insights from the Field 13.3, we discussed how Carlsberg used an interesting combination of AI technology and storytelling to help consumers find the perfect beer, and in Insights from the Field 13.4, we illustrated how museums are increasingly relying on social media to engage visitors and increase accessibility.

In terms of wondering where we go from here, it is important to remember that, regardless of how fast technology is changing our world, our consumer behavior models and theories discussed throughout this text still provide invaluable guidance for creating a better understanding of consumer behavior and predicting what they might do next. The trends that we discuss do not invalidate any of those models or theories, but instead make them even more relevant precisely because we can see that they are still informative in a variety of contexts. Indeed, because the pace of cultural and technological change is so fast, a solid understanding of consumer behavior models and theories is even more important. In the end, new, innovative methods of consumer research, an appreciation for important consumer trends, and advancements in technologies can help us develop better insights into what occurs in the hearts and minds of consumers.

KEY TERMS

automated text analysis p. 485	quick response (QR) codes p. 506	sustainable development and
frugal consumers p. 495	radiofrequency identification	operations p. 500
Internet of things p. 504	(RFID) technology p. 505	telepresence p. 507
neuromarketing p. 482	search engine optimization p. 486	transformative consumer
quantified self p. 504	sharing economy p. 494	research (TCR) p. 489

REVIEW QUESTIONS

1. Outline and discuss the three main trends in consumer research.
2. Explain what neuroimaging is. What can this technology tell marketing managers that other research methods cannot?
3. What do we mean when we say that marketers engage in continuous data collection?
4. What are some reasons behind the trend away from ownership toward borrowing and renting?
5. What is meant by the expansion of research focus in consumer behavior?
6. Why do we say that the empowered consumer is one of the most important consumer trends?
7. What is the quantified self? Why is this concept important to consumers today?
8. What is the Internet of things and why would it be of interest to marketers?

DISCUSSION QUESTIONS

1. We learned that consumers are subject to continuous data collection. What concerns about privacy may arise from this? What could a consumer do about it?
2. In what ways might neuromarketing techniques be superior to traditional consumer research techniques? In what ways may they be inferior?
3. The scope of consumer research is expanding to be more holistic. However, is it really the responsibility of a marketer to do this? Construct an argument for why it makes sense to expand our focus and an argument for why it does not make sense to do this.
4. Many people become quite frugal when they attend college. What money-saving strategies have you used? Being frugal doesn't necessarily apply across all contexts. In which areas of your life is it harder to be frugal? Why? In which areas of your life is it easier to be frugal? Why?
5. Many people are fascinated with their family histories and want to sign up with one of the DNA testing services, like Ancestry.com or 23andMe. However, as discussed, there are some very real privacy concerns associated with these testing services. Using concepts from utilitarianism and the common good (see Chapter 12), how could a marketer reconcile this dilemma for consumers who are skeptical of their services?
6. Concerns about privacy emerge when we think about who has "ownership" of the data that are recorded by health-related tracking apps. On the one hand, some people believe that information about a consumer's own heart rate, activity levels, calorie intake, etc., should rightfully belong to that consumer. On the other hand, some would argue that the app developer owns the data because the developer provided the tools to the consumer and the consumer freely entered the data into the app. Further, these individualized data are valuable because they can be sold to marketers who can use them for targeted communications. Who should own the data? Why? Select one side of the debate and construct a strong argument to support your case.

Your DNA Can Help Catch A Criminal

One out of every twenty-five Americans has submitted a sample for genetic testing to one of the many DNA testing agencies. However, once the testing has been completed and the results have been compiled, there are some very real, unintended consequences for consumers. First and foremost, DNA data provides information not only about the customer who submits the sample, but also about all of that customer's relatives. This results in a host of privacy concerns for all involved.

Yes, your DNA can help catch a criminal. Unfortunately, it might be your cousin Bill. You never know what might turn up in a DNA profile. In early 2018, police detectives were able to track down and arrest a serial killer in California who had been responsible for at least twelve murders and forty-five rapes in the 1970s and 1980s. He was able to avoid capture for decades, that is, until one of his relatives submitted DNA to one of the many DNA testing services. This DNA matched some DNA that was left at several crime scenes, and police were able to quickly track the suspect down and arrest him (May 2018). In another instance, when one woman received a "match" notification from Ancestry.com, she thought that there must have been a mistake. The notification said that there was a "parent–child" relationship between herself and a local doctor. It turned out that her parents had undergone fertility treatments in the late 1970s and, unknown to the woman's parents, the fertility doctor's own genetic material was used to fertilize her mother's egg. After this discovery, the woman and her parents sued the doctor (Gray 2018).

When most people sign up for DNA testing services like 23andMe and AncestryDNA (a division of Ancestry.com), they want to learn more about their family tree. Was grandma from Ireland or Scotland? Do we have any Native American blood in the family? Where did grandpa get his blue eyes? Some services like 23andMe even offer information about a person's likelihood of contracting different genetically transmitted diseases and disorders, such as cancer, heart disease, and diabetes. This information can alert customers to be on the lookout for any health problems. Not

surprisingly, DNA testing is big business. Testing kits are advertised heavily and are easy to use. While most kits normally cost about $99, they often go on sale for much less around the holidays and other times of the year, like Mother's Day and Father's Day. AncestryDNA has claimed to have tested ten million people and be worth $2.6 billion, while rival firm 23andMe reports that it has tested five million people and is worth $1.5 billion (Rodriguez 2018) (see Photo 13.15).

While DNA testing might be offering a valuable service and satisfying a lot of curiosity for individuals, there are some very real concerns that primarily involve how others could use or even exploit the data. What makes these privacy concerns particularly complicated is that unlike a simple medical test that provides information about you, DNA testing provides information about other people too. These privacy concerns stem from several conflicting goals, ineffective technology, and a scarcity of laws and regulations.

CONFLICTING GOALS WITHIN TESTING ORGANIZATIONS

The first issue with DNA testing that provides fertile ground for privacy concerns centers around the fact that DNA testing companies operate under conflicting goals within their own organizations. That is, on the one hand, these companies want to protect their customers' data so that customers remain happy and recommend the services to others. Testing companies also have elaborate privacy clauses that promise that the data they collect will be protected, and they would be violating their own policies if they did not take very concrete measures to

● **Photo 13.15** *DNA testing can unlock your family history ... and much more*

protect those data. It simply makes sense for DNA testing companies, from a business standpoint, to offer the high-quality private services they advertise. However, on the other hand, genetic testing companies are for-profit organizations that also want to sell these data to other companies, such as pharmaceutical firms who are searching for drugs and treatments for a host of genetically related diseases and disorders. The DNA testing firm 23andMe recently signed a $300 million agreement with pharmaceutical giant GSK to provide "genetic data for drug discovery" (Rodriguez 2018). To be as useful as possible, the data need to contain as much detail as possible. DNA testing companies promise that the data are aggregated (combined with the DNA data from a lot of other customers) and deidentified (all of the personal information like date of birth, name, and address are removed) before being sold. However, testing companies still have a strong incentive to include as much detail as possible in the data files when they sell them to these third parties. In addition, individual genetic data provide so much detail that an unscrupulous person with the correct cross-matching data and some skillful analysis can still discover an individual consumer's identity. Thus, conflicting goals within DNA testing companies provide a fertile environment for privacy concerns.

CONFLICTING GOALS BETWEEN CUSTOMERS AND FIRMS

A second issue that leads to privacy concerns is that individual consumers have conflicting goals with both the testing firms and the firms that purchase the data. When agreeing to share their data, consumers are making the altruistic decision to help a pharmaceutical company find cures for potentially life-threatening diseases. Both 23andMe and AncestryDNA provide users the ability to change their privacy settings by "opting out" of sharing the results of their DNA tests with others (Gray 2018). However, the default option for the privacy agreement is for consumers to "opt in" and agree to share their data. Not surprisingly, almost 80 percent of individuals agree to provide their data for "research purposes" because many reportedly think that it will benefit society at large (Rodriguez 2018). Pharmaceutical companies certainly do a lot of good for society. The reality is, however, that big pharmaceutical companies are still for-profit organizations that want to utilize these DNA data to develop new drugs and treatments. Pharmaceutical companies can certainly pay individual consumers for their DNA data, but it is cheaper for them to buy it in bulk from DNA testing services. Further, both 23andMe and AncestryDNA have disclaimers saying that they can change the terms of their privacy agreement at any time (Rodriguez 2018). In short, consumers provide the data to help out humanity, and for-profit companies buy the data to streamline the research process and increase their profits. There is another potential conflict in goals between customers and firms that can be traced to the background of at least one of the big DNA testing firms. 23andMe received much of its initial startup money—$3.9 million—from Google (Primack 2015). Because of this relationship, will Google be able to access the massive database that 23andMe has compiled to sell ads to customers? Could it take some of the health findings and send targeted ads for pharmaceutical products to them? Could it sell the data to others? No one knows.

TECHNOLOGY HAS NOT KEPT PACE

A third characteristic of the DNA testing industry that raises privacy concerns is that the technology needed to protect a consumer's privacy has simply not kept pace with the increasing need to protect the data from the escalating threats of data breaches. Unfortunately, as frequently seen in the news, hackers have become increasingly sophisticated and have gained access to data from some of the most well-known global organizations. Compared to other customer data, DNA data need to be even more carefully protected behind several layers of firewalls and other security devices. Further, individuals who do not even participate in these services are now also being exposed to privacy violations, simply because they are relatives of individuals who do participate. Despite some technological safeguards by the testing companies, data breaches do happen. In 2018, genealogy and DNA firm MyHeritage experienced a data breach in which the information of ninety-two million users was compromised (Paul 2018).

SCARCE LAWS AND REGULATIONS

Another issue that raises privacy concerns is that federal laws and regulations have not kept up with this DNA testing and its related privacy implications. For their part, both AncestryDNA and 23andMe confirm that they will not provide any data to law enforcement authorities, unless there is a court order to do so (May 2018). It is admirable indeed that the industry

has agreed to protect these data. However, current laws are woefully underequipped to deal with these issues because they do not consider the far-reaching implications or the implications to others (not just the customer, but also all of that person's family members). Although health-related results and summaries are provided to customers of the testing services, unlike other information that you and your doctor share with one another, the testing companies are not bound by regulations of privacy in the Health Insurance Portability and Accountability Act (the federal law that protects a patient's private medical information) (Rodriguez 2018). There are currently no federal laws that regulate how DNA data in the possession of these companies should be protected, used, saved, or deleted. Further complicating things is that neither legislators nor citizens know enough about genetic testing or its privacy implications to start the process of formulating comprehensive laws that protect the privacy of consumers of DNA testing services. Simply put, genetic testing is currently not a top-of-mind concern for most citizens or legislators.

DNA testing organizations provide a fascinating service to customers. Not only do these companies provide data to users about their history, but also they provide data on a host of health-related findings. If these personal data are sold or otherwise released, could an employer deny someone a job because there is a propensity for alcoholism? Could someone be denied health insurance because of a propensity for cancer? Could this information be used for targeted advertising? The privacy implications of DNA testing suggest that marketers, consumers, consumer advocacy groups, and public policy makers need to proceed very carefully into this uncharted territory.

QUESTIONS

1. Approximately twelve million adults (one in twenty-five Americans) have had their DNA tested with one of the DNA testing services (Regalado 2018). As we learned throughout this textbook, consumers make decisions with their heads and with their hearts. What are some rational or logical issues that someone would consider when signing up for a test? What are some of the emotional considerations? Be specific.

2. As we learned in Chapter 6, perceptions of the self are powerful motivators for individuals. How could DNA test results confirm or disconfirm important parts of a person's self-concept? How could results alter perceptions about possible selves?

3. Chapter 3 discussed institutional review boards and some ways in which research participants were supposed to be treated and the ways in which their data are supposed to be protected. Using details from that discussion, imagine that you are a marketing manager at one of the big DNA testing services. What specific operational changes would you take to ensure the privacy of the 80 percent of your customers who agree to share their DNA data? How would you communicate these changes to your customers?

4. Many people are fascinated with their family histories and want to sign up with one of the DNA testing services, like AncestryDNA or 23andMe. However, as discussed, there are some very real privacy concerns associated with these services. Using concepts from utilitarianism and the common good (see Chapter 12), how could a marketer reconcile this dilemma for consumers who are skeptical of their services?

Sources: Gray (2018);; May (2018); Paul (2018); Primack (2015); Regalado (2018); Rodriguez (2018).

REFERENCES

About Turo. 2020. Turo. Accessed September 20, 2020. https://turo.com/us/en/about

Ariely, D., and Berns, G. S. 2010. "Neuromarketing: The Hope and Hype of Neuroimaging in Business." *Nature Reviews Neuroscience* 11 (4): 284–92.

Bagozzi, R. P. 1991. "The Role of Psychophysiology in Consumer Research." In *Handbook of Consumer Behavior,* edited by T. S. Robertson and H. H. Kassarjian, 124–61. Englewood Cliffs, NJ: Prentice Hall.

Barr, A. 2016. "Mobile Devices Upend Search—Companies Include Opening Their Apps to Google's Computers." *Wall Street Journal,* Eastern edition, February 26, 2016, B4.

BBC Newsbeat. 2018. "Netflix's History: From DVD Rentals to Streaming Success." *BBC News,* Entertainment, January 23, 2018. http://www.bbc.co.uk/newsbeat/article/42787047/netflixs-history-from-dvd-rentals-to-streaming-success.

"Beer around the World." 2018. Travel Channel. Accessed July 25, 2018. https://www.travelchannel.com/interests/food-and-drink/photos/beer-around-the-world.

Block, L. G., S. A. Grier, T. L. Childers, B. Davis, J. E. J. Ebert, S. Kumanyika, R. N. Laczniak, et al. 2011. "From Nutrients to Nurturance: A Conceptual Introduction to Food Well-Being." *Journal of Public Policy & Marketing* 30 (1): 5–13.

Blocker, C. P., J. A. Ruth, S. Sridharan, C. Beckwith, A. Ekici, M. Goudie-Hutton, J. A. Rosa, et al. 2013. "Understanding Poverty and Promoting Poverty Alleviation through Transformative Consumer Research." *Journal of Business Research* 66:1195–202.

Bloem, C. 2017. "84 Percent of People Trust Online Reviews as Much as Friends. Here's How to Manage What They See." Inc. July 31, 2017. https://www.inc.com/craig-bloem/84-percent-of-people-trust-online-reviews-as-much-.html.

BNP Media. 2016. "Yogurt, Fluid Milk, and Gelato Are Winners." *Dairy Foods* 117 (5): 23.

Cascone, S. 2020. "Meet the Woman Who Beat out Hundreds of Applicants to Manage the Metropolitan Museum of Art's Commanding Social Media Presence." Artnet News. January 8, 2020. https://news.artnet.com/art-world/met-social-media-manager-claire-l-lanier-1737846.

Dean, D. H. 2013. "Anticipating Consumer Reaction to RFID-Enabled Grocery Checkout." *Services Marketing Quarterly* 34 (1): 86–101.

Deibert, A. 2017. "Why Authenticity in Marketing Matters Now More Than Ever." *Forbes,* May 26, 2017. https://www.forbes.com/sites/forbescommunicationscouncil/2017/05/26/why-authenticity-in-market-ing-matters-now-more-than-ever/#663757117982.

Gannon, M. 2016. "Vintage Brew: Carlsberg Recreates Historic Lager with Old Yeast." Live Science. May 27, 2016. https://www.livescience.com/54916-carlsberg-recreates-historic-beer.html.

Giesler, M. 2012. "How Döppelganger Brand Images Influence the Market Creation Process: Longitudinal Insights from the Rise of Botox Cosmetic." *Journal of Marketing* 76 (6): 55–68.

Gillett, P. 2018. "A Marketer's Guide to GDPR." *Marketing News* 52 (6): 4–5.

Graham, J. 2018. "You Are Being Tracked. Deal with It." *USA Today,* February 10, 2018. https://www.usatoday.com/story/tech/talkingtech/2018/02/10/you-being-tracked-deal/325504002/.

Gray, S. 2018. "Ancestry.com Revealed This Woman's Father Was Her Family's Fertility Doctor. Now She's Suing." *Time,* April 5, 2018, 1.

Hall, J. 2017. "The Era of the Empowered Consumer: Insights from the Gartner Digital Conference." Inc. May 15, 2017. https://www.inc.com/john-hall/the-era-of-the-empowered-consumer-insights-from-the-gartner-digital-conference.html.

Harris, J. M.,J. Ciorciari, and J. Gountas. 2019. "Consumer Neuroscience and Digital/Social Media Health/Social Cause Advertisement Effectiveness." *Behavioral Sciences* 9 (4): 42–67.

Haselton, T. 2018. "How to Use the New Google App That Matches Your

Face with Famous Paintings." CNBC. January 16, 2018. https://www.cnbc.com/2018/01/16/how-to-use-the-new-google-app-that-matches-your-face-with-paintings.html.

"Here's Why We're So Unique." 2019. Bag Borrow or Steal. Accessed August 20, 2019. https://www.bagborroworsteal.com/howitworks.

Heron, M. 2019. "Deaths: Leading Causes for 2017." *National Vital Statistics Reports* 68, no. 6, June 24, 2019. https://www.cdc.gov/nchs/data/nvsr/nvsr68/nvsr68_06-508.pdf.

Hubert, M., and P. Kenning. 2008. "A Current Overview of Consumer Neuroscience." *Journal of Consumer Behaviour* 7 (4/5): 272–92.

Humphreys, A., and R. J. Wang. 2018. "Automated Text Analysis for Consumer Research." *Journal of Consumer Research* 44 (6): 1274–306.

Jones, M. 2016. "The Recession Mentality: 3 Ways Frugality Has Shaped Today's Consumer." *Forbes,* May 31, 2016. https://www.forbes.com/sites/michaeljones/2016/05/31/recession-mentality-modern-deal-seeker/#1d1838e04b85.

Kitchen, M. 2018. "The Death of the TV Remote—and What's Coming Next; with the Speedy Adoption of Voice Command We're on the Verge of Smashing the TV Clicker's Hold on Us. Will Anyone Miss It?" *Wall Street Journal (Online),* June 15, 2018.

Lee, N., A. J. Broderick, and L. Chamberlain. 2007. "What Is Neuromarketing? A Discussion and Agenda for Future Research." *International Journal of Psychophysiology* 63 (7): 199–204.

Levin, S. 2017. "Uber's Scandals, Blunders and PR Disasters: The Full List." *Guardian,* July 27, 2017. https://www.theguardian.com/technology/2017/jun/18/uber-travis-kalanick-scandal-pr-disaster-timeline.

Malnight, T. W., and T. S. Keys. 2012. "A Top Ten for Business Leaders." *Economist,* November 26, 2012. http://www.economist.com/blogs/theworldin2013/2012/11/global-trends-2013.

Marr, B. 2018. "Netflix Used Big Data to Identify the Movies That Are Too Scary to Finish." *Forbes,* April 18, 2018. https://www.forbes.com/sites/bernardmarr/2018/04/18/netflix-used-big-data-to-identify-the-movies-that-are-too-scary-to-finish/#3c2071993990.

Martin, I. M., M. A. Kamins, D. M. Pirouz, S. W. Davis, K. L. Haws, A. M. Mirabito, S. Mukherjee, J. M. Rapp, and A. Grover. 2013. "On the Road to Addiction: The Facilitative and Preventive Roles of Marketing Cues." *Journal of Business Research* 66 (8): 1219–26.

Mason, M. J., J. F. Tanner, M. Piacentini, D. Freeman, T. Anastasia, W. Batat, W. Boland, M. Canbulut, J. Drenten, A. Hamby, P. Rangan, and Z. Yang. 2013. "Advancing a Participatory Approach for Youth Risk Behavior: Foundations, Distinctions, and Research Directions." *Journal of Business Research* 66 (8): 1235–41.

May, A. 2018. "Took an Ancestry DNA Test? You Might Be a 'Genetic Informant' Unleashing Secrets about Your Relatives." *USA Today,* April 27, 2018. https://www.usatoday.com/story/tech/nation-now/2018/04/27/ancestry-genealogy-dna-test-privacy-golden-state-killer/557263002/.

McClure, S., J. Li, D. Tomlin, K. S. Cypert, L. M. Montague, and P. R. Montague. 2004. "Neural Correlates of Behavioral Preference for Culturally Familiar Drinks." *Neuron* 44:379–87.

McLaughlin, K. 2016. "Want to Airbnb Your Luxury Home? These Companies Will Handle Everything; the Rapid Growth of Third-Party Management Services and Tools Is Enticing More High-End Homeowners to Try Short-Term Renting—for the Right Price." *Wall Street Journal (Online),* September 8, 2016.

Mick, D. G., S. Pettigrew, C. C. Pechmann, and J. L. Ozanne. 2011. *Transformative Consumer Research for Personal and Collective Well-Being.* New York: Routledge Academic.

Microsoft Reporter. 2017. "The Beer Fingerprinting Project—How Artificial Intelligence Could Create Your Next Pint." Microsoft News Centre Europe. May 12, 2017. https://news.microsoft.com/europe/2017/12/05/beer-finger-printing-project-artificial-intelligence-create-next-pint/.

Milne, R. 2017. "Carlsberg Turns to AI to Help Develop Beers." *Financial Times,* December 26, 2017. https://www.ft.com/content/be042eb2-e4cf-11e7-97e2-916d4fbac0da.

Morin, C. 2011. "Neuromarketing: The New Science of Consumer Behavior." *Society* 48 (2): 131–35.

Mounts, N. S. 2015. "Why Are Teen Brains Designed for Risk-Taking?" *Psychology Today,* June 9, 2015. https://www.psychologytoday.com/us/blog/the-wide-wide-world-psychology/201506/why-are-teen-brains-designed-risk-taking.

Mullan, L. 2018. "How Carlsberg Is Using AI to Help Develop New Beers." Food Drink & Franchise. January 9, 2018. https://www.fdfworld.com/drink/how-carlsberg-using-ai-help-develop-new-beers.

Narayanan, A. 2018. "GM Hopes Buyers Will Buy Pricier Cars That They Can Rent out for Money." *Investors Business Daily,* July 24, 2018, N.PAG.

"One Subscription. Unlimited Style." 2019. *Rent the Runway.* Accessed August 20, 2019. https://www.renttherunway.com/.

Ore, J. 2017. "How Historians Helped Recreate Ancient Egypt in *Assassin's Creed: Origins.*" CBC News. November 1, 2017. https://www.cbc.ca/news/entertainment/assassins-creed-origins-historian-1.4382255.

Paul, K. 2018. "Some Experts Say You Should Think Twice Before Using Online DNA Testing." *MarketWatch.* June 6. Accessed September 20, 2020. https://www.marketwatch.com/story/myheritage-dna-site-hack-reveals-risks-associated-with-genealogy-sites-2018-06-06.

Plassman, H., J. O'Doherty, B. Shiv, and A. Rangel. 2008. "Marketing Actions Can Modulate Neural Representations of Experienced Pleasantness." *Proceedings of the National Academy of Sciences of the United States of America* 105:1050–54.

Press Release. 2019. "Met Welcomes Nearly 7.4 Million Visitors in 2018. The Metropolitan Museum. January 4. Accessed September 20, 2020. https://www.metmuseum.org/press/news/2019/2018-calendar-year-attendance#:~:text=Met%20is%20open-,Met%20Welcomes%20Nearly%207.4%20Million%20Visitors%20in%202018,million%20it%20reported%20for%202017

Pressman, A., and A. Lashinsky. 2018. "Data Sheet—Why Netflix Really Isn't a Tech Company." *Fortune,* Data Sheet, April 17, 2018. http://fortune.com/2018/04/17/data-sheet-netflix-privacy-data-facebook/.

Primack, D. 2015. "23andMe Is the Startup Word's Newest Unicorn." *Fortune*, July 14, 2015, pN.PAG, 1.

Regalado, A. 2018. "2017 Was the Year Consumer DNA Testing Blew Up." *MIT Technology Review*, February 12. 2017. https://www.technologyreview.com/s/610233/2017-was-the-year-consumer-dna-testing-blew-up/.

"Rent Luxury Cars in Europe." 2019. Elite Rent-a-Car. Accessed August 20, 2019. https://www.eliterent.com/en/.

"Reserve and Borrow." 2019. Borrowed Time Watch Company. Accessed August 20, 2019. http://borrowedtimewatches.com/how_it_works.

Riddle, M., and E. Hengel. 2019. "Love Your Melon Brand Launches National TV Ad Campaign." BusinessWire. October 30, 2019. https://www.businesswire.com/news/home/20191030006092/en/Love-Melon-Brand-Launches-National-TV-Ad.

Roddy, M. 2014. "Minecraft Video Game to get Tate Art 'Worlds.'" *Reuters*, November 20, 2014. https://www.reuters.com/article/us-gamesware-minecraft-tate-idUSKCN0J41BU20141120.

Rodriguez, M. 2018. "You discovered your genetic history. Is it worth the privacy risk? *Fortune.com*. September 10. p. 1.

Rosenbaum, S. 2015. "The New World of the 'Empowered Consumer.'" *Forbes*, July 16, 2015. https://www.forbes.com/sites/stevenrosenbaum/2015/07/16/the-new-world-of-the-empowered-consumer/#1adc38474aab.

Royal Flying Doctor Service. 2018. "History: The Royal Flying Doctor Service has a Rich and Vibrant History." Accessed September 20, 2020. https://www.flyingdoctor.org.au/about-the-rfds/history/

Shelton, K. 2017. "The Value of Search Results Rankings." *Forbes*, October 30, 2017. https://www.forbes.com/sites/forbesagencycouncil/2017/10/30/the-value-of-search-results-rankings/#769fcacf44d3.

Small, D. M., R. J. Zatorre, A. Dagher, A. C. Evans, and M. Jones-Gotman. 2001. "Changes in Brain Activity Related to Eating Chocolate: From Pleasure to Aversion." *Brain* 124:1720–33.

Smith, A. 2017. "Pepsi Pulls Controversial Kendall Jenner Ad after Outcry." NBC News. April 5, 2017. https://www.nbcnews.com/news/nbcblk/pepsi-ad-kendall-jenner-echoes-black-lives-matter-sparks-anger-n742811.

Statista. 2018. "Number of Groupon's Active Customers from 2nd Quarter 2009 to 2nd Quarter 2018 (in Millions)." Accessed August 28, 2018. https://www.statista.com/statistics/273245/cumulative-active-customers-of-groupon/.

Steimer, S. 2018. "Wading through a Data Swampland." *Marketing News* 52 (6): 68–77.

Sustainable Brands. 2017. "Nespresso Launches First Major Sustainability Campaign." September 19, 2017. https://www.sustainablebrands.com/news_and_views/marketing_comms/libby_maccarthy/nespresso_highlights_sustainability_strategy_choices_.

Taylor, P. L. 2016. "Millennial Start-up Love Your Melon: Giving Back Is Sweeter Than Making Millions." *Forbes*, December 12, 2016. https://www.forbes.com/sites/petertaylor/2016/12/12/millennial-startup-love-your-melon-why-giving-back-is-sweeter-than-making-millions/#4d1454ea3bd1.

United Nations. 1987. *Report of the World Commission on Environment and Development: Our Common Future.* New York: United Nations.

Wall, R. 2017. Personal interview, August 10, 2017.

Watrous, M. 2016. "Danone Making Progress in U.S. Dairy." *Food Business News*, February 24, 2016. http://www.foodbusinessnews.net/articles/news_home/Financial-Performance/2016/02/Danone_making_progress_in_US_d.aspx?ID=%7BB2BCDE02-BBFC-490C-A22D-48D0EAA234ED%7D.

Web Staff. 2018. "Virginia Living Museum Reveals Name for Newest Sea Turtle." CBS News3. August 9, 2018. https://wtkr.com/2018/08/09/virginia-living-museum-reveals-name-for-newest-sea-turtle/.

"What Is GMD?" 2019. Girl Meets Dress. Accessed August 20, 2019. https://girlmeetsdress.com/#.

Wolf, G. 2010. "The Quantified Self." Accessed February 7, 2020. http://www.ted.com/talks/gary_wolf_the_quantified_self.html.

Wolverson, R. 2011. "The Lipstick Index." *Time* 178 (4): 39.

Glossary

Absolute threshold is the smallest level of stimulus that can be picked up by our senses.

Acceptance/rejection occurs when the consumer considers existing choice criteria and elaborates on the information received to reach a point of acceptance or rejection of the information.

Acculturation describes the process by which an individual learns about a new culture; it concerns the movement of meaning and the adaptation to new cultural contexts.

Active learning involves the deliberate and extensive acquisition of knowledge before purchase.

Actual self refers to the core sense of self, that sense of self which is enduring and stable across situations.

Adaptation is the extent to which an individual's sensitivity to a stimulus diminishes over time.

Addiction occurs when an individual (1) has a low degree of self-control, (2) spends a great amount of time and frequency engaging in the behavior, (3) has low levels of enjoyment (because the behavior is driven by need), and (4) results in a high likelihood of harmful consequences.

Affective component (of attitudes) concerns all of the emotional connections the consumer has with the attitude object.

Anchoring helps consumers start the choice process by helping them focus on one product attribute (which is, unfortunately, sometimes arbitrary).

Approach–approach conflict occurs when an individual must select between two or more equally attractive alternatives.

Approach–avoidance conflict occurs when a goal is likely to result in both positive and negative consequences.

Archetypes are the stable characters that capture basic ideas, feelings, fantasies, and visions that seem constant and frequently re-emerge across times and places.

Aspirational groups are composed of individuals with whom the consumer can identify or admire (often from afar) and to whom they aspire to be like in some way.

Associative network is a collection of files of information that are connected by linkages.

Attention is focusing mental concentration on a given stimulus.

Attitude is a learned predisposition to respond in a consistently favorable or unfavorable manner in relation to some object.

Attitude object is the thing about which the attitude is held and can include brands, services, ideas, people, and behaviors.

Attitudinal loyalty involves a liking or a commitment to the brand that is often based on some perceived value obtained from consumption of the brand.

Attributes are the characteristics or features of the product.

Attribution theory describes how consumers attempt to find a reason for a consumption outcome or a behavior. Attributions occur along two dimensions internal/external and stable/unstable.

Automated text analysis is the systematic interpretation of large amounts of textual data into meaningful patterns and themes.

Automatic mode of thinking means that individuals do not deliberately or consciously think before they behave.

Availability heuristic refers to a situation where people judge the likelihood or frequency of something happening based on how easy it is to remember similar events.

Avoidance–avoidance conflict is when the choices available all have a negative consequence.

Balance theory of attitudes suggests that consumers seek balance between themselves, an attitude object, and some other important person or object.

Behavioral component (of attitudes) refers to the action or behaviors associated with the attitude object.

Behavioral economics is a branch of traditional economics that proposes that an individual's behavior is complex and is influenced by rational, emotional, contextual, and sociocultural factors.

Behavioral intention is a consumer's desire to enact a given behavior.

Behavioral learning is concerned with changes in behavior that occur as a result of changes in the environment.

Behavioral research (also buyer behavior) is an approach to consumer research that examines what consumers do. It does not account for the underlying motivations for those behaviors.

Beliefs are the thoughts an individual has about some object, idea, or person.

Belmont Report (1979) describes the ethical principles and guidelines for the protection of research participants.

Bicultural individuals can identify with two distinct cultures.

Brand addiction is an unhealthy mental and behavioral preoccupation with the brand in which the consumer experiences almost uncontrollable urges to possess any new product from the brand, and once the brand is acquired, the consumer experiences positive emotions.

Brand affinity occurs when there is a strong emotional tie between the brand and the consumer.

Brand community refers to a non-geographically bound community that is connected through brand admiration, with a structured set of social relations.

Brand love is stronger than brand affinity and describes a passionate emotional attachment to a particular brand.

Brand loyalty is the preference for purchasing one brand over another.

Brand personality scale identified five key brand personality traits sincerity, excitement, competence, sophistication, and ruggedness.

Brand relationship occurs when a deeper level of connection is forged between the self and the brand, such that the relation grows and develops in a way that is similar to a personal relationship.

Buyer behavior (also behavioral research) is a field of study that examines what consumers do. It does not account for the underlying motivations for those behaviors.

Caveat emptor is an approach to the buyer/seller relationship that says that the buyer should beware.

Caveat venditor is an approach to the buyer/seller relationship that says that the seller should beware.

Choice architecture describes how marketers may influence the choice context by presenting two or more choices such that consumers make the "preferred" choice.

Choice criterion is a rule or a standard by which a decision will be made.

Choice heuristics is a process that allows people to reduce the number of attributes to be considered for possible alternative choices.

Chunking is the grouping together of similar or meaningful pieces of information.

Classical conditioning is a theory of behavioral learning that occurs when an individual learns a connection between two stimuli that are paired with one another.

Closure is the tendency for people to fill in the "missing" elements of an incomplete picture.

Coercive power is the opposite of reward power and occurs when conformity to the group happens because of the threat of punishment.

Cognitive component (of attitudes) encompasses all of the beliefs, knowledge, and thoughts the individual has about the attitude object.

Cognitive dissonance is the state of having inconsistent beliefs, attitudes, or behaviors, which results in a feeling of unease.

Cognitive learning occurs as a result of internal mental processes and conscious thought.

Cognitive research is an approach to consumer research that focuses on how consumers learn, remember, retrieve information, process information, and form conclusions.

Collectivism is characterized by strong group cohesion and little emphasis on individual needs or wants.

Collectivist cultures are characterized by a focus on collective well-being.

Commodity products are those products that are mass-produced and are not distinctly different from one another.

Common good is an ethical framework that allows for a common set of beliefs and general agreement about what is right and wrong. Here, the most ethical choice is the one that provides the most benefits to the group.

Compensatory models (in attitude theory) are made up of a number of components and are calculated in such a way that a low score on one component is compensated by a higher score on another.

Compliance is a form of conformity and refers to publicly changing behavior to fit in with the group, but privately disagreeing.

Compliance heuristics narrow down a consumer's choice to those involved with complying with a request.

Comprehension occurs when the consumer interprets and understands the meaning of the information.

Compulsive buying is an unusual obsession with shopping such that it significantly affects the life of the person afflicted.

Confirmation bias happens when researchers look at the results of the data analyses as a way to confirm a conclusion they have already made.

Confirmatory consumer research seeks to find a specific answer to a specific question.

Conformity is the adoption of a group's beliefs, attitudes, and behaviors in an effort to comply with the group.

Conjunctive decision rule is when a consumer chooses the brand that achieves the minimum level for each key evaluative attribute.

Connectors are individuals with a large circle of friends and associates, many of whom are from other subcultures.

Consensus rule is a persuasion heuristic whereby a majority opinion is used for guidance.

Consequences are the benefits that the product attributes provide to consumers.

Consideration set is the subset of brands from the evoked set that the consumer might actually consider buying.

Conspicuous consumption is a pattern of consumer behaviors where products are utilized by some consumers as a way to compete in the social sphere and gain social recognition.

Consumer acculturation is the process of movement, translation, and adaptation of a consumer from one cultural environment to another cultural environment.

Consumer behavior is a field of study that examines the behaviors of consumers, as well as the motivations behind those behaviors.

Consumer culture theory (CCT) is a broad collection of models, perspectives, and research methods for studying the social and cultural aspects of consumption.

Consumer misbehavior is a behavioral act by a consumer that violates generally accepted consumption rules and disrupts the consumption order.

Consumer research process is a deliberate series of steps designed to answer key questions about consumer behavior to develop insights that will be helpful to marketing managers.

Consumer theft refers to stealing as a way to acquire consumer objects.

Consumer tribes consist of a group of consumers, emotionally connected by similar consumption values and usage, who utilize a brand as the link to create a community and express identity.

Consumers are individuals who use a product.

Consumption occurs when individuals or groups acquire, use, and dispose of products, services, ideas, or experiences.

Consumption function maps the relationship between disposable income and level of wages.

Contactual or associative groups are generally close membership groups with which we interact regularly (we are in contact with them) and with which we associate.

Contexts of decisions recognizes that the circumstances and the environment where a decision takes place are critical to the decision itself.

Continuous innovations are innovations that tend to create little change in consumption patterns and generally involve the introduction of a modified product rather than a completely new one.

Conventions are a specific form of custom and relate to the norms for the conduct of everyday life.

Corporate social responsibility (CSR) is a set of standards and procedures for running a business that takes into account the needs of stakeholders and works to achieve economic, social, and environmental success.

Crowdsourcing happens when a company or organization takes a task or a problem that normally would be performed by employees and gives it to a group of people to solve.

Cultural ecology refers to the physical geography of a place and the way individuals and the cultural system have adapted to that environment.

Cultural ideology reflects the mental characteristics of a group of people, building on the assumption that members of a society possess the same worldview, ethos, ideas, and principles.

Culture is the sum total of learned ideas, beliefs, values, knowledge, and customs that together regulate the behavior of members of a particular society.

Customers are individuals who purchase a product.

Customs are the norms of behavior that have been passed from generation to generation.

Data refer to numbers or other descriptors that are used to define a phenomenon.

Data visualization is an important graphical tool to help managers see patterns in data.

Decision criteria are rules for making a final purchase decision.

Decision rules are strategies that consumers use to help them make consumption choices.

Declarative memory consists of a collection of facts and events. It is made up of two types of memory systems, episodic memory and semantic memory.

Default is a preselected option that a consumer makes without active thought or consideration.

Dependent variables in consumer research change because of the influence of another factor (the independent variable).

Desacralization happens when a sacred item, person, place, or experience is no longer special and is downgraded to the realm of "everyday" in the minds of consumers.

Descriptive methods in consumer research are used to describe a group of consumers or their perceptions about a product, an advertisement, a store, etc.

Differential threshold is the point at which we notice a difference between two stimuli.

Differentiation means that, from the consumer's standpoint, the brand must stand out as being different in some way from the competition.

Diffusion of innovation is a model that is used to describe the way in which a new innovation is accepted and spread throughout a group of consumers.

Disclaimant group is a group to which we currently belong or to which we belonged in the past, but to which we no longer want to belong.

Disconfirmation paradigm is the difference between a consumer's prepurchase expectations of the product's performance and the actual postpurchase experience.

Discontinuous innovation has a disruptive effect and will require the establishment of new behavioral patterns by consumers.

Dissociative or avoidance groups are groups we have negative feelings toward and with whom we do not wish to be associated.

Distinctive brands have unique colors, logos, tag lines, or celebrities that are associated with the brand.

Divestment rituals involve those actions related to removing meaning from a product.

Double jeopardy is where brands with smaller market share have fewer buyers and those fewer buyers buy the brand less often.

Duplication of purchases principle is the extent to which brands in a given category share their customers with other brands in that category.

Dynamically continuous innovations create some change in behavioral patterns, but the magnitude of change is not very big.

Early adopters genuinely enjoy the process of discovering new technologies and love talking to others about it. They are likely to embrace new social technologies before most people do.

Early majority consumers deliberate a little longer over adoption and take their cues from innovators or early adopters they know personally. They tend to look for innovations offering incremental predictable improvements on existing technology. They do not like risk, care about the reputation of the innovator, are fairly price sensitive, and like to see competitors entering the market so that they can compare features.

Ego is the human consciousness that attempts to look out for the interests of the individual by balancing the demands of the id and the constraints of the superego.

Ego-defensive function (of attitudes) performs the function of defending or enhancing a consumer's self-image.

Ego involvement occurs when consumers perceive products or brands as relevant to their personal interests.

Elaboration continuum describes the amount of thought given to an advertising message/communication.

Elaboration likelihood model describes a process by which consumers think about and process information. If they are highly involved, they use the central route to persuasion; if they have low involvement, they use the peripheral route to persuasion.

Elimination-by-aspects decision rule ranks evaluative aspects by importance and establishes a minimum cutoff point for each attribute.

Emotional methods of consumer research are designed to assess consumer feelings and emotional states.

Encoding refers to how information enters the memory.

Enculturation concerns the process by which individuals learn about their own culture.

Endogenous word of mouth springs up naturally when consumers, as a part of a normal conversation, share consumption-related information.

Endowment effect is the tendency for individuals to value the things they own.

Enduring involvement is the preexisting relationship between the customer and the product.

Engrams are the trace of the memory in the brain; the encoding of the neural tissue that is often located within a neural network.

Episodic memory refers to our memories of specific events and experiences that have formed our autobiographical timeline.

Ethics describe a set of standards by which we can judge behaviors and ourselves.

Ethnicity refers to a variety of cultural factors such as nationality, ancestry, shared customs, and language.

Ethnographic studies are a descriptive consumer research method that provides an in-depth, comprehensive description of a group of people, culture, or situation.

Evaluative criteria are the conditions or benchmarks that are used to compare the alternative offerings to help make a choice.

Evoked set includes a broad set of possible brands that first come to mind when the consumer is faced with a choice.

Exchange is the process of giving up something of value and getting something of value in return.

Exchange rituals involve transferring items, such as gifts, between two people.

Exchange value is how much the product is worth to the consumer, which is usually expressed as the product's price.

Exogenous word of mouth only occurs because of a firm's marketing efforts; the organization does something that is interesting, exciting, and worth talking about.

Expectancy-value model says that attitudes are based on the belief that a product has a set of attributes and the evaluations of those attributes.

Experiential marketing is a way for researchers to better understand marketing. It is a shift in emphasis from the consumer as a rational decision-maker to a model where the consumer is viewed as an experience seeker.

Experiments carefully control everything in a laboratory environment to obtain a precise assessment of the relationship between independent and dependent variables.

Expertise rule is a persuasion heuristic whereby consumers rely on the advice of an expert.

Expert power comes from a group or individual because of special experience, skills, or expertise. Doctors, scientists, and professors have expert power.

Explicit memory is the intentional, conscious recollection of information.

Exploratory consumer research is interested in finding out broad trends or patterns of behavior.

Exposure means that the stimulus had the ability to be detected by the individual.

Extinction in operant conditioning occurs when the desired behavior is no longer reinforced or when the reinforcement is no longer motivating.

Extrinsic need is externally focused and is a drive toward some kind of external recognition, such as prestige or money.

Eye tracking is a test in which researchers monitor the movements of the eyes and determine what images consumers like.

Feminine refers to one of the key dimensions of culture that is more sympathetic, understanding, and compassionate.

Fetishism of commodities refers to the domination of objects or things in the market and relates to the idea of masking the human activity that is critical to, and lies behind, the production of consumer goods and services.

Financial risk is the perception of a likely economic loss.

First-order conditioning occurs when a conditioned stimulus acquires motivational importance by being paired with an unconditioned stimulus that is already seen as positive (like food) or negative (like pain).

Fixed interval schedule in operant conditioning is when reinforcement is provided after a specific, known period of time.

Fixed ratio schedule in operant conditioning applies reinforcement after a specific number of responses.

Focus groups are a descriptive consumer research method where a group of eight to ten people sit around a table with one interviewer and answer a series of questions about a topic.

Formal groups are reference groups that have a highly-defined structure, a set of rules, a hierarchy for membership where some people are designated leaders, and a set of clear goals.

Framing describes how a consumer makes a decision within different contexts; it is the perspective from which the consumer considers the decision.

Frugal consumers are careful with their money and alter their behaviors because of monetary considerations.

Functional (or biogenic) needs enable us to survive and include the need for food, water, and shelter.

Functional theory of attitudes seeks to identify and understand the motives and functions of attitude formation.

Galvanic skin response test measures electrostatic changes in the skin.

Gambling disorder happens when someone engages in repeated and problematic gambling. People who are suffering from gambling disorder experience a "high" that is similar to one that comes from alcohol or drugs.

Gamification is a method that uses a variety of gaming tactics to increase consumer engagement.

Gender refers to the biological reality of a person—male or female.

Gender identity refers to how an individual perceives themselves, their roles, and rules for behavior within the broader social context.

General Data Protection Regulation (GDPR) is a set of regulations that applies to any non–European Union company that collects and processes data collected from residents. These strict guidelines specify how, when, and where a company can collect, distribute, and use customer data.

Generalizing the findings of a research study means that the researcher is able to extend the findings from the smaller research sample to a broader group of consumers.

Gestalt means "whole" and refers to how people look for meaning and patterns in the stimuli in the environment as a whole, rather than in terms of the individual part.

Global consumer culture (GCC) is a connection (via shared beliefs, ideas, behaviors, etc.) with other people around the world based on the brands and products that they enjoy.

Grooming rituals are those private behaviors that consumers undertake to aid the transition from the private to the public self (and back again).

Habit-persistent consumers are those who make decisions based on their previous purchases.

Heart rate test measures a participant's heart rate; when the heart rate goes up, the participant is more excited or stressed. When it goes down, he or she is more mellow and calm.

Hedonic aspects of consumption involve multiple senses, emotions, and even some fantasy. Consumption is designed to provide pleasure, fun, or enjoyment.

Heuristics are methods to simplify decision-making that are based on past experiences. They are often referred to as mental shortcuts or rules of thumb.

Higher-order conditioning occurs when two conditioned stimuli are paired.

Holiday rituals refer to the rituals associated with both vacations (tourism holidays) and culturally bound holiday seasons.

Id is a force that focuses attention and energy on primary needs, immediate gratification, and pleasurable acts without regard to the consequences.

Ideal or idealized self relates to the self we aspire to be like.

Identification is a form of conformity and occurs when individuals like or admire an individual or group, so they try to be like that individual or group.

Image congruency proposes that consumers select products, brands, and retailers that correspond with their self-concept.

Implicit memory is remembering without conscious awareness.

Impulse purchases occur when a purchase is made because of a sudden powerful urge to buy a product with little regard to the consequences.

Incidental learning is the nonpurposeful acquisition of knowledge.

Independent variables in consumer research change on their own and are not dependent on other factors.

In-depth interviews are a descriptive consumer research method where a single interviewer discusses a topic with a consumer.

Individualism is characterized by a focus on the self, with little regard to interpersonal connection or collective responsibility.

Individualism–collectivism is one of the key dimensions of culture, as defined by Hofstede.

Individualistic cultures emphasize an individual's personal motivations and goals.

Indulgence represents the tendency for a society to be open to the gratification of basic and natural human motivations to have fun and enjoy life.

Industrial Revolution refers to the period when the economy transitioned from agriculture to manufacturing. Experts generally agree that this transition happened in the late 1700s and early 1800s in the United States.

Inept set are those brands that the consumer has rejected from consideration because of a negative previous experience or other negative information. They are not under consideration at all.

Inert set includes brands in the product category that the consumer has neither a positive nor a negative opinion about; they're simply not even thought about.

Influencers (or opinion leaders) are individuals who, compared to others, exert more influence on the decisions of other individuals.

Informal groups are reference groups formed by individuals who share a common set of interests or goals.

Information refers to data that have already been organized and analyzed.

Informational group influence occurs when individuals utilize the reference group to get information from influencers or experts, which then alters their own behaviors.

Informational power is based on logical argument and knowledge someone may have acquired from experience or know-how.

Informational social influence is a form of conformity and occurs when individuals rely on the expertise or knowledge of other people to help with a decision.

Information search is the process by which we identify and gather appropriate information to aid our choice in a decision-making situation.

Innovators are visionary imaginative individuals who are technology enthusiasts. They want to be the first to get new technological products.

Insights are useful interpretations of the data that are gathered from the consumer research process.

Institutional review board is a group of people in an organization whose purpose is to review all research studies before they are conducted to ensure the rights of research participants.

Instrumental values are the means, paths, and behavioral standards by which we pursue our terminal values.

Internalization is a form of conformity and involves both an attitudinal and a behavioral change in favor of the group.

Internet of things is a term used to describe the vast collection of wireless-enabled devices that collect data and share that data with one another, with consumers, and with others.

Interpretation involves attaching meaning to the stimulus; consumers understand the message and are likely to connect this new information to other information they already know.

Interpretivist perspective stresses the subjective meaning of the consumer's individual experience and the idea that any behavior is subject to multiple interpretations rather than one single explanation.

Intersectionality is a cultural definition whereby multiple identities exist at the same time.

Intrinsic need is an internal drive that all humans have, such as the need for food, water, and shelter, as well as emotional needs such as love, friendship, and acceptance.

Involvement is the perceived relevance of a purchase to the consumer.

Irrational escalation happens when new data happen to be in conflict with a decision that has already been made and managers are reluctant to "cut their losses."

Just-noticeable difference (JND) is the minimum difference needed for a stimulus to be noticed by the majority of people.

Knowledge refers to familiarity with people or things, which can include understanding, facts, information, and descriptions gained through experience and education.

Knowledge bias is the tendency for participants to prefer a product, advertisement, or spokesperson with which they are familiar over one that is unfamiliar.

Knowledge function (of attitudes) relates to the human need to have an accurate, meaningful, stable, and organized view of the world.

Laddering is a research technique designed to uncover a consumer's means-end chains.

Laggards are consumers who exhibit similar characteristics to the late majority (traditional, skeptical), but even more so. Likely to be found among older consumers and consumers with lower socioeconomic status.

Late majority consumers are conservative, somewhat skeptical, and cautious of new products and progress, preferring and relying on tradition. They fear high-tech products and usually adopt new technologies only when forced to do so.

Law of buyer moderation is the tendency for light buyers to become heavier and heavier buyers to become lighter.

Learning is the relatively permanent change in behavior that occurs as a result of studying, practicing, or experiencing something.

Legitimate power rests with someone who has a particular position of authority in a particular context.

Lexicographic decision rule is when customers rank the product attributes by their importance, select the most important attribute, and then pick the brand that performs best on that attribute.

Long-term memory is the memory system where information from short-term memory moves so that it can be stored for later use.

Long-term orientation concerns a culture's time orientation and the extent to which it is concerned about the future as well as the past.

Loss aversion describes the fact that most people dislike losses more than gains of an equivalent amount.

Malleable self refers to the idea that people will act differently according to the situation, influenced by social roles, cues, and the need for self-presentation.

Market mavens are active information-seeking consumers or smart shoppers, and they like to provide information to others on a broad variety of goods, services, and marketplace characteristics.

Market penetration is the proportion of people who buy an item in a given period.

Market share is the proportion of the total sales for one brand versus the other brands in the market.

Masculine is a cultural motivation that is more action oriented, assertive, and analytical.

Masculinity–femininity is one of the key dimensions of culture, as defined by Hofstede.

Maslow's hierarchy of needs is a model for understanding a person's motivations. It is based on the idea that there is an ordering of needs, from the most basic physical needs (physiological) to higher-level self-actualization needs. People satisfy their needs one level at a time, moving up toward self-actualization.

Materialism is a value that places a strong emphasis on material goods as a way in which consumers can reach important life goals.

Maximizers are consumers who carefully consider all the alternatives and purchase the brand with the best combination of features and benefits.

Means–end chains are a series of connections consumers make that link product attributes to their own closely held values.

Memory is both a system and a process whereby information is received, sorted, organized, stored, and retrieved at a later time.

Mental accounting occurs when individuals allocate assets, such as their finances, into separate groupings to which they assign different levels of utility.

Mere exposure effect happens when the more often you are exposed to a stimulus, the more you will like it.

Message-response involvement reflects the consumer's interest in marketing communications.

Mindful consumption is a recognition that there are consequences to a consumer's consumption choices. Consumers then alter their consumption behaviors in an attempt to have fewer negative impacts on their own lives as well as the lives of others.

Morality can be thought of as a state of virtue and is often connected to strongly held religious beliefs.

Mores are a particular type of custom and have a strong moral overtone.

Motivation is a drive that causes an individual to behave in a particular way.

It is rooted in an individual's goals, desires, and wishes.

Motivational research is an approach to consumer research that focuses on underlying influences on consumer behavior, such as desires and emotions.

Motivation to comply is the extent to which the individual feels driven to comply with or conform to the subjective preferences of these important people.

Multiattribute attitude models acknowledge that attitudes are a combination of beliefs and evaluations about several different attributes, or features, of a product.

Multicultural individuals can relate to or identify with more than two cultures.

Multiplicity of the self holds that different self-concepts motivate us to behave in different ways at different times and in different contexts.

Multitrait approach (to personality) is where researchers are concerned with a number of personality traits taken together and how they combine to effect consumption.

Myth is a story that contains symbolic elements that express the shared emotions and ideals of a culture.

Near-stationary (static) markets are established, mature markets that appear stable over a period of several months or a year.

Needs are the things that are necessary for life. We become aware of needs when there is a difference between our actual and desired states.

Negative reinforcement in operant conditioning occurs when something unpleasant is removed following a behavior.

Negative self refers to the person you are not and do not want to become.

Neuromarketing is a branch of research that uses scientific methods involving the functioning of the brain to understand and predict consumer behavior.

Neutral operants in operant conditioning are responses from the environment that neither increase nor decrease the probability of a behavior being repeated.

Noncompensatory models of attitude formation describe the situation when one overriding component is dominant in the choice process.

Non–gender binary is a self-definition for some individuals that rejects the simple, discrete definitions of gender and gender identity. Instead, they prefer a fluid definition whereby they can be feminine, masculine, both, or neither.

Nonphysical methods of cognitive consumer research attempt to map the thought processes of consumers to infer, or draw conclusions about, the consumer's cognitive processes.

Nonstationary (dynamic) markets are markets in which the forces change quickly and dramatically.

Normative beliefs are the consumer's overall perception about relevant or important others' beliefs that the individual should or should not engage in a behavior.

Normative social influence is a form of conformity when you feel pressure to go along with people around you to fit into the group.

Norms are a set of informal rules that society imposes to guide individual behavior.

Novelty is something that is unexpected and out of the ordinary, based on previous experience and knowledge of that stimulus or event.

Nudging happens when subtle cues are used to help consumers or citizens make choices that are better for them or their families.

Obese individuals have a body mass index greater than or equal to thirty.

Observation in research occurs when researchers simply watch and record what customers do.

Observational learning (or social learning theory) says that behavior is learned from the environment when we watch what other people do and the outcomes they receive.

Observational methods describe a broad set of methods to observe the actual behaviors of consumers or the results of those behaviors.

Ongoing information search occurs independent of a specific, immediate purchase problem.

Online behavior is an observational research method that assesses behaviors such as click-through rates, time spent on a site, search terms used, how a customer navigates through a site, and where the customer went after leaving the site.

Operant conditioning is a theory of behavioral learning that occurs when an individual's behavior is changed through reinforcement that follows a desired response.

Opinion leaders (or influencers) are individuals who, compared to others, exert more influence on the decisions of other individuals.

Opinion seekers are people who search for information and advice to assist in their decision-making.

Parental yielding is when a parental decision-maker is influenced by a child's request and "surrenders" the decision-making authority.

Pareto principle suggests that about 80 percent of a company's sales come from 20 percent of its customers (also called the 80/20 principle).

Passing off is the marketing of a good in a way that enables it to be mistaken for another brand; it relies on the phenomenon of stimulus generalization.

Passive learning is the acquisition of knowledge without active learning.

Perceived behavioral control is the consumer's assessment of his or her own ability to successfully perform the behavior.

Perceived obsolescence happens when a product goes out of date because of its fashion or style.

Perceived risk is the amount of uncertainty or doubt that a consumer has when buying a product or service.

Perception is the process through which information from a stimulus is received by the senses and is then organized, interpreted, and experienced.

Perceptual defense is when a consumer avoids exposure to potentially threatening or unpleasant stimuli.

Perceptual (or positioning) maps are visual representations of the marketplace from the consumer's perspective.

Perceptual vigilance occurs when an individual determines that a stimulus may or may not be relevant.

Performance or functional risk is the perception of how well the product will perform its expected task.

Personality is a person's identity, which can be viewed from either a psychological or a sociological perspective.

Persuasion heuristics are used by consumers to challenge or change their opinions.

Physical methods of cognitive research examine the functions and reactions of the brain.

Physical risk is the perception of harm that a product or service might have.

Planned obsolescence happens when products are designed to break down or become out of date before they should.

Positive reinforcement in operant conditioning occurs when an individual learns as a result of noticing that their previous behavior has produced a positive outcome.

Positivist approach emphasizes the objectivity of science and the consumer as a rational decision-maker.

Possession rituals are the rituals associated with transforming mass-produced products from the marketplace to the home or workplace.

Possible selves are personalized representations of one's self in future states.

Postmodern consumers do not seek a unified theme to their consumption but instead explore different and separate identities that match fragmented markets and different products.

Power distance (PD) is one of the cultural dimensions proposed by Hofstede. It describes how differences in power influence interpersonal relationships.

Prediction heuristics are used when the consumer is trying to predict a future outcome. The two types of prediction heuristics are the availability heuristic and the representativeness heuristic.

Primacy effects describe the phenomenon where it is much more likely for an individual to remember the first piece of information provided.

Primary data are collected to specifically answer the question at hand.

Priming is a phenomenon in which exposure to a stimulus, such as words, images, or sounds, alters an individual's response, without conscious awareness.

Principle of figure and ground states that we are more likely to notice things when they stand out from the background in which they are placed.

Principle of proximity states that things we see close together are perceived to be more related than things that are seen as farther apart.

Problem identification is the first step in the consumer research process. It involves the careful articulation of the exact question a consumer researcher needs to answer.

Problem recognition occurs when a consumer realizes that there is a difference between what is actually happening and what ideally could happen. It is the start of the consumer decision-making process.

Procedural memory is memory involved with knowing how to do things.

Product attribute is a feature or characteristic of the product.

Product involvement is the perceived personal relevance of the product based on needs, values, or interest.

Profane consumption is the term used to capture those consumer objects and events that are more "everyday" in nature; they do not share the "specialness" of sacred consumption.

Psychographic segmentation is based on building a picture of the consumer based on activities, interests, and opinions..

Psychological perspective of personality argues that an individual's persistent and characteristic reactions to environmental stimuli make up an individual's distinctive identity.

Psychological risk is the risk that reflects the potential to damage an individual's self-perception.

Psychology is the "scientific study of the behavior of individuals and their mental processes" (American Psychological Association 2017).[1]

Punishment in operant conditioning is a way to decrease behavior by applying a negative response to the undesired behavior.

Pupil dilation test measures the extent to which a participant's pupils dilate, or open up and become bigger.

Purchase frequency is the average number of times consumers purchase a brand in a given period.

Purchase loyalty involves the repeated, often habitual, purchase of a brand.

Qualitative data describe qualities of a situation, product, consumer, etc.

Quantified self refers to the idea that tracking metrics can lead to self-improvement in some way.

Quantitative data use numbers, ratios, and other measurements to describe a situation, product, consumer, etc.

Quick response (QR) codes are optical, machine-readable barcodes that record and store information related to items.

Race refers to the color of a person's skin and other physical features.

Radiofrequency identification (RFID) technology relies on small electronic tags that are attached to products. It can be used to track inventory and help consumers make consumption experiences more efficient and seamless.

Reactance occurs when consumers perceive that their decision-making freedom is limited, so they reassert their freedom.

Recency effects describe the phenomenon where it is much more likely for an individual to remember the last piece of information provided.

Reciprocal view of family decision-making and consumer socialization recognizes that there is a significant amount of influence that flows back and forth between parents and children.

Reciprocity is a compliance heuristic that involves the return of a favor.

Recognition requires the memory to retrieve information by experiencing it again.

Recollection is the simple act of retrieval of a piece of information from memory.

Reference groups are sets of individuals that other individuals use as a basis for comparison and guidance when forming their beliefs, attitudes, and behaviors.

Referent power stems from an admiration of the qualities of another person or group and results in the individual trying imitate those qualities by copying the behavior.

Reflective mode of thinking means that individuals exert deliberate effort to their thoughts and decision-making before they behave.

Relearning occurs when information that was previously stored in memory has been forgotten after a certain amount of time and the individual needs to relearn the material.

Representative research samples have the same core set of characteristics as the larger group of consumers.

Representativeness heuristic occurs when consumers judge something based on how similar it is to some stereotypical case.

Research participants are the group of consumers who take part in a research study.

Retention has occurred with the successful storage of a new piece of information; success can be measured by the ability to retrieve the information.

Retrieval is the process whereby we gain access to our stored memories.

Reverse socialization is where parents acquire consumer skills from their children.

Reward power occurs when a person or group has the ability to provide benefits for conforming to the group norms.

Rites of passage rituals are those rituals that mark a change in a person's social status.

Ritual refers to a symbolic and expressive activity, often comprising multiple behaviors that occur in a fixed sequence and are repeated over time.

Ritual artifacts are the objects and products that accompany or are consumed in a ritual setting.

Ritual audience is the group that witnesses or participates in the ritual in some way beyond those involved in the particular performance roles.

Ritual performance roles are the roles performed by people involved in the ritual as they perform according to a "script."

Ritual script guides the use of the ritual artifacts—which artifacts to use, by whom, the sequence of use, and the types of comments that accompany the ritual.

Sacralization happens when we attach sacred meaning to profane consumption so that everyday products, people, places, and events are elevated and have a distinctiveness and specialness in the eyes of consumers.

Sacred consumption describes those consumption activities that are set apart from everyday consumption activities and are treated with some degree of respect or awe.

Salespeople (relating to opinion leaders) are artful at persuasion and are often charismatic. They do not resort to strong-arm tactics to influence others. Instead, their influence is subtle.

Salient beliefs are those beliefs that are most important or relevant to consumers.

Sample refers to a smaller group of consumers who represent the target market and are used in a research study.

Satisficing occurs when a consumer buys a product that is "good enough," rather than the best decision.

Scanner data is an observational research method that collects data from products scanned at a retail store's checkout counter.

Scarcity is a compliance heuristic that is based on the notion that consumers will respond when they perceive that a product is rare or scarce.

---

[1] *American Psychological Association. 2017. Accessed May 20, 2017. https://www.apa.org.*

Schemas are cognitive frameworks that are used to organize and interpret information.

Script is a type of schema that contains information on what to do in certain situations.

Search engine optimization is a tool used by consumer researchers that focuses on what consumers do when they conduct a search on Google, for example. It utilizes key words, phrases, links, apps, etc., to deliver higher rankings on the search engine results page.

Secondary data have already been collected for another purpose.

Selective exposure is the act of purposely seeking or avoiding exposure to stimuli.

Self is a person's feelings, beliefs, knowledge, and attitudes about his or her own identity.

Self-concept refers to the sum total of our thoughts, feelings, and imaginations about who we are.

Self-congruity refers to the extent to which a product (or retail) image matches a consumer's self-image.

Self-gifts are a specific example of gift giving, where consumers purchase self-gifts as a way of regulating their own behavior.

Semantic memory consists of specific details, facts, and knowledge about the world.

Semiotics is concerned with exploring the links between signs and symbols and the meanings they signify and convey.

Sensory aspects of consumption involve the experience of sensations that enter one's consciousness through one of a consumer's five senses (sight, smell, hearing, touch, taste).

Sensory memory is the memory system that receives sensory information for a very brief time before it moves to short-term memory.

Shared value is a concept in which an organization creates economic value for itself and its investors, while also creating social and environmental value.

Sharing economy is a term used to describe an economic system that is based not on the purchasing of products, but on the sharing of products.

Shopper marketing is a research perspective that focuses on what consumers do by examining purchase data, observing how consumers interact with a product, and analyzing consumer panel data.

Short-term memory is the memory system where sensory information is briefly processed before it is moved to long-term memory.

Similarity refers to how items that have similar physical characteristics will be perceived as belonging together.

Single-trait approach (to personality) presumes that in a given situation, a single personality trait will be predominant force.

Situational involvement is involvement with a product class or brand dependent on some other event or time in our lives.

Situational self recognizes the self-concept as a dynamic entity, where different aspects of self are activated depending on the different situations the consumer is in.

Social class is a classification system that divides groups of people based on a composite measure of income, occupation, and education.

Social desirability bias happens when research participants provide answers to make themselves look good or provides answers they think the researcher might want to hear.

Socialized inhibition refers to a behavior that society tells you is inappropriate.

Social power is the degree of influence an individual or organization has among peers and within society as a whole.

Social risk is the risk of damaging your standing in your social community.

Social self sometimes referred to as the *looking glass self*, is how consumers believe they are seen by significant others.

Social structure tells us about the way that orderly social life is maintained in a culture.

Sociological perspective on personality suggests that both internal and external factors impact how individuals view themselves.

Sociology is a field of study that examines all the external influences on a consumer, such as social class, gender, and family.

Statusphere refers to the process by which consumers communicate their specialized consumption knowledge or expertise to one another in order to attain status within their social group.

Stimulus is a piece of information that is available for the consumer to pay attention to and later interpret.

Stimulus discrimination occurs when an individual can distinguish between two stimuli.

Stimulus generalization occurs when a stimulus that is similar to a conditioned stimulus elicits a similar conditioned response.

Storage is how the encoded information is retained in the memory.

Subculture of consumption is defined as a group of consumers connected through a shared consumption activity.

Subcultures are smaller, cohesive groups of people who share similar values, beliefs, tastes, and behavioral patterns.

Subjective norms represent a person's perceptions of specific significant others' preferences as to whether the person should or should not engage in the behavior.

Subjective (or psychogenic) needs are socially acquired needs and include the need for status, affiliation, self-esteem, and prestige.

Subliminal exposure occurs at a level that is below the level at which it can be consciously perceived.

Sumptuary laws are laws that attempt to control and regulate permitted consumption activities.

Superego reflects the rules, values, and norms imposed by society and works to prevent the id from seeking selfish gratification.

Surveys are a descriptive consumer research method that provide research participants with a very structured set of questions that they must answer.

Sustainable consumption starts with a recognition that our consumption choices impact one another and the planet. It encourages sustainable actions.

Sustainable development and operations "meet the needs of the present without compromising the ability of future generations to meet their own needs" (United Nations 1987).[2]

Symbolic consumption describes the meanings that are attached to products, as well as the process by which those meanings are transferred between the product, the consumer, and the broader society.

Symbolic interactionism states that relationships with other people play a large part in forming the self.

Symbolic value is the collection of deeper meanings consumers attach to products.

Telepresence is a sensation that is very close to the actual experience and often happens when a consumer uses virtual reality technology.

Terminal values are our life goals and motivate our behavior.

Theory of cognitive dissonance is based on the belief that people need consistency or consonance between their behavior and their attitudes.

Theory of planned behavior (TPB) is a multiattribute model of attitudes that says that behavioral intentions are determined by attitudes, subjective norms, and perceived behavioral control.

Theory of reasoned action (TRA) is a multiattribute model of attitudes that says that behavioral intentions are determined by attitudes and subjective norms.

---
[2] United Nations. 1987. Report of the World Commission on Environment and Development: Our Common Future. New York: United Nations.

Time risk is the risk embodied in the uncertainty regarding the amount of time required to buy or learn to use a product.

Trademarks are the legally protected and distinctive words, phrases, logos, and other symbols that consumers use to identify one product from another.

Tragedy of the commons is a problem that exists with the common good framework of ethical decision-making. It predicts that when individuals attempt to maximize their self-interest in using a common resource like a park, the value of that resource is reduced for everyone.

Trait-based approach (to personality) suggests that personality is the sum of an individual's traits or qualities, which can be used to predict or explain a variety of different behaviors.

Transformative consumer research (TCR) refers to a stream of research that focuses on benefiting consumer welfare and quality of life across the world.

Trendsetters are a special kind of influencer; they start popular movements in music, fashion, food, drinks, and entertainment.

Triangulation of research happens when the findings from several different research techniques all lead to the same conclusion.

Two-step flow of communication is a model that says that influence flows from the media to opinion leaders, who then pass on information to the broader public.

Uncertainty avoidance (UA) is the extent to which a cultural group is tolerant of uncertainty, ambiguity, and risk.

Utilitarian function (of attitudes) is based on the idea that consumers seek maximum utility and value from their consumption.

Utilitarian group influence occurs when individuals utilize the reference group to get information from influencers or experts, which then alters their own behaviors. Much of this influence is exerted by groups with which consumers socialize, like family, friends, or work colleagues.

Utilitarianism is an ethical framework that holds that the choice leading to the greatest good for the greatest number of people is the most ethical one.

Utility (or use) value is a measure of what function the product performs for the consumer.

Value-expressive function (of attitudes) is concerned with the drive to express important aspects of the actual self and possible selves.

Value-expressive group influence occurs when individuals use the reference group to enhance their self-image, build their self-concept, or improve their self-esteem.

Values are a consumer's deep-rooted and enduring ideals and guiding principles.

VALS™ uses a custom-designed survey to identify an individual's primary motivation (self-perception), the extent of resources available to realize their self-perception, five key demographics, and a proprietary algorithm to place individuals into one of eight predetermined consumer groups.

Variable interval schedules in operant conditioning occur when the reinforcement occurs at some unknown but consistent rate.

Variable ratio schedules in operant conditioning occur when the reinforcement is provided after an unknown and often changing number of responses.

Variety-seeking consumers are very interested in trying different brands and product attributes.

Voluntary simplicity refers to a lifestyle choice where individuals opt to limit material consumption and free up resources, such as time and money, which they believe will raise the quality of their life.

Wants are things that we would like to have, but are not necessary for our survival.

Warmth monitor is a knob or device like a joystick that is used to measure emotions.

Weber's law suggests that the stronger the initial stimulus, the more difference would be required for a change to be noticed.

Word of mouth (WOM) is an informal communication, either positive or negative, about products, attributes, retailers, or consumption experiences.

Credits

Chapter 1

p. 2: Pixabay; p. 6: Panet Pompeii; p. 8: Pixabay; p. 12: Courtesy of the Advertising Archives; p. 15: courtesy, Diane M. Phillips; p. 16: Courtesy of the Advertising Archives; p. 17: courtesy, Diane M. Phillips; p. 18: © iStock.com/kokkai; p. 20: © iStock.com/AndreiStanescu; p. 23: Courtesy of the Advertising Archives; p. 26: courtesy, Jen Drexler; p. 27: courtesy, Jen Drexler; p. 38: Source: iStock.com/Evgen Prozhyrko

Chapter 2

p. 42: Anton Gvozdikov/Shutterstock.com; p. 45: Pixabay; p. 46: courtesy, TerraCycle; p. 50 (top): Pixabay; p. 50 (bottom): © iStock.com/Daisy-Daisy; p. 51: Pixnio.com; p. 53: Surfrider Foundation; p. 54: courtesy, Josefa Wivou; p. 55: Tourism Fiji; p. 59: © iStock.com/monkeybusinessimages; p. 62: © iStock.com/RichVintag; p. 74: McDonald's; p. 75: Engadget

Chapter 3

p. 78: © bluedog studio/Shutterstock; p. 82: Pixnio.com; p. 86: © iStock.com/akesak; p. 88: Bark & Co.; p. 89: Bark & Co.; p. 91: © iStock.com/FatCamera; p. 92: © iStock.com/PeopleImages; p. 95: © iStock.com/Afavete; p. 98: courtesy, Joan Hoenninger; p. 99 (top): Wawa, Inc.; p. 99 (bottom): Wawa, Inc.; p. 101: © iStock.com/andresr; p. 104: © iStock.com/Yuri Arcurs; p. 105: © iStock.com/monkeybusinessimages; p. 106: © iStock.com/joeygil; p. 111: © iStock.om/ferrantraite

Chapter 4

p. 114: © Noob Pixel/Shutterstock.com; p. 116: © iStock.com/JoeChristensen; p. 119: Image used by permission of Oxford University Press; p. 120: Pixabay; p. 121 (top): Pixnio.com; p. 121 (bottom): © iStock.com/nicolamargaret; p. 122: Pixabay; p. 128: courtesy, Alice Ping; p. 129: Campbell's; p. 130: Courtesy of the Advertising Archives; p. 133: © iStock.com/slearmonth2; p. 137: Audi and courtesy of Bartle Bogle Hegarty (www.bartleboglehegarty.com); p. 139 (top): Pixabay; p. 139 (bottom): Ogilvy & Mather; p. 142: Image courtesy of Nutcase-Helmets; p. 146: Courtesy of the Advertising Archives; p. 147: Courtesy of the Advertising Archives; p. 148: Courtesy of the Advertising Archives; p. 152: © iStock.com/20fifteen

Chapter 5

p. 156: © WAYHOME studio/Shutterstock; p. 162: Breyer's, Inc.; p. 163: © iStock.com/20fifteen; p. 164: © iStock.com/Pattanaphong Khuankaew; p. 166: Courtesy of the Advertising Archives; p. 168: Girotti Shoes; p. 169: Pixnio.com; p. 171: © iStock.com/Mlenny; p. 176: courtesy, Adriane Randolph; p. 177: Courtesy, Adriane Randolph; p. 185: Pixnio.com; p. 186: Ben Molyneux/Alamy Stock Photo; p. 189: © monkeybusinessimages/Shutterstock; p. 191: Courtesy of the Advertising Archives; p. 194: © iStock.com/davidf

Chapter 6

p. 198: courtesy, Jason Phillips, CEO, ICEE; p. 201: © iStock.com/Hung Chung Chih; p. 202: Vectorstock.com/moibalkon; p. 204: courtesy, Ann Ryan; p. 205: Brownstein Group; p. 207: Courtesy of the Advertising Archives; p. 210: © iStock.com/Enes Evren; p. 213: courtesy, Jason Phillips, CEO, ICEE; p. 214 (top): courtesy, Robert Spangle; p. 214 (bottom): Courtesy of the Advertising Archives; p. 215: © RMC42/Shutterstock.com; p. 216: Courtesy of the Advertising Archives; p. 222: © iStock.com/noblige; p. 225: Pop Chips (www.popchips.com); p. 228: © iStock.com/KangeStudio; p. 230: Belk, R. W. 1988. "Possessions and the Extended Self." Journal of Consumer Research 15 (2): 139–68. With permission of Oxford University Press.

Chapter 7

p. 240: © oneinchpunch/Shutterstock.com; p. 242: © iStock.com/gpointstudio; p. 245: courtesy, Diane M. Phillips; p. 252 (top): © iStock.com/DebbiSmirnoff; p. 252 (bottom): © iStock.com/jfmdesign; p. 253 (top): © CapturePB/Shutterstock; p. 253 (bottom): © Stokkete/Shutterstock; p. 255 (top): © Ken Wolter/Shutterstock; p. 255 (bottom): © iStock.com/ExtremeMedia; p. 262: courtesy, Marta Insua; p. 262: courtesy, Marta Insua; p. 266: Pixnio.com; p. 270 (top): Courtesy of the Advertising Archives; p. 270 (bottom): adforum

Chapter 8

p. 278: © Andre Luiz Moreira/Shutterstock.com; p. 285: Courtesy of the Advertising Archives; p. 290: © iStock.com/galinast; p. 295: Courtesy of the Advertising Archives; p. 296: © Photo Oz/Shutterstock.com; p. 297: © iStock.com/jimkruger; p. 299: Courtesy of the Advertising

Archives; p. 300: courtesy, Cindy Stutman; p. 301: Philadelphia Flyers; p. 303: courtesy, Diane M. Phillips; p. 305: © iStock.com/Worayuth Kamonsuwan; p. 307: Courtesy of the Advertising Archives; p. 310: Courtesy of the Advertising Archives

Chapter 9

p. 318: © Elizaveta Galitckaia/Shutterstock.com; p. 327: Pixnio.com; p. 328: © iStock.com/dkart; p. 333: Pixnio.com; p. 335: © iStock.com/TakYeung; p. 336: Pixnio.com; p. 338 (top): © iStock.com/Pavliha; p. 338 (bottom): Courtesy of the Advertising Archives; p. 339: Pez, International; p. 340: Pez, International; p. 342: courtesy, Dennis Moore; p. 343: The Denver Broncos; p. 344: courtesy, Michael Brown-DiFalco; p. 354: Pixnio.com

Chapter 10

p. 365: © RawPixel.com/Shutterstock.com; p. 358: Chipotle; p. 359 (top): Courtesy of the Advertising Archives; p. 359 (bottom): © iStock.com/LeoPatrizi; p. 360: © iStock.com/korhil65; p. 362: Courtesy of the Advertising Archives; p. 364: Courtesy of the Advertising Archives; p. 365: Mourey, J.A., Olson, J.G., and Yoon, C. (2017), 'Products as pals: Engaging with anthropomorphic products mitigates the effects of social exclusion,' Journal of Consumer Research, 44 (2), 414-431. Courtesy of Oxford University Press.; p. 371: Courtesy of the Advertising Archives; p. 373: Wegmans; p. 379: Courtesy of the Advertising Archives; p. 380: courtesy, Andrew Speyer; p. 383: Courtesy of the Advertising Archives; p. 389: © iStock.com/PeopleImages; p. 393: courtesy, The Facts Now Campaign; p. 394 (top): courtesy, The Facts Now Campaign; p. 394 (middle): courtesy, The Facts Now Campaign; p. 394 (bottom): courtesy, The Facts Now Campaign

Chapter 11

p. 399: © Luvin Yash/Shutterstock.com; p. 401: Courtesy of the Advertising Archives; p. 403: Courtesy of the Advertising Archives; p. 405 (top): Courtesy of the Advertising Archives; p. 405 (bottom): Pixnio.com; p. 407: © iStock.com/Tammy616; p. 409: Pixnio.com; p. 410: © Federico Magonio/Shutterstock.com; p. 412: © Andrea Raffin/Shutterstock.com; p. 414: Courtesy of the Advertising Archives; p. 416: Courtesy of the Advertising Archives; p. 420: Pixnio.com; p. 421: © iStock.com/rightdx; p. 426: courtesy, A. Bruce Cawley; p. 427: Millennium 3 Management; p. 437: courtesy, Free People, LLC

Chapter 12

p. 440: Youth.gov; p. 445: © iStock.com/JunZhang; p. 449: © Nelson Antoine/Shutterstock.com; p. 451: © iStock.com/SDIProductions; p. 452: Pixnio.com; p. 452: © iStock.com/GoodLifeStudio; p. 458: courtesy, Ken Nwadike; p. 463: Pixnio.com; p. 466: © iStock.com/djwoody; p. 467: courtesy, Bill Simon; p. 468: courtesy, McCormick & Company; p. 475: TerraCycle; p. 476: TerraCycle

Chapter 13

p. 480: © supparsorn/Shutterstock.com; p. 483: © iStock.com/yacobchuk; p. 484: © iStock.com/wenht; p. 488: courtesy, Ryan Wall; p. 489: courtesy, Ryan Wall; p. 490: © iStock.com/mphillips007; p. 493: © iStock.com/metamorworks; p. 495: © iStock.com/ablokhin; p. 496: © iStock.com/DejanSredojevic; p. 498: © iStock.com/Ballun; p. 499: © iStock.com/amesy; p. 503: Love Your Melon; p. 505: © iStock.com/SeventyFour; p. 506 (top): © iStock.com/vetkit; p. 506 (bottom): © iStock.com/alexsl; p. 508: © BiksuTong/Shutterstock.com; p. 509: © iStock.com/alvarez; p. 513: Pixnio.com

Index

social identity function, of attitudes, 252,
     254–56
social influence, 364, 365
socialization, 379–80, 400
socialized inhibitions, 22–23
social justice, 442–43
social labels, 500
social learning theory, 171–72
socially conscious companies, 251
social media
     attention and, 134
     behavioral intention of posting, 265
     celebrity endorsements, 298–99
     checks on consumer misbehavior, 449
     children's advertising, 383–84
     complaining behavior, 289
     demographics of platform users, 378
     enhancing engagement with, 507–8
     ethnic subcultures on, 428
     information flow, 370
     Method Products ads, 314–15
     as news source, 256
     sharing via, 494, 506–7
     and social experience of shopping, 303
     tribes, 368–69
     in two-step flow of communication, 367
     variable ratio schedules, 169, 170
     virtual displays of self, 211
     word of mouth, 373, 377–78
     see also specific platforms
social motives for shopping, 303–4
social movements, tribes in, 368
social needs, 226, 227
social networks
     company-sponsored, 69, 70
     consumer behavior and, 67–71
     weight loss, 58
social norms, 48–49, 449
social power, 358, 365–66
social responsibility, 441, 466–72
social risk, 141–42
social self, 209
social structures and processes, 357–97
     case study: "The Facts Now" antitobacco
          campaign, 393–95
     cultural system, 412, 413
     family, 378–87
          advertising to children, 382–84
          sociocultural trends and, 384–87
          structure and roles, 379–81
     opinion leaders and opinion seekers,
          366–72
          expert influencers, 371
          information flow, 370–71
          trendsetters and coolhunters, 371–72
     reference groups, 357–66
          influence, 361–65
          social power, 365–66
          types, 358–61
     social class and consumption, 387–90
     word of mouth influence, 372–78
          electronic (eWOM), 376–78
          power of, 372–76
sociocultural context, of technology, 60
sociocultural trends, 384–87
     age of first-time parents, 386
     birth rates, 386–87
     and family, 384–87
     multiculturalism, 385
     single-parent households, 385–86
socio-historic patterning of consumption, 57
sociologic perspective on personality, 207–8
sociology, 4
soda tax, 86–87
sommeliers, 166
Songkick, 15
songs, incidental learning of, 172, 173
Sony, 486
sophisticated researcher myth, 81
SoulCycle, 406
sound, 123, 135
soup consumption, 334
South Africa, 70, 386, 447

South America
     conspicuous consumption, 15–16
     energy drink sector, 146
     excessive alcohol consumption, 457
     family, 384
     locally-themed Starbucks locations, 122
     marriage rates, 384
     see also specific countries
Southdale Center, 16–17
Southeast Asia, 456, 457
South Korea, 18, 48, 164, 298
Southwest Airlines, 337
spacing, advertisement, 190
Spain, 70, 288
Spangle, Robert, 212, 214
special interest shops, 303
Spectator, 426
Spectre (film), 172
spending self-control, 203
Spenner, P., 102
Speyer, Andrew, 380–81
Spice Route, 6–7
spices, 6, 129
Spizike, 152
Spotify, 15, 135
spreading activation, 182–83
spring break, 457
Spurlock, Morgan, 28
Sri Lanka, 6
stable causes, attributions to, 287
staged personalized experiences, 302
stakeholders, in transformative consumer
     research, 491
Stamos, John, 488
Standard Chartered Bank, 124
standard learning hierarchy, 246, 247
standard of living, Indian, 235–36
Stanford prison experiment, 93
Stanley, T. L., 75
Stanley Cup, 300
Staples, 315, 475
Starbucks, 122, 143, 158, 257, 328, 472
Star Trek franchise, 106–7
static markets, 323–25, 334
status, 15, 16, 153, 303
statusphere, 15, 16
steampunk movement, 360
Steam Workshop, 377
Steinmetz, K., 37–38
STEM (science, technology, engineering, and
     mathematics) programs, 68
Stets, J. E., 207
Stewart, Kristen, 297, 299
Stiller, Ben, 106
stimulus, 116–17
     conditioned, 160–63, 166
     measuring physical reaction to, 104–5
     neutral, 160, 161
     unconditioned, 160, 161, 166
stimulus discrimination, 165–66
stimulus generalization, 162, 164–65
"Stop it… or cop it" campaign, 268
storage, memory, 178–79
store intercepts, 99
storytelling, 229, 297, 299, 404–6, 502
Strategic Business Insights, Inc., 218
strategic memory protection, 178
streaming services, data collection by, 490–91
Street Art Cities, 15
stress, indicators of, 104
Strivers, 219
"Stroll" campaign, 161–62
Stroop test, 179
study abroad programs, male participation
     in, 213
Stutman, Cindy, 300–301
subcultures, 423–32
     consumption communities, 429–31
          brand communities, 431
          consumer tribes, 432
          subcultures of consumption, 430–31
     defined, 423
     demographic characteristics, 423–29

     age, 423–25
     gender and gender identity, 428–29
     race and ethnicity, 425–28
     Free People, 436
subcultures of consumption, 430–31
subjective features of perception, 115, 125
subjective needs, 221–23
subjective norms, 259, 260
subjectivity, in interpretivist perspective, 84
subliminal exposure, 117–18
subscription services, 49
suburban shopping malls, 16
Subway, 333
sugar, 7–8
sumptuary laws, 9
Sundblom, Haddon, 145
sunglasses, 411–12
sunshine movement, 413
Super Bowl, 100, 134, 135, 177, 294, 296,
     297, 301, 418
Supercon, 394
superego, 201
Supersize Me (film), 28
supply chain, 346
survey myopia myth, 81
surveys, 104, 105
Survivors, 219
sustainability, fashion and, 302
sustainable consumption, 460–65,
     500–501
sustainable development and operations, 500
Sweden, 70, 74, 132, 288, 415–16
Swift, Taylor, 164, 373
Switzerland, 288, 348, 353, 403, 466, 494
Sydney, Australia, 18
symbolic consumption, 214–15
symbolic information needs, 282
symbolic interactionism, 207–8, 211–12
symbolic value, 44–45
synchronization, 161
Szaky, Tom, 475

T
tactile shopping, 126
tagging, 409
TAG Heuer, 191
tailgating, 59
Taiwan, 298, 413
Taj Mahal, 420
TalkToChef, 362
Target, Inc., 101, 144–45, 315, 461, 475
target audience, 377–78
targeted ads, 500
targeted promotions, 347
tariffs, 11
taste, 125–29
taste preferences, 483–84
TAT (thematic apperception test), 230
Tata Motors, 66
Tate Museum, 507
tax payments, norms to encourage, 49
TCL, 486
TCR (transformative consumer research),
     489, 491–92
tea, 8, 401, 410
technology(-ies)
     and access, 376
     consumer advocacy, 28
     customer empowerment, 61
     historical perspective, 12–13
     maintaining customer privacy, 514
     new, 482–86
     sociocultural context, 60
     trends in, 504–9
     wearable, 62, 110–11, 504–5
telepresence, 507, 509
television
     adoption, 62
     antitobacco messaging, 393
     commercial breaks, 190–91, 211
     continuous data collection by, 486
     media multitasking, 132